SUSANNA
historian and
of Queenslan
studied art history, literature and history
at the Sorbonne in Paris and the
University of Madrid. She came to
Australia in 1975. She has been the
recipient of a Churchill Fellowship to
study Renaissance art in Italy and has
written extensively on art and history
both here and overseas. She was made a
member of the Order of Australia in
1996 'for services to art and literature'.
In 2001 she was awarded a Tyrone Guthrie Fellowship to write in
Ireland by the Literature Board of the Australia Council. Her
biography of Joice NanKivell Loch, *Blue Ribbons, Bitter Bread: the
Life of Joice NanKivell Loch, Australia's Most Decorated Woman*, won
the Sligo Non-Fiction prize and was short-listed for the Queensland
Premier's Non-Fiction award.

Susanna is the author of the following books, several of which have
won awards: *Historic Brisbane and its Early Artists*; *Historic Sydney:
the Founding of Australia*; *Pioneer Women, Pioneer Land*; *The
Impressionists Revealed*; *Conrad Martens on the 'Beagle' and in
Australia*; *Ethel Carrick Fox: Travels and Triumphs of a Post-
Impressionist*; *Strength of Spirit: Australian Women 1788–1888*;
Strength of Purpose: Australian Women of Achievement 1888–1950;
(part-author) *Raising Girls* and *Parenting Girls*; *Blue Ribbons, Bitter
Bread: the Life of Joice NanKivell Loch, Australia's Most Decorated
Woman*; and *Great Australian Women: From Federation to Freedom*.
She is currently working on her next book, which is about Australian
women in war.

July 2003 Dear Mum
We hope you enjoy this book devoted to women achievers. All our love and best wishes Colin & Marina

SUSANNA
DE VRIES

THE COMPLETE BOOK OF GREAT
AUSTRALIAN
WOMEN

THIRTY-SIX WOMEN WHO CHANGED
THE COURSE OF AUSTRALIA

HarperCollins*Publishers*

HarperCollins*Publishers*

Great Australian Women Book 1 first published in Australia in 2001
Great Australian Women Book 2 first published in Australia in 2002
This combined edition published in 2003 by HarperCollins*Publishers* Pty Limited
ABN 36 009 913 517
A member of the HarperCollins*Publishers* (Australia) Pty Limited Group
www.harpercollins.com.au

Copyright © Susanna de Vries 2001, 2002, 2003

The right of Susanna de Vries to be identified as the moral rights
author of this work has been asserted by her in accordance with
the *Copyright Amendment (Moral Rights) Act 2000* (Cth).

This book is copyright.
Apart from any fair dealing for the purposes of private study, research,
criticism or review, as permitted under the Copyright Act, no part may be
reproduced by any process without written permission.
Inquiries should be addressed to the publishers.

HarperCollins*Publishers*
25 Ryde Road, Pymble, Sydney, NSW 2073, Australia
31 View Road, Glenfield, Auckland 10, New Zealand
77–85 Fulham Palace Road, London, W6 8JB, United Kingdom
Hazelton Lanes, 55 Avenue Road, Suite 2900, Toronto, Ontario M5R 3L2
and 1995 Markham Road, Scarborough, Ontario M1B 5M8, Canada
10 East 53rd Street, New York NY 10022, USA

National Library of Australia Cataloguing-in-Publication data:

De Vries, Susanna.
   [Great Australian women]
   The complete book of Great Australian women.
   Bibliography.
   ISBN 0 7322 7804 X.

   1. Women–Australia–Biography. 2. Feminism–Australia–Biography.
   3. Feminism–Australia–History. 4. Women–Australia–History.
   5. Women–Australia–Social conditions. I. Title.

994.04092

Front cover: Portrait in oils of Jessie Street courtesy of the Street family.
Photograph of Fanny Durack from the author's private collection.
Photograph of Nancy Bird courtesy of Nancy Bird.
Rupert Bunny portrait of Henry Handel Richardson by permission of the National Library of Australia.
Back cover: Gordon Coutts *Waiting*, 1896 oil on canvas, 90.2 x 59.7cm, Art Gallery of New South Wales.
Photograph: Jenni Carter for AGNSW
Unless otherwise stated, all photographs are from private collections
Author picture © Jake de Vries
Cover design by Gayna Murphy, HarperCollins Design Studio
Typeset in 11/15 Stempel Garamond by HarperCollins Design Studio

Printed and bound in Australia by Griffin Press on 79gsm Bulky Paperback White

6 5 4 3 2 1   03 04 05 06

CONTENTS

ACKNOWLEDGEMENTS

To Marusia McCormick, whose ideas and office organisation have been invaluable; to my literary agent, Selwa Anthony; to Barbara Ker Wilson and Veronica Miller for editorial assistance; to the staff of BRISQ at the State Library of Queensland; to Sir William Deane, former governor-general of Australia, and to Elvie Munday of the Churchill Memorial Trust for details on the life of Dame Roma Mitchell; to the Hon. Peg Lusink for details on Joan Rosanove; to Professor Sir Frank Calloway, CMG, GBE, and Deirdre Prussak for help with the chapter on Eileen Joyce; to Alan and Belinda Cox for permission to publish the diary of Martha Cox; to Joyce Welsh for details on Joice Loch and to publishers Hale and Iremonger for permission to use Joice Loch's story as told in my biography *Blue Ribbons – Bitter Bread;* to the pictorial staff at Canberra's National Library and Graham Powell and Valerie Helson in the National Library's Manuscript Department, which archives my research. Thanks to Sir Laurence Street on behalf of the Street family, for permission to use the cover portrait of Jessie Street; Nancy Bird Walton and Father Paul Gardner for their co-operation and to Stuart Abrahams of the Hamlin Fistula Trust, and the Mary Ryan bookshop for launching the book. And finally, huge thanks to my husband, Jake de Vries, who as an architect provided valuable insights into the career of Florence Taylor, Australia's first woman architect, and also did some of the photography. Without his help this book would not have seen the light of day.

Susanna de Vries, Brisbane, 2000

INTRODUCTION

THE CHANGING ROLE OF AUSTRALIAN WOMEN

These stories of three dozen significant women reflect the changing role of women in Australia from pioneering days to the present.

To realise just how much life has changed for women today look at those faded photographs of the Colonial and Federation eras. They show the master of the house, resplendent in mutton-chop whiskers and Sunday suit, standing proudly beside his wife and row of children with ringlets or well-brushed hair. The housewife or 'Angel of the Hearth' sits passively, her latest babe on her lap, careworn and exhausted. The message conveyed by many of these family photographs is of the male as breadwinner and dominant member of the household, who makes all the decisions. And so he did in most cases. Property and children belonged to the husband, the wife was nothing but a chattel. Divorce for most women in abusive marriages was impossible. If divorced by her husband for desertion or adultery (his was allowable, not hers) she was entitled to absolutely nothing but a sewing machine.

Colonial Australia was no place for a nervous woman. Only the strong survived. Annie Caldwell migrated from Ireland during the Great Famine and took up arid land around Adelaide. When widowed and still desperately poor, Annie took her ten-year-old daughter, Martha and six other children across Australia in a horse-drawn wagon in search of better land and settled on a selection at Holbrook in New South Wales. After helping her mother establish a dairy farm, nineteen-year-old Martha married David Cox and helped him drive a covered wagon to the harsh country between Cobar and Bourke. Fifteen years later, widowed Martha, with children of her own to care for, took over the running of three large cattle properties, survived bush fires and droughts and established a pastoral dynasty.

In 1849 young Mary McConnel, was one of the first women to migrate to Brisbane, then a shabby frontier town. After Mary's baby son died of typhoid she worked hard to raise the money to found the first children's hospitals in the north of Australia. Mary's present-day equivalent is the remarkable Dr Catherine Hamlin from Sydney, who, in 1974 founded a hospital for 'fistula women' in Ethiopia and runs literacy programmes for those patients unable to read or write.

Annette Kellerman, born in Marrickville of migrant parents, grew up in poverty, broke international swimming records and achieved stardom on Hollywood's silent screen. Nellie Melba had to fight with her father to be allowed to sing on concert platforms, made more money from the stock market than from her golden voice, married and divorced, then fell in love with the heir to the French throne but could never marry him. Melba had a good business brain and acted as her own manager and publicity agent. Having felt initially exploited, she was one of the first women in the world to market her own talents to maximum effect.

Many women's achievements have been ignored because their husbands were automatically given the credit or took the credit. Mary Penfold of Grange Cottage founded South Australia's most important winery but her husband has been credited with her achievements.

Other memorable stories in this book are those of talented Florence Taylor, Australia's first woman architect; or the equally feisty Nancy Bird Walton, Australia's first woman commercial pilots and Dame Roma Mitchell, Australia's first woman high court judge and state governor. Reading about these dedicated, talented and compassionate women will make you laugh, weep and wonder at their bravery and determination.

By the 1890s the British Married Women's Property Act enabled married women to inherit or earn money in their own right. This was later incorporated into various state laws, for those who had money to inherit or could find suitable work. Yet with or without this assistance, women so often rose creatively to meet their circumstances or challenge the male-dominated institutions that defined them so narrowly.

Pioneering women were far too often the unsung heroines. Such were the two generations of the Caldwell women. In the colonial and Federation eras, marriage was the only career available to the majority of women. Both church and state regarded sex on demand as a husbands right. Women were constantly reminded that Australia needed populating and it was their duty to have children.

In the colonial era, any woman not married by twenty was deemed to be 'on the shelf', and a great many girls married when they were still in their teens. Stories in this book reveal how Alice Joyce, mother of pianist Eileen Joyce married at twelve; Mary Richardson, mother of the writer Henry Handel Richardson married at sixteen; Mary Penfold, founder of Penfold's winery, married at fifteen; Enid Burnell, (the future Dame Enid Lyons) married Australia's future prime minister Joseph Lyons on her seventeenth birthday.

Passionate seventeen-year-old Sarah Miles Franklin was urged by her mother to marry as soon as possible. Instead she wrote a novel that highlighted the injustice of boys being given an education while girls were expected to marry young and raise large families. In 1901, Miles Franklin ironically titled her first novel *My Brilliant Career* to highlight the fact that, in the year of Federation, any career other than marriage was nearly impossible.

This was a period when young Women could not travel around unchaperoned and were expected to cover their knees and ankles at all times, as the sight of a well-turned ankle 'might inflame the passions of men'. Women in Australia's cities were even forced to swim at specific hours or in segregated pools. In 1907 Annette Kellerman risked a jail sentence by cutting the knee-length skirt off her bathing costume when trying to break a long-distance swimming record, thus asserting women's rights to wear suitable clothes for sport.

In Ancient Greece women were routinely stoned to death if found inside the sports arenas where the Olympic Games took place. When Baron de Coubertin revived the Olympic Games in Europe in the late nineteenth century, he allowed women to watch, but did not permit them to compete. He quaintly believed women should not be allowed to perspire in public. In 1908 the Baron finally relented and allowed women to compete but only in the archery competition. At the 1912 Stockholm Olympics, women were permitted to compete in swimming events for the first time and, against overwhelming odds, Australia's determined Fanny Durack won Olympic Gold, a major landmark for women in sport.

This book tells the story of women who demanded something different from the restricted lives of their mothers and grandmothers. It becomes apparent that gaining the right to vote (as a spin-off from of Federation), did not change women's lives nearly as much as Vida Goldstein and Catherine Helen Spence and other intrepid campaigners for female suffrage had hoped. In fact gaining the vote had very little effect on the life of the average Australian woman, as married women on the whole voted the way their husbands told them to. For twenty years not one single woman entered Parliament – Edith Cowan being the first woman to do so in 1921. When this happened, a male journalist accused her of neglecting her home and family, even though Edith's youngest child was thirty! The introduction of vacuum-cleaners, domestic refrigerators, piped water and tinned foods did considerably more to liberate women than did the right to vote or to sit in parliament.

Enid Burnell (the future Dame Enid Lyons) battled male prejudice to become Australia's first female Federal Cabinet minister. In her first decade of marriage, Enid suffered severe pain from an undiagnosed pelvic disorder while coping single-handed with six children under the age of ten, mountains of housework and no money to employ help. Her husband, Joseph Lyons (at that stage a member of the Tasmanian Government at a time when politicians were poorly paid), was away from home most of the time. Between doing the household chores, which included a huge weekly wash without a washing machine, Enid wrote her own and her husband's speeches and complained 'No man would put up with this kind of life.'

Against a background of heckling from male parliamentarians, Edith Cowan and Enid Lyons managed to introduce Bills that secured shorter hours and better conditions for women working in shops, domestic service and factories, as well as pensions for widows and single mothers. Enid Lyons also introduced our modern system of child endowment.

A constant thread that runs through many of these stories is of the struggle by women to gain access to higher education and careers. Women had to disprove the nineteenth-century theory that because they had smaller heads, their brains were smaller and incapable of logical thought. This pseudo-scientific absurdity propounded by some doctors reinforced the male belief that women should stay home and leave the running of the world to men.

By the 1890s Sydney and Melbourne universities were reluctantly accepting young women such as Constance Stone and Dagmar Berne into their arts faculties where they gained first-class honours. However the Deans of both medical schools were horrified when Dagmar and Constance and several of their friends announced their wish to enrol as *medical* students. Eventually Dagmar was admitted to Sydney University's medical school, passed her first-year exams with flying colours but was deliberately failed in later years by a biased dean of medicine at Sydney University, who informed his colleagues that only over his dead body would a women ever practise medicine. He must have thought he was one of the immortals.

Dr Agnes Bennett offered her services to the army in World War 1 but was told by a pompous general to stay home and knit. Agnes ignored him, joined an all-women field hospital and won medals for bravery.

Our first women doctors were appalled by the medical treatment received by the poor. Doctors Constance Stone and Lucy Gullett opened free clinics – other pioneer women doctors established all-female hospitals in Sydney and Melbourne.

Excessive prudery meant that male doctors were expressly forbidden to ask women to disrobe for gynaecological examinations. An engraving

from a medical textbook of 1880 shows a doctor performing a perfunctory gynaecological examination on a fully clothed woman. This picture would be funny if the consequences were not so tragic; because of this social convention many serious conditions went undiagnosed.

The introduction of better obstetric and gynaecological care by women doctors helped cut the shockingly high rate of maternal deaths in childbirth.

Because most women lacked access to reliable contraception there were many unwanted pregnancies. We owe a huge debt of gratitude to an unsung heroine named Sister Lillie Goodisson who fought to establish birth control clinics for Australian women. She battled both church and State authorities who insisted that contraception was something no respectable women should use – condoms were regarded as the preserve of prostitutes. Sister Goodisson broke the law and risked imprisonment by selling contraceptives in her birth control clinics and providing contraceptive advice free of charge to married women.

Before Australian homes were connected to electricity, housewives spent a great deal of time trimming and changing wicks on oil lamps or making candles from tallow. The urban poor and women in the bush made do with 'slush' lamps which used cotton wicks floating in a saucer of mutton fat. Candle grease caused stains – slush lamps smelled terrible and stained walls, which meant even *more* housework.

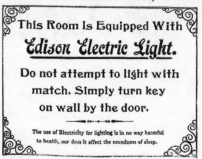

Gas lamps arrived in 1902 (along with Australian women's right to vote) but the thin gauze mantles of the lamps broke easily, so electric light soon became far more popular. Electricity was such a novelty that the power supply companies had to issue a printed notice informing householders not to strike a match but to turn on the light using the key or switch provided.

The introduction of refrigerators saved housewives endless work salting down and preserving food. Another major force for change in women's lives took place during the 1930s with the arrival of piped mains water to kitchen, bathroom and laundry. In remote rural areas today many householders still rely on tank or bore water.

Prior to the introduction of labour-saving devices, most housewives spent up to an *hour* each day fetching water from a stream or remote tank in buckets and even longer on washdays. What with boiling water for the wash-copper (or for baths), scrubbing and removing stains from clothes on a ridged metal washboard, and starching petticoats and shirts, doing the family laundry took up the whole day. The first washing machines to come on the market were not much help: they resembled miner's cradles and had to be rocked by hand to clean the clothes. Doing the weekly ironing was time-consuming as it involved filling flat irons with glowing embers. As flat-irons lacked temperature controls they frequently scorched the clothes.

A study carried out by the British Electrical Association for Women (BEAW) estimated that a healthy woman running a house without electricity spent an average of 32 hours a week on housework (not counting the hours she devoted to child care).

Before the arrival of domestic electricity, regular chores performed by women, such as cleaning and refilling paraffin lamps, trimming wicks, sweeping floors with a birch broom, dusting ornaments, mopping out the kitchen, cleaning grease-laden iron ranges and ovens, cleaning out fireplaces and setting new fires, disinfecting rooms, baking bread, preserving jams, fruit and vegetables, and salting meat, occupied their days. The BEAW study proved that electricity with its new domestic appliances, as well as running hot water, shortened the average housewife's working time by 75 per cent. It was the fact that housewives now had some free time coupled with smaller families and access to higher education, which freed them to turn their attention to spheres outside the home and changed women's lives so dramatically.

A 2002 BBC TV series, 'The Edwardian House', revealed the full horrors of housework in the era between Federation and the start of World War 1. During the shooting of the programme a young girl, who had volunteered to act in the role of a maid of the pre-World War I era became seriously ill from overwork. Rising at daybreak, setting fires, taking buckets of water up three flights of stairs, and long hours of sweeping and polishing seriously affected her health. This drudgery coupled with frequent pregnancies resulted in many actual women of the time dying young.

Pioneer aviator Nancy Bird Walton spent her teens keeping house for her father in rural New South Wales. In her story she recalls how she had to work a sixteen-hour day six days a week carrying buckets of water from a tank in the backyard, filling kerosene lamps, cooking, doing the laundry and book-keeping at night.

Louisa Lawson, Mary Gilmore, Miles Franklin and Ethel [Henry Handel] Richardson also experienced tough childhoods in poverty-stricken households but they survived and emerged as strong characters with the determination to accomplish great things.

Before the motor car became popular, Louisa Lawson, as editor of *The Dawn*, Australia's first women's magazine published by women, advocated the use of bicycles by women as a relatively inexpensive form of transport which would give women a new sense of freedom.

'Bloomers' for cycling were invented by Mrs Angela Bloomer to provide freedom and safety from long flowing skirts. However, to the horror of some authorities 'bloomers' revealed women's ankles and calves sparking a church-led campaign to have them banned as immoral.

World War 1 brought huge social change as young women took over jobs once done by men. Joice NanKivell Loch abandoned life as a household drudge on a farm in Gippsland to take on employment as a journalist and book reviewer on the Melbourne *Herald*; Florence Taylor, a qualified architect, obtained a job in an architect's office when the males went off to war – work almost unobtainable by women in the pre-war era.

The advent of the typewriter and the paid telephonist provided fresh opportunities for bright young women who, revelling in new-found financial independence, shortened their skirts and bobbed their hair.

The other side of this, however, was that women who had gone out to work or driven ambulances and run canteens for soldiers during both World Wars, had difficulty adjusting to a purposeless life once men came home. Many affluent families refused to allow their daughters to work and so they turned to voluntary work to absorb their energies.

Nevertheless, things would never be the same. The diggers came home and found that Australian women had become like 'lions who had tasted blood'. Women had gained a sense of self-esteem and knowledge of how to handle money and operate bank accounts.

With the new appliances of the century came advances such as the motor car. Although women had worked as ambulance drivers in the war in France and Serbia, women drivers on Australian roads were still a rarity. Driving in that period needed a complex skill known as double de-clutching in order to change gears, which inhibited many women from learning to drive.

For unmarried middle-class women, the long voyage to Britain and Europe became a rite of passage before settling down, having a white wedding and bearing children. Families became smaller due to the poverty, hardship and the homelessness imposed by the Great Depression of the 1930s as described by Kylie Tennant (Chapter 25).

World War II brought a new generation of women back into the work force and made them reluctant to relinquish new-found independence once again. Determined to consolidate hard-won freedoms, Jessie Street organised important Women's Charter Conferences in 1943 and 1946. At these, representatives of over ninety women's groups demanded input into government plans for post-war reconstruction, equal opportunity with men, equal pay, child endowment and a network of childcare centres; her conferences also supported rights for Aboriginal and Torres Strait Islander people. Jessie Street was a member of a distinguished pioneering family, and all her life she battled prejudice against women in all its forms. It seems entirely appropriate that the portrait of such an inspiring woman (by Jerrold Nathan, president of the Australian Art Society) adorns the cover of this book.

Following World War II families grew in size and then became smaller, even though the contraceptive pill did not arrive in Australia until 1962. Due to improved medical care the perils of childbirth decreased and women's life spans increased.

In 1959 the Commonwealth Arbitration Court ruled that women's wages should be lifted from 54 per cent to 75 per cent of the male wage. Nine years later in 1968 the ludicrous ban against married women working in the public service was lifted. In 1969 equal pay for equal work was finally instituted.

In the 21st century women form an integral part of our universities, and as many women study medicine, architecture and law as men. How pleased Dagmar Berne, Constance Stone and Joan Rosanove would have been.

Today the wheel has come full circle. Women are represented in all the professions, have a better representation in Parliament and some even hold ministerial posts. Women predominate in the publishing industry and in a recent intake of journalist cadets at the ABC there were more female cadets than male.

Australia has had three outstanding and very popular female State governors, including lawyer and university chancellor Leneen Forde, Dame Roma Mitchell, a former judge and university chancellor (Chapter 15); and Dr Marie Bashir, a psychiatrist of Lebanese background. It is heartening that a woman has been appointed to one of the top positions at Qantas. However the November 2002 report of the Australian Census of Women in Leadership shows that there are still too few women in top positions in our business institutions and women still do most of the lowest paid jobs.

As the heart-warming stories in this book reveal, women have come a long way since the days of female pioneers such as Martha Caldwell Cox, Mary McConnel and Mary Penfold. No longer are the female sex despised as over-emotional and intellectually inferior; today's girls are being educated and encouraged to take on whatever roles they choose – to enter the workforce or remain at home to bring up children or a combination of both. The choice is theirs.

The role of women has changed greatly since they were granted the right to vote, and gained access to higher education, contraception and careers. Thrust into the workforce during the two world wars, droves of women returned to their kitchens during the 1950s only to see their daughters invade the jobs market in the 1970s, and their grand-daughters gain the highest marks at university today.

The two-income family is now becoming the norm, but women's role in child-bearing still produces conflicts when combining career and family life. However, in spite of the 'glass ceiling', which still limits their rise in certain careers, women have become a source of entrepreneurial power within Australian society.

CHAPTER ONE

Sarah Frances 'Fanny' Durack
(1889–1956)
FIRST FEMALE SWIMMER TO WIN OLYMPIC GOLD

Annette Kellerman
(1886–1975)
THE LONG-DISTANCE SWIMMER
WHO BECAME A HOLLYWOOD STAR

Fanny Durack was the first female swimmer in the world to win Olympic Gold. Her father, Irish-born Tommy Durack, was a popular publican with a fondness for the horses. Fanny inherited both his temper and his muscular physique. Fanny's mother had been a domestic servant before her marriage. Mary's parents had emigrated to Australia to avoid rural Irish poverty and could neither read nor write. Fanny's mother had six children. Whenever she could she helped her husband run the rough, tough Sydney pub he leased from the brewers.

Fanny and her brothers and sisters grew up in an atmosphere of beer, sawdust and the six o'clock swill, when men drank themselves into a stupor as fast as possible before the pub closed. Educational achievements were valued less than survival.

Tommy Durack was a very distant relative of the famous Duracks, who opened up vast areas of land in the Kimberleys and whose exploits are recorded in Mary Durack's epic biography, *Kings in Grass Castles*.

Unlike her more famous relatives, Fanny was not taught ladylike accomplishments. She attended the local State school, where she and other working-class children learned reading, writing and simple sums. Fanny and her girlfriends had no ambitions for a career; they left school at twelve or thirteen to do mundane work which would bring in money. At home Fanny shared a bed with her younger sister in a cramped bedroom above the pub. Fanny was a tomboy and a daredevil. SP betting rings, peroxided prostitutes, two-up schools and fist fights in the pub yard formed the background to her adolescence, enlivened by the sound of the pub's honky-tonk piano. Fanny watched her father act as 'bouncer' and intimidate drunks twice his size: early in life she learned the need to stand up for herself against aggressors.

In the summer of 1898, when Fanny was nine, the family spent a summer holiday in Newcastle. An adventurous child fascinated by the surf, she ignored her parents' warnings about keeping close to the beach and was knocked down by a large wave. Fanny might have drowned had not a large St Bernard dog seen her struggles, plunged into the surf and rescued her. The dog held the drowning child above the waves until her father could arrive and drag her back onto the sand.

Horrified by the fact that Fanny, his favourite, had nearly drowned, her father insisted she must learn to swim. At that time State schools had no swimming classes or pool facilities. Fanny was taken to

Sydney's only organised bathing establishment for girls and women, run by Mrs Page at Coogee.[1] The swimmers had to wear heavy knee-length costumes in navy or black wool with short sleeves.

Having paid Fanny's entry fee to the exclusive Coogee Baths, the Duracks lacked the necessary money for swimming lessons. But by watching the other girls and clinging to a rope, strung across the shallow end, Fanny soon taught herself to dog-paddle.[2] As soon as they saw she could stay afloat, her parents allowed her to visit the Domain baths at Woolloomooloo Bay, where part of the harbour was roped off against sharks as a swimming enclosure. A flight of rough, rock-hewn steps led down from the Domain. In one corner females were allowed to swim, sheltered by the overhanging branches of a big Moreton Bay fig tree from the prying eyes of male swimmers. It was thought the men's passions would be aroused by the sight of women in bathing dress.[3]

Fanny's strong arms and powerful shoulders were ideal for swimming and she was totally fearless in the water. At the Domain baths she watched the men swim while the other girls larked around giggling and splashing each other. Fanny soon saw how to adapt her rapid dog-paddle to a breast stroke – then the only style in which women could compete for a championship.

Competition presented problems for girl swimmers in the early days of the 1900s. The ubiquitous and powerful Rose Scott[4] was President of the NSW Ladies' Amateur Swimming Association and she frowned upon mixed bathing. Women and girls could only swim in public places in what was known as the 'ladies hour'. The skirts and the weight of female swimming costumes slowed them down in the water. Hampered by constricting costumes, most girls did not take swimming seriously and were happy to frolic around or dog-paddle in the shallows. 'Real' swimming was a sport for men in a male-dominated world that prized 'manly' pursuits and denigrated women's achievements.

At the beach many girls often remained fully clothed, while young men showed off in front of them, performing in the surf or flexing their biceps.

However, soon after Fanny learned to swim, Sydney Council opened a free bathing area which had separate bathing enclosures and changing areas for men and women. Annette Kellerman had not yet struck her blow for women by wearing her revolutionary boy's costume. Fanny and her girlfriends continued to wear bathing dresses made from coarse wool or even flannel, with a high neckline and bloomers or knee-length skirts attached. Men swam naked in all-male sessions in pools; at the beach they wore black wool costumes that covered their chests and torsos.

To earn pocket money for swimming coaching, Fanny persuaded her father to pay her for doing some jobs usually done by her brothers. She helped them hose down the tiled bar of the pub and collect the empty bottles worth money when returned to the brewers.

Fanny's love of the water, her adventurous nature and determination to succeed and her potential as an athlete were recognised by swimming champions Peter Murphy and F. C. Lane, who decided they would coach her. They introduced Fanny to a revolutionary new stroke, the 'trudgen'.[5] This was a mixture of over-arm and breast stroke. Instead of using leg strokes that mimicked the arm movements of the breast stroke, the trudgen used a kick stroke. But it was deemed 'unladylike', no one thought lady swimmers would even attempt it. In 1902 the inaugural New South Wales Ladies' Championships were held at the St George Baths in Cleveland Street, and for the first time the organisers included a race for schoolgirls.

Fanny felt confident enough to enter this inaugural ladies' competition and planned to use her newly acquired trudgen stroke in public. It was her first race and she was nervous. In the general scrum when the starting gun went off, she swallowed a mouthful of water, starting coughing and came last in her heat. That night she cried bitter tears in her pillow but vowed it would never happen again. The next day she forced herself to return to the water and train again, using the trudgen stroke. But it would take another two years before she felt confident enough to enter another public competition. By that time swimming carnivals had become popular in Sydney. When Fanny arrived at the front entrance of Sydney's Lavender Bay Baths, she found it had been closed because the stands were overflowing with people.

However, she was not prepared to let this hindrance prevent her entering the race. Running around the perimeter to the far side of the swimming baths, Fanny persuaded a startled passer-by to give her a leg-up. She scaled the wall, slithered down the other side and made her way through the hordes of spectators to the end of the pool, where the girls were lining up for the race. She explained the situation to the judge, who delayed the start of the race so that Fanny could dash into the changing rooms, tear off her clothes and put on her cumbersome bathing dress.

She ran back, breathless with exertion, and joined the line-up. At the sound of the gun she dived in, swam her trudgen stroke, at which she was now expert, and finished a close second to Dorothy Hill, the leading female swimmer in Australia. A new champion had arrived. At her next swimming carnival Fanny beat all her female rivals and won the New South Wales Hundred Yards Championship.

That win began a long series of successes for Fanny Durack. One of her younger rivals was Wilhelmina ('Mina') Wylie, whose father ran Wylie's Baths at Coogee. Mina was seven years younger than Fanny and had a more retiring nature. A common passion for swimming united them; they trained together and became life-long friends.

By 1911, when Fanny was twenty-one, she and Mina had refined and adapted the trudgen stroke and turned it into an even faster stroke which would later become known all over the world as the 'Australian crawl'.

From the start of her career Fanny defied the prudish conventions which governed female swimming. While most girls only swam during the 'ladies' hours', she braved the sharks and trained in Sydney Harbour, competing against male champions to acquire that competitive edge. Fanny used her own particular adaptation of the trudgen stroke competing against champions like Cecil Healey, Alex Wickham and other male swimming stars of her time. The men treated her in a sisterly fashion and made no special allowances for her. It was a tough school in which to compete, but down-to-earth Fanny Durack had that happy Australian characteristic of 'giving it a go'. She found she flourished in this world of swimming and soon set new records for women's swimming.

But Fanny's training sessions with men aroused the wrath of that powerful member of the New South Wales swimming authorities Rose Scott, who had extremely firm ideas on how young women should behave in public. (Rose was a strange mixture of prudery and fiery feminism, as related in the story of Louisa Lawson.) Rose Scott saw sexual danger in mixed bathing and on several occasions publicly denounced girls for swimming in the presence of males. Scott prudishly complained that 'any girl ... exposing herself at public swimming carnivals was liable to have her modesty (i.e. her marriage prospects) hopelessly blighted'. Scott's reactionary opinions were backed up by Catholic Archbishop Kelly, who told the press that mixed bathing was offensive and promiscuous and could undermine the fabric of society. The Archbishop denounced in the Sydney papers

> the indelicacies of the so-called up-to-date woman, who moves like a man and has no proper sense of decency ... mixed bathing in pools and on the beach is destructive of that modesty which is one of the pillars of Australian society.

Fortunately for Fanny, the Mayor of Randwick, Maxwell Cooper, defied the Archbishop. The Mayor declared that swimming was a coming sport; furthermore, the beauty of the female form had appealed to the world's great painters and sculptors and should not shock Australians.

Although from a Catholic background, Fanny ignored the grim warnings of both Rose Scott and the Archbishop. To her, marriage seemed light years away. All she dreamed of was swimming for Australia in the Olympics. She wanted to follow in the footsteps of the male athletes with whom she trained in Sydney Harbour – although at this time, entering the Olympics seemed a highly unlikely ambition for any young woman, however talented.

In 1894, Baron Pierre de Coubertin, who was responsible for reviving the ancient Greek formula of the Olympic Games, was voted President of the World Olympic Federation. The Baron, like many other swimming authorities down the ages (including those who penalised Australian champion Dawn Fraser), was a reactionary. He stuck to the formula of the Greeks, who had never allowed women, on pain of death, to compete in or even to watch the Olympics. The Baron drew the line at putting women to death for watching, but he detested the idea of seeing them competing and perspiring in public, and forbade women to take part.

Baron de Coubertin saw 'his' revival of the Olympic Games as a masculine celebration of virile sports. Every athlete had to be an amateur, scorning all monetary reward: otherwise they would be termed professional and unable to compete. For years he refused to listen to protests that women (and blacks, as he called them) should be allowed to compete. His first revival of the Games took place in 1896, at Athens with exclusively male Caucasian athletes competing.

By 1904, at the St Louis Olympics, the American Committee insisted that eight female archers should be allowed to compete, provided they wore long skirts and blouses with long sleeves and high necks. The lady archers proved a star attraction: they behaved demurely and managed not to offend anyone. Women were seen as lending grace and interest to the spectacle.

The 1908 Olympics were held in London. 'Lady' athletes were now allowed to participate in gymnastic displays as well as figure-skating and tennis. They had to be sedate, graceful and chaperoned at all times. Their participation and the interest they aroused among spectators were important in allowing women to participate in spectator sports.

But competitive swimming for women was still not accepted. Australia's first female champion, Annette Kellerman, born in Marrickville, Sydney, in 1886, was never allowed to compete in the Olympics. She had originally learned to swim because it was thought the exercise would strengthen her leg muscles, wasted by a disease which may have been infantile paralysis. She went on to become a champion swimmer years before Fanny Durack.

Annette's father was a German musician who spent long periods out of work. Annette felt she *had* to make money to support her mother and sisters, and became a professional long-distance swimmer. Funded by various newspapers, she broke all previous long-distance records by swimming down the River Thames and along the Danube. In 1907, accompanied by her German-born father, Annette attempted a long-distance swim in America wearing a less constricting boy's costume, a one-piece design in black wool which covered the entire body and had short legs. It lacked the constricting sleeves and bloomers of women's bathing dresses. She was arrested for 'indecent exposure' on a Boston beach.

Kellerman had no money to pay a lawyer, but she defended herself in court by protesting that attempting to break swimming records in a regulation women's costume equipped with sleeves and heavy bloomers was 'like swimming in a ball gown'. The judge proved understanding and dismissed the case.

Overnight, Annette Kellerman became a sensation. She had struck a blow for women in every sport, and one that would change the future of women's swimming.[6] She had made history.

Annette's photograph was splashed across the newspapers worldwide. Spotted by a Hollywood producer, she became a star of silent movies such as the very popular *Neptune's Daughter* (1914) and *Daughter of the Gods* (1919). In one film the courageous Annette had to dive into a tank full of alligators. She succeeded in coming out alive but this daring feat gave her nightmares for many years. However, by now, she was adored by millions of fans in America and Europe.

Her movie career ended with the advent of talking films. She then went into vaudeville and became a music hall star, singing in five languages. She returned to Australia, then lived for a time in Britain, where she wrote a children's book, *Fairy Tales of the South Seas,* for her Australian nieces.[7] Annette and her American husband, James Sullivan, lived in California. When widowed, she retired to Australia and settled in Queensland.

Annette died on the Gold Coast in 1975. In accordance with her wishes, her ashes were scattered close to the Great Barrier Reef. 'Neptune's daughter' had returned to the sea.

Annette Kellerman's courageous stand against ridiculous rules for women swimmers would be an encouragement to young Fanny Durack in her endeavours to obtain better treatment from domineering sports officials.

In 1912, five years after Kellerman had appeared in public in her boy's one-piece swimming costume, the organisers of the Stockholm Olympic Games decided, against de Coubertin's express wishes but with approval from the International Olympic Committee, to include two swimming races and a diving contest for women. Baron de Coubertin was horrified but was outvoted by the rest of the Committee. This historic decision finally opened the way for women swimmers from Europe and America to compete against each other.

Ten thousand miles away in Australia, young Fanny was breaking records against other women, but to compete overseas she had to struggle against the prejudice of committee members of the New South Wales Ladies' Amateur Swimming Association, including the formidable Rose Scott. The Association strictly forbade female members to swim in competitions or swimming carnivals where men were present either as spectators or competitors. (Scott and her supporters feared men might catch a titillating glimpse of female thighs and ankles and become sexually aroused.[8])

By today's standards, Fanny's competition swimming costumes were modesty personified, made from coarse (and sometimes scratchy) black wool with cap sleeves, a round neckline and short legs, a little like Annette Kellerman's long-distance swimming costume. No one could accuse Fanny of immorality when wearing such a costume. But Rose Scott and her supporters were determined to enforce the rules.

There was a head-on collision. Fanny and *her* supporters realised something had to be done to change public opinion: they wrote letters to members of the Association demanding a change in the rules. A public debate ensued in swimming clubs around Australia. Challenged, the New South Wales Ladies' Amateur Swimming Association reluctantly reversed its ruling against mixed competitions.

This landmark decision meant that Fanny Durack, and eventually her friend Mina Wylie, could be the first Australian women swimmers to represent their country at the Olympics. But although in theory women swimmers could compete, no money was provided to pay their fares and expenses.

Male officials organising Australia's team of swimmers to compete in the 1912 Olympics in Sweden agreed with the ultra-conservative members of the Ladies' Swimming Association that women should not compete. But the men had totally different reasons for their stance. They wanted all the available funding in order to get to the Olympics themselves. They felt threatened by the idea of women competing and raised all the old objections that 'nice' girls swam only for pleasure, not to compete: competition swimming was and should remain an exclusively male sport.

When the names of the five men chosen to represent Australia at the Stockholm Olympics were announced, a furore erupted. Fanny Durack and Mina Wylie had been excluded. Not one single official sporting body would put up money to pay for them to go to Sweden.

Women from all over Australia deluged Australia's Olympic officials with letters of protest. Women's organisations and swimming clubs organised petitions and rallies. Fanny's lack of sponsorship and chances of success were hotly debated in the newspapers. But there was still not enough money to pay her fare and her chances of competing seemed slim indeed.

Then, totally unexpectedly, Fanny had a stroke of luck. Her cause was championed by a family friend, Margaret McIntosh, the Irish-born wife of Hugh McIntosh, a former pub owner who was now a major sporting and theatrical entrepreneur. Hugh McIntosh had excellent 'political' connections and his wife used them to open a public fund to help Fanny to travel to the Olympics and to pay the expenses of her sister to accompany her as chaperone. (Provision of a chaperone was insisted on by the Olympic Committee; at this period 'nice girls' did not travel alone.)

The popular press championed Fanny's cause and she became famous Australia-wide. Thousands of warm-hearted, generous Australians (including customers at Tommy Durack's pub) passed around the hat to send Fanny to the Olympics. Cheques and money orders poured into newspaper offices from all over the country.[9] Only the men's swimming associations refused to make any contribution whatsoever to Fanny's costs.[10]

The New South Wales Ladies' Swimming Association made a last-ditch stand and queried the costs of sending a woman to compete in only one event, but it was hopelessly outvoted, and so Fanny was officially allowed to represent her country with their reluctant blessing. But even after such an outcry in the press, no official help was given to Fanny. It was ordinary Australians who raised the money to send Fanny, and her sister, to Stockholm as Australia's first female Olympic swimmer.

To Fanny the fact that she was actually off to the Olympics seemed like a dream. She and her sister boarded the gleaming ocean-going liner at Circular Quay in a fever of excitement. As they leaned over the rail coloured paper streamers were thrown to the ship by well-wishers: a local brass band serenaded Fanny as the ship slowly moved from her moorings and steamed away through the Heads.

This was Fanny's first visit abroad, her passport to adventure, fame and self-discovery. She enjoyed every moment of the voyage while training hard in the ship's pool every day. When the Durack girls arrived in the port of London they transferred to another ship bound for Sweden.

Totally unexpectedly, three weeks after Fanny had sailed from Sydney, the Australian Olympic Committee suddenly changed their minds and allowed Mina Wylie, who was only fifteen, to follow Fanny to Stockholm. Mina's father was to act as official coach to the two inexperienced girls who formed Australia's Olympic Ladies' Swimming Team.

Fanny and Mina met up in Stockholm. They had been provided with uniforms – green swimming caps, green woollen swimming costumes with short sleeves and legs and long green cloaks to cover their legs and bodies. The Olympics took place in a seawater pool on Stockholm Harbour. The world male swimming record for the 100 yards then stood at 1 minute 26 seconds: Fanny and Mina were determined to break it. With the eyes of the Australian press upon them they were both scared, knowing they had to do battle for Australia against the world's best female swimmers.

Fanny and Mina found the water in Stockholm Harbour far colder than that in Sydney. They were dismayed when they were only permitted to train for half a mile a day in the Olympic Pool.[11] They requested permission to enter the relay race, each girl volunteering to swim two laps instead of the standard one lap. Fanny began to develop a hatred for organisers when their request was brusquely refused.

In Stockholm the two Australians found themselves competing against girls with rich indulgent parents who had trained in luxurious heated pools and spent their lives being driven around by chauffeurs. Yet all that swank and swagger counted for nothing when the starter's pistol went off.

Fanny Durack, the battling publican's daughter, broke the Olympic male swimming record on that eventful day in July 1912, and it made her world-famous. In her first heat she recorded a time of 1 minute 20.2 seconds, winning against the more experienced British champion, Daisy Curwen. For the finals Fanny and Mina lined up against a German and two other English champions, Daisy Curwen having withdrawn through indisposition.

The atmosphere was tense with excitement. An Australian reporter at the scene recorded:

> All competitors present got away to a good start. Miss Durack at once went to the front. At fifty yards, she was leading by three yards from

11

the English and German girls, who were neck and neck with Mina in the rear. Durack swam into the side of the pool, recovered and using a beautiful Australian crawl won by four yards in the excellent time of 1 minute 22.2 seconds.[12]

At twenty-three, Fanny had won the world's first Olympic Gold presented to a woman swimmer. The press acclaimed her as the world's greatest woman swimmer. Mina came in second, passing the English and German girls at the 80-yard mark and winning a silver medal. Fanny chose a long white dress and a flower-trimmed hat to accept her medal from King Gustav of Sweden and the press was allowed to take photos of her in her Olympic regulation swimming costume.

There was national hysteria in Australia when it was announced that the first gold and silver Olympic medals for women's swimming had both been won by Australians. Fanny had clipped four seconds off the previous world record held by a man. By modern standards the girls' world records were slow, but in 1912 they were something to boast about.

Six days after Fanny won her gold medal, at the request of Olympic officials she gave a solo exhibition of the Australian crawl and set another world record of 4 minutes 43.6 seconds for 300 yards. Australia's Gold and Silver Girls were then invited to tour Europe and give swimming exhibitions. In the process, Fanny once more broke her own record for the 100 yards. The two girls, still accompanied by Fanny's sister as chaperone and with Mina's father as their trainer, returned home to more brass bands and speeches and still more exhibition swims.

Her time overseas had changed Fanny. She had now seen how other people lived. Although not well educated, she was quick and intelligent. She realised that Australia was antiquated and narrow-minded in its ultra-conservative views: one of the few modern nations to have an irrational fear of mixed bathing. Fanny spoke out against the practice of segregated bathing both in public and private. Her frankness won her powerful enemies who feared 'contamination for the Australian way of life from overseas'. Fanny was told in no uncertain terms by her critics that things went on overseas that 'very properly should not be allowed in Australia'.[13]

Such was the level of public interest in Fanny Durack that additional women's events in swimming were scheduled for the next

Olympics, to be held in 1916. Newspapers boasted how Fanny would win even more medals. But before Fanny and Mina could exploit their remarkable talents in the next Olympics, World War I broke out.

'The lamps are going out all over Europe', proclaimed Britain's Foreign Minister, Sir Edward Grey. He was right.

The war against Germany and her allies meant Fanny and Mina gave up all hope of more travel and international stardom for the duration of a war which shook Western Europe to its foundations.

But in those war years 1915 to 1918, Fanny broke twelve world records over distances varying from 100 yards to 1 mile, swimming in Sydney pools. Mina partnered her, pacing her friend closely.

When the Germans surrendered and the war finally ended, the next Olympic Games were planned for Antwerp in 1920. Once again Fanny and Mina hoped to challenge the women swimmers of the world and bring back gold to Australia.

The Americans were quick to respond to the challenge. This caused some surprise in swimming circles; up to that time the Americans had produced no major female swimming stars of their own.

In 1918 Fanny and Mina, the two super-girls of Australian swimming, were dispatched to America with an Australian manager to swim for their country. Things did not go as planned with this tour. Through some curious oversight, the officials of the Australian Swimming Union had failed to complete the necessary entry papers and the Australian girls suffered the mortification of being banned from entering competitions which they knew they could easily have won.

Another point raised against them was the fact that while Fanny and Mina were unpaid and had amateur swimming status, Mina's father, as their manager and trainer, was paid for his time and effort. The critics implied that he was acting in a professional capacity. The Americans, eager to get rid of foreign competition which threatened their own swimmers, claimed that if the Australian girls were associated with a professional, their amateur status was forfeited and they could not compete. So Fanny and Mina were forced to return home to Australia without even getting their costumes wet. Fiery Fanny neither forgave nor forgot.

On 12 August the following year, another pre-Olympic contest was arranged between Australian and American women swimmers in

Chicago. On that occasion the Australian girls triumphed with ease. Fanny won the 440 yards freestyle and Mina took the 100 yards breast-stroke championship. Back home their success was announced over the radio and in newspaper headlines. Australia celebrated and everybody awaited the next championships with confidence.

The American organisers were furious: every possible help had been lavished on their women's team, who were now using a new type of crawl. Fanny was fascinated by this American crawl with its faster leg beat and wanted to have an opportunity to practise it in private – she hoped to be able to use this stroke in their second contest in New York. But the American organisers gave her no opportunity. For five days Fanny and Mina were forced to attend a series of swimming galas and boring official dinners, and were driven long distances to make exhibition swims at various clubs. When they protested to the American race organisers that they were being asked to perform in public too often, when all they wanted was time to practise for their Olympic events, no one would listen.

The second American-Australian contest took place on 17 August 1919 in New York. Once again the race organisers found many reasons why Fanny and Mina's practice time in the pool had to be curtailed. Fanny began to scent a plot. She was worried and slept badly. Worn out by travelling and confrontation, she did not swim her best and failed to win.

The results reached Australia by cable.[14] Readers learned that their very own 'unbeatable' Fanny Durack had only managed third place in the 100 yards. The Americans were jubilant. They boasted that their girls had established superiority over the Australian Olympic stars. American swimming officials decided to capitalise on the mood of national jubilation by announcing a third swimming contest, to take place at a special meeting scheduled in Philadelphia for 30 August 1919.

By now Fanny and Mina were thoroughly unhappy with the organisation of their visit. At Philadelphia they still were not allowed sufficient time to train in the Olympic-size pool. The administrators who controlled Philadelphia's sporting events were powerful, wealthy businessmen intent on their own glorification through sport. They were totally uninterested in the complaints of two 'difficult' young women from the other side of the world. Mina was still in her teens, unsure of herself and a more pliant character than Fanny, who loathed pompous officials and decided it was high time to teach the hostile American organisers a lesson in fair play.

As soon as the Australian swimmers arrived at the pool, Fanny coolly announced that as an amateur she would not be taking orders from anyone. She declared that she had not been given time to train properly for the race.

'I'm not going to swim,' she said firmly.

A furious American organiser towered over her. 'Listen, sweetheart', he shouted, 'You get right out there and swim ... or pay your *own* expenses to get home'.

Fanny glared at him. She had already formulated a plan to make the organiser look foolish, but wisely did not say a word. The stadium was crowded with excited spectators and press. A lesser woman would have been daunted ... but not Fanny.

At the start of the race Fanny removed her green cloak, threw it down and stood demurely on the blocks with the other competitors, awaiting the starting gun. Just before the gun went off, Fanny dived into the pool, took off in a whirl of threshing arms and legs, reached the steps halfway down the pool and climbed out.

Flash bulbs flared and cameras clicked as angry race officials surrounded the Australian girl in her green costume, her long hair streaming around her. Fanny kept cool. She waited till the hubbub died away and said laconically, 'Well, I got in there and swam, didn't I? What more do you want? Now I'm going home to Australia.'

Fanny won her battle. The rest of her tour was cancelled by furious officials. A defiant Fanny was shipped back to Australia entirely at the expense of the American Swimming Federation.

On her return the Australian press insisted Fanny was still the greatest swimmer in the world. Had she not broken over twelve records? The American press picked up the story and retaliated that she was not. Everyone in swimming knew the real test would come at the next Olympics, to be held the following year in Antwerp.

Fanny was determined to show her superiority over the American girls. She trained almost non-stop, swimming miles every day in Sydney Harbour as well as her marathon running sessions and physical training in the gym. She had always had a typical Australian laconic sense of humour. She laughed and joked with the press who came to interview her and watch her training sessions telling them that by now she had swum the equivalent of the entire circumference of the earth.

Australians were convinced she would succeed. But only a week before her boat was due to sail for Europe, Fanny developed severe pain in her left side. She was rushed to hospital. The surgeon who operated found that her appendix had burst. Fanny developed post-operative complications. With her resistance lowered, she caught pneumonia, followed by typhoid fever. It was the end of her dreams of further Olympic glory.

To add to her misery, an American swimmer at the Antwerp Olympics, Ethelda Bleibtrey, won the Women's 100 and 300 yards races, beating Fanny's previous world records.

At thirty-one, Fanny realised that she could not hope to maintain her form for another four years until the 1924 Paris Olympics. Sorrowfully she retired from competitive swimming.

Shortly after she reached her decision, she accepted a proposal of marriage from a family friend, Bernard Martin Gately, a horse trainer. They were married at St Mary's Cathedral in Sydney. Crowds lined the route to cheer Fanny. The marriage was a happy one, although Gately was not a very successful horse trainer – so in addition to his activities as a trainer, Fanny and her husband ran a pub together. In her spare time Fanny still swam for pleasure and devoted herself to coaching deprived and gifted children in championship swimming. Her sorrow was that she and Bernard never had children.

Bernard Gately died in 1942, and as a way of conquering her grief, Fanny threw herself into organising her favourite sport. Ironically, she became one of the sporting administrators she had once fought so vigorously. She was appointed a life member of the New South Wales Women's Amateur Swimming Association.

Pubs were the only thing Fanny knew apart from swimming. So, like Dawn Fraser, that equally famous and controversial Olympic swimmer, she became sole licensee of the Newmarket Hotel, Elizabeth Street, in the centre of Sydney.

In 1955 it was announced that the following year, Fanny Durack would attend the Melbourne Olympics as an official guest and a race official in the swimming events. But Fanny was taken into hospital for an operation where it was revealed she had cancer. There was no further treatment the doctors could give her. She accepted that her days were numbered with her customary spirit, and continued her daily swims and her coaching sessions with small children. Brave and determined as ever, Fanny announced she would attend the Melbourne Olympic Games even if she had to hire an ambulance to take her there.

She never got the chance. Fanny Durack, game to the last, died during the night of 20 March 1956. Her funeral took place at St Michael's in Stanmore, Sydney. Champions from every era of Australian swimming attended along with the public who had loved and admired Fanny Durack. She was buried at Waverley Cemetery.

Nearly twenty years later, Fanny's old enemies, the American Swimming Association, archived her swimming triumphs for posterity in the International Swimming Hall of Fame at Fort Lauderdale, Florida, and placed a photograph of her on display beside one of Annette Kellerman.

Fanny and Annette represent the archetypal Aussie battler, embodying virtues that Australians hold dear: a strong sense of fair play, courage, determination, a laconic sense of humour and the ability to make the best of life. Every woman in sport today should be proud of these outstanding women.

CHAPTER TWO

Portrait photograph: National Library of Australia, Canberra.

Louisa Lawson
(1848–1920)

Mary Gilmore
(1865–1962)

POETS AND JOURNALISTS WHO CHAMPIONED
THE RIGHTS OF WOMEN AND THE DISADVANTAGED

Louisa Lawson and Mary Gilmore had a great deal in common: they both tried to improve the lot of women, the poor and the disadvantaged. They both experienced unsatisfactory marriages. Yet what started out as friendship between an older writer and a younger one (Mary was seventeen years younger than Louisa) turned into mutual loathing and a bitter feud. As Louisa Lawson's star waned, that of Mary Gilmore ascended. Louisa Lawson went to a pauper's grave, unmourned and friendless: four decades later Mary Gilmore, having achieved literary fame, would be mourned by hundreds and given a State funeral.

Louisa was born into rural poverty. Her father, Henry Albury, attempted various occupations without success before running a shanty pub. Her mother, Harriet, English-born daughter of a Methodist minister, was embittered by her husband's financial failures. She insisted on removing Louisa from school at thirteen, even though the young girl always had her head in a book and dreamed of becoming a teacher. Louisa would always yearn after the literary glory she never achieved.

Both women had tough bush childhoods which formed their characters. Mary Ann Cameron was born in a slab hut near Goulburn belonging to her maternal grandfather. Her first years were spent surrounded by gum trees and wattles; she would love the land with a passion all her life. She came from a long line of clever, talented Orangemen and Scottish crofters. Her father eventually became a building contractor and travelled all over outback New South Wales and southern Queensland in search of work.[1] Sitting beside him on the horse-drawn wagon, or on the front of his saddle as he rode, at the age of five, Mary learned at first-hand about the hardships endured by settlers, drovers and teamsters, and their ruthlessness towards the Aborigines, with whom she sometimes played. (Her father became a 'blood brother' of the Waradgery tribe). During her childhood, Mary absorbed a store of experiences which would surface decades later in her book *Old Days, Old Ways*, in which she wrote about rural povety, families whose children lived on damper and treacle and the odd roast possum leg, and the hardships of the bush.

Unlike Louisa Albury's poverty-stricken family in which no one valued education, Mary Cameron's father encouraged her to read and to become a pupil-teacher in a tiny bush school at Cootamundra, run by one of her uncles. By the age of twelve, she was fluent in ancient Greek and Latin.

Louisa Albury, also highly intelligent, did not study Greek but was taught at school to appreciate and write poetry. She too wanted to become a pupil-teacher, but instead she had to leave school at thirteen. Although her father was practically illiterate, he had a tremendous gift for storytelling which both Louisa and her eldest son would inherit.

Louisa shared Mary's sympathy for the poor and disadvantaged: like Mary, she had lived among them. Louisa was the eldest daughter in a family of nine surviving children. While Mary's mother encouraged her daughter to read and study, Harriet Albury bitterly resented her eldest daughter's love of learning and her passion for poetry. She burned her daughter's first poems as well as some of her favourite books. Louisa never forgave her. Her mother also deplored what she regarded as Louisa's radical ideas, and forced her to look after her younger siblings and do housework.

Louisa's father, basically a kind man, had a weakness for alcohol. Like Mary Cameron's father he became a small-time builder but failed dismally. After his only horse broke its neck pulling an overloaded cart across a creek, Henry Albury consoled himself with drink. Too poor to buy another horse, he stopped working altogether. There was no unemployment benefit, and Louisa and her siblings were reduced to begging or fossicking the local mullock heaps for specks of gold, until finally her father opened a shanty pub.

Surrounded by insecurity, stress and poverty, Louisa and her mother argued constantly. Domestic service in the city would have presented one avenue of escape for Louisa, but her mother refused to let her seek work in the city. Louisa bitterly resented her life of drudgery; marriage to anyone at all was the only way left to escape from her nagging mother.

Henry Albury's general store and pub catered for rough, rowdy goldminers. To attract customers, her father encouraged Louisa, who had a fine voice, to sing in the bar. The miners enjoyed Louisa's singing and suggested that they should pass round the hat to collect money so that she could have her voice trained. But Louisa's mother also prevented her daughter from taking this opportunity to make something of her life.

Louisa's loveless marriage to a man with a lust for gold

Louisa's spirit was unquenchable: she dreamed of becoming a writer and being involved in the world of books. Her father's drinking bouts and her mother's nagging prompted her to seek escape by making a hasty marriage to a man obsessed by the idea of finding gold. At eighteen, Louisa was a relatively unsophisticated but attractive bush girl. After yet another row with her mother, Louisa was sitting crying in the bush when she was consoled by a sturdy bearded gold prospector named Niels Larsen. Larsen, born in Norway, was a sailor who had jumped ship in order to join the gold rush in Australia.

Niels was not Louisa's first suitor. Decades later, she would dedicate some beautiful poems on love and loss to a man she did not marry, for reasons which remain unclear. All we do know is that on 7 July 1866, tall, statuesque auburn-haired Louisa walked to the Wesleyan church in Mudgee to marry a man almost twice her age whom she scarcely knew.[2] Niels Larsen was kind-hearted and generous, but if his temper was roused and he had been drinking, he could become physically violent, something Louisa failed to realise when she accepted his proposal. Niels Larsen's lack of education was in sharp contrast to Louisa's hopes for a career of her own. She married in haste and repented at leisure – although lack of money would ensure she enjoyed little leisure for the rest of her life.

Accounts differ as to how Niels Larsen became 'Peter Lawson'. Either at their wedding or at her eldest son's christening, the officiating minister 'Australianised' his name.

Louisa joined her husband in his tent on the diggings. In spite of months of backbreaking labour he failed to find gold. Soon Louisa, to her dismay, found she was pregnant. They had no income, no savings, no furniture and not enough money to pay for a doctor to deliver her baby.

Legend has it that Louisa's first son, the future poet Henry Lawson, was born in a tent on the Grenfell goldfields. The birth was difficult. Louisa had post-natal complications known then as 'milk fever', which made breast-feeding extremely painful.[3] Bringing up a baby in a tent in the muddy goldfields, having to cart all drinking and washing water by hand from the nearest creek and boil it, and having little money for food proved stressful and exhausting for Louisa.

The Lawsons and their baby son moved from goldfield to goldfield living in various squalid, fly-ridden, cockroach-infested slab huts and shanties, blazing hot in summer, and cold in winter, when the wind blew in gusts through the gaps between the roughly cut slabs. Meanwhile, Peter Lawson's constant search for gold yielded virtually nothing.

When Louisa fell pregnant once more Peter Lawson finally listened to his wife's pleas and became a selector, buying a small block of land on a low-interest mortgage. Lacking any capital, the Lawsons had no choice but to take whatever land was allotted to them, however harsh. Wealthy squatters had usually tied up all the best land and the waterholes. Louisa exchanged life in a tent for life in what was virtually a shack, surrounded by rural squalor and poverty on forty acres at Eurunderee, near Mudgee (then known as New Pipeclay). Louisa's husband chose this area because it was part of the goldfields; he hoped some small pocket of undiscovered gold might remain on this scarred land, pitted with trenches from previous mining. Most of the trees had been cut down to build pit props and shafts. Their little wooden house had a dirt floor, and no piped water or sanitation. Louisa cooked over a wood stove which provided heating in winter. Their furniture was made from packing crates; their diet consisted of bread and dripping, treacle and salt beef.

Louisa, like all women of this period, which viewed women's role as bearing child after child, lacked access to reliable contraceptive advice. All she had were old wives' remedies which failed. Under these extremely squalid living conditions she soon bore her husband two more sons.

Her third pregnancy and birth proved difficult and dangerous. For months after her child was born she could not sleep at night, dozing off for only short periods, and had no desire to eat. Almost anorexic, trying unsuccessfully to breastfeed, the normally hardworking Louisa would sit motionless for hours on end, crying to herself and rocking backwards and forwards while baby Peter howled and Charlie and Henry fended for themselves. This period of mute inactivity exasperated her husband. At that time no one knew anything about the dangerous and distressing hormonal disturbance we now call postnatal depression. There were no antidepressant drugs to treat Louisa's condition. Some women who suffered from it would fill their pockets with stones and jump into the dam, but Louisa resisted the temptation to commit suicide. Still devout and religious, she found comfort in prayer. As her sons grew older and were less work, she recovered – but throughout her life bouts of depressive illness would recurr when she was under extreme stress, and her postnatal depressions coloured her view of sex and child-rearing.

She was now able to take over the running of the property again and drive their horses into town to buy provisions. Horses held no fear for her: on one occasion she halted and subdued a team of bolting horses, an incident Henry Lawson would later recount in a short story.

Peter Lawson spent a great deal of time away from home, chasing his dream of finding gold, which for him was a true gambling addiction. It finally became obvious that the proceeds from farming their small selection were as negligible as those from his gold-prospecting, and Peter decided to work with Louisa's father as an unskilled 'humpy' builder. Lacking any transport he had to walk to distant building sites and camp there overnight. This meant that most of the farm work was thrown onto Louisa's shoulders.

When he did return home, Peter worked hard on digging the unyielding soil of their selection and over the course of a year constructed a large dam. To earn more money Louisa took in sewing in addition to looking after the children, cleaning the house, cooking the meals and doing the washing. She also milked the cows night and morning, sold milk and butter, helped to harvest hay and fattened the calves, bottle-feeding those that were sickly. The strain of hard physical work and the constant money worries took their toll in blinding headaches and renewed attacks of depression.[4] Her only escape lay in writing poetry and reading favourite poems aloud from her old schoolbooks.

Louisa did not want any more children until they could afford to rear them. At that time a husband 'owned' his wife's body; she could not by law deny him 'conjugal rights'. The only form of contraception available to Louisa was *coitus interruptus*.[5] She was soon pregnant once again, following physical violence when she had sought to resist her husband. In later life she would describe married bedrooms as 'chambers of horror'. The same sad drama was played out all over the bush by women reluctant to bear children and their husbands: at this time many bush women commonly bore six to sixteen children, many of whom died young.

After another difficult pregnancy, Louisa gave birth to twins, Gertrude and Annette. The Lawson babies became the marvel of the district, the first twins to be born in Eurunderee. Annette was fair, plump and placid; Gertrude dark, bad-tempered and grizzly. Louisa adored Annette and called her 'a golden child'.

One day in January 1878, while Peter was away from home, Annette ran a high fever. Louisa harnessed the horses and drove her fretful baby to the hospital at Mudgee where she had given birth to the twins. Sick with terror, she waited in the passage outside the ward until the nurses told her there was nothing more they could do. Annette, her 'golden child' was dead. Another depression followed; once more Louisa could neither sleep nor eat. It was feared that she might die. Her mother was summoned and reluctantly arrived to care for the three boys and little Gertrude. The only advice Louisa received was provided by her unsympathetic mother, who told her it was high time she 'pulled herself together'.

Louisa turned to writing poems to relieve her misery. She sat at the rickety table and wrote a moving poem, 'My Nettie', dedicated to the memory of Annette. It was later published in the Mudgee *Independent*. Other poems followed, including 'Mary! Pity Women', describing a mother's desperate journey on foot with a sick baby to a doctor, in which the baby dies en route. These were followed by other verses about lonely, depressed bushwomen, based on her own experiences.

Louisa had a talent for writing poetry but she was a working-class woman who had been denied education: she would never have the time or leisure to develop her talent to its full extent. In spite of their back-breaking years of toil and drudgery, Peter and Louisa Lawson never managed to achieve even a modicum of financial security. It was a fate from which Louisa attempted to escape in vain.

When Henry was eight, Louisa realised he was exceptionally talented and sensitive, a child apart. She was desperate that somehow Henry should receive the education she had been denied and a chance to escape rural poverty. The nearest bush school was over five kilometres away; Henry was a sickly child and she feared he could not manage the walk. Louisa campaigned fiercely for a school to be built in their own area, but as she was 'only a woman' she was not allowed to enter a public meeting about it, although *she* had organised it. She was told that the subject of a school could only be discussed by men, and was forced to stand outside the hall and attempt to hear her own arguments poorly presented to the meeting by her husband. This experience taught Louisa a lesson about women's lack of power she would never forget.

Eventually the campaign she had originated did succeed and a tiny bush school opened at Eurunderee. Henry was one of the first pupils, but at the age of nine he suffered an unknown fever which left him near death, and caused him to miss a great deal of schooling. By the time he turned fourteen he had suffered major hearing loss. A diffident and withdrawn boy, he aimed to become a writer. Louisa encouraged him and gave him what little extra schooling she could.

Her second child, Charlie, had severe personality problems and a terrible temper. His aggression and bad behaviour at school caused his father to beat him so severely that he nearly killed his son – whereupon Charles ran away to live with his maternal grandmother. He turned into a teenage hoodlum in trouble with the law. Young Peter was a gentle, musical boy, somewhat withdrawn. Gertrude's black moods and explosive temper were perhaps inherited from Louisa's mother.

Now thirty, Louisa was desperate to avoid having more children. The arguments and violent episodes when she refused to have sexual relations with her husband continued. Years later she would write with deep feeling about women subjected to domestic violence and advise them to gain some form of financial independence through paid work.[6]

Peter Lawson, equally desperate to escape the hard life of a small farmer, still frequently left home to search for gold. Years later, Henry Lawson's stories would describe incidents based on his mother's exploits when she was left to run the selection alone. In one story a woman single-handedly extinguishes a bushfire and saves her wooden home. In another the wife tries to prevent their dam bursting. Henry described how the bush wife stood 'for hours in the drenching downpour' and dug an overflow gutter to save the dam, hurting her back. It was all in vain: the next morning the dam was broken. The wife thought how her husband would feel when he came home and saw the result of years of work swept away overnight, the ruin of their hopes, and she broke down and cried. In other stories, Henry describes how a woman left to cope alone 'fought' crows and eagles that wanted to carry away her chicks by aiming a broomstick at the birds and screaming to frighten them off. On another occasion the woman in his story protects her children from a mad bull by shooting him through a crack in their slab hut. The bush wife then skins the bull and sells the hide to a dealer. Henry Lawson described how his mother 'fought pleuro-pneumonia – dosed and bled the few remaining cattle and wept again when the two best cows she had reared from birth died'.

The problems between Louisa and her husband worsened and badly affected young Henry, who was old enough to feel the resentment between them. Henry was fascinated by the ethos of 'mateship' in the bush and usually sided with his father, although it was his mother who encouraged his literary talents. Louisa was convinced that Henry would become a writer of great power and originality. (In later life, embittered against Louisa after he had left his own wife and children and become an alcoholic, Henry would refuse to acknowledge her influence in his writing.')

Louisa and her husband parted company after her husband took on a building contract in the Blue Mountains, together with a partner. Although the farm still did not pay, Louisa was not yet prepared to walk away from it after all the backbreaking work they had put into their 'selection'. The children now needed less supervision: she felt she had the time and energy to earn extra money. One of the few opportunities of employment open to women without much education was offered through the rural post offices. Louisa became a country postmistress and ran a small general store. Discrimination against women in the workplace meant that she had to obtain the licence to run the post office in her husband's name rather than her own. Now she found herself working double time. She still had domestic duties, responsibility for her children, Henry, Gertrude and Peter, farm chores, a vegetable garden to maintain and all the accounts to pay.

After a couple of years of this drudgery, to Louisa's dismay she found that in spite of all her additional work, she and her children were still living in poverty. Then a long drought set in. Their selection gradually turned into a dustbowl. Reduced to skin and bone, their cattle stood around the homestead lowing pitifully. Lacking money to pay for agistment, there was nothing Louisa could do to save the poor beasts. As henry later described, she had to watch the calves she had raised to maturity die a painful death.

It was the end of her dream of independence. Her husband, with whom she kept in contact, viewed her intending departure from the property with relief and promised financial support if she and the children sold up and moved to the city. They could not sell out. In 1882 Louisa, now thirty-five, walked off the selection empty-handed and moved herself and the children – Henry, Peter and Gertrude – together with their few sticks of furniture to Sydney, renting a house close to Circular Quay. She had nothing to lose and a specific goal: to make life easier for her children than it had been for her.

Life in The Rocks, Sydney

Louisa has left us no descriptions of The Rocks and Circular Quay but Mary Cameron, arriving there about the same time to take up a teaching post, described the Quay as: 'full of masts as a pincushion is of pins. The sky was pierced to heaven with masts.'

In the days when Mary and Louisa made their separate ways to Sydney from the bush The Rocks area was a slum, a far cry from the up-market tourist area of today. In their day sewers overflowed into the gutters, rats abounded, prostitutes lingered on street corners and pale-faced women worked over their sewing machines as 'sweated labour' to feed fatherless children.

Louisa knew all about rural poverty; she now experienced at first-hand the grinding hopelessness of the inner-city poor. Both Louisa and the sensitive, talented Henry, who shared his mother's left-wing views, were distressed by the numerous derelicts and alcoholics they saw. In those days there was no supporting mother's benefit. Her husband only sent maintenance money sporadically. Louisa made and remade their clothes, and they lived on bread and dripping, bread and jam and black tea.

Henry was not cut out for office work. He was hopeless at bookkeeping and other administrative duties. Writing for a living was insecure and poorly paid, so out of the question. Finally he took up work as a coach painter, and, urged on by Louisa, attended night classes to obtain his matriculation. But his workmates teased him about his deafness and he failed his matriculation examination. His frustrating deafness made Henry even more shy and reserved than he was already.[8] After work he took to drinking alone in dockside pubs and hotels.

The indefatigable Louisa decided to try to make money by running a lodging house. Once again they packed up their few possessions and moved to a larger house in Enmore Road, Marrickville, where she rented out rooms. Peter Lawson's financial contributions became less and less frequent, and Louisa considered taking legal action against him.[9] But lawyers were expensive; instead she began to take in washing and sewing as well as lodgers. To spare her children pain, she kept up a pretence of being separated from her husband by misfortune. But in truth the marriage was over.[10]

In 1887, Louisa was so worried by Henry's drinking bouts and subsequent fits of depression that she used money she had managed to scrape together from her lodging house to buy a share in a small left-wing monthly news-sheet, *The Republican*. It was owned by William Keating, one of Henry's left-wing radical friends. Louisa hoped to train Henry to become the magazine's editor.

Just as Mary Cameron (later Gilmore) would throw her energies left over from teaching into writing for the newspapers, so Louisa now threw herself heart and soul into publishing *The Republican*, as though to make up for all the lost, lonely and embittered years that lay behind her. Determined that women should have a voice in an all-male world, she and Henry together wrote and edited the struggling political news-sheet under the pseudonym 'Archie Lawson'.

Louisa was a quick learner. She soon realised that while *The Republican* was too radical to pay its way, the 'hole in the market' was for a paper designed for women. She saw clearly that with hard work such a newspaper could make a profit and inspire other women to escape unhappy marriages and seek financial independence. She approached potential advertisers and sold some space: soon she was in business – Australia's first female publisher. Symbolically, she called her newspaper *The Dawn*. The cover featured a young woman blowing her own trumpet.[11]

On 15 May 1888, Louisa produced the first issue of this historic paper designed specifically for women and staffed by women. She was both publisher and editor. Henry was now often away working with his father. Using the ground floor of 138 Phillip Street as a combined office and printery, she worked long hours. Once Louisa took over the printery, she replaced the male staff with women, who she felt would work harder and appreciate their jobs.[12]

Bearing in mind the difficulties women encountered in business, she used a fictitious name as editor, calling herself 'Dora Falconer'. This lasted until January 1891, when she felt confident enough to use her own name.

When Henry returned from working with his father in the Blue Mountains, he helped to produce *The Dawn*. After a hard day's work Louisa would go out to dinner with her female staff, leaving Henry to turn the handle of the press with a faraway look in his eyes as he composed poetry in his head.[13]

Louisa was creative and hardworking. But it now became apparent that like many creative people, she suffered from manic depressive illness. She alternated bouts of furious creativity with deep depression. She would work half the night to bring out her paper, and the following day, once it was mailed out to subscribers or on the news-stands, she would collapse with exhaustion, wondering if it had all been worthwhile. Depression would set in. Her daughter Gertrude tried to help her mother. She described how in these black periods Louisa would withdraw 'into herself' and refuse to speak or eat.

Louisa employed several experienced female typesetters on the paper. She campaigned tirelessly for women's rights at a time when they had very few. Most married women still surrendered any property or money they earned or inherited to their husbands (as the British Married Womens Property Act of 1875 was slow to take effect). Women could be divorced for lapses in fidelity (considered totally normal in a man) and children of the marriage were considered the property of the father if the mother defied society and requested a legal separation or divorce.

On New Year's Eve, 1888, shortly after she had started the paper, Peter Lawson, still working in the Blue Mountains, died. In his will he left his wife 1103 pounds, a considerable sum of money for that time. But to obtain her bequest, Louisa had to bring legal proceedings against her husband's business partner, which drained her funds and was stressful.

After she received the money, she improved her printing plant and moved to larger premises in Jamieson Street. She proved to be a shrewd businesswoman as well as a skilful editor. By the following year she was employing ten women working in shifts, including editors, printers, binders and unskilled hands. She also took in outside work on contract to keep her presses running constantly.[14] There was even a messenger girl rather than the usual messenger boy.

Women were delighted to see subjects that interested them in print; from its first issue *The Dawn, A Journal for Australian Women* was a success. The subscription price was three shillings per annum and it was also sold on news-stands. The magazine highlighted the achievements of women and their struggles to enter the workforce. Louisa had enough business sense to realise that a purely political journal would not survive. She wrote or commissioned feature articles on household management, cookery, fashion, gardening and farm work and included some literary criticism. Poetry was also featured (some written by Louisa) and short stories by both Louisa and Henry Lawson.

The Dawn was designed as a publication that women would keep for future reference, so Louisa insisted it was printed on high-quality paper.[15] Subscriptions were received from readers as far away as Longreach, Hobart and Darwin, from the Librarian of Sydney University and from wealthy women such as English-born Margaret Scarlett (who became Mrs Quong Tart, wife of the famous Chinese businessman and philanthropist), and from women physicians such as Dr Dagmar Berne (see Chapter 4) and Dr Ida Carlson.[16]

In *The Dawn*'s first year of publication a series of feature articles dealt with Sydney's destitute children, inequities facing women under marriage and property laws, the need for life insurance to protect families and the importance to women of the Divorce Extension Bill.

There were grave problems when Louisa's female employees sought admittance to the powerful all-male New South Wales Typographers' Union, which had previously refused to accept women as members. Men sacked by Louisa instigated a boycott, through the Trades and Labour Council, of all printing establishments employing women. They intended to punish her. In a clumsy attempt to force her to replace women with men, male union members picketed and harassed Louisa's female staff as they arrived and departed from the printing works. The union even appealed to the paper's advertisers to boycott her paper.

Louisa fought back like a lioness. One trade union official who visited the premises received similar treatment to the old bush remedy she had meted out to tramps who harassed her on her selection. The union man, who was wearing a smart pair of white flannel trousers, refused to leave the printery; he kept telling her how the union could close her down. Undaunted, she threatened to pour over him the contents of the sludge bucket, containing ink washed down from the printing presses. The union official realised he had met his match and departed.

In the October 1889 issue of *The Dawn* Louisa wrote a powerful leading article demolishing the arguments used to exclude women from Unions. She thought deeply about the problems facing working women and was one of the first to advocate provision of childcare facilities for overworked mothers of large families. Slowly she won her battle for survival in a man's world.

Articles in her magazine helped to raise money for Ragged Schools, designed expressly for poor children, for whom she organised collections of cast-off clothing. She became actively involved with campaigning for a refurbished tomb for Henry Kendall, her favourite poet, canvassing subscriptions from politicians such as Henry Parkes and from Lady Carrington, the Governor's wife. She raised enough money to buy an additional plot on which to build a much grander monument, but this was never used. What would now be termed 'the blue rinse set' took up Henry Kendall's cause as their own and Louisa was sidelined from their committee. This experience taught her a sharp lesson about colonial society and its class-ridden structure. She decided that never again would she work with middle-class 'do-gooders', but would run her own organisations. Louisa's strength lay in the fact she appealed to women of *all* backgrounds. No one could accuse her of being 'a rich do-gooder in a posh hat' (as working-class women dubbed some upper-crust suffrage committee members who advised them how to run their lives).

In May 1889, Louisa launched her campaign for votes for all women, rich and poor. She was not in favour of Australian women chaining themselves to railings, slashing paintings, destroying property or throwing themselves under racehorses, as Mrs Pankhurst's suffragettes in Britain had done. Instead, Louisa hoped Australian women would achieve their goal by peaceful means. She used her magazine to pioneer the Australian suffragist movement. Australian suffragists like Rose Scott ruthlessly tried to eclipse her influence by founding their own uppermiddle-class movement. However, Louisa Lawson, from a more humble background, was truly the 'founding mother' of the Votes for Women campaign in New South Wales, while Vida Goldstein was Louisa's equivalent in Victoria.

'Who ordained that men should make the laws which both men and women must obey?' became Louisa's rallying cry for women seeking the vote. That same year Louisa announced the formation of the Dawn Club, an organisation for women concerned with social reform. Quong Tart's English-born wife, a founder subscriber to *The Dawn*, [17] persuaded her wealthy husband of the rightness of the women's cause. Quong Tart kept his Pitt Street tearooms open in the evenings for the Dawn Club's monthly meetings.

Most of the members of the Dawn Club had been denied the right to a similar education to their brothers' and were always expected to defer to the opinions of men. Louisa found them timid and lacking in the self-confidence or experience needed to speak well in public. She realised that public speaking was important – she, too, needed tuition. She persuaded the debating club of the Sydney Mechanics' School of Arts to admit her as a member and encouraged other women to join so that they could gain the necessary experience.

Louisa also supported the entry of women into the professions and their becoming prison warders, factory inspectors and magistrates. Her campaign for prison reform was designed to protect women against rape in gaol: she wrote articles demanding that female prisoners be guarded by women warders rather than by men, something now taken for granted. She wrote about domestic violence:

Women seem to bear the brunt of society's burdens – especially in marriage ... But it is not only in the poorer classes that women have been driven by unkindness, ill-usage or cruelty, to ask why the love which seemed so strong a security before marriage so often becomes hate when the bond is tied ... Men become demoralised by the absolute rights over women which, after marriage, law, custom and opinion give to them ... Women must learn that if they do not claim personal respect neither can their sisters. Women's habitual self-effacement leads to all manner of weakness. An [abused] woman will tell lies to shield her husband – or perhaps her own pride if she is bruised or injured ... she will swear it was not her husband but purely the result of an accident. If he squanders the money, she works harder to replace it. If he drinks she hides the fact and shelters him with lies. The result is that in time she does not own her own body or mind.[17]

Through the Dawn Club and her influential editorials Louisa helped to change public opinion towards enfranchising women and giving them more independence. She believed deeply that women must support and help each other and was in advance of her time in pleading for refuges for homeless or battered women to be established in Sydney. She asked:

Is there any place in our town in which a homeless woman could shelter? And have we taken pains to have its location and purpose so well advertised that no one could fail to know of it?[18]

Politicians did not wish to devote funds to such a cause. They ignored Louisa and her newspaper. But all through 1890 and 1891 Louisa steadfastly continued to hammer away for refuges for battered women, describing how:

We could quickly fill the largest building in Sydney with women and children who now, in order to receive food and shelter ... are bearing blows, insults, servitude and degradation.

Women were overjoyed to find a magazine that expressed their concerns and *The Dawn*'s circulation increased. By now Louisa realised she had the necessary 'gut instinct' for publishing possessed by most media barons. To increase circulation and keep up the ratio of advertising to editorial, she gave away thousands of sample copies to prospective advertisers. She was an excellent editor and along with political articles continued to include items which the *Australian Women's Weekly* would later use effectively – recipes, fashion, health and childcare. She herself wrote over 200 of the journal's leading articles.[19]

During the economic depression of 1891–95, Louisa urged women to seek office employment in the then male-dominated fields of shorthand and typing. She campaigned fiercely for improved factory conditions and encouraged tailoresses and seamstresses to form a union to improve their working conditions and hours. These unfortunate women either did piecework at home or were used as 'sweated labour' by factory bosses. Often there were no proper eating or toilet facilities in their workplaces.

In October 1896 Louisa wrote an article urging women to learn to ride bicycles. She defied some members of the clergy, who thundered against the indecency of women wearing long socks and knickerbockers known as 'bloomers', which many of the clergy considered both indecent and immoral because they revealed women's ankles in public. Louisa, who had spent years in the bush with only a horse and cart, realised that the bicycle was a far easier means of transport and would give working-class women, as well as female doctors, nurses and teachers, mobility. Bicycles were cheap to maintain and did not require feeds of corn or hay or stables. The bicycle would give women more control over their own lives.

The Dawn, Vol. 4, No. 3, dated 1 July 1891, contains an article in Louisa's distinctive style suggesting that to cut the amount of housework for women:

> Greater simplicity of life, dress, food and surroundings would at once mitigate, if not abolish, the evil … Our forefathers ate too much and drank too much (especially the latter).

She attempted to free women from the cult of consumerism, to simplify their lives and to conserve their health through natural remedies and self-sufficiency. This makes her seems startlingly modern for her time, but her paper contained no hint of New Age vegetarianism, mantra chanting or crystal gazing.

The Dawn aimed to free women from the tyranny of fashion rather than lure them into buying ready-made clothes to make factory owners rich. There were articles on how to make simple but tasteful clothes and how to renovate dresses or hats. The paper occasionally supplied readers with paper patterns – until a rise in postage rendered this impractical.

Louisa used her imagination and drive to pioneer many of the publishing gimmicks routinely used by magazine publishers today to increase circulation. She turned *The Dawn* into a household journal by including articles for children.

Because poverty and an embittered mother had denied Louisa a formal education, she was keen that other working-class women should be able to take advantage of the newly won right to higher education for females. *The Dawn* raised funds to pay for residential accommodation for young women at the new Women's College of Sydney University. In 1892 she instituted a scheme for subsidised courses of study in technical colleges for her readers. Provided the women brought in twenty new subscribers to the magazine, Louisa's publishing company would pay their fees.[20] The women could select from fifteen subjects ranging from arts and crafts to philosophy. Louisa's originality was amazing.

She championed a new view of marriage as well as paid employment for women inside or outside the home. She wanted the divorce laws liberalised so that they were fairer to women.

Louisa Lawson meets Mary Cameron

In 1894, Louisa published Henry Lawson's first book, *Short Stories in Prose and Verse*. The book failed to make money in Australia's restricted market, but its publication helped Henry to obtain a two-book contract with the publishing company of Angus and Robertson. A couple of years earlier, Henry Lawson had been encouraged to continue writing verse when, through his mother, he met a young schoolteacher and aspiring poet named Mary Cameron.

Mary and her mother, Mrs Mary Ann Cameron, were lodging in a Sydney boarding house in Sydney's Bligh Street, in the city centre. Like Louisa, Mrs Cameron had left her husband, Mary's father, because she'd had more than enough of the hardships of bush life.[21]

Mary Ann Cameron was working on Sydney's *Daily Telegraph* as one of Australia's first female journalists, writing fairly conventional accounts of social events under the pen-name 'Busy Bee'. Her tall and fairly prim daughter, Mary, had been teaching at Silverton, near Broken Hill. At a time when most young women were married by the time they turned twenty, Mary foresaw herself as a spinster, left 'on the shelf' ... although some of her poems show that she was longing to have a husband and a child. Mary described herself as 'a gawky country girl dressed in a home-made frock'. Her photograph shows a pleasant-faced girl with softly curling hair which she kept unfashionably short, wearing a prim high-necked blouse.

At the time Mary was introduced to Louisa Lawson by her mother, she was looking for a teaching job in a state school and was sharing her other's room. The two mothers without husbands and with a great deal in common became friends, as did their children.

Mary, following in her mother's footsteps, had already written a few articles for the Wagga papers (illegally and under a pen-name because teachers in the State system who wrote for the press could be dismissed.) For a brief period while her mother returned to the bush to wind up her affairs, Mary moved into the Lawsons' tiny spare room as a paying guest. Initially Louisa, worried about Henry's lack of drive, saw Mary as the making of him and encouraged their friendship.

This is how Mary described Louisa's dark-eyed son when she first met him:

> Henry [Lawson] was in the sappy twig stage ... The face was weak, the chin underdeveloped, the look effeminate.[22]

Henry was scarcely good husband material at this point, but he was interested in Mary.

Henry and Mary, thrown together in the small house while Louisa was away for long hours at work, discovered that as aspiring poets they had a great deal in common – although Henry was a year younger than strong-minded Mary and far more immature.

They became good friends. Henry had a poem accepted by the *Bulletin,* known as that time as 'the bushman's friend', and was paid ten shillings for it. Louisa was outraged that they paid her son so little but Mary was impressed. She longed to be published by the *Bulletin.* Arm in arm the two poets, an unlikely couple in many ways, took long walks around The Rocks area where they saw babies abandoned in doorways, drunken men, and prostitutes lurking in alleyways swarming with rats.[23] These images of poverty shocked Mary deeply.

Louisa started to become alarmed. Much as she liked Mary Ann Cameron and had to admit that Mary (who seemed about to become a teacher at Neutral Bay Primary School), with her strong character and principles, might well be the making of her weak, vacillating but talented son, Louisa realised from her own experience that marriage meant children. At that time, when married female teachers had to stop working, Mary would not be able to continue as the breadwinner. If they married, what would Henry and Mary – and their children – live on? Louisa remembered her own poverty-stricken bread-and-dripping days surrounded by grizzling toddlers and crying babies. She had not made all those sacrifices to see Henry and Mary repeat the story of her own marriage.

Louisa concocted a plan that would nip any incipient romance in the bud. The goldfields of Western Australia were luring young men in search of gold. Paying their fares, she would send Henry there together with his younger brother, Peter – a slight fellow without ambition – to fulfil their father's dream of finding gold. That should solve the problem: doubtless clever Miss Cameron would find someone closer to her own age if Henry were not there.

Approaching absence intensified the situation between Henry Lawson and Mary Cameron. In her later years Mary would claim that Henry Lawson had begged her to elope, telling her that all three of them would go to Western Australia, far away from his mother's domination.

This proposal (often doubted) could well have been made in the shadow of long parting. However, an ambitious young schoolteacher like Mary, accustomed to seeing wives of poor men scrubbing, cleaning, baking, digging gardens, concocting toys for children out of scraps and being continually exhausted, and aware that an impoverished Louisa had given birth to Henry in a tent, was not going to put herself into the same position.

It would seem more likely that at the dockside Mary and Henry kissed and said fond goodbyes. Perhaps they promised faithfully to write to each other, but Mary may well have been relieved that a situation which could have got out of hand would now be resolved by a long parting. Mary's mother was still away and Mary continued to board at Louisa's untidy home. In later years, Mary claimed that she did write often to Henry Lawson in Western Australia, but never received an answer. Perhaps the letters *were* of an amorous nature. However, Mary, her pride deeply wounded from receiving no replies from Henry, stopped writing. She was accepted by Neutral Bay Primary School, threw herself into her new teaching post and started attending meetings of a utopian socialist group who met at McNamara's bookshop, where they were addressed by the charismatic socialist William Lane.

Much later, Mary Gilmore would claim that Louisa Lawson intercepted and destroyed all letters to her from Henry, which was why their relationship came to nothing, and that young Gertrude Lawson knew that her mother had done this but was too scared to say so in front of Mary.[24]

Certainly Mary did turn against Louisa – but if she was not physically attracted to Henry Lawson, considering him 'callow and immature' (ironically enough confirming Louisa's opinion of her son), would she have been writing him love letters? Of course, Mary may well have described Henry as immature in a fit of pique because she thought he had not responded to her letters.

By the time she met Henry again, he was back from Western Australia, having failed to find gold. By now he had taken up with flighty, insecure eighteen-year-old Bertha Bredt, daughter of one of his mother's feminist friends. Bertha, whose German father had died leaving her mother badly off, resented the authority of her stepfather, William McNamara (the socialist bookshop owner), and the fact that her mother had had another baby. Mrs McNamara, busy with her radical Labor work and a new baby, had no time for Bertha, who was looking for a way of escape from the McNamara household. Henry, now a published poet, seemed to provide the answer. Bertha slept with him, though it is doubtful if she loved him but, believing she was pregnant, they agreed to marry.

By now Mary was spending a great deal of her free time at McNamara's Bookshop, where William Lane's socialist group was planning to found a commune in South America. At the bookshop she saw Henry Lawson from time to time, and they resumed their earlier easy friendship ... although Mary maintained her unforgiving attitude towards his mother. In this way, she learned about his engagement to Bertha Bredt and did not appear upset by it.

In May 1891, young Mary Cameron was transferred to Stanmore Public School. Tall and upright in her usual high-necked white blouses and long skirts, Mary was by now deeply involved in supporting the miners' and shearers' strikes and helping William Lane raise the money to send members of his New Australian movement, inspired by left-wing principles, to start an idealistic utopian settlement in Cosme, Paraguay. She was attracted to a special member of the group, a tall, muscular bushman called Dave Stevenson, who was a cousin of the famous writer Robert Louis Stevenson. Like many handsome men, Dave flirted with many women, but Mary thought they had a special understanding. He was going on the first group to South America with

William Lane. She had made up her mind to sail with the second group and take over running a school in the commune once a schoolhouse had been built.

We have no way of knowing whether Henry, feeling trapped by McNamara, who was anxious to get rid of the cost of supporting his stepdaughter, wanted to escape from marriage with the emotionally unstable and immature Bertha. Did he make a last-ditch appeal to Mary Cameron, the woman who could possibly have saved him from alcoholism and guided his literary talent? If he did he would not have been successful: by now she had set her heart on Cosme and Dave Stevenson.

On 31 October, Mary resigned from her teaching post and sailed from Circular Quay on the *Ruapehu*, bound for Paraguay. The party arrived at the Cosme settlement in January 1896.

Back in Sydney, Henry did the decent thing and married Bertha. They lived a hand-to-mouth existence as Henry wrote poems and short stories and turned increasingly to drink.

Out in the wilds at Cosme in the jungles of Paraguay, far from the nearest village, Mary Cameron lived in a grass hut which she shared with lizards, toads and tarantulas, and taught the dozen or so children of her fellow pioneers. She had been disappointed on arrival by whispers among the women that Dave Stevenson had had a passionate affair with the only unmarried girl in the settlement, a young nurse called Clara Jones, who had very quickly married someone else and was now rumoured to be grieving for the devil-may-care Dave. Cosme was a tightknit community; like many communes it was riven by dissensions and jealousies. Unmarried girls were in short supply, and Mary's feelings for Dave waned.

The commune lived on a monotonous diet of home-grown vegetables, gluey grain and monkey stew. Mary, busy with her teaching, wrote a few short stories about life in Paraguay but longed to marry and have a child. She wrote to her mother but received no answer. She also wrote to Henry, telling him about the commune. Months later she learned that her father had died of kidney failure, all alone, while her ambitious mother was pursuing her career in the city. Mary felt bitter remorse that she had lost contact with her father after her mother had left him. Her guilt about having lost touch with her father may have meant that she later greatly exaggerated his importance as a bush historian and an expert on Aboriginal lore. Certainly the way that she described his role on George Grey's expedition is grossly exaggerated. But by now no one questioned a word she said.

By this time Mary was seeing a great deal of another handsome young bachelor, Will Gilmore. With her literary and journalistic ambitions, Mary made a strange choice of husband; it is most unlikely that had she remained in Sydney she would have married anyone like uneducated Will Gilmore. He was a burly shearer from a down-at-heel property in Victoria, who possessed all the charm of the Irish and a kind heart. He had left school at twelve, had no use for books and poetry, but was regarded as a good, steady man, well suited for pioneering the tropical mosquito-ridden jungle that surrounded Cosme.

They got to know each other when Will was injured while saving some of Mary's pupils in an accident, and she was asked to read him to sleep. Mary, demurely dressed as always, read an excerpt from one of Dickens' novels. A little later she wrote a poem showing her sexual attraction to Will after he had kissed her for the first time:

'He kissed me twice today, He took me in his arms, O God! The flesh of light! I cannot sleep, I will not sleep, I shall not sleep tonight.'

Will and Mary married on 29 May 1897 and for a time were blissfully happy, even though life at Cosme was primitive in the extreme and group morale so low that forty of the colonists departed.

Mary's first and only child, William Dysart Cameron Gilmore, was born at Villa Rica, the nearest town to isolated Cosme with a trained midwife. Mary went there alone: there was not enough money to pay the train fare for both Will and herself. She was horrified to find that the hospital was riddled with fleas and flies, and the 'expert midwife' turned out to be drunk.

She returned to Cosme with her baby son to find the defections and expulsions within the commune continuing. Life eventually became so difficult at Cosme that the penniless Gilmores left the commune in November 1899 and moved to Villa Rica. During this period Mary, a devoted young mother, was still very much in love with her husband.

Then Will went further south, to Rio Gallegos in southern Patagonia, where he obtained a labouring job on a ranch. It was a hard and isolated period for Mary, who helped to support her adored baby son by giving English lessons. She wrote to her mother but received no reply, and she also wrote to Henry Lawson, telling him of the failure of her hopes and dreams for the community and of the birth of her son.

In September 1899, Mary Ann Cameron, Mary's mother, died after a brief illness, but it was weeks before the news reached South America. Mary, by now quite disillusioned by William Lane's experiment, wrote to her husband on 25 February 1900 saying that she now realised that 'Communism is a failure – not attainable – and enforced Communism is *worse* than none.'

It was time to go home. The Gilmores returned to Sydney via Liverpool and London, where they found a letter from Henry Lawson awaiting them – he and Bertha and their two children were living in London. Mary and Will stayed with Henry and Bertha in their cramped apartment; Mary observed that their children, Jim and little Bertha, seemed sad and cowed. Henry was elated that Blackwood's of Edinburgh were to publish a volume of his short stories and delighted to share the news with Mary, a fellow writer. For her part, Mary took a violent dislike to Bertha. It appears that, unwilling to marry Henry herself because he did not physically attract her, she nevertheless resented Bertha for having done so. It raises the question: did Mary want Henry Lawson for herself because Will Gilmore was proving intellectually her inferior – or did she want some of Henry Lawson's soaring literary reputation to rub off on her so that she too could enter the literary life which had such a powerful appeal for her?

The Lawsons' marriage was now in deep trouble. Bertha accused Henry of drinking the money she needed for the children. She also claimed that he had hit her when he was drunk, though Mary could see no bruises. Jim and little Bertha Lawson were moody and difficult. It appeared that Bertha had had some kind of nervous collapse and been admitted to a lunatic asylum for a month after threatening to harm her own children.

Henry turned to Mary in his time of trouble, asking her if she and Will would take Bertha and their children back to Australia, as he did not feel his unstable wife should travel alone. He planned to leave on another ship as soon as his next book had gone to the printer.

Mary hesitated then agreed, believing this plan was in the best interests of the children. They travelled steerage, the cheapest class. Bertha was often hostile to Mary, blaming her for the break-up of her marriage. She flirted openly with one of the officers and neglected her children, who attached themselves to Mary. After the ship's propeller was damaged in mid-ocean they had to turn back and head for Bombay; they were held up for so long that Henry joined them there. He was glad to see that Mary and Will seemed content with each other (after the horrors of Cosme the Gilmores seemed to be happy enough during this period), but he wept when he discussed his own marriage. He now saw Mary as an ally, someone who would not judge him. He confided in Mary that he feared Bertha's mental condition was so unstable he could not face old age with her. He showed Mary a crumpled letter from a pregnant young woman called Hannah, whom he had fallen in love with while in Melbourne. He hoped he could start a new life with her. With Bertha's history of mental illness he believed he would get custody of their children.

However, when their ship reached Melbourne Henry learned that Hannah, tired of waiting for him, had formed another relationship, and their baby had died as a result of a backyard abortion. He continued drinking heavily.

Back in Australia, three years after leaving Cosme, with only ten shillings in their pockets, life did not look so rosy for the Gilmores. It wasn't long before their differences became apparent. Mary yearned to enter the world of journalism which had meant so much to her mother, and to publish books and poems like Henry Lawson. But Will's only experience was on the land, so this was where they must live.

Very unwillingly, but feeling it her duty as a married woman, she accompanied her husband to the bush at Strathdownie, near Casterton, in Victoria. Will's ageing and frail parents had an isolated rundown property there which Will, a dutiful son, proceeded to run for them.

Mary felt lonely and isolated at Casterton, yearning for the literary world of Sydney that she had hoped to join one day. She and Will moved out of his parents' tiny home to a cottage eaten by white ants which Mary named 'Hilltop'. It was from Hilltop that she observed the poverty-stricken rural world that she would describe so well in her poems and in her narrative writing. Will was often away working as a labourer on other properties. Mary was devoted to her son, little Billy, but felt lonely and isolated in the bush. The resulting mood of depression made her irritable with Will on his return and recriminations ensued. She submitted a few poems to the *Bulletin* and began a correspondence with A.G. Stephens, literary editor of the famous 'Red Page', which pulled her through a bad patch.

But life was hard as a bush wife without help. Mary complained to A.G. Stephens that by the time she had washed and baked, ironed and scrubbed, swept, cleaned and dusted, cooked three meals a day, darned and stitched and made Billy's clothes by hand, 'there was not much time left for writing'. During this time, however, she was building up a store of bush lore which would be her literary capital for years to come. Her depression lifted after being given the hope that the *Bulletin* would publish some of her poems.

The week of 1 October 1903, when the *Bulletin* published an *entire page* of her poems, would change Mary's life. She always maintained that what made her as a writer and a poet was Stephens' lengthy critiques of her poetry, which made her strive to do better and better. (Mary's first collection of poems, *Marri'd and Other Verses*, written in Cosme and Casterton, was finally published in book form two years later in 1910.)

In 1908 she was delighted when the editor of the *Australian Worker* magazine invited her to write a special page for women: she would do this for the next twenty years. Henry Lawson was also writing occasional pieces for the same paper. He and Bertha were now living in Manly. Henry was drinking heavily and had attempted suicide.

Finally Will's father died, his widow went to stay with her daughter, the property was leased and Mary and her husband were free to leave Casterton. Billy was nearly thirteen and Mary was longing to live in Sydney and be part of the literary life. It was decided as a temporary measure (a measure that would last for the rest of Will's life) that Mary would go and live in Sydney with Billy while Will would go to Queensland with his brother and investigate what the possibilities were of obtaining farming land there. Their separation would be reasonably amicable. Will Gilmore, in view of all the support Mary had provided at Cosme and at Casterton, agreed to give her a monthly income from the property he took up in Queensland.

From then onwards, Mary and her husband saw each other only for brief periods. He faithfully paid her monthly maintenance, unlike Louisa's husband Peter Lawson – who provoked Louisa continually by his refusal to pay maintenance for his children. Although Will Gilmore could not share his wife's literary and reformist interests, he was a steady, hard-working man who provided her with a small income.

A few years previously Louisa had financed Henry's publication of *When the World was Wide and Other Verses* and his most famous collection of poems, *While the Billy Boils.* Henry's marriage to Bertha was now over except in name; he was seldom at home, spending nights in his favourite pubs or drunk in some gutter. Bertha was eventually admitted to a mental hospital once more, which seemed to aggravate Henry's alcoholism, possibly through guilt. He was then put in prison for failing to pay maintenance to Bertha. A public subscription was raised for the release of Henry Lawson, who now wrote that he was 'weary, very weary of the faces in the street'.

Billy Gilmore, Mary's teenage son, was beginning to show the same alcoholic tendency as Henry Lawson (a fact Mary tried to cover up all her life). Mary still blamed Louisa for her broken romance – but by now she must have realised what a gruesome fate would have awaited her as the wife of Henry Lawson. After 1907 Henry was jailed several times for failing to pay maintenance for his children. He also spent several periods in a mental hospital, but at the same time his fame as the alcoholic but brilliant poet of the bush was growing fast. Although Mary often claimed in her old age that she and Henry Lawson had been romantically involved, it seems that the romantic involvement had been more from Henry's side, and that Mary had seen herself as a caretaker of Henry's remarkable talent. She resented Bertha's neglect in nurturing it. Mary chose to ignore the fact that it was *Louisa* who had been the major formative influence on Henry Lawson's unique style.

As Louisa Lawson declined in health and descended into poverty once more, Mary Gilmore went from strength to strength, her features becoming craggier, her reputation increasing, and her readers loving her more and more.

Mary composed short poems which went straight to the heart of her readers. *The Passionate Heart* (1918) reflects her horror of the slaughter of young men in the trenches of France, and can be read alongside lyrical poems such as 'Never Admit the Pain', 'Gallipoli' and 'The Flight of the Swans'. Another of her books, *The Tilted Cart* (a pioneering name for a covered waggon) appeared in 1925, when she was in her mid-sixties. In *The Wild Swan* (1930) Mary expressed her anguish over the destruction of the land by white farmers as well as the loss of Aboriginal folklore, and she took up the same themes in *Under the Wilgas* (1932). In what has become an Australian classic book, *Old Days, Old Ways* (1934), Mary wrote down accounts of pioneers, with special emphasis on the life of pioneer women. The book was a great success and the following year Angus and Robertson published a second volume, *More Recollections*.

'Fear not the years, They have gifts to bring,' wrote Mary triumphantly – and for her they did. Mary's weekly page for women in the *Australian Worker* brought her into contact with many working men's wives with sad tales to tell. She printed their heart-rending letters and wrote back to the women, who were deeply grateful to her. They came to trust Mary Gilmore as their friend. The *Australian Worker* magazine saw the printed correspondence as a useful political tool for its cause.

When Billy Gilmore was old enough to live and work with his father he set off for Queensland. This left Mary living alone in a series of Sydney boarding houses. She suffered periods of loneliness and depression, which may explain her claims that she was responsible for Henry Lawson's genius. It was now that Mary publicly claimed Henry *had* loved her and asked her to elope with him to Western Australia.[25]

After Henry's premature death in 1922, Mary, understandably upset by the whole affair, made more claims about his love for her. She started saying that were it not for her, Henry's poetic genius would *never* have flowered at all. These exaggerated claims may have been prompted by her hatred of Louisa and Bertha Lawson as well as her wish to increase her own standing in the literary world. She insisted on spending a night in the room in which Henry Lawson had died, and suffered psychologically as a result. Henry had died in poverty, but Mary was determined he would not go to a pauper's grave. She declared she would go to Canberra to tell the Prime Minister, Billy Hughes, that Australia's greatest poet was dead. In the end money was provided for a State funeral and Henry's coffin, covered by the

Australian flag, was buried with due pomp and ceremony. Mary was one of the many people who raised contributions for a statue in his memory in Sydney's Domain.

Mary Gilmore became even better known after she wrote *Hound of the Road* and *The Rue Tree* (signifying the Holy Cross of Calvary) which made her a great favourite with Catholic readers. By now she was established as an important literary figure: the dream she had nurtured all these years. On occasions she wrote very average verses, but in her best poems she shows a truly lyrical gift. She had a way of writing in simple language which went straight to the heart. Aborigines, the Australian landscape, its wildlife and the people of the bush evoked the best in her and she wrote about them with sincerity, simplicity and strength. *Tunes of Memory* contains the memorable line: 'The world begins anew in every child.' *The Tilted Cart* contains poems filled with childhood memories and images of the bush. 'Botany Bay', her compassionate verses about an old convict, would have ensured her immortality, had she written nothing else:

> I was the conscript sent to hell
> To make the desert the living well
> I split the rock, I felled the tree,
> The nation was – because of me.

The tragedy of Gallipoli sparked some of Mary Gilmore's greatest poems and made her the conscience of the nation. In her book *The Passionate Heart*, Mary dared to tell in verse the story politicians did not want told. *A Mother's Lament* compares the wounded at Gallipoli to wounded dogs – left out in the hot sun where they were covered in flies and eventually died from their injuries.

Honours and fame for Mary Gilmore

The Great Depression of the 1930s was a terrible period for so many readers of the *Australian Worker* but for Mary Gilmore it was a successful time. She was now a literary icon, to whom who younger writers applied for advice.

In 1934 her most famous book, *Old Days, Old Ways*, was published. Three years later she was awarded a DBE (Dame of the British Empire) in recognition of her literary achievements and her community activities. She cherished this hard-won recognition which had come late in life.

In World War II, during the tense months of 1942 after the fall of Singapore, when the Japanese forces advanced ever closer to Australia, her stirring poem 'No Foe Shall Gather Our Harvest' made her a symbol of Australian defiance of Japanese power. By this time most of Australia's fighting men were overseas, and this poem had a huge effect in boosting morale on the home front. Perched high in a tiny apartment in the heart of King's Cross – in those days Sydney's Bohemia – and looked after by a succession of housekeepers, she continued to write and encourage other writers and to gather tales of pioneering days.

Mary outlived her husband and son, who both died in 1945. Both were affected by the alcohol which had destroyed Henry Lawson. The shock caused Mary to fall ill, but her brain remained clear and her spirit undaunted. At eighty-one she maintained her firm belief in social justice and continued her crusade against power and privilege. Her column titled 'Arrows' still appeared each week in the *Tribune.*

She had been born in the days of sailing ships, when the *Cutty Sark* and other clippers berthed at Circular Quay surrounded by wool drays and teamsters in cabbage leaf hats. By the time she was old and frail, commercial aeroplanes were circling the world. In 1954, when she was eighty-eight, she wrote a poem called 'The Lesser Grail', which simply but powerfully expressed her belief that:

Age changes no one's heart, the field is wider, that is all
Childhood is never lost, concealed, it answers every call.

By now, Mary Gilmore had become a living legend, while Louisa Lawson was forgotten. Over 600 people attended Mary's ninety-first birthday party, which was organised by the committee for founding the first chair of Australian Literature. The sum of 500 pounds was collected for this project which Mary had long advocated.

She was one of the founder-members of Sydney's Lyceum Club for women; a founder and vice-president of the Fellowship of Australian Writers and a life member of the Royal Society for the Prevention of Cruelty to Animals. Streets, buildings and old people's homes were named after Dame Mary Gilmore. Journalists, scholars and politicians as well as aspiring writers sought her advice. Her image was perpetuated in portraits by Joshua Smith and Mary McNiven, but the most outstanding one was painted for her ninetieth birthday by William Dobell, donated by Mary to the Art Gallery of New South Wales. Regarded initially by some critics as a 'caricature' but loved by Mary herself, this portrait has become one of the Art Gallery's best-loved paintings.

Disaster for Louisa once *The Dawn* was silenced

Louisa Lawson had worked just as hard as Mary Gilmore to improve social conditions for women. She urged parents to educate their daughters so that they could earn a living in case of bereavement, financial disaster, marital separation or divorce. She was a staunch advocate of women gaining the vote, although Rose Scott and her clique of upper-class ladies refused to give Louisa credit for this, and for all her years of support for women's suffrage in *The Dawn* magazine.

Louisa was also way in advance of her time in advocating the setting up of government hostels or refuges for alcoholic women or women wishing to leave prostitution; she assured her readers that these women were 'more sinned against than sinning'. She also suggested that idealistic young women offering themselves as missionaries overseas should first turn their attention to improving the terrible conditions suffered by Aborigines.

Louisa Lawson published the final issue of *The Dawn* when she was fifty-seven. As her biographer Brian Matthews has observed: 'What finally silenced *The Dawn* in 1905 was not the perceived or actual failure of its idealistic visions – although the women's movement was beginning to lose some momentum – but a collapse within Louisa herself.'[26]

The reasons for Louisa's collapse were many. Henry's alcoholism and periods in jail and her lack of money to help him were major components. Louisa had constantly campaigned against the evils of drink – now she realised that her adored son, whose brilliance she had fostered from childhood, was destroying himself through drink. Slowly, before her eyes, the drama of Henry Lawson's alcoholism unfolded: after wild nights in pubs and drinking clubs, tearful promises never to touch a drop again were followed by a few days of abstinence, black moods, withdrawal symptoms, then more wild nights followed by sleeping it off on a park bench or in the gutter. Louisa feared, quite rightly, that alcohol was turning the writing of her brilliant child into maudlin sentimentality and the rehashing of old themes.

Her son Charlie was no more comfort to her than Henry. Occasionally he returned to the family home, especially when he was in trouble with the police. He spent many nights in gaol or in the gutter. Although no formal diagnosis was ever made, Charlie Lawson was probably schizophrenic. He could on occasions be tender and thoughtful towards his mother but on bad days he would sit for hours in his room at her house, arranging and rearranging his collection of knives, vowing vengeance on those he felt were plotting against him. Several times he threatened to turn his mother out onto the street.[27]

Louisa's third son, Peter, also suffered psychiatric problems. She had always hoped he would become a musician, but with a wife and children to support he was forced to accept odd jobs as a piano tuner rather than as a performer.

Apart from severe family problems, Louisa had been driven to the limits of her endurance by the pirating of her invention of an improved mailbag fastener, a buckling device she had realised was necessary during her time as postmistress at Eurunderie. Louisa had patented her invention in New South Wales and sold her fasteners in quantity to the New South Wales Post Office, intending that future sales should provide a retirement income when she gave up publishing. But a male rival copied her invention and destroyed Louisa's market. To protect her patent she became involved in a costly and stressful legal battle. She was awarded a small amount of compensation, reduced on appeal to a very meagre sum. Louisa felt the justice system had failed her. The stress of this case caused her blinding migraines.

Her second stroke of bad luck came in 1900 when she was thrown from a tram as she was boarding it, much hindered by her long, clinging skirt. She suffered a fractured knee and spinal injuries and was bedridden for almost a year. Once again there was scant compensation. Her daughter, Gertrude, took over running the magazine but everyone wanted to deal with Louisa rather than her deputy. Advertisers fell away in droves. When Louisa returned to work, her old fire, inventiveness and vitality seemed to have ebbed away.

In spite of these disasters, Louisa's desire for women's emancipation was as strong as ever. She joined the council of the Women's Progressive Association and continued to campaign for the appointment of women to public office and the right to advance in professions from which they were virtually barred.

Louisa Lawson's long fight was finally over when she closed down *The Dawn* because of her bouts of ill health and depression.

Louisa Lawson: the final years

Louisa kept herself busy in her retirement and wrote articles and short stories on a freelance basis for other publications. She also wrote a series of poems about the grief and pain of love; it was now that she indicated that she had loved another man before she met her husband. Some of the poems, published in a volume titled *The Lonely Crossing*, are haunting in their intensity.

We will part now, you and I,
With a frozen smile and a faint good-bye …
For we each could save it, but neither will,
As we stoop to injure and strike to kill.

Louisa Lawson's life was one of unremitting struggle and family disaster. If she had had the educational advantages and the stable income from a separated husband that Mary Gilmore enjoyed, would she also have become venerated as a poet and writer? As it is, her reputation has been growing steadily since her death.

Towards the end of her life Louisa created a garden and decorated her final home, a small stone cottage in Renwick Street, Marrickville. In her retirement she spent a great deal of time with her grandchildren and enjoyed writing *Dert and Do*, a novel based on the amusing doings of two lovable children.

Over the next decade she faced increasing loneliness and impoverishment. Although she had been reasonably successful as a publisher and managed to save money, she lost much of it in the 1892 crash of the Australian Joint Stock Bank. She still suffered badly from migraines, aggravated by her fall from the tram. Her daily routine was often disturbed by harrowing visits from the volatile and sometimes violent Charlie. There was no pension to support her and her precious savings were dwindling rapidly. She still managed to sell a few poems and short stories to newspapers, but she was paid a pittance. As a result of her financial problems and family sorrows, her old 'abstracted fits' of depression and lack of concentration returned, accompanied by a reluctance to eat properly. Louisa was further distressed when the local council placed an embargo on her property at Marrickville, preventing her from selling her land, which she had also acquired as investment for her old age.

Her son Peter lived from hand to mouth, going off to the country to take piano tuning jobs. He had by now become a relatively harmless religious maniac, but like Charlie he suffered from a sense of injustice and a persecution complex. Eventually Peter was admitted by his wife to Gladesville Hospital suffering from 'melancholia and delusions'. His admission statement noted that the cause was 'heredity and worry'. He was discharged three months later as his condition had improved, but when his mother fell ill there could be no room for her in his already overcrowded household.

Gertrude had married, but after her husband was killed at Gallipoli she had to raise and educate her two sons on very little money. She lived far away from Louisa and could be of little assistance to her mother in her approaching senility. Henry Lawson was now a frail, legendary, pathetic figure, well known on the streets of Sydney.[29] He died of a cerebral haemorrhage two years after Louisa.

Louisa attempted to keep track of Henry's whereabouts from 1896 onwards. The last half-dozen entries in her private papers are lists of Henry's visits to gaol or his periods in mental and other hospitals. She notes that in February 1910 he was found drunk 'in the gutter'.[30] Louisa still had her 'good' days, but on her 'bad' ones she exhibited classic signs of depressive illness coupled with the onset of senile dementia. As her health deteriorated, she stopped cooking, ate only at irregular intervals, and did not clean the house or take baths. She let her beloved garden go to rack and ruin and became very forgetful. On one occasion she totally failed to recognise her own grandchildren.[31] At other times, she would be found wandering in the street, unclear about her own identity or where she wanted to go.

At the end of her life, Louisa Lawson who had tried so hard to care for her wayward children, had no one to care for her. At 4 pm one hot, humid afternoon in early January 1920, the resident doctor at Gladesville Hospital for the Insane recorded the admission of Louisa Lawson by her son Peter and his wife, Elizabeth, who had too many problems of their own to be able to care for her.

In the days before psychiatric drugs became available to control symptoms of madness and mania, mental asylums were terrible places, staffed by poorly trained nurses, positively Dickensian in their cruel treatment of patients. Little money was spent by politicians on State mental hospitals. The wards reeked of unwashed bodies, urine and faeces.[32] Surrounded by raving, screaming, incontinent patients, some of whom had to be forcibly tied to chairs to restrain them, Louisa lived out the final eight months of her life. Like most patients with dementia, she was more often than not unaware of her surroundings or how she had come to spend the end of her life in such a place. In her lucid moments she cried bitter tears and begged to return to her home.

Louisa Lawson died in Gladesville Mental Hospital in August 1920. It was a tragic end for a truly inspiring woman who had worked so hard to improve the lot of other women. She was given what was in effect a pauper's funeral and is buried in the Anglican section of Rookwood cemetery. No statue or monument – other than a block of Housing Commission flats in North Bondi named after her – exists to commemorate Louisa Lawson, who, when the vote was granted to Australian women in 1902, was publicly acclaimed as the originator of the suffrage campaign.

Mary Gilmore died on 3 December 1962, the anniversary of the historic Eureka Uprising. Unlike poor Louisa, she was granted the honour of a State funeral at St Stephen's Church, Macquarie Street. In accordance with her wishes, her ashes were buried in her husband's grave at Cloncurry, Queensland. This seems a fitting gesture, for he had faithfully supported her during the hard years while she established her place in Australian literature.

CHAPTER THREE

Martha Caldwell Cox
(1854–1947)
PIONEER OF THE 'NEVER-NEVER'

Martha Cox represents all those pioneer women who went out with their husbands into wild country and managed to survive drought, bushfire, loneliness, deprivation, and childbirth without medical aid. They all helped to make Australia what it is today. Martha was intelligent and diligent but had little schooling: her memoirs are no literary masterpiece but are entertaining and written in a distinctively Australian voice.[1]

Martha deserves to be as well-known as Jeannie Gunn, author of *We of the Never Never*.[2] Jeannie, a Melbourne 'lady schoolteacher', horrified her family and friends by marrying Aeneas Gunn, part-owner and manager of The Elsey, a vast cattle property hundreds of miles south of Katherine, in the Northern Territory. Jeannie described Elsey homestead as 'mostly verandahs and promises' but those rooms that were finished were 'neat and well-cared for'. Jeannie, who had no children, was provided with a cook and Aboriginal women as domestic helpers; she had ample free time to keep a lively and entertaining journal.

Martha Cox, on the other hand, was a working-class battler with five children. Jeannie Gunn spent only eighteen months in the 'Never-Never'; following her husband's tragic death she returned to Melbourne. After Martha's husband died she battled on and ran his three properties successfully, staying in the 'Never-Never' until she was in her seventies. In addition to caring for her family, Martha drew water, cooked, cleaned, and broke in horses. When necessary she acted as camp cook for shearers and tank sinkers. She helped her husband to clear land, grub out stumps and build fences.

Selectors' wives rarely wrote about their experiences. Squatters' wives, on the other hand, were fond of writing journals, some of which have become part of the canon of early Australian literature. They went to the bush with pianos, silver cutlery and porcelain dinner services. Martha Caldwell was the daughter of two penniless Irish migrants, Annie and Matthew Caldwell, who leased a small mixed farm in the Adelaide Hills. Martha had no silver or porcelain and certainly no piano. Taught by her elder brothers to handle a gun, Martha was also a fearless horsewoman.

She wrote her memoirs in her old age when finally she had the time to sit down and take up her pen. The journals of most squatters' wives complain about the servant problem, the flies and a monotonous diet of mutton and damper. Martha does not mention these. Instead she writes with authority about the price of sheep and wool, how to mend a fence, how to hand-rear a lamb. Her love of dogs and horses shines through her memoirs, which reveal without a trace of self-pity the grim realities of life on a small selection.

I was first shown Martha's memoirs when I was a guest on a historic property in New South Wales named Livingstone Gully, owned by Belinda and Alan Cox. Alan is the son of the nephew of Martha's husband, David Cox. Martha Cox's memoirs are significant historically, written from the selectors' point of view at a time when selectors and squatters were at loggerheads.

Martha's two elder brothers were William and John, and she had four younger sisters – Olive, Sophia, Agnes and Priscilla, the youngest of whom was born a few months after their father's death in 1864. Martha felt a special responsibility for her youngest sister.

In 1860–61 the New South Wales Government passed two Selection Acts which made it easier for those lacking capital to purchase land on easy terms. When Martha was ten, her widowed mother sold off their stock, packed a covered horse-drawn wagon with food, water and bedding and set off from the Adelaide Hills to southern New South Wales. They took eight weeks to reach the Murray River. Whenever the going was rough, Martha and her sisters walked in front of the wagon to ease the load on the horses. Stones cut their feet until they bled, bramble bushes tore at their pinafores and bare arms. Each night the girls and their mother slept on mattresses inside the covered wagon while the boys took turns to keep watch against bushrangers. They lived on salted meat and game, tinned fish, potatoes, jam and flour, washed down with billy tea.

Annie Caldwell took up a 'selection'[3] of 230 acres at 'The Billabong', 9.5 kilometres from the present-day town of Holbrook (then known as Germanton) in her son's name: in the 1860s women were regarded as chattels of men and were not permitted to own land.

The family worked together to build a slab hut large enough to act as a dormitory for their mother and the eldest girls; the rest of the family continued to sleep in the covered wagon. The hut with its dirt floor also served as a dining room and as the kitchen when it was too wet to cook outside. The children and their mother cleared 10 acres (4 hectares) of trees and undergrowth in order to get in a crop of wheat. There was a demand for home-made cheese at Albury, so Annie Caldwell and her daughters worked hard milking and making butter and cheese to bring in additional income.

Lack of money and a huge workload meant that Martha's schooling was minimal. At first there was no school; eventually one opened at Fern Hill, some miles away, but the schoolmaster turned out to be an alcoholic. Martha writes in her memoirs:

> Our schoolroom was in the rear of the [shanty hotel] premises and our schoolmaster often found his way round to the bar. [In his absence] the more studious among us read our books, or worked on our sums. We worked on slates, but had to copy our figure work into an exercise book and take it home each night to show our parents some evidence of our progress. It was five miles to school, and I rode there side-saddle every day on Cocky, my bay pony, on a man's saddle.

(It was regarded as 'improper' for females to ride astride at that time or to wear trousers.) As soon as Martha was fourteen she left school to help her mother.

Five years later, at the age of nineteen, Martha met a young selector, David Cox, one of five brothers. David was the son of Joseph Cox and his second wife, Mary (née Maloney), who owned a fine property named Livingstone Gully, also in New South Wales.[4] Martha's memoirs are very discreet about the details of her courtship[5] but it is clear that the young couple were very much in love. David Cox was tall, muscular and fair-skinned.

His father 'Joseph' had been born at Cashel in County Tipperary. David Cox was born at Brungle, near Tumut, in 1839. Although Joseph's first wife, who had died on the ship coming to Australia, had been Anglican, Mary was a Catholic and David had been brought up a Catholic. Martha's family were devout Catholics, also from Ireland, so her mother raised no objection when David asked permission to marry Martha, knowing he also came from a hard-working, highly respected pioneering family. David was not the eldest son, and since there was not enough land to support all five sons, Richard Cox bought out his younger brothers' interests, which meant David had the capital to buy stock and set up his own property but not to buy vast tracts of land. So he too became a 'selector' – selecting uncleared acreage bought at a low rate of interest from the New South Wales goverment.

Martha related that:

> David had already selected two adjoining blocks on Ingram's run, near Book-Book, before I married him. He had built a temporary home for me out of wooden slabs with a dirt floor and I went there to start housekeeping on my own. We had hopes of extending our holding but the squatter on the big station wanted rid of us. He selected [took a lease on] the land around us where the water came from and so 'peacocked' us out. We stuck it for twelve months with our stock dying from lack of water and then decided all we could do was to sell out at the cheap price the squatter up at big station offered us and look elsewhere for a better farming proposition.

Wealthy squatters with capital were determined to lock up the land and squeeze out poorer selectors. They adopted devious tactics to block off selectors' access to water, and got them off the land by 'dummying' or 'peacocking'. The squatters could also force selectors off 'pre-emptive' leased land by these measures.[6]

After the disappointment of losing land on which they had worked so hard, Martha and David took up another selection, this time on a pre-emptive lease, which in return for a deposit gave them the right to buy the land once it was subdivided. This time David was more cautious; he did *not* build a home on the land – instead, he and Martha slept in their wagon. But after six months of backbreaking work cutting down trees and grubbing out stumps, the Lands Department notified David that he must select another block: 'their' land had been gazetted as an agistment block for cattle on the move. David would get his money back eventually, but he and Martha would have to start all over again the backbreaking toil of clearing the land on another block.

Martha was convinced that a wealthy squatter had bribed the Lands Department to get them removed on a pretext. She wrote bitterly:

> Those rich squatters always find the means to beat working people like us in the end. David was disgusted by the whole affair. He was forced to forfeit our cleared block and it took twelve months before our money was refunded. So back we were, in the covered wagon and on

the road again searching for a property. But now I was with child so went home to my mother on The Billabong, to wait the turn of circumstance and my first child.

Martha's first son, Joe, was born at The Billabong, with her mother acting as midwife.

Grubbing out stumps to clear land by the sweat of your brow and then losing the land for the second time was soul-destroying. The Coxes decided to take up their third selection in partnership with someone who had capital and political influence, so that the squatters could not throw them off 'their' land again. David chose as his partner his brother-in-law James Gormly, a shrewd businessman with good contacts and a seat on the local council (eventually he would become Mayor of Wagga). On the tacit understanding that he would look after their interests with the Lands Department, Gormly put up the capital for a large block of land adjoining the Cox's selection. For their part, David and Martha Cox agreed to supervise Gormly's stock as well as their own.

They 'selected' two 10-acre blocks known to have water between Cobar and Bourke, then uncharted wilderness in the western district of New South Wales, lacking any road or rail connections. The land was known as Corongo Peak, in the Condobolin district, which suffered from harsh winters and searingly hot summers. There were no schools or medical facilities. Martha, accustomed to having her mother and siblings around her, now found herself several days' horseback ride from the nearest white woman and even further from a doctor. She wrote:

> We decided I should stay out at Wollongough Station, two days ride away, while Dave would go to our new land at Corongo Peak, get a water tank made and a hut built, which would take time. Wollongough was owned by a distant relation of my husband, named King.
>
> Our journey to Wollongough Station took a week. Dave drove a team of twelve horses in the wagon, while I drove the lighter vehicle, which was big enough to seat six people. So there I was driving the tilted wagonette with young Joe on my lap. I had loved driving horses since childhood. One horse was good but Jess, a jibbing chestnut mare, gave me a lot of trouble whenever we came to a hill. Dave always drove ahead so that I would be able to follow his tracks. Sometimes he would

have to ride back and deal with Jess when I failed to get her to budge. She played up badly, seeming to know that I was handicapped by having young Joe on my lap. We picked up supplies of meat and fresh milk at stations as we journeyed along. When we reached Wollongough Station, Dave departed for Corongo Peak in the wagonette leaving the wagon and team with me at the station.

Mr and Mrs King were kind and considerate; but my thoughts were always in the west with Dave busy making a home for us in isolation.

Then came a terrible drought. Every green blade of herbage was gradually burnt off. Six months passed without a drop of rain. Cattle and sheep gathered round the homestead, the sheep bleating piteously as the tanks were low and the heat was insufferable. Mr King and some men set off on the droving track with the sheep in search of grass. Mrs King, who was new to the bush and its hardships, went home to her parents in Victoria to await the breaking of the drought. Only Mrs Daly, the housekeeper, and I were left to battle through as best we might.

The days grew hotter and hotter. The ground was cracked and dry as ashes. There was not a green blade to be seen as far as the horizon and the nights were stifling. Strange as it may seem in such dry conditions, at twilight mosquitoes attacked us in myriads from their haunt in the saltbush and we had no mixtures to spray rooms against then. A plague of fleas made things still worse. The little wretches would swarm onto my legs and attack me when I had to collect the eggs from the hens in a shed some distance from the homestead. If only we had had a decent supply of water things would not have been so bad, but by now the station-tank was dry. Only by digging down two or three feet in the bed of the tank were we able to get a bucket of thick sludgy water which had to be boiled and clarified before we could use it.

Kangaroo rats, or paddy melons, arrived in droves looking for water. Little Joe, who was just able to toddle, used to have great sport among the poor creatures. But the kangaroo rats were no sport for us women as they threatened to foul our limited water supply. Mrs Daly and I got hammers and put in stakes and covered the whole tank with wire netting.

Only the arrival of 'Red Jack' the mailman, tired by his long and blistering journey through drought-stricken country, relieved the monotony. His bulging saddle bags were crammed with letters. He would stay and rest a few hours, and get refreshment for himself and a feed for his jaded horse. He brought letters occasionally from Dave and the Kings but his visits were few and far between. I learned that Dave had to cart water from Kildary Station, over 20 miles away, and there was no sign of rain. A tank was being sunk by Dave and men he had engaged. They were making the first tank on Gormly's lease and then building a temporary slab hut for us.

The drought continued. There was no water to spare for Martha's vegetable patch so the plants withered and died and they found it impossible to buy dried vegetables. Martha perseveres with her story of heroic endurance.

Mrs Daly and I were often left without meat as the sixteen-year-old delivery lad seemed to forget our delivery day, or jibbed at a fifteen-mile trip in the heat. Then we had to fall back on tea and damper with a little dripping to help it down. Mrs Daly was good at 'beggars on the coals', as she called the thin dampers that she baked. If we only had had a drop of real, fresh pure water to make a decent cup of tea. At first we managed to get along without serious ailments but I fretted over little Joe, on our limited and monotonous diet.

At long last the rain came, the King family came back, and with them the stock, with more bought to replace losses. The yellow-baked land became green again in a surprisingly short space of time, the tanks were full once more. Dave wrote to say that he had made things ship-shape at The Peak, as we called it, and was returning for me in a week or two. I began to put things together for the big journey.

Eventually Dave returned, bringing 600 merino ewes he had bought at Forbes. He and Martha then started out on their six-week journey by horse-drawn wagon to Corongo Peak.

Dave drove the wagon with the team and I drove the tilted wagonette. Two old shepherds we had engaged brought the sheep and a few cows for fresh milk. Unfortunately the ewes began lambing much earlier than we had expected, giving us much trouble. I often had two or three sickly lambs to care for behind me in the wagonette.

When we reached the Lachlan River, we found it swollen from the recent rain and we traversed the old narrow bridge with great difficulty. We both had to unload our goods from the wagon and take our stuff across in a boat. Dave hitched the wagonette behind the wagon, I rode ahead and led one horse across the stream. The water rose well over the deck of the wagon by mid-stream. Somehow we landed high and dry without damage or loss of any of our provisions.

The stages [distance between places of rest on the journey] were far drier now, and at stations we had to pay a shilling a bucket for water for the thirsty horses which meant paying ten shillings a drink for the team [a great deal of money at that time]. But it hurt me to see horses suffer. On several occasions Dave took them in the darkness five or six miles, and gave the poor animals a real blow-out with no one the wiser.

A shower fell about 20 miles from Cobar, filling little hollows and giving the sheep a drink. I will never forget the bleating of those poor famished animals when they smelt the water. At Cobar we struck a friendly settler who allowed Dave to water the sheep at his new tank, a hundred at a time. From there on we had free water and plentiful grass all the way. After six weary weeks, we and our belongings arrived at our future home. With a tank full of water and plenty of grass for our stock, it looked as if good luck had greeted us at last.

The next morning I went out for my first look at Corongo Peak. As far as the eye could scan the plain stretched away to the skyline. A world of mulga, wilga, box, but not a sign of a stringy bark, which would have been helpful for our building operations. Our cabin being still incomplete, we slept in the covered wagon. But as it was impossible to keep the cockroaches away, we took meals in the open air.

Our dining table consisted of a sheet of box bark, sap side up, supported upon four stakes driven into the ground. Our tablecloth was a length of unbleached calico, and cooking utensils included a camp oven, frying pan, a few pots and sundries, a couple of kerosene tin boilers, one for cooking purposes, and the other for boiling the clothes in on washing day.

Under primitive conditions, Martha cooked for shearers and tank sinkers, and carried out household tasks and farm work without any of the household aids and appliances we take for granted today such as hot and cold running water, electricity and refrigeration, or a local shop. Martha made her own butter, cheese, jam and soap. By spending every penny they earned on developing their property, she and David would finally achieve what her mother had never known: a proper homestead with a kitchen and real furniture instead of packing cases to serve as tables and chairs.

Keeping clothes clean in hot, dusty conditions was difficult, as Martha describes:

> A couple of iron tubs, a lump of common soap, and unlimited elbow grease completed our laundry equipment when a set of old-fashioned flat irons were added.
>
> Each night we sat at our camp fire where the outback firewood glowed brightly. If we wished to read, we could retire to the covered wagon which served as our bedroom till the cabin was ready for us. Illumination was supplied by a tin slush-lamp. The tin was half filled with dirt and then rendered mutton fat was run in till it was full. A wick was inserted consisting of a thin greased stick wrapped in one of my old cotton stockings, which had been well greased also.
>
> We were too far from civilisation to indulge in the luxury of kerosene lamps. When your nearest neighbour is nearly 30 miles away it is difficult to replace a broken lamp glass or replenish the stock of kerosene. Many people wonder how women, many of whom had enjoyed every domestic comfort before coming to Australia, could endure such a hard and isolated life in the bush where there was no possible escape from nervous strain and constant backbreaking work.
>
> All our food was of the simplest kind and not always overflowing in quantity; the work was strenuous, and, to a woman, often unusual, to say the least. But for the sake of husband and childen and the fulfilment of their shared plans, most selectors' wives tackled the job with sleeves rolled up, and a smile on their face, although hard work and harsh conditions turned many young women to skin and bone or sent them blind from the sandy blight.

Gypsum in the drinking water, (a hydrous calcium sulphate which acts as a clarifying agent) kept it clear. Martha continues:

> It was decided to sink two more tanks on Gormly's land and one on our own lease. Five men were employed. In due course the tanks were made ready for the downpour, which we expected from day to day.
>
> Alas! The winter slipped by. Six months passed, and still no rain. The summer heat returned, each day hotter than the last. The sky remained cloudless. Day by day the water went lower in the tank. The sides and

beds of the new tanks gaped with cracks. Our flock of sheep was now over a thousand, if rain did not come soon it meant ruin for there was no chance of shifting the poor sheep. Every green thing disappeared and only the dry grass seed, which the sheep licked up, stood between them and starvation. We had no thermometer to test the heat, but the temperature must have ranged from 37–48 degrees Celsius [100–120 Fahrenheit] for weeks together. It was the Wollongough drought over again – but worse. I used to pity Dave and the men building a bark-roofed shearing shed in all that glare. We lived off meat and damper, our vegetables had long since withered and died. I was now feeling the strain a good deal. My nerves were getting jumpy and my gums started to bleed. I could not sleep at night with thoughts of our poor sheep, and what might happen to them, whirling through my brain.[7]

It was terribly hot outside, and I was just about to step out of the door of our hut when I saw the head of a large black snake at the doorstep. I stood stock still, stiff with fear. Three minutes or more passed while the ugly brute kept darting its tongue and staring at me. I stood near the table, trembling and praying I would find something to hit it with.

Eventually the snake moved its head round as if it were about to crawl away; then swerved round again, and crawled behind one of our three legged stools along the back wall. Quick as a flash I slipped out, secured a stick and came back and killed the wriggling brute. I sank down on a stool quite exhausted after I had nearly battered the creature's head off. As luck would have it, Dave chanced to come in for the tape measure just after, and gave me a nip of brandy which revived me.

So great was the heat that magpies fluttered down in front of the hut. They would hop timidly to the door, and then, one after another enter and betake themselves under the table to escape the rays of the sun, which had already killed numbers of smaller birds. In a short time, finding no opposition, birds came in greater numbers, and though I might be moving round they remained unafraid. When I went out to scrape a dish, I would tap the plate with a knife or fork. Down those poor birds would come, hopping around, and greedily picking up the scraps of food. I grew very fond of them. The poor birds seemed grateful for food and shelter. They would perch on the roof of the hut in the late afternoons and sing for us. I had never heard magpies carol like them; they sounded like silver flutes.

The rays of the scalding sun would almost fry a steak in the open glare. A hot wind blew most days. Eventually Gormly arrived in his little buggy with a team led by 'Red Rover', a lively mare. He wanted to inspect the tanks that were under construction at different places on the property, and he asked me to pilot him through the trackless bush to them in his buggy. Gormly was a splendid driver, but I must confess that I sometimes felt scared at the pace he drove through the bush.

'Hang on to my arm, Mrs Cox, if you're afraid of being shaken out of the buggy,' he would say after a particularly rough jerk.

I managed to guide him to the tanks. When we arrived, he told me that I was better in the bush than most men, which was certainly a compliment coming from Gormly, who was never known to praise anyone.

Gormly came across two men with horses and drays about four miles down who had cut through our fence and 'pinched' a night's feed. Gormly flew into a rage accusing them of bushranging the grass. The men laughed and asked when did Gormley last see grass there? There was an angry exchange of words.

Gormly, a huge hot-tempered man, threatened to thrash the drovers should they touch his water tanks. Martha's love for horses made her defy Gormly. She told the men to give the exhausted and gasping animals a good drink and that she would take responsibility for her actions, adding: 'I don't suppose we ever missed that drop of water.'

She described two diversions in her hard outback life:

One day an Afghan peddler with his cart arrived. How I longed for the pretty ribbons and laces he offered, but each of us needed a pair of stout laced boots and a new pair of scissors was essential for me as I had lost mine. I made all our clothes and when they wore out, remade them for my child. In those days there was no money to spare for anything that was not considered essential.

Our next visitor was unexpected. A teamster called at a pub at Tindary Station, near Cobar, went on a drinking spree, and in a bout of 'the horrors' walked off into the bush without food or water, drunk and not knowing what he was doing. The shanty keeper reported the matter to Tindary. A station hand and a black tracker sent out to locate him found a pocket knife and a length of string under a gum tree. In the meantime the poor wretch had arrived at our place, his tongue too swollen to speak. He pointed to his mouth and groaned. His eyes were rolling and he kept darting a look behind and around, as though he feared violence. 'The horrors' were still on him.

Fortunately I had seen this before so I gave him weak tea in spoonfuls, then soup in the same way. Little by little I got a bit of nourishment into him, and in time he was able to tell us his story.

He had found himself hopelessly bushed, sat under a tree and saw devils coming after him. In terror he tried to cut his throat, with his blunt tobacco knife, but was only able to make a scratch, as we could see. Then he tried to choke himself with a bit of string, but couldn't manage it. He then must have become unconscious for he could not remember how he reached the track to our place.

Martha nursed the unfortunate man and when he was well enough to be moved, Dave harnessed the horses and Martha held their heads while Dave lifted him into the wagon. It was not an easy manoeuvre:

As one horse reared in panic, Dave shouted to the teamster to take me away as I would be killed. But I hung on; I knew our horses were not vicious, only frightened. Dave set off for the bush inn at Tindary. When he returned that night he smiled and handed me a bottle of port wine, 'A present from our late guest,' he said with a smile.

It was roughly seventy miles to Bourke, our nearest business centre. It took Dave over a week to go there and back. In the drought it was impossible to buy preserved vegetables which we relied on with our water supply so short. When my husband was away at Bourke I had to manage the whole place entirely on my own. Our old shepherd camped in a hut not far away, but he was away with his sheep all day. I became used to roughing it in time but I was always very pleased to see Dave's wagon heave in sight again.

The drought continued and the sheep had nothing to eat but dried trefoil seed. Things were becoming desperate. Dave talked about killing sheep and boiling down their carcasses for their fat to make tallow and sheepskins before our water gave out and forced us to abandon the place, losing everything for which we had worked so hard.

Night after night we talked the matter over. Day after day the sky remained cloudless. That sun burnt the very souls out of us and tried our courage to the limit. It seemed as if the earth would never receive a downpour of rain again. We found piles of dead sheep each morning. There was no railway communication from Dubbo to Bourke then so it was impossible to shift the sheep.

Our sheep were good merinos and had been expensive to buy. It seemed terrible to slaughter the poor things and I had raised some as bottle-fed lambs. But water in the tank was shrinking day after day. What was to be done? The heat sometimes soared as high as 120 degrees. Our shepherd had lost a number of sheep the day before, and Dave had ridden off that morning to search for them. The sky was clear and the sun was roasting. I was washing clothes in a kerosene tin and young Joe was playing close by the door of our hut. Towards noon clouds began to gather in the sky, but I took no notice of them – we had had clouds like that before. By now I had lost hope that the drought would ever break and jumped in fright at the sudden roar of a thunder-clap. The sky was as black as ink. Again the lighting flashed in jagged streaks across the sky, followed by crashes of thunder. I ran outside and brought my child into the hut. A raging wind had sprung up and a red fog of dust made it impossible to see anything. The wind was so strong I was scared lest our tiny hut would keel over. The wind shipped a sheet of bark from the roof, then another and another. The rain came down in streams. I never saw or heard anything like it. I was terrified, and little Joe was crying in my arms. I felt like crying myself when I thought of my husband out in the midst of it all.

The torrents of rain continued. Sheet after sheet of bark was torn from the roof and whirled away. Water from the tank overflowed into a gully and entered the hut and I feared my child would drown. All I could do to save him was stand upon an old stretcher bed holding little Joe in my arms.

An hour later, McGoobery, one of the tank sinkers who had run down from his tent a mile away rushed into the hut. Only one sheet of bark still remained on the roof. He stood on the table and hung on to the sheet till the wind slowed.

All I remember was McGoobery shouting above the wind, 'It's a mercy that little Joe and you are alive!'

In an hour the wind dropped, the rain ceased, and the sky was blue again. My terror passed. I felt overjoyed, knowing that the drought had broken so we did not have to kill the sheep or leave our land.

About 5 o'clock that afternoon poor old Dave turned up on foot, drenched to the skin, but wearing a smile that I had not seen on his face for over twelve months. McGoobery and he would shift all the provisions up to the shearing shed and would stay there till the hut had been fixed. I was not bothered because drought had delayed our plans to build a proper house and so, in spite of the cockroaches, we were still sleeping in the covered wagon, and only used the slab hut for cooking, eating and washing.

The water was knee deep, so Dave had to carry me and Joe to the wagon where we found our bedding dry as a bone, thanks to that good tarpaulin tilt that covered the wagon.

By next day the waters had retired. We were filled with happiness and felt like Noah and his family after they came out of the Ark. What astonished us was finding frogs in thousands. I shall never forget the noise of their croaking. I could never have believed so many could have suddenly sprung up from nowhere, like a plague of mice. On the morning before you could not have found a single frog, and now they covered the ground, little and big, young and old. Little Joe had the fun of his life catching them and seeing them hop around. In a short time we had three tanks full of water and plenty of grass.

However our remaining sheep got 'the scours' [persistent diarrhoea] from the sudden change in diet to rich young grass.

Learning of the rain, James Gormly despatched 2000 sheep out in charge of his eldest son, who landed them in fair condition on their block. He then went back leaving Dave in charge. Gormley had not stocked up before the drought. Had that rain not come when it did, we would have lost all our sheep.

Dave, relieved of worry, set to work to build a comfortable house for us. That rain had made all the difference, giving us some guarantee of permanent occupation. Dave worked with a will, and before very long we had a comfortable habitation which proved a blessing, especially to me, after the roughing I had experienced sleeping in that wagon, where clouds of red dust settled on everything as soon as I cleaned up.

In October our shearing started. We had three shearers. I had to cook for all hands and I remember how fussy those shearers were over their tucker. Shearing is very trying work, bending so long over greasy, smelly sheep puts men off their appetite, and they need something tasty to tempt them to eat.

We had no butcher, baker or storekeeper so I was hard put 'to make a do of it'. But the men seemed to like my bread and brownies. Our great drawback was lack of vegetables because our tank water was too precious to use on a vegetable garden. All I could do was to give our shearers some preserved vegetables which Dave bought at Bourke and which came originally from Adelaide. I used to pour boiling water on those preserved vegetables and heat them up in the pots; they were not a bad substitute for the real thing. [This is the second mention of the fact that they were not eating fresh vegetables.] Dave was a splendid shearer and I was always up at the shed helping the men out when shearing started. Dave shore a ewe first and told the men that that was the way he wanted his sheep shorn.

'Pink 'em, but don't cut 'em,' he would say. The fleece was light and naturally a bit broken after such a season, but it was merino and fetched 9$\frac{1}{2}$d [pence] a pound, which was reckoned a good price at that time. But the clip took a long time to reach the market and it was another three months before I could finally send our wool cheque to the bank.

Jim Gormly came out to us again. I must say he now changed his tune and showed a deal of consideration for me in many ways. As well as cooking for the shearers, I had been doing the cooking for the tank sinkers but Gormly soon put an end to that, saying that the men should cook for themselves and that I was doing 'far too much altogether'. He warned that I would break down. [Martha must have been showing signs of illness.]

One day our old shepherd reported he had lost twenty sheep. The shepherd was eating his breakfast next day in the lean-to along with the rest of us, when Gormly swore at him. The old shepherd answered back that he had done his best to look after them and could not help it. Gormly began to shout at him. Jumping up in a rage, he stormed over to the man, grabbed him by the neck and told the shepherd to hold his clapper [tongue] or he would leave him in such a state he would only be fit for the hospital.

Next day the old shepherd asked Dave for his money. David tried to make the old man see reason but nothing would dissuade that shepherd, who was terrified of Gormly and his threats and insisted on departing. So Dave and Gormly had to take over the task of shepherding for a whole month. I laughed to myself, knowing that Gormly's temper had ensured he would have to work hard for a change. It took a month to obtain the services of another shepherd as our part of the outback was considered 'the back end of the world' in those days.

White shepherds used to buy the sexual favours of black women by giving them, their fathers or husbands tobacco and tea. The Aboriginal men, who often had several wives, did not object to pimping for their wives if enough incentive was provided.[8] The white shepherds often infected these full Aboriginal or part-Aboriginal women with venereal disease and then they returned them to their tribe, who did not nurse them, but abandoned them to their fate, a practice that sickened Martha, who brought food to sick and abandoned Aboriginal women on several occasions.

At this juncture Martha was also worried about little Joe.

I couldn't think what was ailing our child. He lost his appetite. His skin was dull and flaking and his face as pale as putty. His legs became puffy and sore, and his teeth were in a bad state, bleeding at the gums. I had never seen anything like it, and all the usual medicines that we used in the bush did him no good. I was far too worried about Joe to think of myself.

Joe was showing the classic symptoms of scurvy, caused by lack of vitamin C, normally derived from vegetables and citrus fruits. Martha was too busy worrying about her husband and child to notice her own declining health. Her usual optimistic, energetic personality changed and she became weepy and irritable. At that time little was known about scurvy in the bush (although mariners had been aware of its danger for a long time).[9] Eventually Joe's leg became infected and Dave took him and Martha to the nearest doctor, in Bourke, which meant a drive of more than two days. Martha recalls:

We stayed at Sprowl's Hotel. After the loneliness and isolation at Corongo Peak, Bourke seemed like a big city to me. Mrs Sprowl had gone to Sydney on a trip, so Miss Pierce was housekeeping for her while she was away. She was the first woman I had seen for two and a half years. I cried with relief to talk to a woman again after so long on my own. However that doctor was a real fraud and gave me little satisfaction. He said that Joe had evidently injured his leg in some way and advised me to take him home and keep him in bed with his leg bandaged.

On the way home we stayed a night at Davidson's Station. Mrs Davidson immediately noticed Joe's poor condition. She asked what the doctor had said so I told her. She said that the doctor was very wrong, that my poor child had scurvy. She told me that David should go on home, and I should stay there with Joe while she did what was necessary to cure him, and that it was our child's diet that needed attention. She gave him plenty of vegetables, both cooked and raw, which surprised me as normally doctors said raw foods were too hard for children to digest.[10]

Martha herself was also suffering from the onset of scurvy but neither she nor the doctor recognised the early warning signs, which included bleeding gums, fatigue and irritability. Little Joe sickened long before she did; young children have less resistance and show pronounced symptoms of the disease much sooner than adults.

The Davidsons could afford to keep a Chinese gardener on their station who managed to grow them fresh vegetables. Martha records:

In a week Joe was much better, and ere long, Dave came back and took us home. Mrs Davidson filled up the back of the trap with vegetables to keep Joe going for quite a time. It was a blessing to see little Joe running round bright and happy again after such a long spell of sickness. Joe's bout of scurvy made me understand just what the poor sailors used to suffer on long voyages in sailing ships.

Some months had passed since our return from Bourke, when one day, a handsome gentlemanly-looking man rode up to the house inquiring if this was Mr Dave Cox's place. When I answered it was, he politely asked if I was Mrs Cox and introduced himself as Mr McDonald, a friend of Miss Pierce, whose acquaintance I had made some months ago out at Bourke. Mr McDonald had ridden over from Tindary Station where he had seen Miss Pierce, who was employed to teach the children, but finding the company too rough, she had asked

Mr McDonald to call and convey her kind regards and say that she would very much like to spend a week or two with me. The poor lass was wretched where she was. I said that I should be glad to see her and that Dave would take a spare horse and bring her back. Mr McDonald thanked me, and rode off.

Eventually Miss Pierce arrived exhausted by the long journey. We were as happy as could be together. Miss Pierce was a lovely young woman, thoughtful and capable, without a bit of nonsense about her. Although born in the city she adapted to outback life very well and I became like a different woman by reason of her company while she said she felt like a bird liberated from a cage after working for horrible people as a governess. She only came for 'a week or two', but it was six months before we parted.

Not surprisingly, Martha, who had not had the chance to speak to another women for nearly two years and had survived illness and drought, burst into tears of joy at the thought of having a woman friend. She continued:

Mr McDonald came again for a visit, stayed to dinner, and had a long chat with Miss Pierce that afternoon before riding away. He told us he was managing a station out between Davidson's property and Bourke, about twenty miles from that place. He seemed to be in the girl's thoughts, for she often spoke of him. Then a month after his visit, she 'let the cat out of the bag' and admitted they were engaged to be married.

Their marriage took place at Davidson's station. I was her matron of honour and Dave gave her away. The clergyman had to come all the way from Bourke to marry them. The Davidsons made a grand affair of the wedding, and champagne flowed freely at the feast that followed. I felt the parting from my friend deeply, like losing one of my own family. When they drove off in their fine buggy, drawn by a spanking pair of horses, I faced the lonely Corongo Peak with a heart as heavy as lead and Joe felt her absence greatly too. She had been teaching him all the time she had been with us, and he had become attached to her.

Now Martha was pregnant again. She records:

My second child, Mary Ann, was born at Bourke in 1879.

Returning again to The Peak with my daughter, I faced the old lonely life once more and was beginning to feel the long strain of isolation and hardship on my health. I suffered severe headaches and pains in arms and legs and often could not sleep. I tried to battle against weakness and fatigue, but at length it threatened to get the best of me, and Dave began to feel anxious.

Martha's headaches and joint pains from lack of vitamins indicated the slow onset of scurvy. It would all be part of her disease that she slept badly. It is possible that she was suffering symptoms of clinical depression in which energy decreases. Physical illness and a harsh life had now changed her totally from the optimistic, tomboyish girl with flowing dark hair who set out jauntily for a pioneering life at Corongo Peak. Yet her loyalty to Dave, who accepted her as his partner in this enterprise, makes her loath to let him down and leave. She continues bravely:

Good rains fortunately put a little fresh life into me. The tanks filled, the grass grew with its usual quickness, and the flocks soon regained condition. Gormly arrived and the two men held a conference as to the best course to pursue. I was sleeping even worse and the pains were worse and my hair started to come away in handfuls. They could see that my health was breaking under the strain, and both were agreed that they would never be able to sell out to better advantage. They felt that if they missed this chance they might not get another like it for a couple of years more and so they decided to get out while the going was good. And I was inwardly glad to think I might soon be able to say good-bye to Corongo Peak.

As soon as Gormly got back to Wagga he set things moving with the agents, who got into touch with a man named Attenborough who had come from Melbourne to Wagga in search of grazing land. After a full inspection of the two blocks, tanks, sheep, etc., Mr Attenborough decided to buy us out, lock, stock and barrel, as they say, and the sale was completed. Gormly and Dave were well satisfied with the price obtained.

What would Dave and Martha Cox do now? Martha goes on:

Meanwhile my mother, now in her fifties, and my brothers had sold the property at The Billabong, and had gone cattle-raising in Queensland.

Dave and I made up our minds to try our luck in Queensland too. We had been kept informed of my family's experience there while we were at Corongo Peak and they wrote that it was useless to think of taking sheep up there as the dingoes proved too serious a problem. David proposed that we go up to Queensland and see what the country was like. If my mother and brothers could make good money farming cattle in Queensland, there was no reason why we should not do the same.

I asked about the blacks. David assured me that the blacks were all right if you treated them with a little consideration. He added, 'They haven't wiped your folks out, have they? Some settlers start off by pumping lead into the poor devils, and only then wonder why their cattle were speared and folks got killed.'

So we packed our household effects into that old tarpaulin-covered Yankee wagon and headed off.

Our way lay west at first to Wilcannia on the Darling River, then slowly over sandhill country north till we crossed the border in the north-west corner of New South Wales. We had a team of twelve good horses. We halted after a long trek and camped out in the wilds of Queensland. There was plenty of coarse feed with cotton-bush and saltbush which the horses seemed to fancy. Having rested a few days, we pushed along through the strange bush, steering for my brothers' property[11] where at length we arrived, delighted to end such a tiring journey.

It was a joy for me to be with my dear folks once again. We rested there for a week or so. Life seemed to begin all over again with my mother and my brothers around me. We talked over old days when I'd been a happy girl full of life and spirit and eager to have a farm of my own. I knew that many brave women had gone out into the wilderness with their men, resolved to overcome all hardships, worked themselves to the bone and ruined their health. I hadn't thought it would happen to me.

Dave and my brothers had long talks over our prospects in Queensland. They had been cattle-raising there for some time, and were able to give my husband good advice. We had a fair amount of cash in hand, and it was now only necessary to find good land and obtain stock to put on it. By now I was feeling stronger.

My brothers had two good Aboriginal servants, who they had named Jimmy and Judy. We became very friendly with the pair of them. When at length Dave had made a tour of inspection of the country and had secured two ten-mile pastoral leases, and we were about to make a start for our new home, my brothers offered to let us take Jimmy and Judy with us as interpreters, should any blacks appear, as well as being able to assist with the work on the place. Judy was a fine help in the house, and I was glad to see that she was eager to come away with us. Jimmy turned out to be a very good stockman.

It took us a good many miles of travel to reach our new home after leaving my brother's place. We settled about 90 miles from Charleville. Dave located a freshwater spring in a rocky basin a foot or two in depth in a knoll which afforded sufficient water for domestic use and for the horses. The spring seemed permanent and clear. We called one block 'Chester', and the other 'Woodbine'.

We were now in the wilds of Queensland with some twenty square miles of rough country at our disposal. We had no roof to shelter us and no furniture beyond the few things we had been able to stow away in the wagon. We had been so long on our journey from Corongo Peak that our rations were running low when we reached our leases. It was not a very cheerful prospect for me, being so far away from civilisation and camping once more in the heat of the wagon until we could build another hut and with no vegetable garden until I could make one. So there we were back to damper, salt beef and dripping.

David was worried about the future. But I told him we had roughed it before and supposed we could rough it again. He was concerned that it wasn't much of a place to bring me to and I hadn't been in good health for some time – perhaps the right thing would be to take me back to my mother's and leave me there for twelve months and give the game a try-out by himself?

I felt guilty about letting him down with my share of the work. All I wished for was a little more strength to carry me along. I tired easily and was just not the same woman who went out to Corongo Peak so full of enthusiasm. All that work and worry had taken it out of me.

Dave had to go to Charleville for supplies to carry us along. He greased the trap and got things ready for the Charleville trip on Wednesday morning, taking Jimmy in case he ran across some blacks.

We were told there were some pretty wild tribes in the Queensland bush and it would take him a week to get back.

I must confess that my heart trembled within me when I saw the wagon disappear from sight in the grey-green of the bush. David's words with regard to the possibility of encountering hostile blacks on his journey came back to my mind. If there might be danger in that direction what about me, left in the wilderness with poor elderly, helpless Judy? I had not spoken to Dave of my own fear, lest it upset his plans and I didn't wish to make things harder for him.

In spite of her weakened state, Martha's courage and determination shone through. She must have been constantly aware that medical help was over a hundred miles away and it would take at least a week by covered wagon to reach a doctor.

We were there to rough it, Dave had said, and it would not do for me to cave in right at the start of a new adventure. So I choked back my fears, as best I could, and tried not to think of the pain in my knees and elbows. I turned my attention to the camp, trying to make things more ship-shape with good old Judy's help.

That night Judy roasted a snake she had caught for supper. She begged me to eat a bit of the flesh, which, truth to tell, was as white as cooked eel. Needless to say, I declined Judy's tempting offer.

The night closed on us and I was dead tired. Life must go on I told myself. I lifted my sleepy children up into the wagon and, climbing in myself, was soon asleep. Fortunately that night passed without incident.

I awoke at dawn the next morning to see Judy lighting the fire with dry bark and sticks. I watched her through a hole in the canvas. Gazing across the bush towards a clearing, she saw a large party of blacks armed with spears approaching. Dropping her bundle of sticks she uttered a cry, and running quickly to the tail of the wagon, screamed to me to come quickly. I looked where she was pointing and saw black forms moving forward in the timber. I felt weak in the limbs. I did not know what to do and thought only of my sleeping children, who were just beginning to stir. What if the blacks should murder them and me, loot the wagon and take Judy away with them? David would never find us then. But I knew this was not time to faint or think of possible horrors to come.

Determined to protect the children, I leaped down from the wagon. Knowing that the blacks dread guns, I seized a longish smooth stick lying at the fire, and wrapping the greater part of it round with one of Dave's old coats, I leaned it against a wheel of the waggon and returned to comfort the little ones.

On came the blacks, fully fifty of them, brandishing their spears and nullahs, and uttering wild yells. My heart almost ceased to beat. They came nearer and their yells frightened little Joe, who began to cry. I felt that we were doomed and started to pray. The mercy of God was upon us, for the next moment Judy thrust her head in at the back and cried, 'No be afraid Martha. That fella black people belong my tribe. They woan hurt you Martha. I go yabber longa them blackfella, tellem you good fella longa me.'

Up they swept while Judy went out to meet them. While she talked to them they calmed down and dropped their weapons. I asked Judy to tell them to go away. Seeing them doubtful I called Judy back to the wagon and gave her Dave's tobacco to give them and to ask them again to go away.

How their eyes sparkled when they saw the tobacco. Judy broke the thin sticks in two and gave each of them a piece. Picking up their weapons, they made off into the bush and disappeared from sight. Judy informed me that her tribe were on their way to Pittagaroo for their annual corroboree. I had heard of hostile tribes along Cooper's Creek (which was no great distance away), and had originally believed they must be from there. The shock made me vomit and I was head-achey for the rest of the day. What a mercy it was that we had brought Judy along.

Meanwhile, Dave had left Jimmy to guard their camp while he completed his journey to Charleville. On his return, he found that Jimmy had been menaced by another very hostile group of Aborigines. Dave threatened them with his gun and they ran away – much to Jimmy's relief. He was more afraid of his fellow Aborigines than he was of David.

Martha continues her story after her husband's return:

During the next month my health broke down completely. My weak condition reacted upon my baby. As we were over one hundred miles from medical aid, there was nothing for it but to give in. David drove me and the little ones back to my brothers' place, leaving Jimmy and Judy in charge of our things.

Martha's brothers later brought back to their property the faithful Judy and Jimmy, together with the wagon and goods the Cox's had had to leave behind. Martha describes how when she reached her brothers' place she:

> ... had to take to bed for a fortnight. My mother cared for and weaned the baby. Soon we were able to start for Melbourne, taking my younger sister, Priscilla, with us to help us through.

David chose the longer route to Melbourne rather than Sydney, as they could follow the Darling and other rivers and be assured of water. The route to Sydney meant transversing large tracts of land between the rivers and the Great Dividing Range. Martha's 'nerves' were symptomatic of her illness. Her physical symptoms included joint pains, weakness and fainting, and she was suffering from skin flaking away on face and hands, tender gums and hair loss. In the last stages of scurvy sufferers bleed from hair follicles and develop large black bruises beneath the skin from the tiniest knock. Her menstrual periods may well have stopped. At this time, fertile women gave birth on average every two years but Martha's cycle of birth was probably interrupted by deprivation of vitamins C and B. Just as she gives us no details of her childbirth experiences, so she does not dwell on her painful symptoms. But it is evident she was seriously ill and even she acknowledged 'there was nothing for it but to give in'. The journey to Melbourne was 800 miles in searing heat, travelling in a double-seated buggy.[12] This is how she describes it:

> ... there I was, a sick woman with a young child as well as a freshly weaned baby to feed and without a drop of milk most of the time.
>
> It is a marvel that I did not lose my baby. I had none of those special nourishing preparations for infants, no soothing syrups out there in the land of the Never-Never in the middle of nowhere. I fed the baby on sops [bread and water], arrowroot or cornflour, mixed with milk, whenever we could get it, which was seldom.
>
> On that nightmare journey little Joe, Priscilla, David, myself and the baby slept beneath the buggy at night, or beside the camp fire if a cold snap came. It was risky for a woman. Drovers or bushrangers

passed by while we were sleeping. Some unfortunate women had their husbands held to ransom with a gun while the men had their way with their wives and daughters so I stayed quiet as a mouse while the drovers passed by.

Several times, when the sun was at its highest, I nearly fainted from weakness in that awful heat on the road. Dave and Priscilla had to lay me down under a cotton bush to rest and revive before I could go on.

At last we struck a coach at a wayside inn just before we reached Wilcannia. Dave put us aboard and left the buggy and horses at the inn.

At Wilcannia I had to rest for a week before I could continue. Then on we went by coach to Hay, where we met with great kindness and consideration at the hands of the landlord of our hotel, who gave us a letter of introduction to a hotel keeper in Melbourne.

We left a week later, crossing the Murray River at Echuca, where we took a train for Melbourne and I lost no time in consulting Dr Fitzgerald, one of the leading doctors. I felt very ill and weak the morning David took me to see him. I was disappointed to find that doctor gruff in manner. He told me that my system was completely run down with the hardships I had been through and the lack of nourishing food, especially green vegetables and pure water and insisted it would take some time to recover my health.

'If you take your wife back into the wilds again you'll soon have to bury her there,' Dr Fitzgerald warned my husband. The doctor prescribed medicine and gave strict instructions that I was not to travel for some time.

So I remained in Melbourne with Priscilla and the children and David went back to get the buggy, intending to travel across country to join us at my sister Olivia's place near The Ten Mile later.

At the end of a month, my health having somewhat improved we left Melbourne on Cobb and Co's coach bound for Albury and from there to my sister Olivia's home at Germanton [Holbrook].

I was overjoyed at returning to civilisation once more. Coronga Peak had been bad enough but the wilds of Queensland and that terrible journey had almost finished me. My husband was feeling the strain and was also far from well but managed to pull through. He had brought the buggy and our few possessions safely from out Wilcannia way and it was a great joy to me that we were all united once more.

The old Cox homestead was at Livingstone Gully, near Wagga. David and his sister, the late Mrs James Gormly, had been born at Tumut but the rest of the children (from Mr Cox senior's second marriage) first saw the light of day at the old homestead at Livingstone Gully.

David's mother was well advanced in years and in failing health. Dave had been anxious about her condition for some time. So, after staying a while at my sister's place, Dave drove us down to the old family homestead at Livingstone Gully. That good old lady [Martha's mother-in-law] was looking very feeble, but was delighted to see her son again after such a long absence. We were not privileged to have her long, however, for she grew weaker each day, and soon she passed away.

By now I was sufficiently recovered to take up my domestic chores once more. Dave cast his eyes around for a piece of suitable country available for selection and found one on Murraguldrie Creek, a few miles from Humula. Dave's brother, Laurence, owned a property on Kyeamba, nine or ten miles away and had married my sister, Agnes, and so things fitted in nicely from a family point of view.

In 1880 we made a start on a property we named 'Woodburn' where David took up 640 acres. Later we got 320 acres in addition. We also bought an adjoining farm of 150 acres soon afterwards, and these, with pre-leases, gave us over 3000 acres of country. Rough and hilly it was, to a great extent, and heavily timbered, but the flats were suitable for cultivation, and, best of all, we had no worries about water so there was no tank-sinking to pay for. The rainfall ranged from 20 to 25 inches per annum, and we felt that, now, at long last, we might be able to build a permanent home. Our previous undertakings had been more like gambling experiments but now we would make ourselves a real home at last.

As usual, great trees had to be grubbed and burnt off, or hauled away out of the road before we secured a clearing for our home, following ringbarking and constant suckering off the big trees. The biggest cost (after our new and commodious house was built, the home I had dreamed of owning for so long) was our fencing. This ran into a lot of money for wire. Outback we practically did no fencing at all, but here, owing to closer settlement on smaller areas it was compulsory, or there would have been constant boxing [mixing of stock] and trespassing. Some of the hill country was extremely rough, but it suited the sheep, being high and dry and sheltered, more or less, in the cold weather. As far as the living and general conditions were concerned we were better off than before, and I was gradually growing stronger again.

'Plenty of green vegetables and the best spring water you can get,' the Melbourne doctor had impressed upon me. Now, at long last, I would have both. David fenced in a good vegetable patch with three wires and a top rail, and I soon had it under cultivation. What a change to see green cabbages and lettuce and other vegetables, not forgetting good potatoes, flourishing in plenty. Those vegetables and that spring water just about saved my life, and enabled me to live long past the allotted span – I passed my 84th milepeg[13] of life in April last (1937).

David stocked up with a thousand merino ewes. The lambing ran to eighty per cent and the flock settled down and was doing well. However, when mustering came, David was surprised and disappointed to find only 500 lambs. We had branded with an earmark, Dave hated the idea of fire branding, although it was really necessary. However things went better with the next lambing, and we had no further worry in the matter of loss of stock.

My third child, Frederick (Andrew Frederick), was born in 1882, Louis (David Louis) in 1885, and Margaret Clare was born in Wagga in 1890. Our Joseph was now a big strapping lad of 16 years, well able to help his father about the place. The seasons were fairly good, an improvement on what we had experienced. The lambing was mostly good and our flocks increased until we received quite a tidy cheque in wool proceeds every year and the nearer railway communications helped us considerably.

Wagga was a fine business town within easy reach of us, even before the coming of the motor car. There was no slipping away then from a farm to get a supply of goods before breakfast and being back by noon. It took us a whole day with a buggy over shocking roads. In wet spells one would often see loaded wagons covered with tarpaulins, waiting at camps for a week for the road to dry and harden enough for them to reach Wagga.

We made all our own candles, soaps, jams and preserves and raised our own poultry and eggs, our milk and butter. We killed our own beef and mutton, so there was little to buy as regards food supplies, and, as for vegetables, we always had more than we needed. I made all our bread. Apart from shoes which I found I could not make, there was little to buy in the matter of household requirements, while there was mostly something to realise upon for a bit of cash. Industrious people were able to 'make a do of it', and save money on their properties, especially when the seasons were good. There was always plenty of work, but we bush folks who had pluck and wished to get on didn't care a button about the backbreaking toil. We were hard at work early and late. Now we and the children had our health and strength back, we even found time to make a bit of simple social fun and recreation with the neighbours. I loved our home and our free bush life and little thought it would ever change.

The first of our misfortunes was the death of my youngest sister Priscilla. Only the year before[14] she had married Mr Meredith and gone to live at Albury.

Our dear mother had been brought down from Queensland by my brother, as she was advancing in years, and wished to be amongst us all in the Riverina. She stayed first with one married daughter and then another, but she spent most of her time with Agnes. Mother passed away at the residence of my sister Agnes (Mrs Laurence Cox) at Tea-tree Creek, Kyeamba. She had been a good, devoted mother to us all. Mother's birthday was on May 24, the date of Queen Victoria's birthday, and she would have been 70 years of age had she lived a month longer. She was buried in Wagga cemetery.

And now I come to the part of my story which is hardest of all to tell, the death of my beloved husband. Fifty-nine years of age seems early for such a strong and apparently robust life as his to terminate. It was a cruel blow to which I found it hard to reconcile myself; we had been partners in life and all our undertakings. Dave died in September, the spring of the year. He was away on 'Kookoona', the property we had recently purchased and he had temporarily moved there during the lambing season. Fully 90 per cent of the lambs lived, the best we had so far had. Dave had taken our sons Joe and Louis up to help him with the work and written to tell me that 'I will go into Wagga on Saturday morning and buy a pony for Clare. Tell her I am bringing the pony home for her.' Clare [their youngest daughter] was nine years of age. She was a good rider, and the thought of the promised pony filled her with joy.

But on that very Saturday, David suffered a fatal paralytic stroke and was taken into a private hospital in Wagga. My old friend, James

Gormly, informed me by telegram and sent his son to Currawarna with a vehicle to bring me into town.

I sat by his hospital bed for two days before my husband was able to recognise me. He was unable to speak (nor was he ever to utter a single word to me, one side of his body being completely paralysed). I did not leave his beside for any length of time. On the ninth day he passed peacefully away. On September 25, 1898, my husband was laid to rest in the Wagga cemetery.

Now I was all alone facing the problems of life on the land with five children, three boys and two girls.

Joseph was now 25 years of age, Mary Ann 21, Frederick 17, Louis 14, and Clare 9. All of them were devoted to me and eager to do their best, so that although sorely stricken I had my children to console me and help me to struggle on. The management of the property was left in the hands of three executors until Clare should reach the age of 21, when everything was to revert to me to manage as I thought best. In the meantime I was to live wherever I liked, and educate the children as I wished to. It all seemed unreal. I was carried along as though in the grip of a terrible dream. It seemed so hard that after planning more intense farming operations at Kookoona and a move there David should be so suddenly and so unexpectedly stricken.

There was no time to sit and grieve. I *had* to be strong for all of us. The whole of the estate was to be under the general direction of the three executors of my husband's will for the time being but I had to do much of the running of the properties. Clare was being educated by an excellent governess. She would reach her majority in a little over 12 years and when she turned 21 I would have a free hand to make my own decision as to the disposal or retention of any portion of the estate. I was able to exercise a certain personal authority in conjunction with the executors, and certainly stood up for my own judgement where I thought it was to the advantage of the properties.

I was sad to leave the home we had built. But it was now vital we took up residence on Kookoona, our Currawarna farm, so that with the hard work of us all, we could build it up. My sons worked splendidly. No doubt they felt that it was up to them to show their mettle now that their father was gone, and so much depended upon their efforts. Now and again I found time to slip up to the Woodburn property to see how things were going along there and visit the old homestead and my garden, now much neglected. When I found it necessary to complain of defects in the management I did not hesitate to speak my mind to the executors.

In the spring of 1904 good rains followed winter and there was a lush growth of grass everywhere in September and October, promising ample feed for the summer. The country looked a picture and stock was rolling fat but the grass ripened and dried under the fierce summer heat. Christmas was so hot we could eat little of our Christmas meal. The standing harvest crops were a source of worry. What if a spark should ignite a fire? What about my much loved home in case of bushfire? I tried to drive such thoughts from my mind, but each day brought greater heat and glare.

The last day of 1904 with its New Year's Eve associations was an awful day of heat and scorching wind. James Angel, one of our neighbours at Woodburn, had driven down to Wagga in the morning to attend to some business. The heat was almost insufferable. The thermometer registered 112 degrees at 2 pm, but the wind sweeping up from the north-west to the south-east made matters more trying. Mr Angel, with his sharp eyes, was one of the first to notice smoke in the north-west. He knew what that meant with so much dry grass a foot in height. Mr Angel put his horses into the buggy and started back for Humula at a fast pace. He had 42 miles to cover, but his thoughts were not merely for his own safety, but also for the safety of his neighbours. He yelled out a warning to each and all as he raced by, telling them of the onrushing fire. It was dark when he reached home and sent warning messages to other land holders in the neighbourhood.

At midnight, as New Year arrived, so did the bushfire. The dryness of the country and the excessive growth of withered grass fed one of the most disastrous fires ever known in the State of New South Wales. A terrific gale fanned the flames and the fire travelled at a speed of 15 miles per hour in spite of the efforts of men to save their homes and sheds.

I and the rest of the family were at our Kookoona property, near Currawana, when the fire broke out. Fortunately it did not cross our side of the river, but we knew the Woodburn property must be right in the course of the onrushing flames. I felt my heart sink at this next dire misfortune. What of the poor cattle and horses up there? They would all perish. An old acquaintance was keeping a friendly eye on the property, said he would do what he could but little could be done by one man against a galloping fire. Our neighbours would be worked to death trying to save their own stock and homestead. The fate of our family homestead and the stock was too dreadful to think about.

It was the worst fire ever experienced throughout the State of New South Wales. Many declared that the intensity of the fire was not only due to the gale behind the flames, but to the phosphorus distributed by the rabbit poisoning that had been carried on for years. Even in broad daylight, when matches were struck, they burned with a white flame. We were afraid for both properties.

Woodburn adjoined Mr James Angel's property. Joe raced off on horseback to see what could be done to retrieve any stock that might have escaped and soon discovered what ravages the fire had wrought. Our neighbour had done his best to safeguard our horses and cattle by rounding them up into the stockyard, thinking, as the ground was fairly bare around the yard, that the flames would not approach it. But he could do nothing for our unfortunate sheep. The fire roared up as a rolling wave of flame. Red hot fragments of bark and timber were born by the wind through scorching air, across roads and over streams, setting up fresh lines of fire which advanced on that disastrous New Year's Day, 1905.

Joe found not one stick of our home at Woodburn left. Flames had made a clean sweep of the place. Here and there the iron frame of a bedstead, or the remains of a sewing machine, arose above the ashes. Not a woolshed or outhouse remained, all our farm machinery destroyed, all our fences gone. For me there was a double blow. All the labour, all the cost of raising up a comfortable home after years of patient waiting had been wasted. Like hundreds of others in a similar plight, we were not insured. Tragically some of our neighbours were burned to death while others narrowly escaped with their lives by rushing to ponds and creeks, and submerging themselves while the flames swept over them, often crouching in the water beside kangaroos and other bush creatures.

One corner of our paddock was blackened and the fence I had helped build, nothing but a row of stumps. In piles, five or six deep, lay 1400 charred bodies of a flock of prime fat wethers [castrated rams] for which I had recently refused 15/- [shillings] per head in cash. Those poor panic-stricken animals had clambered over each other desperate to escape the flames. (At the shearing a few months earlier, the tally had been 3600). Now only 1600 wethers, less than half our stock, remained. Fortunately the cattle and horses in the stockyard escaped, though a few of the young cattle died after we got them back. Those sheep that had survived were now faced with starvation, as not one blade of grass was left to graze upon. Joe got in touch with me and told me that he would have to take the sheep away to grass as soon as he could as they would soon become too weak to travel. I discussed terms with a neighbouring grass-owner for agistment, as we had as much stock at Currawarna as the place would carry.

Joe went round and notified the neighbours of his intention to take our sheep away and asked them what he should do about 'boxed' sheep [Sheep mixed with those from other properties.] Not one raised the slightest objection. 'Take 'em away, Joe, quick as you can, and get them to grass; we can easily whack up [settle up] afterwards,' they said.

I was now faced with the onerous task of reconstruction at Woodburn and a heavy outlay of money as sheds and fences had to be replaced. My bankers proved most kind and considerate. So the hard job was tackled, and in the course of time most of the damage was repaired and I could pay off the debt. I had been through rough experiences but that fire was quite the worst I had known.

It took time to put things back in the flourishing state they had been in before the fire. Twelve years passed by. Martha resumes:

At last my youngest daughter, Clare, was of age, and no longer needed the executors who acted as her guardians. Now the total responsibility of managing both properties was on my shoulders. The seasons were fairly good, I had learned a great deal about farm management, enjoyed the help and companionship of my children after my husband's death but, of course, in the natural order of things they all married with only my eldest son, Joseph, remaining single.

I had completed life's allotted span of three score years and ten … My children were making their own way in life. They had been so good and so devoted that I resolved to provide for them before the time of the final parting came. Before making my final decision I consulted with my banker who approved of the plan and gave me sound advice in all important particulars. I called the children to a family conference, and told them what I proposed to do. It certainly afforded me pleasure and ease of mind.

My next step was to dispose of the Woodburn property with all the stock it carried. In the final disposition of my estate, Kookoona went to Frederick and Louis, while to each of the other children was apportioned cash in equal shares. I managed to arrange everything and it was good to feel myself free from business cares at last.

Martha went to live in Wagga Wagga with her eldest son Joseph in a comfortable home in Wollundry Avenue. She was 93 when she died, outliving her eldest son by three years. The death certificate gives the cause as 'arteriosclerosis' leading to a fatal heart attack. She was buried on 10 March 1947, in the Cox family tomb at the Roman Catholic Cemetery, Wagga Wagga, beside her husband and children.

I have read at least a hundred journals of pioneer women but Martha Caldwell Cox's account of her life is certainly one of the most remarkable. Her fortitude, resourcefulness and endurance through natural disasters are distinctly Australian attributes. These memoirs are her true memorial.

CHAPTER FOUR

Dr Dagmar Berne
(1865–1900)
and
Dr Constance Stone
(1856–1902)
FEMALE PIONEERS IN MEDICINE

Today around half the students in Australian medical schools are female: many of them receive the highest marks as well as student prizes and awards. How ironic then that Australia's first women doctors were despised by their male colleagues for their lack of intellect and had to struggle to obtain hospital residencies and registration once they had qualified. But once women finally *did* manage to register as doctors, many had *outstanding* careers in medicine, working calmly under stress to save the lives of thousands, in peacetime and during wartime.

It is sad to discover that among this bright and dedicated group of pioneer women doctors how few received the honours accrued by their male peers. While Dagmar Berne is commemorated by the Dagmar Berne Medal, which is awarded to the top female medical student at the University of Sydney, neither Dr Constance Stone nor Dr Lucy Gullett have an award or a statue in their memory. These remarkable women doctors were the driving forces that founded the first all-women hospitals in Melbourne and Sydney, designed expressly for women who could not afford medical treatment.

The history of European medicine shows that male prejudice against female doctors is, relatively speaking, a modern phenomenon. *Diseases of Women*, one of the earliest texts on gynaecology and obstetrics pre-dated the Italian Renaissance. It was written before Gutenberg's printing press was invented by a *female* academic named Trotula, who taught medicine at Salerno University in the eleventh century. Trotula's text was written for nuns and abbesses as they acted as midwives and obstetricians.[1] As the rich began to demand physicians who specialised in delivering babies, men took this up as a profession. From the fourteenth century obstetrics and gynaecology passed into the control of male physicians and 'barber' surgeons who lined their hoods with fur and set up colleges and professional associations to regulate just who could deliver babies and charge for their services.[2] They insisted women had to pass an examination run by six male surgeons and six male midwives or *accoucheurs* to deliver any baby, rich or poor, and soon it became the accepted wisdom that *men* were in charge of healing women's bodies and delivering their babies.

In 1874, Dr Henry Maudsley, writing in the London publication *Reproductive Medicine*, argued that women should not be allowed to enter the profession of medicine. He declared that their skulls were smaller than those of men, therefore they lacked the necessary brain power to study and could become sterile if they attempted something so difficult. Maudsley (in his day a well-known doctor with an interest in psychiatry) also claimed that if women were allowed to practise medicine, their menstrual cycle would make them 'irrational' during their monthly periods. He described how women were *far* too delicate to deal with the drunks, prostitutes and raving tertiary syphilitics, who filled the hospital outpatients departments of major cities.

The influx of men into gynaecology was difficult for women in the prudish nineteenth and early twentieth centuries as many women experienced embarrassment discussing any medical complaint that occurred 'below the waistline'.[3] At the time of Federation modesty demanded that women's legs and ankles had to be kept covered. Amelia Bloomer's 'bloomers' for women cyclists were considered an outrage. The Victorians even swathed the legs on pianos out of modesty. Therefore problems of an 'intimate nature' such as vaginal discharge from thrush or cystitis referred as 'uterine catarrh' could not be discussed with a male doctor. Vaginal and pelvic examinations were a source of deep embarrassment for both doctor *and* patient. Modesty dictated that women remained fully dressed while the gynaecologist poked and prodded away under the long skirts, unable to see anything at all. One result was the large number of women who died of untreated cancers before women were admitted to medical practice who might have been able to examine them.

To understand the struggles of Australian female pioneers of medicine it is necessary to know something about the women doctors who encouraged them to seek medical registration at a time when this was hard for a woman. Dr Elizabeth Blackwell (1821–1910), whose family emigrated from Britain to New York when she was sixteen, was the first woman in the world to register as a doctor. She described how 'the whole idea of winning a doctor's degree assumed the aspect of a great moral struggle and the fight possessed immense attraction for me'. Elizabeth Blackwell founded the New York Infirmary for Women and Children to treat poor and disadvantaged women and to train women doctors before returning to England to help other women in their fight to qualify in medicine. One of the girls she talked to at a public lecture was Elizabeth Garrett (Garrett Anderson after marriage), bored by an idle life at home. Dr Blackwell's example changed her life.

In 1870 Dr Elizabeth Garrett Anderson (1836–1917) became the second woman in the world to register as a doctor but was refused entry to a British medical school due to her gender. She had the necessary funds to qualify as a doctor in Paris. Having struggled herself she was very sympathetic to the difficulties placed in the path of Australia's first women medical students like Dagmar Berne and Constance Stone.

Dr Garrett only gained the right to practise medicine in England through legal advice that a loophole in the constitution of the Society of London Apothecaries (which used the word 'person' rather than 'man' in their admission regulations) could admit her as a doctor. The society found it could not legally prove that Dr Elizabeth Garrett was not a 'person' so was forced to admit her as a practising doctor. In 1874, Dr Garrett and Dr Sophia Jex-Blake founded the London School of Medicine for Women. Remembering her own experiences of male prejudice, Dr Garrett gave pioneer women medical students Dagmar Berne such as jobs in the first London women's hospital at a time when such training positions, essential to secure medical registration, were denied to women in Australia. Constance Stone would also seek Dr Garrett's help when she qualified in medicine and surgery but could not obtain registration in Australia

Male doctors defended their monopoly on healing by insisting that childbirth (then conducted without anaesthesia) was so gruesome that women would faint if they had to watch children being born – a strange statement, considering that women had to *undergo* childbirth. The Vice-Chancellors and Deans of Sydney and Melbourne university medical schools were totally opposed to women practising medicine of any kind. They said so, *very* loudly.

In the early 1880s, women were admitted to arts and other courses at Sydney and Melbourne universities, but ultra-conservative professors in the Faculty of Medicine still refused to admit females. By 1884, Sydney University's medical school caved in and admitted women from other disciplines to its courses. In 1887, Melbourne University's Medical School received applications from seven young women studying for arts degrees. Next women's right to study medicine was put to a vote and carried by a majority of ten. The Vice-Chancellor voted against admitting any female students to the medical school, claiming that male students as well as medical staff would be embarrassed if women dissected naked bodies in front of men and that 'decent young women' would be embarrassed at lectures dealing with 'intimate parts of the human body'.

The Dean of Sydney University's medical school, Professor Thomas Anderson Stuart, argued that women should not become doctors. Women, he claimed, were physically and mentally unsuited to the physically and mentally demanding life that medicine entailed. Facing pressure from more enlightened colleagues, the Dean was forced to admit that Sydney's Faculty of Medicine had one excellent female medical student, a Miss Dagmar Berne, who had been studying medicine for two years and whose 'presence had neither inconvenienced nor embarrassed male students or teaching staff'.[7]

Professor Anderson Stuart was out of date in his thinking. Surgery and on occasions childbirth had been harrowing before the introduction of chloroform in the 1840s for doctors and patients but both changed dramatically after the invention of anaesthetics and the introduction of more sanitary conditions in operating theatres. Before anaesthetics were used, patients were primed with laudanum (opium) or alcohol, strapped down on the table and subjected to the surgeon's knife or bone saw, their screams muffled by a gag or leather strap on which they were told to bite hard. Conditions were insanitary – sawdust was used to catch blood and the bandages covering amputated organs and changed only once a week. Operating theatres and hospital wards reeked of putrid flesh, urine and excrement, and bed linen was rarely changed. The use of carbolic as a disinfectant, coupled with Semmelweiss's discovery in Vienna that infection was reduced if doctors and medical students washed their hands before examining wounds and pregnant women, would change the entire practice of medicine.[8]

From 1891 onwards, a handful of determined and dedicated women managed to get themselves admitted to medical schools in Melbourne and Sydney,[9] and eventually, decades later, admitted to study medicine in other Australian states. (The Medical School of the University of

Western Australia was only founded in 1957 and most other Australian medical schools in the 1960s.[10])

Australia's first female medical students were initially awarded good marks by male professors. But gradually it became apparent that however hard they worked, they would not be allowed to qualify. At Sydney University, Professor Anderson Stuart consistently failed *all* women medical students in their final year, however good their previous marks had been, effectively preventing all women from graduating in medicine for years. Only in 1893, when the professor went on leave overseas, was the first woman allowed to graduate. For years Sydney University medical school applied a hidden quota system for female medical students (as did many British medical schools) although this was always denied.

Lack of finance or any scholarships for women ensured they gave up and entered a different course. Some, like Constance Stone and Dagmar Berne, had to travel overseas to gain a degree, which would admit them to practising medicine. Even then many teaching hospitals flatly refused to accept female graduates and effectively banned them from the wards where the most valuable experience was gained.

Dr Kate Campbell would become one of Australia's most respected pioneer paediatricians and save the lives of hundreds of Australian babies. Her efforts would be honoured by the award of DBE (Dame of the British Empire) but when she was newly qualified, she faced enormous prejudice against women in medicine. Dr Campbell described the prejudice:

> At the end of our course there was fierce competition for residentships. The Alfred Hospital *refused* to take any girls at all, even the brightest. Always the same excuse, if any of us women protested: 'We haven't any toilet arrangements!' the administrators would say. Women were admitted to the Melbourne Hospital but somehow 'accidentally' given all the dirty work ... Only men were assigned to work for 'leading lights' in medicine ... There was no social life ... At night, you might have a confinement, get to bed for half an hour and an hour later be called out again.[11]

In order to get a job, women like Constance Stone ran their own all-women hospitals. Many pioneer women doctors never married, or, if they did, often decided against having children because their work was so demanding. Those who could afford the time for raising children usually had mothers, aunts or unmarried sisters who took their place in the family – or else they simply gave up medicine.

All doctors before World War I worked eighteen-to-twenty-hour shifts, day in, day out. All hospital residents, male and female, were paid a pittance and regarded as being lucky to be there at all, as the only entry into medicine lay through getting good references from their consultants. Female residents were paid even less than their male counterparts although women doctors worked hour for hour with their male colleagues and were 'on call' virtually round the clock.

Dagmar Berne

Dagmar Berne was the first woman to study medicine in Australia. Today, the Dagmar Berne prize is presented each year to the female medical graduate obtaining the highest marks in final year, from money donated by Dagmar's mother after her premature death. Few of those to whom it is awarded know the sad story which lies behind this coveted medal.[12]

The short life of Dagmar Berne held the promise of a brilliant career, but was blighted by male prejudice, ultimately responsible for her death. A photograph taken when she was a medical student reveals Dagmar as blonde and typically Scandinavian in feature, with an open face and candid eyes. She had an equally attractive, caring personality and was universally liked by her fellow students at Sydney University.

Dagmar's Danish-born father had emigrated to New South Wales and died when she was young while attempting to save a drowning man in the Bega River. Her mother married again; her second husband, a pastoralist, died when Dagmar was in her teens. Her mother then took her eight children (Dagmar was the eldest daughter) to Sydney, where she insisted that her girls as well as her boys should attend private school. Dagmar was sent to the exclusive Springfield Ladies' College in Potts Point. Here marriage and motherhood were considered of prime importance and the curriculum specialised in dancing, deportment, conversational French, needlework and other handicrafts. To Dagmar, who was studious by nature and fascinated by science, the social ambitions of most of the girls, who dreamed of debutante balls, wedding dresses and wealthy husbands, were entirely foreign. She spent only two terms at the college before letting her mother know that she thought the fees were too high for the 'little amount of real learning that I am getting'. She begged to be allowed to study chemistry with a private tutor, so that she could enter Sydney University, which had just opened its doors to women.

At seventeen, Dagmar left school and studied science privately. The following year, convinced that she had failed her university entrance exam, she was so despondent that she decided to set up a private girls' school in Sydney's Tempe, aided by her sister Florence, who was only sixteen. Dagmar hoped the school would bring in some funds as well as provide education for her other sisters. Dagmar interviewed parents of potential pupils, found premises, bought desks and schoolbooks. A few days before the school opened she was astounded to receive a telegram from the Registrar of Sydney University, congratulating her on passing their entrance exam. So it was left to her younger sister Florence to open the school. There were six pupils, including two of their younger sisters.

Dagmar Berne arrived at Sydney University in 1885 and studied arts for a year before she was allowed to switch to medicine. The staff of the University's medical school were deeply divided over admitting women students. Some were in favour, but the Vice-Chancellor, Sir Henry N. McLaurin, as well as the Dean of the Medical School, Professor Thomas Anderson Stuart, both bitterly opposed the decision to admit women into medicine.

Professor Anderson Stuart was so bigoted that he stated in public: 'I think that the proper place for a woman is in the home; the proper function for a woman is to be a man's wife, and for women to be the mothers of future generations.'[13] He had nothing against Dagmar personally. He and her other teachers found her a model student, intelligent and hard working. Fellow students described her as quiet and reserved; men admired her courage for attempting the medical course. As the eldest girl in her large family, Dagmar had many duties at home so she mixed little in university activities.

While Professor Anderson Stuart outwardly accepted women in his medical course, inwardly he was smarting that the university authorities had forced him to accept Australia's first woman medical student. He was determined that no woman would qualify as long as *he* was in charge. Dagmar optimistically believed that, having at long last been admitted to the university medical school, she was now on an equal footing with the male students.

At the end of her first year in medicine, Dagmar obtained honours in botany, chemistry, zoology and anatomy, which indicated that if she continued with the same grades she would have a good medical career.

In her second year of medicine, Dagmar attended Professor Stuart's lectures. He never told her that he planned she would fail examinations he marked but this was his hidden agenda. After her outstanding success in first-year exams, Dagmar was never allowed to pass another examination at Sydney University. Following exhausting weeks of study, she would seek out the examination results on the notice board. She saw men who had received far lower marks in the first year examinations achieve a pass, but somehow her name was never on the pass list. She would tell her mother in despair: 'Mama, I've failed again. I know I work hard enough, but sometimes I think it's just because they don't *want* to pass me.'

After four years of hard and intensive study at Sydney University, Dagmar finally realised that male prejudice was too strong and she would never be allowed to qualify in medicine.

In 1888, Dagmar met Britain's Dr Elizabeth Garrett Anderson, who was on a lecture tour of Australia. Dagmar explained the difficulties of her position to Dr Anderson. She told Dagmar that she had suffered from *exactly* the same prejudice in England – and won by finishing her exams abroad. She encouraged Dagmar, telling her that the battle had been won in Britain and advised her to confront the authorities who ran Sydney University's medical school in order to clarify her position and her prospects.[14] If qualifying seemed impossible she should come to London and work in Dr Anderson's all-women hospital.

Fired by Dr Garrett Anderson's support, Dagmar and her mother did confront the Vice-Chancellor. He flatly refused to help Dagmar and made it quite clear that so long as he was vice-chancellor *no woman would graduate in medicine.*

Dagmar now clearly realised that as long as leading authorities in the medical school were against women qualifying she would *never* pass. The authorities reckoned she would soon become so depressed and ashamed by her continuing failure that she would abandon the course.

Sailing ten thousand miles to London seemed her only option if she wished to continue studying medicine. Dagmar was encouraged to finish her studies in London by the fact that Dr Garrett Anderson had offered her a training residency in her hospital. Dagmar's determination was strengthened by the fact that her sister Florence had had enough of running a school and also wanted to study medicine.

Mrs Berne was very supportive of the idea and agreed Dagmar and Florence should go to London. Both girls had been left a legacy and could afford to live there, provided they chose inexpensive lodgings and allowed themselves few luxuries.

Dagmar, who had a kind, forgiving nature, even went to farewell the man who had failed her, Professor Thomas Anderson Stuart. After the interview, she told her family that he had been positively avuncular and begged her to give up the idea of practising medicine. 'You're far too *nice* a girl to do medicine,' he had said, patting her on the head and dismissing her. But Dagmar, undaunted, replied quietly but firmly that she was *determined* to qualify as a doctor.

Mrs Berne was unhappy at the suggestion that her daughters should transfer their entire capital to London. She advised them to take only a portion and leave the balance in Sydney, where it would earn a much better rate of interest. Both girls readily agreed.

Dagmar's years at Sydney University gained her matriculation to London University's medical school. Florence had to sit the first year entrance exam, which she passed. The girls found cheap lodgings and lived modestly, working steadily towards their goals. In 1889 Dagmar entered the Royal Free Hospital; two years later she passed the Society of Apothecaries' exams in anatomy and physiology with flying colours. But years of poor diet, damp accommodation in a London basement and foggy, chilly winters took their toll on a girl accustomed to Sydney's warmer climate. Dagmar suffered recurring bouts of pleurisy and pneumonia; on one occasion she rose from her sickbed to sit an exam, which she passed. But her health was seriously weakened. She knew that once she had gained clinical experience she must return to the milder winters of Sydney.

In her last year of training, Dagmar received a letter from her mother informing her that their Sydney bank had failed in the financial downturn that characterised Australia in the 1890s. The girls' capital was lost, along with the rest of the Berne family money. Her brother Frederick had to leave school and was looking for work; her younger sister Eugenie was helping support the family by teaching. By this time the money the two sisters had brought to England had nearly run out. This news signalled the end of all their hopes. Florence realised that Dagmar was so near to completing her course that loss of income to support her was a tragedy. There were no government grants, no scholarships available for women to study medicine.

'There's not enough money to carry us through', Dagmar declared.

All night long, her sister's phrase haunted Florence. She realised she had teaching experience, which Dagmar did not.

The next day, without telling her sister, Florence went to an employment agency and found herself a resident job as a governess. She arranged with the bank to transfer her remaining money to Dagmar's account. Florence countered Dagmar's ensuing protests by saying that they could not let their mother down. There was only enough money for one of them to qualify as a doctor. It had to be Dagmar, who was now able to continue studying in spite of her weight loss and a persistent cough.

Dagmar finally qualified as a doctor in 1893 and went to work at the North Eastern Fever Hospital in Tottenham, just outside London, as a resident. After two years there she returned to Sydney.

On 9 January 1895, Dr Dagmar Berne registered her Diplomas from the Royal College of Physicians and Surgeons of Edinburgh, the Faculty of Physicians and Surgeons of Glasgow and the Society of Apothecaries, London, with the Registrar of the Medical Board of New South Wales. She was only the second Australian woman to register with the New South Wales Medical Board, the first being Dr Constance Stone who had also had to go overseas to get her degree.

Dagmar Berne set up a practice in rooms in Macquarie Street, the most fashionable area for doctors. She worked hard to help support her mother. Her sister Eugenie, who was teaching, came to live with her. Eugenie was worried by Dagmar's pallor and her racking cough and persuaded her sister to undergo the appropriate clinical tests, which showed that she had tuberculosis.

Family friends, the Morrisseys, who owned Yarrabundie Station at Trundle, in New South Wales, suggested Dagmar should move out there to work, hoping the dry climate might halt her illness. Dagmar stayed with the Morrisseys, from whose home she continued to practise. She saw practising medicine as a vocation and would often refuse to accept fees from those she considered needy or destitute.

According to one of her patients, Mrs Long:

> Dr Berne was very frail and sick and was sometimes so weak she could hardly shake a bottle of medicine. She was still very pretty with a neat slim figure. As a doctor she was very conscientious and capable and everyone in Trundle loved and respected her, for she was so kind and took such a great interest in all her patients, especially the children. She was always very concerned in the treatment of mothers following childbirth, insisting they have plenty of rest ... before they began their ordinary domestic work again. She was probably far in advance of her time as far as this was concerned. She believed that far more women doctors were needed as women understood these things far more than any male doctor could.[15]

Dagmar Berne knew she had not long to live, but she was happy in the career she had sacrificed her own health to undertake. She did not return home in her last days but worked unselfishly right to the last, caring for her patients.

She died at midnight on 22 August 1900, a martyr to male prejudice against women qualifying in medicine.[16]

Although baptised an Anglican, Dagmar worked tirelessly for patients of all denominations. Catholic patients and friends in Trundle presented their local Catholic church with a pair of altar vases in her memory. Dagmar's coffin was returned to her grieving family in Sydney and she was buried in Sydney's Waverley Cemetery. The Dagmar Berne Medal ensures that her name lives on among women medical students.

Dr Constance Stone

The first woman to be registered as a medical practitioner in Australia was Dr Constance Stone (married name Jones). Ironically this woman, who never sought publicity for her work but heroically toiled away to save the lives of others, had initially been turned down as a student by the medical school of the University of Melbourne due to her gender, because they thought she would not be strong enough to cope with medical work.

Constance was born in Hobart in 1856, the eldest child of an English mother and Welsh father, who earned a modest income as an organ builder. Constance's mother had been a governess before her marriage. Books were greatly valued in their household and Constance and her sisters were educated at home by their mother. Like so many of the Welsh, the family were keen chapel-goers and had a strong sense of the Protestant work ethic. Constance was given books but no luxuries as the Stones saved their money for their children's schooling and university, believing strongly in the power of education to transform lives. In later life, Constance Stone described her parents as 'broadminded, especially for those days. They allowed us to make up our own minds as to what we wanted to do.' One of her sisters followed her into medicine, while her brother William became a well-known engineer.

Like Dagmar Berne and other middle-class girls around the pre-Federation and Federation era, Constance Stone started her career as an untrained primary teacher, running a small family school until she was twenty-eight. But anatomy was her passion; she dreamed of becoming a doctor. By now women were admitted to all faculties of Melbourne University except Medicine. Undaunted by a stiff rejection letter when she applied to the Medical Faculty at Melbourne, strong-minded Constance Stone would not take 'no' for an answer. She wrote to the Dean of the Women's Medical College in Philadelphia, an institution inspired by the example of Dr Elizabeth Blackwell. Constance enclosed copies of her teaching qualifications, asking if the Women's College would admit her. She was overjoyed when they agreed and sailed to America to study. Constance did not have the money to return to Australia so would not see her family again for many years.

In 1885 she graduated with an MD from Philadelphia's Faculty of Medicine. But at that time Philadelphia could only provide a three-year medical course. The Australian medical authorities, horrified at the thought of a woman doctor in their midst, informed Constance Stone she would need British qualifications in order to gain registration in Australia – which did not have reciprocity with America at that time.

While sitting her American finals, Constance was also enrolled at Trinity College in the University of Toronto. In 1888, the year of Australia's centennial celebrations, she was awarded first-class honours in Medicine and Surgery from Toronto University.

The remarkable Dr Stone was now in her early thirties. She sailed for London with two aims. First, to obtain a higher degree and her British qualifications, and second, to work with the famous Dr Elizabeth Garrett Anderson, who had by now been joined by Dr Mary Scharlieb, an outstanding surgeon. Their 'new' Women's Hospital (later the Elizabeth Garrett Anderson Hospital) was entirely staffed by women and, of course, admitted only women patients. It was considered a Mecca for women doctors all over Britain. At this unique hospital Dr Stone gained valuable insight not only into the practice of medicine but also into hospital administration. She made up her mind that one day she would found a similar hospital in Melbourne.

In 1889, Constance Stone gained her British qualifications by sitting the examination of the British Society of Apothecaries, still the only English body at that time which would grant a medical qualification to a woman (due to the 'person' rather than 'man' clause under which Dr Garrett Anderson had registered as a clinical practitioner).

The following year, Dr Stone became the first woman to be registered with an Australian Medical Board and was placed on the register in Victoria.[17] She was now one of Australia's best-qualified doctors. Fortified with this knowledge, she rented rooms in Melbourne's Collins Street, and hung up her brass plate. But it proved hard to attract paying patients, even though she charged only a minimal fee. Mainly she saw women and children. Australian working-class men felt threatened by the notion of women examining their bodies.

Constance Stone was in single-handed practice; she had to be on duty every night as well as every weekend. No male doctor would do a swap and accept clinical responsibility for her patients in return for covering for her, as men in private practice did.

However in the surgery Dr Stone's pleasant yet highly professional manner and her feminine appearance overcame much of the initial distrust felt by patients, both female and male. She was dismayed to find that so many poor families were unable to afford even the smallest fee: through contacts in the church she set up a free dispensary and clinic known as the Collingwood Free Medical Mission. At that time Collingwood was a slum area. Large numbers of people attended her clinical sessions as free patients, the only medical service available to them.

In 1893, Constance Stone was joined by her younger sister, Clara, one of the seven pioneer women who demanded the right to attend lectures at the Melbourne University Medical School, basing their demand on the fact that the rest of the university was open to them. Clara Stone became the second woman to qualify from Melbourne's Medical School. She and her sister, two remarkable women, now treated working-class women in Melbourne and its surrounding suburbs. Since they found it impossible to carry a medical bag on a bicycle, they did their rounds by horse and buggy. As so much of their work was for free medical missions, unpaid, they lacked the money to employ a full-time groom. Both sisters became expert at handling horses. Moreover, Melbourne could be dangerous; they were advised to take pistols with them during night calls in the slums.

Through her medical missionary work in slum areas for the City Mission, Constance Stone met and married the Reverend David Egryn Jones, who shared her sense of purpose. He was the minister of St David's Welsh Church in Latrobe Street. (Dr Clara remained single for the rest of her life, believing, like so many pioneers of medicine, that it was too difficult to combine medicine and family duties.) Both the sisters ran clinics from the hall of St David's Church. They saw, without payment in their clinics, sixty women in a single day, three days a week, helped by female volunteers.

Inspired by the work of Dr Elizabeth Garrett Anderson in Britain, the Stone sisters and other newly qualified women who found it difficult to gain hospital residencies decided to set up the first Australian women's hospital. They aimed to treat working-class women free of charge and to abolish the ordeal of ward rounds, where women who could not afford fees had no option but to endure examinations by physicians and their medical students, who often treated working-class women in a patronising manner. Women doctors saw how these women suffered in childbirth and sought to improve conditions for them.

Many churchmen had a patronising attitude to women, seeing the pain of childbirth as the punishment meted out to Eve for feeding

Adam the apple. Male doctors who were influenced by biblical attitudes accepted pain as part of women's lot in life. They and their pastors quoted God's words to Eve in the Book of Genesis: 'I will greatly multiply thy sorrow and thy conception: in pain shalt thou conceive and bring forth children.'

In 1896 Melbourne's Queen Victoria Hospital was founded by twelve medically qualified women, on the instigation of Dr Constance Stone. To combat this defeatist approach to pain and to give working-class and other women a chance of good treatment, Dr Constance Stone invited eleven other women who shared her vision for women's health services to cooperate in setting up the Women's Hospital. She had seen Dr Garrett Anderson's hospital in London and wished to duplicate this dedicated approach to women's health in Australia. It was to be entirely staffed by the voluntary labour of women doctors and be known as the Queen Victoria Hospital for Women and Children. The group used Dr Constance's home as their base in order to raise funds for the new free hospital; from there they also established the Victorian Medical Women's Society.

Before the establishment of free hospitals for women in Sydney and Melbourne, many male doctors flatly refused to treat poorer members of the community or the destitute and homeless unless a fee was paid in advance. There was, of course, no State or Commonwealth medical insurance. Now in Melbourne for the first time Australian working-class women (many too poor to pay to visit the doctor) were treated free of charge or for a tiny fee by women doctors, and if they needed it, provided with contraceptive advice. This was revolutionary since in America, Margaret Sanger's pioneering family planning clinics had been raided by the police, prams and babies scattered in disarray and women attending the clinics taken to the police station.

A committee, headed by Women's Suffrage leader Annette Bear-Crawford, was appointed to run the new women's hospital and to secure permanent premises with inpatient facilities. As treasurer, Annette Bear-Crawford established a 'Shilling Fund' and spoke about the hospital at suffrage meetings. Women throughout the State of Victoria donated a shilling to help set up the hospital.

In July 1899, the Queen Victoria Hospital for Women and Children was officially opened. Besides Clara Stone who was in charge, other dedicated doctors such as Lilian Alexander, Edith Barrett, Constance Ellis, Mary de Garis and Janet and Jean Greig formed the teaching staff.

Dr Helen Sexton, a close friend and supporter of Clara Stone, specialised in family planning (a euphemism for birth control) and in treating sexually transmitted diseases, including syphilis, something 'nice' women were not supposed to speak about, let alone treat. This fatal disease was rampant in Melbourne and Sydney around the time of Federation and women with it were treated like criminals rather than attempts made to contact the men who had infected them. Dr Sexton felt that it required a special clinic to treat women who had been infected by their husbands or boyfriends. Later Dr Sexton's work in Melbourne providing contraceptives to married women would be taken up in community clinics in Sydney by the courageous Sister Lillie Goodisson (See Chapter 11).

Grim sanitary conditions in housing for the poor resulted in epidemics of typhus and typhoid and an overload of patients in the Queen Victoria Hospital. Smallpox was another problem that doctors had to face when dealing with working-class patients. The fault lay in bad housing for the poor, which had either appalling sanitary conditions or no sanitation at all. The governments of the day thought it cheaper to send in rat inspectors, provided with a pack of small dogs to hunt the rats, rather than allocate funds to vaccinate the children of the poor. It was only through pressure applied by women doctors that many humanitarian measures in preventative medicine were forced through around the time of Federation and later that century.

All the women doctors worked extremely hard to establish the Queen Victoria Hospital, which was responsible for saving the lives of countless women and children. Dr Constance Stone, the woman who had the vision and the energy to set up the hospital, did not live long enough to see the full success of her all-women's hospital. Worn out by an enormous clinical and administrative workload and by working long hours, she contracted tuberculosis from one of her women patients, suffered a prolonged and high fever and died. This remarkable woman was still in her early forties. She had saved countless lives by her unstinting dedication to her patients at the expense of her own life.

CHAPTER FIVE

Dr Agnes Bennett
(1872–1960)

Joice NanKivell Loch
(1887–1982)

DISTINGUISHED WOMEN WITH MULTIPLE AWARDS

FOR HUMANITARIAN WORK

Dr Agnes Bennett: Order of the British Empire, Order of St Sava and the Royal Red Cross of Serbia

Agnes Bennett was born in Sydney. Her father was a doctor who had migrated from England with his American-born wife. Agnes's much-loved mother died in childbirth when her daughter was only five. Her father worked very hard at his medical practice and Agnes and her brothers were brought up by a housekeeper. When Agnes was ten, her father married again, choosing an Australian, a widow with her own children to rear, from a rather different social background to his own. Agnes, upset at seeing this woman replacing her own mother in her father's affections, was moody and rebellious. Perhaps if her stepmother had handled the situation better, things might have been different but conflict ensued and her stepmother turned against the highly intelligent but strong-willed little girl.

Agnes loved her father very much but he was rarely home until late. However, during the time they did spend together he encouraged her to believe that she could go to university when she was old enough, like her brothers.

Tragically for Agnes, her father had a fatal heart attack when she was only fifteen. By this time her stepmother actively disliked her clever but argumentative stepdaughter and made her life a misery. Agnes's only support at home was Bob, the brother closest in age to her. In later life Agnes reckoned that being an orphan disliked by her stepmother had the effect of making her more self-reliant than most girls of her own age.

Her father's will had left the necessary money for Agnes to continue attending the Sydney Girls' High School. In Agnes's class were two future authors, Ethel Turner and Louise Mack. Like them, Agnes loved study and books. Agnes topped the class in several subjects, including science. At that time young women had very limited choices: the only degree courses open to women at Sydney University were arts subjects. Agnes enrolled in the Arts Faculty, although she longed to do medicine like her eldest brother.

After years of conflict with her nagging stepmother, Agnes delighted in the freedom that university offered. In her second year she was able to switch from arts to science subjects, including geology, in which she was the only woman in her year. She was tall, athletic and sun-bronzed in summer and attractive to men. She enjoyed sport and became a university tennis champion. In second year she fell in love with a fellow student and her love was reciprocated. They planned to marry once they had finished university. It was a terrible shock when her fiancé, a strong swimmer, drowned in a freak accident. A sand bar collapsed beneath him and he was sucked down by a rip.

Agnes was desolated.[1] This was the third death of someone close to her and she was not yet twenty. She channelled her grief into her studies: perhaps the experience of grief and loss made her wary of loving again, for she never married.

In 1894 Agnes became the first woman at Sydney University to gain a science degree and was awarded first-class honours.

But her dreams of a scientific career were soon shattered. All her letters replying to job advertisements remained unanswered: it seemed that male employers did not want a woman, even one with a first-class degree. Somehow or other she had to earn money so that she could escape from her stepmother's constant nagging and become independent.

The only paid jobs for middle-class women in the 1890s were as teachers, governesses or nurses. Agnes answered an advertisement for a governess and went to the outback of New South Wales to work on a remote property. Then she read in a newspaper that because British female medical graduates had experienced similar problems obtaining the right to use the dissecting rooms at Edinburgh University, a Scottish doctor, Elsie Inglis, had founded Edinburgh's Medical College for Women. Agnes made up her mind to travel to Edinburgh, study at this college and follow in her father's footsteps. Her stepmother told her she was ridiculous, and that she should marry one of the men in the local tennis club. She flatly refused to provide any financial help for Agnes to study medicine, although there was enough money in Dr Bennett's estate to have done so.

So Agnes borrowed the necessary money for board and tuition by enlisting the sympathy of her late father's bank manager. He trusted her and loaned her money which she agreed to pay back with compound interest once she had qualified as a doctor. Agnes departed on a ship bound for Britain; as the liner pulled away from Circular Quay and the paper streamers thrown down by the passengers snapped, Agnes realised she was embarking on a new life.

In London, her father's birthplace, Agnes stayed at the Lyceum Club in Piccadilly, a home away from home for professional women and women in the arts. She explored the city, delighted to be seeing places she had only read about. Then she took the night train north to Edinburgh.

It was autumn. She found Edinburgh Castle and the stone buildings of 'Auld Reekie' fascinating and revelled in their historic associations. Then winter came and with it snow and sleet. Accustomed to the sub-tropical climate of Sydney, Agnes soon pronounced Edinburgh the 'coldest grimmest, grimiest place I've ever seen'.

She rented a damp, cheap basement apartment in an old stone tenement near the medical school, caught bronchitis and was unable to study for several weeks. Dr Elsie Inglis, worried that such a promising student as Agnes had not attended lectures for some weeks, came to visit her and insisted that Agnes should take better care of herself. Dr Inglis took a liking to the young Australian and began to invite her out on Sundays to high tea at the Inglis family home.

Elsie Inglis, a pioneer responsible for giving jobs to many young women in medicine, became Agnes Bennett's role model, her inspiration and mentor. Agnes studied very hard, passed her exams with flying colours and received excellent letters of reference from her lecturers. She dreamed of becoming a surgeon at the Edinburgh Infirmary, a hospital where many great discoveries in medicine had been made.

To her dismay she discovered the same prejudice she had encountered when she applied for scientific posts. The men who sat on hospital appointments committees turned her down and accepted men with much poorer exam results than hers as trainee surgeons.

In spite of Agnes Bennett's first-class degrees in medicine and surgery, the only institution that would employ her was Larbet's Mental Hospital. This was a grim stone pile miles from Edinburgh and civilisation. In the era before the development of psychiatric drugs and anti-depressants, seriously ill patients were treated with a strange mish-mash of dubious remedies, such as cold-water treatments, restraining chairs and strait-jackets, or else kept in padded cells. She worked at Larbet as a house officer for fifteen months to get her medical registration. Agnes now realised that medicine was just as restrictive and anti-female as science or geology. The powerful and very conservative male doctors who ran the teaching hospitals would never allow her to specialise in surgery. She would never be a surgeon. It had all been in vain.

She decided the only thing to do was sail home again, hoping that, in a new country like Australia, the situation for women in medicine would be easier. Back in Sydney, Dr Bennett applied for various hospital appointments but no one bothered to reply.

Refusing to be beaten, she had her name and degrees engraved on a brass plate, rented a room in Macquarie Street, engaged a secretary and went into private practice. But as she had few contacts who would send patients to a mere woman, she had very few patients. Eventually she realised she did not have the money to pay the rent for her expensive consulting room. Moreover, the repayments on her bank loan were due. There was nothing else to do. She had no option but to close her practice, sub-let her premises to a male doctor, and take another job that no one else wanted, at a mental hospital in New South Wales. Here, the 'difficult' patients were treated very harshly by the nursing staff. Dr Bennett wanted to do her best for the patients, which put her in conflict with the male Superintendent. At this juncture a friend of her father's came to her rescue: he wrote from New Zealand offering her a position as Registrar in a maternity hospital in Wellington. Agnes accepted and spent several satisfying years in New Zealand delivering babies.

In 1915, the year after World War I broke out, Agnes turned forty-two. By now almost every able-bodied man had gone away to war and each day the newspapers printed fresh horror stories of young Australians and New Zealanders fighting in the terrible trench warfare of France. Agnes's two brothers were in France and she badly wanted to help in the war effort, but her offer to enlist was refused. She was told that neither the New Zealand nor the Australian Army wanted women doctors. 'Stay home and knit for the war effort!' the army recruiting office advised.

Knitting was not on Dr Bennett's agenda. Undaunted, she offered her services to a French Red Cross hospital where an old friend from university days, Dr Helen Sexton, was working. Dr Sexton put in a good word for her and Agnes Bennett was offered a job as a surgeon. She booked her passage on the next boat sailing for Europe.

When Dr Bennett's ship arrived in Port Said, she looked over the rail and saw stretchers bearing wounded soldiers in what looked like Australian and New Zealand uniforms being carried down the gangplanks of some ships flying the Australian flag. Port Said was in chaos. Men wounded at Gallipoli lay around on stretchers on the dockside, many crying out in pain. There was only one army doctor to help the thousands of wounded men, many of whom seemed on the point of death.

Agnes asked a medical orderly where they had come from and was told, 'Er. Galy-poly … some funny name like that. They're Anzacs wounded in the Dardanelles poor sods.'

Dr Bennett was a volunteer and did not have to answer to anyone for her actions. All she saw were wounded men in pain who desperately needed her operating skills. She went below to her cabin, packed her bags, then marched down the gangplank and buttonholed the first high-ranking officer in British uniform she could find.

'You need me,' she said. 'I'm a surgeon.' His jaw dropped but she was right: they needed every surgeon they could find.

Using a storage shed as an emergency operating theatre, Agnes operated throughout the night, helped by a young medical orderly. There was no anaesthetic so she gave shots of morphine until that ran out, then had to operate without any pain relief. The patients had to be restrained by medical orderlies. Their cries of pain made her feel sick but she saved hundreds of lives.

By ten o'clock next day she had signed all the necessary papers and become the first woman doctor commissioned into the British Army. The army top brass had previously refused to accept women doctors into the armed forces, because they thought them incapable of shouldering the responsibilities and duties involved.

Issued with British Army uniform complete with leather Sam Browne belt and army boots, Acting Captain Agnes Bennett, RAMC, accompanied a trainload of wounded, bound for Cairo. As a member of the Royal Army Medical Corps, she had temporary accreditation to the staff of the British Army Hospital in Cairo.[2]

At last she had found her true *métier* – surgery. In Cairo she proved herself a brilliant surgeon as well as an excellent administrator. At the British Military Hospital she found overcrowded wards, long operating lists and stretchers of wounded lining the corridors. Typhoid and dysentery were common. Beds were scarce until she and two male doctors commandeered an army lorry, drove to some abandoned tourist steamers on the Nile, ripped out the bunks and returned in triumph.

Agnes was overjoyed to hear that Bob, her favourite brother, was now in Alexandria. At this point she had spent nearly six months in an operating theatre or on the wards with little free time. She boarded a train to Alexandria and spent an entire day with him.

By now most Gallipoli survivors were on their way back to Britain. The workload was easing. It was time to move on. Dr Bennett caught the train from Cairo to Port Said and boarded the next ship bound for London. She arrived just in time for the night raids by German Zeppelins.

She was assigned on a temporary basis to the RAMC's Millbank Hospital. Then a chance reunion with Dr Elsie Inglis changed the course of Agnes Bennett's life once more.

The redoubtable Dr Inglis had also been rejected by the British Army for war service. But Elsie Inglis refused to take no for an answer. She formed the Scottish Women's Field Hospitals, which she funded from the proceeds of a lecture tour in America. Now she was in London buying equipment for several tented field hospitals to go to France, complete with operating theatres and mobile ambulances which would be driven by women.

She told Agnes Bennett that a female senior surgeon and administrator was urgently needed to run a new unit which would be leaving for Ostrovo, in Serbia, as soon as the French units were away. In Serbia, Serbian and French forces were fighting as Britain's allies against a combined enemy force of Austrian, German and Bulgarian troops. Would Acting Captain Bennett (recently gazetted for an Order of the British Empire for her heroic rescue work at Port Said) take command? Of course she would.

Agnes Bennett went off to Edinburgh where she assumed control of the employment of ward orderlies and cooks as well as shipping arrangements for all the personnel and medical and camping equipment. At Ostrovo medical orderlies were to be provided mainly by the Serbs. Foreseeing language problems, she engaged a bunch of high-spirited 'gels' from wealthy Scottish and English families keen to get away from home on war service and arranged for them to receive training in first-aid for work as volunteer ambulance drivers, along with the other women who had volunteered as cooks and ward orderlies.[3]

It was a huge task to organise the shipment of people, equipment and all the medical supplies for the field hospital from Edinburgh to the northern Greek port of Salonika, as the British Army called Thessaloniki – a city of cobbled streets and ancient churches built in the days when the city was second in importance to Constantinople, capital of the Byzantine Empire. Thessaloniki was a clanging, teeming city of metalworkers, throbbing with life.

From 1916 onwards Dr Bennett had total control of a medical unit on the Serbian front. In addition, Dr Bennett (her temporary British Army commission now ended) was in charge of setting up a base outside Thessaloniki on which they could fall back if attacked by the enemy. Accordingly, the Scottish Women's Base Hospital in the Balkans was set up on waste ground connected by a dirt track to Thessaloniki. The nearest village was Charilaos. No one else wanted the land because it was the preserve of thieves and murderers. (Today it lies close to the busy Thessaloniki airport.)

Once the Charilaos hospital was running, she left behind enough personnel to cope with special cases which would be evacuated from Ostrovo. Then, from an office near the Thessaloniki docks, she set about organising the transport of seventy large tents and hundreds of crates of medical equipment and tinned food to the front line near Monastir (today's Bitola) in Serbia – a huge task rendered more difficult by language difficulties, potential theft of the supplies and the usual privations of war.

The Balkan War had begun with the assassination of Grand Duke Ferdinand, a relative of the Austrian Emperor, at Sarajevo. This had acted as a powder keg for the rest of Europe. By now food was scarce and very poor in quality. The French had already established two tented hospitals in the area, but one had been sacked and looted by Bulgarian troops and all the personnel killed.

Just as Dr Bennett arrived at Ostrovo Field Hospital, the Serbs, brave guerrilla fighters disastrously short of guns and ammunition, began to retreat before an attack by the well-trained troops of the Austro-Hungarian Empire. Serbian casualties were enormous. Dr Bennett and her fellow doctors were appalled by the enormous number of wounded men who died in the lorry-ambulances that carried them from the front line over pot-holed roads to the Scottish Women's Field Hospital.

During World War I, nearly 2000 courageous Australian women doctors and nurses travelled to Britain at their own expense, having been refused entry to the medical forces of the Australian Army due to their gender. At great risk to themselves, Dr Bennett and her assistant, Dr Elsie Dalyell (a Sydney-born pathologist who had been a junior at the Sydney Girls' High School when Agnes Bennett was a prefect) moved their small operating unit close to the front lines. This had the effect of saving more lives but meant Dr Bennett and Dr Dalyell were operating under the most primitive conditions, often without running water.

The Ostrovo field hospital commanded by Dr Bennett consisted of a row of huge tents and a long, low shed, formerly a barn, divided into two compartments. This housed the operating theatre and emergency X-ray room. Wounded Serbian soldiers, often screaming in pain, arrived in the lorry-ambulances driven by girls who were no longer bored debutantes but heroines. They drove over dirt tracks and roads pockmarked by shell holes and bomb craters to the Scottish Women's Field Hospital where patients lay on straw palliasses or stretchers on the ground in the hospital tents. Other tents acted as camp kitchens. Food was often in short supply once the tins brought from Scotland ran out. Lack of food and medicines coupled with savage rats, so bold that they gnawed patients' wounds and ran across their faces, made the work of the medical orderlies all the harder.

In the midst of this horror the women doctors were surprised to find such dramatically beautiful views of Lake Ostrovo and across the valley. 'The mountains are twenty miles away but in this clear air it seems more like five miles. The line of dazzling snow on the peaks against a clear blue sky is the most wonderful sight I have yet seen'[3] – so Dr Elsie Dalyell described the view from Ostrovo.

Agnes Bennett was eventually joined by another woman doctor from Australia. British-born Dr Lilian Cooper had travelled to Serbia from Brisbane. She too had faced stiff opposition from male doctors to become the Queensland capital's first female doctor. She arrived at Ostrovo with her long-term companion, Jean Bedford, a teacher turned ambulance driver. They were both exceptionally brave. Jean Bedford soon took command of the ambulance runs, which were frequently strafed from the air by German fighter planes. In addition, German aircraft regularly bombed the area.

Heavy bombardment and the stream of ambulances which arrived each night from the front lines with more wounded patients meant that none of the doctors got much sleep. On urgent cases they operated by candlelight far into the night: it was vital that shrapnel should be removed immediately from festering wounds. In summer the heat was blistering; in winter the cold was so biting in the unheated and draughty tents that staff and patients became frost-bitten. Doctors and nurses alike were forced to wear heavy greatcoats taken from dead soldiers or battered old fur coats over their uniforms. Dr Bennett wore an ancient sheepskin coat over her winter uniform and sported a distinctive Australian bushman's hat. All three doctors wore woollen mittens rather than rubber gloves when they operated.

Danger was all around them. No one knew when the Germans and Austrians might attack or bands of Bulgarian guerrilla fighters arrive by stealth in the night and shoot the lot of them; this had happened in several other field hospitals. The Australian women doctors were greatly admired by the Serbs and the French for their coolness under fire, their laconic sense of humour and their acceptance of horrific working conditions.

Summer brought dense clouds of malarial mosquitoes: they did not have enough mosquito netting to combat them and anti-insect sprays had not yet been invented. As a result malaria decimated staff *and* patients. Those staff members who died were replaced.

One of the replacement cooks was the Australian writer Miles Franklin (whose real name was Stella Franklin, see Chapter 21). After the publication of her ironic autobiographical novel *My Brilliant Career*, she had gone to work in America but returned to Britain at the outbreak of war. She enjoyed using assumed names and enrolled as a ward orderly at Ostrovo under the highly improbable name 'Franky Doodle'. Miles Franklin soon applied to switch from ward orderly to camp cook, hoping to write a novel about her war experiences. But the Australian writer contracted malaria, and was shipped back to Britain as a casualty. Back in London, she wrote a few chapters of her proposed book about her time in the Balkans but was unable to get the projected novel published, a fate that would dog many of her manuscripts. In fact, Miles Franklin is probably best known today for the leading literary prize she bequeathed to Australians, rather than for her published work, other than *My Brilliant Career*.

By the time Miles Franklin was evacuated from the Ostrovo field hospital the seventy khaki tents were leaking like sieves onto the patients' stretchers. It was impossible to obtain new ones. In summer the tented wards were filled with fleas and flies as well as mosquitoes. Many patients arrived from the trenches crawling with lice and had to be deloused by orderlies before the doctors could operate on them.

Dr Bennett, known as 'The Chief' by her Serbian medical orderlies, who spoke little English and with whom she had to communicate in schoolgirl French, was greatly admired for her surgical skills and her fairness as a commander.

Life was not easy in a field hospital. Digging camp latrines was a repetitive and highly unpopular chore. Eventually the water supply ran out. A new well from a neighbouring village turned out to be polluted and typhoid and dysentery broke out. The disease of trench foot among soldiers who had lived for months in open shell holes or trenches as the rain fell or the snow melted around them and water soaked through their boots was appalling. The men's toes swelled, blackened and if untreated they fell off.

The Crown Prince of Serbia visited the Ostrovo Field Hospital on several occasions, deeply grateful to the courageous women doctors who risked their lives operating on Serbian soldiers. He awarded Dr Bennett, Dr Dalyell and Dr Cooper the highest Serbian medals 'for valour' – the Order of St Sava and the Royal Red Cross of Serbia.

Shortly after one of his visits, the booming of big guns warned that the Germans and Bulgarians were advancing rapidly. To avoid wholesale slaughter, plans were made to retreat to the Field Hospital at Charilaos, on the outskirts of Thessaloniki. At this stage Dr Bennett had been feeling ill for some time but refused to admit it. As commander of the field hospital she attended a farewell dinner with the Serbian and French commanders, and returned to the Field Hospital to find that although the Bulgarian troops had halted their advance, low-flying German planes had bombed the tented wards. Orderlies and patients had been severely wounded. The operating theatre set up in an old barn was blazing and had to be hosed down to extinguish the flames. Dr Bennett was exhausted but joined in to help douse the flames and save the precious equipment. Adrenalin kept her going but once the danger had passed she went to her tent, feeling faint and nauseated. Catching sight of her pale face in a small mirror on her wash-stand, she saw a lined and elderly woman looking back at her, like a total stranger. Then she blacked out and collapsed.

The next day they struck camp and loaded everything onto lorries to take to Thessaloniki. The Serbian orderlies lined up to kiss the hand of their beloved 'Chief'. Dr Bennett was feeling so weak she could scarcely stand, but she managed to speak a few words of farewell to each of them. Although burning with fever she was determined to leave 'her' field hospital on her feet rather than be carried out on a stretcher. Her Serbian driver and some of the orderlies had tears in their eyes as they saw her being driven away down the bumpy dirt road. Once the car was out of sight, Dr Bennett collapsed completely, her teeth chattering with fever, feeling alternately boiling hot or freezing cold. It was obvious she had a very severe case of malaria. Would she survive the journey?

At Thessaloniki she vainly made the attempt to get out of the car and walk. She was too ill to protest when burly orderlies lifted her onto a stretcher and put her aboard a lorry bound for the Scottish Women's Hospital at Charilaos, which she had set up over a year ago. There she made a good recovery, but was told that she had had a lucky escape. At Charilaos she learned that the Serb orderlies who had stayed on at the Ostrovo Field Hospital had been massacred by the advancing Bulgarians.

Like Agnes Bennett, Dr Elsie Dalyell got away safely, joined the British Royal Army Medical Corps and worked in Thessaloniki. From there she went to a teaching hospital in Vienna, where she published a number of papers in medical journals and was widely respected in her profession. After the war, on her return to Sydney however, she had huge difficulty finding a job suited to her qualifications.

Finally Agnes Bennett was thought to be well enough to be shipped back from Thessaloniki to Sydney on a troop carrier. While she recuperated at her sister-in-law's home, bouts of malarial fever returned from time to time. She wept to learn that Bob, her favourite brother, whom she had last seen in Alexandria, had been killed at Passchendaele, in France. It made her all the more determined not to give up her wartime service.

As soon as she was well enough, Agnes Bennett volunteered for active service once again. She returned to Britain as medical officer on a troop-ship, in charge of a regiment of soldiers, and had a narrow escape when the convoy was torpedoed. Then she went back to Scotland to work at the Glasgow Infirmary, now flooded with casualties. Normally the hospital had a staff of fifteen to twenty doctors. Now Dr Bennett and one other doctor had to cope only assisted by a couple of third-year medical students. Dr Bennett's administrative workload, as well as her operating list, was enormous. Along with war casualties she operated on women workers from the local munition factories, several of whom had arms and legs blown off in accidents.

'I had to do the major operations myself without the assistance of an anaesthetist,' Dr Bennett wrote. 'There was no option but to let third-year medical students give the anaesthetics.'

In 1919, after the war was over, Agnes Bennett returned to Sydney. In spite of her proven dedication and courage, her Serbian and British medals and her years of operating experience, because she was a woman she *still* failed to get a post in a Sydney hospital.

The New Zealand maternity hospital where she had worked wanted her back, so she stayed there until her retirement. Then she returned to Sydney, her birthplace, where she lived quietly in a small house on the North Shore until her death in 1960, by which time her heroism was all but forgotten.

Joyce NanKivell Loch: Order of St Sava, Order of the Redeemer, Order of the Phoenix, the Polish Cross of Virtue, the Polish Cross of Merit, Member of the Order of the British Empire and other medals

Like Agnes Bennett, Queensland-born Joyce NanKivell, journalist, author and aid worker, was a member of the Lyceum Club. She too was honoured with the Serbian Order of St Sava, awarded for her work on malaria prevention carried out at the American Farm School near Thessaloniki, where she worked during what became known as the Greek 'refugee crisis', which followed the massacre of Greeks at Smyrna.

The influx of a million and a half Greek refugees who had lived outside Greece for generations took place in 1922, after some 200 000 Greeks had been murdered by the Turks at Smyrna. As a result of this Turkish 'ethnic cleansing', Greek men, women and children, including hundreds of thousands of widows and orphans, fled from Turkey and Asia Minor and arrived as homeless refugees in Greece, one of the world's poorest countries.

The amazing life of Joice NanKivell Loch is told in my biography, *Blue Ribbons, Bitter Bread: The Life of Joice NanKivell Loch, Australia's Most Decorated Woman*.[5] It is impossible to tell her full story in a single chapter.

Joice NanKivell Loch was as outspoken, compassionate and dedicated as Agnes Bennett. Both women wanted to become doctors but lacking funds for university fees and without a sympathetic bank manager to give her a loan, Joice became an author and journalist instead. Later she worked as a volunteer medical orderly with worldwide Quaker Famine Relief, although she never became a Quaker herself.

Joice NanKivell was born in 1887 at Farnham, a huge cane plantation owned by Fanning NanKivell, in which her grandfather, Thomas NanKivell, was a partner. Her father managed the plantation, and his brothers managed other plantations nearby. As her mother went into labour at the height of a cyclone, without a doctor or midwife, Joice was brought into the world by Daisy, an indentured Pacific Islander. Daisy, kidnapped from her island home by 'blackbirders', had been brought to Queensland as an indentured labourer and became Joice's adored nursemaid. Joice and her brother, Geoff, had a favourite playmate called Tinker, a part-Aboriginal boy who had been abandoned by his mother. Both the NanKivell children were witnesses to Tinker's death in a terrible accident when he was taken by a crocodile during a duck shoot. Joice's early contact with Daisy and Tinker nurtured her deep and enduring concern for the homeless and displaced.

When the Queensland Government insisted that the 'Kanaka' indentured labour system must cease, the NanKivells' heavily mortgaged plantations became unproductive and virtually valueless. In searing heat, amid mosquitoes, scrub ticks and disease-bearing rats, Joice's father, his brothers and their white overseers attempted in vain to cut the cane themselves but were infected by rat bites and several men died of leptospirosis.

Joice's mother, Edith, struggled to run the huge homestead with dwindling funds and staff. The NanKivells' menu changed from beef and imported French wines to kangaroo stew and parrot pie. In desperation they had to sell off their furniture and even Joice's much-loved Shetland pony.

Joice's parents now discovered to their horror that the sugar plantations owned by Fanning NanKivell and Company had been heavily mortgaged by Thomas NanKivell. Foreclosing, the bank took everything in settlement of outstanding mortgages – Joice's parents were ruined. Her grandfather, Thomas NanKivell, survived as he had put his assets in his wife's name; by doing so he sacrificed the future of his children and grandchildren. Joice and her parents had to walk off the property with nothing but a few books and clothes.

Joice's father accepted a job as 'manager' of a sheep property near Morwell in Gippsland, working for a miserly uncle. Joice's mother was horrified to find that the manager's house was nothing but a dirt-floored hut, lined with newspapers. Their new residence was crawling with mice and snakes, and lacked running water or any form of sanitation.

Joice had to grow up fast. She worked hard, baking, cleaning, tending lambs and calves, and cooking for seasonal workers such as shearers and fencers. She realised that her dreams of becoming a doctor would never came true – there was no money to pay university fees.

During the bank crash of the 1890s the Gippsland property fell into debt and had to be sold. Joice's father bought a heavily mortgaged rundown farm at Myaree. Here Joice and her family experienced the tragic consequences of severe drought and bushfires in which Joice's pony burned to death. Once again the NanKivells failed to make any money.

As things went from bad to worse Joice's father took refuge in alcohol and her once-genteel mother, worn out by house and farmyard chores, suffered periods of depressive illness. Joice and her younger brother, Geoff, worked as farmhands and stockmen and never forgave their grandfather for the effect the bankruptcy of Farnham in Queensland had on her parents.

Joice's Uncle Harry, a general practitioner, came to spend a holiday with the NanKivells. During his stay at Myaree Uncle Harry was called in for an emergency operation: since the nearest hospital was over a hundred miles away, he had to operate on a little girl on the NanKivells' dining-room table. Joice assisted him during the operation, her first experience in medical procedure. Encouraged by her uncle, she started to read his old medical books and learned about anatomy and basic medicine. As a result she became proficient at stitching up wounded animals and the NanKivells saved on fees for veterinarian services, an expenditure they could ill afford.

Joice attempted to make money by writing a children's book, *The Cobweb Ladder*. But with the outbreak of World War I in 1914, paper rationing meant the book's publication was delayed. When it was eventually published, it found few readers as everybody was preoccupied with the war.

Joice's brother Geoff (like Agnes Bennett's brother) was killed in action in France. Joice's father was so distraught by the loss of his son and heir that he decided to sell their farm. This decision meant Joice was now free to leave the land and the drudgery of farmwork and cooking for shearers and escape to Melbourne. Geoff's death and the struggle of the past years had seriously affected her mother's health and almost broken her spirit.

Joice wrote a second book in memory of her brother, *The Solitary Pedestrian*. As a published author, at a time when male journalists were away fighting in France, she obtained a part-time job reviewing books in Melbourne's *Sun-Herald*. She also worked as secretary to the Professor of Classics at Melbourne University, a 'learning experience' as she called it. Her deepening knowledge of classical Greek history and literature gave her a yearning to visit Greece.

Joice NanKivell was introduced to Sydney Loch, a tall, distinguished hero of Gallipoli, after she reviewed a book he wrote about the Dardanelles campaign. The two become good friends and it was not long before they fell in love. In 1918, just as the war ended, they married. Their marriage angered Joice's father, who believed writing was a useless occupation, but it pleased Joice's mother, who wanted her daughter to leave Australia and find a new life in the wider world. She gave Joice a farewell gift of a small Australian flag, which Joice promised to keep always on her desk.

The newlyweds sailed to London, where they planned to work as freelance authors and journalists. They were both working as Fleet Street journalists when Sydney met an old schoolfriend, who had been recruited as an undercover agent in Dublin by British Military Intelligence, under the name of Major X. Coincidentally, Joice and Sydney were planning to go to Dublin, as they had been commissioned by their publisher to write a book about the 'Troubles' there.

In Dublin, the Lochs were befriended by the Irish literati, who supported the rebel Sinn Fein in its demand for home rule in Ireland. At that time Dublin was swarming with armed thugs, nicknamed the 'Black and Tans', recruited by the British.

Bombs were planted in public places by Michael Collins and his followers in Sinn Fein and the fledgling IRA. Joice narrowly escaped death when a bomb was thrown in her direction, killing several babies and young mothers. Meanwhile, the Black and Tans were conducting house-to-house searches for gelignite and guns stored in secret IRA 'safe houses'.

The Lochs had rented a dingy furnished apartment in the house of a widow, Mrs Slaney, unaware of her strong IRA connections. They were horrified when the Black and Tans raided the widow's house and found guns under her bed and gelignite among her pot plants. Forbidden to arrest a woman, they arrested Sydney Loch instead. Suspected of treason, for which he could have been hanged, Sydney was imprisoned in Dublin Castle, headquarters of the British forces in Ireland. Joice successfully pleaded for her husband's release, but Michael Collins' men were now convinced that he was a British spy.

On 'Black Sunday', undercover British agents were shot in their beds by Michael Collins' gunmen – but their friend, Major X, managed to escape. The situation became so dangerous that when their room was once again searched by Sinn Fein, Joice and Sydney contemplated leaving Ireland immediately. However, they decided to stay on at Mrs Slaney's and finish their book about the Troubles, *Ireland in Travail*, which they hoped would be fair and reflect the viewpoints of both sides.

They finally left Ireland after being warned by Major X and other friends that Sinn Fein had put a price on their heads unjustly believing that Sydney was a British spy. In London, just before *Ireland in Travail* was published, they heard on BBC radio that Michael Collins had been assassinated. It was time to leave Britain. But where should they go?

A friend suggested eastern Poland, where Quaker Famine Relief was providing free train fares, board and lodging to volunteer aid workers. The Lochs decided that Poland would provide excellent material for another book. Their British publishers, John Murray, encouraged them to go there, hoping that from Poland they would be able to travel into Russia and obtain an eyewitness view of the activities of Lenin and his Bolsheviks for inclusion in the new book.

At Quaker headquarters they were interviewed by stern, dour Miss Ruth Fry, who expressed the opinion that the Lochs would not 'mix well' with Quakers. However, so many aid workers had died in Poland that replacements were urgently needed. Eastern Poland had been devastated by Lenin's troops: pursuing their 'scorched earth' policy, they had burned Polish and Ukrainian villages to the ground, slaughtering the inhabitants or sending them to work camps in Siberia. Those refugees who survived were now returning to find their homes burned to the ground, their cattle gone and their fields turned into wasteland. These refugees, as well as Quaker volunteers who had come to help, were dying of malnutrition and typhoid. All they had to eat was bitter bread made from roasted acorns and tins of sardines sent out by Quaker relief trains from London. Each night bands of starving children beat on the door of the old railway carriage Joice used as her office and sleeping accommodation. She wondered how the Quakers could so fervently believe in a God that allowed such misery. In a desperate attempt to raise money for Polish famine relief, Joice tried to interest the British press in articles she had written on famine in Poland – in vain. Most Fleet Street editors preferred to publish articles about Lenin's triumphs in Russia.

In the midst of so much misery and hunger Joice became pregnant. Sadly, three month into the pregnancy she collapsed from malnourishment and overwork and lost the baby. At the time of the miscarriage Sydney was away, organising teams of horses to plough the refugees' land. To ease her pain the Quakers provided tickets for her and Sydney to visit Moscow, which sparked Joice to write an ironic novel set in contemporary Russia, *The Fourteen Thumbs of St Peter.*

On their return to Poland Sydney's horse teams continued to plough the land and to distribute seed corn to the villagers to ensure their survival. Slowly things improved. President Pilsudksi's fledgling Polish Republic got back on its feet and the need for assistance from the Quaker volunteers became less acute. In gratitude for their contribution to the restoration of eastern Poland, both the Lochs were decorated by the Prime Minister of Poland.

On a visit to Quaker headquarters in Warsaw Joice heard about the horrors of the massacre of Greeks at Smyrna and the need for trained medical orderlies to help the million and a half Greek refugees, victims of the Turks' 'ethnic cleansing'. These Greek refugees had inhabited Turkey and Asia Minor for centuries. Joice remembered her time in the Classics Department at Melbourne University and her desire to visit Greece. When the call came for volunteers, both Joice and Sydney raised her hands, as did their friend Nancy Lauder Brunton, an American heiress turned humanitarian.

Nancy departed for Thessaloniki while Joice finished her work in the

Polish medical centre. Sydney still had several months of work to do in Poland, setting up an orphanage and farm school for Polish children.

On a warm evening in May 1923, Joice climbed down from the train that had brought her to Thessaloniki onto a crowded platform, all her worldly possessions contained in a single suitcase. All around were dazed Greek refugees, carrying their few possessions bundled up in sheets and pillowcases. Many had lived in Turkey for generations, and spoke only Turkish.

The next day Joice travelled by horse-drawn cab to the huge refugee camp in the grounds of the American Farm School, not far from Thessaloniki. On the way she passed by the old Scottish Women's Hospital, established by Agnes Bennett, now being used as a camp for the thousands upon thousands of refugees who were pouring into Thessaloniki from Asia Minor.

At the Farm School, Joice and Nancy Lauder Brunton worked side by side, giving inoculations against typhoid, feeding the starving and tending the sick and dying. In addition Joice wrote articles about her experiences for the British and Australian press. A few months later, Sydney arrived from Poland. The Lochs worked tirelessly for the refugees, who were gradually rehoused in villages of tiny concrete-block cottages, built by the cash-strapped Greek Government.

On a camping holiday by the sea Joice and Sydney visited one of the new refugee villages. Pirgos (today called Ouranopoulis) was named after the huge fourteenth-century Byzantine tower which dominated the skyline. The villagers lacked medicines of any kind and were facing starvation because the olive saplings and vine cuttings provided by the government had died in the fierce summer heat. The Lochs brought seeds and medicines to the villagers the next time they visited. At the request of the Mayor of Pirgos, Sydney shot a wild boar which was devouring the villagers' few chickens.

In gratitude, the mayor offered the Lochs the old Byzantine tower by the sea for a peppercorn rent. Joice and Sydney were ecstatic: they had been planning to look for a place to settle down, now that the worst of the Greek crisis was over. Villagers helped them clean out the donkey manure that had accumulated on the ground floor. After electricity had been installed in two rooms, the Lochs moved in, planning to become full-time writers.

Fate thought otherwise. Knowing that Joice had a well-stocked medicine chest, poverty-stricken villagers, who lacked even an aspirin or a bandage, began to come to the tower, seeking her assistance for their sick children, their aged parents and themselves. Bent over her typewriter, hard at work, Joice used to mutter a few exasperated words, but would always go out to help those in need.

One day Joice visited a sick old man, living with his daughter and her husband. The old man, a former rug weaver, was dying of malnutrition (most of the family's meagre income went towards feeding the bread-winner). Joice, horrified by their poverty, asked the village carpenter to build a loom and commissioned the old man's daughter (who was also a rug weaver) to weave and sell her a rug. Soon it became clear that many rug weavers were living in the village. They were all desperate to earn extra money, so Joice ordered more looms and purchased wool and dyes. So the Pirgos Women's Rug Weaving Cooperative was born.

Joice started to design the rugs herself as she felt that Byzantine rather than Turkish motifs had to be used in their design.[6] She learned from the village midwife-cum-witch the secret of dyeing wool, using local plants. During the years that followed, Joice sold many hand-woven 'Pirgos Rugs' to friends in Britain, Australia and America. (Pirgos Rugs are no longer woven but now command high prices from Greek collectors.)

In 1939, as Hitler threatened to invade Poland, the village celebrated a wedding. The bride was a beautiful young woman whom Joice had saved from death some sixteen years previously. The young men performed the threshing dance in memory of Greeks slaughtered by the Turks. The Lochs were guests of honour, and everyone rejoiced that the days of acorn bread and famine were over and the olive harvest safely gathered.

Their joy was short-lived. That night the Lochs heard on the BBC that Hitler had invaded Poland and Britain had declared war on Germany. They believed Greece would remain neutral: Greek friends assured them that Hitler had no intention of invading Greece.

Once again the Lochs offered their services to Quaker Refugee Aid to Poland. Sydney was appointed head of Friends' Relief Mission in Bucharest to look after thousands of Polish men who had fled from the Germans and the Russians to neutral Rumania. Joice was made responsible for aid to Polish and Jewish women and children who had also fled there.

They said sad goodbyes to friends in the village and to holy men from the monasteries of Athos, as well as Quaker and Farm School colleagues. Joice packed her battered typewriter, her medical books and the miniature Australian flag her mother had given her before she left Australia. Once more they headed into danger.

Joice and Sydney took the overnight train to Bucharest, a city of huge contradictions: lush restaurants and cafes, elegant boutiques and fashionable women ... and emaciated women and children begging in the streets outside the city centre. Male Polish refugees were being interned by Rumania's King Carol, who was anxious to curry favour with Hitler. Many escaped on skis and fled across Europe to join the Free Polish Army in Britain. Joice tried to raise money for exit visas for the women and children without success.

That Christmas, the Polish women and children sang carols and gave Joice small dolls they had made themselves. Jewish refugees, caring for thousands of orphans who had lost their parents in the concentration camps, thanked her for providing them with clothes sent from Britain. Joice was overworked and badly needed an assistant, preferably someone middle-aged, caring and sensible. Instead, Father Ambrosius, the Polish priest to the internment camps, recommended Countess Lushya, who turned out to be young and beautiful.

At twenty-two the charismatic Countess Lushya was the sole survivor of a family of Polish aristocrats. She had no typing skills but possessed a quick mind, a flair for organisation and aristocratic friends in Rumania. She told Joice that she could persuade these friends to open their homes for benefit concerts in aid of the Polish refugees. Lushya was hired and within a few weeks had taken over the fund-raising.

Lushya recruited a group of Rumanian princesses, resplendent in Chanel and Dior clothes and ropes of pearls, to raise funds for exit visas for Polish refugees. Benefit luncheons with French champagne and Russian caviar were held to raise money for the Polish women refugees and their children, whose escape Joice was planning. The British Foreign Office had meanwhile agreed to fund the escape of the remaining male prisoners, who included some members of the Polish Government in exile.

Sydney and Joice each received a medal from King Carol, whom Joice described as having 'the saddest eyes' she had ever seen. The King, whose late mother was British, was under huge pressure from Hitler as well as his own cabinet ministers and the pro-Nazi Rumanian Iron Guard. His position was further aggravated by the Russians, who were planning to invade on the western front of his oil-rich country.

The Iron Guard began to round up high-profile Jews and hang them from meat hooks. Suddenly German officers appeared in Bucharest and the British and French flags outside the Lochs' hotel were replaced by the red-and-black Swastika. Joice and Sydney were caught in the crossfire of street fighting but managed to escape. In the meantime the Russians invaded oil-rich Bukovina.

By now Rumania's royal palace was under siege by the jack-booted Iron Guard and King Carol was forced to abdicate. He departed into exile, taking with him his Jewish mistress, Magda Lupescu. It was rumoured that he had also shipped out much of the country's gold bullion.

The Lochs knew they *must* get the Polish refugees and the Jewish orphans in their care out of Rumania immediately. Sydney departed aboard a chartered river steamer with his group of male Polish refugees on forged visas. Joice was desperate to get her group of refugee women and children out before the Nazis sent them to concentration camps. Fortunately, the day before the German Army entered Bucharest in full force, money was provided by a wealthy Jewish couple who pleaded with Joice to smuggle their young daughter and orphaned nieces out of the country to an aunt in Haifa. Joice agreed to take the children to Israel, as long as their forged passports were sufficiently convincing.

The large-scale escape she planned was code-named 'Operation Pied Piper'. The cover for the exodus of hundreds of women and children was a Quaker Mission day excursion to Constanza, a beach resort on the Black Sea. On arrival in Constanza they did *not* go to the beach; instead, they boarded a ferry that took them to Constantinople and freedom.

Their escape was fraught with danger. At one stage the ferry was ordered to turn back by the Iron Guard. Lushya and Joice feared they would all be arrested and taken to a concentration camp. But all the Iron Guard wanted were the crates of Rumanian gold being shipped out aboard the ferry, destined for King Carol, now safely exiled in Portugal.

The full story of the dangers and tensions of Operation Pied Piper and Joice's heroic spy mission to Budapest on behalf of British Intelligence is related in my book, *Blue Ribbons, Bitter Bread: The Life of Joice NanKivell Loch, Australia's Most Decorated Woman*. From

Constanza, Joice took her party of refugees to British-run Palestine via Constantinople (Istanbul) and Cyprus. Their ship was bombed and shelled by German planes, but, miraculously, the vessel did not sink. The Lochs brought almost 2000 refugees from Bucharest to Cyprus in two separate parties and then took them to Palestine.

In the final years of World War II, the Lochs cared for thousands more Polish orphans whose parents had been murdered in Stalin's gulags. The Polish children were released after Britain started to give aid to Communist Russia. Joice wrote a report to Quaker Refugee Aid in London begging for funds to feed them. She described how 'their shaven heads appeared too large for their emaciated bodies, their eyes burning with fever and starvation, their feet chafed by army boots far too big for them.' She fought for 'her' orphans to receive clothing, food, accommodation and a special school – for which she was awarded another medal by the Polish Government in exile. (Twenty years later in London, I met a Polish woman who had survived childhood due to Joice Loch and her 'Camp of a Thousand Orphans'.)

After World War II ended, the Lochs returned to northern Greece to find their tower home and the village of Pirgos (now renamed Ouranopoulis) ravaged by the Andartes, the Greek Communist rebels. Joice succeeded in raising funds to rebuild the village and re-opened Pirgos Rugs, which once again saved the village from starvation and saw her awarded another Greek medal.

Tragically, in 1955 Sydney Loch died at the age of sixty-six. Joice lived on in widowhood for another twenty-seven years and continued to care for the people of Ouranopoulis. She brought exhibitions of Pirgos Rugs to Australia and wrote several more books, including the bestselling children's book *Tales of Christophilos*, which raised enough money to bring a continuous supply of unpolluted water to Ouranopoulis.

At the age of 95 Joice Loch died in her tower home, mourned by hundreds of monks and Greek villagers, by Australian, British and American diplomats and the governor of Macedonia. A Greek Orthodox bishop, who was also an Oxford don, gave her funeral oration and named her as *'one of the most significant women of the twentieth century'*. She is buried beside her beloved husband in the cemetry of Ouranopoulis.

The Byzantine Museum's Authority have now restored the exterior of Joice's former home, the Tower of Prosforion in Ouranopoulis. There are plans to open a room inside the tower to act as a Joice Loch Memorial Museum and even for a film on her life.

Joice's birthplace of Ingham in north Queensland has also honoured her. In December 2002, in the presence of Greek consul for Queensland Alex Freeleagus, who has done a great deal to establish Joice's reputation in Australia, the mayor of Ingham and a representative of the Queensland Government unveiled a brass plaque in Ingham's Botanical Gardens. The plaque commemorates the birth of Joice NanKivell and details her achievements.

Joice NanKivell Loch remains Australia's most decorated woman and one of the world's most decorated women for humanitarian work. She was awarded eleven medals in all, the first of which was Poland's Gold Cross of Merit Work for work with Polish refugees in 1922. Then came the Serbian Order of St Sava, awarded for Joice's work on mosquito eradication programmes. In 1926 she became the first foreign woman to be awarded the Greek Order of Pheonix for aid work with Greek refugees. For her 'exceptional service to the Greek nation', she was later awarded the Greek Order of the Redeemer for setting up a free medical clinic in Ouranopoulis. the second and higher grade of the Order of the Redeemer was awarded for establishing Pirgos Rugs, for which Koice was also awarded a Gold Medal from the Greek National Academy of the Arts.

The British awarded Joice an MBE for saving earthquake victims, and she was honoured by Romania's Order of Elizabeth for her work with Polish refugees exhiled to Romania after the Nazi invasion of Poland. The Free Polish Government awarded her Poland's Gold Cross of Virtue for saving Polish women and children from the Nazi's. Joice also received two different grades of the Greek Orders of Beneficence, a medal awarded to 'men or women providing outstanding service to Greece'. The first Order was awarded for re-establishing Pirgos Rugs following the devestation caused by the Greek Civil War; the second and higher grade of the Order for donating money to bring a supply of unpolluted water to Ouranopoulis, which saved countless Greek children from dying of typhoid.

CHAPTER SIX

University of Western Australia Department of Music.

Eileen Joyce
(1908–1991)
THE GIRL FROM BOULDER WHO BECAME THE WORLD'S
MOST LOVED CLASSICAL PIANIST

On the platform of New York's Carnegie Hall, Eileen Joyce played her favourite piano concerto, the Rachmaninov No. 2, to a huge audience. Her shapely shoulders and arms gleamed pale as alabaster against the black silk organza of her evening gown with its plunging neckline. Her reddish-gold hair provided a striking colour note in contrast to the sober plumage of the orchestra. Caught up in the joy of performing, she played the lyrical yearning melodies of Rachmaninov with passion, panache and elegance. For Eileen Joyce, music was a union between the brain, the soul and the hands.

Once the last chords of the concerto died away, her audience burst into a frenzy of applause. Dozens of red and white roses were thrown onto the stage. An hour later, wrapped in a fur coat, Miss Joyce left Carnegie Hall and autographed a few programs as eager fans threatened to engulf her. Guards kept them back as she walked to a waiting limousine. Fame, applause and constant praise were the spurs that drove her to continue performing: by this time, the self-styled 'barefoot miner's daughter' from Boulder, Western Australia, was a very wealthy woman indeed.

Musical genius (defined by the Oxford Dictionary as 'natural aptitude') is not chosen by its possessor: many virtuosos lead frenetic and often solitary existences travelling around the world, in and out of different hotels, adored by their public but rarely enjoying harmonious relations with their husbands and children. Genius is a jealous god and demands sacrifice, especially from women endowed with it. Perhaps Eileen Joyce needed the applause, the fame and prestige as compensation for her deprived childhood spent in dusty shanty towns in outback Australia. 'I had to fight for everything,' she explained to journalists, 'my artistic rise came through toil, illness and suffering.'

Eileen Joyce was a twentieth-century Cinderella. She married Prince Charming, acquired an elegant Mayfair apartment in London, a beautiful country house, a wardrobe of gowns designed by leading couturiers. Yet, underneath her beauty and her wealth, Eileen could never forget her teenage insecurities of her looks and background. As compensation for them, she always sought to be the centre of attention. As though to reassure herself she had good looks and money, she commissioned no less than *nine* portraits by different artists.[1]

She dreaded the thought of ageing, and always claimed that her birth had not been registered because she was born in a tent in northern Tasmania 'in 1912'. She also claimed that her parents had led a gypsy-like life as itinerant fruit pickers. Wearing bearded or hand-embroided silk or satin gowns designed by Norman Hartnell, dressmaker to the Queen of England, Eileen would say that as a child she wore ragged dresses and ran barefoot through the bush with Twink, her pet kangaroo, at her heels. It was a charming and romantic fairytale that Eileen never tired of telling. If journalists asked probing questions and asked for names or dates, she would deflect their interest with questions of her own – if they persisted, she became defensive and claimed a slip of memory, or else she terminated the interview.

The truth was just as strange as the legend Eileen embroidered about her barefoot days as Raggedy Eileen with a pet kangaroo on a leash. She *was* a miner's daughter, but there the truth ended. She *did* have a birth certificate, but did not want anyone to see it and learn her real age. In very old age, cosmetic surgery, skilful hairdressing and her lively personality made Eileen appear decades younger.

It has been difficult to piece together the story of Eileen Joyce's childhood because she laid false trails and told stories which contradicted each other. It would appear that when Eileen was born, her father was working in the silver-lead mines of Zeehan, an isolated area north-west of Hobart. Convinced that a birth certificate must exist, I contacted the Registrar of Births, Deaths and Marriages, for Tasmania, who arranged for a search to be made. If it could be found, he agreed to send me a copy. He added that Zeehan, Eileen's birthplace, was by no means the idyllic bush setting she claimed – and as it appears in the 1951 British film *Wherever She Goes*. Zeehan had no orchards in which her parents could have worked; at the beginning of the last century it was a landscape of disued pit heads and mullock heaps.

When the copy of Eileen Joyce's birth certificate arrived from Tasmania, it revealed that she was born on 1 January 1908 (she claimed her birthdate as 21 November 1912.) Hence she was four and three-quarter years older than the date shown in all the reference books. Numerous stars of film, stage and the performing arts routinely lop a few years off their age for the sake of their careers. But *why* did Eileen Joyce give herself an entirely different birth date? This was the first of many paradoxes and unanswered questions I encountered about this enigmatic, complex and insecure genius of the piano.

The remote silver-mining community of Zeehan, at one time Tasmania's third largest town, lies 291 kilometres north-west of Hobart. Joe Joyce, Eileen's father, was illiterate and had emigrated from Southern Ireland without a penny in his pocket. (For some unknown reason he is called 'Will' Joyce in the film *Wherever She Goes.*) Joe was thirty-one when Eileen, his first child, was born. He had married Eileen's mother, Alice Gertrude (née May), when she was only fifteen, a decade younger than himself. Neither of them could read or write; they were hard-working, unpretentious people, though Eileen's mother told her that the Joyces were related to the great Irish writer James Joyce. Eileen's mop of reddish-brown hair, her blue eyes and freckled nose were distinctly Irish, but she was led to believe that her love of music and strong rhythms stemmed from the Spanish descent claimed by her slim, dark-haired mother.

By the time Eileen had learned to walk, Zeehan's profitable deposits of silver were running out. Like most of the miners' families, the Joices lived in a wooden shack, lacking sanitary facilities and electricity. There were no medical services or rubbish collections provided. Instead of the beautiful bushland Eileen conjured up in later years, they were surrounded by mullock heaps, abandoned pit heads, and bush huts infested by flies and cockroaches. Most of the huge Tasmanian trees had been chopped down to build pit props. When the mining company laid off Joe Joyce, there were no unemployment benefits: for a pair of illiterate migrants who now had children to feed, this spelled ruin. Eileen told journalists that her father had 'a passion for finding gold'. Convinced that he could find gold in booming Western Australia, where his brother had immigrated, Eileen's father left Eileen, her mother and her infant brother, John, in the family shack at Zeehan and went off to Kununoppin in Western Australia, to work a claim with a fellow gold miner, convinced – like so many others – that he would strike it rich.

With no money coming in life was hard for Alice Joyce as she waited for her husband to send for them to join him.[2] Later, Eileen would claim that her father's brother sent money to pay their fares to Kununoppin, telling them that Joe Joyce had found gold on his claim. Believing their years of deprivation were over, Alice packed up their few possessions and took the children on a ship from Burnie (sometimes Eileen said Hobart) to Melbourne and then on a different ship to Adelaide. By the time they reached Perth their money had run out and they were forced to hitch a ride on a carrier's covered wagon over the next 600 kilometres to Kununoppin.

Describing this journey to her biographer, English author Lady Claire Hoskins Abrahall, Eileen claimed that they slept under the stars and in farm sheds, but made no mention of Twink, the pet kangaroo Lady Abrahll assigns her. In *Prelude* (a book written for children), Lady Abrahall somewhat improbably has Twink, wearing a collar and lead, accompanying Eileen all the way. However, in her introduction, the author admits that 'Eileen Joyce had lapses of memory', so she had to invent some of the story. Another of the author's inventions was an imaginary character, a writer called Daniel (in *Wherever She Goes* he appears as an artist) who gives Eileen a mouth organ.

Lady Abrahall's book described how, when finally they arrived at arid, dusty Kununoppin, Eileen's mother was horrified to find that the seam of gold had proved disappointing. Joe Joyce and his perpetually optimistic partner had not struck it rich: on the contrary, Joe had now run out of money.[3] At Kununoppin each miner worked his own claim, usually with a partner who helped him lower the bucket on a windlass to haul up rocks and take them to the crushing machine to see if they contained gold. Alice and the three children had to live in Joe's cockroach-infested tent, lacking water or latrines, while he toiled at his claim from dawn to dusk. Traditionally miners lacking cash lived off damper and any rabbits they managed to shoot. Each night the miners drank, gambled and brawled over their claims – fist fights would erupt all round.

Eileen hated Kununoppin. According to Lady Abrahall, Eileen attended a small bush school run by a stern, gaunt teacher, Miss Blenheim. The little girl had a long walk through the bush to reach school. She went barefoot, as she had outgrown her only pair of shoes and her parents could not afford new ones. She claimed she had nothing to wear other than a ragged dress which she had found in a garbage bin. Eileen hated Miss Blenheim, who caned her for some trifling misdemeanour, and became an unwilling and difficult pupil.[4]

Joe Joyce finally decided that he could not subject his family to such a hazardous and primitive life. Much to Alice's relief, he found a job working for wages with a gold-mining company in Boulder, where his brother ran one of the town's twenty-six pubs. The area between Boulder and Kalgoorlie was so rich in gold it was known as The Golden Mile.[5]

Like Kununoppin, Boulder was flat, arid and dusty, without a blade of grass. All the trees had been cut down to build pit props and the tall towers housing the wheels that operated the mine machinery. Faded sepia photographs show Boulder as a shanty town with row upon row of miners' tiny weatherboard cottages. Hastily constructed by the mining company, these shacks lacked running water or sanitation and were built so close together that if a drunken miner walloped his wife, the noise would reverberate through the hessian-lined walls of the next-door cottage. Miners who had made their fortunes and the mine managers lived in brick houses in Kalgoorlie, not in Boulder. An able-bodied man working on the Golden Mile for wages could earn a good living wielding a pick, or gathering wood for pit props or to fuel the mining machinery. Poverty-stricken Italian and Irish migrants flocked to Boulder. So did French and Japanese prostitutes, lured by the prospect of earning good money in the many brothels operating from tumbledown wooden shacks along the Golden Mile. Eileen saw it all too closely to blot out the memories.

Remote Boulder was an unsanitary dust bowl, scorching hot in summer and freezing cold in winter. The clatter of the mining machinery, the long conveyor belts rattling overhead, the clouds of dust that settled everywhere: these were the backdrop to Eileen's formative years. Men were intent on making quick money or else drowning their sorrow at *not* making it. Life was rough and tough: brothels, alcoholism, gambling and wife-bashing were rampant.

Doubtless, Eileen did not care to reveal the gritty realities of life in a dirt-floored wooden shack lacking running water or indoor sanitation, surrounded by hordes of flies, fleas, cockroaches and rotting rubbish. Lady Abrahall relates how the Joyce family ate simple meals at a table made from an old crate and owned little more than a few truckle beds. Neighbours lent them wooden chairs. Eileen and Alice carried buckets of water from the standpipe at the end of their street, water that had been piped in 300 miles by the mining company. They heated water for washing or laundry on a wood-fired stove. Boulder's red dust had to be beaten out of clothes with a stick before they could be washed. Even so, garments which had been white became pink-red, and they soon learned to wear coloured clothes.

Joe worked very hard and made money, so that his family would be financially secure.

In spite of her family's relative affluence in later years, the story of that barefoot, raggedy child earning pennies for playing a mouth organ was firmly entrenched in Eileen Joyce's mind and she kept repeating it. (In later years, however, among trusted friends, she would sometimes laugh about the 'wilder excesses of journalists' and admit that the stories about her childhood 'had gone too far'.) Eileen's younger sisters,[6] born at Boulder a few years after the Joyces settled there, claimed that the family was never destitute and homeless or forced to beg for food as Eileen had told journalists. There was always enough food on their table, although initially their home was far from luxurious.[7]

Eileen's cousin, John Joyce of Kalgoorlie, relates that while Alice was having her second daughter, Eileen stayed with him and his parents in their cottage in Vivian Street, Boulder. Mr Joyce insisted that as far as he knew, Eileen's father was never out of work: he saw no reason why Eileen would ever have had to beg for money to feed starving siblings as she sometimes claimed. Local historian Miss Rika Eriksson grew up in Boulder with Eileen and she states that Eileen's father owned a butcher's shop during Eileen's childhood.[8]

Boulder was working-class and proud of it but some people wanted a better life for their children. Joe wanted his children to attend school and paid the few pence a week charged by the nuns at St Joseph's Primary School. Eileen walked to school, not barefoot as she claimed but wearing white socks and sandals and a clean cotton frock made by her mother. On her way to school, she would have seen semi-naked prostitutes lounging outside their shacks – something else she carefully omitted from the edited tales of her childhood.

During her journey from Tasmania to the west, Eileen claimed she heard a piano for the first time in her life and it had made a great impression on her. Now she was eager to take the piano lessons offered as an optional extra at St Joseph's.

As part of her own legend, Eileen maintained that in order to find the money for the sixpenny lessons, she played tunes on her mouth organ to the miners, who showered her with pennies. She said her father was furious and forbade her to do this again.

Sister Augustine, the piano teacher at St Joseph's, recognised Eileen Joyce's talent, and she was then given free music lessons. She was also encouraged by Sister Ita and Sister Vincent. She used to practise from 4 am to 8 am on the battered old honkey-tonk piano in her uncle's hotel, and described how she would 'transfer tunes she had learned to play on her mouth organ' onto the chipped keys. Eventually, when her uncle moved his old piano into her parents' cottage, it was properly tuned.[9] What Eileen omitted from her legend was that once her extraordinary talent was recognised, she was allowed to practise on a far better piano in Nicholson's music store at Boulder, free of charge.[10]

Eileen's character was one of huge contradictions: she could be confiding and warm or very secretive. She could be tight with money or extremely generous, according to her mood. In mid-life she could be warm and outgoing with friends but guarded, secretive, even prickly, with strangers, with whom her mood could swing from a larrikin sense of humour to the *froideur* of a theatrical *grande dame* and she could be extremely difficult when things did not suit her. To her friends she was loyal and loving, someone very special indeed. Only when she finally became world-famous did Eileen feel secure enough to reveal some aspects of the truth about her childhood. In a taped interview with Felix Hayman, producer of the ABC's morning music program, Eileen told him that her father eventually had made money and invested it and revealed that in later life she had fallen out with members of her family over what they regarded as 'inaccuracies' in her press interviews. During the final years of Eileen's life, Eileen's sister said that Eileen 'outgrew' her family in Boulder, that they felt slighted by her and that she and Eileen had *never* been close.[11]

Eileen never revealed the full truth about her childhood to either of her husbands, to friends or to her biographer, Lady Abrahall, who was a keen patron of music and drama.

When Eileen turned ten she was entered for a music exam set by Trinity College, Dublin. Sister Augustine had wanted her to sit for the Primary Grade but Eileen insisted on going for the more difficult Intermediate Grade. She performed so well that the visiting examiner gave her the highest pass marks possible. He told Sister Augustine and the Mother Superior at St Joseph's that Eileen should be sent as a boarder to the much larger Loreto Convent in the Perth suburb of Claremont, some 600 kilometres from Boulder. This would give her far greater opportunities to study classical music. Privately the examiner thought it was high time Eileen left this rough, tough area if she was to accomplish anything.

Father Edmund Campion, the distinguished historian, recounts how Eileen's examiner talked to Father John T. McMahon ('Father Mac'), the Catholic Diocesan Inspector of Schools. The next time Father Mac visited Boulder, he interviewed Eileen and her parents and arranged for her to board at the wealthy Loreto Convent in Perth. Eileen was allowed reduced fees but additional money had to be found for her music lessons as well as school uniform and sports equipment.

According to Eileen, the warm-hearted miners of Boulder were determined to support Joe Joyce's daughter, who played the piano for their sing-songs in the pub. Over the next few nights gambling parties were held around the town, after which many miners tipped their winnings into the hat to pay Raggedy Eileen's expenses 'in the big city'.

Eileen also claimed that Mrs Swift, a kind elderly widow for whom she used to run errands to earn pennies, died at this time. A black leather handbag was found in Mrs Swift's dresser containing the then considerable sum of fifty pounds, together with a piece of paper bearing the words: *For Eileen Joyce's music.*[12]

The archivist of St Joseph's Primary School and Father Campion both related that a fund was opened in Boulder to which people subscribed their pennies and sixpences to send little Eileen Joyce to Perth, and that the miners *did* pass around the hat in their pubs, so that Eileen would have the necessary money.

Joe Joyce, dressed in a suit and tie for the occasion, accompanied his shy, red-headed daughter on the train to Perth to enrol at the convent, which stood surrounded by grounds that sloped down to the Swan River. Years later Eileen would tell friends and journalists the untrue story that she was embarrassed when her father told the Mother Superior that he did not know on which day his daughter was born, that she had no birth certificate and that neither he nor his wife could read or write, a statement that doubtless had some truth.

As 'a charity child' the skinny girl from Boulder was teased by her schoolmates. She was no good at sports; as someone who preferred to perform individually she hated all team games. However, the school had a swimming pool and Eileen found that she loved swimming. But the constant teasing and bullying she received made the insecure miner's daughter even more determined to study hard and excel at the piano so that her life would be different to that of her parents.

She was fortunate to have been taken under the wing of Loreto's dedicated and exceptional music teacher, Sister John. Eileen's musical talent was a gift from God, Sister John insisted.

By now Eileen, craving friendship and attention like most deeply insecure children, realised that as soon as she sat down at the piano and played, her classmates and teachers paused to listen to her. Lonely and homesick, Eileen's craving to be the centre of attention would last all her life. Like many sensitive creative artists she was subject to severe mood swings. When she was under stress or frustrated she could explode into rage and then burst into floods of tears. Sister John was the only person she really trusted, her only friend.

At the Loreto Convent Eileen practised for many hours a day. Sister John Moore developed a special relationship with the talented but prickly little girl and helped her to cope with the other girls' teasing. Eileen was small for her age, with a pale complexion and delicate physique, highly sensitive and volatile, an easy target for bullies. Sister John taught her she must not burst into tears or fly into a rage but hold her ground and tell the bullies they would be in trouble if they hurt her. She gave Eileen a sense of self-worth, told her she was special and that God had chosen her to give pleasure through her music. For the rest of her life Eileen mingled her devotion to the piano with her devotion to Roman Catholicism.

At the convent Eileen was exposed to refinements she had never dreamed of in Boulder: meals served by maids; the importance of using the right knife and fork, of speaking 'nicely', of brushing her wild mop of chestnut hair each night. Life became a learning curve, essential for her future success. Among the affluent girls from Perth's leading Catholic families, Eileen felt ashamed of her lack of table manners, her roughened, reddened hands and her freckles. She attempted to remove the freckles on her nose and cheeks with lemon juice, which cracked her delicate skin.[13] (In the film *Wherever She Goes*, the director chose a British actress, Suzanne Parrett, to play the child heroine. A blonde, round-faced little girl, Suzanne's hair is neatly plaited into two little pigtails tied with satin ribbons and she speaks with the plummy accents of a posh London suburb – nothing like Eileen's description of herself as possessing a strong Aussie accent.)

Sister John stopped Eileen from using slang picked up in Boulder and taught her to speak clearly and distinctly. She insisted on the importance of good table manners: 'No, Eileen, no elbows on the table.' 'Don't hold your knife like that.' 'Sit up straight, Eileen, ladies don't slouch.' 'Eileen, use your handkerchief, not your sleeve!' Most nuns of that period threatened purgatory and hellfire for children who told fibs; if Eileen received such a message, it does not seem to have got through to her, judging from her later difficulty in distinguishing fact from fiction. Deportment lessons, in which the girls had to walk down a long passage with a book on their heads would enable Eileen to walk gracefully onto concert platforms wearing beautiful evening gowns that swept the floor. The one attribute Eileen *never* lost was her down-to-earth Aussie sense of humour.

It was stressful to adapt to a new way of life. Eileen remained deeply grateful to Sister John, who behaved like the traditional fairy godmother, turning her into a different person to the tousled-haired child who had arrived at the convent with her illiterate father. She also encouraged Eileen to read a great deal in order to learn about other countries and their customs, telling her that one day she would study overseas. She took Eileen to a concert attended by Percy Grainger and persuaded the famous Australian composer to visit the convent to hear Eileen play. This marked another turning point in Eileen's life. Grainger listened intently as she played and then examined Eileen's hands and fingers, 'noting their firmness, the already strongly developed fingertips'.[14] Grainger pronounced Eileen 'the most transcendentally gifted child' he had ever heard. He tried to raise money to send Eileen to America to study but was unsuccessful.[15]

From then on Eileen was determined to become a concert pianist and travel the world. Another famous visitor to the Sisters of Loreto Convent was German pianist Wilhelm Backhaus, then in his mid-forties. After hearing Eileen play he commented: 'I have heard no one to equal her in the past twenty years.' He recommended that she should further her studies at the Leipzig Conservatorium of Music. In the period between World War I and World War II, Leipzig was regarded as Europe's premier conservatorium of music. Eileen learned that the conservatorium had been founded by the composer Felix Mendelssohn, and that one of her favourite composers and pianists, the Norwegian Edward Grieg, had attended it.

Alice and Joe Joyce had three other children to support and educate. There were no musical scholarships in those days for talented young Australians. Eileen would need financial assistance for her passage to Europe and expensive board and tuition fees in Leipzig. A series of benefit concerts were held at the convent and in the homes of various parents of girls attending the school. Eileen's talent for the piano meant that she was now viewed by teachers, parents, and fellow pupils as the mascot of the school rather than as a social outcast. At big houses with smooth green lawns sloping down to the Swan River, afternoon tea and cool drinks were served under colourful umbrellas. Then, wearing a pink tulle party dress made for her by the nuns (pink being her favourite colour in spite of her reddish hair), Eileen would play Beethoven sonatas and romantic works by Schumann and Chopin.

Eileen would claim that once again the warm-hearted gold miners of Boulder passed round the hat in the pub to help her attain her goal. However, a sizeable portion of the money needed to send Eileen to Leipzig was raised from the wealthy city of Kalgoorlie. Kalgoorlie's Catholic churches and their congregations, as well as local dignitaries and their wives, helped the 'Eileen Joyce to Leipzig Fund Committee' raise money. Perth's Battye Library holds the minute book of the committee dated 1926, which would indicate that Eileen, born in 1908, went to Leipzig when she was in her late teens, rather than at fourteen, as she later claimed.

Although she rarely mentioned this to the press, Eileen was also helped by the wealthy West Australian Sir Thomas Coombe. He owned a chain of local cinemas and arranged for Eileen to play between films. These performances, besides helping to publicise the Eileen Joyce to Leipzig Fund, gave her valuable experience in playing in public. In the end, just over nine hundred pounds was raised by the committee's efforts – a relatively large sum in 1928, enough to buy a small house.

The money would cover Eileen's fare, board and lodging and her tuition fees, providing she did not live extravagantly. An inexpensive boarding house was found for her by German nuns who were in correspondence with the Mother Superior of the Loreto Convent.

Eileen wore the pink dress given to her by the nuns for her farewell concert, a fund-raising event organised by the convent. Her mother, unused to cities or public events, came to the concert and Sister John ensured that Alice Joyce was seated in the front row. Making a little speech and dedicating the next piece to her mother, Eileen played Alice's favourite piece, Schumann's Liebesträume No. 3 (rather than the more difficult Liszt piece of the same name) followed by McDowell's 'To a Wild Rose'.[16]

After the concert, Eileen was the centre of attention, no longer the miner's daughter who 'didn't fit in' but the talented pianist the whole school was proud to have helped to send overseas to fulfil her potential. That evening Eileen said a sad goodbye to her mother. Alice realised that her daughter had grown away from Boulder: the piano was now her future. Quiet and self-effacing, she had no intention of standing in Eileen's way. Until this moment, Eileen had not understood the effect that living over ten thousand miles away would have on her and her family. Now it dawned on the unsophisticated girl that she would no longer return to Boulder for holidays.

That night, Sister John, worried about her favourite pupil, visited Eileen's bedside. She found her crying, filled with doubts and fears about leaving Australia for an unknown future.

'I don't want to go. Please let me stay here and continue learning the piano with you,' Eileen sobbed.

Sister John reassured her, telling her she had nothing left to teach her about music. She reminded Eileen how lonely she had been when she arrived at Loreto. Now, after only a few years, she had finally made friends among her classmates. Of course she would find new ones in Leipzig.[17]

The next day Eileen embarked on the long sea voyage to London. From there she went by train to Paris and on to Leipzig. In press interviews, Eileen Joyce would describe her arrival in Leipzig as a shy, skinny teenager in a school uniform: 'a homesick waif-and-stray without warm clothes or knickers'.[18]

According to Sister Ann Carter, the current archivist of the Sisters of Loreto Convent, it was unthinkable that the nuns would have sent their most promising pupil to Europe lacking warm winter clothes *or* knickers. In the 1920s, with their extreme prudery, they would have *insisted* that Eileen did not arrive knickerless in Leipzig.[19] One can only imagine that the nuns bought Eileen 'suitable' underwear, probably thick blue serge bloomers so hideous that Eileen, whose love of beautiful clothes would become legendary, threw them overboard in disgust once the ship left Perth.

A study of press cuttings shows Eileen enlisting journalists' sympathies, repeating the story about arriving at Leipzig with no knickers and telling them how surprised the reception party greeting her at Leipzig station was when they saw her red hair and freckles, because they had been led to believe she was a black-skinned Aborigine.[20]

Eileen was grateful that the nuns had taught her a few simple German phrases to prepare her for Leipzig. However, the boarding house the nuns had chosen was inhabited by office workers rather than students, and she felt homesick for the convent and Sister John. At Leipzig, language and cultural barriers effectively isolated her: she found communication difficult with her teachers and her fellow boarders.

Initially her piano lessons did not go well. Her first teacher, Max Pauer, was exacting and highly critical: his students were in awe of him. His command of English was poor and he often reduced girls to tears by yelling at them in German, as he did to Eileen on occasions. Fortunately for Eileen, the following year she was transferred to a more sympathetic piano teacher who spoke fluent English.

Leipzig itself she found an attractive city of gabled houses and narrow cobbled streets. Some 145 kilometres south of Berlin, it lay beside the muddy, winding River Pleisse. Leipzig, like neighbouring Dresden, would be bombed flat during World War II; today, little of the city that Eileen knew remains.

It was considered very important for pupils of the piano to have the desired strong 'piano hands'. They needed adequate finger pads and strong sinews: much time was spent on exercises developing these sinews and the necessary 'stretch' to play difficult pieces.

Eileen soon found that the German city which had produced Bach, Mendelssohn, Schumann and Wagner was saturated in music. Leipzig was the premier music academy in Europe, with special courses for singers and players of all major instruments.[21] There was a magnificent opera house, and students at the conservatorium could attend concerts by some of the world's leading performers at the city's famous concert hall, the *Gewandhaus*, where they received a discount on tickets. Eileen longed to go to all the concerts, but even though her fees at the conservatorium had been paid in advance, she realised that money remaining in the 'Eileen Joyce to Leipzig Fund' had to last for three years until she would be ready to go to London to make her debut on the concert platform. She was aware that promoting herself as a concert player there would take even *more* money than she had.

In order to compensate for her insecurity, loneliness and language problems Eileen immersed herself in study. She rose at five each morning and practised for at least six hours. She went to bed very early, unless she had a concert to attend. Her moods swung between elation at her teachers' praise and despair at the thought that she would never reach the standards of the pianists she heard perform at the *Gewandhaus*.

As her funds ran lower, Eileen became more and more worried about her future. She moved to an unheated room in a cheaper boarding house where meals were not included. To save money to attend concerts and buy sheet music she ate less and less. Winter brought snow and ice, a novelty to the girl from outback Australia, but the cold sapped her energies. She went for long walks in the woods around the city, marvelling at their beauty under layers of snow.

After practising for long hours at the piano, inflammation of the sciatic nerve running from the lower back to the hips gave her a great deal of pain. Finally one foot became so sore that she was unable to use the pedal. An operation was recommended but Eileen delayed, fearing the cost … until one day she fainted from pain and woke up in hospital.[22] The surgeon's fees swallowed up more of her precious funds and left her depressed. She regained the use of her foot but at times the pain from her sciatic nerve was intense. All she could do was to take a couple of aspirin and continue practising, until finally she had to give in and lie on her bed, with a pillow under her knees to give her relief. But still Eileen refused to abandon her dream of becoming a famous concert pianist.

By the time she reached her final year at Leipzig, she was still unsure of herself, her abilities and her looks. She had gained valuable concert experience by performing at the bi-weekly concerts held in the concert hall of the conservatorium. This taught her not to fear an audience of gimlet-eyed student critics, watching like hawks for any mistake. Unlike the futue novelist, Ethel Richardson, who had left Australia to study the piano at Leipzig, Eileen soon overcame the traditional beginner's fears of forgetting music she had committed to memory and having hundreds of eyes watching her perform.

But Eileen was haunted by the fear that after so much hard work, she would be unable to gain entrance into London's snobbish musical world. She worried that once the aristocratic ladies who acted as patrons to many young musicians discovered she was working-class and a 'colonial', she would be as despised as she had been in her early days at the Loreto Convent.

For Eileen the piano and music were her entire life, her 'gift from God'. Sister John had repeatedly told Eileen that 'she had been put on this earth to play classical music'. Eileen knew that if she did not succeed as a concert performer, she would have to abandon her dreams, return to Western Australia, face those kind people who had contributed to her tuition and tell them she had failed. She refused to think about returning to Boulder or Perth as a piano teacher.

To a girl of her spirit, defeat was unthinkable. She forced herself to continue practising in spite of the pain she felt. She spent some of her precious money on master classes given by the great pianists Artur Schnabel and Adelina de Lara – the last surviving pupil of pianist Clara Schumann, wife of Robert Schumann, the famous composer whose work Eileen loved. On days when it was difficult to obtain the vital six hours of piano practice, Eileen would rise at dawn to obtain a free piano at the conservatorium.[23] She worked day and night to improve her knowledge of musical theory.

At the Loreto Convent Eileen had been taught romantic pieces by Chopin, Tchaikovsky and Beethoven. At Leipzig great teachers and pianists like Artur Schnabel insisted that each soloist had a musical 'identity'. Under his expert guidance Eileen broadened her repertoire to include melancholy, introverted works by Grieg (a former pupil of the Leipzig Conservatorium), the melodic works of Rachmaninov (then in exile from Lenin's revolution), and what were then regarded as daring and *avante garde* works by Shostakovich, Prokofiev and other contemporary Russian composers. These were relatively daring works for a young woman but Eileen would have a lifelong passion for playing them.

Before her final exams Eileen was tense and nervous, prone to floods of tears at the slightest criticism. However, she passed with top marks. But she was still riddled with self-doubts and insecurities, worried about her finances and her future. At Loreto she had been a child prodigy. In London she would have to compete against the world's best musicians. Would she succeed? She was reassured when one of her examiners, the gruff Professor Schilsky, not known for giving compliments, told her in his thick Polish accent: 'You are ze greatest performer I 'ave met in all my travels. Believe me, Fraulein, you *will* succeed.'

Other teachers at the Leipzig Conservatorium had warned her that in London, centre of the performing world, there were legions of young unemployed classical musicians, all *longing* for a chance to have their talents recognised. What she needed was an agent to find her concert work. However, without bookings, no reputable agent would take her on their books: it seemed a vicious circle.

The American stockmarket crash of October 1929 had heralded the start of what would become known as the Great Depression and a huge downturn in the amount of money in circulation. It was not an easy time to enter the highly competitive world of professional music, especially for a girl from the colonies who lacked a private income.

Eileen described how she was 'adopted' by a childless New Zealand couple who were spending a few years in Europe, Mr and Mrs Andreae. (Presumably they were of Greek extraction, although Eileen does not say so.) She would tell the story of how she met this music-loving couple at one of the weekly concerts held at the conservatorium. Her piano teacher pointed her out to them, saying: 'There's a lonely little Australian girl over there, can't you take *her* to your hearts?'

In *Prelude*, Claire Hoskins Abrahall gives a different version of their meeting, presumably provided by Eileen. In it, she arrives too late to be admitted to a symphony concert at the *Gewandhaus*, and sits forlornly outside the hall, on the verge of tears, having missed a piece by Tchaikovsky she was longing to hear: the great Piano Concerto No. 1. The Andreaes also arrive late for the concert. Mrs Andreae talks to the young student, who looks thin and undernourished, and realises how badly Eileen needs someone to support her and look after her while she struggles to find her way in London and tries to obtain concert bookings. Eileen always insisted that this kind, music-loving couple took her under their wing, fed her, paid her accommodation, bought her clothes, gave her an allowance and took her to stay with them in their house in England. She described the kind couple as her 'adopted parents'. Yet she does not seem to have kept up with them in later life – possibly by then the Andreaes had returned to New Zealand. (When Eileen became famous, whenever interviewers asked probing questions about her parents, her first patrons and her period of struggle in London, she would change the subject or storm out of the interview.) She perfected the art of becoming vague and elusive whenever dates or details were required. One cannot help wondering *what* she was attempting to hide.

Before she left Leipzig for London, Eileen's favourite teacher, Herr Teichmüller, gave her a glowing letter of introduction to the British conductor Albert Coates. By the time she arrived in London for her first audition, the skinny freckled little girl with the unruly mop of chestnut hair who had arrived at the Loreto Convent had become a slender, titian-haired beauty.

Billed as 'the barefoot girl from the bush', Eileen Joyce leapt to stardom on the London arts scene long before expatriates like Arthur Boyd, Clive James and Barry Humphries had made Australia appear less of a cultural desert to British eyes. Initially, Eileen's Aussie accent proved a drawback to success with the snobbish patrons of amateur music societies who could give struggling musicians an opportunity to be discovered. Trying to obtain an agent, she was told cruelly that the British would regard her as a 'colonial' and she must not mention that her parents were of Irish stock as this would mean doors would remain closed to her, no matter how good her technique as a pianist.

Eileen was no fool. She had the wit to realise that in such circles it would be professional suicide to reveal that her father was an illiterate Aussie battler from Southern Ireland. Irish working-class girls were viewed as drunken and feckless, only suitable to be housemaids or laundresses. Having parents with an exotic gypsy flavour was *far* more socially acceptable than having them called 'bog Irish'.

The Andreaes freed Eileen from financial worry and provided her with a safe and stable home, nutritious meals and a Bluthner piano to practise on. Eileen had no need to look for a part-time job.[24] She wrote to London's leading conductors asking for an audition. And she sent a copy of Herr Techmüller's letter to the conductor Alfred Coates.

She waited and waited but heard nothing. Meanwhile the Andreaes had arranged for Eileen to appear at a concert given by the local music society in Norwich, as a try-out. Mrs Andreae hired a dressmaker to make Eileen a long silk dress, the colour of maize, which set off her auburn hair to perfection. Eileen's youth and good looks charmed her audience and the concert was a big success. But Norfolk was only a provincial city. What mattered was professional success in London, centre of the Empire and the performing arts.

Anxious months passed before Alfred Coates' secretary finally replied, suggesting a time and place for her London audition.

Eileen was very nervous at the idea of such an important occasion. Always so clothes-conscious, it seems strange that she told friends and journalists she wore 'a cheap little cotton frock' for her first audition.[25] Unfortunately, Albert Coates began by telling Eileen he had already booked all the performers he needed for that concert season. Seeing the look in her eyes, he added that her references from Leipzig had been so good he would still like to hear her play something.

Eileen sat down at the piano and played. The result was electrifying. Coates was so impressed by Eileen's talent that he promptly recommended her to his colleague, Sir Henry Wood, the famous conductor and founder of London's popular Promenade Concerts.

She was summoned by Sir Henry for the audition that could make or break her career. This time Eileen was even more nervous. She had had her hair styled professionally but claimed she could still only afford a cheap dress (although in other accounts she claimed Mrs Andreae had bought her an expensive dress for that occasion). Fortunately Sir Henry was extremely impressed by her performance and agreed to include her in one of his next Prom concerts.

Rehearsals with the orchestra followed. From the outset there were battles between the fiery sixty-year-old conductor and the red-headed performer. Sir Henry wanted his beautiful young female 'discovery' only to play romantic 'feminine' works.

'Leave "hard" masculine works by Prokofiev to male performers,' Sir Henry commanded. Eileen objected. What she saw as Sir Henry's patronising approach contradicted everything Artur Schnabel had taught her about selecting concert programs to suit her musical personality. She was terrified of falling out with Sir Henry and jeopardising her fledgling career, but she decided Schnabel's advice was so important she must make a stand. She was a serious musician and had no wish to be regarded as some sweet young thing filling in with a few 'feminine' works.

White-faced, with clenched knuckles, she requested an interview with the great Sir Henry and insisted on playing 'difficult masculine' works by her favourite Russian composers as well as the more feminine pieces he wanted her to play. Surprised by the passion in her voice, Sir Henry amazed her by ceding to her request without further discussion.

In 1931 Eileen Joyce finally made her debut at a crowded Promenade Concert, attended by London's leading critics. Walking up the steps and into the Queen's Hall on her way to her changing room, Eileen was extremely nervous, but Sir Henry Wood's handclasp and his kind words of assurance gave her confidence. After changing into her long maize-coloured silk dress, she sat quietly in her dressing-room concentrating on the score she would play from memory as the hall filled up with excited concertgoers.

As she walked onto the platform, she saw the hall packed from floor to ceiling with faces all turned towards her. Below her huge baskets of rainbow-coloured flowers were banked up below the grand piano. Remembering Sister John, Eileen kept her head high. The audience had no idea how nervous she was. She seemed to glide effortlessly across the platform. The light shone down on her auburn hair as she spread her skirts around her, sat down at the black Steinway grand and started to play.

Sir Henry Wood need not have worried that Eileen would not seem 'romantic' enough to please seasoned Prom goers. Her youth and beauty won their hearts. But it was Eileen's superb technique, the passion and the power of her playing that created a sensation amongst audience and music critics alike. Her choice of 'difficult' music won respect for her eclectic selection among serious musicians. Even the hardened London critics sat up and took notice. Here indeed was a discovery. Eileen's beautiful arm movements and her powerful playing coupled with her sensitive interpretation of the music won their approval.

As she finished the last chord there was a long moment of silence.

Then waves of applause echoed round the hall. Hearing the cries of '*Encore, encore!*' she could have wept tears of relief that she had not failed her supporters in Boulder, dear Sister John or kind Mr and Mrs Andreae.

The meteoric rise of the girl from Boulder had begun.

Eileen's concert promoters found her photographs useful in securing publicity for her performances. Her heart-shaped face, deep-set blue eyes, magnolia complexion and striking figure meant that journalists often compared her to the red-headed Irish-born film star Maureen O'Hara.

An Eileen Joyce tour was booked for various British provincial cities and towns, playing with amateur and professional orchestras. At last Eileen was able to show a reputable agent that she had bookings. For her tour, Eileen fulfilled her long-held dream of buying expensive evening gowns in which to perform. It was the start of her lifelong passion for designer clothes.

Doubtless her agent informed Eileen that the cooperation of the titled lady patrons of various music societies was vital for success at this beginning stage of her career. The legend of 'Raggedy Eileen, the gypsy girl' gained wide exposure in press interviews. Society ladies, patrons of concerts in country areas, who would have scorned to hold cocktail parties for a colonial miner's daughter, willingly organised them for Eileen Joyce, the former barefoot gypsy girl.

The tour resulted in several more engagements with the BBC but no offers to make records. However, what Eileen needed at this critical stage in her career were contracts to perform with *leading* conductors. Determined to succeed at all costs, she used part of her fees from the tour to hire a sound studio and record one of her favourite pieces, Liszt's Study in F Minor. She sent off copies of her 'test' record to all the leading conductors of the day and waited with some trepidation for the results.

Offers of concerts flooded in from major orchestras. She was also given a contract to cut two more records from the sound studio where she made her first recording and a contract from the BBC for regular radio performances one evening a week. These dinner-time concerts became very popular. As the public bought her records so the fame and the legend of 'Eileen Joyce, the barefoot girl from the bush' grew. More and more offers of concerts poured in from Britain, Holland and Germany. She was now performing with some of Europe's leading conductors.

Eileen had an astonishingly wide repertoire. It included seventy concertos which she played entirely from memory – a dozen concertos by Mozart, piano works by Beethoven, the dazzling piano concertos of Prokofiev and her favourite, the soaring and emotional Rachmaninov No. 2, with which she would become identified. Eileen described herself as 'a quick learner'.26 'I could learn a concerto in a week, or in a weekend if I had to. Nowadays,' she added, 'most pianists only have a repertoire of seven or eight concertos from memory.'26

If she felt the occasion required it, Eileen Joyce had no difficulty in mimicking an 'educated' British accent, remembering Sister John and her insistence on the importance of good diction. Among friends, however, her voice had a distinctive Aussie twang. In fact, Eileen had a decidedly larrikin streak on occasions. She was no snob although she now moved in snobbish circles. She was a feisty young Cinderella, fighting against huge odds to succeed. Eileen achieved her celebrity through hard work, and brilliance of technique against overwhelming odds.

In 1936, with her program notes claiming she was only twenty-four, Eileen made a triumphant return to Australia on an interstate concert tour organised by the ABC. Concerts were sold out as crowds flooded in to hear her, proud that an Aussie battler had become so famous overseas.

Arriving back in Perth to a civic welcome and a warm hug from her mother, it seemed that the only person Eileen could *not* please was her father. At an official reception in Eileen's honour, Joe Joyce, by now almost sixty, had arrived at the reception in a shiny new suit, new and squeaky shoes and a bushman's hat accompanied by Eileen's mother Alice, who sported a new perm specially for the occasion. As a special request, Joe asked Eileen to play the Irish folk song 'Believe me if all those endearing young charms'.

When she told him that she could play over a hundred sonatas and concertos from memory but could not play his favourite tune, her father exploded. 'Then what's the point? All that money spent on foreign schooling's been wasted!'

Eileen, in long gloves and an elegant beaded satin gown designed by Hartnell, looked embarrassed. Hastily she promised to learn the song immediately. Alice soothed Joe down so that her father stayed on for the reception, where he heard various speakers praising Eileen and calling her Western Australia's favourite pianist. Eileen's mother said little, overawed by so many civic dignitaries and their wives, all of whom wanted to meet Eileen.

When the reception was over, Eileen's younger sister took her aside and told her angrily that their mother had been deeply hurt when the neighbours told her that the southern newspapers had carried an interview with Eileen claiming the family had been so poor that she was forced to beg for money to feed herself and her siblings and went to school in ragged clothes. Eileen must have been embarrassed when her younger sister reminded her acidly that their parents had *always* provided them with nourishing meals and even though every drop of water had to be boiled, their mother had spent hours at the washboard scrubbing out the clinging red dust so that they both had clean frocks for school, clean socks and clean hankies.[27]

Fortunately, no hint of these family dissensions reached the ears of journalists. The discovery that Eileen had taken great liberties with the truth could seriously have harmed her in Australia. Eileen compared her beaded Hartnell gown, strappy Bond Street shoes and diamond brooch (a gift from the man she would later marry) with the cheap dress and tawdry fake diamonds of her younger sister. How lucky she had been to escape from Boulder!

Requests followed from Sydney impresarios for a second concert tour of Australia but Eileen insisted she must return to London. No hint of romance was made public: it was presumed she was returning to fulfil concert engagements in Europe.

The real reason for Eileen's speedy return to London was revealed when Cinderella married her Prince Charming, the rich stockbroker Douglas Leigh Barratt. Her only child, John Douglas Barratt (at this juncture in her career a baby she probably did not want to have) was born on the fateful day in September 1939 when war was declared and Britain stood alone against the full force of Germany's army and air force.

Neville Chamberlain, the appeaser of Hitler, was replaced as prime minister by Winston Churchill. A few weeks after the Barratts' marriage Douglas enlisted as an officer in the British Navy. Separation from her husband of only a few months meant constant anxiety for the new bride. Each day telegrams arrived from the War Office informing next of kin that their loved ones had been killed.

During London's terrible blitz by the German Luftwaffe, many thousands of civilians were killed and much of the East End was destroyed. Eileen had played several times before King George VI and Queen Elizabeth at fund-raising concerts. Like them, she refused to run away and hide somewhere safe until the war was over.

One night Buckingham Palace was badly damaged by a bomb. The Queen won the undying love of the East Enders when she announced on her next visit to bombed-out families: 'At last we can look the East End in the face!' It was a tense and hectic time for everyone who remained in London. Sirens sounded their warning as the German planes approached on their nightly raids and searchlights raked the night sky. No one could predict if they would be dead or alive the next day. Some theatres and concerts continued to hold performances, although the wailing of the air-raid sirens would mean that everyone in the audience, as well as the performers, rushed to the nearest tube station to shelter from German bombs.

It was an anxious period for Eileen, a young mother with no family to support her other than her mother-in-law, who had never approved of her son's marriage.[28] Her mother-in-law could not understand that Eileen was totally in love with music, driven to perform and filled with a burning desire to create beautiful sound. Eileen now faced a dilemma every supporting mother will understand: whether to continue working or stay at home with her child in reduced circumstances.

For Eileen the decision was simple. She had to continue performing, so she entrusted her infant son to her mother-in-law and to well-trained nannies. Doubtless she believed this was the best thing she could do under the circumstances. Unfortunately separation at this tender age created a rift between mother and son, exacerbated, according to Eileen, by her Scottish mother-in-law who implied that instead of looking after him, his mother was 'gadding about on concert tours'.[30] Eileen later said that she was working extremely hard at her chosen profession in order to support herself and her son, the wages of a naval officer not being overly generous. However the separation and what her son probably perceived as rejection, set a pattern for a troubled and stormy relationship which would never be resolved.

One morning, three years after her romantic wedding to Douglas Leigh Barratt, there was a ring on the door of Eileen's small studio apartment. She answered it to find a uniformed telegraph boy. He handed her the yellow envelope containing a telegram. She went inside. The telegram informed her that her husband had been killed in a direct hit on the minesweeper in which he was serving on the run to Murmansk.

She did not weep immediately, numbed by the news, then broke down into torrents of weeping as she saw her husband's portrait, handsome in his naval uniform. The horror of the fatal telegram stayed with her: even in old age Eileen would recount the story of the telegraph boy's arrival again and again to close friends.

Cinderella had lost her Prince Charming but life had to go on. With her son away from the bombing in the care of his grandmother, Eileen was alone in wartime London, a bleak place of ration books, black-outs, clothing coupons, bombed-out homes, with nightly air-raids and people sleeping in the London Underground stations to escape the bombs. Fearlessly Eileen continued doing what she loved most, giving paid concerts as well as charity performances in hospitals and clinics for victims of the London blitz at a time when many believed the Germans might cross the British Channel and invade Britain.

'We shall fight them on the beaches, we shall never surrender,' Winston Churchill thundered on the radio, effectively raising the morale of Britons weakened by bereavement, air-raids and food shortages. It became apparent to the British that this young Aussie performer had grit and determination which no threats of German bombs could daunt. They loved her for it.

Eileen gave a series of concerts which did much to raise the morale of Londoners. Eileen Joyce and Dame Myra Hess were courageous pianists who insisted on giving concerts in central London, no matter how great the danger. Eileen gave a series of concerts with Sir Malcolm Sargent and the London Philharmonic Orchestra around Britain's worst-hit cities, including Coventry and Southampton.

At one Eileen Joyce concert in London, the concert hall was freezing cold: there was no coal to stoke the boilers for the central heating. To huge applause, Eileen Joyce appeared on the platform in a holly-green silk dress that accentuated her magnolia complexion and titian hair. Later, journalists learned that she wore a double set of woollen underwear underneath the long skirts of her dress and kept a hot water bottle in her lap so that she could warm her chilblained hands.

In spite of the cold her performance was faultless. She lifted the audience's war-dampened spirits with a brilliant performance of Chopin, an affirmation of the spirit of freedom and the triumph of the human spirit. The audience clapped and cheered until their hands were sore and they grew hoarse. Eileen gave encore after encore, ignoring the wailing air-raid sirens outside. Such was the power of her music that no one departed until she had gathered up her music, made a final curtsey to the audience and left the platform.

The strain of performing night after night, coping with continual nagging pain in her lower back and the horrors of the bombing of London in the blitz preyed on Eileen's nerves so much that she turned into a heavy smoker. One day she suffered a third-degree burn to the finger of one hand from a car's cigarette lighter. The doctor bandaged her hand and ordered her to keep her arm in a sling, thinking this measure would prevent her from performing. Being Eileen, she insisted she would not disappoint those who had booked and paid for tickets. She replaced the bandage with a sticking plaster and gave another concert to overwhelming applause.

Eileen Joyce was the consummate professional. More than once she fainted from nervous exhaustion in her dressing-room before a performance but insisted on appearing on the platform. She hated to let her public down. Once she squashed the tip of her finger in a door, but forced herself to give the advertised recital. When she made up her mind to do something, no one and nothing would stop her. Sometimes the pain in her back was so bad that a trained nurse was paid to stand in the wings, in case Eileen collapsed during a concert. One evening the pain was so intense that as she stood up from the piano stool to receive tumultuous applause from 6000 people at London's Royal Albert Hall, she collapsed and had to be helped off the stage. Frequently she gave recitals wearing a full-length plaster cast, which she disguised by wearing an intricately swathed tulle gown.

In the final years of World War II, Eileen Joyce gave a series of concerts with the London Philharmonic in various provincial cities around Britain, which meant hours spent in crowded trains and draughty stations. Crowds would gather at the stage door of the concert hall to see her arrive and depart.

Through good looks, inborn talent and hard work, aided by the haunting legend that she was the barefoot girl from the bush, Eileen Joyce had acquired film-star charisma. Some critics classed her in the same league as Horowitz and Rachmaninov, which was praise indeed. However, she faced stern criticism from some of the older and more chauvinist critics, who found it hard to reconcile Miss Joyce's glamour with her talent and tried to denigrate her achievements. What they failed to realise was that Eileen Joyce was a true virtuoso, dedicated to her career. It was the most important thing in her life.

Eileen was eclectic in her choice of program, always seeking new works to add to her already large repertoire. She declined to slavishly follow popular taste. She was interested in good music no matter from what source it came. Performing works by Russian composers was not a popular choice in wartime Britain; there were already rumours of Stalin's ill treatment of the Poles. Eileen saw great composers as being above politics. She was one of the first pianists in Britain to champion the preludes, fuges and fantastic dances written by Dmitri Shostakovich.[30]

There were plenty of handsome American officers in wartime London, eager for female company. Eileen was invited to play for an audience of American generals and colonels at the Grosvenor House Hotel, headquarters of the American forces. Here she met the brilliant American dancer Ginger Rogers, in Europe to entertain American troops, who became her friend. It may have been here, too, that she first met Christopher Mann, Ginger Roger's London agent. Like many other men, he was fascinated by Eileen's titian-haired beauty and lively personality.[31]

Eileen was honoured by an invitation to play Chopin before leading members of the Polish Government in exile, lodged in style at London's Ritz Hotel. Such a beautiful unattached young widow was bound to attract male admirers (another point which aroused the ire of her Scottish mother-in-law). Eileen enjoyed the attention, receiving bouquets of flowers and invitations to parties. However, as a strict Catholic she was not interested in extra-marital relationships with married officers and was wary about marrying again. She was aware that marriage could tie her down and prevent her performing. Nor did she want more children. Music was her life.

It was Christopher Mann who finally won her heart. In 1945, when the war was over, Eileen claimed she married him.[31] One of the things that drew them together was the fact that he understood the stressful yet exhilarating world of the performer. In this, as in a host of other ways, he was the ideal partner for Eileen. Christopher was very tall, slim in build, with an engaging smile and enormous charm. He too had been married before. A former journalist turned publicist, he had become London's leading film agent. The Christopher Mann agency represented most of the leading British film directors and producers as well as the British and American stars who appeared in their films. The contracts of directors such as Carol Reed, David Lean, the team of Powell and Pressburger, and the populist producer Betty Box made up the bulk of the agency's income. Repeat showings of their best films worldwide would continue to bring in large royalties for years to come.

The late 1940s and the 1950s was the great age of British films, and Christopher Mann was involved in many of the major British films of that era: *Lawrence of Arabia,* with Peter O'Toole; *Zorba the Greek,* starring Anthony Quinn; Alec Guiness's Oscar-winning *Bridge over the River Kwai;* and *Dr Zhivago,* with Julie Christie – films which have enchanted audiences worldwide for decades and still bring in money to the Christopher Mann estate today.[33]

Christopher was well read and loved classical music. Poised and personable, he was equally at ease in high society and in the British and Hollywood film worlds. His agency had offices in Park Lane, and his London apartment overlooked Hyde Park from the top floor of 140 Park Lane, near the Marble Arch. Eileen and Christopher soon acquired Chartwell Farm as a country house near Westerham, in Kent, which they bought from Mary and Christopher Soames, Winston Churchill's daughter and son-in-law. Later they would buy two more farms.

In wartime, when clothing coupons were in force, Eileen repeatedly wore the exquisitely beaded long evening gowns she had purchased from London and Paris couturiers before the war. She was such a perfectionist and so disciplined in her diet that neither years of stodgy wartime food nor the birth of her son had put an ounce of weight on her.

Once the austerity of wartime Britain relaxed, Eileen was again able to buy her long gowns from famous couturiers like Norman Hartnell and Victor Stiebel. She was also loaned dresses by leading couturiers to attend film premieres with her husband. She rarely had to wear the same glamorous gown twice.

One night a zip broke during the first half of Eileen's performance and she had to change in the interval. It was an unusually hot night for London. For the second half of the concert she wore an Empire-style gown with a high waist. To go with the dress and help her keep cool, Eileen's dresser swept her shining auburn hair into an elegant chignon, pinning it with a diamond clasp.

The audience, used to the deprivations of wartime, burst out clapping as Eileen reappeared. This was an innovation. Most female musicians performed wearing plain black dresses perhaps adorned by a pearl necklace. Eileen had started a trend. Today's concertgoers regard it as normal for female performers to look as glamorous as possible at concerts, instead of blending in with the black-and-white of the orchestra.

Eileen's striking good looks and beautiful gowns, coupled with her brilliance as a performer, made her even more popular. A change of costumes midway through the concert became her 'trademark'. Eileen now chose each exquisite dress to match the mood of the piece she was playing – flame colour or lilac for Grieg, Liszt or Chopin, dark greens or her favourite magnolia satin for the chords and arpeggios of Beethoven, red for the bolder music of Prokofiev.

Her husband's constant visits to Hollywood brought Eileen into contact with leading film directors and producers as well as actors like her friend Ginger Rogers, Katherine Hepburn and the young French star Brigitte Bardot. One younger performer Christopher Mann helped to make famous was the multi-talented Russian-born actor, linguist and writer Peter Ustinov.[33]

To celebrate Christopher's birthday[33], there were parties where Eileen played. Sometimes Eileen and Christopher played duets together on two grand pianos which stood close together. Once, as a birthday surprise for Christopher, Ginger Rogers dressed up in top hat, white tie and tails and gave a spirited rendering of her famous routines from the film *Top Hat* which she had made with Fred Astaire.

Unlike some classical pianists who enjoyed playing jazz for amusement, Eileen would *never* play anything but classical music, even at a party. At one party a leading film director heard Eileen play her favourite Rachmaninov Concerto No. 2, filled with emotion and huge sweeping chords. As a result, she was contracted to record the music for *The Seventh Veil*, a major British film. In *The Seventh Veil* viewers saw the young blonde actress Ann Todd pretend to play a silent keyboard, while off-camera Eileen was performing the great romantic Grieg Piano Concerto, with which her public would always associate her.

This and other well-paid film tracks increased her fame and popularity. Eileen spent a large proportion of these fees on her couturier clothes and travelling expenses. Top performing artists were not paid nearly as much then as they are now.

The first film for which Eileen Joyce played the sound track (breaking her commitment to classical music) was *I Know Where I'm Going,* shot on the Isle of Skye. The haunting and unforgettable Highland ballad of that name forms the theme song. It became world-famous after Eileen played it and her recording of the film score was sold in huge numbers in Britain and America. Eileen now belonged to the film world as well as the concert platform. The girl from Boulder had come a long way.

For her second film Eileen played the Rachmaninov Concerto No. 2. *Brief Encounter,* directed by David Lean, starred Celia Johnson and Trevor Howard as star-crossed lovers gazing soulfully at each other in railway stations, fearful their illicit but innocent affair will be discovered.

In the post war period, most people owned far fewer recordings than today, but as prosperity increased so did the market for records. Eileen soon discovered there was a huge public, deprived by the war from concertgoing, hungry for new musical experiences. Her recordings did a great deal to popularise classical music among a wider public.

Now that Eileen was financially secure, she was able to be generous with both her time and her money. She befriended Ann Todd, then an unknown actress, and invited her to Chartwell Farm to help her make her silent playing look lifelike.

By now Eileen Joyce had become a household name throughout Britain. Stories appeared in *House and Garden, Vogue, Harpers* and *Woman's Weekly* describing Miss Joyce's seven grand pianos, her Mayfair apartment, her beautiful country house decorated with antiques and English chintzes, her portraits commissioned from leading artists, her triumphs at the Albert Hall playing before the Queen and the young Princess Elizabeth, and her friendship with the Churchill family.

At the end of World War II, a socialist government under Clement Attlee replaced Churchill's coalition government. Sir Winston Churchill, the man who had saved Britain in her darkest hour, found himself out of office, with more time to spend at his beloved country home at Chartwell. He would spend hours at the easel in his garden studio, then visit his water garden to feed the rare golden orff (a variety of sea-perch) with biscuits, or perhaps walk down to the lake to watch his black swans. Sometimes, when the mood took him, Sir Winston might continue walking the short distance to Chartwell Farm, where he was welcomed as an old friend, and where he would sit and listen attentively while Eileen practised for her next concert. Both Sir Winston and Lady Churchill enjoyed watching the latest British films that Christopher Mann showed in the private cinema at Chartwell Farm.

Eileen and Christopher would often be invited to a meal at the Churchill home, where they might meet other members of the Churchill family, as well as politicians and diplomats, media barons, such as Lord Beaverbrook, and artists and writers. In the evenings the card table was always kept ready in case Winston suggested a hand of bezique, his favourite game, which Christopher Mann also enjoyed. The dining room at Chartwell, with its long Tuscan-style windows, overlooked the magnificent garden, Lady Churchill's pride and joy, which she had designed. Eileen, who had grown up in arid Boulder and then spent years living in a studio apartment in central London, knew little about gardens. Lady Churchill helped her to design a beautiful garden for Chartwell Farm. For the rest of her life Eileen would love green lawns filled with daffodils in spring, massed herbaceous borders and rose beds bordered with lavender.

At Chartwell Farm Christopher Mann employed a manager, Jim Mayne, to run his dairy herd. On Friday nights, home for the weekend, he and Eileen would discuss farm business with him. Saturday and Sundays were spent relaxing and with friends.[34] Eileen loved the peace and beauty of Chartwell Farm. If she had no concerts scheduled she would often stay on, taking a train to London later in the week to have clothes fitted or visit her hairdresser, then lunching with friends in her favourite restaurant on the ground floor of the exclusive department store Fortnum & Mason in Piccadilly.

The lessons in deportment and social etiquette she had learned long ago from Sister John stood her in good stead. Eileen was now a socially adept hostess, a perfectionist in everything she undertook. Her homes were furnished with understated elegance in the English manner. She had acquired the manners of a lady: instead of dirt floors and hessian walls, she was now surrounded by all the trappings of wealth and good taste. However, she always remained proud of being an Australian, and she and Christopher made no attempt to gloss over her huge struggle to become one of the world's leading virtuosos. The nearby village of Westerham, built around a village green, was famous for its antique shops. Eileen would take house guests from America and Australia to Pitt's Cottage, a combined tea room and antique shop with a picturesque cottage garden. She loved the Kentish countryside in spring when the orchards were filled with pink and white cherry and apple blossoms. Show business friends of the couple often stayed at Chartwell Farm. Once Ginger Rogers arrived bringing some inflatable black swans for their swimming pool – a witty reference to the black swans from Western Australia that swam on the Churchills' lake at Chartwell.

Even in Australia, famous for lopping down its tall poppies, no one seemed to grudge Eileen Joyce her achievements. Everyone, that is, except Eileen's siblings and her father, who were always unhappy at the way she presented her 'deprived' childhood to the press. Eileen remained typically Australian in her belief in a 'fair go' and equality of opportunity, topics on which she was never afraid to speak her mind. She was identified with Australia in the same way as her friend Peter Finch, the Australian actor, even though they both resided in Britain.

Eileen spoke her mind fearlessly on racial questions. In Johannesburg, she aroused the wrath of the South African Government when she announced that besides playing to a white audience on a paid basis, she would perform free of charge to a coloured audience.

It was in 1947 that *Prelude,* the children's book by her friend Lady Claire Hoskins Abrahall which purported to recount Eileen's Australian childhood, was published by Oxford University Press. Complaints were received by the publisher. Eileen was asked to explain. The book was withdrawn from sale. *Prelude* aroused considerable mirth when copies went on sale in Western Australia. The illustrations by fashion designer Anna Zinkheisen, who had never visited Australia, portrayed the miners of Boulder like cowboys in a Wild West film, with white sombreros and fringed leather chaps. Other illustrations showed a long-legged, barefoot Eileen running through the bush with Twink, her kangaroo. The book talked of her walking him on a collar and lead.

Even after the book was withdrawn from sale, in the files of countless newspapers and radio networks the legend of 'Raggedy Eileen' running barefoot around Zeehan and Boulder (which is as flat as a pancake) and playing the mouth organ to miners who gave her pennies to pay for music lessons lived on. To cover herself for writing a children's book which was partly fantasy, partly biography, Lady Abrahall wrote in her Foreword:

> Thanks to Eileen Joyce, I have had the privilege of probing back into her childhood days and all the reactions which went with them. At times, it has been a little difficult for her to remember or re-capture the past. On these occasions I have used an author's licence, and drawn upon my own imagination, even conjuring up a few fictitious characters with which to surround her.[35]

Eileen insisted that the book had been written without her cooperation. Given the high reputation of the publisher and the fact that Eileen remained good friends with Lady Abrahall, this seems hard to believe.[36] Lady Abrahall was part of the British arts establishment, one of those leading patrons who had been important to Eileen at the start of her career. Unfortunately, Lady Abrahall had never visited Australia or contacted Eileen's parents or siblings. To give the author her due, Eileen's contradictions over events in her childhood and her unwillingness to describe them in detail would have posed a nightmare for *any* biographer. *Prelude* mentioned the Andreaes, Eileen's kind and generous patrons, and raises a number of questions. Was Andreae their real name? Why did Mr and Mrs Andreae disappear from Eileen's life? Did Mr Andreae resent the money his wife spent on launching Eileen's career or did he become overly fond of Eileen and did his wife end their relationship?[37]

The next attempt to relate Eileen's life was a black-and-white 16 mm film made by London's Faun Films in 1950.[38] Called *Wherever She Goes* (taken from the nursery rhyme 'Ride a cock horse to Banbury Cross/To see a fine lady ride on a white horse/With rings on her fingers/And bells on her toes/She shall have music wherever she goes. The film enjoyed considerable success. It claimed to be *loosely* adapted from *Prelude*. The miners of Boulder were played by Australians; dark-haired Muriel Steinberg played Eileen's long-suffering mother, and a pretty blonde actress Suzanne Parrett played the young Eileen, while Tim Drysdale, son of artist Russell Drysdale, played Eileen's brother John. In the introduction and the final reel Eileen played herself.[39] The film perpetuated the legend of Eileen as a penniless barefoot girl who taught herself to play classical music on a pub piano then went to a Perth convent on money donated by the miners. Boulder is well portrayed but parts of the film are unreal. For example, Eileen calls her parents 'Mummy' and 'Daddy', more like a middle-class English child than the daughter of a Boulder miner, who would surely have called them 'Mum' and 'Dad'.

By now the 'Raggedy Eileen' legend 'owned' the world-famous pianist and she could not escape from it without humiliation. Eileen was also very aware of the advantages of good public relations stories, like those magazine articles that celebrated the Manns' increasingly glamorous lifestyle and their famous friends in show business and the world of international music.

Decades later, ABC producer Felix Hayman related that when he interviewed Eileen Joyce she was very 'prickly' when her early life was mentioned. She was still playing the *grande dame*, flaring up and terminating any interview she did not like. Eileen defended herself by saying that her refusal to cooperate with the author of *Prelude* had been 'because I didn't want to upset my family'. The problem was that she had *already* upset them.

Eileen no longer needed to play for money but her passion for performing and her need to be the centre of attention drove her on. Christopher paid for Eileen's son John to attend a private school and tried to provide him with the good things in life. However, they were never close.

Eileen continued to play to increasingly large audiences. Like Nellie Melba and the Australian pianist and composer Margaret Sutherland,[40] Eileen lacked the necessary time to be a devoted mother. During John's infancy she left him in the care of excellent nannies, as most upper-class women in Britain did during this period. Friends recall that as a child and a teenager John Barratt never wanted for material things. But working hard and touring constantly meant that Eileen was frequently short of time to spend with her son, to the detriment of their relationship. Money spent *on* children rarely compensates for lack of time spent *with* them. Eileen was often under stress and her temper (inherited from her father) could flare up and then end in tears. Such behaviour confuses children. Close friends noted that the relationship between Eileen and her growing son was now stormy.[41] Like Christopher, Eileen had a stressful but fascinating career. She did love her son in her own way, but like most successful performers hers was a driven personality. Being a concert performer, she often claimed, 'demanded the pianist's life and soul'.

The continual striving after subtle nuances of expression and the sheer physical effort involved were emotionally and physically draining to someone as temperamental as Eileen, who was still battling lower back pain after sitting at the piano for long periods. Sister John had told her that God had created her to make music; for Eileen the creation of good music held a religious intensity.

Now that Eileen was seriously wealthy, in addition to paid concerts, she gave recitals free of charge in aid of her 'pet' charity, a home for lepers run by missionaries at Vellore, India. She also generously donated her time to play in churches and schools to raise money for scholarships to enable deprived children to study music. She played in hospitals for the mentally and physically handicapped and on occasions for prisoners in jail. She played on grand pianos and battered old uprights, in hospices for the dying, in small village halls to raise funds for guide dogs for the blind and for visiting dignitaries at Australia House in London.

As the world's highest paid concert pianist, Eileen had never worked harder. She toured Australia in 1948, performing in Melbourne and in Brisbane's City Hall, where the audience was enthralled by her wonderful rendition of the Rachmaninov No. 2 Concerto. It was the first time they had known a performer change in the interval – this time from a blue gown to another of dashing yellow.[42] She did not visit Boulder on this tour. She and her family moved in such totally different worlds that they had little in common. Her family was now quite well off and did not need her money.

Before her sell-out concert at Sydney's Town Hall, Eileen invited a group of excited schoolgirls to hear her practise. Before she started playing, Eileen came to the front of the platform and spoke to the girls 'very sweetly', telling them of her own difficulties and joys as a performer. One of the girls who heard Eileen play (and immediately decided that she too must become a concert pianist) was Deirdre Prussak, who would become a close friend to Eileen in her final years.[43]

Over the next decade Eileen gave concerts all over Britain, in Holland, Russia, South Africa, South and North America as well as Scandinavia. She spent a great deal of time travelling by train, boat and plane. British critics remarked that no other pianist ever filled the Royal Albert Hall more times than Eileen Joyce.[44]

Eileen remained what she had always been: a demanding perfectionist, hard on herself and dedicated to performing. To live up to her high standards of performance meant weeks of constant practice which resulted in bouts of pain, exhaustion and tears. Yet for all her apparent fragility, Eileen was a woman of inner strength and spirit. She was convinced that 'there must be a great deal of hard and mundane practising to achieve anything'. She also said: 'It can't *all* be joy making music, otherwise the joy would be too overwhelming.'[45]

Her decision to retire came in 1960, caused by exhaustion leading to what is now called 'burn-out'. She had made a gruelling concert tour by train around the Indian continent before flying to Hong Kong, where she survived a particularly hazardous landing. She was hot and exhausted. Crossing Hong Kong harbour by ferry to the concert hall, racked with stabs of pain from her lower back, she asked herself, 'Why am I doing all this? What a crazy way to live, rushing around the world at this pace. Why don't I give it all up and stay at home with Christopher?' It should be borne in mind that Eileen's decision to retire took place before jumbo jets made life slightly easier for international performers as they moved across the world from one concert hall to another.

Accordingly, worn out by decades of international travel, Eileen Joyce announced her retirement that same year. She did this at the end of a concert in Aberdeen, symbolically closing the top of the grand piano. Then she turned to the audience and explained that due to muscular pain in her back and fingers this would be her final public concert.[46]

She had injured the little finger of her right hand, which badly affected her ability to 'stretch' (she used to be able to extend her fingers to cover ten notes). At the time she retired Eileen described herself as being 'an empty shell, depleted physically, spiritually and emotionally. I loved the piano which had brought me exaltation as well as despair.'[47]

So give it all up she did.

As a substitute she took up tapestry and gardening. Finally she was freed from the necessity to practise from six to eight hours almost every day – 'blood, sweat and survival' as she now termed it. After she ceased playing professionally and practising for hours on end, and doubtless had some physiotherapy, the pain in her hands and her lower back gradually lessened until finally she was freed from that as well.

She did not touch a piano again for almost six years. Then, pain-free, she started playing again ... and experienced the same sense of magic and awe for music that she had felt as a child sitting beside Sister John. Entirely for her own pleasure and that of her friends, she would play the piano or the harpsichord in the evenings. Eileen was unusual in playing the harpsichord as well as the piano, instruments that require a totally different 'touch'. She performed on her hand-painted harpsichord in concerts at London's Royal Festival Hall.

After six years of silence, the public still loved Eileen Joyce. There were countless demands for her to return to the concert platform. Finally, in 1967 she relented and gave one last charity concert, playing works by her favourite composers to a huge audience. At the end the audience applauded, stamped their feet and cheered. They wanted her back. She enjoyed the experience so much that she did consider returning to the concert platform. But she was now in her late fifties, her back had recovered and she abandoned the idea. Remembering Sister John's words she announced to the press: 'I was put on this planet to play with joy. I did my best.'

Reviewing her final concert, one critic wrote: 'Her old sparkle and crackling vivacity has another dimension, that of an inner radiance.' Eileen herself felt that her interpretation of the works of many composers had acquired more wisdom and understanding. Her long rest from performing had given her time to read and study and this was apparent in her profound interpretation of various works.[48]

In 1971 she was honoured by the award of an Honorary Doctorate of Music from the University of Cambridge. It gave her enormous pleasure to have this very public acceptance from the world of academic music, a compensation for all those years of hard work.

Christopher was also tiring. He had cut down staff numbers and moved his agency to smaller premises. He had been a heavy pipe smoker for many years, and had developed a 'smoker's cough'. Eventually he was diagnosed as having lung cancer.

Aided by professional nurses, Eileen nursed her husband devotedly until his death in December 1979, aged seventy-one.[49] Eileen, now in her late sixties, was deeply distressed by Christopher's death and found his funeral very hard to endure. There is nothing harder for the bereaved than walking away from the last resting place of a loved one. Loyal friends rallied round. Gradually Eileen's strength of character came to her rescue and she recovered her equilibrium.

Christopher Mann bequeathed Eileen some five million pounds in assets and property, making her an immensely rich woman in her own right.

Eileen was a complex and sometimes insecure person. At times she could display an impractical, almost fey attitude, giving away designer dresses, jewels and gifts of money. Fortunately her affairs were looked after by an excellent accountant. Loneliness meant that she was easy prey for sob stories; she was taken advantage of by one particularly charming young man who obtained a large sum of money from her.

She donated large amounts to her favourite charities and to help aspiring concert performers.[50] Nothing could weaken Eileen's determination to continue helping others to create beautiful music. She learned from her Australian friends Professor Sir Frank Calloway and his wife, Kathleen, who used to visit her regularly, that Perth would soon celebrate its 150th celebrations and that the University of Western Australia was to award her an Honorary Doctorate as Cambridge had done, which delighted Eileen. She would commission another portrait in her academic gown to have in her home.

In June 1981, in her seventies, Eileen returned to Perth to inaugurate a very generous and imaginative scheme designed to benefit music students in Western Australia. She told friends that Christopher had urged her to make a donation to honour her parents' memory *now*, rather than bequeath money to the University in her will. Possibly Eileen felt remorseful that she had not been closer to her mother and father, and Christopher had realised this. Accordingly she donated $110 000 to cover the cost of the Eileen Joyce Studio 'in memory of her parents' and to set up an Eileen Joyce Fund which would pay a graduate of the university to study the piano overseas.

The beautiful music studio dedicated to Eileen Joyce's parents is now part of the University of Western Australia's music department. It stands in the university's landscaped grounds, and its glass walls look out onto gardens thick with tree ferns.

Eileen wanted the Eileen Joyce Studio to be used for the teaching of keyboard music, for master classes similar to those she had attended at Leipzig and to house a range of instruments representing the history of Western keyboard music. The instruments Eileen donated to the studio that bears her name included an organ, a spinet, her hand-painted harpsichord built for her in 1959 by the famous instrument maker Thomas Goff, and an old-style or *forte* piano. She also gifted the portrait of herself by Augustus John and the bronze bust by Anna Mahler as well as her correspondence (now available to the general public on the University of Western Australia's website).

On this third and final visit 'home' to Western Australia (having made previous ones in 1936 and 1948), Eileen was her usual bubbly, delightful self. She visited her former convent school in company with Father McMahon (the priest who organised her scholarship to the Sisters of Loreto Convent), and was delighted to have a chance to see her beloved music teacher Sister John, now Mother John Moore.

Eileen never forgot these two devoted people, who had done so much to change her life. She was still a devout Catholic and while in Perth she attended Sunday Mass at Father McMahon's church. She did not visit Boulder. Questioned by the press, Eileen (reluctantly) confessed that due to living in totally different worlds, with some ten thousand miles separating them, she had lost touch with her siblings.[51]

In the summer of 1981 she was thrilled to learn she had been awarded the Order of St Michael and St George, bestowed on her by HM the Queen. Letters and telegrams of congratulation poured in, including one from the Prime Minister of Australia and another from Sir Charles Court, Premier of Western Australia, who had opened the Eileen Joyce Studio at the University. Malcolm Williamson, the Maker of the Queen's Music, was also delighted that she, a fellow Australian, had been honoured in this way. 'Countless congratulations from all musicians and from all true Australians,' he wrote. 'Honours should have been poured on you all your life.'[52]

Eileen also felt honoured when she was appointed a juror at the Sydney International Piano Festival and Competition. With her usual generosity, she donated 20 000 pounds (a large sum for that period) to help mount the Third International Piano Competition and flew out to Sydney to attend it in 1985. Eileen, who did not look her age, was now nearing eighty but refused to acknowledge the fact.

Deirdre Prussak, a former Australian nurse turned magazine columnist, was sent to interview Eileen by *New Idea* magazine. It had been arranged by the magazine that Deirdre would interview Eileen then take her out to dinner. Georgie, Eileen's female secretary, who had been with her for many years, was unable to accompany her to Sydney on this trip. Upon arriving at the hotel, Deirdre learned that without a secretary or a minder Eileen had forgotten she had agreed to do an interview for *New Idea*.

A confused Eileen opened the door of her suite at the Hilton, saw Deidre, apologised profusely and they sat and talked for an hour. When Eileen learned that Deirdre was not just another journalist in search of sensational details about her childhood and that Deirdre's adoptive mother was the famous opera comedienne Anna Russell, so she knew a great deal about music and musicians, Eileen was delighted. She said that fate must have sent Deirdre, an entertaining, intelligent and caring young woman, to interview her at a time when she badly needed someone to help her.

Deirdre saw Eileen practise at the Sydney Town Hall almost forty years ago and felt 'there was something ethereal about Eileen's ability to weave dreams with her music and wrap her audience in magic. I was fortunate that many years later I became her friend. When you have admired someone for so many years it is gratifying to discover that, beside their incredible talent, they are also a truly delightful, gentle and beautiful human being.'[53]

Dinner that night marked the start of a long and enduring friendship between the two women. Eileen, usually so guarded with journalists, opened up and revealed her insecurities about her diminishing memory and the fear she had Alzheimers disease and asked, 'You will help me, won't you?'

Deirdre's heart went out to this valiant women who had come to Sydney because she believed in the aims of the International Piano Competition but who now had problems with her short-term memory and was worried to go out by herself, fearing that she might forget her handbag or get lost.

Eileen had not been provided with an official minder by the competition's organisers. Over dinner that night she confided to Deirdre that on the outward journey she had got lost while changing planes at Singapore. She said she did not like to admit her fears to the Piano Festival's organisers and ask for help, for Eileen took her role as a juror of the piano competition very seriously indeed. 'You feel a sense of responsibility and dedication towards being a juror. You have to give your whole spirit and attention to each competitor. It takes an enormous amount of concentration to fulfil this commitment,' she said, understanding from her own experience just how hard each competitor had worked to get to this point and how disappointed the losers would be.[54]

Deirdre, a former nurse, had enough experience of elderly people with dementia to realise just how vulnerable Eileen was. She volunteered to be Eileen's chauffeur and guide and described how 'each morning I would go to her hotel to be met with "Thank God, Deirdre, you've come!"'

Deirdre found Eileen unpretentious with a marvellous sense of humour and deeply grateful for driving her around Sydney and inviting her to meals at her Balmain home. She did not realise that by now Eileen was a multi-millionaire. She even asked Eileen if she could afford to stay at the Hilton, then Sydney's most expensive hotel. Deirdre was very surprised to learn that Eileen had been able to write a cheque for many thousands of pounds to the Piano Competition's organisers.

Eileen still harped on the 'Raggedy Eileen' legend. She repeated to Deirdre the improbable story that she had arrived in Leipzig without warm knickers and how the Germans had been expecting a black Aborigine. Tactfully, Deirdre suggested omitting this anecdote from her story, but Eileen could not change and went on radio repeating the story. She was very grateful to Deirdre for all her help in Sydney and invited her to stay with her in England.

By now Eileen was tiring easily and found Chartwell Farm and the and pedigree herd of Jersey cows too much to manage alone. She had sold her beautiful home and moved a few miles away to Limpsfield, a very pretty village not far from Oxted. White Hart Lodge, her new home in the High Street, was smaller than Chartwell Farm. Nevertheless, it had once been part of an old monastery and the entrance hall, complete with oak beams and an inglenook, was large enough to house her precious Steinway grand pianos.[55]

'My new home is very strategically placed', Eileen told her friends with her usual sense of humour, 'opposite a booze shop and just up the road from the crematorium!'[56]

At White Hart Lodge, she no longer had live-in staff as both Peggy and Dorothy, her faithful retainers for so many years, had died. Eileen herself suffered a heart attack caused by the stress of the move to Limpsfield, but devoted friends and her own positive approach to life helped her to recover from this, as well as a subsequent car accident.

Now her memory would fail her more frequently, but she was determined not to give in. With the help of friends she organised musical evenings in her new home. In the huge entrance hall her two Steinway pianos stood back to back, beneath a row of portraits of Eileen by various artists. The area was suitable for private concerts. She hosted recitals by young 'finds' whose careers she enjoyed helping to promote, out of her own funds, and with whom she would sometimes play duets.

In 1988, aged eighty (but still refusing to admit to it), her figure trim and taut, her hair tinted to its former auburn and her skin remarkably free of wrinkles, Eileen hoped to be well enough to play in public once again. She was scheduled to appear at a concert at London's Theatre Royal to celebrate Australia's Bicentennary, to be conducted by her old friend Australian-born Sir Charles Mackerras. Sadly, Eileen had to cancel her performance. The muscular complaint which prevented her from stretching the little finger of her right hand far enough had returned. She had intended to perform music by the Australian composer Percy Grainger, but realised she would be unable to play it well enough. Still the total perfectionist, she declined to appear unless she felt that her performance was up to world standard.

Deirdre Prussak was Eileen's guest at White Hart Lodge in 1987 and again in 1988. Eileen, whose memory had once been so superb, now had great difficulty remembering scores and was forced to play from sheet music. Her moods were sometimes badly affected. Deirdre Prussak recalls: 'There were times when I cried with her because she felt lost and could not understand what was happening to her.'

At other times she was still the old Eileen with her impish sense of humour, laughing and joking away. On good days she enjoyed being driven up to London and lunching at her favourite restaurant.

John Barratt, her son, was now married, and Eileen was thrilled to learn that her daughter-in-law, Rebecca, had given her a grandson – especially one with red hair. Perhaps tactlessly, Eileen told the press that she hoped to send Alexander to Geelong Grammar School when he was old enough. John and Rebecca Barratt's reaction to this idea was not reported. At this stage they still visited her and she sent Deirdre photographs showing Alexander sitting on her lap as she attempted to make his baby fingers play the piano. Other visits were not so happy and ended in rows. Then the visits stopped altogether.

Eileen's longstanding friend Professor Sir Frank Calloway, Head of the Western Australia University Department of Music, had written from Perth to say that if she decided to donate her papers to the University of Western Australia, the Agent General for that State would arrange for their shipment to Perth.[57] On 17 October 1988, Eileen replied that she 'had not yet reached a decision about the transfer of this material'.[58] English friends, however, advised her to send off the material and finally she agreed. It was as though she realised that the sands in the hour glass were running out.

Eileen had already made five visits to Australia from London – in 1936, 1948, 1981 and 1985.[59] In 1989, frail but undaunted, she returned to Sydney as a guest of honour to give a brief speech at a concert organised by Mary Valentine, General Manager of the Sydney Symphony Orchestra. The concert was held in the Sydney Town Hall on 10 February.

Frail and forgetful as she now was, nothing could stop Eileen from attending the concert where the young pianist Bernadette Harvey played the Rachmaninov No. 2 Concerto. Actor and writer Nick Enright gave a speech in which he reminded the audience that Dr Joyce had received honorary degrees from the Universities of Cambridge, Melbourne and Western Australia.

Eileen was interviewed by Peter Ross for the ABC *'Arts on Sunday'* program. Yet again she repeated the old no knickers story and the fact that the Leipzig Conservatorium had been expecting a black girl. 'Just fancy, an Aboriginal,' she said. Suavely, Peter Ross never missed a beat and steered her off on another tack. Strangely, Eileen, still looking a decade younger than her real age, told Peter Ross laughingly, 'I was never a great beauty. I had *far* too many freckles and couldn't get rid of them!'

Deirdre Prussak accompanied Eileen to the concert. Eileen, very much the grande dame, seated on the platform, was interviewed, and then read a brief but inspiring speech. It was her last night of triumph.

By now Deirdre was seriously worried by the deterioration in Eileen's memory and concentration and told her so. Eileen was also very worried and asked Deirdre to accompany her to consult a leading Sydney specialist. After a detailed examination, she was told that there *were* signs of Alzheimers disease, just as Deirdre had feared.[60]

Eileen returned to White Hart Lodge, where she lived out her last two years helped by kind and caring friends. She had good days and others when she could remember very little and was totally confused. However, in the good times she gained comfort from listening to music and from her dogs and cats.

Eileen Joyce always confronted life with great courage and generosity. By the time of her death she had given away large sums to various good causes. Her impish sense of humour did not lessen as she aged. On a good day she would even joke about her funeral. 'When I die, Deirdre, I want to be dressed in my red Norman Hartnell and laid out over my Steinway pianos!'

'Surely not the *red* one, Eileen, it won't go with your hair!' Deirdre replied and she and Eileen burst out laughing.

Deirdre worried greatly about her and generously suggested that Eileen come 'home' to live out the rest of her life in her Sydney house, where she would care for her. But the doctor said it was too late for such a move. Eileen's Alzheimers disease had now deteriorated to the point where the long flight to Australia was impossible. The brilliant musician who had once had such a marvellous memory for complex scores was now confused about dates, times and current events. It was a torment for someone who had possessed such a lively mind as Eileen Joyce.

In March 1991, just as the daffodils were coming into flower on the green lawns of White Hart Lodge, Eileen suffered a bad fall and broke her hip, already seriously weakened by osteoporosis. She was moved to hospital and suffered a fatal attack of pneumonia. When she closed her eyes for the last time, all those who loved her could only feel relief that this period of anguish was over, and remember the beauty and the joy that Eileen's playing had brought them.[61]

Eileen had expressed her desire to be cremated. Her wishes were followed. She was given a memorial service in the local church at which the pianist Philip Fowke, who had performed with Eileen in the past, played some of her best loved music and music critic Bryce Morrison gave an emotive valedictory address.[62]

Eileen's loyal friends were saddened that her relationship with her only son had deteriorated to such a point that neither he nor his wife attended Eileen's funeral or her memorial service. The local Rector expressed the wish they would be reunited in heaven.

Her executors chose a simple granite tombstone engraved with the words: 'In Treasured Memory of Dr Eileen Joyce, C.M.G., Concert Pianist, died 25 March 1991.' To the left of her grave is the white marble memorial to the famous conductor Sir Thomas Beecham and to the right the granite slab below which the composer Frederick Delius is buried.

Hundreds of floral tributes were received from many different countries, from musical celebrities and from orchestras Eileen Joyce had played with. The attendance at her memorial service was huge. Ornate wreaths and small posies of flowers from those to whom Eileen's playing had given so much pleasure marked the final chapter in the story of a courageous, talented and dedicated woman. Eileen Joyce, had to struggle to win her honoured place in the world of international music. Her phenomenal technique at the keyboard, her innovative programmes and her huge repertoire made her greatly admired wherever the piano is played.

CHAPTER SEVEN

Portrait photograph: National Library of Australia, Canberra.

Edith Dircksey Cowan
(1861–1932)

FIRST AUSTRALIAN WOMAN TO SIT IN A STATE PARLIAMENT

'Who is that woman with the sad face?' asked a teller at my local Commonwealth Bank, as she handed me a fifty-dollar note bearing Edith Cowan's portrait. I explained that although many women had fought for the right to vote or even stood for election, Edith Cowan was the first woman in Australia actually to gain a seat in Parliament, where she fought for the rights of women and children, the poor and the disadvantaged.[1]

I wondered to myself why, in view of her importance in the worldwide history of women, Edith Cowan had been virtually ignored for half a century following her death.[2] Fortunately we are now rediscovering her achievements. She is the woman whose story all Australians should know.

Edith Cowan's face does appear sad on our currency, but this is hardly surprising. The sadness stems from a childhood and adolescence scarred by tragedy and a blaze of notoriety. Edith's mother, the beautiful and devout Edith Dircksey Brown (born at Wittenoom) was the daughter of a Protestant pastor. She became a governess and married a local hero, a grazier turned explorer. Edith's gentle, intelligent mother died when her daughter was only seven, but her love of learning and her ideals would influence her daughter's future.

Edith's father, Kenneth Brown, soon married again, this time a woman with a strong temper and will of her own. Kenneth Brown was now drinking heavily. Edith's life at home was filled with violent arguments between her father and her stepmother. She was sent away to boarding school when she was only nine.

She returned for school holidays to Glengarry Station, Kenneth Brown's remote cattle property near Geraldton in Western Australia. Edith's father was an aggressive, domineering man who fitted well into a male-dominated pioneer society where masculinity was glorified and married women were expected to provide sex on demand. By law, women were the property of husbands or fathers – a man's authority over his wife and children was absolute. Tolstoy described the position of all married women at that time in Anna Karenina's lament, 'I am a married woman, my husband owns me'.[3] The distinguished jurist Sir William Blackstone, on whose codification of laws Australian justice depended, insisted that:

... the very being of legal existence of the woman is suspended during marriage ... incorporated and consolidated into that of the husband under whose wing, protection and cover she performs.

In 1876, the studious Edith turned fifteen. Her fellow boarders at the Misses Cowans' boarding school in Perth were horrified to learn from newspaper reports that Edith's father had shot his second wife during a drunken argument. His trial for murder created more headlines. It was the murder of her stepmother in a bout of drunken rage that opened Edith's eyes to women's lack of power in marriage. Edith had no wish to be the slave of any man and would insist on using the name Dircksey, her mother's middle name, for the rest of her life.

Edith suffered agonies of shyness when she was forced to appear in court to give evidence at the sensational murder trial. After her court appearance she was besieged by journalists demanding answers to the most intimate questions. She shed tears of humiliation and despair in the privacy of her room at school.

Kenneth Brown was found guilty and hanged. His execution brought sensitive, retiring Edith face to face with the realities of death. Unsavoury stories about her father and stepmother were whispered behind her back and some girls in her class were told by their parents to shun her. She was thrown into the adult world prematurely.

Edith buried herself in books. She had no close relatives in whom to confide her inner feelings, and in those days there was no bereavement counselling. She now had no home to go to and spent the holidays at school. She read widely, preferring works about social and political reform to the novels read by her contemporaries.

Edith would have loved to go to university. But in the late 1870s, when she was in her teens, a university education for girls was almost unheard of. Her only choices were to stay on at school as a pupil-teacher or to marry. A suitable marriage for Edith Dircksey Brown, daughter of a murderer, seemed impossible. Perth was a snobbish place where middle-class families all knew each other: Edith was now virtually beyond the pale.

However, one eligible and attractive man who visited the school was not discouraged. James Cowan, younger brother of Edith's joint headmistresses, found tall, willowy Edith fascinating; her sweet but sad face had haunted him since the day he first met her. Edith studiously ignored him. It took nearly a year for her to realise that James Cowan was as serious-minded as she was. Cowan was a book-loving lawyer with an interest in social reform. He brought the sad, confused young girl presents of books he thought would interest her. At first she refused them, so he left them with his sisters.

At long last, Edith stopped avoiding her suitor: they began to converse and she realised they had much in common. James Cowan was considerably older than her, and had the wisdom to take their relationship slowly. Their friendship ripened and finally Edith accepted his proposal of marriage. She was only nineteen.

On 12 November 1879, Miss Edith Dircksey Brown married Mr James Cowan in St George's Cathedral. James Cowan was Registrar of the Supreme Court and worked long hours. Before children kept her at home, Edith attended some court sessions and saw and heard the sad stories of battered wives and abused children. She visited the homes of women whose stories had touched her, trying to help with advice and financial assistance.

But family demands soon took over her days. In eleven years Edith bore four daughters and a son and took a long time to recover from each pregnancy. She was a devoted and proud mother who adored children and gave them all the love she had missed when growing up without a mother herself.[4]

In 1890, James Cowan was appointed Police Magistrate in Perth. Their last child was born the following year. By now, the elder children were growing up and Edith could afford domestic help. She wanted to do something to help the women she had seen appear in the courts, but was held back by her shyness and lack of experience.

Invited to become a founding member of the famous Karrakatta Women's Debating Club in Perth, Edith realised that speaking in public might help overcome the problem of her shyness. She was terrified when she mounted the platform for the first time, confronted by hundreds of women's faces beneath fashionable hats, all staring at her. Her soft voice wavered but she continued talking, telling her audience about the abused children and battered wives she had seen in the Magistrate's Court, and saying how much she wished the laws could be changed so that abused women were no longer slaves and prisoners in their own homes. She talked of the need for women's refuges and for pensions for widows and single mothers. She conquered her reticence about the past and told her audience about her murdered stepmother. Her audience listened, wide-eyed. At the end they applauded. Edith Cowan's career in public speaking had begun.

The Karrakatta Club (named after an affluent Perth suburb) had been formed by and for women from a similar background to herself. They were intelligent but most had acquired accomplishments rather than education and, like Edith Cowan, had left school young, married and raised families. All these women were keen to improve their education: all were determined that women should have the vote.

Edith made friends with strong-minded Bessie Rischbieth and Roberta Jull. She persuaded Rischbieth, wife of a millionaire wool broker, to take on some voluntary social work.

Edith proved herself an excellent and tactful organiser with an ability to handle committees and paperwork. The Karrakatta Club increased in size and importance. Their lectures covered areas such as women's health, women's rights, the arts, and legal reform.

Edith was eventually voted chair of the club's Education Section; from there she progressed to chair of the Literary Section, then to chair of the Legal Section, informing women about their lack of legal rights in cases of domestic violence, separation or divorce, when most would forfeit the right to see their children again. She became the club's secretary in 1894, vice-president and then president.[5]

Members of the Karrakatta Club knew that the women's vote was vital to their cause. Between 1910 and 1917, Vida Goldstein bravely but unsuccessfully stood as a Victorian parliamentary candidate. Many women were supportive of Miss Goldstein's bravery in trying to enter the male-dominated world of politics. Australia was then an intensely conservative country, where muscle, machismo and virility were glorified and the 'White Australia' policy prevailed. Women were told they should leave all decision-making to husbands, fathers or brothers. Male perceptions of women as weak and unintelligent proved hard to erode. Although Vida Goldstein was a brilliant public speaker, she never managed to gain a seat in Parliament. The Karrakatta Club members would have had no idea at that time that Edith Cowan would become Australia's first woman Member of Parliament.

Over the years, Edith developed more confidence in her own abilities. She had become involved on a voluntary basis with raising the money to found a District Nursing Society, to provide home nursing for women who could not otherwise afford this. She was also deeply involved with running a convalescent home for children and helping to fund and build the Alexandra Home for Women, a refuge for unmarried mothers with a maternity hospital attached.

The Alexandra Maternity Hospital was unique for its period because it would admit unmarried as well as married mothers. At this time, unmarried mothers, known as 'fallen women', were shunned in public maternity wards and pressured to give up their babies for adoption. Unmarried pregnant women were treated like petty criminals. During the latter stages of their pregnancy they were made to scrub hospital floors and empty garbage bins. No one cared if they lost their children. They were often denied access to anaesthetics, in the belief that a painful birth would prevent them repeating their sins. In order that the mothers should not bond with their newborn babies, they were forbidden to touch, hold or feed them. Adoptive parents were found for as many illegitimate babies as possible. Adoption was not popular and babies who did not find adoptive parents were sent to orphanages or 'domestic training' homes, especially if they were of mixed race. These unfortunate children received only the scantiest of education. Many would be sent out as labourers or domestic servants in their teens, and some were horrendously abused in their workplaces.

Edith became involved in finding suitable adoptive parents, and rescuing battered or neglected children from abusive parents. In the days before State or Commonwealth governments employed social and welfare workers, Edith's voluntary work took her into some of Perth's worst slum areas, where there was poor sanitation and no hot water on tap. She removed abused babies from horrific 'baby minders' who took care of the children of prostitutes or unwanted children for a fee. She found babies lying on filthy blankets or on the floor, some dying from dysentery, typhoid or other contagious diseases, spread by the lack of sanitary facilities. She walked up tenement stairs lined with urine and faeces. She found babies born deaf and blind to mothers with syphilis.

In many cases, a single cold-water tap on the ground floor was the only supply of water for several families: she soon realised that the majority of Perth and Fremantle's poor and disadvantaged lacked access to hot water. Open drains proliferated and lavatories, where there were any, were small reeking sheds in backyards.

Edith was determined things must change. But what influence did she have as a mere woman when men shaped the laws?

She decided she would have more authority as a paid employee than as a 'lady volunteer' and accepted a post as a 'lady almoner' (as social workers were then called) with the North Fremantle Board of Education. This was a landmark. Edith had broken the rigid middle-class barrier that prevented 'ladies' from working for money. The North Fremantle Board of Education was one of the few public offices to employ middle-class women. Edith Cowan quickly gained a reputation as a tireless and selfless worker who donated her income to help those less fortunate than herself. She was invited to serve with the Children's Protection Society,[6] which campaigned against the employment of child prostitutes in brothels. Child prostitutes, often as young as eight or ten, were eagerly sought after by the brothel madams; their male clients demanded 'virgin' prostitutes because syphilis, the disfiguring and ultimately fatal sexually transmitted disease, was so widespread.

Edith saw things that no 'nice' woman of her era even dreamed existed. They fired her indignation and she was determined to ensure that destitute and abandoned children would not be lured into prostitution or used as sweated labour, working long hours for a pittance at looms or sewing machines under terrible conditions.

To achieve her aims Edith organised public rallies, wrote letters to the press and lobbied politicians. In 1906, her courage and hard work helped in the passing of the first State Children's Act, granting children some measure of protection. But much more needed to be done. Aided by her husband's legal expertise, she and other female colleagues successfully campaigned for the establishment of a special Children's Court.

Through working in the new Children's Court, Edith's friendship with Bessie Rischbieth flourished. Childless Bessie, a decade younger than Edith, was imposing, statuesque, expensively dressed and often domineering. Edith Cowan was petite and invariably polite and tactful, securing decisions on committees through consensus. Bessie had considerable artistic talent, enjoyed the limelight and loved to be surrounded by art and artists. She lived in splendour surrounded by domestic staff in what is now known as Perth's millionaires' row, Peppermint Grove.[7]

In 1915, when many men were away fighting in World War I, Edith Cowan was appointed a justice of the Children's Court. In 1920, she and Bessie Rischbieth were among the first women to be appointed Justices of the Peace. Edith, who had constantly urged the appointment of women to such positions, was delighted. Both of these remarkable women shared the same aims – to secure better conditions for children and to raise the status of women, both nationally and internationally.

Edith also worked with Rischbieth and with Roberta Jull on specific projects, such as the setting up of free kindergartens for the children of working-class women, which provided these needy and often hungry children with meals and clothes. Roberta Jull and Edith Cowan had been friends since they had worked together to create the Western Australian National Council of Women in 1912 (Edith was its president from 1913 to 1921). Among other aims, the council wanted the age of sexual consent to be raised to eighteen, a measure aimed to prevent child prostitution. This was finally achieved in 1914, ensuring that any man or woman who introduced a girl under the age of eighteen to prostitution could be prosecuted and sentenced to years in gaol.

By now Edith Cowan knew only too well the enormous toll syphilis was exacting on a hypocritical society which refused to talk about this disease – just as terrible in its consequences as AIDS. But 'nice' respectable women simply did not mention such matters. Only in response to even higher rates of infection after the troops returned from serving in France during World War I did most State governments finally introduce controversial Health Acts. For decades, the West Australian Parliament had ignored the problem, hoping it would go away. Urged on by activists like Edith Cowan, a special Act designed to protect women and children from venereal diseases was finally introduced in 1917. The Act made all cases of venereal disease notifiable and prostitutes liable for inspection. Infected prostitutes were subjected to compulsory confinement in Lock Hospitals where they received treatment. Many of the children of prostitutes or returned veterans were born with syphilis. They were either blind or deaf, or both, and after a decade of intense physical suffering, their bones and teeth rotted away, they became incontinent and eventually died insane.

Edith was appalled at the rapidly mounting numbers of women infected by soldier husbands and lovers who had contracted syphilis from French and Egyptian prostitutes during the war. At that time, the only treatment was by injecting the patient with mercury, which caused their hair to fall out, or prescribing an arsenic compound known as Salvarsan, which could only delay the onset of the final and fatal symptoms.[8] But the end was always the same: dementia, paralysis, gangrene and death. Only the work done by Adelaide-born Howard Florey on treatment with granules distilled from the penicillin mould would finally provide a cure for syphilis. But penicillin was not produced commercially until the final years of World War II.

Bessie Rischbieth felt that the West Australian Health Act of 1917 made women victims of the men who had infected them: she spoke out against the Act, insisting it was the men who should be confined to the new Lock Hospitals rather than the women they had infected.

Edith was a realist: she considered the Health Act far from ideal but knew that male politicians, some of whom were clients of Perth's many brothels, would never agree to lock up men. After a long struggle with her conscience, she finally decided to support the Health Act as 'the fairest solution yet offered between men and women' and her supporters followed her lead. The Act split the Women's Movement in Western Australia into two opposing camps. It also affected the long and close friendship between Edith Cowan and Bessie Rischbieth and gave rise to bitter arguments between them. However, in public they were careful to gloss over their differences for the sake of their common aim to improve the lives of all women.

Bessie's husband died in 1925, leaving childless Rischbieth a lonely and wealthy widow. She wished to reform attitudes to sex through theosophy, which entailed comparative study of world religions, belief in man's innate goodness and reincarnation in future lives. On her travels around India, Rischbieth almost became a 'New Ager', announcing that the world was on the verge of a 'new spiritual order' where woman would 'claim her place in the sun'.[9]

Down-to-earth Edith did not share Rischbieth's beliefs that mysticism, mantras and theosophy would save the world from sexual abuse and disease. Long ago, Edith had received terrifying insights into the darker corners of the human psyche and had seen with her own eyes dire poverty, alcohol addiction and violence. Like Louisa Lawson, Edith believed firmly in education, so that women could earn their own living. She had carried out voluntary work and fund-raising for decades and knew from bitter experience that the rich did not always like to give to those less fortunate than themselves. She insisted that taxes must be raised so that governments could undertake reforms. She saw no point in Rischbieth and her followers spreading woolly concepts about the innate good in all mankind and begging for a few crumbs from the tables of the rich to give to the poor. Something had to be done by Parliament: voluntary work by dedicated women was not enough. She petitioned her Member of Parliament to support more social reforms, but without success.

Edith's ideas were seen as revolutionary. In the right-wing circles in which Rischbieth moved, including the Women's Service Guild, Edith Cowan was criticised for holding 'dangerous' ideas. But Edith, inspired by Christian ideals, had the courage to act on them. Whenever she received money for paid work she gave it away to poverty-stricken women and children.

Edith considered sex education programmes in schools more important than locking up diseased prostitutes (an approach now taken in AIDS education). She was a woman of vision and commonsense and knew it was impossible to suppress sexual urges, as some idealistic members of Bessie Rischbieth's group in the Women's Services Guild urged. Eventually Edith was criticised so bitterly that she resigned from the Women's Services Guild, to which she had devoted so much time and effort.

Edith now aimed to reduce the spread of syphilis using posters, leaflets and educational programmes, including a specially written play, *Remorse, or the Red Scourge*. This play contained a similar message to Ibsen's *Ghosts*, but lacked Ibsen's dramatic talent. Edith helped to fund performances and supported the play against a storm of opposition from women who felt it 'unladylike', improper and even immoral to discuss contraceptives or sexually transmitted diseases in public.

Edith stood firm against attack: she continued to press for sex education in schools to make teenage girls aware of the fact that syphilis was rampant at all levels in the community. She needed to get her message across to single supporting mothers. She demanded refuges for abused women and children. Entering Parliament now seemed to her a logical step towards changing the laws and public opinion.

Women had won the right to vote in Western Australia in 1899. Edith was used to addressing women's meetings, but the idea of speaking to a hostile audience of jeering men terrified her. The idea of entering Parliament seemed impossible. But how else could things change, she wondered.

In 1921, exactly a year after the ban on women entering the Western Australian Parliament was removed, Edith became one of only two Nationalist candidates endorsed for the seat of West Perth. She found herself on the hustings opposing an experienced Cabinet minister, Mr T. P. Draper. Her whole campaign seemed absurd. How could she, a mere woman, hope to make political history and win a seat against such opposition in an all-male Parliament?

By this time, Edith Cowan was relatively well known. The previous year she had been honoured with the Order of the British Empire for her vast amount of voluntary work during World War I.[10] Edith's supporters now realised she must have the backing of the whole Women's Movement, and for this she needed the support of Bessie Rischbieth, who had no political ambitions herself. Fortunately, Bessie realised it was vital for women to have a voice in Parliament if they were to achieve anything: somewhat reluctantly she agreed to support Edith's attempt to win a seat.

Mrs Cowan campaigned on her record of providing unpaid service on twenty-four councils and committees, which impressed many of her women voters. On the other hand, some women voters deemed it 'unfeminine' of Mrs Cowan to stand for election; they believed they should put their efforts into lobbying male Parliamentarians for change rather than voting for a woman. Edith also encountered jeers and hostility from some working-class women when she knocked on their doors in her campaign. They believed that such an educated 'lady' could not possibly understand the problems of the poor.

Undaunted, Edith campaigned on draughty street corners and at meeting after meeting. She told the women in her audiences that she was fighting to improve conditions for all women and asked them to support her by giving her their votes. James Cowan supported his wife loyally by leading the applause at most meetings.

During one doorknock campaign, Edith was accused by the lady of the house of neglecting her children and home. The lady informed her that a friend had told her 'that poor Mr Cowan was so distressed by his wife campaigning that he was dying of a broken heart'! James Cowan took it upon himself to explain to the lady in question that he was *not* dying of a broken heart. Edith's political opponents also spread false rumours that she was neglecting a brood of young children in order to campaign. Whenever possible, her husband defended her against these charges, informing hecklers that their children were grown up and no longer dependent on their mother.

No one expected willowy Edith, inexperienced in State politics, to beat a smooth-talking, highly experienced Cabinet minister into Parliament. But when the votes were counted, the confident Attorney-General, Mr T. P. Draper (sitting Member for West Perth), was in for a big shock. He discovered that fifty-nine-year-old Edith Dircksey Cowan, whose chances of election he had not taken seriously at all, showed a lead when the first preferences were counted. It came as even more of a shock to Mr Draper when, after counting the third candidate's preferences, Mrs Cowan was found to have a majority of forty-six. The figures showed that 1760 women had voted in her electorate, compared to 1325 men.

Edith Dircksey Cowan was now the first female member to take her seat in any Australian Parliament – and women voters had put her there.

The Nationalist Party were furious with Edith. They had lost a Cabinet minister and in return they gained nothing but a problem: a woman Member of Parliament.

Inwardly nervous but outwardly composed, Edith took her seat in the House, wearing an elegantly simple black dress. Her maiden speech addressed the concerns of women and the need for social reform. Naturally, there was scant applause from male members of Parliament. Edith Cowan soon found Parliament a complex, arcane organisation with its own rules. The male members made little or no effort to help her with Parliamentary procedures. She found sex discrimination and patriarchal attitudes to women deeply engrained. Some Parliamentarians snubbed her, others tried to humiliate her. One male member even asked the House in her presence (amid roars of mirth from the floor) to specify exactly how much money had been spent on modifying the toilets so that she could use them.

Edith worked hard and used her time in Parliament to promote the cause of women and children. She found that male politicians (who formed a vested interest group) were extremely reluctant to share power with women. This was one reason many had not supported the female vote.

Male members did not wish Edith to bring in any measures that could change the balance of power in favour of women. Most of them supported the doctrine of separate spheres for men and women – men at work earning money and status, wives confined to the home and childcare, left powerless to make decisions and lacking access to paid work.[11]

Edith Cowan entered Parliament with the full support of her husband. But that fact did not stop a male journalist on the Melbourne *Age* writing acidly: 'If holding political office for women becomes the latest fashionable craze ... there would be many dreary, neglected homes through the country, sacrificed on the altar of women's political ambition.'

Her enemies thought the best method of denigrating tall, distinguished-looking Mrs Cowan was to ridicule her. Edith Cowan, Member of Parliament, soon became the target of cartoonists such as Percy Leason of *The Bulletin*. Cartoons pictured her dusting the mace, smacking sleeping Members for not paying attention, sweeping the floor of Parliament House or knitting socks while debate raged around her. Only the cartoon that showed her knitting held a grain of truth. Whenever male members screamed insults, cursed or became particularly obnoxious to each other, Edith Cowan, who hated displays of malice, bad manners and insults, would sit in the House calmly doing her embroidery.

In 1919, American-born Nancy Astor had become the very first woman to sit in the British Parliament. But Nancy Astor had one asset Cowan did not. Nancy's husband, Waldorf Astor, was an experienced politician who helped her to understand the arcane language and obscure rites of Parliament which could prevent members having their say.[12]

Edith's debating skills soon became formidable. But she was at her best as a committee worker. She lacked a 'background' in State politics, was not given a paid research assistant, and had to struggle against the introduction of endless amendments and other delaying tactics to prevent her raising important questions about women's rights.

Edith Cowan fought her enemies in the State Parliament who tried to prevent her speaking. She managed to contribute substantially to debates on the Shops and Factories Act, which affected working women, and the State Children's Act. She stood fast and refused to be shouted down by male members during acrimonious discussions on the Nurses Registration Bill and the Industrial Arbitration Bill. At every opportunity, Edith spoke eloquently for equal rights for women, for migrant welfare, for funding of infant centres and for child endowment. She also pressed for more sex education in State schools.

Unlike most politicians, Edith resisted the iron control of the whip's office on Members. When she thought it necessary, she voted according to her conscience, even if it meant voting against her own Nationalist Party, something which made her many enemies in Parliament.

Mrs Cowan outraged male members of both sides of the house when she argued that a wife should be legally entitled to a share of her husband's income – at that time a revolutionary concept. She also wanted child endowment to be given to unmarried as well as married mothers, something we take for granted today, but at that time a concept many people found totally unacceptable. They wished to make mothering as hard as possible for unmarried 'fallen women'.

One of Edith's most outstanding achievements in Parliament was the passing of the Women's Legal Status Act, a Private Member's Bill, which she introduced in 1923. She found it totally unjust that qualified women who had obtained their degrees were being denied the right to practise their chosen professions. It was entirely due to the work of Edith Cowan that in 1930 the pioneer lawyer Alice Mary Cummins, previously banned from the Bar because she was a woman, was finally permitted entrance.

Mrs Cowan's second successful Private Member's Bill was to ensure that married women could inherit property from children who predeceased them. Before the passing of Edith Cowan's bill, all property in a marriage was automatically bequeathed to the husband, even if he had abandoned his wife years previously and she was destitute.

Edith Dircksey Cowan believed that she was not put into Parliament to court popularity from the other members. She was there to represent women who had voted for her. Her courage and determination to remain true to her beliefs was impressive. She dared to challenge male Parliamentarians who yelled abuse at her or schemed against her.

In the 1924 election campaign, Edith's political enemies, some from her own party, determined to see the back of her. They urged every male voter in her constituency to vote against her and provided free transport to get them to the polls. In addition, Edith found that some of her ideas for social reform had been leaked to her opponents, and the Labor candidate hijacked them. This meant that some people who would have supported her now voted for her opponent. The result was that in the next election she failed to win the seat.

The third time she stood for election her opponents were still up to their dirty tricks. Once more she was defeated at the polls, so she decided to turn her lively mind and organising abilities to fresh fields.

She was one of the first Australian women to gain recognition from international Women's Movements, travelling overseas in 1903 and 1912.[13] In 1925, in her mid-sixties, Edith Cowan was invited to the United States as one of Australia's delegates to the Seventh International Conference of Women.

Even in her old age, Edith continued to speak at meetings all over Australia arguing the case for equality for wives before the law (at the time custody of children was always awarded to the husband in divorce cases), for the establishment of free kindergartens, for a hygienic water and milk supply. She also supported qualifications for hospital nurses and the banning of unqualified nurses (who were sometimes alcoholics or even part-time prostitutes), and she demanded (in the absence of a widow's pension) a rent allowance for widows and orphans.

Before the provision of pensions for widows, single mothers and the disabled, Edith Cowan supported the causes of the war wounded, those born with disabilities, widows and single mothers – some of whom had been forced into prostitution solely through lack of income and job prospects. A true Christian in the full meaning of the word, Cowan struggled against the dogmas of conservative clergymen as well as the selfishness of the rich and powerful in her quest to improve the lives of the poor and destitute. All her life, Edith Cowan was pragmatic and practical: a 'doer' as well as a talker. She gave away almost every penny she earned to those in need and supported several orphans while they studied at school and technical colleges. She changed lives.

Edith Dircksey Cowan lived to eighty-one, adored by her husband and children as well as her much-loved grandchildren. By now, the long struggle had worn her sad but beautiful face into a sombre mask. Her achievements were immense and should never be forgotten. She initiated a social revolution in her term in Parliament and caused an ultra-conservative, reactionary, male-orientated society to become more responsive to the needs of its women and children.

Finally the long struggle took its toll. Her last whispered words were: 'I'm so tired.'

Hundreds attended at her burial in the Karrakatta cemetery. A plaque on a clock tower in a quiet corner of Perth's Kings Park bears witness to the fact that Edith Dircksey Cowan, politician, devoted wife, mother and grandmother, was truly 'One of Australia's Greatest Women'.

CHAPTER EIGHT

Edith and Joseph Lyons and family.
Photograph: National Library of Australia, Canberra.

Dame Enid Burnell Lyons
(1897–1981)
AUSTRALIA'S FIRST FEMALE FEDERAL CABINET MINISTER

At the 1913 Tasmanian Labor Party rally held on the outskirts of Hobart, Enid Burnell, a petite fifteen-year-old pupil-teacher from Burnie State School, climbed onto the seat of her chair to obtain a better view of Tasmania's craggily handsome Minister for Education.

From the platform draped with the Australian flag, The Hon. Joseph Lyons was propounding what many of his listeners considered as radical ideas about reforming the Tasmanian school system. Joe Lyons was speaking to a poorly educated rural audience where women were deemed inferior to men in everything but the ability to bear and rear children. The Minister was putting forward what were then very advanced ideas. He suggested that women teachers should be paid the same salary as their male counterparts and be allowed to continue teaching after marriage if they wished.

A frisson of horror ran round the hall. 'Wives leaving *home* to work. Whatever next?' muttered elderly men in the audience.

Edith Burnell, an overworked and underpaid pupil-teacher, already knew a little about the Minister's background. Almost nineteen years older than herself, Joe Lyons was a bachelor, although it was rumoured a few women had tried to snare him into marriage. A deprived childhood had turned Joe into a fighter for left-wing and humanitarian causes. What Edith Burnell did not know was that Joe Lyons' father, a gambler by nature, had lost his entire savings in an unsuccessful bet on a 'safe' horse to win the Melbourne Cup.[1] The shock of near bankruptcy brought on depression and a nervous breakdown, and his father spent the rest of his life in and out of mental hospitals.

At the age of nine, Joseph Lyons, the brightest boy in his class, was forced to leave school to help support his brothers and sisters – there were no welfare allowances at that time. The only work he could find was as a baker's delivery boy and occasional farm labourer; he had to grow up fast. Then, rescued by two maiden aunts who offered to maintain the family, and having missed a year at school, Joe went back to the classroom. He was determined to make something of himself, get the necessary qualifications to become a teacher in the State system and eventually be able to provide proper family support. His radical views, formed by harsh experience, led him into politics. Ability and charm, together with the Irish gift for public speaking, meant that he rose rapidly through the ranks of the Tasmanian Labor Party to become

Minister for Education, deeply committed to a variety of left-wing causes.

While Joe Lyons endured a poor Catholic childhood, with all that entailed, Enid Burnell had been raised in a slightly more secure working-class home in Smithtown where there was little money but where books and education were greatly valued. Her parents were Methodists, suspicious of anything Catholic, and had strong Labor Party affiliations.

After the speeches ended that night in 1913, tea and biscuits were served by volunteers at the rally. Enid plucked up the courage to approach the Minister and ask his views on improving hours and conditions for pupil-teachers like herself, girls from working-class homes whose families could not afford school fees. It was a method whereby working-class children could receive additional years of education which would help them to become teachers. Pupil-teachers were mainly female, bright and intelligent, and were used by the staff to keep order at playtime, fill inkwells and attend to children with reading problems. In return for many hours of unpaid work, if they were lucky they received additional tuition themselves, aspiring one day to be accepted as teachers in their own right.

In spite of the fact the Minister was almost nineteen years older than herself, Enid found him disturbingly attractive in the dimple-chinned devil-may-care way that is so typically Irish. At thirty-four Joe Lyons had a mop of unruly dark hair, a craggy profile, broad shoulders, deep blue eyes and an infectious grin. He had been so busy acting as the head of his family and building a career in politics that he'd lacked the time or the energy to think about marriage. He was wedded to politics ... that is, until he met Enid.

As Joseph Lyons answered Enid's probing question, he saw an outstandingly attractive young girl with long golden-brown hair, a delicate heart-shaped face and a smile which revealed perfect teeth and brought dimples to her cheeks. Although many others were waiting to talk to him he stayed chatting to this delightful young girl whose brimming enthusiasm for his plans was so infectious.

Over a cup of tea and a biscuit Enid found her normal shyness had vanished. Reforming the work situation for pupil-teachers was a topic dear to her heart. Joe Lyons expanded under the warmth of her smile and told her of his own early struggles to become a teacher. Enid was enthusiastic about the Minister's plans to abolish school fees and pay female teachers the same wage as their male counterparts. Joe realised that Enid's left-wing convictions were as strong as his own. She, for her part, was flattered that the Minister treated her as an adult rather than some naive teenager.

Meanwhile, a long queue had formed, all waiting to speak to the Minister. The Hon. Joe Lyons' secretary caught his eye and pointed to the queue. The Minister apologised to Miss Enid Burnell. He was sorry but he must end their talk as others were waiting. At this her smile faded. Joe could not bear the thought he would never see her again. Hastily he told Enid he would be delighted to answer the rest of her questions the following day. He suggested a time and place. Her dimples returned, she smiled up at him and agreed.

Their second meeting, away from the staff who normally accompanied the Minister on his speaking tours, was a turning point in their lives. Joe and Enid felt themselves to be in love and realised that this was something very special indeed for them both.

Enid dared not admit her feelings for the Minister for Education to her parents. She feared their opposition which would be based on the difference in their ages as well as the Roman Catholic–Protestant divide. She remained silent, keeping her secret to herself. The budding romance blossomed in letters which were tender but formal: Joe must have feared the results had they been opened by Enid's parents. Everything seemed against a permanent relationship. At fifteen, Enid was underage and needed her parents' permission to wed. A highly intelligent and hardworking girl, she had just won a scholarship to attend the Hobart, Teachers' Training College and her parents were determined she should have a career to fall back on for the rest of her life.

To understand the couple's predicament it is important to realise that at that time the Australian Labor Party was riven by religious strife. Irish Catholics could not abide Protestants and vice versa; Methodists had been reared to honour the Bible as the Word of God.

Enid's mother, Eliza Burnell (born Taggart), had emigrated from a depressed tin-mining area in Cornwall, a hive of Methodism. She was a devout member of the congregation of her local Methodist chapel as was Enid's father, who worked hard as a leading hand in a Burnie sawmill. Edith's parents were hard-working, decent folk who had been brought up to despise the Irish and distrust everything Catholic as 'Popish nonsense'.

When Enid finally plucked up the courage to tell her parents about her feelings for Joe Lyons, they were so shocked and distressed that they forbade her to see him ever again. Eliza was horrified at the mere thought of her much-loved daughter marrying a 'Mick' (as Catholics were known), even if this particular 'Mick' *was* the Labor Minister for Education. Tears and recriminations followed. Enid's parents stood firm; they loved her and had her best interests at heart.

Undaunted, Joe arranged a secret tryst on deserted Co-ee Beach, where they strolled hand in hand along the sands, kissed and swore to love one another forever and to get married as soon as they could. Mores were strict; the virginity of young girls was jealously guarded. It is most unlikely that they had sex before marriage even though they were both head over heels in love for the first time.

In spite of strong opposition from Enid's parents, who saw the age and religious differences as an insoluble problem, and firmly believed they were doing the right thing, Joe and Enid got engaged once she turned sixteen. Enid's parents made them promise that they would not marry until Enid turned seventeen. Their engagement year was one of constant separation; to Enid it seemed like an eternity, but she and Joe were determined to marry.

Joseph Lyons and Enid Burnell were finally married on 28 April 1915.[2] They had kept their promise and waited until Edith had celebrated her seventeenth birthday.[3]

There was other opposition to their marriage. Joseph Aloysius Lyons had the undying support of the Irish Catholic lobby in the Labor Party. He knew that marriage to a Methodist, however devoted to the Labor cause, could spell political ruin for him, since Irish Catholic influence was predominant in the Labor Party. He was warned of the dangers of marrying Edith Burnell by most of the people around him. The circumstances surrounding their marriage forced Enid to convert to Catholicism, causing great distress to her parents. However, as her Catholicism deepened, she derived great strength from her faith.

Enid had been warned by her mother and her chapel-going friends that marriage to a Catholic meant bearing numerous children. Did she want to spend the rest of her life dragging around a brood of snotty-nosed children and playing second fiddle to an important man, her mother asked. Enid smiled, this was not going to happen to her. Joe was different from other men.

In spite of prophecies of doom from family members on both sides as well as Joe's Labor Party colleagues, their marriage surprised everyone by proving to be splendidly happy – a partnership of equals.

They honeymooned at a Sydney hotel where Joe was attending a premiers' conference. This was Enid's first introduction to the Byzantine complexities, blood feuds and shifting alliances of life in the Labor Party.

Enid proved to be an astute judge of character and had an excellent grasp of the main issues facing the Labor Party, as well as an understanding of the feelings of the average working man and woman. And she soon discovered that she had a gift for writing down-to-earth yet emotional speeches. Joe perceived Enid's talents. He too was a good speech writer but was totally overworked. So he encouraged Enid to write some of the speeches which won him acclaim. He was by now firmly convinced that Enid herself could achieve great success in politics. But who would pre-select a *woman* for a Labor Party seat? Whenever they were apart Joe wrote Enid moving letters telling her, for example, that 'my faith and confidence in you is supreme. That's one of the reasons why I care so much for you. I not only love you but I *believe* in you too.'

In Tasmania, the couple lived at first in rented accommodation. In 1916, they commissioned a builder for the then princely sum of 375 pounds to build them a simple white weatherboard house, which they named Home Hill, in Devonport. At that time, before the advent of commercial airlines, Tasmania was isolated from the rest of Australia and deficient in many amenities that other Australian cities took for granted. Amazing as it seems for a politician's household, the telephone was only connected to their home in 1938.

Enid soon discovered she was carrying her first child. Lacking a phone, she wrote Joe long letters whenever they were apart. In return, he would reply in even more passionate vein, telling her how much he loved and missed her and how he valued her opinions.

They hated being apart so much that Enid joined Joe on the arduous campaign trail of 1916, travelling around the wilder areas of Tasmania.

At that time it was not thought 'quite nice' for pregnant women to appear in public. However, Enid's trim figure masked her pregnancy until the secret was finally out. Then she returned home to Devonport for the birth of their first child.

Enid may have suffered from rickets, due to vitamin deficiency in her childhood, like many working-class women of that era. The birth of her first child took place at a time when little was known about the complications of pregnancy. It was an agonising birth which left her with a badly damaged pelvis, causing intense pain and difficulties with walking.

Enid finally made her first public speech in 1920 and continued to do so in between bearing and raising twelve children, one of whom died in infancy, causing them both intense distress.

Raising and educating a large family in the days before automatic washing machines meant piles of soiled nappies and children's clothes to wash and iron.[4] 'We never had much money,' Enid revealed many years later in her autobiography. 'At one stage we had six children under six. I'd wash out the back in an enormous copper, meanwhile trying to work out my next speech in my head. No helper, no washing machine, and *what* a wash!'

She herself had been brought up in a small family: now she realised what life was like for so many women raising numerous children without help. This gave her a valuable insight into what life was like for married women and the many war widows – who as yet lacked social security payments. She was determined to do everything in her power to improve the lives of ordinary women.

Even the pain from her damaged pelvis did not daunt Enid, who had conquered her initial shyness about public speaking and soon became a powerful and persuasive speaker. Joe realised that his wife's good looks, astute brain, and exceptionally warm personality made her a valuable ally and a great asset to him. He encouraged Edith to speak at Labor rallies and meetings wherever possible.

This was an era when politicians' wives were expected to kiss babies, wear decorative hats, bake lamingtons and remain silent on public platforms. Enid Lyons broke the mould of the typical politician's wife by doing all of that as well as delivering her own speeches. She was an extremely well-organised person; somehow she managed to combine preparing and delivering electioneering speeches with caring for her children. Her sincerity was obvious; like her husband, Enid had a natural gift for public speaking.

In her memoirs, Enid describes how she juggled her political activities with the needs of her large family. When asked to speak at the opening of a Federal election campaign, she felt how unfair it was that she had no one to organise things for her and settle the children down; when her husband was writing a speech she kept all the children quiet to allow him to concentrate. Her heartfelt cry echoes down the ages to all working women with children: 'At five o'clock on the day of the meeting I was totally unprepared ... I sat down at the dining table with pencil and paper to write a speech. I felt tired to death. The baby on my knee was crying with fatigue, the other children were quarrelling noisily. Suddenly I burst into tears. It was not fair. No *man* was expected to endure such things.'

What Enid needed was a secretary or else a housekeeper or nanny to organise the household – but there was no one. She was on her own for much of the time with a huge family and not much money.

With Enid's devoted support Joseph Lyons eventually became Premier of Tasmania. Concerned that his wife should have the chance to fulfil her potential, Joe persuaded her to make her own foray into politics by standing as a candidate in the 1925 Tasmanian elections. This was a revolutionary step for a married woman with young children. Enid was seen by the men in the party as no threat. They were convinced that she had little chance of winning. However, fielding a woman candidate was deemed 'good public relations' for the Labor Party, which campaigned heavily on the fact that they were supportive to women's causes (although, of course, some chauvinistic males devoutly hoped no woman would take a seat in Parliament. Why should such seats be wasted on women, they demanded among themselves.)

While coping with several sick children at home, Enid kept up a rigorous schedule of speaking engagements. A passionate believer in equality and women's rights, she managed to demolish opponents who accused her of 'doing a man out of a job'. Her appearances on the hustings boosted her confidence in her speaking abilities. It also made her even more aware of the prejudice against women achieving *anything* in a man's world. Interestingly enough, Edith's mother, Eliza Burnell, by now reconciled to her daughter's marriage to a Catholic, also stood as a Labor candidate in this election.

Both women failed to win a seat, Eliza by a large margin, Enid by a mere sixty votes. Losing did not upset Enid unduly: in some ways she was relieved that she was not forced to abandon her young children to spend long days in the State Parliament. Campaigning had taught her one important lesson: whatever working-class men might think of her, working-class women would vote for her in droves. It was the down-to-earth quality of Enid's approach to politics coupled with her fresh, unspoiled beauty and her evident sympathy for others that gave her a huge appeal at the ballot box.

From the first Enid spoke her mind about women's domestic roles, especially in rural Tasmania: she knew how hard farmers' wives worked, on household and farm tasks, rearing calves and lambs, cooking for shearers and harvesters in addition to running their own homes. She astounded a rural meeting, composed mainly of men, by drawing on her own childhood experiences of living without gas, electricity or running water, observing: 'While farm life might be very satisfactory for farmers, it may not be as rewarding for their wives. I can't help myself wondering whenever I meet a farmer's wife, if her kitchen still needs a sink with running water and if she still has to boil the washing over an open fire in a kerosene tin.'[5]

Enid describes in her memoirs how her husband was very unusual in that he helped her with the housework as they lacked servants because money was always short raising a large family: 'Joe was determined that I should not sink into a sea of domesticity. If he wasn't away on business, he would be at home with me. If I was ironing, he would talk or read to me. On Sundays he would cook dinner for the family, while I had some time to myself.'

Joe would shop for school clothes for the children whenever she was sick and was proud of his domestic skills. 'You see I can be quite a good mother, when I have to,' he wrote without embarrassment in a letter to his wife.

During Joseph Lyons' second term as Premier of Tasmania, from 1923 to 1928, he began to realise that more money was needed if he was to reform the education system and he began courting big business and industry to donate funds. In her memoirs, Enid describes how 'Joe mellowed with the years'. They no longer subscribed to the trade union journal *The Australian Worker* because they both found it 'too bitter in its denunciations, far too intolerant and too biased'.

The fiery left-wing couple were both softening their views as they grew older. Now Tasmania began to seem like a very small pond indeed. With Edith's blessing, Joe switched to Federal politics. Elected Federal member for Wilmot in 1929, he joined the Scullin Labor Government as Postmaster General and Minister for Works and Railways, and from August 1930 was Acting Treasurer – not an easy position to hold at this juncture. The country was soon in a ferment due to the American stockmarket crash of October 1929, which led to the start of the Great Depression. Thousands of men were thrown out of work and the Labor Party was divided against itself on many important financial issues. Joe's alarm at the Labor Party's unconventional financial policies was shared by a group of fellow conservatives.

Like most Australians of their era, both Joe and Enid were imbued with respect for conventional economics. They favoured following the ultra-cautious advice of the economists Giblin, Copland and Melville. This trio, like many foreign economists, believed that inflation and the soaring deficit would bring economic and political chaos. Joe soon fell out with his own party over how to manage the worsening financial situation caused by the New York stockmarket crash – which, somewhat like Australia in the 1990s and Paul Keating's 'recession we had to have', caused soaring rates of unemployment and a galloping financial deficit, breeding lack of confidence internationally. Joe and Enid believed that Australia should pay its way out of recession – Joe insisted all financial commitments should be honoured. They agreed with the economists that depression could be cured by tightening the belt, balancing the budget and reducing government spending. There were fiery caucus meetings with those in the Labor Party who wanted to increase the deficit, create thousands of new jobs and *spend* their way out of trouble.

As Acting Treasurer, Joe Lyons defied them, demanding both a reduction of government spending and a reduction in the salaries of leading public servants. He won on the last issue but the larger conflicts of economic policy remained unresolved.[6] By now the stockmarket had totally collapsed in Britain and Australia, financiers were jumping out of windows, men were laid off in droves. There was a world trade slump and scant prospects of the situation improving.

Despite the famous 'Don't do it, Joe, don't do it' plea of a Labor colleague, after considerable soul-searching Joe Lyons resigned from his Cabinet post in January 1931, and finally left the Labor Party for which he had worked so hard. He had Enid's unwavering support. In May that year he became leader of the newly formed United Australia Party. The new party was vigorously supported by press baron Keith Murdoch, who felt Joe Lyons was the man to solve the economic crisis; he sensed his ability to unite different groups and opposing factions, a skill which Enid also possessed.

In a snap election in December 1931, as things were going from bad to worse, 'Honest' Joe Lyons, as the papers styled him, became Prime Minister of Australia with an absolute majority, just nine months after he had left the Labor Party. By now the 'golden couple' of Labor politics had acquired some very powerful political enemies. Joe Lyons would need all his skills as a consensual politician to manage a difficult Cabinet and the worsening economy of the Depression.

On 6 January 1932, Joseph Aloysius Lyons was sworn in as Prime Minister of Australia in Canberra. Honours never went to Joe's head and that night he found the time to write to Edith, who had stayed at home to nurse a sick child. 'Whatever honours or distinctions come are *ours* not mine … it is grand to know that our love for each other is still our most cherished possession … It has been a great day for me, but I would be happier on Home Hill with you and all the children.'

Joe and Enid moved into The Lodge with their younger children; Enid had to divide her time between Canberra and Tasmania where the older children were at school. She found coping with lengthy separations from her husband and older children stressful and longed for the time when they could all be together once more. The Lyons still cherished their ideal marriage. After the birth of their twelfth and last child, Joe wrote to Enid: 'Remember that the chap who came to you at Co-ee Beach because he loved you. He still loves you more than ever tonight.'

Few people expected Joe Lyons would last more than one term as prime minister. However, supported by excellent speeches written by Enid, and using her suggestion to contact the nation by speaking more frequently on the radio, Joe won three successive elections. At the time, this was a record unmatched by any other Australian prime minister.

Prime Minister 'Honest' Joe Lyons remained in power from 1932 to 1939, a very difficult time in Australian politics. He implemented the 'equality of sacrifice' plan to combat the Depression, consolidated an alliance with the Country Party, cracked down on Communism, and, faced by the threat of another world war, remained fiercely anti-conscription.

Despite her large family and the loss of a stillborn child, which depressed her considerably, Enid travelled all over Australia for official speaking engagements during those Depression years.

A young Liberal politician named Robert Menzies actually suggested that she should not be making speeches but instead stay at home in the kitchen. Edith ignored his patronising advice but never forgave Menzies and blamed her husband's subsequent heart problems on him. Curiously enough, her anger did not extend to Dame Pattie Menzies, whom she both respected and liked.

As the Prime Minister's wife, Enid aimed to win support from women Australia-wide and was frequently invited to address women's associations and conferences, both religious and secular. Women's organisations such as the Victorian Women Citizen's Movement and the Sydney Feminists Club sought her as an ally in various causes because she was known to be deeply committed to 'women's rights'.

When Enid Lyons accompanied her husband to England in 1934 to 1935 they attended a large number of official functions at which her intelligence and grace won approval even among the snobbish British, who tended to sneer at Australian accents. Wearing a borrowed ballgown, Enid looked magnificent at an official reception hosted by King George V at Windsor Castle. She remained engagingly fresh and unspoiled by all the pomp and ceremony that surrounded them as representatives of the Australian people. She described how, at times, she felt a sense of unreality – as though she was in a dream. She and Joe were an ordinary Australian couple from working-class backgrounds, being entertained by leading politicians and by royalty.

As Catholics, they had always dreamed of an audience with the Pope. Their wish was granted. They travelled to Italy and visited the

Vatican before sailing to America to stay at the White House with President Roosevelt and his wife. There they had the chance to see first-hand how Americans were dealing with the Depression before returning home to Australia.

In 1937, they sailed to Britain for a second visit, to represent Australia at the coronation of King George VI. Once again, Enid's unspoiled nature and dignity in her official role aroused favourable comment. She found time to speak at a number of feminist rallies and Catholic meetings in Britain. And this time Enid was put up for an honour of her own. Returning home via a brief visit to Venice, which she loved, Enid received a telegram advising her she had been made a Dame Grand Cross of the Order of the British Empire, an honour she would cherish for the rest of her life.

Serious problems awaited the Lyons on their return home. Long hours of argument and invective in Parliament and in Cabinet meetings, and disloyalty from party members were extremely stressful for them both. There was also the looming menace of war in Europe as Hitler revealed his ambition to gobble up the smaller nations of Europe. Australia, as a Commonwealth member, was pledged to support Britain if war broke out.

Enid, worried about her husband's health, urged him to visit the doctor, something he was reluctant to do. Eventually, he did and was diagnosed with high blood pressure. No drug treatments to combat high blood pressure or cholesterol were available at that time; as prime minister, charged with a heavy workload, he was advised either to slow down or resign.

Each time Joe Lyons attempted to resign, however, colleagues pressured him to stay in order to give the appearance of party unity. Enid was extremely worried about him but did not like to interfere. Both Enid and Joe placed their own happiness second to the good of the party. Joe's blood pressure went up rather than down with the long hours and the tension. He continued to reassure Enid that once the next crisis was over he would resign ... but always another one arose.

The result was that Prime Minister Joseph Lyons suffered a massive heart attack while travelling to Sydney in April 1939, just as the situation concerning Hitler and Poland was worsening. Joe was rushed to hospital but died a few days later.

The obituaries praised Joseph Lyons for his honesty, saying that he believed in politics as a vehicle for creating a better world for all Australians. At the same time they noted that he had made many enemies in his career, including the formidable Robert Menzies. Many of his colleagues felt guilty that they had persuaded him to stay on rather than resign as Enid had wanted.

For Enid it was a terrible time. At the age of forty-one, she found herself a sole supporting mother with a huge family to educate, no private income or savings of her own and at times suffering severe pain from her damaged pelvis. Joe's will revealed just how little money or investments he had. There were no large superannuation payments for politicians then, as there are today, and scant financial provision for Parliamentarians' widows and children. In addition, Enid had the constant feeling that she should have overridden the wishes of her husband's colleagues and insisted he resign.

The United Party Government tabled a bill proposing an annuity for Enid and her children. This modest provision evoked outrage among many Labor members who felt Joe had betrayed them by joining the Liberals. There were angry speeches in the house, reported in the press and over the radio. Enid received carping critical letters and hate mail, even death threats, all of which greatly upset her. She was unable to sleep and scarcely ate. She lost weight dramatically and became clinically depressed, an illness now treatable with Prozac or other anti-depressants but at that time not properly understood. She was told to 'snap out of it', that things would get better – but clinical depression does not respond to such injunctions. Enid's worries about finance and her children increased and her grief and despair worsened.

She soldiered on, sometimes in severe pain, becoming more and more depressed. Finally she collapsed, overwhelmed by exhaustion, grief, and guilt that she had not defied her husband's colleagues and insisted Joe resign from politics sooner. Taking her doctor's advice she retired completely from public life and devoted herself to her children.

Slowly, over a period of time, her strong and stable personality reasserted itself as she came to terms with her grief and guilt. She eased her grief by making notes for a book about her years in politics and discovered that writing was cathartic, that writing about their lives lessened the pain of Joe's death and that she had a real talent for it.

World War II was still raging in the Pacific and in Europe and North Africa where Australians were fighting. Many men were away in the armed forces. Women were needed to take their place. In 1943, when the Tasmanian Federal seat of Braddon (not her husband's old seat of Wilmot) became vacant, one of Enid's daughters persuaded her to contest it for the United Australia Party.

Ironically, although women had achieved the right to vote and Australian women had been granted the right to sit in Federal Parliament in 1902 – even before women in Britain had the vote – twenty years later they *still* experienced huge difficulties gaining preselection. As yet, no Australian woman had been elected to Federal Parliament, ensuring women had little influence on Federal politics. In a male-dominated world many of them were still told by their husbands exactly how they should vote.[7] Men of both parties refused to admit women through the preselection process. This scandalous state of affairs would continue unofficially for the next forty years – and continues today in certain electorates.

Enid campaigned vigorously, determined to win, buoyed up by Joe's vision of her as someone ideally suited to politics. Her seat was by no means a safe one, and only after the distribution of preferences from four other candidates was she finally declared the winner. On 21 August 1943, Enid was doing some ironing at home when she heard over the radio the announcement that history had been made: Dame Enid Lyons had become the first women elected to the Federal House of Representatives.

The United Australia Party, then led by Sir Robert Menzies, was now in Opposition; as Enid took her place in Parliament, the entire country waited to see how a woman would perform in Federal Parliament. Enid did not disappoint the country, winning support from the press and the general public. She used her maiden speech to make the point that women entering Parliament had to 'attack the same problems and ... shoulder the same burdens' as men because 'every subject from high finance to international relations, from social security to the winning of the war, touches closely on the home and the family.'

In politics, Enid Lyons was motivated by a firm belief in the right of women to a place in government. She saw her role in government as a nurturing one and enjoyed fostering talents in others. She was known by male parliamentarians as 'The Mother of the Parliament', a sobriquet with more patronising overtones than 'The Father of the Parliament', traditionally bestowed on the longest-serving male MP. She had to grin and bear the title in public but among close friends she used to joke about it.[8]

In spite of all her commitments, Enid Lyons remained a devoted mother, who had to work hard to provide for her numerous brood, all growing up and needing education. She was always a loyal friend and colleague but a great hater of those she felt responsible for her husband's premature death, including Sir Robert Menzies, whom she regarded as 'the enemy within the gates'. She felt that he had unjustly attacked her husband in a speech he made in 1938, for which she never forgave him.

Five years later, by which time the UAP or United Australia Party had become the Liberal Party, Sir Earle Page, the leader of the Country Party, who had been deputy prime minister in the Bruce—Page coalition, suggested to Dame Enid Lyons a way of bringing Menzies down. Page insisted the Country Party would follow Enid if she broke away from Menzies and the UAP and formed a separate party.

Enid was cautious and inquired from the politicians how she would fare as Leader of the Opposition in place of Menzies. They told her: 'You wouldn't have to do a thing. *We* (the men) would do all the work. You would only be a *figurehead*'. Not surprisingly, even though it would have defeated Robert Menzies, she indignantly rejected what she now realised was a patronising offer. Dame Enid Lyons was her own person and would not be a puppet leader for anyone.

In certain respects, Enid bore a resemblance to Elizabeth Bowes-Lyon, the Queen Mother. Both women were greatly loved by the general public for their charm, radiant smiles, innate dignity and naturalness. Like the Queen Mother, Enid Lyons derived evident enjoyment from meeting and talking with people from all walks of life. But while the Queen Mother rarely spoke in public, Enid Lyons delivered her speeches with great feeling. She is supposed to have been the first Australian politician who could move her fellow politicians to tears.[9] She dressed simply but with good taste in her younger days, choosing striking but tasteful colours; Billy Hughes described her on the historic day when she nervously walked into Parliament for the first time as 'a bird of Paradise among carrion crows'.

Even a woman as hard working and well organised as Enid Lyons found it hard to cope with all the commuting by boat and slow train between home and family in Tasmania and her busy parliamentary office in Canberra. She was still battling constant pain; the fact that this was due to a fractured pelvis was not discovered for some years. She also suffered from an undiagnosed thyroid deficiency which caused her to tire easily.

Wartime civilian rail services were infrequent. Returning to Tasmania by ferry and train took two days from Canberra and was dangerous: during the overnight trip across the Bass Strait, her ship had to pass through mined waters.

Although she asked for no special favours, Prime Minister John Curtin granted her permission to travel by air whenever possible. This gave her additional time to spend with her children, which she greatly valued. However, juggling work and home duties, organising her large family, coping with their childhood illnesses and medical problems, liaising with their teachers, keeping herself well-dressed (photographers delighted in taking pictures whenever she appeared), fulfilling social duties in her constituency, without the support of a husband, were extremely tiring. Her heart-felt cry touches a nerve in women today: 'I would sometimes look at the men about me and envy them 'for having wives. Were there any of those politicians, I would ask myself, who even washed their own socks?'

During her first term of office as Member for Braddon, Edith Lyons made her Parliamentary speeches before hostile male chauvinists who chattered and joked while she spoke seriously on the need for extended social services, including maternity care for women in the city and in the outback, for increased child endowment, widows' pensions and more government housing for those in need. She spoke with first-hand knowledge about the difficulties which war-induced inflation and shortages of essential foods and clothing posed for the nation's wives and mothers. She retained her concern for the poor and underprivileged and, as a devout Catholic, opposed divorce and abortion.

Dame Enid Lyons continued to enchant the public and win elections. She easily trebled her majority in the post war 1946 election and quadrupled it in 1949. Turning her attention towards consumerism, she saw beneath the hype that accompanied salesmanship and realised how easily women were being manipulated by advertising to enrich manufacturing firms. She observed: 'The trouble is that we live in a commercial world geared to keeping women appearing trivial and light-minded. They are made to feel that they must do what they're told by men and that they haven't got minds of their own.'

In a parliamentary chamber known for male histrionics and searing insults, Enid Lyons was always firm but courteous. Rather than ranting like some of her male colleagues, she managed, by explaining the matter under discussion in a pleasant way, to persuade people to do things for her. She upheld the need for ante-natal care, sought to raise widows' pensions and always tried to eliminate discrimination against women at work.

She spent years lobbying for the rights of Australian women to retain both their nationality and citizenship when they married foreigners, and this legislation was finally passed in 1948. She also secured government endowment for *all* children. (Previously the first-born child was omitted and child endowment granted only for second and subsequent children.) She joined with other MPs to secure the free distribution of certain life-saving drugs to those most in need.

At first, Dame Enid could not afford a secretary and had to write all her correspondence by hand. Eventually she managed to secure the services of a secretary but could not afford a live-in housekeeper. Sometimes she was so busy she had to dictate letters to her secretary while preparing a family meal.

She spoke out on sex discrimination when she discovered that government plans for re-employment, demobilisation and training allowances for returned servicemen would be far higher than for returned servicewomen. 'Is the cost of living any lower for a woman?' she pointedly demanded of her male colleagues in Parliament. During her second term of office she used the same argument over equal pay for women. Her opponents found it difficult to answer her logic – a quality they had previously believed was rarely found in a woman. They were forced to respect her.

Dame Enid Lyons' second term in parliament with the Liberal Party – as the United Australia Party was now known – was marred by an undiagnosed thyroid deficiency which caused a painful goitre in her throat. She struggled on, but a few weeks before the 1949 election she was admitted to hospital. She made a dramatic pre-election appearance with her slender throat swathed in bandages. She could only whisper her speeches, yet by now she was so well loved by voters of both sexes that she quadrupled her majority.

In the new Liberal-Country Party Ministry, Prime Minister Menzies appointed her Vice-President of the Executive Council. Enid Lyons entered the pages of history once more as the first Australian woman to break into the all-male world of a Federal Cabinet. Unfortunately, her thyroid deficiency now made concentration difficult; she tired easily and began to believe she was doing Australian women a grave disservice by remaining in office. She felt she could no longer lobby effectively for them.

Enid Lyons retired from Parliament in 1951, due to illness. Even her bitterest opponents had to admit she had been a charismatic leader who had accomplished a great deal. She had been an exceptional minister, always loyal to her staff and mindful of their problems. Without exception, her staff members were devoted to her and very sad to see her go.

Eventually advances in medicine resolved the thyroid problem and finally Enid's fractured pelvis was diagnosed and repaired by means of a number of complex operations. For the rest of her life, Dame Enid remained involved with family and women's issues. In 1951 she chaired the Jubilee Women's Convention. She was also a member of the Australian Broadcasting Commission from 1951 to 1962.

Other honours followed. She became an Honorary Fellow of the College of Nursing, Vice-President of the Elizabethan National Theatre, which was responsible for bringing many important actors to prominence, and held high office in the National Trust of Australia.

From 1951 to 1954 she contributed to an influential newspaper and found she enjoyed writing so much that she produced three books of memoirs. In the first, *And So We Take Comfort*, published in 1965, she related the story of her remarkable marriage, describing it as one in which 'two people who loved each other ... set out on the great adventure together when she was only seventeen and he was twice that age ... They laughed and knew sorrow and great happiness and it all happened in twenty-four years.'

The Old Haggis (1970) was her second book. The title was based on a family joke. Once, when Dame Enid recounted how she had been given a salute by a group of Highland pipers, one of her many grandchildren quipped: 'And I bet the crowd probably said "Here comes the auld haggis!"' Her third volume of memoirs, *Among the Carrion Crows,* appeared in 1972 and concentrated on her experiences in Federal Parliament.[10]

Her final book, *Once on a Windy Hill,* was all about her beloved family home at Devonport, which had been enlarged over the years as her family grew. At the age of seventy-five she created a small fish pond complete with water supply and drainage outlet at Home Hill, her Devonport house, emphasising that she had done it all 'with my own two hands and a bucket'. She wrote: 'As you grow old, you become conscious that happiness is something you create for yourself. *Creating* something gives a real sense of achievement.'

In 1971, when her son Kevin finally retired from the position of deputy premier of Tasmania, she observed wisely: 'Politics is a nerve-wracking business. If you want life without anxiety, keep out of it.'

Dame Enid still played the organ each week at Our Lady of Lourdes Church. She also continued, when asked, to make speeches to women's groups, at which she insisted:

> Women have special attributes, special insights of immense value. Of course, they also have special problems too. But these problems must be solved in *partnership* with men if women are to fulfil their public and private roles. I don't think that we should lose those attributes and priorities that are natural to us as women ... We shouldn't imitate men, the world's far too male already. Nor should we lose our sense of humour. I say to girls – don't abandon marriage. For women the sexual revolution can mean a loss of human dignity. A lot of people have a false idea of freedom. Even in a society of three you can't be free to do exactly as you like. Life has ... taught me that real freedom lies in the control of self.

In 1980, Dame Enid was delighted to be awarded the highest grade of the Order of Australia, a magnificent gold sunburst on a blue-and-gold ribbon. She died the following year, on 2 September 1981.

Honours heaped upon her, Enid Lyons left a legacy of over one hundred children, grandchildren, great-grandchildren, nieces, nephews and grand-nieces. However, contrary to expectations, she did not leave the family home to any of them but to 'the people of Tasmania'. Her will contained the wish that Home Hill would be kept 'as a place for the public to visit and enjoy'.

Throughout her long and productive life, Enid Lyons had always believed that 'we owe the public something. Many things that have occurred in my life would never have happened if the public had not had confidence in my husband and myself.'

The women of Australia owe her a great debt.

CHAPTER NINE

Portrait in oils by Rupert Bunny. National Library of Australia, Canberra.

Ethel Florence Lindesay
(Henry Handel) Richardson
(1870–1946)
AUSTRALIA'S FIRST INTERNATIONALLY ACCLAIMED WRITER

As a medical student at the University of Edinburgh, Walter Richardson must have been aware of the dangers of catching syphilis. Did he catch this then-fatal disease from one of the many prostitutes that haunted Edinburgh's Grassmarket and the courtyards of the High Street, or years later in the gold-rush town of Ballarat? Syphilis takes four to five decades to develop into what was then known as 'grand paralysis of the insane'. Decades later, Walter's eldest daughter, Ethel, would write three novels about the life of a fictitious doctor who marries for love, achieves great wealth in Australia's mining boom but is finally overcome by madness and mania as he realises he will die of syphilis.[1]

In real life, Walter Richardson also made his fortune in Australia in the gold rush. After qualifying from Edinburgh Medical School, he was engaged for a very low salary (as there was then an oversupply of medical graduates) in a practice near London. A disagreement with the local Board of Guardians (Medical Board) made Walter restless, as did the premature death of his younger brother, so he decided to emigrate.

The discovery of gold in New South Wales and Victoria in the 1850s meant that many gentlemen of good education sailed for Australia to try their luck at the diggings. When the son of the doctor for whom Walter Richardson worked announced that he was off to look for gold in Australia, Walter decided to join him.

He arrived in Melbourne in June 1852, and set off for the goldfields at Ballarat, the sort of gentleman digger complete with top hat, gold fob watch and waistcoat observed by the goldfields artist S. T. Gill. Walter soon found the physical effort of digging, cradling and panning dirt unpleasant and had no success at it. He was proud, lonely and withdrawn, unable to fit in to the rough and tumble of life on the goldfields. Looking around him and seeing everyone in the mining settlement of Ballarat busy making money out of the miners, he started a general store in a timber shed to the south of the tented shanty town. He realised that if the gold rush continued, Ballarat would soon become a thriving city. The crudity of the miners and the way they drank away their money appalled him. He made few friends but was kind-hearted enough to gave credit to miners' families down on their luck. Richardson's General Store had many debtors and Dr Richardson felt homesick.

On trips to Geelong to buy more supplies for the store, Dr Richardson stayed at Bradshaw's Family Hotel. There he met Mary Bailey, an ambitious eighteen-year-old English girl from Leicestershire, employed by the Bradshaws to look after their young children, and do housework and other odd jobs. Mary, who came from solid yeoman stock, had left school at fourteen; she was impressed that a doctor in his thirties should take an interest in her. She was a handsome dark-eyed girl. Walter, lonely for female company and convinced that he could educate her and make her into a suitable wife, proposed marriage. Doubtless he believed that having treated with mercury the small chancre that denoted syphilis, he was cured of the disease. Sadly, this was not the case.

Walter Richardson and pretty Mary Bailey were married in Geelong in August 1855, then lived in Ballarat over his general store. The following year, the store was flooded. Since he was making little money, Walter prudently obtained a licence to practise medicine in the colony of Victoria.[2] He was saddened to discover that sturdy, practical Mary completely lacked his own lifelong love of literature. Physically in love with his hardworking young wife, he was disappointed they had so few interests in common. Dr Richardson set up his shingle as a general practitioner, and channelled much of his energy into helping found Ballarat's first hospital. But he was both too outspoken and too erudite to be successful in a country that worshipped mateship and money. At this point, like so many others at this time, he and his wife discovered a common interest in spiritualism.

Like the general store, the medical practice had bad debts from the families of failed miners. Despite their hard work he never made much money. However, in the booming economy of the gold rush, Walter bought a bunch of mining shares on the advice of a barrister friend. These soared in price when gold was found: suddenly the Richardsons found that they had become very rich indeed.

They moved to Melbourne, which was prospering in the mining boom. They made several visits to England, but Irish-born Walter Richardson now felt himself to be an outsider there as well. Undecided whether to remain in Australia or return to Britain permanently, the Richardson's rented a house in Melbourne's Fitzroy.

After fifteen years trying to conceive and several miscarriages (possibly due to Walter's latent syphilis), the Richardsons, who had despaired of having a child, were delighted by the birth of a daughter, born on 3 January 1870. They called her Ethel Florence, names she would come to hate; she preferred to be known as 'Ettie'.

By the time Ettie could walk, Dr Walter was in his late forties, worn out by years of hard work. His wife had aged well: she was a tall, strikingly handsome woman, with dark glossy hair, an ivory-white skin and black eyes.[3] Mary fell pregnant again and the Richardsons moved to a larger rented house in Chapel Street, St Kilda. Keen to keep their money in their very profitable shares, they did not buy a house. They named their second daughter Ada Lillian – she was known as Lil. Sunny, blonde and cuddly, everything dark-haired moody Ettie was not, Lil became Mary's favourite.

Now that mining shares had made him rich, Dr Richardson retired from general practice and devoted himself to his young daughters' upbringing and his study of spiritualism. He was a kind, affectionate father. Ettie was his delight, his 'heart's darling'. He taught her to read at an early age and was delighted by her progress.

When out riding one day, Dr Richardson suffered what he believed to be a fit and fell off his horse. He told Mary of his hidden fear of insanity, which she refused to believe. However, he did not reveal his other secret fear, that he still had syphilis. Mary nursed her husband devotedly, but as Ettie would write in *The Fortunes of Richard Mahony*, whose central character is based partly on her father, 'things would never be quite the same again.'[4] Dr Richardson developed *tic douloureux,* a facial twitch that embarrassed his patients and Ettie, a symptom that can be associated with tertiary syphilis.

Ettie was intelligent, quick-tempered and ultra-sensitive. When she turned four, her father took his family to Britain so that his children could meet their English and Irish relatives. Like so many migrants, Dr Richardson was caught between cultures, unable to feel truly at home anywhere – not in Ireland nor in England or Australia.

He was in denial over the warning signs of the disease he dreaded and planned a romantic holiday with his wife, touring Italy, France and Switzerland in grand style. They left Ettie and Lil in the care of a devoutly Protestant cousin who lived in Cork, whose husband was

Registrar of the Court of Probate. Ettie, used to her parents' sceptical attitude towards organised religion, was dismayed by her church-going Bible-thumping cousins.

The Richardsons' 'second honeymoon' became a nightmare when Walter read in a newspaper that shares in the New North Clunes Mining Company, in which most of his money was invested, had crashed. Suddenly he was worth very little. They had been spending a great deal in Britain and he feared his finances were now in very poor shape indeed.

Dr Richardson travelled overland to Bombay and from there took the first available ship back to Australia. Meanwhile, Mary returned to Ireland, collected Ettie and Lil, and the three of them sailed back to Australia aboard the *Sobraon*. In Melbourne, Dr Richardson came out of retirement, put up his brass plate again and tried desperately to persuade former colleagues to send him patients. He was worried that his family did not own a house, and somehow managed to purchase a block of land at Burwood Road, Hawthorn, then an outlying district of Melbourne. There, on money borrowed from the bank, he built a five-bedroomed mansion with wide balconies and a playroom so that 'the children can have a decent home to grow up in'. In later life, Ethel remembered the Hawthorn house as having 'huge empty rooms'. The reason for this was that before visiting Britain, her parents had sold off most of their furniture (but not Walter's precious collection of books), planning to buy handsome antiques overseas.

However, they still had a piano. By this time, Ettie's musical talent had shown itself; she loved playing the piano.[5]

Re-establishing himself in practice in his fifties proved harder than Dr Walter Richardson had imagined. By now, his undiagnosed illness was making him ill-tempered and eccentric, which offended his patients. Hawthorn was isolated, 'full of new roads, running nowhere', Ettie noted. The few patients Walter did have complained that he was behaving very strangely. At this point, he became obsessed about the large port-wine birthmark that extended from shoulder to wrist on one of Ettie's arms. Possibly, he feared it was a sign of syphilis, which it was not. He photographed the birthmark and then made an unsuccessful attempt to remove it surgically. This made Ettie feel that her birthmark was something to be ashamed of.[6] The birthmark embarrassed Ettie more and more as she grew older, especially in summer when everyone wore sleeveless dresses. She felt ugly (later she described herself as 'a thin lanky child adorned with a crop of black curls'), and suffered agonies of jealousy of her younger sister, pretty, sweet-tempered Lil.

Dr Richardson continued to buy books, something that his wife bitterly resented, she said she needed the money to run the household. Economy became the chief topic of their arguments. Apart from her piano playing, the only bright spots in Ethel's young life were the evenings when her father was well enough to read to her. Later she remembered him as: 'a thin, stooped figure coming up the path, carrying a big carpet-bag full of books, which was plainly too heavy for him. Such a sight would bring me running downstairs, for there was usually something for me in the bag, some child's story suited to my age which he had gone to the trouble of picking out for me.'[7]

The Hawthorn practice made no money; Dr Richardson had strong competition from a younger doctor who was more popular with the patients. When Ettie was six and Lil five, the family moved again, this time to the isolated mining town of Chiltern, where the local doctor was retiring from practice and there was talk of a mining boom. Valiantly, Dr Richardson attempted to run a surgery from their new home, Lake View, but patients were scarce. Now Walter Richardson began to behave even more eccentrically. He tired easily and worried about his large bank loan. Ettie heard her parents arguing bitterly. Failing finances meant there were no more presents of books from her father. Instead, she made up stories to tell to Lil – an excellent start for a future novelist.

Years later, when Ethel Richardson was living in England, she described Chiltern: 'There for the first time I saw wattles in bloom. It was an unforgettable sight. To this day I have only to catch a whiff of mimosa in a dingy London street, and I am once more a small girl, sitting on a fallen tree under the bluest of skies, with all around me these golden, almost stupefyingly-sweet masses of blooms.'[8]

The Richardsons' debts were helped by rent from a tenant Mary had installed in the Hawthorn house, which proved to be unsaleable at anything near the cost of building it. Mary engaged a governess for the two girls, not wanting them to attend the local State school and mix with what she called 'rough children'.

Summer at Chiltern was blisteringly hot. Mary took the two girls to the beach in Melbourne and they stayed with friends at Queenscliff. Alone in Chiltern, terrified that the symptoms of tertiary syphilis were setting in, but unable to share his fear with his wife, Dr Richardson suffered an attack of aphasia, reeling like a drunken man and unable to talk, he wrote to his wife and finished by saying, 'I hope you will come home soon before I go *quite* mad.'

To Mary he blamed his symptoms on a severe attack of sunstroke suffered years ago. By now the Chiltern practice was very low on patients. Walter's physical and mental health was deteriorating so badly that he could no longer run it single-handed. Sturdy Mary had to cope with her husband's mental decay and try and do her best for the children.

In 1877, when Ettie was seven, her father applied for what he thought would be a relatively easy government job. He was appointed as quarantine officer at Queenscliff, a small harbour situated on Port Phillip Bay. His strength was failing, he had rheumatic stiffness and swelling in one knee and found climbing the long ladders up to the sailing ships to check on the crews and passengers extremely tiring.

As the fatal disease progressed, he started to suffer from memory loss and delusions, and people laughed at him in the street, which was agonising for Ettie and Lil. At eight years old, the sensitive Ettie was called to fetch her father home from the main street when he forgot where he was. She saw that people were laughing at her father. She became rebellious and petulant. Lil, on the other hand, was timid and clung to her mother. Ettie's mother realised she had to find a job or they would be forced to live on charity.

Finally, Dr Richardson collapsed completely and was sent to a private asylum, where his condition deteriorated to such a point that he was committed to the Yarra Bend Asylum. Here doctors made the diagnosis of general paralysis and insanity. (At this stage it is a conjecture; not until 1913 would two doctors establish definitively that general paralysis of the insane is caused by syphilis acquired decades previously.)

It was generally rumoured that Dr Richardson was dying of syphilis and the shame would haunt Ettie for the rest of her life. As was customary with a dying patient, Mary Richardson's husband was released into her care in February 1879. For the next seven months Mary bravely nursed her paralysed husband until gangrene set in and he died a harrowing death on 1 August that year. Nine-year-old Ethel saw it all but she blocked those memories in an attempt to forget. Decades later, under the influence of Freudian theory, she would recall her memories of her father when she was creating a major work of fiction set in Australia during the gold rush, *The Fortunes of Richard Mahony*. But all she remembered about her father's funeral was how she and her sister were made to wear scratchy black crepe dresses. She would close her famous trilogy with an account of the burial of the fictitious Dr Mahony, writing how 'the rich and kindly earth of his adopted country absorbed his perishable body'.

Dr Walter Richardson's widow had little schooling, no training and now possessed only a tiny income. How would she manage to feed, clothe and educate her daughters? There was no social security, no government support systems for widows and children. The only paid job she could apply for was that of a housekeeper, which could mean it would be difficult to keep the girls with her.

Thanks to the kindness of a family friend, the Post-Master General of Victoria, Mary secured a job as postmistress at the remote village of Koroit in the Western Districts of Victoria. It came with a two-bedroom primitive stone cottage where she had to manage the post-office in her own sitting room. The house and the job spelt salvation. Mary could keep her daughters, rather than farming them out to relatives. But Ettie and Lil were no longer the doctor's adored daughters, wearing white muslin dresses, black stockings and boater hats: they were 'those poor girls whose father died of syphilis'.

Mary was given some training for post office duties, holding her head high that she now had to work for a living at a time when middle-class ladies did not work outside the home except in dire need.

It was still impossible to sell the Hawthorn house – due to the general economic downturn, so Mary continued to rent it, saving the income for Ettie and Lil's school fees. Mary found her highly-strung, temperamental elder daughter difficult to manage but recognised her musical talent and high intelligence. Ettie withdrew into herself, making up stories and telling them to Lil or reciting them out loud.

Indoors, she fought with her strong-minded mother but, at other times, she tried to protect both her and Lil against the savage gossip that surrounded them. Ettie admired her mother for her strength and determination but found her difficult to live with. Years later she would recognise her mother's strength and write: 'Undaunted, Mary Richardson, who had previously lived the cloistered life of a Victorian lady, trudged daily to the local Post Office for instruction in telegraphy and account-keeping. Bravely she faced the loss of caste that must inevitably follow in a community where a woman who worked for her living was considered definitely outside the pale.'[9]

By now most of their possessions had been auctioned off. Little remained of their former prosperity.[10]

Mary was good at her job, and was soon promoted to run a much larger post office at Maldon. Ettie described Maldon as:

a lovely spot. Trees abounded. The main street was lined with great gums and almost every house had a garden. Blue ranges banked the horizon and to the rear of the little town rose its own hill, old boulder strewn Mount Tarrangower, an hour's climb up a trickling gully. Round our back veranda hung a muscatel-vine, in season so laden with grapes that neither we nor our friends could cope with them and they ultimately went into the pig tub ... Vegetables were supplied by Chinamen, who trotted from door to door with their hanging baskets ... The result of Mother being away at work was that I ran wild, letting out all the rowdy, tomboy leanings till then held in leash.[11]

She continued to make up stories and write them down. Without her mother to supervise her, she read everything she could get her hands on, not all of it appropriate for her age.

By working hard and saving money, Mary managed to send clever Ettie, now thirteen, to Melbourne's Presbyterian Ladies' College, which had an excellent academic record and was attended by girls from leading professional and pastoral families in Victoria. The education Ettie received was based on the curriculum offered in boys' private schools, something very unusual at that time. The staff encouraged the girls to attend university and take up careers at a time when most girls' schools were only interested in teaching ladylike accomplishments such as drawing, French, music and deportment.

Ethel Richardson arrived at the Presbyterian Ladies' College in 1883. Her father's illness had made her a precocious, moody teenager. She was argumentative, believing she had musical talent, and her mother had told her she was sure to top her class. However, she was sensitive about her appearance and her hand-me-down clothes, and underneath her pushy exterior, Ettie was ashamed of her clumsy feet and port-wine birthmark, which she tried to hide by wearing long sleeves. She was deeply convinced that Lil was pretty and she was ugly. This was far from the truth. Ettie was described by one of her classmates as 'a dark, distinguished looking girl with a peculiarly high and rounded forehead and most intelligent eyes. She had a grave almost melancholy expression and a somewhat cynical way of talking.' Receiving nothing but 'snubs and sneers as she came in for a very bad time', Ethel described how she was deeply wounded by the reaction of her classmates. She became a good student in every subject except mathematics, geometry and algebra, which totally defeated her. She managed to survive the teasing she received due to her sharp tongue by burying herself in her books and spending hours practising the piano. Her only friend was a much older girl, beautiful Connie Cochran.

The college had been established to educate the daughters of Presbyterian clergy, and the students had to learn chapters of the Old Testament by heart. Ethel always maintained that the sonorous cadences of the King James version of the Bible formed her prose style. Surprisingly enough, her teachers did not spot her remarkable talent for creative writing. Instead, the school's principal advised Mary that Ettie should take up a musical career. As a widow left to fend for her family as best she could, Mary Richardson was determined the same would not happen to her girls. They would have brilliant careers.

Decades later, in 1910, Ethel published an ironic novel, *The Getting of Wisdom*, based on her time at the college. The novel tells the story of tall, dark, ungainly Laura Rambotham (aka Ettie) and the turmoil of her adolescence. Laura is teased by the other girls and tries to enhance her standing by inventing a romance with the handsome married curate, Mr Shepherd. After spending a short holiday at the curate's home Laura discovers that he is odiously bad-tempered and treats his wife appallingly. Laura's lies about her 'romance' are exposed by a girl who loathes her. She is ostracised by her classmates but is saved by the friendship of older Evelyn Soultar (aka Connie Cochran). Ettie's relationship with Evelyn becomes a passionate one, undetected by the teachers who allow them to share a room. Finally Evelyn leaves school for her 'coming out' season in Melbourne, from which Laura's poverty excludes her. Laura's pride is such that she cannot bear to be dropped; so it is she who abandons Evelyn rather than the other way round. A girl, rather than Mr Shepherd, is the *real* subject of Laura's infatuation.

In real life, Connie Cochran, like Evelyn in The Getting of Wisdom, was everything Ethel was not—beautiful, rich, sophisticated and about to have a coming out season in Melbourne. In her memoirs, Richardson described her passion for the older girl, 'who stirred me to my depths, rousing feelings I hadn't known I possessed and leaving behind a heartache as cruel as the new and bitter realisation that to live meant to change'. She also expressed her surprise that they were allowed to share a room,

> 'when it must have been clear to the blindest where I was heading. Some may see in my infatuation merely an overflow of feelings that had been denied a normal outlet. But the attraction this girl had for me then was so strong that few others have surpassed it. The affinity was mutual and hard to understand for Connie was eighteen and fully grown up while I was still skinny and half-grown. It was Connie's last year at school and she went to considerable lengths to keep things going. But I felt myself an interloper in her family circle, a sort of pariah among her new and stylish friends, I, poor and unsuitably dressed and always on the watch for slights and patronage ... And so we gradually drifted apart.[12]

In *The Getting of Wisdom*, the failed relationship with Evelyn convinces the lonely Laura of the eternal 'fleetingness of things'. She left school with the 'uncomfortable sense of being a square peg which fitted into none of the round holes of her world'.

Some sixty years after the book's publication, an Australian film based on the novel aroused worldwide interest in its author. In the final scene in Bruce Beresford's film, Laura, having come to terms with losing Evelyn and about to leave school, celebrates her freedom from the restrictions of boarding school by running at top speed down an avenue of trees until she is lost to sight.

Ethel Richardson published all her novels under the pen-name Henry Handel Richardson (Handel being a family name on her father's side). When *The Getting of Wisdom* appeared in 1910, British reviewers couldn't imagine why 'Mr Handel Richardson' should wish to turn 'his' attention to a story about a bullied girl attending a boarding-school in Melbourne. They claimed the title was misleading and that 'this novel tells us *nothing* at all about education'. One reviewer remarked that the book was 'far too concerned with the sexual obsessions of a group of nasty minded schoolgirls' and was nothing like the usual stories of girls at boarding school.

What Ettie enjoyed most about the storm aroused by the publication of *The Getting of Wisdom* was the fact that not one of her critics guessed the book was by a woman. Not all the critics were unfavourable. Gerald Gould, in the London *Observer* of 20 April 1924, described *The Getting of Wisdom* as 'the best of contemporary school stories' and urged his readers to buy a copy.

In real life, unlike the fictitious Laura Rambotham, Ettie did well at PLC. She was a champion tennis player, won a scholarship for her piano playing and prizes in French and history.[13] However, she was led by her teachers to believe that music was her forte.

Before becoming infatuated with Connie she had a teenage crush on the handsome vicar of Maldon, and (like Laura's 'romance' with Mr Shepherd) Ettie made up stories about an imaginary affair with him. These gained her some prestige among the girls, but were finally perceived as lies. Ettie was ostracised, sent to Coventry, and scarcely anyone would speak to her for the rest of that term. Telling stories was all part of her creative talent.

Towards the end of her life, after it was revealed that 'Henry Handel' was a woman, readers wanted to know *why* she had called herself by a man's name to write a book about schoolgirls in a lesbian relationship. The answer was that she wanted to be seen as a serious writer at a time when it was believed that women could only write sentimental trash. Ethel Richardson published under the name Henry Handel Richardson for the same reason Charlotte Brontë called herself Currer Bell in order to write about a love affair between a governess and a married man, the central theme of *Jane Eyre*. The same criteria applied to painting as writing. Women were only good for painting flowers and children, 'high' art was reserved for men. Doctors like Henry Maudsley, founder of the London psychiatric hospital that bears his name, claimed that 'men's bodies are bigger than women's so their brains must be bigger', explaining that women should not study hard or it might affect their menstrual periods, making them infertile. An absurd theory, but at the time, people believed it.

Ethel Richardson could never be accused of writing romantic trash. Her style was powerful and polished and her novels compared by literary critics to those of Flaubert or Dostoyevsky. Her books dealt with what were at that time regarded as 'shocking' topics such as homosexuality, lesbianism, suicide and syphilis, which were deemed highly unsuitable for the delicate ears of ladies. The horrific circumstances of her father's madness and death, and the permanent sense of insecurity it inflicted on Ethel Richardson, would affect all her relationships and permeate her writing, which was often concerned with the darker side of human nature.

Another topic Ettie wrote about from bitter experience was jealousy eating away from within. Clever little Ettie had been her father's favourite, the daughter who shared his love of books. After his death she had to share a bedroom with Lil, the pretty little girl with the sunny nature whom her mother obviously preferred. Ethel's intense jealousy of Lil, bottled up for decades, made her even more insecure about her looks, her future and her chances of marriage. Relations between the three females during school holidays often reached boiling point.

In 1887, her final year at school, Ethel turned seventeen. By now her mother had been promoted to postmistress in the Melbourne suburb of Richmond, so now both Ettie and Lil attended the college as day girls. Lil was also musically talented and played the violin.

After leaving school Ettie spent a few months teaching music at a small private school in Toorak, a job she hated. She spent her afternoons alone at home. She read Tom Paine's *Rights of Man*, the novels of Walter Scott and the poetry of Tennyson. She also wrote gloomy entries in her diary and surreptitiously pored over her father's papers, which must have been a revelation to her, since he often expressed sexual desire for her mother with extreme frankness. Reading this material marked the end of innocence. Ethel was fascinated by sex and these letters and diaries would furnish her with material for her three novels about the fictitious Richard Mahony.

In 1888 Mary Richardson resigned from the postal service. At last she had been able to obtain an excellent price for their huge Hawthorn house, which they had despaired of selling and called 'the white elephant'. Mary's aim was to 'finish off' her girls in Europe using the money from the sale of the house to support them. She was anxious that no one should know she had been a humble postmistress, and determined that her teenage daughters should be seen as clever, accomplished and eligible: once they had carved out careers, she hoped they would make 'good' marriages.

Aboard the ship taking them to Britain, Ettie was mortified that all the eligible men were attracted to pretty Lil rather than herself. Only one elderly Australian showed any interest in her but she was not interested in him.

They visited English relatives, who insisted on taking the girls 'to every museum in London', believing them to be 'raw colonials'. In reality, the excellent education received at the Presbyterian Ladies' College meant that Ettie and Lil were far better educated and more cultured than their English relatives. After spending some time in Britain, which Ettie found dismal and dirty, the three Richardson women went by boat and train to Leipzig, the pleasant university town in eastern Germany. Here, in April 1889, both Ethel and Lillian enrolled at the famous Conservatorium. Ethel was to study the piano while her younger sister studied the violin. They were soon immersed in the musical and social life of the town and Ettie described her three years there as 'the happiest I had yet known'. Leipzig, then the most highly regarded centre of musical studies in Europe, was saturated in music. Young composers such as Richard Strauss and Gustav Mahler came there to conduct their first symphonies at the local concert hall. The two high-spirited Australian girls had the time of their lives, attending lectures, concerts, the opera and the theatre. Weekends were devoted to tennis, swimming and walks in the woods surrounding the city. Ettie was filling out and becoming far more attractive, while beautiful Lil shrugged off her shyness and became something of a flirt. Unlike her older sister, she was not seriously interested in a musical career. Ettie was not good at dealing with young men; she tended to be competitive and aggressive, which put them off. Jealously she watched as men swarmed around Lil.

Ethel worked hard at the conservatorium but feared her slender fingers were not strong enough for performance playing. Uneasy about her future she was flattered to receive two proposals, unfortunately from men she found unattractive. Meanwhile, at several parties she had observed a tall quiet Scot, George Robertson, who had what she described as 'a gentle face and keen blue eyes hidden behind spectacles'. The penniless Glaswegian postgraduate was three years older than Ettie. After gaining his degree in science, as his parents wished, George had come to Leipzig to study German language and literature – to the concern of his father, a lecturer at the Glasgow Church of Scotland Training College, who was convinced that his son's best hope of a good academic job lay in science.

George invited Ettie to accompany him to the autumn cycle of Wagner's operas, the highlight of the opera season in Leipzig. Ettie found the life of a student in Leipzig liberating and intellectually stimulating. With Robertson's help she discovered the richness of German literature and learned German to please him. With his help she was able to read the works of Sigmund Freud, which at that time were scarcely known outside Germany. They shared a passion for writing. Her developing friendship with George gave her self-confidence: now men were eager to dance with her at student parties.

She and George began a clandestine romance within that free-living student community and their relationship deepened. But Mary, Ettie's mother, soon discovered where her elder daughter's interest lay. Appraised that the Robertson family had little money, she did *not* view George Robertson's interest in Ethel with favour and remained blind to any sort of prospects his academic studies might bring. Meanwhile, flirtatious Lillian's heart remained untouched.

Mary Richardson had no doubt that her elder daughter had the makings of a professional concert pianist. Initially Ettie yearned to pursue a musical career and became deeply interested in great musicians, such as the composer Edward Grieg, whom she saw perform at Leipzig's concert hall, the *Gewandhaus*. She was heartened by the news that fellow Australian Nellie Melba (Nellie Armstrong) had enjoyed a huge triumph singing at the Paris Opera and longed to emulate her.

However, she was receiving warning signs that although her 'stretch' was good, her lean long fingers were deficient in staying power. She spent hours practising, but completely lost confidence in her ability after a disastrous student concert. Finally she admitted to her mother that she couldn't bear the thought of hundreds of pairs of eyes staring at her as she performed in public. After all these years of study, she realised that she was temperamentally unsuited to the concert platform. But she had absolutely no intention of becoming a music teacher. Instead, she would marry George Robertson. Her mother was disappointed and angry, as were some of Ettie's teachers. Tantrums and recriminations ensued.

Ettie was no longer the 'musical genius' and far more distressed by her failure than she admitted in her memoirs, *Myself When Young*, written at the end of her life. In reality, she was distraught. Her father had failed and so had she. Her only consolation was that George adored her. By now she had turned into a handsome young woman, whose heavily lidded sensual eyes and Roman nose give her a patrician appearance. She realised that she was now attractive, to women as well as men. Mat Main, an admiring young Scottish girl who had shared the Richardsons' rented apartment on Leipzig's Mozartstrasse developed a hopeless crush on Ettie and even threatened suicide when she learned of her engagement to George, which was formally announced in 1891.

Miss Ethel Richardson graduated from the conservatorium with honours in all branches of her subject. At her *Hauptprüfung* on 25 March the following year, she received 'great and well-deserved applause' for her performance of the first movement of Beethoven's Piano Concerto in C Major. Yet in *Myself When Young*, her (sometimes unreliable) memoirs, she says she did not complete her course at Leipzig. Ettie was always prone to lies and silences when recounting her past.

George Robertson did not want to tell his parents about their engagement; having switched from a career in science to studying German (which at that time had few career prospects) he knew they would fear for his financial future and try to talk him out of marrying Ettie. So while the Richardsons returned to England, George had to remain in Leipzig to complete his thesis, hoping he would be able to find a lecturing position in the German department of a British university after he had a postgraduate degree.

Meanwhile, the Richardsons drifted around Britain staying with friends, then rented rooms in Cambridge, where once again Ettie had to share a room with Lil, who was recovering from an unhappy affair in Leipzig. Lil had lost her virginity (a huge step in those days and enough to render a girl unmarriageable in certain cases) to a German who now refused to marry her. Both sisters were lonely, and miserable and felt cold uncomfortable and alien in England.

However, Ettie cheered up after discovering a capacity to write articles, and found a good market for her writing in English magazines. Her first published work was a short story, 'Christmas in Australia'. Away from her fiancé, she was tortured by jealousy and desperately worried that his parents would talk him out of the marriage. She saw herself and George as twin souls and was longing to be involved with him in literary work; she felt this was the one hold she had over him which other girls could not share. So she undertook a paid translation of Jens Peter Jacobsen's influential bestselling novel *Niels Lyhne*, lent to her by George. By now, the Richardsons were living with Australian friends in London. George arrived from Germany to carry out research work in the British Museum Reading Room. He was beginning to realise he would not be able to get a post in the German department of any British university, since they only employed German-born lecturers. He helped Ettie with her translation, and their work on this awakened in her a passion for writing. (Her translation, *Siren Voices*, was eventually published in 1896.)

George went home to Scotland, hoping to find work there. Ettie's insecurities that the marriage would never take place due to pressure from his parents caused her real anguish and jealousy. Without a job, George could not set a marriage date, and Ettie was very aware that her mother did not want them to marry either. She alternated between delight when she sold an article and floods of tears whenever she did not receive a letter from George. She said she hated London and wanted to return to Germany after her marriage.

Although Mary Richardson had desperately wanted her daughters to have careers before they married, Ettie's tantrums and scenes wore her down and eventually she offered Ettie a sum of money to pay for a quiet wedding and support her and George for the first year of their marriage. Ettie was now twenty-five; in that era of young brides, she was in danger of being regarded as 'on the shelf'. This explains why Mary gave in to her wishes; it also explains Ettie's fear that George might find a younger, prettier girl – a fear that was lifelong.

As George had predicted, his parents were furious that all their financial sacrifice had been in vain and that their clever son could not get a job in a department of German language and literature. They blamed him for not continuing with science and were scathing about his proposed marriage. Ettie swore over and over again she could not live or write without him: she urged that they should use the money from her mother for a quiet wedding and 'at least enjoy some years of happiness before they were old'. George was flattered by her need for him. He, too, was feeling lost and insecure. Finally, they were married at the Church of St John the Baptist, Clontarf, Dublin (her father's birthplace) on 30 December 1895.

Close family friends hosted a champagne breakfast for the wedding reception. There were thirteen places laid at the wedding feast, a bad omen it is said, but their marriage confounded the dismal predictions by proving a remarkably happy and productive relationship. They received over 200 wedding presents from friends and relatives, some of which were cheques to help support them until George found a university job.

They honeymooned along the Rhine and spent time in Munich, where George at last obtained work in the university there. Mary and Lil joined them there, until the married couple moved to Strasbourg (then in Germany) for the next seven years. George had secured a lectureship there. They both loved living amid the German/French ambience of this university city. With the appearance of Dr George Robertson's monumental *History of German Literature*, his career as a scholar of considerable repute was established. Ethel was overjoyed that after all her mother's gloomy predictions, her adored husband was now widely respected in the academic world. Their love, based on mutual respect and intellectual companionship, endured. It seemed that neither Ettie nor Lil wanted children when they married, doubtless because they feared passing on their father's dreaded affliction. One has only to read Ibsen's *Ghosts* to realise that before Alexander Fleming and Howard Florey discovered penicillin, syphilis, the 'Red Plague' and its inheritance by children who risked being born deaf, blind and crippled, was one of the preoccupations of the era.

Mary continued to write to Ettie each week – homely letters giving household hints and recipes which fell on deaf ears. Ettie *hated* housework and hired a housekeeper.

She was earning money from her translation of Björnson's *The Fisher Lass* and a published article on Jacobsen, 'A Danish Poet' – both works aided by her husband. When he suggested that she should write a novel dealing with their student days in Leipzig, Ethel immediately started plotting the storyline and creating characters based partly on students and musicians they had known. She would write during the morning, take walks or play tennis in the afternoon, and after dinner George would read what she had written and make suggestions for cuts or alterations. It was the bond that held them together. 'My twin soul,' she called him, 'my rock'.

In the autumn of 1896, a telegram arrived from Lil in Munich with the news that Mary was ill 'with an inflammation'. It was followed by a second telegram saying that Lil was also ill and Ettie must come. Ethel could not believe that her mother, the mainstay of all their lives for so long, could be seriously ill. She took the train for Munich and learned that the doctors thought Mary had an internal blockage in her intestines. They gave her an enema which made Mary writhe and scream with pain. Her condition did not improve but Ettie went back home to Strasbourg, then returned with George. Lil blamed her sister for leaving her to deal with their mother alone. It now appeared that the doctors suspected Mary had cancer of the stomach or the bowel. Her condition worsened; her lips, covered in sores, were bluish-black, her eyes sunk deep into their sockets. It was clear she had not long to live.

Ettie ventured to say, 'Don't worry about us, mother.'

'You're all right, dear,' Mary replied. 'You have George to take care of you. It's Lil I worry about.' These were her final words before she cried out, 'Hold me up, hold me up,' and died.

Later, they learned that Mary died of undiagnosed appendicitis followed by peritonitis. Both her daughters were distraught. Ettie was consumed by remorse that she had not showed more love for her mother while she was alive. Lil still blamed Ettie for leaving her mother and going back to Munich. They quarrelled and all their old bitterness re-emerged.

In an attempt to resolve her feelings of grief and her anger towards the doctors she felt should have saved Mary, Ettie wrote an account of her mother's death. She was rundown and emotionally at a low ebb. As a result, she suffered a severe attack of bronchitis; for the rest of her life she would suffer from a 'weak throat' and severe attacks of bronchitis each winter.

In 1903, Dr Robertson accepted the first chair of German and Scandinavian studies at the University of London and proceeded to set these subjects on a firm foundation in Britain. The honours bestowed on him by the German, Swedish and Norwegian governments were well deserved. Ethel, the professor's wife and aspiring author, basked in reflected glory. However, she did not enjoy living in London, where she felt patronised as an 'uncultured colonial'. She thought of herself as Australian and European but not British. The Robertsons' German housekeeper had accompanied them to London and Ethel was able to devote her mornings to writing her first novel. During the university vacations the Robertsons took walking tours in the Rhineland or went skiing in Austria, visiting the opera and concerts, staying with friends or in small *gasthauses*, leading a very European and cultured lifestyle.

In London they lived in a narrow, five storey house in Regents Park Road, a pleasant tree-lined street close to the park. What Ettie most enjoyed were the evenings she and George spent together at home, reading and discussing books. In her emotional dependence on her bookish husband there are echoes of Ettie's relationship with her bookish father. She wanted her husband's academic career to prosper and conquered her usual feelings of shyness at meeting new people to entertain his colleagues at dinner parties. However, she always refused to discuss the novel she was writing with anyone but George. She was working hard at what turned out to be an extraordinarily powerful first novel. Begun in Strasbourg in 1897, *Maurice Guest* was the result of prodigious research, meticulous writing and rigorous re-drafting. 'Henry' was both disciplined and imaginative. She required a tray of freshly sharpened pencils to be lying on her desk when she began work punctually at 9.30 each morning. Nobody was allowed to enter her study once she had started to work. If anything was required she would summon her German secretary and housekeeper, Irene Stumpp, or a maid on the house telephone.

In 1908, five years after their move to London, *Maurice Guest* by 'Henry Handel' Richardson was published by Heinemann. The publishers had accepted *Maurice Guest* and its 'daring' passages dealing with homosexuality and explicit sexual references because Ethel's editor believed that this was a major work of literature.

Maurice Guest is about a talented young English music student in turn-of-the-century Leipzig who abandons his musical studies at the conservatorium for the sake of Louise Dupleyer, an amoral Australian woman. She is having an affair with a leading conductor famous for his womanising (partly based on the famous composer Richard Strauss), and at the same time she consoles her vanity by sleeping with the naive and inexperienced music student Maurice Guest. She does not feel any love for him. Maurice, an extremely talented musician, has problems defining his sexuality. He experiences the same intense stage fright at performing in front of hundreds of people that Ethel suffered. Deeply in love with Louise (his first affair), he is tortured by feelings of jealousy and self-doubt – as Ettie had been. But for the probably bisexual Maurice there is no happy ending. He puts an end to his financial problems and his doubts about his sexuality by committing suicide. It is a very psychological novel, an extraordinary first novel for anyone at that time, let alone a woman.

To Ethel's extreme dismay, the critics hated the topics treated in *Maurice Guest*. 'An intolerably long book about people not in the least worth writing about,' pronounced the *Sheffield Independent*, a provincial and very conservative paper, 'when the person who gives the title to the tale commits suicide, the reader feels relieved.' Another critic called the book's candid story about love, lust and student life in Leipzig 'morbid, verbose and erotic'. It seemed the British had problems dealing with the world of music students living the Bohemian life, as sexually liberated as the artists of Montmartre.

Ethel's editor had led her to believe that her work was modern, psychoanalytical, in the spirit of the times, and would be acclaimed for its lack of hypocrisy, its characterisation, for revealing how a group of students and aspiring musicians really behaved. Now, to her horror, 'Henry' became the subject of attack over a book which was not seen as great literature but as morally degrading, an outrage against decency. All her old insecurities surfaced. Was she always to be the outsider, mocked and humiliated, just as she had been at school? Ethel claimed that reading the reviews left her speechless, unable to communicate even with her domestic staff, physically nauseated by mortification every time she thought about the critics' acid comments, yet unable to retaliate. No criticism would ever wound her again like those first reviews. Childless by choice, Ethel regarded her books as her progeny, and suffered deeply when critics attacked them.

What the critics were not prepared for was the wildly promiscuous life of most of Richardson's young musicians. Men and women competed for the affections of the same lover. One character was definitely bisexual, conducting affairs with partners of different sexes at the same time. At that time, same-sex relationships were taboo, unmentionable in polite society. Before the theories of Sigmund Freud were bandied about by the chattering classes and emulated by a host of psychologists and counsellors, homosexuality and lesbianism were regarded as unmentionable in novels. Although the upper classes indulged in countless affairs after marriage, both heterosexual and homosexual, and country house parties consisted of endless bed-hopping around stately homes, the status quo of marriage contracts, based on property and possession, was maintained. The horrific fate of Oscar Wilde, who had died only eight years previously, gaoled then exiled to France for love of Lord Alfred Douglas as well as mindless couplings with guardsmen, was at the back of everyone's mind. Homosexuality was still a prosecutable offence. *Maurice Guest* was condemned for its 'lack of moral tone'. 'The book will have little general reader appeal,' critics predicted correctly. Some copies were withdrawn and a second, expurgated edition was published; by now the publishers were scared they could be prosecuted for immorality for the homosexuality revealed in Ethel's novel. Many bookshops flatly refused to stock it.

A German translation was published in 1912, also heavily cut but it was highly praised. Edited American and Danish editions followed. In the end the second English edition of *Maurice Guest* was reprinted seven times. Those broad-minded and well-travelled people who *did* buy 'Henry's' book and enjoyed it appreciated the deeper understanding she gave them of men, women, human sexuality and human frailties. She wrote perceptively about jealousy, a subject she understood very well. Fellow writers, such as Hugh Walpole and Somerset Maugham, praised Henry Handel Richardson's first novel and became her friends. But for Ethel, the damage had been done. She had always been reserved when meeting people for the first time, especially those with whom she felt she had little in common. Some people thought her proud but it was insecurity and shyness rather than pride. Now, bitterly hurt by the critics and averse to discussing the reviews or the topics she had chosen to write about, she became a virtual recluse, even though the true identity of 'Henry Handel Richardson' was still not revealed. Now she allowed very few visitors to the tall, silent house. George Robertson, who had always urged his wife to 'aim high' in her writing, shared her dismay – but although he had advised her over the years it was taking shape, it was not his book: he was one step removed from the anguish the author endured.

The Robertsons' move to London suited George better than his wife. The onset of World War I distressed both of them greatly as they had many German friends in universities and musical circles there. Lillian, too, was living in Germany, having married Dr Otto Neustatter, a Munich eye specialist. The marriage was initially a happy one and eventually Lillian's only son, Walter Lindesay Neustatter, was sent to school in Britain, where he lived with the Robertsons and was like a surrogate son to them. The war caused divided loyalties for Ethel's nephew, who would remain in Britain and study to become a psychiatrist, influenced by his aunt and uncle's fascination with the writings and research of Sigmund Freud.

The war changed pretty effervescent Lillian. Her loyalties, too, were divided but her Australian background won. She left her husband, came to live in London with Ettie and George and her son, Walter. After a period of loneliness, she met a charismatic young teacher and writer named Stuart Neill, and after the war she helped him to set up a school in Austria with progressive ideas on education and the teaching of music. Lil was still married to her very Germanic husband, whom she now found safe and dull, and started an affair with Neill. She and her husband and Neill spent a great deal of time together. Eventually this strange *ménage à trois* broke up, and Lil and Neill then opened a school in England similar to the one they had run in Austria, backed by Dr Neustatter's money. An amicable divorce was arranged: Lil married Stuart Neill and devoted the rest of her life to running Summerhill School.

Besides his lecturing workload, Professor Robertson conducted intensive research and undertook extra work to maintain the large house and staff at Regents Park Road. He and Ettie spent long vacations walking, bicycling or skiing in Germany, Austria and Scandinavia. At home, Ettie continued to compose songs in English and German and to play the piano for her husband's pleasure but writing and involving her husband in critiquing and editing her work became the focus of her life.

No man could have done more than Professor Robertson to ensure that his wife was free to devote herself to her writing. He was in a good position to advise her. By now, his knowledge of literature, music and the arts was immense; in Ethel's novels there are distinct traces of his literary criticism: for example, his knowledge of Freud's research, which Ethel shared, and of the works of Wagner (on whom he lectured). 'Henry' as he affectionately called his wife, sometimes in jest, sometimes in tenderness, learned from her hardworking academic husband the habits of prolonged application and the dedication required to research and write her books. He always found time to discuss her work with her. She wrote in longhand for a few hours each day and employed a typist. Then, very conscious of maintaining her svelte figure, she kept to her regime of walking in Regent's Park, playing tennis and swimming. She was a member of the London Society for Psychical Research, the London Spiritualist Alliance and the International Society for Psychical Research, consciously or unconsciously echoing her father's interests.

Ethel's childhood had been spent moving from one home to another. She craved stability, security and her husband's undivided attention. She was jealous of his female students, hated change and insisted they should remain in the house at Regents Park Road which had become her refuge and her work place. They lived there for the next thirty years. By now 'Henry Handel Richardson' was making a name for himself. 'Henry' had no intention of changing her name and her image, especially not to the name Ethel, which she had always hated. She said that the idea people would call her Ethel Richardson, the *lady* novelist, 'made her flesh creep'. She wanted to be known as a *literary* writer on contemporary themes.[14]

Used to the wide open spaces of country Victoria and the woods surrounding Leipzig, Ethel Robertson never felt entirely at ease in London and often felt homesick for Australia, the country she had left as an adolescent. In 1912, the Robertsons visited Australia to allow Ethel to research her next book, a fictionalised account of the life of her father in Australia during the gold rush. Young children are rarely concerned with their parents' lives and Ettie, while her father was alive, had never asked questions about his past.

Ethel was now forty-two, an age when most people attempt to make sense of their own lives. She became fascinated by the history of her own family and by the huge social changes brought by the gold rushes in Australia. This, she realised, was a great turning point, the period that changed Australia from a penal settlement into a thriving rough-and-tumble male-dominated society linked by the concept of mateship, where Jack was as good as his master and the theory of the 'fair go' for all was born.

The trip was a success and as her research continued, she realised that she now had enough material for three separate books. They would take her almost twenty years to complete. Her parents' story had sparked a deep creative wellspring within her and turned her into a fine writer, although not always a *truthful* one.

Now, decades after her father's death, she unleashed, from the hidden depths of her consciousness, the details of her father's madness and horrific death. *The Fortunes of Richard Mahony* was the first novel in the trilogy; the three books are now called *Australia Felix*. Together, they tell the story of a doctor who dies of syphilis. *The Fortunes of Richard Mahony*, published in 1917, brought the Victorian diggings to life as no other contemporary novel had succeeded in doing.

In it, Ettie managed to communicate her father's passion for finding gold (a passion, shared by so many, which resembled a craving for heroin), as well as his eventual disillusionment. She wrote perceptively on this topic, describing how: 'A passion for gold awoke in them an almost sensual craving to touch and possess. The glitter of a few specks at the bottom of a pan or cradle came to mean more than home or wife or child ...', and how:

> This dream ... of vast wealth ... had decoyed the strange motley crowd in which peers and churchmen rubbed shoulders with the scum of Norfolk Island, to exile in this outlandish region. The intention of all had been to snatch a golden fortune from the earth; and then hey presto back to the Old World again ... But many became prisoners to the soil. The fabulous

riches amounted to a few thousand pounds: what folly to depart with so little, when mother earth still teemed. Those who drew blanks laboured all day for a navvy's wage. Others broken in health, could only turn to an easier handiwork.

She wrote about people who became addicted to digging for gold, describing how: 'Those, who, as soon as fortune smiled on them dropped their tools and ran to squander the work of months in a wild debauch before returning, tail down to prove their luck anew.'

Writing as 'Henry Handel Richardson', Ettie was able to define the Australian experience. She saw how Australians worshipped Lady Luck. She described how those new Australians who succeeded were not viewed in the same way as their American counterparts, as being talented or hard working. Luck – in property speculation, the stockmarket, the race track, in a game of two-up – became part of the Australian ethos. Luck is the reason for Australia's fabled egalitarianism.

In describing the role played by luck and gambling in the Australian psyche, 'Henry Handel' had just written an important passage in Australian literature.

World War I was still in progress when *The Fortunes of Richard Mahony* was published. London was in the midst of Zeppelin raids and bombs, and the horror of young Britons and Australians dying in the trenches of France. During wartime, paper was rationed and the book did not have huge sales. Few copies were shipped to Australia.

Nor did her second novel, *The Way Home* (1925), achieve much success. Some critics and fellow authors in Australia considered the chapters that dealt with Richard Mahony's return to England the most revealing expose of English snobbery and social attitudes they had ever read. When the time came for the third novel of the trilogy, *Ultima Thule*, to be sent off to the printers, Heinemann baulked at the prospect of having another novel about syphilis by Henry Handel Richardson left unsold on their shelves. Only the direct intervention of Professor Robertson, and his undertaking to guarantee the publishers against loss and to cover the cost of printing, saved the day for Henry Handel Richardson's latest novel.

Review copies of *Ultima Thule* were sent out late in 1929. Two agonising weeks went by, during which the author and her husband anxiously awaited the final verdict on a work which had been nearly two decades in the making. Finally, the influential critic Gerald Gould wrote in the *Sunday Observer*: 'The book is a masterpiece, a work of genius worthy to rank with the greatest and saddest masterpieces of our day.' Reflecting the feelings of hundreds of thousands of readers in England, Australia and America, the eminent music critic Ernest Newman described how the illness and final break-up of Richard Mahony had moved him 'as much as any passage in Beethoven'. Reading the review one can imagine that, after the mauling she received from previous critics, Ettie would have wept with sheer relief.

To the surprise of the publishers *Ultima Thule* sold well. The monumental tragedy of the author's theme was recognised. The book was quickly reprinted by Heinemann in Britain and by Norton in America. There were several European language translations. Heinemann hastily bought back all rights from Dr Robertson. Today the *Australia Felix* trilogy has become an Australian classic, taught in university literary courses and helped to literary prominence in Australia by the writer and critic Nettie Palmer.

Australia Felix describes the great upswing in nineteenth-century Western capitalism fuelled by Australia's gold discoveries as well as the sense of cultural alienation and isolation experienced by British migrants in a land ten thousand miles away from Britain. She saw Australia as a land where different social values prevailed due to the harshness of life and the cult of mateship.

The three books deal with issues which were to define the direction of white Australian society from the 1850s onwards, set within the framework of a troubled marriage and an inevitable and horrific death from syphilis – an illustration of what Tolstoy called 'the universal human vulnerability to pain and loss'.

Richardson's three Dr Mahony works are powerfully written, haunted by images of guilt, separation, alienation and death. English novelist Somerset Maugham greatly admired the Richard Mahony trilogy and described it as similar in its imagery and layers of meaning to Dostoyevsky's *Crime and Punishment*.[15] The sins of the fathers visited on their children is a theme common to both authors. The Richard Mahony trilogy has also been described as 'one of the great inexorable books of the world'. Dostoyevsky's medically qualified father had been brutally murdered by serfs at his country home in revenge for his treatment of them, a tragedy that haunted the Russian author in the same way that the harrowing death of Dr Walter Richardson haunted his daughter.

What Dostoyevsky, Zola, Flaubert, Balzac, Dickens and other great writers, including Henry Handel Richardson realised in their writing is the infinite complexity of human nature rather than the black-and-white version portrayed in much popular fiction and films. They see no good or bad characters but realise men and women may commit heinous crimes and yet be brave, generous and loving towards their fellow beings. There are no villains or heroes here, only complex people coping with problems that face *all* humanity. This is where Ettie's talent as a novelist lies – 'character drawing' she called it.

Heinemann had published John Galsworthy's hugely successful *The Forsythe Saga*. They realised that in Richardson's trilogy they had a family saga with bestseller potential, as well as a literary success. By now, British newspapers were clamouring to know the identity of the author. Journalists eventually ferreted out the truth. The writer, it transpired, was a *woman, and* one born in Australia.

Interviews were scheduled but Ethel declined to speak to journalists. The professor's wife continued to hold herself aloof from London society and would not sign books or speak at literary lunches. When a brash journalist almost cornered her on one occasion in a department store, she took refuge from him by hiding in the ladies' lavatory for so long that he left. It made a good story.

The vulnerable insecure schoolgirl had not changed very much. She still disliked talking about her work and did not make friends easily. Her second live-in secretary, Olga Roncoroni, and her nephew, Walter, were her closest companions apart from her adored husband. She received the Australian Literature Society's gold medal for *Ultima Thule* as the best novel of 1929, and now that the trilogy was completed, her husband and other literary figures gave her hope of being nominated for a Nobel Prize for Literature. Then, without warning, her husband became ill and grew steadily worse.

In 1933, the sudden death of Professor Robertson from cancer was a huge shock to his wife and an irreparable loss. Writing had been her hobby, her career, her passion and had left her little time to cultivate many other interests or intimate friends. Ethel remained in the Regents Park Road house with Olga for a year after her husband's death, then they both moved to the south coast. But Ethel never became reconciled to living in England.

When she was sixty-four, Ethel's book *The End of Childhood*, a collection of short stories about young Cuffy Mahony, son of Dr Mahony, was published. It was 1934 – a year after her husband's death.

Richardson and Roncoroni loved visiting the cinema. Ethel belonged to a private film club which enabled her to see films proscribed in England, which then had very tight censorship – as did Australia. She had contacts in Germany and Paris, and in what was a very restrictive era, they supplied her with banned novels, including works by D. H. Lawrence.

Ethel's letters and diary entries for this period show that she suffered a long period of depression after her husband's death. Her letters mention neuralgia, sciatica and influenza. She wrote how 'a weariness of things in general ... sometimes takes possession of me' but 'it goes hand in hand with a vigorous hold on existence and with the unyielding toughness of the born fighter'.

She was helped in her fight against a reactive depression, sparked by her husband's death, by Olga Roncoroni. Olga had battled to overcome severe panic attacks – she was agoraphobic, a neurotic condition defined as a morbid fear of entering public spaces. The sufferer only feels safe at home and becomes progressively less able to venture outside. In the 1920s and 1930s, little was known about this condition. Olga, whose parents were friends of Lillian and her second husband, had been encouraged to seek treatment by the Robertsons, whom she met in 1921, when they were staying with Lil and Stuart Neill at their home in Lyme Regis.

Appraised of her difficulties, the Robertsons had invited Olga to stay with them in London so that she could seek psychiatric treatment. She had consulted a psychiatrist who had helped her, and she had also been helped by her friendship with Lil and her son, Dr Walter Neustatter, who was staying with the Richardsons while doing his postgraduate training in psychiatry. Eventually, Olga had recovered sufficiently to continue her teaching of Dalcroze Eurythmics at a London school. The Richardsons liked her and found her vivacious, intelligent and very European in her approach to life, as well as an accomplished pianist. And so she remained at Regents Park Road, and in time became invaluable to Ethel as a secretary. Olga's sense of fun appealed to Ethel's lighter side and they became good friends, so Olga agreed to a deathbed request by George Robertson 'to look after Henry' when he had gone.

Much speculation has surrounded Ettie and Olga's friendship, often erroneously based on the premise that Ettie's literary interest in homosexual relationships meant she had a lesbian relationship with Roncoroni after her husband's death. There is no concrete evidence to support this view. Handel Richardson's greatest novels *Maurice Guest* and *The Fortunes of Richard Mahony* deal with heterosexual as well as homosexual relationships. While it is not possible to deny that Olga and Ettie were more than good friends, when Ettie was widowed, she had spent almost forty years in a loving relationship with her husband with no more than the usual conflicts of a married couple. She was devastated by his death, and her constant wish to get in touch with him through the spirit world does not suggest someone in a lesbian relationship.

Ettie continued pursuing her father's interests in spiritualism and the paranormal. Her sessions at the Ouija board and attendance at séances were a desperate attempt to get in touch with her husband 'on the other side of death' and re-establish what she insisted was 'a permanent marriage', claiming that their souls were 'twinned for eternity'. She 'discussed' her writing with her husband in expensive séances with various mediums, who claimed they were in touch with him in the spirit world. The grieving widow told her dead husband about problems with her latest book, even played the piano to him and continued the co-dependent relationship, which had lasted nearly forty years. She even read him part of her unfinished novel *Nicky and Sanny*.

This novel was supposed to be based on Lil's first marriage to the German doctor. Notes by the author indicate that its plot hinged on a marriage breakdown. It seems logical to assume that, like almost everything she wrote, *Nicky and Sanny* was based on something she had seen unfold, a contemporary middle-class drama. It would seem that Ettie, for so long jealous of Lil's hold of her mother's affections, had avenged the wounds of their past in *Nicky and Sanny*. She described in detail Lil's marriage breakdown, based on intimate details she knew about Lil's engagement and marriage to Dr Otto Neustatter, their initial happiness and growing prosperity, and their divided loyalties as tension mounted in the 1930s between Germany and Britain. As war seemed inevitable and the forces of the Third Reich increased in power, venting their hatred of the Jews, Lil realised it would be impossible for her to remain in Hitler's orbit, even though she had helped to establish a school in a beautiful part of Austria. She attempted to resolve an impossible love triangle with an Englishman who shared her views on education. She had genuinely loved her husband when she married him but experienced distaste for sex with him after she became involved with her new lover. The novel detailed the death of love in a marriage that convention ordained must survive for the sake of the child, and the eventual divorce and remarriage of the female protagonist to a more compatible man.

Doubtless Lillian and her son, Dr Walter Lindesay Neustatter, had every reason for wishing this novel would never be published. (It has been assumed that this was the reason that Olga Roncoroni, possibly at the request of Dr Walter Neustatter – Lil's psychiatrist son, who had done so much to help combat Olga's panic attacks and agoraphobia – destroyed the manuscript after Ettie's death.[16])

In 1934, Ethel and Olga moved to Fairlight, near Hastings on the Kentish coast. Ettie bought a large touring car, an old Armstrong-Siddeley. In it they visited Austria and Germany, Ettie happy as ever to be in the mountains and lakes she loved. But all too soon came the long hot September of 1939 when Hitler invaded Poland and the wireless message was relayed over the BBC that Britain was at war with Germany. Like Virginia Woolf, Ettie was extremely depressed to think that war with Germany was about to erupt once again. This, on top of George's death, depressed her spirits and badly affected the quality of her writing.

Now, at the age of sixty-nine, Ethel's final published novel, *The Young Cosima*, appeared. Unfortunately, it fell far below the standard of the Richard Mahony trilogy. It deals with the tortured relationships between Cosima von Bulow, Wagner, Cosima's father Lizt and her husband, the conductor Hans von Bulow. The novel provided an opportunity for Richardson to re-examine the themes of genius, passion and intimacy and the universal human vulnerability to pain and loss.

Ettie and Olga remained at Hastings all through heavy bombing raids by the German air force on south-eastern England, where in 1940–41 German planes would off-load any remaining bombs after they had devastated London. The dreaded 'doodlebugs', the V1 rockets which menaced southern England in 1944, were another hazard. 'The one that would kill you and destroy your home,' Richardson dryly observed, 'was the one you did not hear.' Her complex personality remained surprising resilient. She was as sharp-eyed, shrewd and caustic as ever.

At the age of seventy-four, frail, grey-haired and in poor health, especially in winter when her bronchitis caused problems, Ettie insisted on keeping a log of all flying-bomb attacks that occurred in the Hastings area. The house was often shaken by the bombs, which gave her severe migraines. There was rationing of food and clothing, and a lack of new books or concerts. Surprisingly, Ettie claimed that she found the war 'intensely interesting. It's *far* more relaxing than writing books,' she claimed wryly. Because of the bombs, she abandoned work on the new novel but she managed to write part of her memoirs, *Myself When Young*.

In her memoirs, *Myself When Young*, Ethel claims that she was refused entry to the Presbyterian Ladies' College when she made the trip to Australia in 1912, but this claim is now known to be grossly exaggerated. As a pupil she had often *felt* rejected – by Connie, by other students and by her teachers, and this probably coloured her feelings towards returning to her old school and the scenes of her childhood.

Her unreliable memoirs were completed by Olga after her death and published by Heinemann in 1948. They are very important in understanding the way she used her own life and her family history to create fiction.

'Henry' died of cancer at Hastings on 20 March 1946, a year after peace with Germany was declared. Olga's own health was failing; the eighteen months she spent caring for her friend and employer, who by now could afford to pay very little for her care, was a heroic gesture. Ettie was cremated at a dismal funeral service held in chilly wintry London: her ashes were scattered out to sea along with those of her husband as she had requested.[17]

In 1957, the Robertson house in Regents Park Road acquired a blue memorial plaque to 'Henry Handel Richardson, novelist', but the building was later demolished. The Victorian Fellowship of Australian Writers saved Ethel's Australian birthplace from demolition and the Victorian National Trust restored the former Richardson home, Lake View, at Chiltern.[18] Among the relics on view there is Richardson's Ouija-board. Three portraits of her by the Melbourne-born artist Rupert Bunny are in the National Library of Australia. Portraits and photographs usually show her in profile; they all reveal a strong nature and a handsome young woman.

Ethel Richardson's Richard Mahony trilogy (later republished as *Australia Felix*) suffered from the long intervals between the publication of its volumes. World War I badly affected sales of the first volume, *The Fortunes of Richard Mahony,* published in 1917. All three volumes were published in one large edition in 1930. Ethel signed a contract for a film during World War II but the film's production was halted due to lack of funds and never recommenced. The trilogy was translated into Danish, reprinted in 1931, 1934, 1937 and 1939. In 1941 an American edition was produced with an introduction by the eminent writer Sinclair Lewis, and an Australian edition by Heinemann in 1947. (Even in 1977, when London's feminist Virago Press republished *The Getting of Wisdom,* several British literary journals still referred to the author as '*Mr* Richardson'.)

Henry Handel Richardson is surely Australia's most significant woman author of the early twentieth century. Because Miles Franklin funded a well-known and sometimes controversial literary prize, she is often considered more important – we hear her name more often. But Miles Franklin, after the initial success of the ironic *My Brilliant Career* and her prize-winning account of pioneering on the Monaro, *All That Swagger*, wrote little else of significance.

Some Australian critics have sought to downplay Handel Richardson's significance as a great Australian writer on the grounds that 'she spent so much of her life overseas'. Yet art critics happily call long-term expatriates Arthur Boyd, Sydney Nolan and Geoffrey Smart 'great Australian creative artists', and the novelist Christina Stead, who left Sydney in 1928, married an American and *never* returned to live in Australia, is always viewed as an Australian writer.

Henry Handel Richardson's place in Australian literature remains a very important one.[19] She wrote *major* novels about big issues and created unforgettable characters that haunt the mind. In Britain, she is viewed as an Australian author, a foreigner living in London and writing in English, as Joseph Conrad did. This has militated against Henry Handel Richardson in the British literary stakes. As Henry Handel Richardson she made little effort to become part of British literary life, although she enjoyed close friendships with H.G. Wells and several other notable British authors.

In 1932, at the height of her fame, Henry Handel Richardson was finally nominated for a Nobel Prize for Literature, one of the first women to be so honoured. However, the prize went to a male author. 'Australia's greatest female novelist,' as her obituary called her, died at the age of seventy-six over ten thousand miles away from the Australian bush she had loved. Her reputation as an author lives on.

CHAPTER TEN

James R. Lawson, Rare Books Department, Sydney. Now author's collection.

Sister Elizabeth Kenny
(1880–1952)
WHO GAVE HOPE TO POLIO VICTIMS

Elizabeth Kenny was born in Warialda, New South Wales, in 1880. Her father was a farmer who, when necessary, practised as an untrained bush vet. Later the family moved to Nobby, on Queensland's Darling Downs. As a young girl Kenny had dreamed of becoming a doctor, but such chances were denied to women. She had been taught bush nursing techniques and a knowledge of human musculature by Dr Aeneas McDonnell, a Toowoomba general practitioner who admired her bravery when he had to set her broken arm. He had taken her on as his assistant.

For a nurse to practise at that period, formal nursing qualifications were not mandatory. Initially, Elizabeth Kenny never registered as a nurse and her subsequent problems with the medical profession stemmed from this.[1]

In her youth, Elizabeth Kenny may well have suffered the pangs of unrequited love but she never recorded her feelings. She loved children and adopted a young girl named Mary Stewart at a time when adoption was not the popular option it is today. She did this so that Mary could take her place and fulfil Elizabeth's responsibility of caring for her widowed mother when she went to America. Elizabeth Kenny never married. Her work was her passion and would always come first.

At the time of Federation, the Darling Downs was desperately short of hospital facilities and to reach Brisbane meant a long journey by horse-drawn ambulance. In 1913, at the age of thirty-three, Nurse Kenny set up her own tiny hospital on the Darling Downs, at Clifton. That year she was called out to treat a two-year-old girl, Amy McNeil. The child was suffering from a mysterious fever, previously unknown to Nurse Kenny who telegraphed her former mentor Dr McDonnell. He replied that the child must be suffering from infantile paralysis, a relatively unknown illness which was rapidly becoming a scourge for children in the southern states of Australia and proving difficult to treat. This was the first mention Elizabeth Kenny had heard of infantile paralysis – or polio, as it would soon be called, by which time the disease would have reached epidemic proportions.

A few years earlier, Elizabeth's own young brother had suffered from a mysterious attack of paralysis and she had alleviated his pain and restored movement to his limbs by soaking strips of blanket in hot water and applying them as poultices. She did the same for Amy, after which she was able to move the girl's rigid limbs and alleviate the child's pain.

Amy's father was a stockman and the family lived in a bark hut with a dirt floor. They were far too poor to pay Nurse Kenny, but money was never her principal interest. In her teens she had dreamed of being a medical missionary and her overriding aim was to cure her patients, regardless of whether they could pay or not.

Kenny's success with little Amy (as well as her own brother) led to her formulation of a radical new treatment for polio. Her remedial treatment was contrary to the instructions of many doctors, who refused to let their patients move their limbs and kept them with their arms and legs in splints.

Sister Kenny treated her patients by immersing the stiffened limbs in hot baths, and giving them hot packs and intensive massage. The prevailing medical theory held that patients' limbs should be kept immobilised to avoid further damage to their muscles. Kenny insisted that her patients discard the splints and braces prescribed by their doctors as soon as possible and strengthen their muscles by moving around and exercising.

In 1915, Elizabeth Kenny joined the Australian Army Nursing Service and made twelve sea voyages between Britain and Australia with returning wounded. During World War I, nearly 3000 Australian nurses volunteered to serve in areas ranging from the British Isles to France, Italy, Egypt, Palestine, the Persian Gulf, Burma, India, the Balkans, Vladivostok and Abyssinia. Many, like Nurse Kenny, served with great dedication aboard hospital ships. On board the cramped, overcrowded hospital ships, Kenny observed that those wounded men who were encouraged to get up and move around stood a far better chance of regaining the use of their limbs than those who remained bedridden. She was in advance of her time in understanding the psychological effects of encouraging patients to move their limbs.

After the war, Sister Kenny, who had adopted the title of 'Sister' in view of her seniority rather than by examination, returned to the Darling Downs. Now she gave her polio patients remedial exercises to perform as well as hydrotherapy treatment, and stressed the psychological importance of instilling in her young patients the idea that their condition was curable.

Sister Kenny was strong-minded, authoritative and commanding, attributes which would have been highly admired had she been male and medically qualified; but in a nursing sister (even one running a large clinic), they were deemed by doctors to be assertive and unfeminine. Nurses were meant to be in awe of doctors, not to contradict their advice when they recommended immobilisation or surgical operations for polio patients. She made powerful enemies by airing her opinions. Soon Sister Kenny's methods and philosophies and her suitability to be treating patients at all were seriously challenged by medical authorities. Her big mistake was that initially, Sister Kenny implied that she was able to *cure* polio. This caused many doctors to view her with grave suspicion. Her later experience taught her that she was able only to *alleviate* the symptoms of the disease.

Terrifying epidemics of polio occurred all round Australia during the long hot summers of 1931–32 and 1937–38. At that time, there was no vaccine against polio.

Queensland farmers christened it 'cow disease' because they believed that it had been started overseas in cattle and could spread from humans into their herds. Everywhere she went in the bush, Sister Kenny encountered hysteria and fear of the dreaded disease. Many quaint bush remedies were recommended to halt its progress, none of which worked. These included painting fences with creosote 'to kill the germs', hanging camphor blocks around children's necks and sending them to school with sulphur in their socks.

Sister Kenny now had some measure of financial independence, receiving a small pension for war service and having made money from inventing what became known as the 'Sylvia stretcher' – a cushioned stretcher which became popular for transporting patients over bumpy unmade roads in the outback.

After years of crusading for children to throw away their splints and braces and refusing to let them lie in the wards with their limbs immobilised in metal cages, in 1934 Sister Kenny set up a small polio treatment clinic in Townsville.[2] Parents turned to her in desperation. They brought their paralysed or semi-paralysed children to her clinics rather than going to doctors. Naturally, the doctors were not amused. They claimed that when they sent Sister Kenny patients for exercise and hot baths, she would brush them aside and take over the case completely.

Over the next four years, Sister Kenny received assistance from the Queensland Government to set up small rehabilitation clinics in other towns, including one in the grounds of what is now the Royal Brisbane Hospital.

In 1937, Sister Kenny aroused even more wrath from leading members of the medical profession when her book *Infantile Paralysis and Cerebral Diplegia* was published in Sydney. In it she deplored the prevailing medical treatments for the effects of polio. She claimed that muscles atrophied in splints or cages and bones were drained of vital calcium, leaving the patients deformed and pain-ridden. She described their muscles as being 'in spasm'.

Some doctors called her 'an untrained charlatan', ignoring the fact that paralysed children treated by the Kenny method were no longer bedridden but walking to school. One of the patients she helped was a boy named Johannes Bjelke-Petersen, who would become premier of Queensland. Dr Aubrey Pye, the Medical Superintendent of the Brisbane Hospital, had no choice but to recognise her success.[3] But other doctors made certain that nurses trained by Kenny working in the small clinic in the grounds of the Brisbane Hospital were not allowed to mix with regular hospital nurses or wear the same uniform, claiming she lacked sufficient knowledge of physiology.

Sister Kenny claimed that she was denied valuable hospital space and given only long-term cases, patients already deformed through months of 'orthodox' immobilisation. Kenny's enemies were powerful members of the Queensland medical establishment. In 1935, doctors and administrators insisted on a Royal Commission headed by the eminent medico Sir Raphael Cilento to investigate Sister Kenny's 'radical' treatment and its outcome and to oversee a full report.

While the judge and medical specialists on the panel of the Royal Commission were preparing their report, Sister Kenny went to Britain, where a polio epidemic had broken out. She found herself treated with far more respect by the medical profession there than in Queensland: a Kenny Polio Treatment Clinic was opened in Carshalton, Surrey. On her return from Britain, she was invited to Melbourne by the Victorian State Government. The rapid spread of polio terrified it and it also considered trying the Kenny method.

The day after Sister Kenny arrived in Melbourne, the Royal Commission released its long-awaited report. She was horrified to find that the report damned her treatment methods in favour of hospital treatment by immobilisation. Ironically, some of the doctors who condemned the Kenny method would quietly adopt some of its techniques when, years later, they discovered that total immobilisation in splints had failed with many patients.[4]

Despite the Royal Commission's findings, Sister Kenny continued to receive support from the general public, many of whom saw her as an angel of mercy and a victim of medical conservatism. Kenny continued her work; she remained as dedicated as ever. Sometimes, after working all day, she would keep watch by the bed of a sick child through the night until, at dawn, totally exhausted, she fell asleep.

When Annette Kellerman, the champion swimmer and Hollywood film star, returned to Australia, the land of her birth, she heard about the polio epidemic and saw the fear it inspired in parents living in the bush and small towns. Sister Kenny's clinics were often featured in the press, and many journalists who had seen paralysed children walk again supported her.[5]

Nearly thirty years after Sister Kenny's first success, Annette Kellerman visited several Kenny Clinics and offered her services for voluntary work with the young patients. The children were delighted to meet her. Endorsement by Annette Kellerman, a star of the sports world in a nation that was sport mad, did no harm to Sister Kenny, either.

Bruised by the harsh verdict of the Royal Commission, Sister Kenny had toyed with the idea of going to the United States with its willingness to embrace new ideas. A few Australian doctors did support her, and in 1940, six Brisbane doctors signed a letter on behalf of Sister Kenny to the prestigious Mayo Clinic in Rochester, Minnesota. The Queensland Government offered to pay Sister Kenny's fares to the United States and she was also supported by Annette Kellerman, who was well known to Americans for promoting exercise as the way to health. A polio epidemic had erupted in Minnesota, which prompted the American authorities to give Sister Kenny a teaching position at the University of Minneapolis Medical School and beds for her patients in the university teaching hospital.

In 1942, the Elizabeth Kenny Institute opened in Minneapolis to give therapists a thorough training. The National Polio Foundation of America gave her an allowance, and a Minneapolis club voted her $416 a month for life, so that she now felt financially secure. She gave up her Australian war pension and bought a house in Minneapolis, donating all gifts she received to the Kenny Foundation. In 1952, during another epidemic of polio in America, a Gallup poll found that she was even more popular than Eleanor Roosevelt.

After this, Sister Kenny's methods were widely accepted: she became famous beyond her dreams, additional Kenny Clinics were opened and she received honorary degrees from Rutgers University, as well as the Universities of New York and New Jersey.

Like Annette Kellerman, Elizabeth Kenny was idolised and feted in the United States. The film *Sister Kenny*, starring Rosalind Russell, was released in 1946. Billed as 'the life of the woman who brought hope to the hopeless', it was based on her autobiography, *And They Shall Walk*, written in collaboration with Martha Otenso three years previously. The film was a success: Sister Kenny became a household name across America. She was invited to the White House and presented to President Franklin Delano Roosevelt, himself a victim of polio. The American public adored her. With her striking appearance and commanding and charasmatic presence, she was in huge demand as a public speaker. Kenny, with her bluntness of speech, could still arouse controversy. The medical profession argued over her concept that the disabilities in poliomyelitis are caused by the virus invading peripheral nervous tissues, rather than the central nervous system – the accepted medical opinion.[6] But to the mass of people the doctors' arguments seemed irrelevant. In their eyes, Sister Kenny was simply the woman who saved children from the terrible after-effects of infantile paralysis. They flocked to her treatment clinics and her public lectures.

Kenny declined to relinquish her Australian citizenship. She received many offers to lecture around the world, and to enable her to travel freely throughout the United States, Congress passed a special Act which enabled her to come and go in America as she pleased without having to obtain a passport or visa.

Towards the end of her life, Elizabeth Kenny discovered that one of her feet was dragging and she could not prevent her hands shaking slightly. A motor neurone disease was diagnosed for which there was no cure. She yearned to see the mauve plumes of the jacarandas once again in springtime in Queensland, and to be cared for by Mary McCracken (née Stewart), the girl she had adopted way back in 1926. Mary had looked after Kenny's widowed mother, and after Mrs Kenny's death had run one of Queensland's Kenny Clinics before she married. In an interview in 1996, Mary McCracken said that Sister Kenny showed the same devotion to her patients as Mother Theresa and Albert Schweitzer.[7] Mary welcomed her back home.

By now the Queensland nursing sister, who had cured so many others that she was known as 'the lady with the blessed hands', was suffering from Parkinsons' Disease. Gradually this independent woman became totally dependent.

Sister Kenny died in November 1952, at the age of seventy-two. Friends who were with her in her last hours reported that just before she died she prayed that a vaccine might be found to abolish infantile paralysis forever.[8] She was buried at Nobby, on the Darling Downs.

Soon after, an American doctor named Jonas Salk produced the answer to Sister Kenny's prayer: the Salk vaccine against polio.[9] Within two decades, thanks to the Salk vaccine (which would eventually be replaced by another preventative which could be hidden in a sugar lump), poliomyelitis virtually disappeared in the developed world. The Sister Kenny Institute in Minneapolis still exists, but has been changed into a rehabilitation centre for victims of spinal cord injuries.

Today, Sister Kenny remains a legendary figure, especially in Queensland where so many people still have relatives who were treated by her.

CHAPTER ELEVEN

Sister Lillie Goodisson
(1860–1947)
PIONEER OF FAMILY PLANNING CLINICS IN AUSTRALIA

'*I am convinced that our lives are not in vain. We, and other women like us, have been forces of change. We can depart the world in the belief that we leave it in a better condition than when we first encountered it.*'[1] – Dr Aletta Jacobs, pioneer of the use of the 'Dutch cap' pessary, which Sister Lillie Goodisson imported and sold in her Sydney family planning clinics.

Lillie Goodisson is very important in the history of family planning in Australia. Her invaluable work in promoting birth control contributed to the acceptance of today's contraceptive techniques. Sex education and condoms have, in the age of AIDS and the sexually transmitted and often lethal disease hepatitis B, saved the lives of many girls and young women. Today, with relatively reliable contraceptives available, the average age of a white Australian woman bearing her first child is around twenty-eight.[2] Better nutrition and sanitation, better obstetric care and new forms of contraception have extended women's lives.

At the time of Federation, women married young and died relatively young. They were taught by Church and State that women's role was to have sex with husbands on demand, 'be fruitful and multiply', preferably raising as many sons as possible.[3] While the rich wanted sons to inherit, the cry of poor working-class mothers of families, on learning they were pregnant yet again, was heartfelt: 'Oh no! Not another mouth to feed and another bottom to wipe!' Yet in the Federation era, when no government support was given to the poor, providing such women with contraceptives or contraceptive advice was punishable by imprisonment.

Lillie Goodisson became a campaigner for birth control (then known as family planning) because she had nursed many women dying from botched backyard abortions. Condoms had been available for centuries, firstly made for the rich out of silk and then out of vulcanised rubber or fish skins. However, most husbands refused to wear them, believing that they ruined the pleasure of sex and should only be used with prostitutes to avoid catching venereal disease, rather than with their 'innocent' wives. There was also an old wives' tale that using a condom could make the wearer epileptic: even men as intelligent at the philosopher Bertrand Russell were told this by their fathers as children.

Lillie's greatest challenge was providing women with reliable information about contraception when this was a punishable offence. Most working-class women bore their first child in their late teens or early twenties, raised a family of at least eight or nine children, were considered old at forty and faced death in their fifties. Many women still died in childbirth due to unsanitary conditions and complications in the pregnancy or labour.[4]

In hypocritical and censorious colonial Australia, the sale of contraceptives was illegal in most States. No respectable woman was supposed to know much about family planning. Many married women wished to limit their families, but church and State frowned on doctors or nurses giving out sample contraceptives or advice on their use. Anyone who sold them privately or in pharmacies risked prosecution.

In the Federation era and after, childbirth was hazardous, even for the rich. Lack of contraception and male disinterest in using what was available meant women of all classes were likely to die in childbirth, as activists such as Miles Franklin and Rose Scott (Chapter 21) recorded. Mid-life crises and divorces were rare in married men: deaths in childbirth meant many were widowers and free to mary again.

Single mothers were seen everywhere. Some 'fell' pregnant because they had received no family planning advice; they were regarded as little better than common criminals and shunned. Male employers abused their positions, taking sexual liberties with hired help without their wives' knowledge, believing that lowly paid maids or washerwomen had no rights. Once the servant's pregnancy became apparent, the husband would disclaim any responsibility, or else insist the girl had 'led him on'. The unfortunate girl (often Irish or a mixed-race Aborigine and barely literate) would be thrown on the streets without a character reference to find *no one* would employ a single mother. Most working-class families rejected daughters who fell pregnant. Many of these young women were left to take their pathetic little bundle onto the streets and beg for a living or become prostitutes.

Church and State treated single mothers as 'fallen women'. In the Lying-in hospitals for unmarried mothers, or in segregated wards in general hospitals, single women were made to give birth with a cloth over their faces, or else held down by nurses so they never saw their newborn babies and could not bond with them. Adoption was the recommended course of action for single mothers.

Governments in Britain, Australia and America did nothing to help working-class mothers limit their families because they needed cheap labour. Australia was extremely exploitative in this respect. As a developing nation fearful of an invasion by its Asian neighbours ('the Yellow Peril'), cheap, unskilled male labour was required to build the Lucky Country.

State governments (and after Federation, Australia's Federal Government) wanted uneducated youths for army service in case of war. So the authorities issued colourful posters urging all patriotic women to become mothers 'for the good of Australia'. 'Australia *needs* populating by white people' was the catch-cry of men in power. To encourage this, in the 1920s a Commonwealth grant, roughly equal to one week's basic wage, was paid to every new mother. This baby bonus was not specifically intended to help poorer women but to encourage procreation of the white races in Australia.

Just after Federation, the average family size in New South Wales was nine children. In spite of the 'baby bonus' or motherhood grant, Australia's birth rate began to fall. As the birth rate fell, fewer women died in childbirth, yet government spokesmen *still* urged women to have *more* children as their patriotic duty.

Before the advent of family planning clinics, many working-class women, debilitated by annual childbirth and rearing children, lost all interest in sex after a few years of marriage, causing problems in many marriages – yet hardly surprising when the end result was yet another mouth to feed on very little money. A hidden army of prostitutes and child prostitutes helped to sate the sexual appetites of married men.

Medical authorities did not help, especially if they were Catholic. In 1907, in his presidential address to the Medical Society of Victoria, Dr Michael O'Sullivan thundered that:

> when a wife defiles the marriage bed with the devices and equipment of the brothel [condoms] and interferes with nature's mandate [sex on demand by husband] by cold-blooded preventatives and safeguards [pessaries]; when she consults her almanac and refuses to admit the approaches of her husband except at stated times ... can it be otherwise that estrangements and suspicions of wifely faithfulness should occur? Many husbands will ... be tempted to seek elsewhere those pleasures denied them at home. Such are Nature's reprisals.[5]

Dr O'Sullivan referred to 'the devices of the brothel' as he did not wish the dreaded word 'condom' to appear in print. Lillie Goodisson and a handful of other significant women defied male-dominated authorities, to demand reasonably reliable methods of contraception. There was much trial and error, but in the end contraceptive advice became freely available to married women and finally to everyone.

The fact that by the end of the twentieth century, most Australian women were limiting their families with the cooperation of their partners, shows how important was Lillie Goodisson's battle with the authorities for family planning advice.

Today women live longer. Crones in black have disappeared; women no longer automatically put on dark colours on the death of their child. In fact, by the time they reach forty-five, many have launched off into starting a business or have gone to university as mature-age students, where they often perform exceptionally well. Healthy women who reach the age of fifty can expect to see their eightieth birthdays. For most Australian women, fifty is not what forty used to be, due to fewer pregnancies and better obstetric care.

Before contraceptives were widely available, popular (but usually unsuccessful) ways of procuring an abortion consisted of drinking gin in a hot bath or throwing oneself down the stairs in a desperate attempt to detach the foetus from the lining of the womb. The latter was also a face-saving measure: the woman concerned could tell her neighbours she had slipped and suffered a 'miscarriage'. Many women died from illicit back-street procedures in unsanitary conditions, using unsterilised knitting needles. Australian city women could buy a bottle of Widow Welch's pills. These could only be sold in pharmacies to women who claimed they needed them to 'regulate menstruation'.

Working-class wives were often more prudish about sex than their middle-class contemporaries. Sex was something few people talked about, mostly performed with the light turned off. Women would sometimes ask male doctors what they could do to prevent having another baby. They received unsympathetic replies, such as: 'Get your husband to sleep out on the veranda' or 'Lock the bedroom door till you want another baby'. Women doctors, horrified by the misery of worn-out or battered wives, were often pioneers of sex education, especially in the new all-women's hospitals which opened in Sydney and Melbourne. By the time of Federation, women's 'temperance' leagues were formed to guard women against alcoholic husbands, syphilis and other venereal diseases. However, the societies issued their message in such guarded language that it was often hard for unmarried girls to understand exactly what the pamphlets or speeches were driving at.

Lillie Price was born in Britain, on the Welsh coast, where her Methodist father was a doctor. Urged on by her father, Lillie trained as a nurse but would have preferred to have studied medicine.[6]

At the age of nineteen, she stopped her nursing studies in order to marry a Welsh doctor named David Evans. In search of a better life for their as yet unborn children, the newlyweds migrated to New Zealand, where they worked long hours establishing a general practice in which Lillie was the practice nurse. There and in Britain, Lillie had seen young women made old before their time from bearing enormous families in stark poverty. Like Margaret Sanger, the pioneer of birth control in America, Lillie had nursed many women dying in childbirth or who, destroyed by numerous and unwanted pregnancies, had been desperate enough to resort to the services of backyard abortionists and had paid for this with their lives.

Eventually, Dr and Mrs Evans moved to Melbourne. When the children were old enough, in 1897, just before Federation, Lillie set up a small private hospital in St Kilda where she acted as matron.

Dr David Evans died in 1903. Widowed, and with her son and daughter married, aged forty-three but still full of energy, Sister Lillie Evans sold her share in the St Kilda hospital and immigrated to Western Australia. Here she met and fell in love with an Australian businessman named Albert Goodisson, whom she married the following year. From their pleasant Geraldton home, Lillie continued her crusade for married women to be able to control their own fertility. Providing birth control for unmarried women at this period could have put Lillie in prison but she did what she could to provide information to women in need.[7]

It is interesting that Britain's pioneer of birth control, Marie Stopes, had a dark secret in her first marriage which inspired her to help other women and so did Sister Lillie Goodisson. Lillie's dark secret was syphilis.

Decades before Lillie married Albert Goodisson, a man in his sixties, he had had unprotected sex, caught syphilis and like Ethel Richardson's father and countless other men of the period, now the symptoms of tertiary syphilis, the nervous symptoms and strange behavioural patterns, manifested themselves. He knew what the end would be, and the scandal that would be attached to his family, so he went overseas to die in a mental asylum without telling his wife. Lillie only discovered too late the cause of his illness, as syphilis was a topic no one wanted to mention. The shock turned her into a campaigner for preventative measures like condoms.

As a result of her husband's tragic death, Lillie became preoccupied with the prevention of sexually transmitted disease, a topic then banned from polite conversation.

Emotionally and financially drained by her husband's illness and death, and fearing the syphilis might have infected her, Lillie borrowed money from Belle, one of the famous Goldstein sisters, returned to Melbourne and set up a small medical lending library to alert women to the horrors of syphilis and other venereal diseases. At this time, penicillin, which would eventually provide a remedy against syphilis, would not be discovered for another twenty years or so. Lillie's lending library shocked some people and failed to make money, ensuring she had to cut her losses and close it.

Lillie corresponded with Britain's Marie Stopes, who had a first-class degree in science. Marie had married a botanist named Reginald Gates, who was impotent and unable to consummate their marriage. At that time, sex was never discussed and there were no marriage guidance clinics. Marie struggled to understand what was happening in her marriage, which eventually broke down, and later she would write a book of advice for women called *Married Life*, copies of which reached Australia.

Marie married again, this time a wealthy man willing to support her crusade to help women everywhere. Humphrey Verdon Roe's fortune helped his wife set up marriage guidance clinics which she felt were necessary after receiving pathetic and harrowing letters from women denied access to birth control, such as this one, which Marie ensured received wide publicity:

I have had 7 children, lost my eldest girl with consumption about three months ago and have six children living. My youngest eleven months.

Three of them are consumptive. My husband is only a laburer [sic] and has been out of work 4 years. I don't want any more children and it seems how[ever] careful I try I seem to fall wrong. I am three days past my time and feel worried because I am 43 in October. Of course it might be the change but I want to be on the safe side. I thought I would write and ask you [for information] … It is a shame that pore [sic] people should be dragged down with families, fed up with life [and] keep having children. I hope you will oblige me by writing return of post. Yours sinculy [sic].

In 1926, Lillie moved interstate to join her daughter from her first marriage, now married herself and living in Sydney. In that city, five years after her friend Marie Stopes founded the first birth control clinic in Britain, and ten years after Sister Margaret Sanger opened America's first birth control clinic for poor women in Brooklyn, Sister Lillie Goodisson founded her association in New South Wales to promote sex education, give clear and accurate information on birth control, limit mentally defective girls being drafted into prostitution, and in doing so attempted to limit the spread of venereal disease which was then widely prevalent in Australia. While some of Lillie's ideas are considered extreme in the light of our knowledge today, as a dedicated nurse she was motivated to do *something*, knowing that sufferers often unwittingly passed on syphilis to their wives, who could die from it, and to unborn children, who could be born blind and deaf or crippled as a result of the disease.

In 1933, Sister Lillie Goodisson's family planning association established Sydney's first birth control clinic, selling condoms and fitting contraceptive devices (probably the Graffenberg ring and Dr Rutgers' diaphragm imported respectively from Germany and Holland) to married women unable to give 'a decent upbringing, proper food, clothing and education to their children'. She also tried to prevent women and girls from undergoing illegal and life-threatening abortions, and wherever possible arranged private adoptions for their children.

As well as the unpopular condoms made of thick vulcanised rubber, the clinic sold thinner ones made from fish skin, sold under the 'Fiskin' brand label. Fish skins may not have been ideal but at least they were an improvement on the dried sheep's intestines, always readily available in the bush, which had served as condoms, usually tied on by a ribbon.

Sister Goodisson's family planning society did valuable work, selling subsidised contraceptives to whoever wanted them. In the Great Depression of the 1930s, when so many working men and their families were thrown out of work onto the streets, Lillie was a tireless worker. She campaigned for contraceptive devices to be available and for measures to prevent the spread of venereal disease until she was in her eighties. When she started giving women advice, charging a small fee to help run the clinics, there was *no other* source of free birth control information. The clinics were visited by desperate women (some of whom had played Russian roulette with the 'rhythm method' of contraception and lost), and who were prepared to risk their lives to abort children whose birth might kill them or drag them into destitution. At that time a husband had the legal and moral right to force his wife into having sex, even if he was drunk, violent or suffering from venereal disease.

In Sister Goodisson's clinics, she trained her all-female staff to give advice to women whose children had been born mentally defective through inherited syphilis. She fought against the 'double standard', whereby well-off men infected by syphilis visited prostitutes but the authorities only treated the female prostitutes whom they accused of spreading the disease, ignoring the fact that legions of infected Australian soldiers had returned from Egypt and France after World War I. The only recognised treatment for syphilis then was repeated application to the vagina or penis of an ointment containing mercury, which, in fact, did not halt the progress of this lethal disease and could cause women to develop kidney disease. Sister Lillie Goodisson donated money to various hospitals to help find a cure for syphilis, but no progress would be made until it was discovered during World War II that penicillin, developed by Alexander Fleming and Australian-born Howard Florey, cured the disease. Thanks to Fleming and Florey and Howard Florey's wife (Dr Ethel Hayter Reed, a graduate of Adelaide University in 1924), who supervised her husband's clinical trials of penicillin at Oxford which resulted in it going on the market but who never received any recognition for her work, penicillin became widely available after 1945. And so, finally, the scourge of syphilis was ended.

It is an interesting fact that 'men fight: women cooperate'. Lillie Goodisson was fortunate to have received remarkable cooperation from strong-minded women who set up birth control clinics overseas. From Dr Aletta Jacobs and Marie Stopes she received the latest information on contraception like cervical or Dutch caps and Graffenberg and Mensinga rings. However, her Sydney clinics did not dare to provide contraceptive advice for unmarried women for fear, in that restrictive period, the Federal Government would have closed them down. The Australian clinics imported the Mensinga ring, invented in 1882 by Dr Wilhelm Mensinga which, like the Graffenberg ring, was a precursor of the IUD or intra-uterine device. Both these devices prevented pregnancy by inhibiting sperm fertilisation.

The fact that we have birth control clinics today, as well as sex education classes in many schools, is due to the pioneering work done by remarkable Australian women like Lillie Goodisson and grocery-store owner Brettena Smyth (who in the nineteenth century sold contraceptives to bush women from the back of a grocery cart). Lillie Goodisson was supported by Dr Aletta Jacobs in Holland, Marie Stopes in Britain and American-born Sister Margaret Sanger, who was imprisoned *seven* times for providing contraceptive advice.

Due to the dedication of these women, we rarely see tired, careworn, pregnant mothers, looking ten to fifteen years older than their age. Most women today look ten or more years younger than women looked at the time of Federation and few women die in childbirth, the part government, part privately funded Family Planning Association of Australia now has branches Australia-wide and provides aid to women in many developing countries.

CHAPTER TWELVE

Ella Simon
(1902–1981)
AUSTRALIA'S FIRST ABORIGINAL JUSTICE OF THE PEACE
and
Kundaibark
(dates unknown)
HEALER OF THE BIRIPI PEOPLE

Ella was born in a tent on the outskirts of Taree and, like so many part-Aboriginal children, her birth was never registered; her father was anxious to keep it a secret. Her mother (whose name, like that of her father, Ella never revealed in her memoirs) was a 'fringe-dweller' with no money and no home. Ella's mother was a pale-skinned Aborigine who worked for a white family in Wingham. She had been 'taken advantage' of by her white employer, an important man in Wingham's ultra-conservative community. After Ella was born, her mother survived on part-time domestic work, but lived in fear that either the police or welfare authorities would be alerted and remove or 'steal' her daughter. Whenever the police inspected the fringe-dwellers' camp, she would black Ella's face to make her look darker, since the police were instructed to remove pale-skinned children either for adoption or to orphanages. In 1902, the New South Wales Aboriginal Protection Board had been given the power to remove mixed-race children if they thought the child was suffering neglect. It was a catch–22 situation for Aboriginal fringe-dwellers. Their camp had no sanitation or piped water, so 'neglect' could easily be defined as the absence of the everyday amenities white people took for granted.[1]

Ella's father was fond of her mother, but already had a wife and five legitimate children. Ella's mother had worked for him and his wife as a resident domestic. Ella had been conceived after a party at which Ella's mother was employed to serve her father's guests.

Shortly after Ella's birth, her mother returned to work as a domestic servant for another white family. She loved the baby and managed to keep Ella with her for some time – this was difficult as unmarried domestics, black or white, were not usually allowed to bring babies with them. Although she was unaware of it, Ella's mother was suffering from tuberculosis, which would eventually kill her. The disease was endemic particularly among the poor whose living conditions were often unsanitary. She then married a young Aboriginal man, but he was unable to care for a young child and an ailing wife and Ella's health suffered.

As a result, around the time of Ella's second birthday, she was sent to live with her maternal grandparents on the Purfleet Aboriginal Mission just outside Taree.[2] Ella's grandparents had been relocated to Purfleet in 1902, the year when it was set up. As members of a Protestant church, for a small sum they were able to purchase a block of land and build their own little wooden house. At that time, jobs on the land were plentiful and the mission self-supporting. Ella's grandfather was a fine Aborigine who had always worked as a stockman on a neighbouring property. But during the Depression years of the 1930s with the rural poverty that resulted, he lost his job due to objections to the employment of low-paid blacks over unskilled whites. Suddenly, in late middle age, he was denied work.

The little girl was too young to understand what was happening to her; for many years Ella believed that her grandmother was her real mother. She had no idea that scarcely a year after she went to live on Purfleet Mission her mother was dead of tuberculosis. Her father's family refused to take her in due to her illegitimacy and her coffee-coloured skin.

Unlike many white men who fathered a child by an Aboriginal or part-Aboriginal woman, Ella's father showed remorse for his actions. He visited Ella at her grandmother's home during her childhood, although initially Ella was not told their visitor was her biological father. He ensured that she was provided with clothes and shoes, but her education at the mission school was very limited. The rest of his family (who were prominent figures in New South Wales) would have nothing to do with Ella and considered her existence an embarrassment.

Ella did not discover the truth about her mother's death and her own parentage until she turned twelve. Her maternal grandparents had always cared for her as though she was their own child. So she was shocked to learn that the couple she believed were her parents were, in fact, her grandparents, that her real father was the white man she was sometimes taken to visit, and that her mother had died of tuberculosis. Ella described her sense of loss and anger:

> The bottom fell out of my world as I sat listening to Kundaibark, my grandmother. Looking back on it I think it's the greatest mistake to wait until an adopted child is set in her ways before telling her the truth. When someone tells you that they are not your real mother or he's not your real father, suddenly you are tormented about who you really are and what you are. You just don't know what to think. Then a kind of rebellion starts to creep into your heart and slowly you begin to lose your love for the person who reared you. Oh it's still there of course

but you have this nagging thought, 'Well you're not my mother, you have no right to say this or that to me.'

Ella was probably better off with her grandparents than living in a tent on waste ground with an ailing mother, but no adopted child is willing to believe this. Adopted children, learning of 'missing' parents, spend nights sobbing into their pillows for what might have been, instead of taking advantage of the love that is offered to them.

Fortunately for Ella, her grandmother, Kundaibark, was a remarkable woman and a traditional healer. Kundaibark had also had a disturbed childhood. Her mother (Ella's great-grandmother) was a full-blood Aborigine of the Biripi people, who lived a nomadic life. While Ella's mother had been seduced by a man she knew, Kundaibark's mother had been raped by a white stranger. She had died giving birth to Kundaibark while going walkabout. At that time, full-blood nomadic Aborigines regarded half-caste children as bringing bad luck and some abandoned their mixed-race babies. In Kundaibark's case the Biripi did not want to take a mixed-race baby with pale skin along with them on their travels. She would hinder their progress and there was no one who could feed her. So, according to nomadic custom, they moved on, leaving the baby under a tree to die. Fortunately, little Kundaibark was found by a passing stockman, taken to the nearest homestead and bottle-fed by the station owner's wife. Kundaibark lived in the household and became the family domestic.

No one bothered to teach Kundaibark to read and write. But she showed a talent for nursing the sick, and being quick and intelligent she learned a great deal about white medicine by nursing sick stockmen and the children of the station owner.

Her own people may have abandoned her, but Kundaibark yearned to return to them. In her twenties, she returned to the Biripi and set herself to learn all she could about Aboriginal lore. She married a Biripi man, Ella's grandfather. He was a devout Christian, whose father had been a Scottish engineer working on the railways.

On the mission at Purfleet, Kundaibark combined her experience of white man's medicine with her knowledge of healing plants gained from the Aborigines. She nursed Aborigines who were sick and dying and acted as a midwife. Kundaibark believed colour was only skin-deep, that it was a person's character that mattered, not the colour of their skin.

Ella was far paler than most of the children on Purfleet Aboriginal Mission. (She was termed 'light-skinned' on her mission papers.) In the mission school, the darker skinned children refused to play with her because of her light colour. Kundaibark brought up Ella not to have a chip on her shoulder about life and to forgive others. She taught Ella to assert her dignity as a human being and gave her a sense of mission to help her fellow Aborigines achieve citizenship and a better life. She taught Ella a great deal, including the bush remedies she knew; she also passed on to Ella a sense of duty, that she should help Aboriginal people even though some of them might reject her, believing her pale skin brought bad luck. Kundaibark had no sense of racial prejudice or inferiority. She reared Ella to believe that *all* people were equal in the eyes of God and to be proud of her heritage rather than ashamed of it.

Ella needed this reassurance. For much of her life she would battle prejudice against the colour of her skin from white people as well as from Aborigines, who resented both her pale skin and her European features. Refusing to say she was of mixed race, Ella described herself as a 'light-caste Aboriginal'. She loathed the fact that white people called the Purfleet settlement 'the blacks' camp'. She was proud that her grandparents had bought the land on which their house was built rather than having it given to them. She hated to think that white people looked down on her.

The knowledge that her mother was dead and that the two people she had believed to be her parents were really her grandparents strengthened Ella's resolve to achieve something more with her life than her mother had been able to achieve. She dreamed of a life as a trained nurse.

At the mission school, the children jeered at her for trying so hard and told her she should be at the school in Taree for white children. She learned only the rudiments of reading and writing. The tuition and equipment provided was dismal and the Aborigines on the mission lacked the knowledge or the will to demand better schooling for their children. Ella left school in sixth grade aged twelve, still unable to write well, although she was highly intelligent and had an extremely retentive memory. At Purfleet she cared for family members who were having babies and performed a variety of resident domestic jobs. She still dreamed of becoming a trained nurse, but her difficulty in reading and writing ruled out nursing, at that time the province of white middle-class girls.

Discipline was strictly enforced on missions. It was impossible to leave without a certificate from the manager. On the other hand, there was always the danger Ella might be removed from her grandparents' care by the police and placed in the dreaded Cootamundra Domestic Training Home.

On the mission the traditional Aboriginal way of life was banned. Corroborees were forbidden and the Aborigines were punished if they swore, gambled or drank. Any mail they might receive from distant relatives (usually written for the senders by well-meaning Europeans) was censored.

In 1915, the NSW Aborigines Protection Act was amended to give the Protection Board the power to remove any child at all without parental consent. Aboriginal children of mixed blood with fair skins were the most likely to be 'stolen' by police and sent to be 'educated' in schools or in white homes. Officially, these children were removed from their mothers to give them 'better chances' in life. For intelligent and sensitive girls like Ella there was scant education and only one kind of employment – as a domestic. When Ella turned twelve her grandmother became too ill to keep her and she was sent to live with a maternal uncle. She travelled by train, then by horse-drawn milk van, the only vehicle that went up into the mountains behind Gloucester, where her uncle lived.

Ella's uncle was poor and his home overcrowded. She was sent to work at Coneac Station, on the understanding she would be trained for a lifetime of domestic service. At the age of twelve, Ella found herself overworked and unloved, virtually an unpaid slave to a white family where the mother was ill and she was left to do most of the work. She had to round up the cows, milk them, feed the animals and do the housework. When the white or Aboriginal station hands got drunk and, as she described it, 'talked stupidly' there was no one to defend her. Ella was a well-developed and attractive girl but sexually innocent and with a strong sense of Christian ethics given her by Kundaibark. The situation at Coneac Station worried Ella.

She wrote to her aunt describing how she had to bar and bolt her room each night and how the men were harassing her at work. Her maternal uncle sent a horse for her and she managed to leave the property, but there was still not enough room for her at her uncle's. She returned to Purfleet Mission, but found the former missionary gone, replaced by an autocratic, overbearing manager, who insisted she go to Sydney to work as a domestic.

Ella's first employers in the city were not very kind to her, but she was smart and hardworking and managed to find herself a different post. Ella found some white employers kind, others not. Using the small portion of her salary she was allowed to keep for herself (the rest being held in trust for her by the Protection Board), Ella wrote away to Britain for books on nursing. She worked from early morning until eight o'clock each night, struggling with the nursing books, determined to improve herself.

Ella's biological father kept in touch with her and came to visit her in Sydney when he visited his legitimate children, who, of course, never wanted to acknowledge Ella and never had anything to do with her.

By 1928, when she was twenty-five, Ella was working as a resident maid in Mosman for a white family who were reasonably kind to her. However, at that time, life for all resident domestic staff, white or Aboriginal, involved long hours, backbreaking work and little regular time off. The hours of work were not regulated by unions. Uniforms with starched collars and cuffs needed frequent ironing – as did other garments in the weekly wash. Vacuum cleaners and refrigerators were in their infancy, housework and food preparation consumed enormous amounts of time and effort.

Ella befriended another fair-skinned part-Aboriginal girl named Margaret, a fringe-dweller like herself who had been torn away from her mother. Margaret had suffered the fate Ella's mother and grandparents feared might happen to her. Margaret and her sister had been snatched by the police as they left school one day and bundled into a waiting car. Her mother had arrived on the scene just as this was happening; in the confusion Margaret feared that the police might shoot her mother, so she had gone willingly. In the end, it turned out that what the child had seen hanging from the white policeman's belt was not a gun but a bag containing handcuffs. Margaret, sent to the Cootamundra Domestic Training Home, felt isolated and depressed. She had never received any tuition in reading and writing. All she had been taught was to sew, sweep and clean. None of the girls at the home had ever seen a proper stove, yet they were expected to cook European recipes. If they made a mistake in the kitchen, using unfamiliar pots and pans and ingredients, their white teacher slapped their faces.

At thirteen, Margaret had been sent to work with a white family who were to pay her board and wages of one shilling and sixpence a week. But her employers had not paid her for five years, and fed her very poorly. The girl had no one to complain to, and, as she could neither read nor write, she had scant redress. Her employer appears to have been mentally disturbed. The woman had three children and must have been suffering from some phobia about cleanliness. If she found a dirty nappy she would rub Margaret's face in it. Margaret's life (and Ella's at this time) consisted of dusting, polishing, sweeping and scrubbing. Coals had to be carted up to bedrooms in buckets in the days before central heating.

Ella, older and stronger in character than Margaret, was outraged at the treatment her friend received and her employer's cruelty. She took up Margaret's cause with the Aboriginal Protection Board, but got nowhere, so she found Margaret a new job with friends of her own employer, at twenty-five shillings a week. The wage was duly paid.

This is how Ella's career as activist for the rights of Aborigines began. An Irish friend told her:

> Ella, you're a fighter. You'll always be noticed because of the colour of your skin, and you'll always feel you have to do things better than everyone else because of it.

When her beloved grandmother Kundaibark became worse, Ella returned to the Purfleet Aboriginal Mission – now designated an Aboriginal Reserve – to nurse her. Kundaibark, a committed Christian, had been nurse and midwife to her people. Although she had no formal training, she had acquired a fair amount of nursing skill which she passed on to Ella. While nursing her grandmother (and taking her place as bush nurse to the Aboriginal community), Ella met Joe Simon, a full-blooded Aboriginal who fell deeply in love with her. She refused to marry him while her grandmother needed constant nursing.

In spite of her fair skin and European features, Ella always felt she belonged among the Aboriginal people. Her grandmother had instilled in her from childhood the maxim: 'It's character that matters: not skin colour.' Now, having been to the city, acquired some self-confidence and more knowledge, Ella was determined to stand up for Aboriginal rights against the authoritarian Scottish-born manager who now ran the former mission. She was determined that with her city experience and her verbal skills, she would speak out for those who could not defend their own interests.

The manager took an instant dislike to Ella. He insisted on his right to enter houses as he wished and to send away any Aborigines who stood up for themselves. They were branded as troublemakers. One of Ella's uncles protested about the 'stolen children' who were brought to Purfleet and warned the manager that if he laid a finger on any of his children he would knock him down. Ella's uncle was ordered to leave the mission immediately. His children were to be sent to a reformatory. Ella raised an outcry to prevent her uncle and his family from having to leave their home. But the manager had by now marked Ella down as a troublemaker.

One day, the manager came barging into Kundaibark's tiny shack without knocking. Ella, standing behind the door, busy turning her grandmother in bed, was nearly knocked over. Tired and stressed, she lost her temper and told off the manager in no uncertain terms. He threatened to expel her. Fortunately, he was replaced before he could carry out his threat and Ella was allowed to stay with her grandmother on the condition she apologised … in writing. Ella, who could scarcely read, was embarrassed by her poor skills at writing. She had to ask someone else to write the letter of apology to the new manager for her. She vowed that one day she would learn to write properly.

When Kundaibark died, Ella was free to marry Joe Simon. They stayed on at Purfleet Reserve, where she continued to nurse the sick and act as midwife to the community.

During the Great Depression of the 1930s, life was hard for all Australians, black and white. As more and more Aborigines lost their jobs they flooded into the Reserve. In 1939, when war was declared, Joe tried to enlist in the army along with some of his Aboriginal friends. But he was rejected on medical grounds: the doctors discovered he had a weak heart.

Joe and Ella were employed by a farmer at Avoca who had been given a contract by the Australian Army to provide one of their camps with vegetables. Growing and picking the vegetables and digging up potatoes was hard, backbreaking work and had to be done in all weathers. To spare her husband, Ella would work all day in the fields with him, then cook dinner for the farmer and his family, and rise at 4 am each morning to pack vegetables ready for the army truck that called to take them to the base.

In 1945, the army camp was disbanded and Joe and Ella returned to their home at Purfleet Reserve with their child. This child seems to have died soon afterwards, but Ella does not give any further information, in accordance with Aboriginal tradition whereby a dead person is not named. After their return to Purfleet, Ella entered into a struggle with the manager for better facilities for her people. She wanted the women to have proper stoves in their houses (at Purfleet the women still cooked in camp ovens on open fires in the backyard) and for the manager to hand over to mothers their unpaid instalments of the recently awarded government benefit known as 'child endowment'.[3]

The manager, a mean and bitter Scot, ignored Ella's claims and hung onto her own child endowment for nearly six months. One day, determined not to be swindled out of money that was rightfully hers, she took a bus into town, went to an electrical store and ordered a cooking stove. Inwardly trembling at her daring, she calmly told the white store owner to send the stove out to her house and the account to the Purfleet manager as 'he has my child endowment and should pay out of that'. By using her head and a degree of daring for those times, Ella got her 'proper stove' and helped others to do the same.[4]

At this time, Ella's biological father was living with her. His wife was dead and his own family had rejected him. He was very sick and Ella had taken pity on him. The manager told her that even if he was her father, no white man could stay on an Aboriginal mission – this was despite the fact that Ella owned the land and house, which her grandparents had bequeathed to her.

In vain, Ella pleaded that her father had no one else to care for him. The manager was adamant. Ella was forced to put her father into a poorly managed all-white nursing home where he died. Having neglected him shamefully while he was ill, his legitimate children refused point-blank to allow Ella to attend her father's funeral. She tried to overcome the considerable pain and resentment this caused her by determining to educate herself better. She and Joe were members of the Presbyterian church. Helped by her local church, Ella taught herself to speak in public and borrowed books to fill the gaps in her inadequate education.

Ella was horrified to find that in order to leave the reserve, she, an Australian, needed a piece of paper which would act as:

> a passport in my own land. I had to have it to go to any place from which an Aboriginal was banned, to take government jobs and to leave the reserve. I could never work this out, in spite of my fight for rights. I had to have this piece of paper like a passport, to give me rights in my own land, to be a citizen of Australia – my own country. That manager told my uncle that the Aboriginal was really nobody – not a human being in the land which should have been his own by right of birth. I was born here, I am in my own right an Australian. But I had to fill in a form to get this passport to become a citizen.[5]

Joe and Ella moved away to the Gulargambone Reserve, where Ella helped the inhabitants to obtain a community hall, in which young people were able to learn to read and write. She dreamed that one day Aboriginal and mixed races would be shown a better life than the one forced on them by the white authorities. On reserves they were denied the right to open a bank account, or to go into town, even for medical reasons, without permission.

Ella Simon showed herself a natural leader. She was occasionally reviled by both sides for the colour of her skin, but continued in her efforts to help Aboriginal people help themselves. She did not wish to retreat to the past but to build a bridge to the future by obtaining citizenship, with its responsibilities and privileges.

In 1957, in her mid-fifties, Ella was finally granted a Certificate of Exemption from the degrading restrictions under which Aboriginal people were forced to live. She was allowed to open a bank account and to leave the reserve when she wanted to. She moved back to Purfleet.

Ella dreamed that one day 'her' people would achieve financial independence through their own efforts and gain proper medical facilities. She was angry that the manager kept their old age pension money and refused to give it to them so they could improve their situations. She lobbied visitors to the reserve, asking for better conditions and a chance for the women to use their skills to earn money.

In 1960, Ella was permitted to form a Purfleet branch of the Country Women's Association and was elected its first president. With a little capital provided by the Association she encouraged the women to continue traditional Aboriginal crafts and organised a committee to open the Gillawarra Gift Shop, selling Aboriginal artefacts. (Gillawarra was the name of the old bora ground, a few miles from Purfleet.)

Through further support from the Country Women's Association, she was able to arrange for electricity to be installed on the reserve. Profits from the gift shop paid for electric stoves for all the houses. It was a great step forward. Ella was now the spokesperson for the women on the reserve. She fiercely resisted the demands the white inspector put on behalf of the 'Protector of Aborigines' (Mr Donaldson) that light-skinned children be sent away. Donaldson painted rosy pictures to these light-skinned children of the delights awaiting them at the Cootamundra Domestic Training Home. Their eyes were opened when one little girl called Daisy believed him and let herself be sent away to be 'trained' at the Cootamundra Home. Daisy caught a chill and without proper care died there of pneumonia. After that women fought to stop their children being taken away from them, sometimes with success. But more often than not the children were removed.

Tourist buses started to call at Purfleet to buy the Aboriginal artefacts produced there. Ella did the shop's accounts and oversaw the staff. Her own baby had died – she had no other children herself, but cared for the children of others. She was a surrogate mother to many of the children on the reserve, determined that they should have better opportunities than she had been offered.

Ella had very little money but was always neatly dressed, even if her clothes were hand-me-downs from white people. She spoke with fluency and passion. It was the way she put her people's cause to the women of the CWA that gained their help in improving conditions for women on the reserve. This, together with her striking looks and warm personality, drew people to the cause.

None of the Purfleet children had ever seen the sea. Using money earned by the gift shop, Ella and a local schoolteacher started a scheme whereby Aboriginal children could spend holidays with white or Aboriginal families in Newcastle and go to the beach. She made sure the children had swimming costumes and shoes for their holidays, paying for them out of shop funds. There was no doctor on the reserve, so when the children needed in-patient treatment she accompanied them down to a hospital in Newcastle or Sydney. When roused, Ella could be a tiger, but as a nurse she was gentle and caring, much loved by everyone at Purfleet Mission.

In 1962, Ella was appointed Australia's first Aboriginal Justice of the Peace, so that she could help to fill in and witness documents for those who could not read and write. In her efforts to improve life on the reserve she concentrated on issues such as poor Aboriginal health and the lack of any medical facilities. These included pregnancy and ante-natal care; high rates of diabetes in adults; blindness in Aboriginal children caused by trachoma; and the segregation of whites and Aborigines in hospitals. Other issues which concerned her were the banning of Aborigines from public places; the meagre 'rations' of tea, sugar, tobacco and bread paid in lieu of wages by the Aboriginal Protection Board; and Aborigines' right to sit where they wanted to in the local cinema, where they were still discriminated against as 'fringe-dwellers from the blacks' camp'.

Ella was viewed as an 'uppity' troublemaker by the manager. When her husband died, she was evicted from her home, even though she owned the land on which her grandparents' house had been built. According to the manager, Ella's home was now under the control of the Housing Commission, and since the house was sub-standard according to their regulations, it was condemned and she had to leave. He was obviously settling old scores and did not offer Ella, now elderly, any alternative housing.

After a period of great anxiety when it appeared that she would be homeless, and as a result of efforts on her behalf by various concerned friends, Ella was eventually given a Housing Commission home at nearby Gillawarra. She continued to nurse old people and work at the gift shop for another year. But she resigned from the gift shop committee when the Black Panther Movement demanded a share of the store's profits to further its own aims. Ella felt saddened that the women who worked in the store on a voluntary basis were being forced to hand over money intended to help their own children.

Ella's health was now poor; she was too frail to carry on fighting. She had blazed a trail through a maze of prejudice and fear. In her final year, she dictated her memoirs to a typist for publication.[6] By then things had changed on the former Purfleet Mission. Ella commented:

> I read all the criticism about money given to Aborigines but I am writing down what happened during my lifetime. I know there are selfish people abusing the privileges my generation had to fight for but that's not because they are Aborigines. That's because they are *people*.

Ella believed that one of the distinguishing characteristics of human beings of all races is that:

> Some grow up to be greedy, grasping and anti-social while others don't. Some, because of trauma suffered in childhood, never sort out their problems and may have to turn to professional counsellors, to religion or drugs in attempts to sort out their problems.

A third group, in spite of suffering deprivation and abuse as children, have a strong sense of identity and a belief system implanted into them. Adversity and suffering strengthens them. They turn bad experiences outwards instead of inwards and convert their anger into determination to help others in similar or worse situations rather than into anti-social behaviour or drug taking. So it was with Ella Simon. 'Skin colour doesn't matter', she always said. 'In the end it's *character* that's important.'

Ella Simon died just before she reached her eightieth birthday. She was cremated and in accordance with her wishes, her ashes were scattered over the graves of Kundaibark and her husband. She had gone home to her people.

CHAPTER THIRTEEN

Florence Mary Taylor
(1879–1969)
AUSTRALIA'S FIRST FEMALE ARCHITECT

At the age of forty-one, thirteen years after she had gained her degree in architecture at the Sydney Institute of Technology, Florence Taylor, rejected by male members of her profession, managed to gain professional accreditation. After years spent trying to gain admission, in 1920 she was finally admitted as an associate (rather than a full member) of the New South Wales Institute of Architects.

Until 1923, there was no Board of Architects in New South Wales to register members of the profession.[1] Before this, when Florence was seeking admission as a member, the male-dominated Institute of Architects determined who gained professional accreditation and won architectural awards. They organised dinners and presentations and acted as the 'boy's club' of the profession of architecture.

In hindsight and in our less prejudiced age, it seems incredible that the Institute of Architects was able to reject the membership application of a truly exceptional woman like Florence Taylor. Not only was Florence a talented architect, she was also a fully qualified structural and civil engineer. But in spite of her excellent results on her architecture course, Florence was discriminated against by the professional body which should have welcomed her with open arms. For years she was able to work only as a designer rather than a fully fledged architect.

In addition to her other skills, Florence Taylor had a flair for publishing, was a good editor and technical journalist and a talented print-maker. She also made the first glider flight recorded in Australia by a woman. Despite this impressive range of achievements, she received little recognition during the early years of her professional life. It is only today that we can see her as a catalyst in the lengthy and tortured process by which Australian women fought for recognition in their chosen professions.

How did Florence manage to become an architect in the early years of this century? It was a male chauvinistic era. Most clients for important buildings believed any architect worth their salt must wear a small pointed beard and sport a bow tie. Florence followed a long and rocky road to gain accreditation and acclaim.

Florence Mary Parsons was born in England on 29 December 1879 at Bedminster near Bristol. She was the eldest of four clever and attractive daughters of John Parsons, a civil servant.[2]

In 1888[3] John Parsons, who suffered from a weak chest, immigrated to Australia in search of a warmer climate. He also believed he could give his daughters a better future in a new and developing country.

The Parsons family settled in Sydney. John Parsons was employed as a draftsman-clerk in the sewerage construction branch of the Parramatta Council, and with a regular income was able to educate Florence, the eldest and cleverest of his daughters, at a private school. Florence attended the Presbyterian Ladies' College, Croydon. At an early age she excelled at mathematics and was soon able to help her father with complex engineering calculations.

At first life in the antipodes went well for the Parsons. But disaster struck the family when John Parsons died prematurely in 1899, before he had had time to accumulate any significant assets. His widow received only a minute sum in compensation and the whole family faced considerable hardship. Australia was just emerging from the depression of the 1890s. There was no social security net to fall back on. Mrs Parsons inherited the family home in Sydney, but with younger siblings to feed, clothe and educate, it was necessary for Florence to leave school and go to work in an office to earn money.

Florence was only nineteen[4] when her father died and had to take on responsibility for supporting her mother and younger sisters. This could have been the death of her ambitions. Like so many young women of her period, Florence could have remained a typist or telephonist, condemned with the rest of her family to a life of genteel poverty.

However, Florence's ambitions remained. She found herself a job as a clerk with her father's friend F. E. Stowe, head of a combined architectural and engineering firm in Parramatta. At that time, construction disciplines were not as specialised as today; frequently the functions of architect and engineer would be combined in one office.

Highly intelligent and creative, Florence soon found menial tasks and clerical work boring. She decided to become an architectural draftsperson instead. As a woman of great spirit and purpose, she did something totally unusual for her period and enrolled herself for evening classes in architecture at the Sydney Technical College. She was the *only* woman studying building construction, quantity surveying and architectural drafting and found herself marooned in the midst of two hundred male students. She worked extremely hard and often topped the class.

Now in her early twenties, Florence was a tall, willowy, strikingly attractive young women. In addition to her architectural studies and her long working days, she managed to attend lectures at the School of Engineering at the University of Sydney as well. Here she was one of the first female students; engineering was also viewed as a tough, 'masculine' profession. But with her family responsibilities, work and study, Florence had attempted to achieve far too much for anyone, male or female. She studied hard in what little free time was available but failed her first year examinations in all architectural subjects.

This setback did not deter Florence. She was determined to repeat the year and set herself the goal of being in the top ten in her architecture class at the Sydney Institute of Technology which she accomplished. At the same time, she was serving her practical apprenticeship (or articles) with the Sydney architect Edmund Skelton Garton. The work she was given in Garton's office was anything but creative. She toiled over the tedious task of technical specification writing, while her male colleagues received all the more stimulating tasks, such as preparing sketches, designs and working drawings.

Florence was always the first to arrive at Garton's office, often as early as 7.30 am. She would work very hard in an attempt to finish her specification writing by lunchtime, hoping she would be given drafting or design work in the afternoon. But however hard she worked, she only received more and more specifications to write. The men continued to receive all the design work. Referring to her time in Garton's employ Florence would describe how 'The (specifications) seemed to be never ending. I thought I would never get around to designing homes and other buildings though I used to get in at 7.30 am every day in a desire to overcome my work load.'

Frustrated creativity prompted Florence to apply for another job as soon as she had completed her articles. She succeeded in getting a job as chief draftsperson in the prestigious office of John Burcham Clamp, the diocesan architect. Unlike her previous employer, Clamp recognised Florence's professional competence and dedication – she was allowed to design and was put in charge of the plans for some very expensive homes on Sydney's North Shore, which she did very well. But the name on the designs was always that of John Burcham Clamp, rather than her own.

But Florence's sense of purpose was strong. She *would* become a qualified architect. Finally, after eight years' arduous study, combined with practical experience in two architects' offices, in 1907, Florence completed her architectural course and graduated from an Arts course at the University of Sydney, gaining a BA. She had already qualified as a structural and a civil engineer: it was unheard of at that time that a mere woman could achieve so much.

Immediately after Florence qualified as an architect, John Clamp nominated her for associate membership of the New South Wales Institute of Architects so that she could receive official recognition by that august professional body. Clamp gave Florence an excellent reference. He praised her architectural skills and excellent design sense. All to no avail. As a woman, her nomination to join the Institute of Architects was rejected by the powerful men on the committee. Clamp was furious when he heard the committee's decision and demanded, 'Why did they reject her? On what grounds? She can design an entire home while an ordinary draftsman is still sharpening his pencil.'

Florence Parsons' male colleagues did not recognise her abilities and made it plain they did not want her to join them. But like other professional pioneer women, Flos Greig, Joan Rosanove and Dr Constance Stone, Florence refused to give up the right to practise the profession she loved and had been trained for.

However, she had to wait another thirteen years before her professional governing body, the Institute of Architects, finally admitted her as the first qualified female architect in New South Wales. In the meantime, the long years of rejection by the Institute did not deter Florence. Working as a draftsperson in John Clamp's office she had designed a large number of private homes in Mosman, Neutral Bay and Darling Point – for which, of course, she could not command an architect's salary.

While Florence was studying engineering she fell in love with one of her lecturers. George Augustine Taylor was as multi-talented, resourceful and adventurous as Florence. He did not feel threatened by her brilliance but admired her work.

George Taylor was an engineer by profession as well as a skilful cartoonist, working in black-and-white as a freelancer for the *Bulletin* and *Punch*. His friends were artistic and literary and he was a council member of the Royal Art Society of New South Wales. By the time he met Florence he had also become interested in the technology of wireless and telephony; he carried out much pioneering work in these fields, particularly for military purposes.

On 3 April 1907, Miss Florence Parsons married Mr George Taylor at St Stephen's Presbyterian Church, Sydney. It was a love match, and husband and wife shared many interests and ambitions.

Shortly after their marriage, George became interested in aviation and learned to fly gliders. He became so fascinated by aeronautics that he established his own factory where he manufactured gliders and light aircraft. In 1909, he promoted the Aerial League of Australia and expressed his view to the government that it was important to establish an air force. Urged on by her husband, Florence conquered an initial fear of heights and gained a pilot's licence. In 1909, she made the first glider flight ever attempted by a woman. There was enormous public interest when she took off in her glider from the Narrabeen sand hills near Sydney and she was cheered by all the onlookers. Flying and the romance with the air became a passion with both of them.

Florence and her husband went into business together and formed their own Building Publishing Company. They published major technical and professional journals such as *The Australian Engineer*, *Building*, *The Commonwealth Home* and the *Radio Journal of Australia*. In these building and engineering publications they promoted the interests of architects, engineers and builders and made the Australian Government and the public more aware of the merit of professionalism in construction activities.

As a feature writer and as the editor of a diverse range of journals, all published by their own company, Florence campaigned for urban planning, improved construction methods and superior material application. The Taylors advocated modernism in architecture and town planning. One outstanding example of their joint achievements was to organise a petition in which support from architects and engineers was enlisted for the acceptance of Walter Burley Griffin's revolutionary designs for the new national capital, Canberra.

Their publications became well known in the field of construction. However, it took considerable time before Florence's journalistic input became as highly respected as that of her husband.

In 1913, the Taylors founded the Town Planning Association of New South Wales. The following year they travelled abroad and spent some time in America. They greatly admired Theodore Roosevelt's progressive outlook, in particular his involvement with the finalisation of the Panama Canal project.[5]

Florence and George Taylor's marriage was a happy one in every respect. They spent many exciting and productive years together, both as business partners and as professional colleagues. George was a devoted husband and an exceptional man, having succeeded in many differing fields, in spite of the fact that he was an epileptic. Florence had to learn to manage his condition and prise open his teeth to free his airways when he succumbed to an epileptic fit. Perhaps the fear that epilepsy was congenital (although now it is believed not to be) was the reason the Taylors never had children, but concentrated on their careers.

Then, after twenty-one years of happy marriage, disaster struck. George died in their Sydney home on 20 January 1928. He had an epileptic fit while taking a bath alone in their house, slumped into the bath water and drowned. Florence found his corpse when she returned home. She was devastated and grief ridden.

Florence was determined she would never marry again. She carried on their joint publishing business and took full responsibility for managing it. But she had to reduce her workload and cease publishing eight out of their eleven periodicals. She carried on producing the most successful of their journals, *Building* (later *Building, Lighting and Engineering*) and *The Australian Engineer*.

Florence was a fighter. She submerged her grief and loss in a surge of creativity, threw herself into a host of professional activities and produced several town planning schemes and civil engineering projects. The time she had to spend on running the commercial side of their publishing firm made it necessary for her to employ draftsmen to draw up the detailed work for the vast engineering projects she designed.

Her biggest challenges were traffic subways for Sydney and an express route from the centre of the city to its eastern suburbs. She also had the foresight to realise that Sydney Airport would eventually become overcrowded and that the city would need a second airport, so she designed one to be based out at Newport, to the north of Sydney.

In spite of Florence's technical aspirations and skills, she remained extremely feminine, and always dressed in the height of fashion. In Australian's male-dominated society it must have been most disconcerting for men that a highly feminine woman like Florence Taylor achieved so much. In descriptions of the period, she appears as a walking contradiction: an extremely attractive and feminine woman, who was highly competent in 'masculine' disciplines. To male colleagues and critics she was often perceived as a threat. Some saw her as far too forceful in personality; other male critics hinted that she must be eccentric in wanting to enter a male world rather than staying home and baking cakes. Art historian John Berger has argued the case that:[6]

> men look, women appear – men are socialised to be active and women to
> be passive models. If this is so, what happens when women begin to
> 'look' as well as to 'appear'? How should women manage the com-
> plexities of 'appearing' when undertaking an active role in public life?

Florence Taylor addressed this tension by accentuating her femininity. She loudly proclaimed her conviction that 'every woman should be able to stand shoulder to shoulder with the men folk without losing the characteristics of her sex.'[7]

Florence's strategy was to wear expensive clothes, French perfume, long kid gloves and carry lace-frilled parasols.[8] In the Federation era, women dressed to kill. She sported sweeping skirts, piled-up hair under eye-catching hats in the style of *My Fair Lady*. Defiantly she continued wearing flowing skirts and the ultra feminine look, even when 'flappers' bobbed their hair and shortened their skirts in the jazz-mad Roaring Twenties, by which time she was in her forties.

Contemporary journalists swallowed the bait she offered them and gave her all the publicity she needed. But instead of reporting her achievements alongside her outstanding good looks, they described how 'despite these exacting occupations, Mrs Taylor's gracious personality is the very essence of femininity.[9] Despite her achievements in male strongholds Mrs Taylor is essentially feminine. She has a weakness for outsize hats with ostrich feathers.'[10]

These statements about 'gracious personality' and 'hats with ostrich feathers' create an impression that Florence Taylor's claim to fame was not her architectural and town-planning design skills, nor in the influence of her articles advocating better town planning and airport facilities for Sydney, but rather in her skill at presenting herself as a beautiful lady in a large and extravagantly feathered hat. This misleading description led some men in power to refer cynically to Florence Taylor as 'The Great Lady of Sydney Town'.

Today, some women in male-dominated professions react to criticism by taking on men on their own ground, deepening their voices and power-dressing. Florence did the opposite. One wonders whether, by wearing the outrageous fashions of an upper-class woman of the Edwardian era, she actually diminished her reputation as an architect, engineer and town planner.

Would Florence have been taken more seriously as a professional woman if she had dressed more like a man? Probably not. Australia was then so male dominated that in the first half the twentieth century Australian women were generally not taken seriously, *whatever* they were wearing. Those were the days when a woman's place was firmly in the home. Most men regarded women as inferior in brainpower, at the mercy of their 'frail' physiques and 'feminine' whims.

Fortunately for Florence Taylor, she lived long enough to experience a marked change in men's attitudes towards women in business and the professions. She was a perfectionist, never satisfied with local knowledge, particularly in respect to town planning and engineering. Consequently, she travelled to Europe and America to broaden her own vision. In America, which was more in love with the new and with success than Australia (where 'tall poppies' in every sphere were constantly denigrated and women seen as totally inferior to men), Florence fascinated all those she met with her knowledge, her design skills and the charm of her personality. She expressed delight with the labour-saving designs of American homes, their excellent plumbing, and the open and easier way of life for women. In return, her hosts gave her a detailed run-down of plans and schemes just completed or on the drawing-board. She proved herself an excellent ambassador for Australia – and, just as important, she and her revolutionary ideas *were* taken seriously by her fellow American professionals. The American architects and town planners were most impressed by the breadth of Mrs Taylor's knowledge on many aspects of architecture and planning, and by the range of technical publications produced by her company.

Enriched with a host of new and progressive ideas, she returned home. Full of enthusiasm for the approach to town planning in Europe and America, she conveyed her newly acquired knowledge through her articles and speeches to members of various professional bodies, trying to convince her largely sceptical and predominantly male colleagues that Australia was lagging behind America in the fields of town and regional planning.

In spite of her outrageous way of dressing, the technical professions eventually started to take Florence Taylor more seriously. Gradually, her progressive ideas took hold. Even the diehard prejudices of some of her male colleagues slowly mellowed as she grew older. And the journals she continued to publish after her husband's death had became highly respected among the engineering and building industries.

In middle age, Florence sponsored and gave financial support to several design awards, some of which were named in her honour. The most important award was that given under the auspices of the Australian Institute of Metals, duly named the Florence M. Taylor Medal.

In 1939, Florence was honoured by King George VI with an OBE (Order of the British Empire). Much later, when she was in her eighties, she was awarded a CBE (Commander of the British Empire), a clear indication that, finally, her enormous competence and dedication were fully appreciated.

Florence's wide interests kept her in close contact with a large number of friends and colleagues. In her later years, she was associated or involved with an astonishing number of organisations, clubs and societies, many of them almost exclusively male. She had become an honorary member of the Australian Institute of Builders and of the Engineering Society of New South Wales; a life member of the Master Builders' Federation of Australia and of the Master Builders' Association of New South Wales (whose Award of Honour she received in 1952); a life member of the Town Planning Association of

New South Wales; a member of the Society of Women Writers; a member of the Arts Club; a member of the International Society of Australia; a member of the Royal Aero Club of New South Wales, and of the prestigious British Royal Society of Arts – an honour granted to few Australian men, let alone women.

All her life she spoke out for women to be taken seriously in whatever field they entered. She also voiced an unpopular opinion at that time, namely that marriage could, and often did, confine women and limit their talents and potential. She dared to speak about the sadness of 'the empty nest' syndrome. She was one of the first to voice an opinion that in their later years, when children had left home, married women with no work experience or qualifications to fall back on often become deeply depressed. (Now we know that many of the symptoms attributed to the physical side of menopause are psychological, caused by this 'empty nest' syndrome.) When Florence was in her mid-seventies she stated her credo that:

> For a woman to marry, to get trapped in the small confines of her home and never be articulate, is a disgrace. There is not enough mental occupation in home duties only and women never get the chance to shoulder life's full responsibilities.[11]

Despite all Florence Taylor's achievements, even in later life she could not avoid the fact that there was often more interest in her appearance than in her remarkable record of activities. A journalist writing in the *Daily Telegraph*, on 30 December 1959, observed:

> It would be hard to find anyone more feminine than Mrs Florence Taylor. And almost impossible to find any woman with less feminine interests. When I dropped in to see Mrs Florence Taylor on her 80th birthday yesterday, I was struck by her beautiful perfume, her frivolous hat, her soft feminine dress. But immediately she began talking about tunnels, bridges, high density buildings and car parks.

It is interesting that the anonymous reporter (male or female?), did not bother to write down one single word Florence uttered about urban planning, architectural design and the problems confronting the built environment of Sydney. Florence Taylor's brilliant ideas and sophisticated concepts – including her important plans for a second airport for Sydney, which would have saved airlines from the long delays entering and leaving that city plaguing them for years – must have been beyond the comprehension of the reporter, who confined their piece to superficial comments on Florence's femininity.

In 1961, Florence's health started to deteriorate. Now in her eighties, she finally retired from her wide variety of occupations and spent her final years living with her younger sister Annis Parsons, who nursed her until her death.

Florence Taylor died in Sydney on 13 February 1969. Like her brilliant husband, she was cremated in the Anglican church. It is interesting to observe that the enquiring and analytical minds of George and Florence Taylor made them change their religious faiths, in George's case more than once.

The achievements of this remarkable woman are commemorated in the annual Florence Taylor Award for outstanding services to engineering, currently administered each year by the Australian Society of Mechanical Engineers.

CHAPTER FOURTEEN

Photograph reproduced courtesy of the Hon. Peg Lusink.

Joan Mavis Rosanove (Lazarus)
(1896–1974)
WHO FOUGHT FOR THE RIGHT TO PRACTISE LAW
ON EQUAL TERMS WITH MALE COLLEAGUES

Joan Rosanove, a woman who battled prejudice against women in the legal profession all her life, commented wryly:

> To be a [female] lawyer you must have the stamina of an ox and a hide like a rhinoceros. And when they kick you in the teeth you must look as if you hadn't noticed.

Charismatic Joan Rosanove, daughter of a Jewish barrister, was more than a match for most men. She endured discrimination because she was a woman in an almost exclusively male profession and because she was Jewish (by race rather than religion). In Melbourne's clubbish Anglo-Saxon Protestant legal circles, the old boy network operated strongly to keep out women and foreigners. Most of Joan's legal colleagues had bonded together as boys. They had played cricket and rugger against each other at Victoria's exclusive private schools. They did not welcome outsiders into their club. In spite of her remarkable talents in the courtroom, it would take over a quarter of a century for Joan Rosanove's intelligence, tenacity and superb cross-examining skills to receive their due recognition.

Joan was born into the law. Her father, Mark Lazarus, was unusual in working as an amalgam, operating both as a solicitor and a barrister, with offices in Ballarat and Melbourne. Joan's mother, born Ruby Braham, came from another leading legal family, who were part-Jewish and part-Irish. Joan's parents enjoyed a happy and stable marriage with seven lively, attractive and intelligent children. Two of their sons entered the law in addition to Joan. She was the second daughter in this large and multi-talented family.

Joan and her sister inherited their mother Ruby's sparkling dark eyes and long dark lashes. As a plump, dimple-cheeked teenager, Joan feared she was destined to play second fiddle to her elder sister Vida, whose slender figure had a devastating effect on the local youth.[1] While Vida flirted with the boys, Joan Mavis, with her dark unruly curls, had to push her younger siblings around the streets of Ballarat in a pram.

Joan and Vida attended Loreto Convent before changing to Clarendon College, Ballarat.[2] Bob Menzies, who attended a neighbouring school, recalled Joan as the more intelligent of the two sisters.

In those days, wives of successful middle-class men like Mark Lazarus were not expected to do housework. They were expected to employ maids, run the household and bring up children. An endless succession of Irish girls lived in as domestic staff, washed, cleaned, cared for the younger children and did most of the cooking. Joan recalled that most of them were called either 'Bridie' or 'Cissy'.

At the time when the majority of the middle-class girls were taught accomplishments and prepared for marriage rather than educated for jobs or careers, both the Lazarus girls were encouraged to study hard by their father. They showed scant interest in learning about household management, although Joan did learn the rudiments of cooking from her mother, who was far more interested in dressing beautifully and attending the races than in being a housewife.

At the age of fifteen, Joan was allowed to accompany her father to the prestigious Selborne Chambers, where Melbourne's leading barristers had their chambers, and to sit in the courtroom. Joan was fascinated by the drama of the law courts: she vowed that one day she would become a barrister with rooms in Selborne Chambers.

On leaving school, she became articled to her father as a law clerk and worked in his Melbourne office. However, her mother felt that Joan was too young to live away from home. So every morning Joan would rise at 5 am, cycle to Ballarat Station, catch the 6.45 train to Melbourne and work in her father's office, as well as studying compulsory law subjects at Melbourne University. Then she would return home to Ballarat by the 8 pm train, eat the dinner cooked for her by one or other of the servants and work on her law assignments. So much hard work in pursuit of her ambition meant little time for socialising.

Cycling to the station slimmed Joan down until she became just as attractive as her mother and sister.

Joan's closest friend at university was a pharmacy student, Annie Cunningham, who was of Scottish Protestant descent. Annie was invited to tea at Queen's College by a male student with Scottish connections. He had a close friend who was a medical student, so Annie took Joan along with her. Both girls were charmed by the lively, amusing auburn-haired medic, Emmanuel (Mannie) Rosanove. Mannie's father was a Russian-born Jew, an agricultural expert who worked in Broken Hill, who had worked in Palestine before migrating to Australia. Annie found Mannie extremely attractive and amusing:

she went out with him a few times while Joan went out with their host, the Scottish student.

Annie, a practical Scot, soon realised that a prolonged relationship with Jewish-born Mannie was bound to bring serious problems. One day they were discussing the subject when Joan, who had also taken a strong liking to Mannie, observed, 'Annie, you have a Jew while I have a Scot. What about a swap?'

So Joan and Mannie started to go out together. Their only means of transport was Mannie's ancient and unreliable motorbike with sidecar, which he expected Joan to get out and push, whenever it broke down. Joan's old friend from Ballarat days, Bob Menzies (the future Prime Minister of Australia), was also studying law at Melbourne University and often helped the pair of them push-start Mannie's motorbike when it broke down on campus.

At the time when Joan started working as an articled clerk in her father's office, only a handful of outstanding women worked in the law. Although Melbourne University's Law School had been operating since 1857, for its first forty years women were denied admittance. The argument men in power used to prevent the admission of women to law school was the hoary old fable that, as their brains were small, studying would have a bad effect on female health and render them sterile – although for some reason this did not happen to men who studied hard! The authorities also claimed that women would not have the necessary toughness to deal with the horrifying details of sexual depravity and domestic violence encountered in legal practice. Joan would prove these arguments wrong on all counts.

In Joan Rosanove's day, there was male prejudice against women lawyers in every State in Australia. When they were employed by the government, women lawyers had to fight for the right to be paid the same as their male colleagues.

In 1917, when Joan Lazarus (as she then was) gained her LLB, most of the male students had been called away to fight in World War I.[3] Possibly Melbourne University authorities were embarrassed at the high proportion of women graduating in law. The ceremony that marked their admission to the bar was delayed for two years until June 1919, so that male students could finish their degrees and make the ceremony seem more 'serious' and less female.

Reporting Joan's entry to the law, the newspapers placed her name at the bottom of the list and ignored her when trying to spot which students would become barristers and judges. Only the *Jewish Herald* commented favourably on Joan's achievements, describing how 'Miss Lazarus was the first Jewess in Australia to be admitted to the law'.

The fact that Joan was Jewish as well as female intensified discrimination against her from Melbourne's Anglo-Saxon Protestant legal fraternity. This tightly bonded clique with their antipathy to Jews and women lawyers would ensure that in later years Joan Rosanove's many applications to take silk (or become a QC) were passed over in favour of less qualified candidates – who were, of course, both male and Protestant.

Ironically, neither Joan nor her husband-to-be actually practised the Jewish faith: both the Rosanove and Lazarus families saw themselves as Australians first and foremost. But multiculturalism had not been invented, Australia was still a racist society and unsympathetic to women.

Mr Ah Ket, a Chinese barrister trying vainly to practise in Melbourne, once told Joan: 'You and I have chosen the wrong profession and will never satisfy our ambitions. Neither of us will ever be made a judge: you because you are a woman, I because I am Chinese.' He recommended that they both return to university and study medicine, because he felt there was less discrimination against doctors from 'ethnic' backgrounds than in the legal profession. The idea of going back to university and studying medicine held little appeal for Joan. The law was in her blood. She was determined to succeed in court, a side of the law that attracted her dramatic temperament and vivid personality. The histrionic side of her character, which stemmed from her mother and her Jewish heritage, might have enabled Joan to become a successful actress. Certainly her acting abilities stood her in good stead in a career in which many theatrical techniques are employed by barristers.

Fortunately, Joan was blessed with a strong constitution, which meant she could stand for long hours in court without tiring. Her deep contralto voice never became shrill when addressing the court; this and her personal charisma would prove an asset with juries, confronted (as Joan described in an interview with *Table Talk*) 'with the spectacle of a comely woman locked in seemingly unequal combat with a man'.[4]

In July 1919, Mark Lazarus instructed his daughter in her first brief. It was nearly a disaster: the prejudiced judge was loath to listen to her evidence. However, Joan held her ground and won her case. Under the laws of the State of Victoria, lawyers were admitted to practise both as barristers and as solicitors and could appear in both roles, although most chose one or other branch of the profession. Young lawyers who did both, the 'amalgams', gained excellent experience in both office and court work.

From the outset Joan encountered strong prejudice from certain judges. Anti-feminine prejudice in court was especially marked in one case, tried by Mr Justice McArthur. Joan was defending Alfred Thomas Ozanne, Labor MP for Corio, who had sued the *Geelong Advertiser* for slander. Mark Lazarus had accepted the case but then discovered he was defending in the Ballarat court. So Joan, still relatively inexperienced and only in her early twenties, had to defend Ozanne in the Supreme Court of Victoria against an experienced barrister twice her age, and cross-examine Billy Hughes, then Prime Minister of Australia.[5]

Hughes was an experienced politician, practised at techniques to fend off awkward questions. He *was* somewhat deaf and played on this, taking care to shield himself from Joan Lazarus's piercing questions behind his hearing aid. As the trial wore on the politician's deafness became progressively worse, allowing him sufficient time to formulate suitably evasive answers. However loud Joan bellowed, Billy Hughes pretended he could not hear her – until he had played for time to consider his reply. Of course the anti-feminist Mr Justice McArthur did nothing to help Joan. The Ozanne case dragged on for months before Billy Hughes' delaying tactics won the day. Joan and her father suffered a humiliating defeat.

But Joan was a fighter. Defeat made her even more determined to succeed. She became smarter, worked harder and won most of her cases in Ballarat and Melbourne. She was astute enough to realise that to succeed as a woman in a man's world she must capitalise on every advantage that offered. She emphasised her femininity, dressing fashionably, wearing very high heels to make her petite slim figure appear taller and hence more imposing. Fortunately for Joan, she had an outstanding personality: her husky contralto voice, combined with a rapier-like wit, made her a charismatic figure and a formidable opponent in the courts. She had a fund of witty stories for every occasion; hardbitten Melbourne courtroom journalists loved writing about her because she was so entertaining and never patronising towards them, unlike some of her male colleagues.

When the proposed marriage of Joan Lazarus to Dr Emmanuel Rosanove was announced, one journalist commented:

> All kinds of cases are absorbed by her brief bag, and among these, divorce cases are most prominent. If Miss Lazarus shrinks from marriage – she is yet almost too young to give the matter serious thought – it will be because of a prejudicial idea born of an extensive experience in the courts, that marriage is a failure; the number of [divorce] cases she has handled tend to prove that it is so.

Although Joan must have realised it would not be easy to combine the joint role of barrister and wife of a young doctor with a busy practice, Mannie Rosanove was the man she wanted. And when Joan wanted something, she usually got it.

On 2 September 1920, Miss Joan Lazarus and Dr Emmanuel Rosanove were married by Rabbi Lenzer. This ceremony probably took place out of deference to Mannie's parents, who were more orthodox than Ruby and Mark Lazarus. The bride and groom, both highly intelligent and hardworking, were obviously well suited. Mark Lazarus could not help feeling slightly antagonistic to his new son-in-law for taking his much loved daughter away from the Ballarat courtroom, where she was now making a name for herself, to a sleepy, isolated country town like Tocumwal, on the Murray River. Mark Lazarus was also worried because he knew Mannie had spent all his savings to buy into a general practice – as was usual in the days before a national health service was introduced.

After a brief honeymoon the new bride found herself in a small wooden house in the centre of Tocumwal. She was no longer a barrister but the wife and unpaid secretary of a country GP. Their little wooden house was extremely primitive, a far cry from her parents' home in Ballarat. Like most bush homes at that period, it had an outside lavatory complete with gigantic huntsman spiders and no piped hot water – only a cold tap set in the kitchen wall, connected to an outside water tank. The kitchen had a temperamental wood-burning stove that demanded patience and cookery skills, which Joan did not possess.

Housekeeping in the bush was not Joan's strong point: her husband soon observed 'as a housewife Joan is a marvellous lawyer'. She had done a crash course in cooking and picked up hints from her mother and the maids, but although Joan was a devoted wife to Mannie, she never took much interest in the details of cooking or housework. In this small New South Wales country town, where the train only ran three times a week, uneducated country girls flatly refused to work at Dr Rosanove's combined house and surgery because they feared they might catch some fatal disease there. The few girls that did apply for jobs were either mentally retarded or too fond of the bottle and provided Joan and Mannie with scorched shirts and culinary disasters.

Adapting to the role of wife of a country GP in a pioneering society, where women were seen as inferior to men, was not easy for a city lawyer. To add to their problems, Joan's first child was stillborn. This was her first serious setback: like women today who experience cot death through no fault of their own, she had to work through a period of intense grief and guilt.

Their second child, Rose Margaret (Peg), was born at Tocumwal in 1922. Mannie's medical practice proved a tiring one. He was constantly on call with little free time and had to make home visits to remote areas in emergencies. In the 1920s, Tocumwal was too small to warrant a commercial pharmacy so Mannie had to spend long hours making up his own prescriptions. Joan missed the drama and excitement of the courtroom and found no friends to share her interests.

When the visiting GP from neighbouring Cobram told them with pride, 'I've been here for thirty-four years tomorrow,' Joan and Mannie looked at each other, each thinking that it was high time to move on. So Mannie put the practice on the market and sold it within a month.

Much to Joan's delight, they moved back to Melbourne.[6] In the northern suburb of Westgarth, Dr Emmanuel Rosanove took out a huge overdraft to buy a combined practice and home only a few minutes by train from the city, so that his young wife could continue with her profession. She was longing to return to legal practice, and she was fortunate that Mannie was an exceptionally understanding husband. In those days, it was considered positively shameful that a professional man would even consider allowing his wife to go out to work. But instead of demanding Joan turn into the 'Angel of the Home', her husband had the wisdom and maturity to encourage her to employ a nanny for her child and return to practising law. This would not prove easy, because by now the legal profession was overcrowded with male lawyers back in practice after fighting in World War I.

On 2 September 1923, the Melbourne *Herald* found it important enough to record that Mrs Rosanove had signed the Roll of Counsel of the Victorian Bar, undertaking that henceforth she would work only as a barrister.

An interview with an admiring journalist for *Table Talk* recorded that the attractive Mrs Rosanove was the first woman in Victoria to work solely as a barrister when she was still only in her mid-twenties. But male solicitors flatly refused to send her work. They rationalised their prejudices by claiming clients did not want 'women to defend them'.

As Joan could not get chambers in the traditional barristers' building, Selborne Chambers, Mannie had to rent a tiny backroom office for her in a dilapidated building in Chancery Lane, where cockroaches lurked in the cracks and rats gnawed Joan's legal books during the night. In between running her house at Westgarth and organising a stream of changing domestic staff and nannies to take charge of Peg, Joan sat alone in her tiny office and waited for briefs. She waited in vain: the only briefs she did receive came from her father's office. And when she did go into court, she experienced discrimination from patriarchal judges like the distinguished Mr Justice à Beckett Weigall, who would either yawn or look bored when Joan was called upon to plead.

This particular judge absolutely loathed the idea of women 'invading law'. He preferred to concentrate on a fly on the wall rather than watch a mere woman perform in court. Joan had no option but to grit her teeth and bear it. Her briefs were few but she made the most of them. Her rare but striking court appearances and her examining skills invariably attracted newspaper publicity.

In 1925, Joan decided to leave the Bar and had her name removed from the Roll of Counsel. Her abrupt departure was sparked by a traumatic incident in which a Jewish legal colleague named Philip Jacobs, on the point of departing to spend a year in England, offered Joan the temporary use of his room in exclusive Selborne Chambers 'to get the fellows used to having a woman there'. Immediately after they heard of Phil Jacobs' offer, the male inmates of Selborne Chambers called a protest meeting. They were *outraged* at the thought of a woman's presence amongst them. Phil Jacobs was informed by the directors of Selborne Chambers (Joan Rosanove's fellow barristers) that if he allowed Mrs Rosanove to use his room, they would have no option but to cancel his lease.

Had Joan Rosanove considered using Philip Jacobs' room as a brothel rather than to practise law, her legal 'colleagues' could not have been more outraged by her proposed presence. This hurtful and public rejection by her colleagues was one of the most humiliating moments in Joan Rosanove's entire career, the 'kick in the teeth' that she did appear to have noticed. After so many 'kicks in the teeth', Joan felt it was pointless trying to continue practising solely as a barrister. She realised she would never receive briefs from solicitors, however good she was in court, if her own professional colleagues would not support her.

Determined to prove herself, she decided to put up her brass plate at home and work from a joint suite of consulting rooms there. She would return to being an 'amalgam' – practising as a solicitor and also appearing in court on occasions as a barrister. She would limit herself to those areas of the law she knew best, criminal and divorce law.

In view of the overwhelming male prejudice which had been displayed against her, this decision proved a wise one. Over the next twenty-two years Joan Rosanove became incredibly successful, handling thousands of cases and earning a very good income. She specialised in defending women and twice appeared for females accused of murder, one of whom was a backyard abortionist. She did not succeed in getting them acquitted, but in both cases the women were found guilty of the lesser charges of manslaughter.

She went to the trouble of designing her own version of the legal costume. Under her barrister's robe Joan added a distinctively feminine touch, a *broderie anglaise* frill around the starched linen collar, from which hung two white bands. In court her beautiful dark intelligent eyes and her dazzling smile were seen to their best advantage set off by her white legal wig.

During working hours, the Rosanoves, Westgarth home was filled with Mannie's patients and Joan's clients. 'Crocks and crooks', as she and Mannie joked in private, were their speciality. Like John Mortimer's fictitious barrister Rumpole with his terrible Timpson family, one curiously inefficient family of burglars now formed the foundation of Joan Rosanove's criminal practice. She soon discovered that getting members of this feckless family off their charges of burglary was a thankless task: no sooner was one free than another family member would be arrested. The parents were always desperately keen for their offspring to be out of gaol by Christmas. It took Joan some time to realise that this antipodean Timpson family's wish for a Christmas reunion was not so they could sing carols together, but because the Christmas holidays (when wealthy Melbournians were away at the beach) were much the best time to do a spot of housebreaking.

Joan's burglar clients combined to protect her home. As long as Joan Rosanove defended criminals, the Rosanove residence was never burgled; but when her divorce cases became so numerous that she had to give up criminal work, their 'magic' immunity from burglary ceased.

Eventually Joan's dual life as wife and barrister became so hectic that she found it difficult to find the time to buy clothes. That is, until the Melbourne *Truth*, which specialised in sensational court cases, reporting her spirited performance in the lower court (where legal gowns and wigs were not worn), commented that Joan Rosanove was a 'haphazard dresser'. From then on, Joan determined to spend on designer clothes, shoes and expensive hats. She paid a small fortune for one particularly flattering red hat, which became her trademark in the lower court. Joan Rosanove always maintained that women in the law should be allowed to tax-deduct money spent on good well-cut clothes, as these formed part of their stock in trade along with their armoury of legal books.

In private life, Joan's good manners remained unchanged. But once she entered the courtroom in her white wig and black gown she took on a different persona: she could become as tenacious, tough and inquisitorial as her male colleagues. At the peak of her legal career, Joan Rosanove was handling one-eighth of Victoria's divorce list.[7] By the end of the 1930s, she had become well known for fighting for women's interests in breach of promise or divorce cases, where the law was often stacked against them. To gain a divorce, women needed to prove cruelty or adultery on *various* occasions by the husband. Faced with an attractive woman in a wig with a charming smile and dimpled cheeks, powerful and wealthy men defending themselves against charges brought by their wives often became tongue-tied, or trapped themselves into admissions they had no wish to make. Joan Rosanove's verbal skills became a legend in the divorce courts, along with her flair for discovering exactly what assets the husband possessed that had not been declared to the court.

Through Joan's burning desire to see that women were not taken advantage of, many men found themselves paying far more in alimony or property settlements than they had envisaged.

At this period, most legal firms looked on divorce cases as being an unsavoury branch of the law. Many male barristers flatly refused to touch divorce and advised their clients to take their business elsewhere. Such an attitude was extremely distressing to women undergoing the harrowing process of separation and divorce. Divorce was a procedure that carried strong undertones of disapproval in the rigid paternalistic society of Australia before World War II.

In contrast to the prevailing attitudes of lawyers, whenever women lacking in self-confidence and distressed by the thought of a court appearance arrived in Joan Rosanove's office, they were greeted with kindness and understanding. But Joan had a totally different way of dealing with arrogant Toorak ladies who looked down their noses at her and announced, 'My normal solicitors are Messrs X and X. But they say they don't deal with *dirty* matters like divorce, so I've *had* to come to *you*.'

Joan found the perfect way to deal with this. She would smile sweetly at the arrogant lady and touch the bell concealed under her desk for her assistant, the faithful Miss Caffrey, to enter. Then she would turn to her and say, 'Miss Caffrey, this lady's usual solicitors are Messrs X and X. But she tells us they don't do *dirty* work; so she has had to come to us to get her a divorce.' Miss Caffrey would give an understanding nod, return to her desk and add twenty guineas to that particular client's account as an 'annoyance' fee.

In 1932, Joan was in her late thirties and her daughter, Peg, was ten. Joan, who had felt she was too old to have another child, became pregnant again. She solved the problem of whether or not to go to work during her pregnancy by planning an extended trip overseas with her husband and daughter, determined not to let her male colleagues have the pleasure of sniggering over her increasing girth in the communal robing room. She planned to have her baby in London. Mannie had been talking about studying overseas for a post-graduate qualification in dermatology, having been appointed as a part-time clinical assistant in dermatology at the Alfred Hospital. She decided they would combine both aims. Naturally the press were not told the real reason for their departure.

Joan asked their old university friend, Bob Menzies, for an official letter of introduction which would open doors for them in London and America. A locum was engaged for Mannie's practice and Joan's father agreed to take care of her legal clients. On 26 July 1932, the Rosanoves boarded the SS *Mariposa*, to find their cabin brimming with red roses and *bon voyage* telegrams from friends and relatives.

The Rosanoves left the ship at San Francisco and travelled by train to Seattle, then on to Vancouver and over the Rockies by Canadian Pacific. They ended their spectacular train journey in New York, then crossed the Atlantic to England. They rented an apartment in London's elegant Buckingham Gate, and found a leading Harley Street obstetrician for Joan. Mannie attended postgraduate lectures at London teaching hospitals, and Peg was sent to a private school in Knightsbridge, while Joan went sightseeing. On 28 November 1932, Judith Anne Rosanove was born in a nursing home in Devonshire Place. Shortly after the birth, Mannie left for Edinburgh to be examined for membership of the Royal College of Physicians. He passed with flying colours.

Joan met three English female barristers who told her that nearly one hundred women were now practising as barristers in Britain. She attended meetings of the Fabian Women's Group discussing Britain's economic crisis where the Depression was causing severe social problems for women and families. Joan, an excellent public speaker, talked to various women's organisations, giving them an Australian point of view on women's rights and conditions of work.

In February 1933, Mannie and Joan took the boat-train to Vienna to attend lectures by leading Viennese skin specialists. The Rosanoves had intended to travel on to Berlin, where friends had offered them the loan of their apartment, but Jewish friends warned them not to go. Hitler's Brownshirts were persecuting Jews, confiscating their assets, beating them up in the streets. The first pitiful flood of Jewish refugees was escaping, others were 'disappearing'. It was too dangerous. So on 7 April 1933, Dr and Mrs Rosanove, an English-trained Norland nanny in her brown uniform, and their two little girls embarked for Australia on the *Cathay*.

Back in Melbourne, the press described how Mrs Rosanove, the famous barrister, arrived with her six-month-old baby in her arms. They said Joan was 'the latest word in smartness – hair immaculately waved and crowned by a tiny hat in the latest style'.

After an absence of ten months, Joan was pleased to return to the courtroom. Mannie sold the Westgarth general practice and took rooms in Collins Street where he put up his brass plate as a dermatologist. Eventually they built themselves another home, a large two-storey house just off Orrong Road.

Joan never refused an invitation to speak out against injustice to women and those from a non-English speaking background. And she was haunted by what she had heard about the persecution of Jews in Europe. On behalf of a committee of left-wing writers and artists, she was asked by the author Katharine Susannah Prichard to handle a clear case of government injustice to a Jewish Czech journalist named Egon Kisch. Katharine Prichard, pale, composed and elegant, visited Joan and handed over money she and other supporters had organised to pay for Kisch's defence at a public rally.

Kisch, who had been living in Germany, had been due to address a series of left-wing meetings about the dangers of Hitler's Germany, where he would plead for world peace. But the Australian Government had become alarmed when King Alexander of Serbia was shot down by a Czech gunman. This led to a series of raids on Czech socialists and the result was that the Australian Government panicked and decided to ban Kisch from entering Australia.

Although Egon Kisch had a British visa, on arrival at Fremantle he had been denied entry to Australia on the grounds that he was actively involved in communist propaganda, and his passport was seized. In Parliament, Menzies issued the unfortunate statement: 'Kisch shall *not* set foot on Australian soil.' Joan was placed in a position of divided loyalties between her support of Kisch as a fellow Jew and her friendship with her old university chum Robert Menzies. She could have backed out at this stage. But having recently returned from Europe, she knew that Kisch could face a firing squad if he were shipped back to Nazi Germany, where he had already spent a terrible period in a concentration camp.

Joan decided her sympathies *had* to lie with Kisch. She had prepared hundreds of cases for her father in attempts to rescue hapless Chinese immigrants who, along with their families, were forbidden to enter Australia by customs officials acting under the 'White Australia Policy' and detained on board ship. She decided to obtain a writ of *habeas corpus* and demand that the ship's master should produce Kisch in court, where Kisch's detention could be argued on legal grounds.

As the *Strathaird*, with Kisch aboard, approached Port Melbourne, Joan was taken out to it by launch. She boarded the ship and demanded that Captain Carter release Kisch, who, she told him firmly, was being detained illegally. She was allowed to meet Kisch, a small, dark-haired man with a moustache, who seemed stunned by the furore that his speaking tour had aroused in Australia. The Captain refused to allow Joan to take Kisch back with her to Melbourne.

The following morning, Joan, along with Kisch's friend Mrs Aarons and a justice of the peace, returned to the ship, now moored against the dock. The affidavit from Mrs Aarons was signed and sealed but once again they had to leave the ship without Kisch. There was no High Court judge available. Joan went into the Practice Court and demanded that Captain Carter show due cause why a writ of *habeas corpus* should not be issued to produce Kisch in court, as he already had a valid entry visa. The writ was issued. The faithful Miss Caffrey sped down to the ship and served it on the Captain. But the Commonwealth Government countered this action by seeking an adjournment, pleading through its solicitor that instructions from Canberra were on their way.

On her return to the courtroom Joan was besieged by journalists and photographers. But now top legal names had been brought in against her. The legal expert acting for the Commonwealth Government insisted that Kisch, as an alien, had no right to claim admittance to Australia. To Joan's despair, and that of the committee which had retained her, the court's decision was telephoned to the ship, the gangway was drawn up and the *Strathaird* made ready to depart. The waiting crowd saw the desperate Kisch, terrified of being sent back, appear on deck, climb over the rails and jump six metres down onto the wharf below. He landed badly, his leg crumpled under him, and he remained motionless. (Later it was discovered he had broken his leg in two places.) The waiting police pounced on the unfortunate Kisch, dragged him screaming with pain up the gangplank and back on board. Those watching felt it was like some terrible scene under a South American dictatorship. All over Australia people of conscience were appalled.

Joan maintained that the police had seized Kisch unlawfully, as by jumping he had actually 'landed' on Victorian soil complete with a valid visa. Her father urged Joan to try to board the ship and accompany Kisch to Sydney. Although she always had at least two domestic staff at home, she did not wish to spend months away from her husband. She feared the case would drag on for months or years. She believed it was better for the extreme left-wing Sydney barrister Christian Jollie-Smith to take over, as she was a close friend of Katherine Susanah Prichard.

Time proved her decision the right one: the legal battle to free Kisch took a long time. Kisch was arrested by New South Wales police, given the infamous dictation test in Gaelic, a language which he had no chance of understanding, and sentenced to six months hard labour as an illegal immigrant. An appeal was made to the High Court and Kisch, now the subject of front-page headlines, was freed. Joan and Mannie followed the case with horror. It was a low point in Australian history.

Joan's starring role in the Kisch affair, and the fact Jollie-Smith had taken over the case, meant that a file was opened on her as a 'suspected person' by some consular authorities. An additional entry was added to her file, claiming that Mrs Rosanove had 'revolutionary tendencies', having chaired an anti-war meeting addressed by Jessie Street, whose father was a member of the squattocracy.

Twenty years later, when applying for a visa to visit America, Joan was shown her top-secret dossier, which contained the text of an anti-war speech by Jessie Street given at the meeting Joan had chaired. It looked as though the authorities would deny her an American visa. Quick-witted as ever, Joan pointed at her elegant hat and fur coat and demanded: 'Do I *look* like a revolutionary? I have defended many criminals, but that doesn't mean I *believe* in crime.' She was granted her American visa – but only after she had filled out a statutory declaration that she was not, and had never been, a communist.

What was 'revolutionary' about Joan was that in the 1930s, when society decreed that wives of professional men who could afford to support them should not work, she insisted on continuing her career. She wrote:

> I look on life primarily as a barrister for that is my chosen career ... I think that every women, married or otherwise, is better with a career. A career, in my eyes, offers an outlet for the enthusiasm and abounding energy of every intelligent woman ... [Her] children are better off, for they learn to be self-reliant and in addition, probably see more of their mothers than those children whose mother [has] so much time on her hands that she is at the beck and call of every bridge-playing and golfing friend. The mother who is engaged in carving out a career for herself tends to give up more of her spare time to her children than would otherwise be the case. Also, I think the woman who is actively engaged in the work of the world keeps young in mind as well as appearance. And both of these things are desirable in her children's eyes.
>
> The statement that a woman has no business taking up a career because her husband is able to support her is utterly ridiculous. We would not dream of saying that a man who is married to a rich woman, however great her riches, was justified in not working. It is my opinion that a woman should enter the field of work on an even footing with men. Her fees should be the same as a man's, not only because her work is equally good, but because she must on no account undercut the work of her masculine rival, who may be the sole supporter of his family.
>
> But even then, success is not allowed to be hers – it is said of her 'she has a brain like a man', although I can never see why it is not considered the hallmark of success to have a brain like a *woman*! To have a career, and at the same time to be a wife and mother requires a cast-iron constitution, an equable temperament and a sense of humour ...

Married life is the most difficult thing in the world as I find out in the course of my work ... Marriage is a partnership, which to be successful ... calls for the deepest commitment on both sides ... and for wisdom, tact and understanding – and once again it is invariably up to the woman to provide them![8]

So that Joan and Mannie could sometimes forget the stress and pressure of work, they bought a block of land close to the beach on the Mornington Peninsula and hired architect Roy Grounds to design them a family weekend retreat. Their main home was called 'Medlore', a clever word play on their joint professions, so they named their beach house 'Little Medlore'.

In addition to her heavy workload, Joan found time to give lectures to women's groups about much needed reforms to the divorce laws, which she believed utterly disadvantaged women. She also campaigned for uniform divorce laws in each State and believed women should be allowed to serve on juries – from which, at that time, they were barred.

Joan's quick mind would often enable her to win a case by turning unexpected evidence to her client's advantage, no matter how unpromising it seemed. One of her clients, a woman suing for divorce on the grounds of her husband's cruelty, explained to the court how he had thrashed her with a whip. The husband's barrister brought in the whip in question as an exhibit, saying it was only a riding crop, not a stockwhip. Joan remembered her childhood, when she had attended race meetings with her parents. When it was her turn to address the court she picked up the riding crop.

'My client *never* implied she had been thrashed with a stockwhip,' she declared, and went on to tell the court how riding crops were used by jockeys for the express purpose of thrashing their horses past the winning post. She held the whip in her hand as she spoke and 'absent-mindedly' cracked it a few times against the mahogany bar table, smiling pleasantly at the judge as she did so.

The judge got the message and Joan's client got her divorce, on most favourable terms.

In 1940, the Rosanoves were delighted when Peg married a fourth-year medical student, Graeme Larkins. The couple had two sons; now in her mid-forties, Joan became a grandmother.

During World War II, Joan practised from rooms in Chancery

House and during the war, because many male barristers were away in the armed forces, her legal practice became busier than ever. The presence of American troops in Australia and the prolonged absence of many husbands led to an increasing number of marriage breakdowns.

After the war, Joan and Mannie took another overseas trip to Britain and Europe, and returned to Melbourne in 1949, just before their old friend Bob Menzies became prime minister.

Joan Rosanove was admitted to the Bar in New South Wales shortly after resigning from the Roll of Counsel of the Victorian Bar. Thereafter, she practised exclusively as a barrister. But she still had her teenage dreams of practising from Selborne Chambers, still Melbourne's most exclusive address for barristers. After her humiliating rejection over twenty years earlier, for her Selborne Chambers became more than just an address on a letterhead: it represented acceptance as an equal by her male colleagues. She could easily have rented rooms in Equity Chambers, where she had many friends; but she had decided that if she was not accepted by her male colleagues in Selborne Chambers, she would work nowhere else.

While she waited for rooms to fall vacant, Joan ran her legal practice from the Supreme Court Library.[9] However, a hint reached her on the legal grapevine that seeing clients in there was frowned upon by the upper echelons of the legal fraternity. Joan thought laterally and came up with a novel idea on how to achieve her ambition to enter Selborne Chambers – by working as 'reader' or pupil to a male barrister, which meant she would have to share his rooms. She believed once she was in chambers she could win the barristers over to accepting her. Edward Ellis, a barrister younger than herself both in years and practice, was greatly tickled by the idea that the famous Joan Rosanove would work as his 'reader'. Although, in theory, Ellis was meant to be instructing her in the practice of law, everyone in legal circles knew this was only a device to get Rosanove into Selborne Chambers. At this stage in her career, there were no objections to her presence. In jubilation she had her dingy room repainted in brilliant Matisse-like colours, which made some of the more crusty old barristers complain that it looked more like a boudoir than legal chambers.

It had taken Joan Rosanove twenty-five years to climb the 'glass ladder' but her persistence had paid off. She had defied prejudice and achieved her long-held ambition to work from Selborne Chambers.

Joan was, above all, a practical person, and she always gave her clients excellent advice on their courtroom appearances, something many barristers did not bother to do.

'If you *look* good, you'll *feel* good', she advised women clients, especially those receiving legal aid. Joan knew only too well that the poor and needy rarely received sympathy in court.

Remembering how Billy Hughes had taken advantage of her inexperience by fiddling with his hearing aid, Joan acquired a long black-and-ivory cigarette holder, which she used as a theatrical prop. During the 1940s and 1950s, no one was aware of the dangers of smoking; everyone smoked, from film stars to factory workers.

At a vice-regal levée in the Queen's Hall of the Victorian Parliament House, yet another public humiliation lay in store for her. An open invitation, requesting barristers to attend the levée, appeared on the notice board at Selborne Chambers. Joan had been appearing in a suburban court; returning to the city, she changed into her black silk legal gown and black high-heeled shoes. An exception to attend an all-male vice-regal function had been made for a Victorian woman MP, Fanny Brownbill, and Joan assumed that this would apply to her as well.

But no. She found that the Victorian establishment was as hidebound as ever. As she waited alongside her male colleagues to be presented to Governor Sir Dallas Brooks, a uniformed Parliament House attendant approached and whispered a firm request for her to leave. Joan allowed herself to be led away through the dingy back corridors and shown out like a tradesman. This time, she was more amused than annoyed. However, the whole affair made her even more determined to continue fighting against male discrimination.

In 1951, Joan Rosanove addressed a meeting of the Legal Women's Association, urging women's organisations and women lawyers to work for more rational divorce laws which would benefit women rather than men. Women had few rights over property when they divorced and stood to lose a great deal. The law was also most unjust when dealing with adultery. A woman could be divorced if found guilty of *one* single act of adultery. But a woman wishing to divorce her husband for adultery had to prove it had taken place *repeatedly*, or else produce firm evidence of adultery coupled with several acts of cruelty.

She had to obtain evidence from a detective who would stand up in court and say he had seen the husband in bed with another woman. Obtaining this evidence was often expensive and difficult.

Joan was outraged by the hypocrisy of this double standard by which men and women were judged. She wrote: 'I feel ashamed that in spite of all my attempts I have never been able to alter the provision that a woman may not sue for divorce after producing proof of one act of adultery.'

In 1954, she compiled an exhaustive survey of the current divorce laws in the various States of the Commonwealth together with her proposed changes. Her report was published in the *Australian Law Journal* later that year. She found curious anomalies in the attitude of each State towards the grounds for divorce for women petitioners. In Queensland, habitual drunkenness did not qualify a woman to seek a divorce. Laws governing divorce for bigamy, sodomy and bestiality varied in each State. However, in male-dominated Australia little notice was taken of Joan's proposed reforms.

Not until five years after her review was published did the Commonwealth Attorney-General, Sir Garfield Barwick, introduce a Matrimonial Causes Bill in Parliament, embodying many of the reforms which Joan Rosanove had recommended. It was not until 1975, the year following Joan's death, that the Family Law Act was passed by the Commonwealth Government, abolishing 'fault' in marriage from the statute book and making family law uniform throughout the Commonwealth.

In 1954, Joan decided to make a valiant attempt to become Australia's first-ever female Queen's Counsel. Male barristers who had entered the profession years after her had taken silk and then been appointed judges. Why should promotion be denied her just because she was a woman?

Joan was now so successful she could afford to take a drop in income if male solicitors would not give her the more expensive briefs normally handled by QCs. When Chief Justice Sir Edmund Herring summoned her to his chambers to discuss her application for silk, he was amazed to learn just how much Mrs Rosanove was earning from legal practice.

The reply from the Chief Justice's office, when it finally came, was humiliating. Yet another 'kick in the teeth' for Joan Rosanove:

I have very reluctantly come to the conclusion that it would be wrong for me to grant your application. I am very sorry to have to disappoint you but personal considerations cannot be allowed to weigh with me in the exercise of such an important function as the granting of silk.

The Chief Justice's decision was certainly a blow to Joan Rosanove's self-esteem. But once again she followed her own maxim: 'When kicked look as if you had not noticed.' She gained additional strength from the fact that her Jewish ancestors had fought for centuries against prejudice and never given up.

Resolutely, she continued to apply to take silk and become a QC whenever a male barrister years junior to her sent her a notice informing her that he had applied. But Joan was continually passed over in favour of more junior male applicants and eventually, at the request of her daughter Peg, who thought it was undignified to continue trying in the face of such prejudice, Joan Rosanove closed her 'Queen's Counsel Application' file.

The general opinion was that Joan Rosanove had been shabbily treated: dozens of her colleagues and even some judges sympathised with her. Premier John Cain (senior) inquired why she had been passed over and was informed Mrs Rosanove's practice was 'too specialised', but everyone knew that other highly specialised barristers had been granted silk. Joan's rejection become something of a *cause célèbre* when the famous poet and feminist Mary Gilmore (See Chapter 2) wrote to the United Association of Women in Sydney requesting *their* support to nominate Joan Rosanove as a judge or Queen's Counsel. Mary Gilmore's submission pointed out that Joan Rosanove had a 'long, stable and notable career in Law. She is of suitable age and her citizenship [possibly a veiled reference to Joan's Jewish background] is impeachable. As a barrister she stands high. I do not know of any other woman whose standing in the Courts is higher.'

In 1962, Joan and her husband were on a working holiday in San Francisco when Peg sent them a cable informing them that the Adelaide 'establishment' barrister and solicitor Roma Mitchell (See Chapter 15) had just been appointed Australia's first female Queen's Counsel. Joan was naturally disappointed she had been pipped to the post by a woman younger than herself and less senior in law (Roma Mitchell had been admitted to the Bar in 1934, seventeen years after

Joan Rosanove). Hiding her hurt Joan quipped that she 'couldn't have heard the news in a nicer place'.

Joan knew full well that Roma Mitchell also specialised in matrimonial and divorce law.[10] She was deeply hurt, although she admired Roma Mitchell for her philanthropic activities.

In 1964, the Chief Justice of Victoria retired. The following year, on 16 November, Attorney-General Arthur Rylah announced the appointment of eight new Queen's Counsels. Among them was the valiant, determined, dedicated Joan Rosanove, undisputed leader of the Victorian Bar in matrimonial and divorce law. Mrs Joan Rosanove, QC: her appointment had taken her eleven years from her initial application.

Getting your wish sometimes has hidden drawbacks. Queen's Counsels command higher fees and are usually only briefed for more important cases. As a QC, Joan Rosanove's actual workload was no lighter. Although she now had fewer cases, the work that did come her way was even more complex and demanding than previously. As Victoria's only female QC, Joan was now a highly public figure in the media. She could not afford to make any mistakes. Because men had the money and the power, her clients, formerly 60 per cent women and 40 per cent men, now became 75 per cent men and only 25 per cent women. Slowly her practice was reduced. As her fees were now higher, many of her clients preferred to employ a man rather than a woman, however brilliant that woman might be.

In 1959, the close-knit Rosanove family suffered a bitter blow when Peg's husband, brilliant Dr Graeme Larkins, died of a brain haemorrhage at the age of thirty-nine. Showing the same courage as her mother, Peg Larkins enrolled at Melbourne University and became a first-year law student while her son was in second year.

Peg would subsequently remarry a Dutch-born lawyer, Theodore Lusink. In 1966, Joan Rosanove QC moved the admission of her daughter Peg Lusink to practise law, her junior in support being Joan's grandson, John Larkins. Peg Lusink went on to have a highly successful career in law and became a distinguished judge in the Family Court and Adjunct Professor of Law at Bond University.

As Joan and Mannie aged, they finally moved to a new home they had built behind their Frankston beach house. On 2 June 1969, Joan celebrated fifty years in the legal profession. Eventually they both retired. Joan, ever the skilled negotiator, reached a peaceable accord with her husband that many married women would envy: Dr Mannie Rosanove, the perfect husband, took over much of the cooking as well as the work of running the household, smiling and saying gently that he was better at housekeeping than his adored wife.

In 1970, when Victoria's first female QC was in her seventies, a female journalist queried why brilliant Joan Rosanove had never received the award of DBE. It is significant that through her long and successful career, Joan Rosanove never received any royal or Commonwealth award, nor any lucrative appointment to a royal commission or any government qango – these being reserved for her male colleagues.

In April 1974, Joan was admitted to the local hospital, ostensibly for rest and relaxation. She was now seventy-eight. But Peg Lusink felt instinctively that something was very wrong with her mother. She took the afternoon off work and she and her husband collected her father from his home and they drove to the hospital. They found Joan in the sunroom. Peg described her mother 'surrounded by four or five obviously enchanted old boys'. Not wanting to alarm her mother, Peg pretended they were only there because her husband had business in the area. Joan accepted that, then berated her husband gently for bringing her the wrong shade of nail varnish. Even in hospital she insisted on looking as immaculate as ever. Mannie promised to bring her the right shade when he came back that evening.

As they were about to leave, Peg Lusink, who describes herself as 'not into fortune-telling, crystals or beads' had a terrible sense of foreboding that she might not see her mother again. She had already kissed her mother goodbye. Now she recrossed the hospital's polished floor and kissed her again.

Joan looked surprised. 'What's that for?' she asked.

Not wanting to sound alarmist, Peg replied: 'Oh well, you're not such a bad old girl! And if I can still entrance the old boys when I'm your age, I'll think I'm doing all right too.'

Joan, with her usual sense of humour, burst out laughing, and on that happy note Mannie and the Lusinks departed.

About 5.30 that afternoon, Peg Lusink entered her Melbourne apartment and found her husband on the phone to Mannie.

'Oh no, Poppa!' he exclaimed.

Peg's heart missed a beat. Her immediate response was: 'Mum's dead.'

'My God, Peg, how *did* you know?' her husband cried out.[11]

The remarkable Joan Rosanove died as she had lived, with style and panache. She had suffered a fatal heart attack while talking animatedly to an admiring audience, her hair immaculate as ever and her face beautifully made up – but with her nails unpolished.[12]

In 1999, a block of barristers' chambers with the name: 'Joan Rosanove Chambers' engraved about its door in large letters opened in Melbourne's Londsdale Street. This granite-faced building was named in honour of the formidable woman barrister who, seventy-five years earlier, was banned from Melbourne's all-male Selbourne Chambers. From the grave, Joan Rosanove, QC, had won her last battle.

CHAPTER FIFTEEN

Roma Flinders Mitchell
(1913–2000)
THE LAWYER WHO BLAZED A TRAIL FOR AUSTRALIAN WOMEN
AND WOMEN INTERNATIONALLY

Over 2000 people attended the state funeral and requiem mass for Dame Roma, which took place on a warm March day in Adelaide's Cathedral of St Francis Xavier. Among the mourners were the Governor-General, Sir William Deane, the governors of most States, politicians and people from all walks of life, representing the many charities and arts organisations with which Dame Roma had been involved. So many people wished to pay their final respects to a woman who had been deeply loved as well as honoured, that crowds of mourners spilled out of the cathedral porch and onto the pavement.

Inside the cathedral, roses and wreaths of late summer flowers sent by relatives, friends and organisations covered the coffin and decorated the cathedral. Eulogies spoken by the Governor-General and the Premier of South Australia were personal and deeply moving. Both men acknowledged Dame Roma's many outstanding achievements. These included her appointment as the first female Queen's Counsel in 1962; three years later her appointment as the first female Supreme Court judge; then as the first female vice-chancellor of the University of Adelaide in 1983 (and the first woman in the British Commonwealth to hold such an appointment). She was also the first chair of the Australian Human Rights Commission and its representative at the United Nations. From 1991 to 1996 Dame Roma was the first female governor of South Australia, the first woman governor to be appointed in Australia.

Roma Mitchell's achievements were all the more remarkable because her rise to prominence took place in a conservative and male-dominated era at a period when women found it hard to gain positions of trust in high places. Roma Mitchell, 'the quiet achiever', was no red radical and initially described herself as 'a conservative sort of feminist'. In later life she frequently expressed the belief that all public appointments should be made on competence and merit rather than quotas. By the 1990s, when I talked to her about the outstanding Australian women whose lives and achievements I had chosen to relate, she acknowledged that she had changed with changing times. She preferred to work from the inside at changing public opinion rather than by confrontation, which she felt solved very little. She would answer traditionalists by saying gently but firmly: 'Yes, I used to think like that but now I've moved on.'

Dame Roma was not born into a background of power and prestige, she achieved them by her own efforts but remained unchanged by them. A deeply religious woman from her youth, she had a delightful sense of humour and scant use for pomp and ceremony. As Governor of South Australia she insisted on walking from Government House in North Terrace to the cathedral in Victoria Square for morning mass, greeting fellow Australians on her walk. Some of the staff at Government House were amazed when each week the Governor of South Australia would put on a battered pair of sneakers and walk to the local shopping mall to make her own purchases; she felt that it was important she should keep in touch with the concerns of ordinary people, and this was one of her ways of doing so.

Roma Mitchell's childhood in Adelaide, city of churches, was far from affluent. She was born the year before the outbreak of World War I, the second daughter of Harold and Maude Mitchell, a couple who had already lost another daughter.[1] Her father was a lawyer who went away to fight in the trenches in France. When Roma turned four her mother received the dreaded telegram containing the news that her husband had been killed in action.

Finances were strained. Maude Mitchell had not been trained for any profession and was unable to earn enough to support her daughters, Ruth and Roma, in the way she and her husband had planned. Maude now realised very forcibly that tertiary education was vital for her clever daughters if they were to achieve good careers, and she encouraged them to study and read in their free time. Roma Mitchell always said how close she had been to her mother.

> Being a widow wasn't easy in those days. The fact that my mother was not trained for any occupation other than home duties was one of the things that influenced her and she was determined that her daughters would have a career that they could follow. For as long as I remember I wanted to be a lawyer and I don't quite know why.[2]

Since her father had been a lawyer, possibly the law was in Roma Mitchell's blood: it would certainly become her passion. The Mitchell girls lived very modestly; their mother made all their clothes, struggling to keep up appearances on very little money. Through her mother's economies and self-denial it was possible for Roma to attend

St Aloysius College in Adelaide. She showed great aptitude and determination from an early age, but described herself as a small skinny girl, poor at sport. She was unsure about her appearance, regarding herself as 'no great beauty'. A keen and conscientious student, she liked French and debating best and eventually became dux of the school. She told me: 'I was always willing at school to push *for* things that I thought were right and to push *against* anything that I thought was an injustice. I was regarded as the spokesperson for our entire class.'

She won the coveted David Murray scholarship to study law at the University of Adelaide and soon proved herself as a hardworking and brilliant student. Roma, still extremely slim, was energetic and highly disciplined in everything she undertook. However, friends told her mother that it was a waste of money for her to study at university. 'A woman can't get anywhere,' they said.

Adelaide was still in the grip of the Great Depression and Dame Roma described how:

> on the way to uni, I would pass Kintore Avenue where men were lined up waiting to get their ration cards. I was horrified to learn that was *all* they got, a ration card which they could exchange for certain groceries … I felt that justice demanded that we shouldn't have another Depression. It strongly influenced me to study law because I thought that through it people could be helped.[3]

Just as she was about to finish her degree she read a Department of Foreign Affairs notice calling for graduate employees; it did not specify gender. Although Roma Mitchell hoped to become a lawyer, it was doubly hard during those Depression years for a woman to be accepted into law. Even though Roma had graduated as the outstanding student of her year, she was not at all confident that a law firm would accept her. So she applied to the Department of Foreign Affairs. She was in fact relieved when they replied saying they only wanted *men* with good law degrees. 'I don't think I would have been a very diplomatic diplomat,' she said in later years.[4]

Women in the late nineteenth and early twentieth centuries had great trouble getting *access* to study law, by the time Roma Mitchell left university, they had considerable trouble gaining *employment* in the law. However, as a young graduate Roma Mitchell was fortunate. In 1934, at the age of twenty-one, she was appointed managing clerk in an Adelaide city practice. Only ten law graduates succeeded in finding legal employment that year: nine men ... and Roma.

One of only a handful of female lawyers practising in South Australia in the 1930s and paid far less than her male counterparts, Roma Mitchell worked very hard and took on cases which male lawyers did not want, such as domestic problems involving drunken or violent husbands and divorce. (Her work, in fact, echoed exactly that of Joan Rosanove in Melbourne – see Chapter 12.) Barristers and judges were always male, middle-class and usually Anglican. Clever, hardworking Roma Mitchell's ambition was to become a barrister; in this restrictive period for women, she did not look further – the mere idea of a woman becoming a judge would have seemed ridiculous at that time.

In 1934, at the tender age of twenty-one, Roma Mitchell achieved her wish. She was admitted to the Bar and for the next twenty-eight years she worked as a barrister representing clients in the courts. It was a tough job demanding long hours and complete commitment. She said:

> You need a fair amount of courage. It's a fearsome thing at first to fight for people in front of a judge and jury. You have to have a certain amount of determination and a certain amount of persistence. ... Even the attire was difficult for a woman. In summertime in non-air conditioned courts I didn't like wearing stiff collars and thick jackets. The men were accustomed to wearing dark suits: I was accustomed to wearing sleeveless dresses. When it became very hot the judge would suggest we might like to remove our wigs ... I was always hoping he might say 'Let's remove our stiff collars' but he never did![5]

Her work was noticed and brought her promotion – eventually she became a partner in the city law firm she had joined. This was most unusual at that period, when the law was considered a male club and law courts 'unfeminine' places. Specialising in matrimonial causes, Roma also lectured on law at the University of Adelaide, her *alma mater*. During her last year in practice as an Adelaide lawyer, Roma Mitchell was chosen as the Australian representative at a United Nations seminar on the Status of Women in Family Law.

That same year she became the first woman in Australia to be appointed a Queen's Counsel. This (as well as her subsequent appointment as a judge) sent shock waves through the legal system; for her part, Roma Mitchell was in turn extremely shocked by such a reaction. Working long hours she became a noted advocate, continuing to specialise – again like Joan Rosanove in Melbourne – in matrimonial law and the breakdown of marriage. She said:

> I was very gratified when I became a QC because that was really the recognition within the legal profession of achievement as a barrister. I was the first woman in Australia to do this and I really did take pleasure in it.[6]

As a QC, Roma Mitchell supported the efforts of the League of Women Voters to change South Australian legislation so that women could sit on juries, and the arguments she put to Premier Tom Playford proved successful. She also advocated equal pay for equal work. She said:

> In my experience, the law client doesn't care two hoots about the sex of the Counsel. What he or she wants is somebody to win the case. But briefs to barristers come from the solicitors, most of whom are men. I have seen far too many women solicitors who give good service to legal practices working as managed clerks or as employed solicitors – but when it comes to promotion they are passed over for young men … And it's not for lack of qualifications. I think these days women have got to have a certain amount of gumption and get out and make their own legal firms.[7]

In 1965, just before she was due to assume office as President of the South Australian Law Society, Don Dunstan, then Attorney-General in South Australia's newly elected Labor Government, recommended to Premier Frank Walsh that Roma Mitchell be appointed a judge of the Supreme Court in that State. This meant that she became the first woman ever to be appointed to an Australian superior court. She said of Don Dunstan, 'I doubt if anyone else in this day and age would have pushed so hard for a woman in this job.'

Even though it was a huge honour to be chosen as Australia's first woman judge, she could not help feeling some regret. She had greatly enjoyed being a barrister – the work, the courtroom, the arguments. In fact she was quite sad to be leaving the Bar.

'A WOMAN JUDGE!' exclaimed the newspaper feature writers, while some of her fellow judges wondered what the world was coming to as they passed around the port in their exclusively male clubs.

Roma Mitchell's own reaction was characteristic:

I was surprised when I was asked to accept the appointment of Supreme Court Judge, because once again there had never been a woman on the bench in an Australian court nor in England at that stage. As far as being a woman is concerned, I am hopeful that, in my lifetime, appointments such as this one will not excite comment.

Sadly, when she retired from the Bench in 1983, eighteen years later, she was *still* the only woman judge of a superior court in Australia. When she was first appointed, there were endless legal wrangles over how she should be addressed. Roma Mitchell settled the matter by firmly refusing to be called Mrs Justice, Ms Justice or even Miss Justice. She wished to be addressed as Justice Mitchell, pure and simple, an appellation which blazed a trail for female judges in other countries. As a judge she was outstanding and a pivotal member of two of the landmark State Supreme Courts in Australia's legal history, the Bray Court and the King Court.

Of her appointment to the Supreme Court Bench in 1965, Justice Mitchell observed:

Women should be able to take whatever place they are fitted to take in the professions. I do not mean that a woman should ever be appointed to any significant office merely because she is a woman. But women's intellectual and other attainments should be recognised objectively. I am sure that they are being more widely appreciated nearly everywhere in today's world.[8]

Sir William Deane related an incident which reveals Dame Roma's sense of humour. During an interview in her early years at the Supreme Court, a journalist interviewing her inquired brashly: 'You are not married?'

'I am not,' she replied.

'And do you drive a motor car?'

'I do not.'

Undeterred by her terse replies, the journalist pressed on. 'The Chief Justice, Dr Bray, is also unmarried. Is there any chance you might get together?'

Keeping a straight face Dame Roma replied, 'No, that would be no good at all. He doesn't drive a car *either*.'

In 1975, after three years as chair of a South Australian Committee of Inquiry into Criminal Law, Justice Mitchell was selected to deliver the prestigious Boyer Lectures, broadcast by the ABC. She chose as her title The Web of the Criminal Law, and her lectures are considered by lawyers to have been among the most insightful analyses of criminal law and its problems in Australia ever made. She rarely gave press interviews and was scathing about magistrates and judges 'who went out of their way to attract the attention of the press'.

Busy as she was, she still found time to do things for other people and think about them. As an instance, she wrote me a letter of congratulation when I was awarded a Winston Churchill Fellowship to study Italian Renaissance Art in Florence, a topic dear to her heart as she had personally funded the Churchill Fellowship in the area of the arts. The Winston Churchill Memorial Trust was founded in 1965, the year in which Sir Winston died, 'to reward proven achievement with further opportunity in the pursuit of excellence for the enrichment of Australian society'. Over the years, Churchill Fellowships have enabled many hundreds of Australians to enlarge their field of practice through travel and study overseas. Roma Mitchell became a member of the South Australian Regional Committee in 1965, then became its chair. Subsequently, she was appointed Chair and then Federal President of the Churchill Memorial Trust, and finally its Patron.

Elvie Munday, the Trust's Executive Officer, and a good friend of Dame Roma, told me that:

Dame Roma had a wonderful way of combining her judicial role with warm personal relationships. She had a great sense of humour coupled with an extreme sense of fair play. The Trust gained much from her wise counsel over the years and she has left a void which I do not think will be filled in my lifetime.

Roma Mitchell held strong views on issues such as the need for changed attitudes towards working wives, refresher courses for women graduates wanting to return to work after raising children, the need for housework to be shared by married couples and a unified retirement age for men and women. In 1994, at a Women's Week meeting organised by the Trades and Labour Council, she said: 'As women's roles in the workforce increase in number and in variety, their influence in the unions should also increase.'

Dame Roma was a staunch advocate of equality, justice and human rights. Here is her advice to women:

If you have a particular ambition, follow it. Don't be put off by thinking it's too difficult. You just *have* to go on trying at the thing you think you do best.[9]

Between 1981 to 1986 she became the first chair of the Human Rights Commission, whose establishment in Australia she had lobbied for over a long period. She believed the Commission had to be controversial in order to be effective and she never shied away from tough topics. She used her influence to advance the human rights of disadvantaged Australians in every field, particularly Indigenous Australians. She created something of a furore when she announced that boys in kindergarten and early primary school should be taught to play with dolls. ('JUDGE URGES BOYS TO PLAY WITH DOLLS!' the newspaper announced.)

In 1983, her seventieth birthday brought with it retirement from the Bench ... and a new beginning. Later that year she was appointed Chancellor of the University of Adelaide, the first woman to be honoured in this way. As chancellor (1983 to 1990), she was always very keen to see more women appointed to university teaching positions and to the boards of public companies. She said:

Women should not be forced to achieve. Why should we? But we cannot afford to be complacent. I think that, on the whole, there is still a problem of prejudice. There is still a problem of power ... I think we have still got a lot to achieve.

Dame Roma always claimed that she had so many interests and friends that she never felt lonely. Why did she never marry? Was the fact that she did not have a husband and children one of the reasons that she was able to achieve so much? She always resolutely refused to discuss her private life, claiming that it was entirely her business. However, those close to her claimed she was very sensitive about a love affair when she was very young with someone she felt she could never marry. In an interview with feminist author Susan Mitchell for her book *The Matriarchs*, Dame Roma denied that she had fallen in love with a man who died in World War II, and abruptly changed the subject. In subsequent interviews with other journalists she refused to mention the topic again.[10] If journalists asked too many personal questions she would clam up. 'I'm of that generation that keeps oneself to oneself,' she would say.

It is possible that the young Roma Mitchell fell in love with a married lawyer or barrister, and her strong religious feeling would not permit the relationship to develop. It does appear that there was someone in her life, years ago, but she steadfastly refused to mention his name. Ruth, Dame Roma's elder sister, was her closest confidante. It is likely Ruth would have known who the man was, but she is no longer alive, so her sister's secret died with her. All this is speculation, but perhaps it makes Roma Mitchell seem more human to realise that such an outstanding woman may have suffered the pangs of love like the rest of us.

Dame Roma often said that the Women's Movement had brought great changes into Australian life, and that what had been very rare when she was young, that a woman could have a career and be a wife and mother, was now possible for most women. She emphasised the progress that had been made, especially in a restrictive area like legal practice, saying that this had benefited women as a whole.

Like Joan Rosanove, Roma Mitchell experienced discrimination during her long legal career, but she dealt with it in a different way. She was less confrontational than Rosanove and lacked the vibrant sex appeal of her Melbourne counterpart. Roma Mitchell never thought of using her femininity in court, as Rosanove did to such devastating effect. She disapproved of such gambits. When I interviewed Dame Roma, she told me firmly: 'I think it's fatal to ask for concessions for being a woman. Never ask or give quarter. *Never* play the sex game at work. It can rebound on you.'

On a lighter note, Dame Roma also suffered from that hairy old excuse proffered to so many professional women during the early years of this century: 'We'd like to give you the job, my dear, but unfortunately we don't have any lavatories for women.'

When Roma Mitchell started practising at the Bar there *were* no lavatories for lady barristers, so she was forced to use the public lavatories, risking a confrontation with a jury member or a dissatisfied spectator from the public gallery. By the time she was acting chief justice she had become much more confident about women's rights issues; she gave instructions for a latch to be put on the door and used the barristers' lavatory, regardless of what anyone thought.

In addition to Dame Roma's interest in the Winston Churchill Memorial Trust, she was an excellent vice-president of ADFAS, the Australian Decorative and Fine Arts Society, an organisation staffed by devoted volunteers which has over thirty branches in Australian cities and country towns. ADFAS is the offshoot of the huge British organisation NADFAS with its pool of specialised lecturers, who make lecture tours of Australia. ADFAS has brought to Australia a deeper knowledge of all the arts; in addition the different branches sponsor art prizes and restoration work in churches, museums and galleries. Dame Roma was a member of the Adelaide branch for many years and attended their lectures.

After being sent by ADFAS to Longreach during a severe drought to give a slide talk about the Australian artist Conrad Martens, I told Dame Roma how much it meant to women in remote country areas to have a chance to extend their knowledge. I added that I felt very humble when some of them told me they had driven for several hours to reach my lecture – and had to drive back that same night. Country members told me about the horrors of drought, including plagues of mice that invaded their homes, and said how pleasant it was to have another topic of conversation. I was finding it hard to continue writing books and lecturing but Dame Roma urged me to continue with art lectures, and gave me the quotes I have used in this short account of her story but politely and firmly refused to reveal any more of her private life. She said that she had grown up at a time when it was considered bad form to explore one's feelings about family and relationships in public and I respect her wishes.

What I most admired about Dame Roma was the fact that, even though she was an incredibly busy person she would become deeply involved whenever she acted as patron to a worthy cause. After retiring from the Bench she *personally* delivered meals on wheels to elderly pensioners. As Governor of South Australia from 1991 to 1996 she always showed a deep interest in the disadvantaged and the homeless and did what she could to help. She was also very much involved in creating opportunities for young people. She travelled around the State attending functions and talking to people at all levels. Roma Mitchell and Leneen Ford (also a lawyer), who was appointed Governor of Queensland in the 1990s, have been two of our most loved and admired State governors. Leneen Forde, another outstanding woman, as a gesture towards gender equality, appointed a woman as her equerry.

People loved Dame Roma's warmth, her friendliness, her generosity, her courage and her spirit of adventure – on one occasion, she climbed the highest peaks in Irian Jaya. She loved life … good food, good wine, music, drama, art. She was a true Christian, staunch in the Roman Catholic faith yet ecumenical.

In 1992, Dame Roma was appointed a Companion in the Order of Australia, the highest honour possible, and received the Order's beautiful sunburst medal on its blue-and-gold ribbon, which she wore with pride on official occasions.

Friends were always hugely important to her. She had the gift of friendship and made close friends in different walks of life. She listed her recreations as cooking, going to the beach, the opera, the theatre, and art and music. She believed firmly in appointment on merit, regardless of gender. By the mid-1980s, men and women had begun to graduate from Australian law schools in equal numbers, yet it is interesting to note that at the time of her death few other women had been appointed as senior counsels or to judicial posts.[11]

Dame Roma was also national president of the Ryder-Cheshire Foundation which, apart from other worthy causes, carries out enormously important work among disadvantaged children. In her will, Dame Roma bequeathed money to the Foundation, as well as to the Winston Churchill Memorial Trust and two other charities. Other influential appointments held by her were those of chair of the Ministerial Board on Ageing in South Australia, and patron of Disabled

People International, the Overseas Aid Bureau, and the Diabetic Association of South Australia. It is a measure of Dame Roma's popularity in the community that every time I have talked about writing this short account of her life, people from all works of life have told me: 'I admired Dame Roma so much, I'm glad you are writing her story.'

Women's causes were always dear to Dame Roma's generous heart. In 1994, she helped launch a tapestry which contained a portrait of herself for the South Australian Women's Suffrage centenary, and remarked:

> I have often been requested to speak at meetings in favour of the proposition that women should receive equal pay for equal work. In theory this was achieved. But in practice, there is still leeway to be made up ... in affording women equal opportunities for promotion and having regard to the fact that women who are mothers ... may necessarily have to put 'on hold' their professional advancement while their children are young.

In June 1999, Governor-General Sir William Deane unveiled a life-size bronze statue of Dame Roma 'as a permanent tribute to her lifetime achievement in South Australia'. The statue stands in Prince Henry Gardens, in front of Government House on North Terrace. Aware of her own mortality but, as yet, unaware that she had a fatal bone cancer, Dame Roma donated her papers and correspondence to Adelaide's Mortlock Library, requesting some restrictions over her private correspondence.

In 1999, Dame Roma, the quiet and discreet achiever, was made a Commander of the French Légion d'Honneur. In the week before she died she was invested as a Commander of the Victorian Order, an honour conferred on her by HM Queen Elizabeth II. She was to have received this award personally from the Queen on her visit to Canberra in the year 2000. Hearing that Dame Roma was not expected to live very long, Governor-General Sir William Deane cancelled other appointments to visit Dame Roma in hospital and made the award at her bedside shortly before she died.

Not only was Dame Roma greatly admired by men and women in high places but she was held in great affection by ordinary folk throughout the country. In her funeral oration Sir William Deane said:

For my part, I venture to suggest that there has been no better loved vice-regal representative in the whole of this land. Her death is an occasion of deep sadness ... but also an occasion for celebration ... A life of wonderful achievements, including an incomparable number of nationally significant firsts, a life which blazed a trail for all Australian women, in law, in government, in academic life, in public and philanthropic service. A life which is truly an inspiration for all Australians.'[12]

CHAPTER SIXTEEN

Portrait photograph: Private collection.

Mary Penfold
(1820–1896)
CO-FOUNDER AND MANAGER OF
A GREAT AUSTRALIAN WINERY

It seems unjust that Mary Penfold, co-founder of a great Australian winery, does not rate an entry under her own name in the *Dictionary of Australian Biography*.[1] Instead of having her own entry, she is included as an afterthought to her husband's. It reminds many of us of the time when women had no role in business, could not get loans or mortgages and everything they owned belonged to their husbands, including their children.

Some people do not wish to acknowledge Mary's importance in co-founding and running Penfolds Wines. Dr Christopher Penfold, having developed financial difficulties, was initially very busy establishing his medical practice in Adelaide and although he prescribed red wine to his anemic patients for its restorative value, he left the work of setting up the winery and overseeing the ploughing of the land to his clever hard working wife.

Attempts have been made by men to denigrate Mary's role in this enterprise. But women should never forget that it was Mary Penfold, aided by her maid Ellen Timbrell, who founded and ran the business which later became famous internationally as Penfolds Wines, now part of Southcorp Wines. Unfortunately Mary's own letters were not preserved, but one major source of information is letters her mother wrote to Australia.

'The wind blew in gales and our days and nights were spent in tears and prayers for your safety' wrote Mrs Julius Holt, a London physician's wife, to her daughter Mary, who had just arrived in South Australia after a nightmare voyage aboard the *Taglioni* in 1844. Terrible storms had lashed the ship and Mary's parents feared that their much-loved only daughter might have drowned. At the time Mary's ship was due to sail Dr Julius Holt was very ill and Mary's mother had accompanied her to the docks to see her off. Mrs Holt goes on to recount her husband's anguish over the fact that he might never see his daughter again, and his fears for the deprivation and hardship which could await her in the new country. In this same letter Mrs Holt deplores the fact that Mary's husband 'would listen to no one but the emigration agents'.

In a letter Mary received in May 1845 from her mother-in-law it becomes apparent that one of the reasons for the young Penfolds leaving England was a debt problem between Christopher and his brother Tom, and possibly other creditors.

…how different everything turns out to be in Adelaide to what we anticipated but you know it was contemplated that you should go to the Bush and you must have endured many hardships from which you are now exempt. Indeed I hear nothing that should induce you to wish to leave Adelaide (excepting to be with those dear to you) and I can say with truth that all our happiness is in yours. Therefore I cannot wish your return at present if I love you or those near and dear to you, because it must be to poverty …

It is very gratifying to hear that Christopher likes the change and is so determined to put his shoulder to the wheel. You say he works so very hard, I trust he will reap the benefit and that your crops will turn out very profitable … I do hope that Christopher will not recover only his profits but think as well of the losses he may meet with as I attribute all his failures in life to have arisen from his being too sanguine …

We went to Notting Hill to see Emma [Mary's sister-in-law] and they tell me they are going out to you the first of June. Emma is all life and spirits with the expectation of seeing you again. I wish you to have her society but I do not know what to say [about] Tom. He says he is forgetting all that has passed and with a good feeling towards Christopher and would be willing to lend him money again if he will but pay the interest — this Emma tells me — but I would advise you to have nothing to do with his money however advantageous it may appear to you. Do pray strive to overcome all difficulties and be independent of him. Remember his irritability he will always take with him and although I would say we must forgive and forget all injuries, you must avoid having your reputation injured as it was at Brighton … There must be something wrong in the man who is at variance with all his brothers and sisters (excepting James) as Tom is … if the mosquitoes bite you must put a bit of honey on as this almost instantaneously cures wasp stings.

I saw the Adelaide *Observer* of December at Tom's [home]. It had the account of your purchase of the farm and the sale that was to take place of a robe and cap and two dressing cases. We expect they were yours.

I shall dine with Tom and Emma on Saturday next and tell them that you say not to bring out more than they want. I tell them only to take one servant, she wants two.[2]

From this letter it became apparent Tom had fallen out with other siblings apart from Mary's husband. Ironically, having been partly responsible for their emigration, he and his wife were now proposing to join the Penfolds in Adelaide.

Mary Penfold had accompanied her husband, Dr Christopher Rawson Penfold, to South Australia with their four-year-old daughter Georgina, and their mother's help and companion Ellen Timbrell, the orphaned daughter of an army captain. The decision to emigrate appears to have been made entirely by Christopher, and Mary, an only child, was obviously torn between her love for her parents and that for her husband and child. When the Penfolds arrived in South Australia on 18 June 1844 they brought with them precious vine cuttings from the Rhône area of France.

At the start of settlement in Adelaide, all ships were forced to anchor a mile downstream and female passengers were carried unceremoniously ashore, slung like sacks of potatoes over the shoulders of burly sailors. They also had to endure the sight of their precious baggage and irreplaceable household possessions being thrown ashore onto the muddy beach, where crates and boxes sank into the oozy slime and many items were broken or damaged beyond repair. For many pioneer women it was not an auspicious beginning to life in a new land, but fortunately for Mary a new wharf had just been built at Port Adelaide and they were able to land in a more civilised fashion.[3] However, some of their household goods were damaged. Mary's family had given her expensive wedding presents and the Penfolds owned Wedgwood and Sèvres porcelain, handsome mahogany furniture and a piano.

On 3 October 1844 the *Observer* recorded that:

Mr [not Dr] Penfold is the fortunate purchaser of the delightfully situated and truly valuable estate of Magill [named after Sir Maitland Magill], for the sum of one thousand, two hundred pounds ... comprising 500 acres of the choicest land, 200 acres of which are under crops. The site of the residence is worthy of a noble mansion ... its woodlands offer a most agreeable background to this highly picturesque and desirable property.

Mary Penfold must have been delighted to live in such a beautiful place, nestling in the foothills of the Mount Lofty Ranges and surrounded by birds and trees but only six and a half kilometres due east of the new town of Adelaide. Grange Cottage, with its white-washed walls and tiny rooms panelled in red cedar, was to be her home and office for the next forty-five years.

Local gossips whispered that Christopher Penfold had emigrated because he was in trouble through financial losses caused by over-speculation. This gossip seems to be substantiated by Mrs Holt's letters. Mary Penfold's missing diary would, no doubt, have thrown further light on the subject but it mysteriously disappeared after her death, possibly destroyed by heirs to the the family's name who feared damage to the family's reputation.

In another letter to Mary her mother repeats her belief that Christopher had always been overconfident, which might possibly confirm this conjecture, but on the other hand Mrs Holt obviously resented her only daughter's forced departure to Australia so she was not a strictly impartial witness. She clearly did not approve of Christopher's brother Thomas, his financial exploits and the way in which he treated his wife. She warned Mary not to become involved with him financially again or she would have more problems with him, and her remarks suggest that Christopher had suffered as a result of previous financial dealings with his brother.

While Mary was a beloved and privileged only child and had received every advantage in the way of education and upbringing, Christopher was a member of a struggling family of thirteen children. His father was the hard working vicar of the Sussex village of Steyning, only 16 kilometres from Brighton, where Christopher eventually went into practice. Although books and education were greatly valued at Steyning Vicarage, there could never have been much money from a vicar's meagre stipend for Christopher's expensive medical books and living expenses when he was studying at the prestigious St Bartholomew's Hospital Medical School. Perhaps Christopher Penfold wished to become a specialist, but the first years of hospital medicine were unpaid and young medical residents worked there for the honour of post graduate study under a famous consultant.

The Penfolds married in 1835, when Mary was only fifteen. It is not known how Mary met her husband, but in the early Victorian period girls married far younger than they do today; however, rarely did girls from a middle-class family marry *quite* that young. At fifteen she would not have 'come out' into the affluent middle-class society in which her parents moved.

Three years after their marriage Dr Penfold set up in general practice in the fashionable seaside town of Brighton, rendered expensive by the patronage of the Prince Regent who had used it as an elegant health resort. In order to make the right impression on his wealthy patients, Christopher was forced to rent or purchase an expensive home with suitable accommodation for his surgery and waiting room. With no family funds available, he would have had to borrow money to finance setting himself up in practice. Presumably he borrowed from his elder brother Tom, and failed to pay back the interest. There was certainly ill-feeling between the two brothers.

It was rumoured that during Christopher's childhood a sister had been sent to live with an elderly aunt to cut the family's housekeeping expenses, and she had later been married off to an elderly man for his money. Obviously there must have been great financial pressures on the Penfold family for them to allow this to happen. Christopher had to make his own way in the world, which may have been one of the major motivating forces for his emigration. Possibly he was too proud to seek financial help from Mary's parents and wished to be totally independent, although young doctors have always had to rely on loans to establish themselves in private practice. He would have studied at 'Barts' (St Bartholomew's Hospital) with the sons of the wealthy, and come to expect that his training would enable him to establish himself and Mary in surroundings of which he felt her parents would approve.

Whatever happened to the Penfolds in England that caused them to emigrate, Christopher Penfold redeemed himself in Adelaide. They took over Grange Cottage on the Magill property, a stone one-storey building with a low-hipped roof and a long verandah. They installed their beautiful furniture and fine porcelain, probably wedding presents from Mary's parents and friends, in the tiny sitting room.

Portraits of Mary and Christopher Penfold are still at their cottage. Dr Penfold was painted in 1835, the year of his marriage, when he was twenty-four. He holds a book in one hand and appears handsome as well as intelligent, with expressive, gentle eyes and a warm and generous mouth. The only existing picture of Mary shows her as an elderly widow, but she was obviously very attractive when younger. In widowhood she looks kind and rather careworn but with a very determined set to her chin. The Penfolds were a devoted couple and had an extremely happy marriage. They had true pioneering spirit and both worked enormously hard to make a success of the farm and the practice.

Once they had moved into the cottage Mary sent her parents a picture of the little house and the outbuildings, showing young Georgina wearing red shoes and stockings and striding 'stick in hand, among the poultry and animals: pigs, cows, turkeys, fowls and pigeons'.[4]

Mary also sent home a small piece of metal for testing, which her father told her in his next letter was a mixture of lead and zinc. South Australia was then in the grip of a mining boom.[5] Christopher was still interested in mining and investments, but Mary's father cautioned them not to 'neglect the fleece and the farmyard to dig a will-o'-the-wisp out of the earth'. Attached to her father's letter was a most moving letter from Mrs Holt to her son-in-law saying: 'I sincerely hope you may realise your expectations. Many thanks for your assurance that you do and will take care of my idolised Mary. I place implicit confidence in your promise and will do my best to be happy. You can judge of my affection by your own for your lovely darling infant.'

Mary's parents were obviously worried that Christopher Penfold would once again do something rash, and a later letter to Mary from her mother says how 'I am glad that Chris, who has always been a little too sanguine, would not give the man fifty pounds [a large sum at that time] to tell him [the whereabouts] of the mine.' Obviously freight was expensive to Australia, as in the same letter Mary's mother described how she had passed on Mary's message to Tom Penfold, her brother-in-law, to bring out only essentials with him, including feather beds.

The Magill estate gradually prospered through Mary's hard work as farm manager in all but name. All the administration fell to *her* as her husband was deeply involved in building up his practice and doing the rounds of his sick patients on horseback. He did not have an assistant and, like any other doctor's wife, Mary would have taken messages and given practical advice to patients in his absence. The surgery was set up in their dining room.

Mary was often busy supervising both Ellen Timbrell in her domestic duties and their manservant, Elijah Lovelock, who helped with the ploughing, sowing and harvesting. She was also involved with her daughter's education. A page from her day book contains varied entries showing her bank accounts, payments to a man for additional ploughing, the purchase of new ploughshares in Adelaide, receipt of cash for a surgery visit from a sick child and other farm work.

Most important of all is Mary's brief statement that *she* 'began making wine'. Wine-making was Mary's special interest rather than her husband's, although his scientific knowledge would have been very useful when it came to the actual process. He prescribed their red wine to his anaemic patients, being firmly convinced of its medicinal powers. Having chosen land with wine-making in mind, they started with port and sherry but soon discovered clarets and rieslings sold better. They certainly planned the vineyard together, as did many other couples. But what had originally been conceived as an adjunct to the medical practice, medicinal wine to be prescribed to patients of Dr Penfold, under Mary's careful stewardship developed into a thriving and prestigious business.

By the end of the 1860s, Penfolds Wines had become a flourishing concern. Because of her husband's heavy workload Mary continued to manage the business virtually single-handed, a fact that was not widely known. In colonial Australia a middle-class woman was not expected to be in charge of any business venture, but to occupy herself with home and children except when her husband was absent. Dr Penfold was a dedicated and popular doctor, although at that time medicine had few cures for major diseases, and general practitioners were seldom wealthy. Like other country doctors, he would also have had many poorer patients who were unable to pay his fees during bad years and whom he treated free. He worked long hours and was also involved with the founding of St George's Church at Woodeford, north of Magill, and chaired meetings of the Burnside District Council. With so many commitments, the doctor had little time available to involve himself in the day-to-day running of the farm and the wine business, although many wrongly believed the success of the winery was due to him.

At first the Penfolds made wine for their own use and to prescribe to patients, leading to the company's slogan: '1844 to evermore'. The Penfolds sold their wine in Adelaide and won prizes at local shows, so that gradually the fame of their product spread. With a keen entrepreneurial instinct Mary found another marketing outlet for their excellent wines in Melbourne, and it was only the high interstate customs duty imposed on South Australian wine in Victoria that prevented greater expansion of the business. Before Federation, each state levied tariffs on the others' produce.

Dr Penfold's medical practice prospered. Their daughter grew into an attractive and intelligent girl. When the Penfolds made an extended visit to Melbourne to find new markets for their wine, Georgina, then nineteen years old, met and married a public servant and capable administrator named Thomas Hyland. He acted as the Victorian sales agent for Penfolds, as he and Georgina were living in Melbourne. The wine business grew and prospered, but it is likely that Mary regarded herself as the wife of a respected doctor with a business sideline rather than as a successful entrepreneur in her own right, although that *was* her role.

In March 1870 Mary Penfold suffered a major tragedy when her husband died at the age of fifty-nine after a long illness, possibly cancer. Dr Penfold was buried at St George's Church, Magill. He was held in great esteem by his patients, and when his funeral cortege passed through Magill the flags which were flying for a local election were lowered to half-mast and all the stores closed out of respect.

In a letter to Mary written just after her husband's death, Thomas Hyland advised her that he had been building up good sales of Penfolds and other wines in Victoria as a sideline to his public service appointment. Rather patronisingly, he added that Mary should now sell out the property and be 'pensioned off'. It appears that at this time Thomas Hyland had not realised that Mary Penfold had been managing the vineyard and wine-making process prior to her husband's long illness, and he seriously underestimated her role in the winery and her business acumen. He wondered if 'you could manage things for six months [as] it would give us more time to sell the property', and suggested that 'if the Border Duty gets settled, we could then sell it [the Grange estate] well in Melbourne'.

Mary had absolutely no intention of selling the home and business she had worked so hard to create. She replied brusquely to her son-in-law's discouraging letter with a well-written and concise report on the prospects for the Penfolds wine business and included a balance sheet setting out the financial situation. Two months later she received a letter from Thomas Hyland stating: 'I am quite pleased at the practical way in which you are taking the business in hand and your resolutions, determination and instructions could not be better. In fact if you go at it determinedly ... you will be alright.'

The letter also contained a proposal for a formal partnership between them. Hyland sensibly proposed that Mary should continue to manage the Penfolds Grange Estate vineyards and that he and Georgina would continue to sell Penfolds Grange wines in Melbourne. Mary accepted his proposals and a most successful partnership was contracted. By now Ellen Timbrell, who had originally helped her with the wine-making, was dead, but Mary's domestic burdens were far lighter since there were no patients to take up her time. Mary continued to work hard; she could no longer be regarded as a doctor's wife making pin money when she was in fact a skilled vigneron running a successful enterprise. Thomas Hyland grew to respect Mary Penfold's business acumen and management skills.

The relationship between Mary, Georgina and her husband was close. In 1872, two years after Dr Penfold's death, Thomas and Georgina entrusted their delicate little daughter, Inez, to Mary, believing that the clear country air of Magill would help her to regain her health. The arrangement was a great success for grandmother and granddaughter, and Thomas later adopted the name Penfold and called himself Thomas Hyland-Penfold.

At the beginning of June 1874 a journalist from the *Adelaide Register* inspected the Penfolds Grange vineyards and cited the estate as an example of good management. From his article it is evident that the writer was impressed by Mary Penfold's personal supervision of the winery and her extensive knowledge of the wine-making process, and noted that Mary must have been doing this for a long time to gain this kind of expertise. The reporter described how:

Mrs Penfold makes four varieties of wine, sweet and dry red and sweet and dry white. Grapes of all kinds are used and the uniformity which is so great a consideration is secured by blending the wines when they are two or three years old. This is done under Mrs Penfold's personal supervision, not in conformity with any fixed and definite rule but entirely according to her judgment and taste. Mrs Penfold is aiming to get such a stock that she need not sell any which is under four years of age. There are now in the cellars about 20,000 gallons of wine of that age ready for market but the total stock is close upon 90,000 gallons.[6]

Mary had expanded her wine-making in a most professional and organised way. The *Adelaide Register* described the exact procedures that she used, together with the type of machinery, and went into some detail about the enormous oak casks which Mary had purchased in spite of gloomy predictions of disaster from her rivals.

These oak casks, each holding some 22,700 litres, and standing 3.6 metres high, were installed in her cellar. There were seven of them, made of Australian red gum or English oak. From the *Adelaide Register*'s article it appears that Mary was experimenting with many new varieties of grapes, apart from the grenache which she and Christopher had originally brought with them on the voyage to Australia. New varieties included tokay, madeira, frontignac, verdelho, mataró, the Spanish pedro ximenez, and muscat; to obtain these Mary must have been involved in correspondence with vignerons all over Europe. She read widely about new methods of wine production and maintenance of vine stocks, as she was keen to avoid phylloxera and other diseases that ravaged vineyards in Europe.[7]

After Christopher's death Mary kept herself constantly busy. Unlike many widows of the period, she did not appear to suffer from a sense of isolation or depression. She had the companionship of Inez, her intelligent and creative grandchild, and her beloved pug dogs Toby and Beppo. The Hyland-Penfolds often visited her when they could get away from Melbourne, and in turn she wrote the family long and amusing letters. Frequently these were addressed to Inez's brother Leslie. In one letter to Leslie she recounted how, with his father and sister Inez, she had taken a trip to the Adelaide Hills where they had encountered men panning for gold: 'I wanted to get out and see what they had got but directly they caught sight of our wagonette they took us for a wedding party and yelled at us in a very Colonial fashion', she wrote.

Mary was progressive in her ideas and evidently welcomed the technological advancement of the time. Rather than taking the steamer on her visits to the married daughter and children, she was one of the first passengers aboard the newly instituted train service between Adelaide and Melbourne.

By 1869 the Penfolds Grange estate had 27.3 hectares of vines under cultivation. On 14 September 1881 a further partnership agreement was signed between Mary, Thomas Hyland-Penfold and her cellar manager, Joseph Gillard, by which she would receive 10 per cent of the profit and in which she agreed to continue to act as wine-maker and wine-seller under the name of Penfold & Co for the next seven years, with Thomas acting as accountant for the partnership. Mary's son-in-law, due to the success of the business and his confidence in its future, left his secure public service job to devote his time and energy to the family enterprise, although he remained in Victoria while Mary ran the winery. The historic partnership agreement is still in Grange Cottage today.

By 1881 the Penfold company was producing over 486 422 litres, equal to one third of all the wine stored in South Australia at that time and selling all around the country.[8] They exhibited successfully at the Colonial Exhibition in London. In 1884, when Mary was sixty-eight, she finally handed over the management of the thriving business to Joseph Gillard. He did not retire until 1905, at which time Mary's grandson, Herbert Leslie Hyland-Penfold, took control. By this time Penfolds had become one of Australia's major wine-makers and Mary's Grange trademark had won world renown for its reputation as one of Australia's greatest wines.

In 1892, Mary's beloved granddaughter and companion, Inez, with whom she had happily shared Grange Cottage for 20 years, died of what was thought to be pernicious anaemia. Although Inez had been shy and retiring, she was well read and an excellent conversationalist with a passion for literature. She had given Mary great joy and mental stimulation in her later years. Inez had written some poems in the rather charming whimsical style, later made popular by the fantasies of Walter de la Mare. Mary devoted her time and energies to collecting her granddaughter's poems and stories and publishing them under the title *In Sunshine and Shadow*, hoping that 'whatever their faults they will meet with no harsh criticism for her dear sake'.

After Inez died Mary no longer wished to remain alone at Grange Cottage and in January 1892, when her garden was at the height of its beauty, she packed up a few treasures to take with her to Georgina's home in Melbourne. She could not bear to witness the disposal of the beautiful Regency furniture which she and Christopher had commissioned in the first years of their marriage, or her much-loved ebony piano and the Dresden, Sèvres and Wedgwood china which had given her so much pleasure. They were sold under the auctioneer's hammer after her departure and most were scattered beyond tracing.

Mary Penfold died in her mid-seventies on a mild January day in Melbourne in 1896. Her body was brought back to be buried at St George's Cemetery, Magill.

It is a significant comment on the way women were viewed in Australian colonial society that her obituary in the *Adelaide Register* of 4 January 1896 mentioned that 'she resided for forty-eight years at the Grange Vineyards'. Neither the journalist who wrote it nor any of the Melbourne papers mentioned her contribution to the wine industry. She was not given any credit for pioneering South Australian wine-growing and wine-making, for trying to lower the tariff barriers between South Australia and Victoria, or for her successful initiation and management of one of the largest and most important wineries in Australia.

Attempts have been made to denigrate Mary's position as the major founder and first manager of Penfolds Wines, because it is felt that the makers of the famous medal-winning Australian red wine Grange Hermitage should have a man as its sole founder. To counteract the false impression of Mary's subsidiary role in the company (which appears in a book by a male author), the following points should be born in mind:

- Without detracting from Joseph Gillard's contribution to Penfolds Winery, he joined the Penfold business in 1869, only months before Dr Penfold's death. Dr Penfold's involvement had been minimal for some years due to illness. Prior to that he was kept very busy running his thriving medical practice.
- Under an 1869 agreement, Thomas Hyland was the accountant and the marketing agent for Penfolds in Victoria, the state in which he continued to live, leaving Mary to run the winery as she thought fit.
- Mary Penfold remained living on the site of the winery at Grange Cottage. It was Mary who continued to run and oversee the expansion of the Adelaide winery and vineyards, not Thomas Hyland, as the book by Dr Phillip Norrie designed to link male doctors with the manufacture of Penfolds' and Lindeman's wines suggests.

Over the next fifty years Grange Cottage deteriorated badly and after World War II it was about to be demolished. It was saved by the exertions of Mary's great-granddaughter and other members of the family. In 1949, the cottage from which the most famous of the Penfold wines takes its name was opened as a private museum commemorating the achievements of Mary and Christopher Penfold. (At the time of writing the museum is no longer open to the public and most of the original Grange vineyard has been subdivided for a housing estate and sold.)

Penfolds wines have won international fame in wine circles due to the vision and enterprise of a remarkable woman. Revealingly enough, a spokesperson for Southcorp Wines (which now owns Penfolds) admitted to myself and Jeremy Cordeaux during an interview on ABC Radio in Adelaide in the 1980s that 'as men are the major buyers of Grange Hermitage, we like to give our premium reds a *male* image'. Hmmm. This wish for a male image seems tough on Mary Penfold.

As I said years ago on ABC Radio and as I still believe, many women who buy fine wines look forward to the day when they can buy a premium white wine bearing a picture of Mary Penfold on the label. This might be some compensation for the decades-long denial of Mary Penfold's *huge* contribution to the founding and managing of what has become a major and very prestigious export industry for Australia. Denying Mary Penfold her rightful position as co-founder and first manager of an important winery is comparable to the Australian Wool Board denying the role of Elizabeth Macarthur in the founding of the Australian wool industry because shearing sheds have a masculine image.

CHAPTER SEVENTEEN

Portrait photograph: Private collection.

Sister Lucy Osburn
(1835–1891)
AUSTRALIA'S FLORENCE NIGHTINGALE

Lucy Osburn, raven-haired, petite and delicately pretty, was widely travelled in an era when most women rarely left the country of their birth. She accompanied her academic father William Osburn, a well-known Egyptologist, on several study tours to Egypt, the Middle East and Europe.

From childhood Lucy suffered chest infections during the British winter, so she had spent many winters in warmer climes and was fluent in several European languages and, through working as unpaid secretary for her father, had a wider education than most women of her time. Both Florence Nightingale and Lucy Osburn were taught the classics and given a broad sweep of history and literature by their fathers, who had degrees from Cambridge and travelled widely in Europe. These two strong-minded young women horrified their families with their choice of nursing over marriage at a time when the nursing profession had a somewhat disreputable image as an occupation for ladies of ill-fame.

In her mid-twenties when most of her friends were married and raising numerous children, Lucy amazed her family by announcing she wished to take up nursing as a career. Lucy's father was unaware of the enormous changes which were currently taking place in British hospitals as a result of Florence Nightingale's reforms and he was horrified at the thought of his cultured, intelligent daughter working with the illiterate and sluttish women who were, prior to these reforms, employed to nurse the sick and dying in dirty, overcrowded public hospitals.

Lucy's desire to become a highly trained professional nurse started when she accompanied her father to Germany. While he carried out his research in museums, Lucy undertook voluntary work for four months in the important Kaiserwerth Hospital, Dusseldorf, and visited hospitals in Holland and Vienna. Her father did not object to her unpaid work, which he viewed as a genteel philanthropic gesture. Like many others of his time, he did not see nursing as a suitable occupation for a young lady and wanted Lucy to continue helping him with his research.

As Lucy had inherited a small legacy, she was able to defy her father. In 1866 she enrolled in the Nightingale Training School of Nursing attached to London's prestigious St Thomas's Hospital, where she gained valuable experience working in both men's and women's surgical, medical and accident wards. Lucy greatly admired Florence Nightingale; for both of these dedicated women, nursing the sick and dying was more than a job — it was a mission. Previously hospitals had been dirty places where only the poor went to die, while the wealthy were nursed by family members at home. However, Florence Nightingale's insistence on hygienic principles was slowly changing the attitudes of patients and doctors towards the profession of nursing.

Lucy was a steel magnolia with a mind of her own. Against a background of family hostility, she steadfastly continued her nursing studies even though her father turned her portrait to the wall in a gesture of disgust. Her sole support in her professional endeavours was her sister Ann, a teacher who dreamed of leaving home and founding her own school based on modern principles. Lucy finished her nursing training in September 1867 and was proud to be known as Sister Osburn, one of Miss Nightingale's nurses. She went on to study midwifery at another great London teaching hospital, King's College Hospital.

After a personal appeal by New South Wales Colonial Secretary Henry Parkes to Florence Nightingale for trained nurses to staff the Sydney Infirmary and Dispensary, Sister Osburn, now in her early thirties, was invited to apply for the job of Lady Superintendent of the Sydney Hospital. Her constitution was not strong and she hoped that the milder winters of Sydney would alleviate her bronchitis and chest infections. She knew little of the conditions at the old Sydney or 'Rum Hospital' (so-called because it had been built with a levy raised on the sale of rum). She was told that she was expected to establish a training school for nurses in the colony based on Nightingale principles of hygienic nursing and train those nurses currently employed there.

Lucy said a sad farewell to her family and she and the five nursing sisters under her charge endured a long and uncomfortable voyage to Australia. On 5 March 1868 the *Dunbar Castle* sailed into Sydney Cove and all six Nightingale nurses disembarked. Wearing their white starched caps and nurse's uniforms they found that cheering crowds had lined Circular Quay and Macquarie Street to greet their arrival.

Lucy soon discovered that the Sydney Hospital in Macquarie Street, founded by Governor Macquarie and his wife in 1816, over half a century before, was old and dilapidated. There had been criticism in

Parliament and in the Sydney newspapers about the poor administration of the hospital by the House Committee and the Superintendent.

On their arrival Lucy and her nurses were shown round the long hospital building with its wide verandahs. They were horrified to find no running water, wards riddled with vermin and kitchens thick with grease. Cockroaches scuttled out of every crevice and were even seen in the patients' bandages. Ventilation was poor and the stench was overpowering. Patients lay unwashed, covered in bed sores, on unmade beds with mattresses rotten from urine and faeces. The fetid odour of putrefying flesh, open sewers and makeshift latrines permeated the hospital. Lucy was appalled and several nurses could not prevent themselves from vomiting. It was not a good start.

To counteract such an unhealthy working environment Lucy knew that she and her nurses must have good living conditions, but she found that the new nurses' residence promised by Henry Parkes in her letter of appointment was not complete. They were hastily found damp and dirty rooms in the already overcrowded hospital. Later that night Lucy's lamplight tour of the hospital revealed black rats that swarmed onto the wards, ran across the patients' beds, invaded the mortuary and even gnawed on corpses.

There was no going back to England. Lucy knew she must stay and fight for better conditions for her patients. Desperate to initiate reform, she found herself trapped between the dreadful conditions for patients and corrupt and uncooperative administrative staff. The 'nurses' she was expected to train to become health professionals were underpaid and clearly unsuitable. Some had been hospital cleaners, while others with their raddled complexions, greasy hair and bawdy language Lucy suspected of being part-time prostitutes.[1] She discovered some of these 'nurses' smuggled alcohol into the patients for a fee; they would sit on the beds and drink with the patients or even have sex with them. Sometimes the 'nurses' became so drunk on the wards that a desperately sick patient's anguished cries for help fell on very deaf ears.

Lucy knew she must act swiftly to establish discipline. She was a fireball in character but from childhood she had never been physically strong and tired easily. She set about her task of reform immediately but had to stop due to severe dysentery which lasted for two months, probably brought on because the hospital's kitchens were so insanitary and running with cockroaches.[2] Lucy felt depressed and isolated. When she remonstrated with both the Medical Superintendent and the doctors they ignored all her suggestions for change, obviously intimidated by the presence of a woman in a senior position.

Sister Osburn's proposed reforms were obstructed at every turn: the cooks, cleaners and storeman ignored her authority and would only deal with the male superintendent. In a despairing letter to Florence Nightingale,[3] Lucy described the Sydney nurses as 'dirty frowzy looking women'. She wrote how 'the younger ones had long greasy hair hanging down their backs' and wore ragged overalls instead of nursing uniforms. She also confided to Florence Nightingale how lonely she found herself, isolated by her position of command.

Lucy's main rival for power and prestige was the very man who should have helped her to reform the nursing service. The Sydney Hospital Board had appointed Superintendent John Blackstone to administer all aspects of the hospital, and he bitterly resented a woman telling him what to do. Unknown to the Hospital Board, Superintendent Blackstone was an alcoholic: he was far more interested in the bottle than in his work, and his supervision of patients and staff was minimal. Hospital gossips told Lucy that, when a patient from the Solomon Islands died, Blackstone had been drunk and no attendant had been instructed to remove the corpse to the mortuary. The dead man's fellow Islanders who, according to one account, had a long tradition of cannibalism, simply pulled the blankets from the bed, placed the corpse on top and began to roast it for a funeral feast.[4]

Superintendent Blackstone felt threatened by a woman issuing orders that showed up his own inefficiency. His sphere of control under the rules of the Hospital Board clashed with the list of duties Lucy had been given by Premier Parkes and Florence Nightingale. He took positive delight in encouraging his staff to defy Sister Osburn and frustrate her as she attempted to clean up the wards. Lucy and her nurses spent hours spraying disinfectant onto walls and floors, but the bugs lurked in crevices or under the floor. All Lucy's appeals for help to the Hospital Board had to go through Superintendent Blackstone's office and were ignored. To make matters worse, Blackstone continually ran down her work and her character when chatting informally to members of the Hospital Board.

But Lucy worked on doggedly. She was able to send trained nurses to the bush and received glowing reports from country doctors praising them. The foundations of nursing training in Australia were being laid. By the end of the year she had dismissed the worst of the local nurses and trained sixteen more local girls in their place. However, some of her British nurses became jealous. Lucy poured her heart out in long letters home to her relations and to Florence Nightingale describing her achievements: 'a nice staff of nurses now — eighteen have passed as nurses and six probationers. I would greatly like to have more sisters. At present we have only four'.[5]

In an attempt to alleviate her loneliness, Lucy bought herself a small black and tan terrier which proved a faithful companion and a deterrent to the rats that infested the nurses' quarters. Superintendent Blackstone seized on her fondness for the dog to harass Lucy further: he demanded she remove her dog from the hospital. Lucy just smiled sweetly at him but continued to keep the dog in her room.

Another dangerous enemy was visiting surgeon Alfred Roberts (later Sir Alfred), with whom Lucy clashed time and time again over the vermin problem. Alfred Roberts operated at the Sydney Hospital and other places and made a handsome living at it. But Roberts resented Lucy's zeal for reform because he thought it cast a slur on his capabilities and so did everything in his power to get her removed from the job.

On a visit to London Roberts visited Florence Nightingale who, he discovered, had received unfavourable letters about Lucy from two of her English Nightingale nurses, Sister Bessie Chant and Sister Annie Miller (who had previously been disciplined by Lucy because Sister Miller allowed a married house surgeon to visit her bedroom at night and Lucy feared reprisals from his wife). On his return to Sydney Roberts spread rumours that Florence Nightingale was disappointed with Sister Osburn's work. Fortunately Henry Parkes championed Lucy, and he wrote to Florence Nightingale defending her. Parkes described how 'Mr Roberts is a respectable professional man but he is … a fusy [sic], officious diletente [sic] in all matters of sanitary reform, who spoils his own efforts to be useful by his desire to be the authority on all occasions'.

In fact Roberts *did* want reform, although he wanted to effect it himself without consulting a mere nurse. He visited London in 1871 with a view to designing a model hospital but, like many medical men who would later object to employing female doctors, he could not bear to share power with a woman and especially one younger than himself.

Capable but power hungry, Sister Haldane Turriff (later to become the first matron of the Alfred Hospital, Melbourne) saw herself as Lucy's successor and wrote letters of complaint to Florence Nightingale, hoping that if Lucy was dismissed she would be appointed Nursing Supervisor in her place.

Medicine was then an exclusively male profession. There were, as yet, no female doctors working on the wards to support Lucy. Many male doctors supported Alfred Roberts in his campaign to make life so difficult for Sister Osburn that she would resign and go back to England. Some even refused to write essential information about patients' diseases on the chart that hung at the end of each hospital bed. When Lucy tried to hold lectures for her trainee nurses, Alfred Roberts or one of his medical colleagues would arrive unexpectedly and disrupt her lectures by demanding the nurses go back on the wards and prepare patients for operation immediately.[6]

Lucy's order to a staff member to burn a cockroach-infested box of damaged and mouldy books and magazines that contained pages torn from an old Bible was 'magnified into a systematic and determined burning of Bibles on my part', Lucy wrote angrily. Distorted accounts in which Lucy had taken a devilish delight in burning a box of Bibles were spread by Sister Miller. Further damage to Lucy's reputation ensued when the Bible-burning story was printed in the *Protestant Standard*.

Following publication of the article, a subcommittee was hastily convened to judge Lucy's actions. They deliberated for six weeks before finally clearing her of the charges. The whole farcical incident seriously affected both staff morale and Sister Osburn's disciplinary powers, but she carried on working tirelessly at great cost to her own health. However, Parkes and others in political and philanthropic circles admired Lucy for her ideas and her dedication and they began to voice a growing discontent with the incompetent and corrupt hospital administrators. The Legislative Assembly appointed a Royal Commission of Inquiry which examined 58 witnesses as well as Lucy herself.

In 1873 the Public Charities Committee under Judge William Windeyer was convened and Alfred Roberts gave evidence stating that Lucy had failed in her duties. Windeyer was not convinced by Roberts' statement, and his wife, Lady Mary Windeyer, a great champion of woman, may have helped Windeyer see things from a balanced perspective by pleading Lucy's case.

After an exhaustive inquiry the Commission condemned the Sydney Hospital's 'horrible' operating room, the stench of rotting flesh and the lice and cockroaches on the wards. The Commission accused the House Committee of 'utter neglect' and 'interfering between the head of the nursing establishment and her nurses'. The Commission blamed the Hospital's Board of Directors and the House Committee and said they were making every mistake in hospital management that Florence Nightingale had warned against in her writings. Sister Osburn was totally vindicated. The final report praised the 'vast improvement in the nursing services' and raised Sister Osburn's salary. [7]

The report on the Sydney Hospital led to a public scandal when it called for the sacking of Superintendent Blackstone. Major reforms were slow to be implemented, but with Blackstone gone Lucy Osburn was officially in charge of wards, patients, nurses, cooking and domestic staff. By now she had made firm friends with Lady Windeyer and her daughter Lucy, and with Emily Macarthur, wife of James Macarthur, and her married daughter Elizabeth Macarthur Onslow, but Lucy found that even supportive friends in high places were no substitute for her sister Ann. It had been more than a decade since Lucy had left England and she longed to return home to visit her.

By 1884 she had spent sixteen productive years in Sydney. She felt that she had reformed the nursing service in New South Wales and laid the foundations for one of the best nursing training systems in the world. Lucy was by then in her forties and suffering from diabetes. She returned to London to seek a specialist opinion about her illness, intending to come back to Australia for good once her health improved. From 1886 to 1888 Lucy succeeded in managing her diabetic condition relatively well. A workaholic, she could not leave nursing although earning money was never her main aim. She worked on a temporary basis as an underpaid district nurse among the sick poor in London's Bloomsbury and was promoted to

Superintendent of the Southwark, Newington and Walworth District Nursing Association.

Lucy still talked of returning to New South Wales but as her diabetes became more acute her doctors strongly advised against it. She became frailer and suffered fainting fits. In 1891, aged only fifty-six, on a visit to her sister's boarding school in Harrogate, Lucy collapsed and died from diabetic complications. Ironically Florence Nightingale, who was fifteen years older than Lucy and had already been a bedridden recluse for many years, outlived the lively Lucy Osburn by almost twenty years.

Money she had left behind in New South Wales awaiting her return was bequeathed in her will to her namesake, young Lucy Windeyer. Lady Mary Windeyer and other friends raised funds for a plaque to be placed in the Sydney Hospital in memory of Sister Lucy Osburn and the nursing reforms she initiated.

Lucy Osburn's battle for professional status for nurses and better conditions in hospitals forged the basis of Australia's highly regarded nursing services. Both she and Florence Nightingale elevated nursing to a level of professionalism that it had never had before and the name of Lucy Osburn deserves to be an honoured one in Australia.

CHAPTER EIGHTEEN

Mary McConnel
(1824–1910)
FOUNDER OF THE ROYAL CHILDREN'S HOSPITAL, BRISBANE

Dark-haired, demure Mary McLeod met her future husband, David McConnel, when visiting her brother, a medical practitioner in Yorkshire. David was also visiting his brother, who farmed near Mary's brother.

David McConnel, a typical Scots Presbyterian and from a farming background, was well-built and athletic and had sandy blond hair. He had just returned from Queensland, then known as Northern New South Wales, where through hard work and initiative he had established the first sheep station on the upper Brisbane River, called Cressbrook.[1] Mary's parents were city dwellers from Edinburgh and the rest of her family were either in medicine or the church. There was instant attraction between the blond young squatter and Mary, whose engagement portrait shows her with her long dark hair demurely fastened into an elegant chignon. She was religious, idealistic but surprisingly practical for one so young and had qualities of gentleness and sympathy which were to make her loved by everyone who knew her.

Mary's father Alexander McLeod gave David permission to marry his daughter the following year on the understanding that the young couple would remain in England to farm near Nottingham but, a few months later, David was urgently summoned back to Cressbrook by his brother John for financial reasons.

In 1848 Mary McConnel, then aged twenty-four, was faced with the difficult dilemma of whether to let her husband return to Australia without her and stay behind to look after her elderly parents or accompany David, who had originally promised her parents that he would stay on in England and let his brother John run the Australian property in his place. If she accompanied her husband to the Brisbane River Valley, Mary would be one of the few white women for hundreds of miles. With her deep faith that God was guiding her life for a special purpose, she chose to go with her husband aboard the *Chasely,* an old, leaky, rat-infested vessel. Mary recounts how:

> ...I was led to decide in favour of going to Australia. The cup was a bitter one, but it had its own sweetness. I wrote to my dear parents, telling them that I must go, and asking them to commend me to God's care. Their hurt, reluctant consent was given and we left our friends and beloved Scotland. Then we went to London to make preparations for our departure on 31 December 1848.

The ship *Chasely* had been chartered, along with two others, by Dr John Dunmore Lang, whose church was in Sydney, New South Wales.[2] These three ships were to convey well-chosen superior emigrants, intended to populate the towns that had been formed about 20 years before in the newly opened district of Moreton Bay. My husband took cabins in the *Chasely* for ourselves and our maid [Hannah].

The emigrants had availed themselves of Dr Dunmore Lang's arrangement with the British Government that on payment of 200 pounds they should have land privileges on arrival in Brisbane. The evening before sailing, Dr Lang came on board, and addressed the emigrants in a fatherly manner, reminding them of their responsibilities in making their home in a new land, and bidding them to be true to their religious principles. My husband made our large cabin in the stern most comfortable. Our bookshelf was well filled; two swinging candle lamps gave a fair light. We had a large double sofa that shut up into a single one for the day.

We set sail on a voyage which was to take four months. The weather continued boisterous, and we crossed the Bay of Biscay in a gale. There we had the misfortune to lose overboard in a giant wave all our poultry and our sheep we had brought with us, save one which was reserved for a sumptuous repast when we arrived in Moreton Bay!

We had a disagreeable experience of rats both by day and night. My husband knew my antipathy to these rodents, and had brought two terriers with us, one from Skye, the other English. One we always had in our cabin; the other was invariably out on loan! At meals I always sat with my heels under me, the only protection I could have at these times. These rats became so numerous that water had to be put out for them to drink as it was found they were gnawing the ship, seeking for water since they were so thirsty.

There was real hardship when our fresh provisions were finished. Salt beef and pork were not at all appetising. We were very badly off for vegetables, milk and butter, as the art of preserving these items was at a very rudimentary stage. The bread was always heavy and dark, so we had to fall back upon mouldy ships' biscuits. We were each restricted to three pints of fresh water daily, for all purposes. We had a saltwater bath, which it would have been hard to do without.

In spite of all these drawbacks, we had pleasant times ... We were all young married women, full of wonderment about the faraway land that was to be our home.[3]

They arrived in Moreton Bay on 1 May 1849. Mary reminisces:

My husband, self and maid were invited to leave the ship in the Customs boat. We took our two terriers with us. We were some hours going up the river to Brisbane. What a dismal waterway it was! Neither sign of house nor man and mangroves the only vegetation visible. Soon we were near Brisbane. The first building by the river was the Customs House, and close by lay Mr Thornton's cottage, from which there was a jetty. In the cottage we could see two ladies using a telescopic spyglass to see who was in the boat. An immigrant vessel landing in the Bay was an object of great excitement in those days. The landing took place and we were introduced to Mr Thornton's wife and stepdaughter. After me came my traps [suitcases etc.], just such things as ladies in England travel with. One lady looked at them in amazement and pointed out to me that they would be of little use in Brisbane as there were no roads. My heart sank.

The houses did not have the luxury of spare rooms, so my husband secured accommodation for us in the only hotel which Brisbane could boast, the Bowes Inn. There Dr Ballow brought his young wife to see me. There were no ladies travelling, so the landlord thought it useless to provide public sitting rooms which would not be used. We were shown into a bare dining room, with a long table and many chairs. Several men were there who left when we entered. The verandah was the great rendezvous. I went into our rooms but when I wanted to shut the door I found that I had to put a chair against it as there was no handle, lock, nor bolt! I looked for a blind to the window, but it was innocent of such a luxury, and I could not spare the one towel to give the room privacy. Other things were equally unpleasant and we decided that we must leave the hotel.

My brother-in-law, Mr John McConnel, was also in the Colony. At the time of our arrival he had two rooms in Brisbane Town. When he heard that his brother David was just married and was bringing his wife to Moreton Bay, he had at once come to Sydney to look out for us. Although John had been told by letter that we were sailing direct for Moreton Bay, it was long after our arrival that he received that letter.

Meanwhile we took possession of his two private rooms in a cottage belonging to Mr Swan, a quiet and respectable man, former owner of the *Courier*. The cottage was in George Street, where it crossed Queen Street, the principal thoroughfare.

The cottage was weatherboard, with a narrow verandah. A French window opened from the verandah into the sitting room. Another door, at the opposite end, led into the bedroom. They were sorry apartments. The sitting room had as its only contents a table, some chairs, and two large packing cases containing the skins of birds and animals which John had preserved with evil-smelling arsenic, to send away to a museum. In this room there was no fireplace. I had become accustomed to bad cooking on board ship. Here it was no better, but at least the food was fresh, which was a decided improvement. It was all very rough and I had not learned to cope with this. Brisbane was a township with no general store. One does not easily get accustomed to such things.

In the evening of the day we moved into the rooms I heard a rustling noise, and a swarm of large, black flying insects hit me on the face. They came from behind the chest of drawers. I called out to my husband in terror. He said they were flying cockroaches! We had no protection from them that night. But next day we made net curtains to hang around the bed. Everything was unpleasant, although my dear husband made the best of it all for me.

There had been no rain for some months; now it began to fall in torrents. No one had a carriage of any sort, not even Captain John Wickham, the Government Resident. His house, Newstead, at Breakfast Creek, was some miles down the river. He rode on horseback into town along what is now Wickham Street, but everyone else came and went by river. There were no proper roads, and in such weather a carriage would have been of little use. My husband had gone to the ship to get our belongings on shore and his absence made it more dark and cheerless, and I was glad to find a fireplace in our bedroom.

When the rain cleared people came to call on me — Captain and Mrs Wickham, Dr and Mrs Ballow, Mr Duncan, Collector of Customs, with his wife and daughter. They were all most cordial in their expressions of welcome. Mrs Annie Wickham was a daughter of Hannibal Hayes Macarthur, of Vineyard, Sydney, who I think was the first to introduce sheep into the Moreton Bay district. Mrs Wickham was young and very charming. Later she became a good friend to me. [Anna Wickham was married to Captain John Wickham, who had been on the voyage of the *Beagle* with Charles Darwin and Conrad Martens. Their home, Newstead House, was then Brisbane's unofficial Government House.]

Before long our brother returned from Sydney. He was glad to have a sister in this new and faraway land, and nothing could exceed the heartiness of his welcome. We had to vacate his apartments and we found a small, wooden, five-roomed cottage on Kangaroo Point, on the south side of the river. The walls were unlined weatherboards and the shingled roof was very leaky. There was a 4 foot wide verandah along the front, enclosed by a wooden paling. We were forced to put most of our imported furniture in a shed, but we had to find room for the piano, one of our wedding gifts. This could only be done by blocking the door that gave access to the verandah, so that all our visitors had to enter through the kitchen. The roof of the sitting room was so leaky that when a shower came I had to place utensils to catch the raindrops to save my pretty things. And yet, how happy we were in that rough little place!

My husband bought acres of land at Bulimba, a few miles down the river on the south side, and set about clearing and building. I accompanied him and the surveyor when they went down to inspect the land. It was too rough for me to go all the way, so they seated me on a log to await their return. It was then that I made my first acquaintance with a snake, lying in a heap of withered leaves. It raised its head, showing a beautiful scarlet throat. I seemed hypnotised and could not take my eyes away from it, but I did not feel any fear.

The work of clearing the land and building Bulimba House became an unfailing object of interest to us. Our only way of going to the spot was by river, so my husband purchased a boat. We took many boat trips, spending days watching the progress of our new home. The house was built of white freestone, brought up in punts from a quarry some miles down the river.

While we were waiting for our new home to be ready we paid a visit to Cressbrook, my husband's station about 90 miles up the Brisbane River. It was a sheep and cattle station found and taken up by him in 1841–42. The journey was a formidable one for a lady to take in those days, especially for me as I could not ride. We had brought out with us a heavy, four-wheeled phaeton which we had used during the few months that we lived in Nottinghamshire, and we travelled in that. It seated four. My husband and I sat in front, and Hannah, with the smallest amount of luggage we could possibly do with, sat behind. The groom led spare horses, carrying saddlebags filled with clothing. As there were neither made roads nor bridges, we had some rough experiences. To save the phaeton's springs, they were bound up with green hide, the untanned hide of a bullock cut up in strips, not very elegant in appearance, but answering our purpose well.

Half way along our journey was a small township called Woogaroo, now the site of an enormous lunatic asylum [Woolston Park Hospital]. The place is beautifully situated on the Brisbane River. A pretty cottage in this early township was the home of Dr Stephen Simpson, the first Commissioner of Crown Lands for the Moreton Bay district. He was a man past middle life and a widower, a doctor of medicine, who had travelled much. We greatly enjoyed his interesting accounts of his travels. This was my first experience of bush hospitality; his hearty welcome was delightful. We were made most comfortable; his arrangements were simple but with an air of refinement.

From here it was an easy journey to Ipswich, or Limestone as it was then called. Being the head of navigation, it was a busy little town. Goods came up from Brisbane by river and the streets were lined with long teams of bullocks and drays that had brought wool, tallow, and hides from the interior. They were reloaded with necessary goods for the stations: flour, tea and sugar, as well as all the contents of a bush store.

The Ipswich Inn we stayed at was a rough little place and very rowdy. We started early next day, a rough way over miles of black soil. It was a feat of dexterity to keep clear of the ruts made by the great wheels of the heavily laden bullock drays. We crossed impossible looking gullies with steep and often slippery banks! I used to shut my eyes, abandoning myself to God. Then we came to 'wattle-tree country', poor soil, but so pretty, for the trees were in bloom, and the air fragrant with their sweet scent. We had to keep zigzagging to avoid fallen trees.

It had been a long, weary day, and it was quite late when we arrived at Wivenhoe Inn. Many drays were camped all about, their drivers carousing inside. The man and his wife who kept the Wivenhoe Inn seemed quite respectable. We had a private room, if one could call such a room private, for the partition separating it from the public room was of wooden boards 6 feet high! It was the same in our bedroom. The landlady brought in our supper of a fine ham, new-laid eggs, good bread and delicious fresh butter. We were very tired, and glad to rest.

Through the space between the partition and the shingled roof every single sound was heard, and, as the night wore on, the obscene talk of the bullock-drivers became unbearable. My husband went to the landlord to ask if he could quiet them. It was no use. Their money was just as good as other people's, they replied, so we had to endure it.

We were off early next morning. A long journey was before us, with nowhere that we could stay the night till we reached Cressbrook. We stopped at the house of Major and Mrs North for lunch. The Major had lost a good deal of money by standing as security for a member of his family. He honourably paid his debt and came to Australia trying to retrieve his fortune. Their cottage was bark, with an earthen floor which was very uneven. His wife went to a box and took out a snow-white damask tablecloth, spread it on the rickety pine table, unsteady because of holes in the floor, and laid out on it some beautiful old silver. I was even more amazed when I saw her take a great pot off the fire, carry it outside and drain the water from the boiled fowls.

After the meal we hurried away as we had to reach Cressbrook before dark. About 8 miles from the head station my husband stopped and bade me welcome to Cressbrook. Neither white man nor black did I see, nor hoof nor stock, and the stories about his sheep and cattle seemed to me all a myth, and I said so. My husband only laughed. As we neared the station the country became very pretty, and the road grew much better.

The crossing of Cressbrook Creek was beautiful. However, the banks were steep and the crossing difficult. Two and a half miles further we came to a chain of lagoons. Here we were met by the super [superintendent or farm manager], Alpin Cameron, a big burly Scotsman, who gave us a hearty welcome. It cheered me to see a pretty, neat cottage and a well-stocked garden with a grapevine. Just in front of the house was a bunya tree planted by my husband in 1843. It is now a giant, called grandfather's tree. I felt rested, glad and thankful, for after the experience of the last two days I did not know what to expect.

We had a suite composed of sitting, sleeping and dressing rooms. The house was quiet and comfortable, though terribly bare. We took our meals in the common dining room. Our first meal was in the evening. The super presided. I sat beside my husband. There was an enormous tin teapot that held at least 8 quarts and it took both hands to lift it. There was an apology made for the sugar, which was as near black as could be. When the super learnt that I was coming to Cressbrook he had ridden to the various stations around, none of them nearer than 12 miles, to try in vain to get white sugar. Master and men shared alike what food was available. In the middle of the long table there was a huge mutton fat lamp which was not pleasant to smell but it gave a fairly good light. I often sat down with 14 men, most of them travellers arriving at sundown, which is never later than 7 o'clock. Cressbrook was on the main road. We often had very pleasant people to dinner, but I was always the only woman.

During that time I witnessed the most sudden and severe storm that I have ever experienced. Everybody was at the woolshed and I was alone in the house. Suddenly the sky become overcast, then black. It was almost dark when the rain, accompanied by hail, came down in torrents. The roofs were not sealed, and through the dry shingles the storm spouted down. There was not a dry spot or thing in the house. I was terrified. My husband and brother-in-law ran as fast as they could since the woolshed was some distance off and the water in places was already up to their knees, incredible as it may seem. They were much concerned as everything was dripping wet. Big woodfires were soon blazing, and Hannah, together with the married couple in the kitchen, set to work to make things better. Of course I did my share, and was glad to be busy. Many sheep were killed by the force of the storm.

I was troubled by the bareness and shabbiness of our sitting room, which had a very old sofa, six old cane chairs, and a square cedar table, but nothing more. One afternoon while my husband had gone to town to see how our house at Bulimba was progressing, my brother-in-law showed me the stores. There were bags of flour and sugar, chests of tea, saddles, bridles, hobbles, men's clothing and tobacco. In the corner of a shelf I spied a roll of unbleached thin grey linen. On my request it was brought into the house.

Mary used this linen to cover the sofa and chairs and her husband's crimson silk handkerchiefs as piping for the covers. Expecting her husband to be angry, Mary rushed to finish the room before he returned from work. Much to her surprise he was delighted with the results of her resourcefulness. In December they were able to move into Bulimba House, which was still not complete.

We moved into one large room, making a dividing partition of strong unbleached calico, the inner division [became] our bedroom, while we made the front part as nice a living room as possible. Beyond this was the store. The servant's room was overhead. No servants could be procured nearer than Sydney, although very soon after immigrant ships came directly to Moreton Bay. Our servants, a man and his wife, seemed respectable and capable. The woman was cook and laundress, the man was an indoor servant and also helped his wife. Hannah was housemaid and generally useful.

As the hot weather increased the mosquitoes became intolerable. I took refuge in our large bed, safely tucked inside the net curtains with my work, books and writing materials. With a swamp close by, the pests could not have been worse. Early in 1850 an immigrant ship arrived. From it we obtained an excellent gardener, James Johnston from Edinburgh. He had a nice young wife and a baby. The interesting work of gardening began and several acres of ornamental grounds in front and at the sides of the house were created. There was also a large and useful kitchen garden. My husband encouraged settlement of respectable families near to him. He had bought a good deal of land, and portions of this he sold to his work people. They had it on easy terms, making regular payment from their wages. Then from time to time they were let off work, allowing them to begin clearing and making their homes. I think our gardener was the first one to start. He was delighted with the new country and wished to bring his father and mother out. To have a house ready for them he worked hard all his spare hours.

Just about this time my first baby was born, and Mrs Johnston was my nurse as there were no special nurses available in those early days. I had a good doctor and all went well. James Johnston, our gardener, rose to own a sugar mill, built on his own land. He was a very intelligent man and well read, a grand type of my own countrymen. Ultimately he became a member of Parliament. These people, who remained with us down to the third generation, were invaluable. About this time my husband set up a large dairy at Cressbrook and had a milking herd of beautiful Devon cows. Another Scottish family was that of Thomas Cairns. Aided by his wife he took over the poultry yard and their daughter became our nursery-maid.

Among Dr Lang's immigrants was a first class cabinet-maker named Towell. My husband engaged him to come to Bulimba to make the furniture for the house, all except the beds which we brought from England. He used cedar and stained pine, and it was much admired by our visitors.

It was a busy time, clearing, draining, ploughing, with everything growing like mushrooms. Thus began the thriving district now called Bulimba. We began to have a considerable population around us. Among them were a number of children and we cast about to devise means for education and Sabbath observance. All the young people and their elders that came from the old country knew their three r's and were very intelligent. There was no teacher to be had in Brisbane, although there were one or two schools. My husband and I each had a large Sunday School class, he of boys and I of girls, and all except the little ones read to us. They were very regular in attendance, prepared their lessons well, and were quiet and attentive.

We also had frequent services on Sunday afternoons. There were two ministers in Brisbane, one Church of England, the other Independent.

They held regular Sunday services at Bulimba. About this time Mary's second son was born, although she does not mention the date of the birth.

On the north side the way was very rough, without a formed road. My enterprising husband bought a strip of land running from our ferry to North Brisbane, fenced it on both sides, and made a road. He also built stables, a little coach-house and a dwelling. There we put our conveyance, two horses and a man in charge, who also had charge of the ferry boat. This arrangement added greatly to our comfort and convenience.

In South Brisbane much business was being done with Ipswich and the bush, so it became a busy place. The Rev Mr Mowbray, who lived in Kangaroo Point, used to have services in South Brisbane when his health allowed him. He suggested to my husband that a Presbyterian church might be built there. A wooden church was erected, seating about 200 people.

In 1852 my youngest brother, Rev Walter McLeod, arrived unexpectedly from Scotland. My joy was unbounded for not one familiar face had I seen since I came to this far off land. In those days when a steamer was coming up the river a bell was rung to announce the event a long way below our reach of the Brisbane River. On the day when this bell heralded my brother's arrival, we hastened down with our little son; and he and I stood by the boat-shed while the boat was rowed out into mid-stream by my husband to meet the steamer. I could scarcely bear my joy when I watched my brother leave it and enter the boat. As it neared the bank I came out of the darkness, and then the moment arrived when we were locked in each other's arms. He was three years younger than I, always delicate and needing tender care.

We had grown a great many pineapples, and I wished to send a hundredweight of pineapple jam to my relatives in England and Scotland. This caused a busy time, the pineapples first had to be reduced to pulp, placed in large earthenware jars and sprinkled with sugar. The work was done in my beautiful large storeroom.

At about one or two o'clock in the morning I awoke and found myself standing on the floor of our room, some way from the bed. I did not return to bed, but was impelled to walk towards the nursery. The moon shone brightly when I entered it. I passed Harry's cot, with its net curtains drawn and tucked in. I then passed the nurse's bed. All seemed still and peaceful. I watched the moon beams playing on the water and then turned again. Repassing Harry's cot I thought the moonbeams were too strong on it, and I went to draw the dimity curtain, when I thought the child looked strange. I instantly threw back the curtain and found he was in a fit, with his face dark purple, foam all round his mouth, his eyes glazed and his body rigid, cold and shaking. I took him in my arms, awakened the nurse and called my husband. The nurse went at once for hot water.

My kind friend and neighbour, Mrs Wickham had written for my benefit a list of rules useful for a young mother. One rule was never to be without hot water. [Mrs Wickham lived at Newstead House.] This I adhered to most faithfully, so that our darling child was soon in a hot bath and he became less rigid. We tried to give him castor oil, the only thing we had for an emetic, but his teeth were clenched and we could not open them. Soon there was no need of an emetic for he brought up a great quantity of pineapple pulp. After this he quickly recovered, and the life of our child was saved. Unobserved, the child had been running backwards and forwards taking each time a handful of the delicious pineapple pulp. He was under two years of age but was very precocious, walking at ten months and speaking early. How glad and thankful I was that I kept the rules given to me by my dear friend Annie Wickham [who would, shortly after, die of an unknown tropical fever].

I had begun to feel contented and happy in my far-away home. The distance caused the only heartache in my otherwise happy life. I had one of the best and kindest of husbands, two boys and my beloved brother. My new home was beautiful, and there was much in which I could take a real interest. Our people were very dependent upon us, and it was in our power to help them.

Mary grew into a confident, well-organised and hard working woman who came to love her adopted land and coped well with the trials of pioneering. Since one of her brothers was a doctor she had some medical knowledge, and she visited any sick woman or child within riding distance. Mary dispensed sensible medical counsel, books to read and medicine when suitable. However, when she developed a lump on her own knee, an alcoholic doctor informed her husband she was dying with gangrene and left her to her own devices. Mary relates the progress of her severe illness:

One day there was a regatta in Moreton Bay. My husband was very fond of boating. I was feeling better, and I persuaded him to go to the regatta while my brother remained with me. Towards evening I became very ill, fainting continually. My brother was anxious and sent one of our men for my husband and for the doctor, who also was sailing on the bay. My husband arrived and every restoration was tried, but still I continued fainting. The doctor was long in coming, so my husband sent again and again. At last he came but was quite tipsy. When he entered my room, the smell of drink made me sick. He looked at me, felt my pulse, and then took my husband aside to tell him I was dying and would not live till morning. He left some foolish prescription, and took his departure.

When day was breaking my brother carried me downstairs to the drawing room. I was laid on a couch by the open French windows. It was haymaking time. The farm servants, who were Germans, sang while they worked. The fresh early morning, the scent of hay and the rhythmic merry singing seemed to work as a charm on me. There gradually came longer intervals between the faintings. My husband, after consultation with my brother, decided to ride to Ipswich, some 30 miles [48 km] away, and fetch Dr Sachs to see me. We parted with the probability of not meeting again on earth. I commended him to God and he started off.

On arrival in Ipswich my husband begged the doctor to come to Bulimba. But the doctor had a most important case on hand and could not leave and suggested that I come to Ipswich to see him. My husband decided to engage a river steamer to go to Toogooloowah [the Bulimba property, as it was also known] to fetch me and he found a furnished cottage with four very small rooms. He returned home to find me no worse. Next morning the steamer arrived and I was carried on board in my bed. A widowed sister of James Johnston came with me as nurse and Harry and a maid also accompanied me. I had to leave my baby behind with his nurse, who was a good and tender woman. My brother, who came also, lodged with my husband at a hotel close by.

I bore the journey well, and my bed was put in the largest of the four little rooms. Dr Sachs came as soon as possible. After examination he took my husband aside and said, 'I cannot undertake this case. Your wife probably will die and I will be blamed for it. I have a reputation to make.' At last he yielded to earnest pleading. On the following day he took charge of my almost hopeless case. The leg was much worse than he had anticipated and he proposed amputation. My dear husband tenderly broke this painful alternative to me. When I said that I would rather die, Dr Sachs agreed to try and save my leg.

For many weeks he poured liquid caustic down my leg but to me it felt like water. However he persevered and twice a day applied the caustic and bandages. I had a cane lounge chair put on wheels and was kept out in the open air all day long, and scarcely had any food, only bread dipped in champagne and herb tea made by the doctor.

One day, while having the caustic poured down my leg, I suddenly had a feeling as if a little red hot cinder was rolling down my limb. Dr Sachs threw down what was in his hand, gave a skip across the floor and excitedly cried, 'Now I can give you hope. Life is coming back to the limb!' From that day there was a steady though slow improvement.

Now I felt stronger I had a great longing to see my baby. He came up from Bulimba with his nurse and he looked so bonnie! It was good for me to have him with me again. However teething problems went hard with him. I do not think the good doctor understood the treatment of infants and my beautiful boy died when he was only seven months old. I tried not to fret, and sought to be resigned to our Father's will. His little forlorn brother wept and fretted. His father brought him a little toy from Brisbane. He looked at it, burst into tears, and returning it to his father said, 'Papa give it to God, and ask Him to give it to my little brother Alick'.

Then the day came when I was allowed to use crutches, but my foot scarcely touched the floor. Gradually it improved and one day I told the Doctor that, if I had a high-heeled shoe, I probably could walk. He replied that I should never have high-heeled shoes since I must compel my leg to get straight and he was right. After about a year and a half I walked as well as ever and my heart was full of gratitude. I prayed that I might become a better woman, with a heart alive to the sufferings of others and able to help them.[4]

Undoubtedly these painful experiences caused Mary to become the motivating force in the founding of what is now the Royal Children's Hospital and increased Mary's faith that God had sent her to Queensland with a special mission in life. Mary's eldest daughter, Mary (the future Mrs Banks), described how a laundry maid got into difficulties in the creek at Cressbrook while the children were bathing. While all around her panicked, her mother, who could not swim, quietly waded out to her in water up to her chin in spite of her heavy skirts and crinoline and saved the hysterical girl from drowning by dragging her to safety.[5] She had that quiet day-to-day courage which characterised so many Australian pioneer women.

Mary McConnel had been brought up in a cultured, academic and sheltered world but at Cressbrook and at Bulimba House she coped with daily emergencies, hard physical work in subtropical surroundings, illness and isolation, acting as manager of all household and dairy activities as well as unpaid social worker to their numerous tenants and employees, behaving as 'to the manor born' since her husband was indeed one of the largest landowners and employers in Queensland at that time. In that era long before the welfare state Mary fulfilled many roles — teacher, counsellor and even medical adviser — and was sustained by her religious faith that her role in life was to help those less fortunate than herself. Some time after recovering from her gangrenous leg she had another accident when her horse bolted and she was thrown from the trap; again she went to Ipswich but she was only badly shaken. Her husband decided they would sell Bulimba House and visit England to give Mary a rest.

The following seven years were spent in England, Scotland and on the Continent. Four more children were born to us during that time, two sons and two daughters, and my husband went once to Australia. While he was away my ten months old baby boy died, which was a great grief to me.

Eventually my husband found it necessary to return to Queensland. As the length of his stay was indefinite, I desired to go with him. Since the summer heat in Australia had such a disastrous effect on my health, it was thought better that I should stay in Europe. My doctor said that I was in perfect health and that he could not see any reason why I should not go with my husband. However he advised that, if my health began to suffer, I should return home without delay. We decided Alpin [an Aboriginal boy they had adopted] should return with us.

In 1862 we again sailed for Australia in a sailing vessel bound for Sydney. I had an excellent nurse for the baby and we had quite a comfortable voyage. About a year before, the Moreton Bay district and all to the north of it had been formed into a new colony called Queensland, with Brisbane for its capital. Sir George Bowen was our first Governor.

On our return we found a great change for the better in things generally, although Brisbane was still in a very crude state. There were more people but no good hotel. Queensland now had its own Parliament and my husband was asked to become [a] member of the Legislative Council. However he respectfully declined the honour. There was no easy way of getting to town in these days, so to accept meant he would have to live in Brisbane while the House was sitting. He did not wish to be so long away from Cressbrook, especially as he had been absent for nearly eight years. In declining he said he would leave the honour to one of his sons.

My husband set himself to make friends with the different tribes that lived on the land of Cressbrook and they soon got to like and trust him. He never failed to do what he promised. I know that one or two of the Aboriginal men speared cattle, once they killed an imported bull from England, but of course they had no idea of the value of the animal.

Mary was an efficient manager at Cressbrook, where the storeroom was kept locked and groceries in short supply were noted down by her on a slate so they could be brought once a month by bullock wagon from Brisbane. Soap, tea, flour and working clothes for the men on the property were all dispensed from the storeroom by Mary. The storeroom was constantly plagued by ants and she insisted that all sweet things be placed on stands with their feet in saucers of water, which the ants would not cross. Behind the house lay the outbuildings with stables for the draught horses and the pure-bred stock, barns for hay and corn cobs, a schoolhouse where a morning and midday bell was rung to summon the children, a blacksmith's forge and a row of little wooden houses where the stockmen, the ploughmen, the blacksmith and an old Irish carpenter lived with their wives and children.

Mary grew attached to some of the Aboriginal women and was distressed when they were ill-treated by their menfolk.

My little Harry, when he was a baby, was very fond of an Aboriginal woman named Long Kitty. She was very affectionate and liked to have charge of him, so I let her go to the river and bathe him. I gave her a comb and a loose red gown and she would come up very smart, with her hair parted — 'likit missus' — and ask for the baby. Another interesting native woman was also called Kitty, the wife of Piggie Nerang. Kitty was very pretty, she came from Durundur, and grew very fond of me and the children; she was very affectionate. Polly was another fine 'gin' who was very cruelly abused by her husband, who had knocked out her front teeth. She was a gentle creature with a little daughter named Clara. Kitty also had a little daughter named Topsy, who was full of mischief. I tried to separate these children a little from the tribes. I arranged a room for them where their clothes were kept and where they had a tepid bath every morning, for although I had provided warm beds I could not prevent them from going off to the camp at night to sleep by the camp-fire. They learned to read a little and to sew, to repeat and sing verses and hymns, but when the tribe went on their nomadic excursions leaving their clothes behind and wearing nothing but possum skins nothing would induce them to leave the little girls behind. So on their return everything had to be learned again. The Aboriginal mothers are certainly very fond of their children.

We had another station, Durundur, about 30 miles away. It had been agreed that by giving a year's notice on either side the partnership would be dissolved and my brother-in-law would have Durundur if he wished, while Cressbrook was to be my husband's property. After the dissolution of the partnership we built a large addition to the old Cressbrook homestead making it our permanent home.[6] When my brother-in-law went to Durundur we made the cottage into bachelor's quarters. [After her husband's death Mary lived for an extended period in the cottage.]

After Sunday school each week we gave the children numbers of *Sunday Magazine* and *Sunday at Home* for their parents. The children got plenty of books and we took a great deal of pains in teaching them to sing. After school they joined their parents in a walk by the river. Many changes took place. Sandy Creek [now Esk], 15 miles away was made a township and most of our people bought land there. The conditions of sale were that the purchasers *must* reside on their allotments and improve the land. The men had not enough money to do that as they could not give up work, so as soon as possible they moved their wives and families down and joined them from Saturday till early Monday morning. But there were neither churches nor schools.

Our silver wedding took place about this time, and my husband bought, cleared and fenced land in Esk for a church and parsonage, in commemoration of our silver wedding. Then we set about building the church and parsonage. State schools were being established and, as there was a sufficient number of children to warrant a school at Esk, we at once applied and got one. Soon the school was built and a teacher placed in it so the children were all right. At Cressbrook there were also enough children to enable us to apply for a provisional school. The conditions were that a schoolhouse and house for the teacher should be provided by the applicants, also that the teacher should be provided with food, firewood, etc. We made application for the teacher we already had at Cressbrook. Her certificates were accepted and she continued for some years.

There was a good deal of immigration from England, Scotland and Ireland, and a number of the immigrants took up land around us. I was interested to visit them and see just how hard they worked homemaking when money was scarce. Trees had to be felled and slabs prepared for the huts. Wives bravely helped their husbands with the cross-cut saw and when the roots of the trees were laid bare to be burnt out, they helped to keep the fire going. Meanwhile the families lived in tents loaned by the government ... There were frequent accidents and sickness among the children of these migrants, sometimes necessitating them to be taken to town. This could be difficult and bad for the patient when transported by a springless cart over rough roads. When they arrived in town there was often a long period of waiting before the doctor saw the patient, prescribed and got his fee of ten shillings.[7]

Due to the tragic death of her two babies and her own illness, Mary had long been interested in infant and child welfare. While overseas she had visited both the Sick Children's Hospital in Edinburgh and the famous Great Ormond Street Hospital for Sick Children and observed their methods. She had seen that during the pioneering days Queensland was no place for a sick child; many children failed to survive to the age of five because of the outmoded attitudes towards childcare and nourishment. There was no children's hospital and no special wards for children between the ages of five and adulthood.

As adequate medical care is today seen as the birthright of every Australian, it is difficult to imagine the heavy burden of responsibility carried by pioneer mothers. They struggled single-handedly to cope with the task of raising large families in remote areas with little recourse to medical or hospital assistance in an emergency. Lack of proper facilities certainly contributed to the appallingly high infant mortality rate in Queensland. Accidents were common, and when a child from the bush required medical treatment it meant a harrowing journey by bullock cart over rough tracks to Brisbane and many young patients died on the journey.

Mary McConnel was the first person to be deeply convinced of the urgent need for a children's hospital and she instigated much fundraising, although later she was helped by other volunteers. Her reasons for this were given in her second book, published at her own expense, entitled *Our Children's Hospital,* which was written to raise additional funding for the hospital. Her own writings reveal a woman of great compassion and determination whose religious faith expressed itself in a practical way.

Before Mary's campaign for a children's hospital began, sick children under five were never admitted to hospital in any state except Victoria. It was believed that sick children were exclusively the responsibility of their mothers and should be prevented from entering hospitals, as this deprived parents of one of their most sacred duties: to nurse their children. This attitude was responsible for the premature deaths of a great many children. Mary set out to change public opinion and awareness in favour of a special hospital where children from the bush and local children would have good clean accommodation and specialist nursing. 'The authorities forgot that mothers, however affectionate, are often totally ignorant of how to cure any kind of disease and when accidents occur are helpless in the treatment of them,' she wrote in a book describing the first twenty-one years of the hospital she had virtually founded.

Although she raised an enormous amount of funds for the hospital over the course of the years and contributed a great deal herself, Mary believed that the children's hospital should not only be a charity but also an institution for children of any nationality or creed, in return for which parents should pay something for the welfare of others, no matter how small, or should contribute help to the running of the wards. Mary was powerfully affected by the words of Jesus, 'Suffer the little children to come unto me'. She believed she had a mission to found the Brisbane Children's Hospital for children of *all* creeds and races.

Mary ran the charity fetes and bazaars which raised much of the money necessary for the building of the hospital. She was helped by a ladies' committee, which organised a display of articles for sale at the Annual Exhibition in Bowen Park in August 1877. Mary undertook the task of obtaining trained staff for the new hospital, which was extremely difficult because the only other Australian children's hospital was in Melbourne. Qualified sisters and a matron were impossible to find in Brisbane, she soon realised. So, using the resourcefulness and ingenuity which characterised all of her actions, she wrote to her brother who worked as a doctor in Yorkshire. His wife became very involved in the project and personally interviewed and selected the first matron, a Miss Hellicar, an Australian sister who had trained at the Westminster Hospital in London, and two further nursing sisters. The necessary medical equipment was purchased and, since funds were low, the McConnels personally paid the matron's fare to Australia.

On 11 March 1878 the new hospital was officially opened in a converted private house in Spring Hill. Mothers from the city and the bush were deeply thankful for the work of Mary and her committee of fundraising helpers. The little hospital rapidly outgrew its premises and moved to its current site in Bowen Hills, where it now forms part of the Royal Brisbane Hospital complex, the largest in the southern hemisphere. Mary McConnel remained the patroness of the hospital and was deeply involved with its work until her death in 1910. In view of her remarkable achievements, it is surprising that she is not better known.

Today the Royal Children's Hospital has a McConnel ward with a bronze plaque in memory of Mary, and a women's committee which raises money for vital projects that has been renamed the Cressbrook Committee in her honour. A large brass plaque also adorns the wall of the little church at Sandy Creek, now Esk, which she and her husband built with their own money. Cressbrook still stands almost in the original form and on the same acreage as when it was built, making the third memorial to this important Queensland pioneer woman, two of whose descendants are practising as doctors today.

She survived her beloved husband by twenty-one years and lived on at the cottage at Cressbrook, which is still occupied by her descendants.

Mary's obituary in the *Brisbane Courier* praised her accomplishments both in developing Cressbrook and the surrounding town of Esk, and her outstanding achievement in securing a children's hospital for Queensland. Somewhat surprisingly, she never managed to rate even a brief entry under her own name in the *Australian Dictionary of Biography*, but many parents whose sick children have been cured in the hospital she founded must look at her memorial plaque and feel gratitude for her dedicated devotion to Queensland's children.

CHAPTER NINETEEN

Mary MacKillop
(1842–1909)

A ROLE MODEL FOR OUR TIME

Bombarded by articles about highly paid and sometimes rather dubious media celebrities and sporting stars, today's girls have a great need for good role models. However, the view of many is that 'good' or 'saintly' people are boring, pompous, cardboard figures. This is something that could never be said of beautiful, lively, strong-minded Mary MacKillop, a truly 'modern' heroine and an excellent role model for *all* women who struggle to be heard by male authorities.

In January 1995, Pope John Paul II declared Mary MacKillop 'blessed', the penultimate step before proclaiming her a saint who has gained wide recognition in the general community; in 2001, as part of Melbourne's official celebrations to commemorate Federation, Mary MacKillop was cited by popular vote as one of a select group of 'outstanding Australians'.[1] The severe difficulties she overcame to bring the advantages of a practical education to all Australian children, regardless of race, creed or colour make Mary a truly heroic woman.

With her sweet face, her bravery and high intelligence, Mary's life story should appeal to girls who read and view countless stories in the press and on television about pop singers, actresses or lavishly sponsored sportswomen, many of whom turn out to have feet of clay and are exposed as anorexic, bulimic or drug-addicted. Mary MacKillop's life sets an example to young people that they *can* have positive rather than materialistic aims in life and achieve goals that benefit others. One of Mary's main aims was to give *all* Australian children a better chance in life by providing them with an education at a time when this was reserved for those who could afford to pay school fees.

Mary's parents, Flora McDonald and Alexander MacKillop, both of whom came from the Lochaber area, south-west of Inverness, sailed separately from Scotland to Australia. They met soon after they arrived in Victoria. Flora's father also emigrated to Australia and became a farmer in Victoria. After Flora and Alexander MacKillop married, they found themselves scraping together a bare existence in rural Victoria, a very different way of life to the religiously orientated one they grew up in the isolated Highland villages of their childhoods. Another very 'modern' note in Mary's story is the fact that her parents were Gaelic-speaking migrants, members of what was then a despised ethnic community. However, their Scottish connections brought them to the notice of another Highland Catholic family, the Chisholms, and some sources suggest that a member of the Chisholm family later became Mary MacKillop's godfather. Caroline Chisholm is, of course, famous for having gained respect for the work she carried out looking after single young girls, mainly of Irish extraction, who came to Australia and found themselves homeless and endangered.

Like the Chisholms, the MacKillops and other Highland families had remained true to the 'old' or Catholic faith. After the defeat of Bonnie Prince Charlie at the battle of Culloden, Catholics and other families who fought for the Stuarts were forced to forfeit their lands and money, but in spite of so much persecution, remained loyal to the Stuart line and what they called 'the King over the water'. This was their way of saying they owed allegiance to Bonnie Prince Charlie and the exiled Stuart line, rather than to the Germanic-Protestant House of Hanover in London. It was the hostility shown towards those of the 'Old Faith' as well as the infamous Highland Clearances, when the clansmen were displaced to make room for thousands of sheep, that forced so many Highlanders to emigrate to other countries.

Alexander MacKillop was handsome, intelligent, passionate but restless, keen to avenge the slights his family had suffered as a result of their loyalty to the Stuart and Catholic cause. He spent many years in Rome studying for the priesthood and as a result spoke fluent Italian. However, after much soul-searching, Alexander decided that he did not have a vocation for the priesthood. He decided to emigrate to Australia with scarcely a penny to his name. Several members of his family would emigrate later, including his father who also established himself in Victoria. Initially, Alexander worked hard and made enough money to buy a house in Brunswick Street, Fitzroy. The house is now demolished although the pavement in front of it bears a plaque recording the fact that Mary, the first of the eight children of Alexander and Flora MacKillop, was born there. By the time Mary turned two, her family had moved, and her father had lost his money in rash speculations and been declared bankrupt, which altered his personality for the worse.

Following this disaster, the MacKillops spent a restless period, living for a time at Glenroy, Marri Creek and Sydney before moving out to Darebin Creek, where Alexander's father took pity on them and gave them a block of land to live on and farm. Unfortunately

Alexander was a dreamer by nature, always involved in some crazy scheme or other. Money slipped through his fingers like water. Mary's mother, worn down from caring for a young family, was scarcely any better as a money manager. Since her mother frequently had difficulty coping with her family responsibilities, Mary, as the eldest daughter, had no option but to care for her younger siblings. This meant a childhood that made constant demands, entailing upon her responsibilities beyond her years. Mary's greatest support came from her adored maternal grandfather McDonald. She loved visiting him and hearing tales of Scottish history and life in the Highlands.

Just before Mary turned six, her beloved grandfather drowned in their local creek as the result of a freak accident, shocking Mary deeply. Her father and brothers had to drag the waters of the creek to retrieve his body; Mary would never forget the traumatic sight of his bloated corpse.

Then came the sudden death from an unnamed fever of Alick, Mary's baby brother. Still in shock, Mary was sent away to Melbourne to stay with an aunt. While she was there she dreamed of a beautiful lady who, Mary said, told her she 'would be a mother to me always'. Mary's aunt believed that Mary had seen a vision of the Virgin Mary.

By now Mary's family was increasingly dependent on the generosity and charity of wealthier relatives. Out of work and lacking the money to have his children educated, Alexander taught them to read and write in English, speak Gaelic, construe Latin, and simple mathematics. Mary also received religious instruction from her father.

At that time it was considered a huge disgrace to leave the priesthood, and Mary wondered how her father could possibly have left his studies in Rome and the chance to serve God to live amidst a bleak pioneering society like that of rural Victoria. Slowly she came to believe that God's plan for her life was to follow her father's original path, dedicate her life to God and become a nun.

This was an especially hard decision for Mary to make. She was a lively, extroverted girl with a great love of life, a brilliant horsewoman and widely admired by the young men of the district for her outstanding good looks. She had long, thick dark hair, delicate creamy skin and huge blue eyes fringed by long lashes.

By now her father had been dismissed from a series of jobs and had mortgaged the Darebin property to return to Scotland for an extended visit. In his absence, the family was unable to keep up the mortgage payments, and the mortgagee (her uncle) took possession and evicted Mary, her mother and the other children from their farmhouse. Alexander MacKillop was totally irresponsible. In today's terms one would probably say he was severely maladjusted. What were his family to do?

At this time, it would have been impossible for Mary to take the veil. As the eldest daughter, she had to become the breadwinner and support her family. She took a post as nursery governess to the children of relatives, before working as a shop assistant at the Sands and Kenny stationery shop in Melbourne, where she made Protestant friends who would remain her staunch supporters throughout her life. From Melbourne she moved to remote Penola in South Australia to work as a governess to the children of her uncle, Alexander Cameron, and aunt, Margaret MacKillop, and live with them at their home, Old Penola Homestead.

On his return home, Mary's father proved no help at all to his struggling family. Instead, he became a liability. He would happily appropriate any money that came his way and spend it on some mad scheme or other. The MacKillop women realised that they must band together to support themselves and the younger members of the family at a time when women rarely worked outside the home. Teaching was one of the few ways for middle-class women to earn money, so Mary and her sisters decided to open their own boarding school, with their mother as the housekeeper.

They borrowed money from concerned relatives, moved briefly to Melbourne and then in mid-1862 moved to Portland, where Mary worked in the Catholic Denominational School. Everything was going well until her father came to visit. He complained arrogantly about the way the school's headmaster treated his hard working daughter, which caused problems for Mary.[2] Mary's father meddled in the running of the school and entered into heated arguments with the parents of pupils. Finally she and her sisters bravely rented an old guesthouse to start a boarding school. Somehow or other, the money for the school and a new piano sent to them by sympathetic relatives found its way into Alexander's pocket, with the result that parents withdrew their children and the MacKillops' school failed. Clever, hardworking, responsible Mary was left wondering what else she could do to support her mother and younger siblings.

Early in 1866 she returned to Penola with the aim of setting up a Catholic school there. She was encouraged in this scheme by Penola's remarkable parish priest; tall, dark English-born Father Julian Tenison Woods, a highly intelligent, largely self-educated man who had only recently entered the priesthood, before that he had worked as a journalist. Father Woods was a visionary who wanted to help Australia's poor by starting a series of free schools and refuges for the homeless.[3]

The charismatic Father Julian became Mary's confessor. She admired him for his dedication to scholarship (he read scientific papers to learned societies, preached brilliant sermons and was one of the first people to recognise that the Coonawarra district's *terra rossa* might produce very good wine). This multi-talented man encouraged Mary to achieve her childhood dream of becoming a nun and founding her own school rather than working as a governess.

In 1865, helped by her younger sisters Annie and Lexie, Mary started teaching children free of charge at Penola. Their first schoolroom was a dilapidated stable which had been converted into a schoolroom by their brother John.

Father Woods told Mary it was possible with his backing (in that male-dominated period a woman could do nothing by herself) for her to found a teaching order of nuns. Like the Franciscan Order, these young ladies (the nucleus of the 'Josephites') would take vows of poverty and chastity. The Josephite Sisters would own nothing but their robes and live in cottages or houses loaned to them free of charge by well-wishers. With no property to tie them down, the Sisters would be free to go wherever there was a need for their services and could set up schools, orphanages and refuges for the homeless in pioneer country areas. Sharing the hardships of itinerant railway workers, fettlers and pioneers on the land at the goldfields, the nuns could minister to their families and educate children who would otherwise receive no schooling at all.

How could they manage to do all this without any funding? Mary wondered.

'God will provide,' Father Julian replied. And He did. There was certainly no shortage of ragged and hungry children to care for and educate around Penola, a bleak settlement just inside the border of South Australia and Victoria. Settlers lived there in squalor in bark or log huts with dirt floors and no running water or sanitation.

Mary's father, Alexander MacKillop, went on to follow other diggers to the goldfields in search of riches and excitement. It was not long before he returned home empty-handed, and this led to even more family dissension about how to pay their rapidly mounting debts. Finally, Father Woods agreed to settle the MacKillops' debts. (Unfortunately this was a promise which, as a priest vowed to poverty, he was unable to keep.)

Mary's father was now behaving in an eccentric manner; and he may have suffered some undiagnosed mental illness. There was no such speciality as psychiatry at that time; all the family could do was send him away to stay with his relatives on a large property near Hamilton in the Western Districts of Victoria. This was a great relief to his long-suffering wife and children, who were now able to get on with their lives at last.

Three years later Alexander MacKillop died. Mary wrote to her mother about the 'humiliations of the past few years' and added: 'I am sure you cannot regard Papa's death as a trial.' This chilling sentence shows just how dysfunctional the MacKillop family had become.[4]

Encouraged by Father Woods, Mary gave away her pretty clothes. According to Mary's biographer, Father Paul Gardner, the Josephites are considered to have come into existence in 1866.[5] From that time onwards, Sister Mary, as she was henceforth known, wore a plain dark dress with a large white collar and signed her letters 'Mary, Sister of St Joseph'. Mary was now the head of a religious order in which the members were vowed to poverty, and dedicated to the service of God and educating the children of the poor. They owed a direct allegiance to Rome. Other orders of nuns ran convents that were under the control of various bishops and used European methods to educate Australian children. Mary believed firmly that in a pioneer country, Australian nuns should be familiar with the stark realities of bush and migrant life, the lack of amenities, the loneliness and absence of close relatives, the frequent droughts and the shifting nature of pioneer society. Nuns familiar with these conditions would be advantaged when educating Australian children to survive in a harsh environment.

It reflects great credit on Mary's ability that she was only twenty-four when she founded the Josephite Order. With the help of Father Woods she drew up a Constitution for the order, which was ratified by Bishop Sheil, the Roman Catholic Bishop of Adelaide. Mary and Father Woods worked together to educate the new recruits who flocked to join them. Parents paid for the education of their children if they could afford it, but many paid nothing at all.[6]

Sister Mary's beauty, her warm personality and her evident happiness in her work, and Father Woods' striking good looks and charismatic personality attracted many young girls to join the order of St Joseph of the Sacred Heart. Supporters donated money, books, food or vacant cottages for the nuns to live in. Somehow they managed — God had provided, just as Father Woods said He would.

Ten years before free State-funded education was introduced in South Australia, Josephite schools gave the children of the poor a basic and very practical schooling to help them earn a living. Unlike the fee-paying educational establishments, Josephite schools did not teach the piano, French or what Mary termed lady-like 'accomplishments'. They taught only basic skills such as reading, letter-writing, sewing, religion, geography, history and simple maths. At the core of their curriculum there lay recognition of the needs of a new and egalitarian pioneer society, based on hard work, justice and a fair go for all.

Mary relinquished the wish to acquire possessions and accepted living in poverty, happy to own nothing except her black dress and her rosary. She devoted her life to caring for the poor, the sick and the destitute, regarding this as the principle tenet of Christianity. What drew people of all denominations to Sister Mary was her kindness and devotion, the warmth of her personality and her wonderful sense of humour, which she kept even in times of hardship and stress.

As more and more recruits joined the order, more vacant cottages and houses were put at their service. The number of Josephite schools, orphanages and shelters for the homeless rapidly increased across South Australia.

In 1867 Mary moved to Adelaide to establish new schools in the city and at Port Augusta. A branch was also opened in Bathurst. Subsequently she went to Brisbane to open a branch of the order there, in what was formerly a public house, a move that evoked fierce hostility from Brisbane's famous Catholic Bishop James Quinn. This expatriate Irish prelate also had great charisma and had brought with him an order of nuns to found what became the prestigious All Hallows School. He firmly believed that any order of nuns should come under *his* jurisdiction.

The American Modern Catholic Encyclopaedia states that 'Mary MacKillop's sufferings in a patriarchal church have made her a heroine to modern Australian feminists'. There is no doubt she and her Josephite Order did endure suffering and humiliation at the hands of certain bishops. The problem started in 1870 while Mary was away in Brisbane and the Josephite Sisters at Kapunda, who were caring for abused and battered children, were informed by Father Woods of certain undesirable incidents (presumeably child sexual abuse) involving a Father Ambrose Patrick Keating and some children. In the absence of the bishop, who was overseas, Father Woods reported the incidents to the man in charge of the diocese in the bishop's absence, Father Smythe, the Vicar-General and Administrator.

Father Woods' complaints were taken seriously and resulted in the expulsion of Father Keating. Father Keating vowed vengeance on Father Woods and the Josephite Sisterhood. He stumped off in a rage to complain to his good friend and fellow Irishman, Father Horan, advisor to the rather unworldly and ailing Bishop Sheil of Adelaide. (Father Horan seems to have been as effective in spreading poison to the Bishop as Anthony Trollope's malicious Rev Mr Slope in *The Barsetshire Chronicles*.) His malicious desire for vengeance contributed to the dramatic and lamentable events leading to Mary MacKillop's difficulties with Bishop Sheil and its disastrous result for her and the Josephite Sisters.

Father Horan was aware that character assassination of the Josephites and Father Woods was the best way to defend his good friend Father Keating on the charge of child sex abuse. Accordingly he used smear tactics to malign Mary's character, claiming that she had a fondness for alcohol which was at times smuggled in to her, to blacken her reputation and that of the Josephite Order.

In fact, Mary MacKillop had suffered for a long time from what is today known to doctors as dysmenorrhoea (distressingly severe monthly period pains) and at that time a mixture of brandy and water was actually prescribed by doctors to alleviate menstrual pains. In that era, women were never even examined internally by male doctors and topics of a gynaecological nature were taboo. Period pains were certainly not a subject that could be discussed with the opposite sex. As a result, Mary could not defend herself and her treatment with brandy for a distressing condition which would have laid her low each month unless she received some alleviation of the severe pain and cramps.

In 1885, writing a confidential letter to her mother, Mary made a veiled reference to her pains as 'the illnesses you know of try me terribly'. The brandy that her doctors prescribed for this extremely painful condition was the *only* alcoholic drink she took. She was careful to do this under self-imposed supervision and some of the Sisters knew of her painful condition at certain times. However, malicious gossip managed to turn her prescribed spoonfuls of medicinal brandy into an issue about temperance and self-indulgence.

The Bishop of Adelaide was unwell and far too unworldly to recognise the poison Father Horan was spreading although he had previously always supported Mary. But the damage was done. Nothing Mary could say to defend herself would make any difference. As a woman trying to run an organisation in a male-dominated world, she was at a disadvantage.

False allegations were made that Mary was alcoholic, power-mad and incompetent. What those around the bishop wanted was for the Josephites to be under the bishop's direct control. The bishop told Mary he planned to change the constitution to which he had previously agreed. The Josephite Order was to come under the control of the Dominicans and have one fixed convent (which, of course, would limit their work in the outback). Unless Mary agreed to the bishop's changes she would be replaced as Head of the Order and the aims of her order would be totally changed. Overcome by stress at the thought that her years of work among the poor and homeless would be destroyed, she collapsed.

Father Horan arrived at her convent and told her she was guilty of the sin of pride in resisting God's will. In 1871, Mary, without a chance to defend her reputation, suffered the disgrace of being 'excommunicated' by the Bishop of Adelaide, who had been so cleverly manipulated by Father Horan into becoming her foe. The offence cited was that of 'insubordination'. It meant that priests who sided with the bishop could denounce Mary from the pulpit but her official biographer Father Paul Gardner says Mary was never *legally* excommunicated.

The bishop's directives were a terrible blow to devout and law-abiding Mary, who had a clear understanding of the nature of authority, of law, and of the 'chain of command'. The internal government of the Josephite Sisters was *not* in the hands of bishops but in those of its Mother General in Australia and of the Pope in Rome. Mary was protecting her Sisters against a few bishops who were trying to ignore the law. She remained respectful but firmly upheld that law. But all to no avail. The ragged schools 'without fees' she and the Sisters had worked so hard to establish and run were closed. Without homes to live in and work from, her Sisters were forced to find resident jobs as governesses or domestic servants. Mary had virtually become an outcast, her dreams of helping the poor shattered by the dramatic turn of events.

Fortunately, the strength of her personality, combined with her charisma and her overwhelming kindness to those in need, however humble, had the power to draw people of all faiths to her. Turned out of their cottages and with no money to pay for other accommodation, Mary and her devoted sisters were helped by a Jewish Member of Parliament and businessman, Emanuel Solomon, who loaned them, free of any charge, an entire row of terrace houses in Adelaide which he had been renting out.

In Adelaide the overworked and dynamic Father Tenison Woods was not only a priest but also Director of Catholic schools, editor of a paper, and a schools inspector. His huge work load affected his physical and mental health and blunted his powers of judgement.[7] Unlike Mary he had *never* seen prudence as a virtue. Now he entered into bitter conflict with some of the Catholic clergy over details of his schooling system. Then he put forward the astonishing claim that several of Mary's Sisters had been visited by the devil. Father Woods had a credulous, almost 'New Age' streak in his character, and was an avid reader of mystical writings. It was this fascination with the paranormal and with Satanic visions that led him to believe reports by several hysterical or morbidly neurotic women connected with the Josephite Order, such as the mentally disturbed Mary Joseph, who was cared for by the Sisters. These unfortunate women genuinely believed they had received Satanic visitations, which may well have been the manifestation of mental illness, and at that period there were no psychiatric drugs to control the visions.

Father Woods totally ignored Mary's views that Mary Joseph was mentally disturbed. He insisted that Mary Joseph had the makings of a saint, which naturally caused problems for Mary and her order when rumours of these 'visitations' and Father Woods' assertions of their validity circulated among members of the priesthood antagonistic to Mary and the Josephites.[8]

Those priests sympathetic to Mary realised that such women and their hysterical visions were isolated cases. They disagreed with the bishop's act of 'excommunication', knowing that his illness meant that he was overly influenced by Father Horan and, believing it to be illegal, gave Mary the sacrament quietly. One influential priest declared publicly he would ruin Father Tenison Woods' reputation because of the part he had played in Mary's downfall. The tide started going out for Father Woods.[9]

Naturally, the bans imposed on Mary by the bishop, which lasted for five long months, caused her intense pain. However they did have one positive effect: they bonded 'her' Josephite Sisters to her but badly affected what had once been a close relationship with Father Tenison Woods. Mary's 'excommunication' was lifted only days before Bishop Sheil's death.[10] It was at this distressing and stressful time in her life that the real goodness of Mary's character shone through. Respecting the authority of the Church, she refused to blame either of the bishops who had caused her such bitter sorrow.

Mary's enemies were gathering in South Australia and in Brisbane, determined to get rid of her. To protect the Sisters of St Joseph of the Sacred Heart, Mary moved their headquarters to Sydney. She resolutely refused to see herself as a victim or blame anyone for what had happened realising that, through no fault of her own, she had been caught in a power struggle and a clash between male church dignitaries. All she and her Sisters wanted was to administer their own religious Order, going out to succour those in new areas, providing free education for children as well as classes for unemployed adult migrants, teaching them new skills such as book-keeping with which they could obtain jobs. Her 'modern' ideas upset bishops who wished to keep the nuns in their convents and dominate religious orders, rather than have them respond directly to the Pope.

Mary MacKillop stood firm and appealed to Church law, although she had no legal training. She was in her thirties, inexperienced in the ways of the world, but she prayed long and hard about her decisions and was deeply convinced that God was on her side. Bravely, she dared to stand up for the legality of the constitution of the Josephite Order. She declared that if the bishops wanted to found convents under *their* control, they were welcome to do so. But the Josephite Sisters had agreed to work under their *own* leadership, serving 'the poor, the homeless and the uneducated and unemployed' rather than the wishes of any particular bishop.

Mary's enemies and those of Father Woods circulated stories about her love of power and continued to fabricate the rumour that she was an alcoholic. Bishop Quinn of Brisbane disapproved of Mary and her nuns. What the bishop wanted in *his* diocese were educated, lady-like nuns, following the pattern set in Ireland, teaching good manners and giving music lessons to middle-class girls. He did not want Mary and her Sisters, who owned nothing but the clothes they stood up in, living in converted public houses or cottages loaned by laypeople, establishing a new Australian-style order and insisting on donating all their money to the poor. Bishop Quinn wrote to his agent in Rome describing Mary as 'this sentimental young lady who is now only thirty-two years of age', when in fact she was down-to-earth and *far* from sentimental.

Mary possessed sound commonsense and a practical approach to life. From adolescence on, she had coped well with her dysfunctional family and with the difficulties of running a religious order with no regular source of funding; ministering to people who lived under pioneer conditions in bark huts and hovels. She could not have accomplished so much without a practical mind, high intelligence and a belief in the power of education plus her boundless faith in God.

When Mary went to Rome early in 1873 there was no Bishop of Adelaide. She went there at the direction of the man in charge in the absence of a bishop, who was the Vicar-General and Administrator. It was he who supervised details of her travel, approved her informal mode of dress and arranged the inconspicuous nature of her departure, travelling under the name 'Mrs MacDonald' to avoid interference from people of ill-will. She hoped to secure an audience with the Pope to try to obtain Papal approval for the Constitution of the Josephites under the control of its Mother Superior and the Pope in Rome. She was still respectfully but firmly upholding the law.

Mary had just enough money to pay for a one-way ticket to Rome and prayed that God would find the money for her return. This was an era when travel was time-consuming and far from pleasant, especially in steerage class, which was all Mary could afford. Women rarely undertook long journeys on their own as Mary had to do.

Once she reached Rome, Mary stayed free of charge in a convent run by French nuns who were sympathetic to her plight. Friends at the Vatican arranged a Papal audience. Through an interpreter Mary told her story to Pope Pius IX. The Holy Father listened to her attentively as she told him how very different conditions were in Australia, and what were the crying needs of the Catholic congregation. He laid his hands on her head and blessed her. Mary described it as 'a day never to be forgotten, a day worth years of suffering'.

Subsequently Sister Mary *did* obtain Papal approval of the Josephite Sisterhood, but they were told to make changes to their Constitution and Rule of Life and officially move their headquarters to Sydney. The tenets of poverty and non-ownership of property as laid down by Father Woods and Mary had to be rewritten. Rome, with centuries of experience of the sudden dispossession of monks and nuns by anti-religious governments and rulers like Henry VIII who had dissolved monasteries and nunneries and turned their occupants out into the street, was eager to secure a permanent home for the Sisters of St Joseph, so that they would not be put out onto the streets again.

Mary had to accept Rome's terms in order to gain acceptance for the Order. However Father Tenison Woods never forgave her for her compromise, hurt and disappointed that his dream of an order of nuns vowed to poverty had been tampered with. In his deeply troubled state of mind, he withdrew from contact with Mary. He never spoke to her again for the next fifteen years. Indeed, he tried to undermine her and to establish an entirely new Order, the Sisters of Perpetual Adoration (which still operates in Queensland today). He also tried to get other groups of nuns going and to divert some Josephites into them but they failed to take root. Such was the loyalty the Sisters showed to Mother MacKillop that all Father Woods' attempts to persuade them into joining his new order met with scant success.

Mary was saddened by Father Woods' change of attitude towards her. Showing Christian charity, she forgave him and continued to praise him in the highest terms and to write pleasant letters to him but her sound Scottish commonsense did not desert her. She was careful to warn new (and vulnerable) recruits to the Sisterhood that Father Woods, while a very charming and intelligent man, was no longer the keen supporter of the Josephite Order that he had formerly been.

Mary worked tirelessly establishing refuges for women, orphanages for abandoned babies and the first permanent Mother House of the Sisters of Saint Joseph in the Adelaide suburb of Kensington. The Josephite Order, under Mary's determined and skilful leadership, went from strength to strength, opening new orphanages and schools in areas that needed them and closing old ones as the population changed. They also housed prostitutes who wished to leave sex work and rehabilitated them. Mary travelled by stagecoach, ship and rail over long distances to visit her Sisters, often under very uncomfortable conditions. In 1876 her friend Sister Laurentia and another sister were badly burned when a lamp exploded where the Sisters lodged at Port Augusta. Mary took the train as far as she could and then tried to get a coach and horses to take her to Port Augusta but the coachman refused to go there at night. Fearing Sister Laurentia might die, Mary asked the man to saddle her a horse to ride there over a lonely and dangerous pot-holed track. Her courage in volunteering to ride all alone in foul weather shamed the coachman into driving her there.

Inspired by Mary, and through perseverance and hard work, by the late 1880s the Sisters of St Joseph had schools, orphanages and refuges of various kinds in many areas of Australia and in parts of New Zealand.

It is important to remember that, all her life, Mary MacKillop believed strongly in the rule of law. Those who had met her said that what struck them most about her was her sweetness of character and extreme kindness to all those in need. She was, however, an excellent administrator and strong when she needed to be. She was a woman in advance of her time, determined to provide the gift of education to all children; including those from deprived backgrounds and those who lived in remote areas where there were, as yet, no schools. Without Mary's vision and energy, many of these children would have remained illiterate.

In her later years 'Mother Mary', as she was then known, suffered health problems but managed to overcome them. An additional cross she bore with fortitude was the appointment of Mother Bernard (described as 'weak and incompetent' by some sources) as Head of the Josephite Order for a period of years.[11] Finally, however, in 1899 Cardinal Moran cleared the way for the Sisters to re-elect Mother Mary as Mother General.

Disappointed that his chances of promotion were blocked by powerful enemies in the Catholic hierarchy, Father Woods channelled his drive, his intellect and charisma into fresh fields. He became a member of the Royal Geological Society in London and the Royal Societies of Sydney and Tasmania. He researched and wrote the two-volume *Discovery and Exploration of Australia* (1865) and the classic textbook *Fish and Fisheries of New South Wales*, which today is a rare and highly valuable volume.

In old age Father Julian Tenison Woods moved to Sydney where he spent his final days severely paralysed and bedridden. Sweet-natured and forgiving as always, Mother Mary, who was then residing at St Joseph's Convent in Mount Street, North Sydney, remembered Father Julian's love of strawberries. When she received the news that the man who had done so much to found the Josephite Order had not long to live, she took a basket of strawberries and caught a ferry to visit him. However the ferry broke down and, to her distress, Father Woods was dead by the time she arrived at his bedside.

However Mary had sufficient greatness of spirit to forgive the cavalier way he had treated her. She suggested someone should write his biography but when those that she approached refused, she researched and wrote a moving and sensitive memoir praising his scientific work and what she saw as his greatness, quoting from many of Father Woods' books and scientific papers, and applied to Cardinal Moran for funds to have it published. But, alarmed by some of Father Woods' more extreme beliefs and utterances, Cardinal Moran replied that he regretted he could not approve the publication of such a volume, which must have been very distressing for Mary.

In May 1901, Mother Mary MacKillop suffered a stroke while she was on a visit to the Sisters in Rotorua, New Zealand. Although she retained her mental faculties, she lost the use of her right hand. This disability sadly curtailed her life, but she met it with a brave front. A period of depression followed, which she overcame by her stable personality, the love and devotion of her Sisters, and by prayer. The Sisters wished Mary MacKillop to remain Mother General of the Order, which she did until her death in August, 1909.

She lay, serene and peaceful in her coffin in the chapel of the Mother House in North Sydney. People from all over Australia, many of whom had been helped by the Josephite Order, flocked to Sydney to pay their last respects. The streets of North Sydney were lined with mourners as her coffin was taken to its resting place.

In a final act of inter-denominational friendship, Mary's white marble gravestone was paid for by her long-term friend and benefactor Joanna Barr Smith of South Australia. Even before the Pope beatified Mary MacKillop for 'heroic virtue', many Australians thought of her as a saint. Mary was heroic in adversity, and showed a truly Christian lack of malice towards those who slandered her and sought to destroy the work of her Order, which continues today. Members of the Josephite Order now work with underprivileged migrants in inner-city areas and with Aborigines in remote regions.

But one thing is certain, the name of Mary MacKillop will *always* be honoured as a great Australian and a great humanitarian.

CHAPTER TWENTY

Portrait photograph (detail): National Library of Australia, Canberra.

Nellie Melba (Helen Porter Mitchell), DBE, GBE
(1856–1931)
THE VOICE OF AUSTRALIA

> 'Her brain made Melba's voice unique.'
>
> Madame Marchiesi to
> Katharine Susannah Prichard, Paris, 1912

A century ago Melba was regarded as *the* greatest opera singer in the world, the first Australian to make a name for herself overseas as a singer at a time when Australia was seen as a cultural desert.

Her name has become a legend. There are *many* Melbas, each one different, so attempting to create a portrait from eye-witness accounts is frustrating. As a legendary figure, people viewed Melba from contrasting viewpoints; some recounted her parsimony, others praised her outstanding generosity. Beverley Nichols wrote a laudatory biography that was paid for by Melba, but once he had left her employ he published unkind stories of an ageing diva obsessed with her own image. Melba's granddaughter, on the other hand, records Melba as one of the most unselfish grandmothers any child could wish for.

Nellie Melba was fortunate in possessing all the elements that a prima donna needs for success: a beautiful voice, a capacity for hard work, a commanding and charismatic presence, a strong constitution, a will of iron. All these combined to help her develop her talent and run her career with remarkable efficiency. Her portrait has appeared on the Australian $100 note, a fitting legacy for a woman who turned her golden voice into a fortune. She owned valuable property in London, Paris and Australia, a magnificent collection of jewels and a wardrobe of beautiful designer gowns.

Unlike many female opera singers, Nellie Melba won her fame without granting sexual favours to opera or theatre managers. She was no prude, but after her only marriage had failed *she* liked to be the one to choose her lovers, rather than the other way round. Melba's huge fortune was amassed with the aid of homosexual financier Alfred de Rothschild, with whom she formed a judicious friendship. Rothschild, a great admirer of Melba, gave her good advice on how to invest her hard-earned money, which Melba followed with spectacular success. In return she never charged a fee when she sang at Rothschild's sumptuous dinner parties.

How *did* an Australian girl with a husband and a baby leave Melbourne in 1886 as an unknown singer and return sixteen years later as Madame Melba, the world's most famous prima donna? The answer lies in her talent, her strong personality and the good relations she fostered with the press.

From Melbourne mansion to a sugar plantation at Marian

'If you wish to understand me at all, you must understand that first and foremost I am an Australian,' Melba said revealingly in her autobiography, ghost-written by Nichols.[1]

'Nellie' was the name given to her by her younger brothers and sisters. She was christened Helen Porter Mitchell and was born in the Melbourne suburb of Richmond, the third child of Isabel (formerly Dow) and David Mitchell, both keen amateur musicians. Dark-haired, dimpled Nellie was the first of the Mitchells' ten children to survive the hazards of childhood in a period when the infant mortality rate was very high. A stubborn and determined child, she often defied her strict and equally determined father, whom she greatly resembled. In spite of all their arguments, Nellie would remain his favourite all his life.

Educated at home by two elderly maiden aunts and given her first music lessons by her mother, Nellie's habit of whistling and humming around the house drove her father mad. Hoping to turn her into a 'young lady', her parents enrolled her as a day girl at Melbourne's Presbyterian Ladies College, where she received piano and singing lessons. This was the school described by Henry Handel Richardson in her novel *The Getting of Wisdom*.[2] Neither Nellie nor Ethel Richardson enjoyed their schooldays, but they both received an excellent grounding in musical theory and piano.

Nellie Mitchell left school at eighteen. She was not expected to train for a career or find a job outside the home, but to lead a domesticated life until she made a 'good' marriage. Her father had trained as a master stonemason in Scotland before emigrating to Australia with only a few pounds in his pocket. Through hard work and good business acumen the construction business he founded flourished and he was able to buy a huge stone quarry at Cave Hill, near Lilydale, as well as a brick works, and undertake major construction work in Melbourne. He also owned a country property at Dalry, where he sometimes took young Nellie on a visit in a horse-drawn wagonette. It was from the shearers and fencers she met here that she learned to swear so fluently, something she would do all her life to the amazement of some of her fellow guests at parties.[3]

Her father intended Nellie to sing in the drawing room after dinner, attract a suitable young man, marry him and bear his children. Strong minded Nellie, however, had other ideas about her future. She had won praise for her singing at school and loved being the centre of attention. She obtained her father's permission to take private lessons with Pietro Cecci, an Italian singer and former member of Melbourne's Lyster Opera Company.[4] Cecci was very taken with Nellie and prepared to overlook her bouts of bad temper when she was thwarted. He encouraged her to believe that she had great talent and that some day her voice would enthral the world.

If Nellie's father had realised that his favourite daughter planned an operatic career he would have been horrified; in his opinion, based on his strict Scots upbringing, singers and actresses were 'a load of painted harlots and strumpets'. He would certainly not permit *his* daughter to sing on the stage. Even the great actress Sarah Bernhardt (later a close friend of Melba) had initially been a 'kept woman', with her living accommodation and her jewels paid for by a succession of powerful men in return for sexual favours.

When Nellie was nineteen her mother fell ill and was nursed at home by Nellie and her younger sisters, Annie and Belle. David Mitchell deeply loved his wife, who died just as Nellie turned twenty. The grief of the Mitchell family increased when Nellie's youngest brother, Vere Mitchell, died four months later. Their family home, Doonside, was plunged into mourning: the girls scarcely ever went out and Nellie's father, a loner by nature, became extremely depressed.

As a means of escaping from a home with tragic memories into a brighter and sunnier environment, David Mitchell accepted a commission to build a sugar mill in the small settlement of Marian, almost twenty kilometres inland from the developing port of Mackay, on the central Queensland coast, where the sugar industry was booming. Huge sugar plantations were being developed using the labour of Pacific Islanders — this was the sorry era of 'blackbirding'. The younger Mitchell children were left at home to be looked after by two nurses and a housekeeper, while the two eldest girls, Nellie and Annie, accompanied their father and boarded a steamer for Mackay. Soon the high-spirited, attractive Mitchell girls with their smart city clothes were the talk of this small town. They were invited to all the best houses, usually owned by wealthy sugar planters, where Nellie was repeatedly asked to sing after dinner. One evening she was introduced to the Honourable Charles Nisbett Armstrong, a good-looking young English aristocrat three years older than herself. Following some wild teenage escapades, he had been sent away to jackeroo in Australia; he now held a more responsible position as plantation manager at nearby Marian.

'Kangaroo Charlie', as he was known, was tall and broad-shouldered, as blond as Melba was dark, with a fondness for wine, women and fast horses and a temper as volatile as Nellie's. The young girls of Mackay and Marian sighed over his good looks and their mothers invited him to supper parties, delighted at the prospect of a daughter marrying a younger son of a baronet. Charles's widowed mother, Lady Armstrong, was rumoured to own a stately home in Sussex.

All her life Nellie would have a weakness for titles and for handsome, self-confident men. She was a sensual woman and there was an intense physical attraction between her and Kangaroo Charlie. For his part, Charles Armstrong admired Nellie's curvaceous figure and her sense of humour and appreciated her father's fortune. They flirted but, on her father's orders, Nellie was always chaperoned by her sister whenever they met. Charles realised that he would have to propose marriage, although they did not know each other at all well. He did so and was accepted.

Like many men of his class, Charles Armstrong enjoyed the music of Gilbert and Sullivan, but cared nothing for grand opera. His true passion was reserved for sport and horses, he was a brilliant rider and an excellent shot. He was *not* a meek husband standing by the piano turning pages of music while his wife sung her way into history.

David Mitchell, the man who had fulfilled the Australian dream by starting out with nothing and founding a fortune, could scarcely object to his future son-in-law's pedigree, although he was worried by the rumours of wild fights and debts that Charles had incurred in England before coming to Australia. But once Nellie had made up her mind nothing would stop her. She wanted Charlie Armstrong for his body and his aristocratic connections, and what Nellie wanted she got.

The young couple married at St Ann's Presbyterian Church, Brisbane, on 22 December 1882. Nellie Mitchell, now the Honourable Mrs Charles Nisbett Armstrong, was twenty-one.

The newlyweds spent their three-month honeymoon in Melbourne at Doonside. In Melbourne Nellie resumed her singing lessons with Pietro Cecci, whose repeated assurances that she was certainly good enough to sing in the great opera houses of Europe unsettled her. Once the honeymoon was over the Armstrongs returned north by steamer, stopping off in Sydney where Nellie gave a couple of private recitals. She was hailed as 'the Australian nightingale', which unsettled her even more.

In spite of the fact that Nellie was David Mitchell's favourite child, he did not help the young couple financially and feared their marriage would not last.

The couple's return to far north Queensland, where they lived in the simple weatherboard cottage built for the plantation manager, was an anti-climax for Nellie. By now she was convinced that she could succeed as an opera singer ... if only she had the chance to do so. Covent Garden in London and the opera houses of Europe beckoned, but how could she get there? She had no money of her own and no way of earning any, and she soon discovered she was pregnant. Her husband had hoped for a submissive wife to run the home and bear his children; instead he found himself married to a frustrated singer with an iron will and a temper as strong as his own.

During the long wet season rain fell unceasingly, drumming on the tin roof of the cottage, ruining Nellie's piano and heightening the tension between husband and wife. Charles's salary was not large and he had no private income. There was little to do in Marian. Nellie had read scores of romantic novels and expected a great deal more from marriage than Charles Armstrong provided. She recorded dismal impressions of Marian during the wet season: 'My piano was mildewed; my clothes were damp, the furniture fell to pieces; spiders, ticks, and other obnoxious insects penetrated the house to say nothing of snakes, which had a habit of appearing under one's bed at the *most* inopportune moments.'[5]

She bore a son, whom they named George. Much as she loved her baby, domesticity held few attractions for ambitious Nellie. By the time George could toddle and utter the word 'Mama', Nellie was scheming how she could leave north Queensland and return to Melbourne. She felt she must have some breathing space from her hot-tempered husband; in one of his rages the Honourable Charles Armstrong had thrown a clock at her head, but had missed. A pattern of domestic violence and abuse was being established. Nellie felt she must get away; perhaps her marriage would improve if they had some distance between them, then as soon as George was old enough she could fulfil her ambition to become a professional singer.

Nellie knew her father would not help her financially so she wrote to the faithful Cecci, telling him how unhappy she was. 'We are as poor as it is possible for anyone to be', she wrote, explaining that she could not practise because her piano was constantly out of tune due to the high humidity. She asked if it would be possible for Cecci to form a small opera company. If he could do so she would come south, go on tour with it and leave her baby to be brought up by her sisters at Doonside.

Alarmed by her letter, Cecci wired money for her fare to Melbourne. Although he knew that David Mitchell would never help his daughter to embrace a singing career, he was convinced that Nellie Armstrong had a voice that would enthral the world.

This was the encouragement Nellie needed. On 19 January 1884, at the height of yet another wet season, she sailed south with George to begin a concert career backed by Cecci. Although she was welcomed back by her father, who was delighted to see his first grandson, David Mitchell still disapproved of anything connected with the stage and remained adamant that he would not support Nellie's fledgling career.

With her adoring younger sisters and the maids at Doonside to care for her small son, Nellie was able to work hard on her singing, practising from six in the morning onwards. In Melbourne she met John Lemmone, a flautist who would eventually become her accompanist, and she gave paid and unpaid concerts in Melbourne's Town Hall to great applause. But this was not enough. Her ambition, reinforced by both Cecci and Lemmone, made her dream of performing at Covent Garden and the great opera houses of Europe seem a possibility. How was she to achieve this with no regular income and an infant to look after?

Then, totally unexpectedly, her father, Melbourne's most successful builder and property developer, was offered the post of the State of Victoria's Commissioner to the Indian and Colonial Exhibition in

London. Excited by the honour, he accepted and prepared to move to England with his family; he told Nellie that to preserve the conventions her husband *must* accompany them.

In March 1886, Nellie, Charles and two-year-old George sailed to London with her father and Annie and Belle. Nellie's marriage was on the rocks, but David Mitchell was determined that she and her husband should preserve the facade of respectability expected of someone in his position. Divorce was out of the question. During Queen Victoria's reign divorce was a major scandal; a divorced woman was about as socially acceptable as a leper, was presumed to be the guilty party and automatically lost custody of any children of the marriage. Going to London was worth any sacrifice to Nellie, who hoped Charles would find a job to keep him busy so that she could pursue her singing career.

David Mitchell was confident that in a new environment, with different activities to occupy her mind, Nellie would stay in the marriage. To lessen her unhappiness with her 'difficult husband', her father held out the carrot that once they were settled in London she could take singing lessons with the best teachers.

In England Nellie met her widowed mother-in-law, Lady Armstrong. Against all expectations, these two strong-minded women took an instant liking to one another. Doubtless Lady Armstrong realised that her hot-tempered son was not exactly an ideal husband; perhaps she hoped that Nellie had a strong enough character to make him toe the line. However, by this time Charles and Nellie were fighting so badly that it was impossible for them to continue to live together under one roof. He joined the militia as an officer and was sent to serve in Ireland. Outwardly at least their marriage still appeared viable.

Paris, Vienna, Leipzig, Rome, Turin and other European cities were where the best singers trained. All Mrs Charles Armstrong's attempts to be 'discovered' as a singer by the London press and by musical impresarios failed, although she was applauded at two small concerts. Her aristocratic connection provided no help and Cecci's name certainly did not impress London's musical establishment, nor did the fact that Nellie had been trained in faraway Melbourne, in the colonies. Nellie's sole success lay in her renderings of popular songs like 'Home Sweet Home' at evening parties. All she could do was to remind her father about the promise he had made in Melbourne and pester him to allow her to study with Europe's most famous singing teacher, the great Madame Mathilde Marchiesi, in Paris.

Eventually her father provided Nellie with a small annual income which would allow her to live inexpensively in Paris with her son for one year. Fortunately, Nellie had an excellent ear for languages and her French was reasonable. But would Madame Marchiesi agree to take her on as a pupil? Nellie was aware that Marchiesi accepted only a tiny fraction of the singers who begged her for tuition.

Nellie knew that the audition she was able to arrange with Madame Marchiesi was her big chance. It was fortunate that before leaving Melbourne she had obtained an enthusiastic letter of introduction from a former pupil of Marchiesi, Madame Wiedermann-Pinschof, otherwise Marchiesi would never have agreed to see her.[6] When the day arrived she was, quite naturally, extremely nervous.

At first Madame Marchiesi seemed bored by the idea of auditioning another hopeful colonial.[7] Nellie had chosen to sing the aria 'Sempre libera' from *La Traviata*. At one point Marchiesi interrupted, telling Nellie not to screech the top notes but to sing them *piano*, but said nothing more, listening intently until the aria ended. Then, without a word of praise, she hurried out of the room. Years later, Nellie recounted that Madame Marchiesi had gone off in great excitement to tell her husband, the Marques Salvatore Marchiesi Castrione: 'Salvatore, I have found a star!'

Nervously Nellie waited. When Madame Marchiesi returned she took Nellie by the arm and led her into a room away from other girls waiting to audition. She sat her down on a sofa beside her and, in what Nellie would always describe as 'the turning point in my life', told her: 'Madame Armstrong, if you are serious and will study with me for a year, I shall make something *extra*-ordinairy of you.'

Nellie would never forget the way Marchiesi accented the word '*extra*ordinary'. At that moment she would have died if anyone had tried to stop her studying with Marchiesi. Fame seemed within her grasp.

Marchiesi was an excellent teacher and showed Nellie how to overcome her faults. Nellie worked very hard; as a result, her low scale 'rippled from low C to top C with never a change in quality'.[8]

Marchiesi told Nellie she was lucky to have been born with an almost perfect larynx and vocal cords. It wasn't long before she became Nellie's confidante and blend of best friend and mother substitute as well as her teacher. When Nellie wrote to her she would address her as 'Dearest Mother'. Unfortunately, through no fault of her own, Nellie alienated Marchiesi's only daughter, Blanche, an aspiring singer of average ability, who envied the time and effort her mother lavished on Nellie.

At this point, having been spurned in London as an unknown colonial and realising that no one in European circles cared a fig about Cecci, Nellie now totally disowned his contributions to her success. Marchiesi played a vital part in this discreditable affair: she wanted the glory of having discovered Melba for herself. Accordingly she claimed Nellie had to unlearn everything she had been taught before and that she, the great Marchiesi, was the sole influence on her voice. Nellie knew very well that Marchiesi had the power to establish her as a great singer, which Cecci, far away in Melbourne, could never do. So she went along with Marchiesi's pretence.

To cope with her guilt over disowning Cecci's professional influence on what she and Marchiesi called 'the voice', Nellie invented a fictitious story: she said that before she left Melbourne, Cecci had demanded the return of the money he sent to enable her to leave Mackay. She told Marchiesi she would never speak to Cecci again or acknowledge him as her teacher. (In the future, whenever she related this story, she would add for good measure that Cecci died of apoplexy when he heard of her success.)

It is difficult to reconcile Nellie's tale about Cecci demanding the return of his money with the fact that in 1886 she wrote a friendly letter to him from London informing him of her success in two concerts, asking him to write back to her care of Lady Armstrong, in Sussex. Did Cecci ever imagine that Nellie would betray his years of work and his influence on her technique in order to succeed? Opinions differ sharply on Nellie's probity in this matter.

Madame Marchiesi described the future diva as 'the pupil of my dreams' and worked Nellie long and hard in her quest to create a perfect singer. Nellie grew fonder and fonder of her teacher, describing her as 'more than a mother to me', and repeating how she was eternally grateful to her. In 1912 Marchiesi would tell the Australian author Katharine Susannah Prichard, who was interviewing her for an article in the Melbourne *Herald*, that 'It was her brain that made Melba's voice.' The phrase impressed Prichard as giving readers the key to Melba's success.[9] Marchiesi was convinced that Melba's high intelligence helped her to control her voice better than any other singer of her era and to develop what became her speciality, her famous 'nightingale trill', which required enormous control.

Through Marchiesi's faith in her and the invitations she received to musical evenings held at her teacher's home, Nellie made friends with several major composers, including Gounod, Delius and Massanet. These composers, especially Gounod, who adored her, would advance Nellie's career by coaching her in important roles and writing arias especially for her unique voice.

As yet Nellie's dreams of fame and fortune were only dreams. As a penniless student living in Paris on money provided by her father and having to support her son, she had no option but to resist the temptations of this elegant city and exist within her modest means. With little George she lived in an inexpensive family *pension* within walking distance of Marchiesi's home. At this period in her life, Nellie (whose name would become a byword for conspicuous consumption as she tried to erase memories of her former poverty) walked everywhere rather than taking hansom cabs. She saved up her monthly allowance to buy the cheapest seats at the opera and always wore the same old blue serge dress to her singing lessons much to Madame Marchiesi's despair: she wanted Nellie to dazzle all those who met her.

By this time Charles Armstrong had found strict military discipline not to his taste and was trying to make a success of farming the family estates in Sussex. On the occasions when he came to Paris to visit his wife and son (for whom he felt great affection), each visit would end in a violent quarrel. Charles was as quick-tempered as Nellie was stubborn. It became obvious they could never live together, whether Nellie was successful as a singer or not. What were they to do? Divorce was very expensive and the scandal would severely undermine her father's official position in London, so their unhappy marriage continued and Nellie did not inquire too closely how Charles spent his spare time in London.

Fame and fortune

Under Marchiesi's guidance, Nellie's debut took place at the Theatre de la Monnaie, Brussels, in 1887, in the emotive role of Gilda, Rigoletto's daughter, in Verdi's opera of that name. She was twenty-six. Before she appeared in Brussels, Marchiesi advised her to choose a stage name that was memorable and sounded European; both 'Armstrong' and 'Mitchell' were far too Anglo-Saxon to impress European opera lovers. Between them they evolved a new name — henceforth Nellie Armstrong would sing under the name of Melba, based on her birthplace, Melbourne. The stage name was short, memorable and Italianate. In addition, Nellie hoped it would make Australians proud of her.

Melba's Brussels debut in *Rigoletto* was a triumph. In Verdi's great quartet 'Bella figlia dell'amore', her remarkable voice with its unique trill was heard to its best advantage. In her interview with Prichard, Marchiesi told the young Australian writer: 'The very next day and for days afterwards there was nothing but a chorus of praise everywhere, the entire press of Brussels declaring the young artiste to be a star of the first magnitude.'[10]

International success seemed within Melba's grasp. She remained deeply grateful to Marchiesi for having given her the opportunity she craved, and she would continue to work on new roles with her teacher for many years. Now she yearned for success in London, knowing that news of it would appear in all the Australian papers; however, Melba found it impossible at this juncture to repeat her Brussels triumph in London. In hindsight it seems incredible, but her Covent Garden debut in the title role in *Lucia di Lammermoor* was not a success with London audiences. Melba had been invited to sing at Covent Garden because Lady de Grey (later the Countess of Ripon), a member of Covent Garden's Board of Trustees, had heard Melba sing in Brussels. The newspaper critics did not bother to attend, viewing her as someone of no importance since Covent Garden had not issued any press notices about her.

Covent Garden's autocratic manager, Augustus Harris, was reluctant to engage Melba, whom he believed was a 'colonial' singer whose success in Brussels was a mere flash in the pan impressing a crowd of excitable foreigners, which was why Harris did not give Melba any advance publicity. However, the Prince and Princess of Wales loyally supported their close friend Lady de Grey and attended Melba's first night. Although like Lady de Grey they admired Melba's silvery voice, the house was half-full and there were only two curtain calls. It seemed as though Nellie's career in London was over as soon as it had begun.

After that disappointing first night Nellie, deeply upset, complained to Lady de Grey and to the Covent Garden management that the conductor disliked her and that Covent Garden's orchestra had 'drowned' her voice. The management refused to give her a more 'sympathetic' conductor or to reprimand the one they had engaged. Lady de Grey also protested at the conductor's treatment of Madame Melba. Melba herself claimed she could not continue to work with him. Tempers flared, as they frequently do in the volatile world of opera. The conductor in his turn refused to work with Melba and the management took his side. By way of compensation Melba was offered a humiliatingly small role in Verdi's *A Masked Ball*, while a more famous singer was offered the lead.

Nellie was furious. She packed her bags and returned to Brussels, having learned a bitter lesson. The high-handed way in which she considered Covent Garden's manager had dealt with her would significantly affect her future behaviour towards opera managers and contracts; from then onwards she was determined to work only with conductors she liked and with publicity specified in her contract.

By fair means or foul, by manipulating contracts to her advantage, she was able to keep potential (and younger) female rivals off the stage. Her behaviour was often devious, but doubtless Marchiesi advised her that this was how other divas kept their positions at the top. Nellie, as intelligent as the best of them and with a will of iron, was determined to employ their strategies. She was her own manager-cum-publicist and dictated the most advantageous terms possible for all her contracts, to ensure that she was always seen on stage to *her* best advantage.

She had a huge success when she was invited to sing the role of Ophelia in *Hamlet* at the Paris Opéra. The critic of *Le Figaro* described Melba as a great new discovery with 'a marvellous soprano voice, equal, pure, brilliant and mellow'. He went on to say that Madame Melba's personal appearance was 'an advantage to her', describing her as 'tall and slender with an expressive face'.

What is interesting is that Melba was far from tall. One of her strengths lay in obtaining from opera companies clever costume designers and hairdressers who were able to create the *illusion* that she was tall and slim. Melba's best features were her large, velvety brown eyes which were indeed expressive; but in fact her personal appearance was not the 'advantage to her' that the music critic described. Off-stage she was short in stature, so she compensated by wearing the highest of heels. She had a very prominent nose and a sallow complexion, which she skilfully disguised with make-up. Nor was she a great actress like her friend Sarah Bernhardt. Melba was what the French call *jolie-laide*: her face was interesting and expressive rather than beautiful, and she possessed the special gift of making her audience *believe* she was beautiful.

In Paris Melba followed her success as Ophelia by again playing the title role in *Lucia di Lammermoor*, performing brilliantly in the scene where Lucia goes mad. To London audiences she had been a 'mere colonial'; to the French she was an exciting new star from exotic, remote Australia. Sarah Bernhardt described Melba's voice as 'pure crystal', while a critic as enthralled as Cecci and Marchiesi had been described it as 'hovering in the auditorium like a beam of light'. Overnight Madame Melba became the toast of Paris.

Meanwhile Nellie's friend Lady de Grey, convinced that Melba had been treated very badly by the management of Covent Garden, was determined to get her back there. It took time but, as a result of all Lady de Grey's lobbying and committee work, in 1889 Melba returned to star at Covent Garden, where she would continue to create operatic history for the next forty years. Her triumphant return to London coincided with a long period of national peace and prosperity and a golden period of opera at Covent Garden. With the gloss of her Paris triumph behind her and *plenty* of advance publicity, this time Melba was a huge success. Covent Garden audiences loved her and could not see enough of her. Success followed success. Soon the management were paying Nellie Armstrong from 'down under', the woman they had scorned, the highest fees of any singer in the world, male or female.

Nellie had a memory like an elephant — she never forgot a slight or an insult. As her own manager she dictated her own terms and she insisted that Covent Garden, although very short of space, should provide her with a private dressing-room for her sole use, which was to remain locked in her absence. Realising they had a star on their hands and fearful of losing her, the management bowed to her demands. Nellie kept that dressing-room for her exclusive use for the rest of her singing career.

The golden years

Success at Covent Garden changed everything. Nellie Armstrong and her inexpensive blue serge dresses and scuffed down-at-heel shoes had vanished, replaced by Melba, the grandest of divas, who wore Paris gowns designed by Worth and pearls the size of a pigeon's egg. She bought a diamond tiara, which she wore at first nights of operas in which she was not starring. She lived surrounded by servants and hot house flowers, her every whim catered for. She was the guest London society hostesses most wanted to attend their parties.

For the next fourteen years, during her annual season at Covent Garden, Melba rented a luxurious suite at the Savoy Hotel overlooking the Thames. She spent so much money at the Savoy that eventually she found it cheaper to buy a house in Mayfair at 30 Great Cumberland Place, which she remodelled to look like a mini-Versailles complete with Louis XIV gilded furniture and mirrors. She spent a fortune on the house, importing plasterers, cabinet-makers and designers from France because she believed British workmen were incapable of carrying out the work. The end result was slightly over the top, to put it mildly, but Nellie was happy. She was *somebody* now and everyone who visited her would know it.

She was clever enough to keep in with the younger, racy members of the Prince of Wales's set as well as the more formal and subdued court of the widowed Queen Victoria, for whom she sang on several occasions at Windsor Castle. Nellie loved royal performances and being on first-name terms with aristocrats. A duchess once asked Nellie if she would rather be a duchess or Melba. 'There are *lots* of duchesses,' Nellie replied, 'but only *one* Melba.'

She appeared at every London opera season (with the exception of 1909–12) until World War I, when Covent Garden closed its doors for the duration. She never forgot that it was Lady de Grey who had been responsible for her return to London; Melba's loyalty to old friends was one of her most endearing qualities. By now John Lemmone had become her accompanist, and she looked after him financially in his old age. She was a true friend to those she trusted, an implacable enemy to her rivals.

Like her father Melba liked money; she was attracted to men who had an abundance of it, as well as the power that money brings. Her friendship with the Prince of Wales and his circle gave Melba huge social clout. The Prince was a complex man who had endured an isolated, unhappy childhood. Once he had his own household he devoted his time to the pursuit of pleasure and sex but bowed to tradition and entered into an arranged marriage with the beautiful and dutiful Princess Alexandra of Schleswig-Holstein-Glucksberg. He was fond of his wife, but she bored him witless and he was notoriously unfaithful to her.

Melba walked a delicate tightrope; she was friends with Princess Alexandra and the Prince's many mistresses, who included Sarah Bernhardt, the Princesse de Sagan, the Duchess Caraciolo, Daisy Brooke, the Countess of Warwick, Lillie Langtry and Alice Keppel (great-grandmother of Camilla Parker Bowles).

By the time Melba met the Prince of Wales he was enormously fat, the result of the huge meals he devoured. He was experiencing difficulties in consummating his *affaires*; each time he selected a new woman for his bed, he always hoped that his bouts of impotence would be cured. It was common knowledge among the Prince's circle that in order to hoist his heavy body in position for lovemaking, he had to use a curious apparatus which featured a cradle and a pair of stirrups. Among those who knew him well, the 'in joke' was that this remarkable piece of equipment was based on one employed for mating the Prince's stallions to his mares in the royal stables at Sandringham. Extra-marital sex was a given in the Prince's circle: Melba, who had a number of lovers, fitted in very well, although she and the Prince never became involved. The Prince had little time for his mother's stuffy court at Windsor; his own set was very *nouveau riche* and its members were often criticised for their vulgarity. The fact that Melba swore like a trooper when she was relaxed and her taste in somewhat gaudy, to put it mildly, interior decoration presented no problems for the Prince and his circle. He had a very limited appreciation of opera and no ear for classical music. What satisfied His Royal Highness was knowing that he had the best performers at his parties. And Melba *was* the best. On several occasions the Prince carried on a spirited conversation while Melba was singing. She was deeply offended but forgave him ... after all, he *was* the Prince of Wales.

This was the era known as the *belle époque,* a period of extraordinary opulence, peace and prosperity when the rich were not burdened with income tax. As a result money flowed freely. It was considered normal for wealthy men to send a diva jewels or huge bouquets of flowers before important first nights. Melba received both in abundance. She once observed: 'If I had only the money that has been spent in flowers for me and *nothing* else, I should *still* be a rich woman.'

Everything Melba did was news. Leading chefs in London and Paris named their latest creations Pêche Melba and Melba toast. Picture postcards (which are today valuable and collectable) portrayed her portraits and photographs in favourite roles. Great composers like Toscanini, Puccini and Verdi were her friends and admirers.

In an era when most women were denied the luxury of their own bank account or were unable to obtain a mortgage or a bank loan because (shades of Hegel) it was thought their little brains could not handle finance, Melba, by her own efforts, became a millionaire (the equivalent of a billionaire today). Her financial acumen, inherited from her parsimonious but astute father, and her days of relative poverty in Paris meant that she was well aware of the value of every dollar she earned and of the pulling power of her voice.

If the mood took her she could be extremely generous, donating large sums to charities or former colleagues in need. To supply her own needs, she employed a retinue of maids, cooks, secretaries and her own hairdresser. All her clothes, including her silk nightgowns, were made by leading designers. She travelled like a queen in her personal train carriage, furnished with monogrammed silk sheets, silken cushions and silver candelabra, its walls hung with several of her portraits and favourite paintings. She could be as autocratic as any duchess, dominating the conversation and ignoring other women at the dinner table, but warm and affectionate to old friends.

Melba was the grandest of divas in the days when opera singers were accorded the adulation now reserved for pop and film stars, possessing a very special charisma. After she performed in St Petersburg the audience cheered themselves hoarse and students took the horses from her carriage and placed themselves between the shafts, pulling it back to her hotel in triumph. The Tsar himself, enraptured by the special quality of Melba's voice, gave her an exquisite diamond and pearl bracelet.

In Vienna, a city dedicated to music and opera, Melba's appearance at the Hofoper was yet another triumph. The Emperor Franz Joseph, widowed ruler of the vast Austro-Hungarian empire, scarcely ever went out after the death of his wife, the beautiful Empress Elizabeth, who had been assassinated by a madman. Nellie was summoned to Schönbrunn, the Emperor's summer palace, and led through mirrored anterooms and immense salons filled with rare porcelain. Finally she arrived at an audience chamber where she was presented to the Emperor, whom she described as 'a dignified, sad, old man in a black coat standing with his hands behind his back'. He presented her with a jewel-encrusted medal and told her that until the previous night he had not visited a theatre for over a year. 'Not once, not since the Empress was assassinated,' he said. He smiled sadly and continued: 'Madame Melba, the beauty of your voice called me from my enforced retirement. It was a great effort to attend the opera but I am glad that I did so.' She felt deeply sorry for him as he pinned the medal on her, so moved she could not reply. Her eyes filled with tears. She was intelligent enough to realise that the ageing Emperor was totally isolated from most people by the pomp and majesty of his position.

Her interview in Berlin with the German Kaiser was not so pleasant. Appearing as Marguerite in *Faust,* she was summoned to the Imperial Box at the Opera House but told she must not bring *anything* perfumed with her, as the Kaiser was allergic to perfume. He spoke to Melba in almost perfect English, saying how he had enjoyed her performance, but he was very critical about the tempo at which she had sung 'The Jewel Song'.

Melba was no great admirer of the Germans. She thanked the Kaiser but said she had sung the song 'according to the instructions of Gounod, its composer, who had been very pleased indeed by her rendering of his aria'. She smiled sweetly as she saw the Kaiser's moustache bristle with suppressed rage and added: 'And furthermore, I would not dream of criticising His Imperial Highness's government.'[11]

Melba had a quick wit, loved being the centre of attention and was adored by many, but it would be wrong to claim that everyone loved her. Her enemies called her ruthless, autocratic, conniving. Perhaps she was, but so were most of her rivals, and to beat them she had long ago decided to employ their techniques. Like most prima donnas Melba knew she must be constantly on the watch for the stab in the back, as well as for younger artistes who might supplant her as she grew older. She made sure that a clause was written into all her contracts stating that she must approve of any other female star contracted to perform. Madame Melba became famous (or infamous) for doing everything in her power to rid herself of potential rivals. She had absolutely no intention of abdicating.

She was a clever self-publicist, cultivating 'friendly' journalists who wrote favourable stories about her. She was always ready to provide journalists with photo opportunities, and to dream up new angles for stories. She never employed a press agent, preferring to handle this side of her career herself. On a cleverly orchestrated visit to the Taj Mahal to pose for publicity pictures Melba burst into song, enchanting the waiting photographers.

Madame Melba (by now separated from her husband) was a wealthy and desirable woman. Rich and highly eligible men sent flowers and jewels and invited her to dine with them after her performances. Sometimes she accepted, mostly she did not, preferring to be surrounded by those she knew already. She lived in a world where lovers (after marriage) were tolerated as long as there was no scandal. Divorce was legal but scandalous. Melba moved in a fast set and acted as they did but kept quiet about it. Still nominally married, she handled her brief *affaires* with discretion. She liked aristocrats and had a fondness for young writers, musicians and painters. Artist Rupert Bunny, handsome son of a Melbourne judge, is reputed to have been one of her lovers and painted one hugely flattering and youthful portrait of her. But hers was not a life dedicated to love; it was a life dedicated to opera. Men came a long way down Melba's list.

The unwritten code of London and Parisian society was that it did not matter what two adults did together 'so long as they did not do it in the street and frighten the horses'. Country house parties in stately homes consisted of a great deal of bed-hopping, the chief bed-hopper being the Prince of Wales; by the time he finally acceded to the throne in 1901 he was known as 'Edward the Caresser'. Yet the Prince and Princess of Wales (later Edward VII and Queen Alexandra) always presented a united front to the world.

Only once in her life did Melba lose her head over a man, exposing herself to an international scandal which nearly destroyed her career. In 1890 at the age of thirty-one, just as she was about to return to Covent Garden for the second time, she met bearded, handsome Louis-Phillipe, Duc d'Orléans, heir to the Pretender to the throne of France, who was engaged to a European aristocrat. He was blond, Melba was dark and sultry. He was ten years younger than she was and more handsome than any duke or king in grand opera: a real-life Lohengrin with a touch of Dumas's Chevalier D'Artagnan. It was instant attraction for both of them, and the duke did not think again about his arranged marriage.

Their romance blossomed in Paris in spring, and continued when the duke and the diva went to Vienna together. They rode through the Vienna Woods and waltzed to the music of Strauss in the Volksgarten. The Viennese, used to glamorous romances, shrugged their shoulders; Austrian archdukes were *always* having romances with ballerinas or singers. However, when Melba and her royal duke shared a box at the Vienna State Opera, this caused some gossip in aristocratic circles. Madame Marchiesi, to whom Melba still wrote, was her confidante in this *affaire*. Perhaps Melba had forgotten that Marchiesi's daughter Blanche, Melba's implacable enemy, was now married and living in Vienna.

After Melba and the duke were seen together at the Opera, Blanche contacted a journalist intent on writing a story about Melba and the duke and they had a long talk. The journalist duly 'broke' the story about Melba's relationship with a member of the French royal family in the *Wiener Taggblat*, Vienna's daily 'populist' newspaper. The resulting scandal made headlines around the world.

'Everyone who has known fame has also known the agonies which fame brings', Nellie wrote with deep feeling after the news of this *affaire* destroyed her hollow marriage and almost wrecked her career. Suddenly she found herself in the real-life role of Violetta from *La Traviata* — she was the woman who in reality lost the man she loved because his family objected to her. Of course Melba was not a penniless courtesan like Violetta, but she was married and on the stage. Even were she divorced she could not marry a royal duke, especially one who was a Catholic and already engaged. The Orleans family could not countenance such an alliance. Melba was making headlines, but they were not the sort of headlines she enjoyed. Local and foreign journalists followed the couple around and produced stories with such titles as 'The scandal of the diva and the duke'.

Far away in Texas, Charles Armstrong learned about his wife's lover from a newspaper. As the injured party her estranged husband announced he would sue for divorce, naming the duke as co-respondent. Melba knew that a divorce would cause great scandal and that should this happen she would be viewed as a scarlet woman, a social outcast, an Australian Anna Karenina, the woman who had broken the unwritten code: 'You may commit adultery but you shall not be found out.'

She returned to London to find journalists besieging her home. She fled to Paris to seek comfort from Madame Marchiesi, who told Melba in no uncertain terms that she must negotiate with her husband and, in public at least, renounce her friendship with the duke. Marchiesi also remarked that there were many attractive men in the world but only one career as a diva. In Britain, Queen Victoria still had the last word. Melba would be ruined if she was cited in a sensational divorce; even the Prince of Wales and his fast-living set would drop her like a hot potato. At the thought of being banned from Covent Garden Melba is reputed to have burst into tears, saying that if she could not marry the duke she would *never* marry anyone.[12]

At this point the duke's engagement was broken off, his future in-laws outraged by the scandal. The French royal family was appalled — it was one thing to have a prima donna as a mistress, but quite another to have their family name dragged through a divorce court.

Possibly some French diplomatic pressure was brought to bear on Charles to drop his petition for divorce.[13] (At that time the concept of no-fault divorce did not exist; Melba would have been declared the guilty party, liable to pay her husband damages and lose custody of her child.) Marchiesi had already pointed out that if she divorced, both her popularity and her income would suffer badly. Lawyers argued at great length and for a great deal of money. They discussed terms for a compromise whereby the duke's name would be dropped from Charles Armstrong's divorce petition on condition that he was given custody of his son and maintenance for the child. Horrified by the prospect that Lady de Grey and other aristocratic patrons would be alienated by the scandal and fearful for her career, Melba agreed.

She sent young George to boarding school in England, but Charles removed him from his school without her consent and took his son to Texas, where he was attempting rather unsuccessfully to run a ranch. In 1901, Charles divorced his wife quietly from Texas; news of the divorce was not featured in the newspapers. Charles taught George to be as good a horseman as he was, but apart from this the boy's education was neglected and he ran wild.

Melba continued to see the duke from time to time during the next few years, until in November 1896 he made a grand but ultimately tragic marriage to the Archduchess Maria Dorothea of Austria. Needless to say, Melba was not invited to sing at the wedding. The Archduchess's subsequent infertility was rumoured to be a result of inherited syphilis contracted from her father. Eventually the unhappy couple separated.[14] The duke consoled himself with other beautiful women and took up big game hunting in Africa. He had been the only man who was really important to Nellie, apart from her father. After he separated from his wife the Duke of Orleans was put in charge of an exploratory expedition to Greenland for several years. When he returned to London he visited Melba.[15] She took good care that no word of their meetings ever got into the press and is believed to have burned all their correspondence.

Although she had other lovers, including an aspiring Australian writer called Haddon Chambers, the Argentine composer Herman Bemberg and (supposedly) Australia's Rupert Bunny, none of them could ever replace the duke in her affections. After this, Melba rarely appeared in public with her lovers and made certain that the press never knew about her brief liaisons.

Melba never seems to have made the slightest attempt to see her son George, but possibly she had had to sign a clause to that effect as part of her secret agreement with Charles. She was not exactly a conventional mother; in the custom of the time George had been brought up by various nannies and housekeepers. Deep in her heart, however, she adored her only son and was devastated by his absence.

She would not see George again until he was grown up. She felt herself alone as she approached mid-life and filled the void by concentrating even harder on her career.

The year after her divorce, Melba returned to Australia after a long absence to undertake a hugely successful concert tour. Once again, scandal followed her. She was supposed to have advised another diva named Clara Butt that on Clara's forthcoming tour of Australia she should 'Sing 'em muck, that's all they understand.' Melba believed a dignified silence was the best response to what she saw as a story deliberately concocted by a spiteful enemy to do her harm. 'They say, what do they say? Let them say', she wrote to a friend.

More scandal followed. Ezra Norton, the vitriolic and alcoholic editor of *Truth*, published a letter accusing Melba (who was always generous to those who worked for her) of underpaying her employees. He also accused her of alcoholism, which was totally unjust: to guard her precious voice she drank only wine and the finest champagne. Those who knew her well assert Melba *never* drank more than a couple of glasses with a meal, her voice being the possession she held most dear.

Eager to see her father, who was now seventy-four, Melba returned once again to Australia in 1902, to a country elated by the excitement of Federation. She left Vancouver aboard the steamship *Miowera* and was due to berth in Brisbane on 14 September, but the ship's ancient engines failed three times on the voyage and Melba had no way of informing the organisers of her tour of the delay. Red carpets, flowers and speeches awaited her. A kind of royal tour had been arranged using a special 'Melba' train in which, with some of her brothers and sisters, it was planned she should pass through country railway stations crowded with cheering people, all longing for a glimpse of Australia's most famous daughter.

At Albury she was to meet her father for the first time in years, and she was longing to see him. However, when the train steamed into the station she was met by a doctor who told her that her father had suffered a stroke after worrying she had been shipwrecked because of her late arrival.

Melba was distraught. She was taken to a house near the station, where her father was lying in bed. Overcome by emotion she knelt down and kissed his hand. Nothing in the world seemed to matter except her father. She told him she would cancel her tour of honour and her appearances, stay at Albury and nurse him until he was better. David Mitchell, a tough Scotsman who believed in duty and hard work, shook his head. Unable to speak aloud, he mouthed the words: 'Nellie, you *must* go on. You can't disappoint your public.'

The train had been halted for over an hour and the crowd was growing restive. Nellie thought of cancelling her whole tour but realised that was impossible. All the railway stations along the route had been specially decorated in her honour, and spectators were lining the route to see her. So like the trooper she was she followed her father's wishes and continued on to Melbourne, albeit with a heavy heart.

The city of Melbourne had proclaimed a public holiday in honour of Melba, its most famous daughter. The *Melbourne Argus* ran a feature calling her 'Our greatest Australian', the only woman to be so honoured in a country besotted with sportsmen.

As though in a dream she drove through streets hung with bright flags and bunting. Bands played; all trams had stopped. There were speeches, flowers, more speeches, more flowers ... Melba's iron control took over and she did not show her agony but presented a calm exterior. The day that should have been her greatest triumph, the return to her home town, had turned to dust and ashes in her mouth. She felt as though she was sleepwalking, part of a nightmare. Finally, alone in her hotel suite, she burst into tears at the memory of her bedridden father in Albury, so near and yet so far away.

That night she was to sing at a special Melba Gala in the Town Hall. She would have preferred to cancel it, but her father had said she must not let her public down. She carried out his wishes. Pale and resolute, wearing a long white satin dress embroidered with jewels and a rope of baroque pearls, Melba made her appearance to wild applause. There were repeated requests for encores, more applause, still more encores.

David Mitchell recovered sufficiently to return to Melbourne and was able to attend her second concert. He sat in the front row, frail but proud, as his daughter announced to roars of applause that she would sing for him his favourite song, 'Comin' Through the Rye'.

After the concert was over her father came backstage in a wheelchair and they talked for hours. What impressed him most was Nellie's account of how much money she had earned from her singing. She told him wi.th justifiable pride that she had earned double that sum from investing her money wisely in property and stocks and shares.

'That's ma guid wee lassie,' her father replied proudly.

On Melba's return to London, she continued to perform for the entire summer season at Covent Garden and at several European opera houses. She was now starting to earn huge sums from her recordings, which in those pioneering days of recorded sound did not do justice to her remarkable voice.

That celebrated Melba trill

Melba employed Beverley Nichols, a young homosexual writer, to act as her secretary and ghost write her memoirs. After Melba dispensed with Nichols's services he wrote *Evensong*, a waspish and sardonic novel about an ageing diva who intrigues and struggles to keep her place at the top, which appeared the year after Melba's death and outraged many Australians. Nichols had dipped his pen in vitriol to describe Melba's 'truly awful' taste in interior decoration and millinery. He was of course familiar with her London house, and told the world how she decorated gilded picture frames with satin bows and furnished her salon with overstuffed divans upholstered in shiny gold satin and gilded French furniture, some of which was reputed to be fake.

Later, under the tuition of an aristocrat-turned-interior-designer, the Marquis Boni de Castellane (described by Beverley Nichols as 'a tiny pomaded creature like a scented meringue') Melba got rid of most of her ornate furniture and overstuffed sofas and replaced them with simple but elegant mahogany chairs and tables from the workshop of the great English cabinetmaker Thomas Chippendale.

The Marquis de Castellane also managed to persuade Melba, now in her fifties, to dye her jet black hair a softer shade of brown, which was far kinder to her complexion. Nichols criticised Melba's increasing girth in middle age and her gigantic picture hats that he claimed made her resemble a mushroom. (Rather sadly, she believed huge hats made her look slimmer.) One thing Nichols could not do, however, was to find fault with her voice, which all those lucky enough to hear insisted was of incomparable beauty.

Unfortunately, the 100 different recordings of arias which Melba allowed to be released out of the 150 or so she actually made are ancient bakelite ones, designed to be played at 78 rpm. Listening to these records crackle and hiss, it is impossible to gain a true impression of what Melba *really* sounded like. Her voice disappoints, often sounding tinny and lifeless, and it makes it hard to imagine how, in her lifetime, critics wept for joy or went into ecstasies, praising that 'silvery voice, pure as that of a choirboy but more powerful' and her 'remarkable ability to trill like a nightingale'. It was her talent for ornamentation, to use a musical term, combined with her beautiful tone and perfect technique that made her internationally famous. It is very sad that we cannot hear her as she sounded in real life.

Beverley Nichols also wrote a first-hand account of the 'filming' of Melba's voice. Nature had given her an almost perfect larynx and vocal chords; her range was three full octaves. Professor A.M. Low was now in the news as the inventor of the world's first audiometer, with which he recorded sound on film. Nichols persuaded Melba to allow the professor to 'film' her voice, telling her that she would be the first singer to be recorded in this way and undoubtedly the British Museum would like a copy of 'her' film. He pointed out that Melba's younger rivals, Patti and Tettrazini, had not got anything of *theirs* into the hallowed halls of the British Museum. Professor Low duly arrived at Melba's house with his audiometer. He was an extremely handsome man, quite young, with a shock of black hair and sensitive features. Initially Melba, who always liked to surround herself with handsome young men, was charm personified.

'What shall I sing, professor?' she asked him with a smile. 'Where should I stand?'

She had no idea that the professor was filming the *sound* of her voice; she was under the impression that he was making a moving picture of her as well. She preened a little in front of the mirror, then asked coquettishly whether the professor liked her dress, or would something simpler be better for 'her' public?

Keeping a straight face with difficulty, Professor Low finally managed to convince her that this was not an audition for one of Hollywood's new silent movies but a scientific experiment he was carrying out. Melba's face fell.

The professor drew the curtains, fiddled about with some wires and then fused all the lights. In the resulting darkness one of Melba's regiment of liveried footmen tripped over an electric cable, fell flat on his face and broke a valuable vase. Melba, upset, left the room muttering angrily. When order was restored and the professor had rearranged everything to his liking, Melba was persuaded to return and stand beside the grand piano on which Beverley Nichols was to accompany her. She started with a middle E, then sang a scale, rather grumpily according to Nichols.

Tactfully he suggested she should sing a 'trill'.

'Why should I?' she snapped. 'A trill wouldn't come out on film.' She turned to the professor. 'Or would it?'

Professor Low assured her that her trill would 'come out'.

'*My* trills,' began Melba. And then she stopped.

'*Please, Madame*, do a trill for the film,' Professor Low implored her.

So she did. And the trill was wonderful. Their session over, the professor packed up his machine and departed. Over the next few days he 'filmed' the voices of other leading sopranos. Then he came back to the house with a roll of film on which Melba's voice showed up as a series of peaks and troughs, which bore some resemblance to the peaks and troughs on an electrocardiogram machine. His scientific rendering of her trill had produced on film twenty feet of undulations between perfectly parallel lines. Melba was famous for the incredible delicacy and precision of her trills, which did not flutter or wobble or wander from the notes like those of other sopranos Professor Low had filmed.

He commented that Madame Melba's results were truly astonishing. Her top A flat was *far* richer and more complex in design than *any* of the other singers, whose trills had reproduced on film in a far more random pattern. Melba's trill was outstanding in its regularity, so uniform in outline that it might have been drawn by a geometrician.

Melba was impressed. Ever conscious of favourable publicity, she asked the professor if he would let the *Daily Mail* publish an article about his machine. What she wanted was for *her* magnificent trill to be featured across three columns of the paper, accompanied by the inferior trills of her rivals.

'*That'll* show 'em,' she said with relish.

Professor Low refused, fearing that publication in a newspaper could lead to libel actions against him ... which is why Melba's perfect trills were never published.

Melba in Manhattan takes on the Metropolitan

Between 1883 and 1910 Melba appeared with the Chicago Opera and sang at the Metropolitan Opera House in New York, where she had a huge following.[16] Then she found herself being wooed by the American impresario Oscar Hammerstein, who wanted her to sing for him at his Manhattan Opera House rather than at the Metropolitan. Melba did not care for Hammerstein's way of doing business and held out for a long time, on each subsequent occasion demanding larger and larger fees.

Hammerstein refused to take no for an answer. He would appear in her dressing-room after a performance or at her home, imploring her to sing for him. On one occasion he carpeted the floor with thousand franc notes while she was out, but still did not succeed. Each time he appeared Melba, well aware of the value of her voice and the Melba legend, increased her demands.

Finally, after years spent pursuing Melba, Hammerstein capitulated and asked her if she would name her terms. She did. He agreed, with the result that Melba was contracted to sing at his new opera house, something which mortally offended the management of the Metropolitan. However, following her disastrous attempt to sing Brünnhilde in *Siegfried* at the Met in 1896, it was not exactly her favourite opera house.

Melba arrived in New York before her first performance at the Manhattan Opera House only to find that for all his bluff, Hammerstein was a worried man. Would his gamble pay off? Would Melba establish his Manhattan Opera House once and for all, or would they both look ridiculous for daring to take on the power of the Met?

For the first time in many years Madame Melba was nervous, fearing the Met might retaliate and hold a rival gala or even an opera ball to steal her audience away from her.

On her historic first night at the Manhattan Opera House, on 2 January 1907, as Melba the diva stepped to the front of the stage to play her role as Violetta in *La Traviata*, there was a storm of applause. The floor of the house was a vast sea of glittering jewels worn by the audience. For a moment Melba stood motionless, as if blinded by the flashing diamonds and gleaming white shirt fronts. The opera house was silent for a moment, and the audience started to wonder if certain rumours were true and Melba had lost her nerve. Then the orchestra started up and that beautiful silvery voice rang out across the theatre, casting its unforgettable spell.

There were rave reviews. Her performance was described by *The Times* opera correspondent as 'One long night of triumph. Melba's voice has its old-time lusciousness and purity, its exquisite smoothness and fullness. It poured out of her with spontaneity and freedom'. Melba had made American opera history; she broke the huge power of the Metropolitan and filled Oscar Hammerstein's brand new Manhattan Opera House with New York society 'names', most of them defectors from the Met.

That night Melba received ten curtain calls. The vast opera house was a storm of waving handkerchiefs and cheering people. The rest of her New York season was a sellout, bringing excellent profits to Hammerstein and record-breaking performance fees to Melba's bank account. The mighty Metropolitan implored her to return to its stage. Her gamble had paid off handsomely.

Return to Australia in triumph

In 1909, at the height of her fame, Melba made another sentimental journey back to her homeland on what was to be a backblock tour of Australia's remote country areas.

Everywhere she went ordinary Australians turned out to see her. In remote areas they arrived by cart, bullock wagon, on horseback or on foot. To the Scots among them she was 'their' Nellie, David Mitchell's lass, who had made good in the big world. They were so proud of her. These were unsophisticated people who knew nothing of Italian opera: for them she sang the old favourites like 'Home, Sweet Home' and 'Comin' Through the Rye'. Each concert was sold out; everywhere she went she was feted like royalty at banquets and receptions.

The enthusiasm with which Australians greeted her affected her deeply. 'In Britain and Europe I am respected for my talent and my money but Australia is where I am loved,' she is supposed to have said. It marked a turning point — she knew now that after she retired she wanted to spend her final years in Australia.

Melba devised a good method for dealing with journalists who asked invasive questions: she simply talked through them about something else as though she was deaf. She refused to answer any questions that she found too personal, especially those dealing with the Duke of Orleans.

For many years she had thought about building or buying a home in Australia and spending more time near her beloved father. On this trip she found the land she had dreamed of at Coldstream, six and a half kilometres from her father's limestone quarries at Lilydale. It was in gentle countryside and was surrounded by low rolling hills. She bought an old stone farm cottage and commissioned Melbourne architect John Grainger (father of the composer Percy Grainger) to design her an elegant country home. Her new house took almost two years to complete with its terraced garden, English-style lawns and a large swimming pool. She called it Coombe Cottage, after a house in which she had been very happy in England.

In 1911 Melba returned to Australia again, eager to see how her house was progressing. She was heading an enterprise to bring to Australians opera of international standard in joint Melba–J.C. Williamson seasons, a project in which she had invested money. She and her accompanist and lifelong friend John Lemmone, who had assumed a managerial role in her later life, engaged all the artistes.

By now David Mitchell was in his eighties; worry about his health was the main reason Melba came back to Melbourne again in the northern summer of 1914. She could not anticipate that the assassination of the Archduke Franz Ferdinand at Sarajevo in a few months time would spark a world war which would see Covent Garden close for five years and put out the lights in all the capital cities of Europe.

The onset of World War I meant that Melba spent several years in Australia, with Coombe Cottage as her base. She threw herself heart and soul into war work, bringing the full weight of her personality, her tenacity of purpose and her legendary attention to detail into fundraising and supporting Australian and occasionally British troops in the field. She was intent on helping to win the war against Germany and allowed her large and luxurious Paris apartment to be used as a convalescent home for wounded Australian soldiers, generously funding it herself.

In Australia Melba gave concerts in every State capital and in wooden halls way out in the bush to raise money for the wounded. She generously financed *Melba's Gift Book,* published as another fundraising gesture, which sold in huge numbers; Melba signed numerous individual copies until her hands and wrists were sore. She personally paid for Red Cross parcels of cigarettes and chocolate to be sent at Christmas to soldiers in the Dardanelles campaign and in the trenches of northern France. The fact that she was no longer able to perform at Covent Garden, coupled with the huge sums she gave away in aid of the war effort, made severe inroads into her capital.

Wartime travel was hazardous and difficult between England and Australia but was still possible by ocean liner to America. Melba travelled three times to America, each time giving concerts after which she personally auctioned flags for huge sums. She made fundraising speeches in which she exhorted the Americans to enter the war on the side of the British, and raised large amounts of American dollars to provide comforts for British and Australian troops serving in the trenches. Her contribution was outstanding, way above what anyone had expected of her and it was this, as much as her voice, which placed her on the British Honours list. On her American tours she feared that German Intelligence had scheduled her assassination because of her fundraising activities. Some biographers have viewed these fears as illustrative of how grandiose she had become, but it does seem an amazing series of coincidences that while Melba was in America she was involved in several car accidents, the engine of a train in which she was travelling blew up (injuring several passengers but leaving her unscathed), and a bomb exploded near her box at the Chicago Opera House. However, no connection between these accidents and German Intelligence was ever established.

In 1916 she received news that her father was critically ill, and set off to see him. David Mitchell, now eighty-seven, went into hospital and died on the operating table. Unfortunately the ship on which Melba was travelling was delayed and did not dock until after his death, which caused her a great deal of heartache.[17]

When the war ended Melba was awarded a DBE, Dame of the British Empire; in 1927 she was created a GBE (Dame Grand Cross of the British Empire).

Proceeds from previous Melbourne concerts had gone towards building a concert hall at Melbourne University, which was named the Melba Hall; it opened in 1913. Now, due to internal disagreements in the music world, Melba joined forces with the English-born composer-director Fritz Hart to start her own all-female singing school at what became known as the Albert Street Conservatorium (now the Melba Memorial Conservatorium at York Street, Richmond).[18] She designed a uniform for the girls which was ornamented with a large 'M' and taught there free of charge. She used what she referred to as the Melba method (which was really the Marchiesi method with modifications) and published a book titled *The Melba Method*, ghosted by Fritz Hart.[19] Melba tried to help young female singers, claiming that she was trying to discover 'a second Melba'. However, by a strange quirk she invariably chose girls who never achieved very much. Winning a Melba Scholarship proved traumatic for Stella Power, whom Melba tried to establish as 'Little Melba' until Power defied her and got married.

Melba was now in her late fifties, still energetic and bubbling with plans for fresh ventures. Her enormous success and fame did make her appear rather grandiose on occasions. For example, she designed a kind of royal warrant for the tradesmen of emporiums she patronised. The warrants, bearing a gold 'M' in place of the Royal Arms, were engraved and framed in gold. She also presented tie pins and diamond brooches to tradesmen who performed valuable services.

She entertained frequently at Coombe Cottage, but not all the guests enjoyed going there. The talented violinist Norah Clench, wife of Sir Arthur Streeton, absolutely detested spending weekends at Coombe Cottage because Melba demanded the full attention of her husband while ignoring her.[20] Yet when Melba really liked someone she was warm-hearted and affectionate towards them and often offered help, just as she did to elderly performers down on their luck.

After the war Melba returned to London to find that practically an entire generation of young men was dead and the ambience of Covent Garden was quite changed. Unfortunately she had gained a great deal of weight during the war and now looked matronly. She continued to sing at her beloved Covent Garden but often lamented how times had changed, that audiences in the stalls and the dress circle no longer bothered to change into evening dress or don tiaras.

In 1927 she came back to her homeland again. As Australia's most famous expatriate, she had been chosen to sing the National Anthem at the opening of the new Parliament House in Canberra.

Her son George, once he reached adulthood, had returned to her from America. After his marriage he and his wife lived in a house which Melba had specially designed and built for them in the grounds of Coombe Cottage.

Like most prima donnas Melba hated the idea of growing old and retiring, especially from Covent Garden, which she thought of as her second home. She gave numerous official farewell performances in London and Australia but always kept coming back to the stage, loath to tear herself away from the world she loved. On 14 October 1924, the Melbourne *Argus* reported one of her many farewell speeches: 'I have done my best. I have tried to keep faith with my art. For all that Australia has done for me, for all the beauty that she has shown me, for all the love she has offered, I wish to say, thank you from the bottom of my heart. I never was prouder than I am tonight to be an Australian woman.'

Her final Covent Garden farewell took place on 8 June 1926, and her performance in *La Bohème* was a triumph. King George V, Queen Mary and Edward, Prince of Wales, were there with other members of the royal family. The auditorium was a sea of jewels, tiaras and diamond-studded decorations, glistening bare shoulders and white shirt fronts. Some opera lovers feared that at the age of sixty-seven, Melba would no longer be capable of giving a good performance. She proved them wrong. At that gala she sang so beautifully that the years seemed to recede and she was once again the great prima donna she had been a quarter of a century earlier. That heavenly legato was still there together with the wonderful technique. Everyone was entranced by her performance.

The applause was deafening; the theatre rang with cheers. Stagehands brought from her dressing-room all the floral tributes that Melba had received and laid them edge to edge. When the curtain rose again, the audience saw Melba standing in front of a pyramid of flowers taller than herself. The clapping and cheering died away as she moved forward to stand in front of the footlights. In a voice breaking with emotion she said: 'This is such a great and glorious evening, but you can imagine what a terrible feeling it is for me to think that I shall never sing within these beloved walls again.'

After thanking all those with whom she had worked Melba's eyes were filled with tears, like those of most of her audience. There would be numerous other farewells, leading to the old saying 'More farewells than

Nellie Melba', but that night at Covent Garden was the one that affected her most. At least she could console herself that she had her beautiful Australian home to return to, and a devoted family and good friends.

Melba spent her final years at Coombe Cottage with her son, his second wife Evie, and her little granddaughter Pamela (later Lady Vestey). She truly loved Pamela, who in turn adored the woman she said had been, in every way, a perfect grandmother.[21]

Following a long illness which stemmed from a fever she had caught years before in Egypt, complicated by septicaemia from a botched facelift, Dame Nellie Melba, Australia's most famous woman of her era, died in Sydney at St Vincent's Hospital, Darlinghurst, on 23 February 1931. Her devoted and lifelong friend John Lemmone was present at her deathbed.

In accordance with her wishes, Melba was buried beside her father. Mountains of flowers and wreaths surrounded the coffin. Her will gave orders that the headstone on her grave should be engraved with Mimi's final poignant words from Puccini's *La Bohème*: '*Addio, senza rancore*' ('Farewell, without bitterness').

Melba left handsome bequests to the Conservatorium she had founded, to those who had served her and to elderly musicians in need. The bulk of her fortune and her jewels were left to her beloved granddaughter. Lady Pamela Vestey still lives at Coombe Cottage and has written a delightfully illustrated memoir of her famous grandmother.[22]

Melba's name lives on in the Melba Conservatorium of Music, while some of her personal effects are preserved in the Lilydale Museum. The name Melba will continue to be celebrated wherever opera is sung.

CHAPTER TWENTY-ONE

Stella Miles Franklin
(1879–1954)

and

Rose Scott
(1847–1925)

VISIONARIES WHO DEMANDED CHANGE
TO THE ROLE OF WOMEN

As part of Melbourne's Federation celebrations in May 2001, Stella Miles Franklin was honoured as one of Australia's high achievers.

Most Australians know Franklin as the benefactor of the Miles Franklin Award, an annual award for literature. Australian, British, American and Irish readers know Franklin's Australian classic *My Brilliant Career*. Several books written about Miles Franklin concentrate on her writing rather than her life, about which she was extremely secretive. In *Great Australian Women* I wrote about the remarkable Dr Agnes Bennett and a hospital in the Balkans she administered during World War I, which was completely staffed by women. During my research into Dr Bennett's life I discovered previously unknown information about Miles Franklin's period of war service in the Balkans. I also explored Franklin's complex relationship with the fascinating Rose Scott, as important a mentor and confidante to Miles as Madame Marchiesi was to Melba. Miles also took Melba as a role model, seeing the diva as the first Australian woman to achieve the 'brilliant career' for which she herself yearned.

Rose Scott and Miles Franklin (whose photograph appears on the front cover) have the longest chapter in this book because what they stood for and achieved has had a huge influence on women today. They dared to question women's roles in the era before domestic appliances freed women from grinding domestic toil. Miles grew up seeing her mother living a treadmill existence of domestic and farm drudgery interspersed with repeated cycles of pregnancy, birth, breast-feeding and weaning. Miles' own life spanned a period of huge change: she saw horses and buggies replaced by motorcars and aeroplanes; contraceptives, previously illegal, become freely available in family planning clinics; and later she watched (albeit with misgivings) the arrival of the contraceptive pill in Australia. Before Miles' death, syphilis, the 'Red Peril' so detested by her and Rose Scott, was finally vanquished by penicillin.

Franklin grew up in the Brindabella ranges south-west of Canberra. Today the Franklin and Lampe families no longer inhabit Talbingo or Brindabella homesteads, but a bronze plaque beside Jounama Creek in the Monaro records Miles Franklin as 'one of Australia's most widely acclaimed and spirited authors, who wrote 21 published books ... reflecting her unflinching belief in equality and social justice'.

Stella Miles Maria Sarah Franklin was descended from two markedly different cultures. From her Irish father she inherited good looks and a Celtic love of words and poetry. Through her mother, Susannah Lampe, she inherited the virtues of thrift and a capacity for hard work.

Miles Franklin's maternal grandparents were Holtman and Sarah Lampe. Holtman had emigrated to Australia as a free settler and become a pioneer of the High Monaro. Sarah was born in England, and her father had been transported to Australia. Granny Sarah Lampe was the woman Miles Franklin loved and admired most in her childhood, a strong-minded matriarch, mother of ten offspring and successful owner-manager of Talbingo Station.[1]

Holtman Lampe had bought the grazing rights to Talbingo Station from his father-in-law, convict-turned-farmer William Bridle. Due to Holtman and Sarah Lampe's hard work and efficiency, Talbingo Station became one of the best-run properties in the Monaro. Unfortunately, while relatively young, Holtman Lampe was paralysed in a riding accident and died a couple of years later, leaving his widow and daughter Susannah to run the station until Susannah fell in love with an impractical dreamer named John Franklin and married him.

Stella Miles' Irish grandfather, the darkly handsome Joseph Franklin, was a teacher's son who emigrated in 1839 from County Clare to escape rural Irish poverty. After spending a profitable period on the goldfields, he married and 'squatted' on land (the phrase 'squatting' refers to land farmed without a lease) in Yass and later in the Monaro. In 1863 he took up the lease on isolated Brindabella Station, in the Goodradigbee River Valley, where his cattle grew fat on summer pastures. His sons swaggered around the High Monaro on pure-bred horses, farmed rich land and married girls capable of bearing fine sons. They earned a good living breaking, training and selling the strong, sure-footed wild horses of the area, which they sold at a handsome profit to the British Army in India.[2]

Stella Miles' father, John Franklin, was in partnership with his three older brothers. They leased grazing rights to the adjacent cattle properties of Brindabella, Bin Bin, Bramina and Oakdale. (A fourth brother, George, ran another large lease on the Murrumbidgee River near Yass.) As the youngest son, Stella Miles' father was given the smallest property, Bin Bin, situated beside the important Brindabella Station. (Stella Miles adopted the pseudonym 'Brent of Bin Bin' as one of her numerous pen names; it seems amazing how few people discovered her secret, especially as she mentions she lived at Bin Bin in her autobiography, *Childhood at Brindabella*.)

John Franklin, blue-eyed, black-haired and descended from a long line of talkative, imaginative but impractical Irish Protestants, was seen as an unwise choice of husband for such a provident, punctilious and proper young woman as Susannah Lampe, whose mother Granny Lampe firmly believed none of the Franklin brothers was 'good enough' for her daughter, whose many accomplishments included playing that colonial status symbol, a rosewood piano.

Although the Brindabella Ranges are relatively close to Canberra, the only way to reach the Goodradigbee Valley and the three Franklin homesteads was on horseback. When Susannah was eight months pregnant with Miles, she made a heroic journey from isolated Bin Bin riding side-saddle through snow and ice. Susannah made this long journey so her own mother could act as midwife at Talbingo homestead, a sprawling weatherboard house surrounded by a magnificent garden and orchards and served by ample domestic staff. The child was named Stella Miles Maria Sarah Franklin. Susannah, a very practical woman proud of her housewifely skills and the Lampe family name, hoped her daughter would take after her; as time passed, she was dismayed to find Stella Miles very different in character to herself.

High in the beautiful valley of the Goodradigbee, Stella Miles spent a happy childhood. She was taught to read by her mother, from adult rather than children's books; Shakespeare's plays, Milton's *Paradise Lost* and sonorous passages from the King James version of the Bible, helped form her prose style.

Like her mother, Susannah's second daughter Linda Lampe Franklin was meek, religious and dutiful, while Stella Miles was strong-willed, energetic and rebellious. Susannah was totally perplexed by her eldest daughter. Susannah, a thrifty bush housewife who worked hard on her husband's farm, did not believe that women should perform paid work *outside* the home. When Stella Miles challenged her mother's views on the role of women Susannah punished her, declaring that women who wanted to have equal chances with men challenged God's laws.

Stella Miles may have been her mother's despair but she was her father's favourite. A brilliant but reckless horseman, John Franklin taught her to ride as fearlessly as he did, to swim in the creek and read aloud from the poetry of mad, bad Lord Byron. In *Childhood at Brindabella*, Miles Franklin noted how different her mother was to her father: 'My mother never indulged in fantasy. Her natural bent was not that way, and she never had a minute of her own free from responsibility from the time she could toddle'.[3]

Following the birth of a second daughter, Susannah's health deteriorated and the precocious, hyperactive Stella Miles, now four, was sent to be cared for by Granny Lampe at Old Talbingo. Granny Lampe also read the Bible, as well as the novels of Charles Dickens, to the four-year-old.

At Talbingo, surrounded by ten young aunts and uncles, Stella Miles became the adored youngest member of the household. She discovered that by being amusing and lively she would receive plenty of attention, and her time at Talbingo proved to be the happiest period of her entire life. She felt far more loving towards her grandmother than she did towards her mother. God-fearing, dignified Granny Lampe lived by strict rules. She was a just and enlightened employer of station hands and a good judge of livestock, but on her property swearing, drunkenness or loose conduct was never tolerated. Granny Lampe would figure in Miles Franklin's novels as the model for a series of wise, widowed matriarchs who ran their pastoral properties better than did most men.

However, at Talbingo there were occasional conflicts between the wilful Stella Miles and her grandmother. She was a stubborn, at times defiant child who enjoyed being the centre of attention. Dressed in a brand new white frock and standing in the yard in front of the homestead, little Stella Miles announced one Sunday that she was *not* going to church. Since she could not see or touch God, how could he exist? she demanded. Scandalised, Granny Lampe picked up a broom and smacked her with it. Miles fell flat in a mud puddle in her new white dress. As a punishment she was shut in a cupboard and denied dinner until she apologised. At first she sulked and refused to say she was sorry. Then, growing hungry, she apologised and was released. But for the rest of her life she remained convinced that God did not exist.

After almost a year Susannah Franklin recovered her health and Stella Miles returned home to her parents at Bin Bin. Mr Charles Blyth, a well-educated but alcoholic Scottish gentleman 'down on his luck', was engaged to teach Stella Miles and her four older cousins. When sober Charles Blyth was an excellent teacher, delighted by little Stella Miles' quick intelligence and her love of books. Dressed in white, topped by a frilly sun bonnet, she walked across the paddocks to the small schoolroom beside Brindabella homestead.

When the Commissioner for Crown Lands arrived at Brindabella to reassess the Franklin landholdings, he was amazed by the little girl's knowledge and breadth of vocabulary. 'You should be an author when you grow up,' he told her, and she always remembered his words.[4]

Stella Miles loved the beauty of the Monaro. She wrote about its mountain ranges 'thrown one upon another like storm waves petrified when the world had cooled', and cattle paddocks bright with flowers. She loved the rivers and their poetic names: the Murrumbidgee, the Goodradigbee and the Yarrangobilly, 'their waters silver in the summer sunlight and dark green where they entered deep granite gorges'. She was a perceptive, sensitive child, observing the platypus that lived in the creek, soaring eagles and the displays of lyrebirds.

Mr Blyth's fondness for alcohol eventually became so pronounced that the Franklin children had to find proper schooling. Expensive boarding schools were out of the question; the golden days of profitable trade in brumbies to the Indian Army were now over. Years of drought meant that although the Franklin brothers were land rich, they had no ready cash. Debts forced the dissolution of the family partnership; Uncle Thomas Franklin and his wife Annie bought out John Franklin's interest in Brindabella.

John and Susannah Franklin decided they should find a new home near a State school so their children could benefit from State-funded education. In April 1889, when Stella Miles was nine, they left Brindabella forever and moved to a small run-down dairy farm near Goulburn, which they named Stillwater after the muddy dam on the property. They were no longer wealthy graziers but had become poor 'cocky' farmers, scratching a living from harsh land like cockatoos.

Watching her mother and grandmother, she realised that, in order to survive, each station homestead had to be virtually self-supporting:

vegetables, milk, eggs, salted beef and mutton, preserves, fruit and tallow candles were all obtained or produced by these resourceful women.

Out at Stillwater, living without piped water, Stella Miles and her mother carted buckets from the well, boiled water to do the weekly wash and did the ironing using flatirons heated on the stove. They baked bread, salted meat to preserve it, made jam and cheese, churned butter, kept hens, scoured tinware and cutlery, cleaned windows, mended clothes and fed poddy calves and sick lambs. The Franklin girls attended the little wooden State school at Thornfield. Stella Miles' teacher, Miss Gillespie, encouraged her to study music and entered her successfully for examinations in singing and music in the Sydney College of Music.

They were unlucky in settling near Goulburn during a seven-year period of drought that lasted until 1902. During this time cows and calves, reduced to skin and bone, stood around the house mooing piteously. Stella Miles' father refused to spend money to buy feed for the animals, knowing they were worthless. Finally the wretched beasts were so weak that crows pecked out their eyes and they died in agony. For Stella Miles, who loved animals, their slow deaths were torture, especially those of the calves she had bottle-fed.

At Stillwater Susannah Franklin bore a son, whom she named Hume Talmadge. Lack of money and the rearing of children had changed the formerly 'genteel' piano-playing Miss Susannah Lampe of Talbingo Station into a domestic drudge. Susannah struggled to maintain standards, but her dowry of fine linen sheets and damask tablecloths was ruined when rain poured through Stillwater's sagging roof. Stella Miles couldn't help comparing her parents' poverty-stricken existence to life at the more luxurious Talbingo homestead. She stopped believing in love matches and began to view marriage as virtual 'sexual slavery', as she would write later. By this time Susannah had given birth to five more children. Most pioneer wives (in an era with no reliable contraception) bore six to ten children as a matter of course because so many children died at infancy. Stella Miles saw her mother struggling to cook, iron and clean in a bark-roofed home surrounded by cowsheds and pigpens. It made marrying for love, as Susannah's mother had done, distinctly unattractive.

Trying to farm on drought-afflicted land with seven children to raise and educate, the Franklin family's position became desperate. Their water supply turned out to be polluted, and Susannah's youngest daughter, Ida, died of typhoid fever. When her mother gave birth to another daughter, Laurel, Stella Miles upset her mother when she declared that the birth of yet another child during the drought was a disaster: another mouth to feed, another bottom to wipe. In a desperate attempt to avoid more children, Susannah denied her husband access to her bedroom. As a result husband and wife fought bitterly over sex and money. Stella Miles overheard fierce, whispered arguments. She decided that if this was marriage she did not want it. A career *must* offer a better life.

When Stella Miles was sixteen she spent one last idyllic Christmas with her beloved grandmother at Talbingo homestead. She was dismayed to realise she was no longer the amusing, youngest member of the family, but had been replaced by a crop of even younger grandchildren.

Like most teenage girls Stella Miles worried about her figure. In the looking glass she saw herself as snub-nosed, short and fat, whereas in fact she had an attractive figure that curved in all the right places. She compared herself unfavourably to her younger sister, blonde, willowy Linda, and despaired. Both girls had their photographs taken to send to their Lampe relatives in northern Germany. They wrote back commenting how very beautiful (*sehr hübsch*) Linda was, with her fair hair curling softly around her face in ringlets, and how elegant was her long flounced dress. They said not a word about Stella Miles, a champion rider who had been photographed wearing a black riding habit and a bushman's hat.[5]

The Lampes added approvingly that Linda looked aristocratic, and if she was not already promised in marriage then one of their sons, Heinrich Lampe, a cavalry officer in a crack German regiment, would be *very* interested in her. To Stella Miles' dismay, none of her male cousins seemed at all interested in her. She craved male attention, for although she did not like what marriage did to women she *did* like men and was hurt by what she regarded as male rejection. Her mother and grandmother had already warned Stella Miles that cleverness was 'a curse', that men felt threatened by a woman with brains. Females were prized for beauty and femininity, for domestic skills and for bearing their husbands male heirs. Miles decided that marriage and domesticity was not the answer to happiness — she wanted a career *and* male attention.

As though to reassure herself she could attract the opposite sex, Stella Miles made a point of flirting with boys she met, earning reproofs from her mother about coquetry and 'being forward with the opposite sex'.

'Do you mean to marry *any* of the young men to whom you are writing flirtatious letters?' Granny Lampe demanded, deeply shocked by what she saw as Stella Miles' scandalously coquettish behaviour. But Stella Miles told her grandmother she had no serious intentions and wanted to remain single. To proclaim the truth, that she *feared* marriage, pregnancy and childbirth, would have given rise to ridicule in the farming culture in which she was raised. To avoid this, the ultra-sensitive girl became expert at dissembling her fears.

Miles would flirt with attractive men and then reject them. In fact Miles' flirtatious behaviour was motivated by fear that she would become 'the girl left out in the cold'. For decades she would be torn between needing male admiration to raise her self-esteem and a complete revulsion against the sex act and its consequences. Today she would have consulted a psychiatrist; at that time she could not tell anyone her fears.

At dances, parties and country race meetings young girls were always chaperoned; the 'flirtations' of which Stella Miles' grandmother accused her were doubtless very mild by today's standards. It was a conservative Bible-dominated era, especially in the bush. Girls had to be virgins when they married: unmarried girls who gained the reputation for being 'forward' or 'loose' with members of the opposite sex would jeopardise their marriage prospects. To become an unmarried mother ensured ostracism. 'Nice girls' went to the altar as teenage virgins, having experienced no more than a chaste kiss on the lips. These were some of the factors that shaped Franklin's puritanical attitude to sex and marriage.[6] Her prudishness appears almost contradictory for a woman who pursued freedom from stifling convention.

Stella Miles Franklin did not complete secondary school and had no qualifications apart from an Honours Certificate in Music. She wanted a career, but teaching, governessing and nursing were the only occupations permitted to young ladies at the time of Federation. Having done well in her music exams, she was inspired by Melba's brilliant career. She was told she had a beautiful singing voice; all it needed was professional training and she could be another Melba. A wealthy local grazier offered to put up the money for her to travel to Europe to train her voice.

However, like Nellie Melba's father David Mitchell, who believed that performing on stage was only for whores and courtesans, Granny Lampe would not hear of her granddaughter singing for money. 'Ladies do *not* sing in public,' she decreed.[7] Instead, she told Stella Miles she had a talent for writing, and this should be enough for her. Years later Miles wrote a novel called *Cockatoos*, in which the central character, Mollye Brennan (based on Melba), becomes a singer in London and returns to Australia as the rich and famous Madame Austra.

Stella Miles was recommended twice for a lowly paid pupil–teacher position which included free tuition from the headmaster, but each time her application was unsuccessful. Was she too outspoken and 'modern'? No reasons were given. She worked briefly as a governess to the unruly brood of her Aunt Margaret and Uncle George Franklin, hated it and returned to back-breaking farm and housework at Stillwater. She observed the wives and daughters of neighbouring farmers working from dawn to dusk, cooking, cleaning, rearing children, milking cows, churning butter and making cheese: all 'women's work'. She saw children dying of typhoid after they drank from polluted wells and streams, including three of her siblings.

Her mother found her eldest daughter a difficult, moody teenager. In an era when girls married very young, to be in one's twenties and unmarried meant being disparaged as a spinster. Susannah Franklin urged both her daughters to marry 'well'. The beautiful Linda was longing to get married, but Stella Miles distrusted romance and marriage as a means of acquiring happiness or financial security.

My brilliant career or my brilliant marriage

A career as a writer seemed the answer for Stella Miles. At sixteen she started writing her first novel, *My Brilliant (?) Career*, in an exercise book. Apprehensive of ridicule, as the question mark in the original title demonstrates, she did *not* tell her family about it. Once it was completed she sent it away to Angus and Robertson, the only Australian publisher of any note at that period. Unfortunately for Miles the managing director,

George Robertson, who had a wonderful nose for a saleable manuscript, was away at the time and the manuscript was sent out to a reader. Miles Franklin's prose would always be verbose; Angus and Robertson returned the manuscript with encouraging comments and some suggested changes but without an offer of publication. Their reader had advised that a great deal of editing would be required to make the novel publishable. Bearing in mind the fact that *My Brilliant Career* without the question mark in its title has gone into at least twenty editions worldwide, Angus and Robertson made a serious error of judgment in not helping Miles carry out the required editorial work.

After this rejection, Stella Miles was brave or desperate enough to write for advice to Henry Lawson in Sydney. She was careful to sign her letter 'Miles Franklin', hoping Lawson would assume she was a man and thus (at a time when women's writing was deemed to be sloppy and romantic) take her first novel seriously. She told him she lacked the necessary money to come to Sydney and politely asked for his help.

Her stratagem worked. Henry Lawson wrote back to 'Mr' Franklin, saying how much he had enjoyed 'his' work and even referring to it as 'the first great Australian novel', and asked for details of 'Mr' Franklin's career. Later, Lawson admitted that he had a suspicion the author might be female.

Eventually Henry Lawson and Miles Franklin met in Sydney. Lawson, beset by lack of money, deafness and a rapidly deteriorating marriage, took Miss Stella Miles Franklin home to meet his wife. Bertha Lawson had been very jealous of the interest Henry Lawson displayed before their marriage in the young Mary Gilmore.[8] This time, however, Bertha had nothing against her husband's friendship for Miles, realising that his interest was not romantic but simply that of one writer for another. Bertha took pity on the young, inexperienced girl, and tried unsuccessfully to find Miles a local publisher.

In the meantime Miles needed a paid job. Before her marriage Bertha Lawson had been a nurse, and she urged Miles to apply to the Sydney Hospital as a trainee. This would mean she could live away from home, as nursing would provide her with an occupation and some money while she waited to see if anyone would publish her first novel.

Miles was accepted by the hospital, given free board and lodging and paid a small wage as a trainee probationer nurse. Only a few weeks into her nursing course, she received terrible news. Her brother Mervyn had died of typhoid fever and her mother was prostrate with shock. Miles immediately relinquished her place on the course and returned to drought-ridden Stillwater. Linda was away at Talbingo with her grandmother, so Miles took over the housework and cared for her boisterous young brothers and baby Laurel, of whom she became extremely fond.

Meanwhile Henry Lawson, who was planning to move to London, asked Miles to post him her handwritten script of *My Brilliant (?) Career* once he was settled there, after she had made all the alterations recommended by Angus and Robertson's reader. He also made a few more changes, including omitting the controversial question mark from the title, and wrote a glowing preface to the work, describing it as 'Australia's first real novel'. In London Henry Lawson found Miles Franklin a literary agent named J.B. Pinker, who finally sold her first novel to a leading publisher, Messrs Blackwood & Son of Edinburgh. They offered Miles a minute advance and a meagre two and a half per cent royalty instead of the normal ten per cent, using the excuse that Australia would be the prime market for this first novel by an unknown writer and it was expensive to ship copies such a distance.

Convinced her book would fail if the critics, all of whom were male, knew it was written by a *girl*, Miles refused to sign the publishing contract as 'Miss Stella Miles Franklin'. She insisted Blackwood should use her chosen pen name, 'Miles Franklin', which derived from her maternal forebear Edward Miles. What her parents omitted to tell her was that Edward Miles had arrived in Australia as a convicted thief, transported for seven years for stealing two overcoats. In an era when convict forebears were considered shameful, Miles might conceivably have selected a different name if she had known this.

The book was finally published in 1901. The influential literary critic of Edinburgh's *Blackwood's Magazine* loved Franklin's novel. He was perceptive enough to realise that its clever portrayal of the feelings of a sensitive teenage girl on the brink of womanhood must have been written by a female author. He compared Miles Franklin to Emily Brontë, who initially wrote her novel *Wuthering Heights* under the masculine name 'Ellis Bell'. Meanwhile, copies of *My Brilliant Career* were shipped to Australia.

When Miles examined the published book she realised that the editor, nervous about bringing out such a 'precocious' novel (ie, one which was sexually challenging and anti-religious), had toned down some of her more caustic comments on marriage, which she had described as 'sexual and domestic slavery'. The comments the editor had *not* removed would still cause a furore when the book appeared in Australian bookshops.

Miles believed that if her first novel proved a success she could become a professional writer. However, she knew that she would have to wait a long time to receive her first royalty statement.

My Brilliant Career was a remarkable book for *anyone* to have written, let alone a teenage girl who had left school before she turned fifteen. Even more remarkable is the fact that Stella Miles wrote much of it by candlelight after a hard day doing household chores and farm work.

Miles had no idea that *My Brilliant Career* would cause a furore in the Franklin family and among their neighbours who, unable to differentiate between fiction and autobiography, believed she had caricatured them in her novel. Her family was mortified by her notoriety and especially by the fact that the novel dealt with the dangers of sex and syphilis, topics considered far too indelicate for ladies. Angry criticism from family members and friends hurt Miles deeply. Alone in her bedroom she wept. Even worse than the rage of her relatives were her mother's angry comments that she had been a 'vexatious' daughter from childhood onwards, that she had disgraced her family and did not deserve to be part of it. The Franklins' lowered social status and lack of money only served to make Susannah Franklin more sensitive. Her father, on the other hand, found *My Brilliant Career* amusing and was not upset by it, even though the heroine's fictitious father was portrayed as an alcoholic.

Angriest of all were Aunt Margaret and Uncle George Franklin, for whom Miles had worked as a governess. They were convinced that in the part of the book where Sybylla Melvyn works for relatives as a governess, Miles had caricatured them as a pair of nouveau riche, bog Irish bumpkins.[9] They believed their neighbours were laughing at them and threatened to sue Miles for damages. Aunt Margaret Franklin, who was not exactly thin, identified with Mrs McSwat in Miles' novel and was furious. The fictitious Mrs McSwat weighs sixteen stone, over-eating to compensate for the stress of a grizzling infant and several toddlers. She sweats away cooking a stew in a greasy iron pot. Her grubby children and slobbish husband eat together at a wooden table while pigs and fowls wander around them.

To make things worse, Miles' opinions about women, that they should receive more education and delay marriage in favour of a career instead of regarding babies as their main purpose in life, were viewed as dangerous and subversive by the Anglican and Roman Catholic churches. Describing her battles with clerics, Miles wrote: 'I put forward my pity for overburdened women dying before their time. I advanced cases where even the doctors said the woman would die if they had *any more* babies'.[10]

Australia's clergy strenuously opposed her point of view. One cleric thundered from the pulpit: 'With common [working-class] people ... if their noses are not kept to the grindstone, rearing families, they would get up to the devil's mischief. We must populate Australia or perish and hold it safe from the Yellow Peril at our doors.'[11]

Both Protestant and Catholic clergy told married women that as part of their marriage contract they had a *duty* to 'submit themselves unto their husbands in all things'. This was interpreted as providing sex *whenever* (and however) husbands demanded their 'conjugal rights'. In the eyes of the law women were mere chattels, the property of their husbands, who were also the sole owners of their children and were automatically granted custody in the rare cases of divorce. Such clerical statements as those quoted above angered Miles Franklin: she would make it her lifework to refute them.

The furore over her first novel scarred Miles. For the rest of her life she would protect herself behind a series of pen names and subterfuges and become intensely secretive. Miles was still extremely thin-skinned about her novel. 'It's only a girl's story,' she claimed defensively, 'tossed off in a matter of weeks.'

By now it seemed as if the entire reading population of the Monaro and Goulburn were gossiping about Miss Franklin and her shocking book. From being considered a 'nice girl', she became a social outcast. For a time she even wished she had never written *My Brilliant Career*. She claimed she had withdrawn her first novel from sale, but in fact it went into three further editions in Britain and Australia in the next two years. Convinced that she could write a better book and by this means kill off the scandal, Miles finally issued instructions to her publisher that *My Brilliant Career* was not to be reprinted until after her death.[12]

In March 1902 Miles Franklin received a letter from 'Banjo' Paterson, the famous poet and author of *The Man from Snowy River*. He invited her to lunch at a suitable place to take a nice young unmarried girl: the ABC teashop in Pitt Street, Sydney. Miles accepted with some misgivings, for her mother told her that he had a reputation as a womaniser.

She brought to their meeting some short stories, hoping to obtain his opinion of them. Banjo (whose real name was Andrew Barton Paterson) turned out to be a tall, muscular, dark-haired man.[13] He had just turned forty and had decided to cut down his work as a partner in a legal practice and take up the challenge of becoming a full-time writer. However, his most recent verse collection, *Rio Grande's Last Race and Other Verses*, had not been nearly as successful as *The Man from Snowy River*. He was desperately looking for new ideas and younger readers. The poet-cum-lawyer saw a lively bright-eyed girl with a curvaceous figure, wearing a trim black costume with a white collar, ankle-length skirt, a bushman's hat, worn at a jaunty angle, and carrying an umbrella. He was charmed by Miles, and they talked at length about books and writing, about horses (which they both loved) and about the Monaro, an area Paterson knew well.

Susannah Franklin had warned her daughter that, as an unmarried girl, she must be careful not to compromise her reputation. If Banjo invited her home she must make it clear to him that she was a house-guest of Rose Scott, the well-known Sydney socialite and feminist. It was only on the condition that she stayed with Rose that Miles was allowed to go to Sydney.

Rose Scott's feminism dated from her first reading of *The Taming of the Shrew*, and her conviction that in this play Shakespeare was unfair to women. Along with Sydney socialites Lady Mary Windeyer and Mrs Montefiore and backed by the educationalist Maybanke Wolstenholme, Rose Scott had formed the revolutionary Womanhood Suffrage League of New South Wales to demand votes for women.[14] After she read *My Brilliant Career* she wrote to Miles inviting her to stay at her house in Sydney. 'Your book is so lifelike, I cannot disassociate you from your heroine,' she told Miles. 'Let me, my dear fellow Australian, my dear fellow woman, serve you in any way I can.'[15]

Rose Scott, who was thirty years older than Miles, owned Lynton Villa at 294 Jersey Road, Woollahra. Like Miles, her father was a grazier who had lost much of his money. On 19 August 1902 Miles wrote to Rose asking if she could stay with her on the night of 21 August and meet Banjo Paterson. 'Mother is in a state for fear I will come to some harm,' she said. Rose Scott replied with a telegram that read: 'Welcome, welcome.' So Miles was allowed to go to Sydney and became a welcome guest at Rose's comfortable home, where she met some of Rose's feminist and literary circle of friends. Doubtless Rose also warned her young guest about the handsome poet's reputation as a womaniser.

After meeting him, Miles felt that Banjo's attitude to her was patronising. She was wary of his intentions and did not want to commit herself to any form of literary partnership, as she was now working on the sequel to *My Brilliant Career.* They parted amicably and she was still feminine enough to be flattered by Banjo's interest in her *and* her writing.

Two months later Banjo wrote to Miles again, asking her to help him 'liven up' a 'racing and sporting yarn' which he feared was 'rather flat'. It transpired that George Robertson of Angus and Robertson had told Banjo that clever Miss Franklin might work on the first draft of his novel and 'liven it up with a little more plot'.

Possibly prompted by Rose Scott, her new mentor, Miles wrote back asking which of their names would appear on the book's jacket if she did rewrite some of Banjo's material. Banjo replied flippantly, suggesting they could toss a coin for the honour. It was tempting to collaborate with such a well-known poet and author, but Miles feared she might become nothing but a ghost writer. Perhaps Rose warned her that she could end up doing most of the work while Banjo Paterson received all the credit.

Banjo now proposed that Miss Franklin should accompany him to Fiji on a six-week lecture tour, something no well brought up single girl could do unchaperoned and hope to keep her reputation. Girls with damaged reputations remained old maids, her mother reminded her; she would be regarded as 'second-hand goods' and become a target for gossip and scandal if she accompanied Banjo to Fiji without a chaperone. Miles turned down Banjo's offer.

At the end of August Banjo sent Miles another letter, praising her writing skills, her mind *and* her looks and enclosing five pounds so that she could come to Sydney and work with him on a play. By now Miles' younger sister, Linda, was married and not available to act as chaperone. To accept this invitation *without* a chaperone would make Miles look 'cheap', her mother maintained (by which she meant sexually available). Having upset her family by writing her book, Miles had no wish to upset them even more. Again, she did not take up Banjo's offer.

Banjo Paterson went to Fiji alone. Before he left, he made the mistake of sending Miles the manuscript Angus and Robertson wanted her to work on *before* she had agreed to do so, and before the question of whose name would appear on the cover had been settled. His high-handed conduct annoyed Miles considerably.

Linda, who was now Mrs Graham, believed Banjo Paterson was attracted to Miles and that he might return from Fiji and propose marriage. She wrote teasingly to Miles: 'When are you going to be Mrs Banjo? My word! The next generation ought to be something. Mum an Authoress and Dad a Poet.'

Banjo Paterson's feelings remain a mystery. Like most men he found Miles attractive, but he needed money in order to abandon his legal practice and become a full-time writer. Miss Franklin's family were no longer prosperous members of the squattocracy but were selectors, 'cow cockies'. A rich wife would be an asset to a writer, and Banjo *was* courting a squatter's daughter at the time. Was he pursuing Miles as a lover-cum-collaborator? Or was he really very attracted by her and might have proposed marriage even though she had no dowry or prospects of inheritance? Did she refuse his invitation to come to Sydney to work with him believing that rejection would make him all the keener? We shall never know the answers to these questions, as there were no more letters between them.

Within a few months Banjo announced his engagement to Alice Walker, the daughter of a wealthy grazier who owned the prosperous Tenterfield Station with its broad acres. By Easter the following year Banjo and Alice were married and about to move into a large house in elegant Woollahra, aided by a handsome dowry from Alice's father. It seemed that Rose Scott was right. The bohemian Banjo probably had planned to take advantage of her, in one way or another. Miles became even more conscious of her family's declining social status and wary of men.

Another bohemian fascinated by Miss Franklin was Norman Lindsay, who was a year older than Miles. Surrounded by sexually available artist's models, he too had acquired a reputation as a ladies' man. After fathering a son (Jack) by a model named Katie Parkinson, he had been forced to marry her but the shotgun marriage was breaking down.

Norman Lindsay, slight, keen-eyed and a great admirer of the female form, was climbing the stairs to see J.F. Archibald, editor of *The Bulletin*, when he encountered Miles Franklin on her way down after visiting Archibald to discuss the sequel to her first novel. She was wearing a dress her mother had made for her which set off her curvaceous figure to perfection. With her generous bust, wasp waist, thick plait of chestnut-brown hair and snub nose, she looked younger than her seventeen years. Norman Lindsay was just as attracted to her as Banjo Paterson had been, and said as much to Archibald. The *Bulletin*'s elderly editor reminded the artist/writer that he was a married man and should keep his hands off the presumably virginal Miss Franklin.

Years later Norman Lindsay described his first meeting with Miles Franklin in a collection of essays, *Bohemians of the Bulletin*. The man who would become famous as Australia's most prolific painter of nude women and a connoisseur of female beauty described the young Miles as 'very short but pleasingly plump, [in] a flowered hat and summery ankle-length frock. Her mass of dark hair reached her pert rump, which matched her pert nose. She had fine eyes, arched eyebrows and an alluring pair of lips'.

Rose Scott and her influence on Franklin

Soon after her brief encounter with Lindsay, Miles Franklin completed her new novel, *My Career Goes Bung*. In a desperate effort to silence the criticism of her family and friends, in her second novel she portrayed a fictitious family living at drought-stricken Possum Gully. However, it is a very different family to her own; the heroine, Sybylla Melvyn, is an only child rather than one of seven. The novel opens where Sybylla, who has just published a scandalous book, insists that she does not wish to enter the state of marriage, which she sees as one of 'unrestricted childbearing'. She then receives an invitation to stay with Mrs Crasterton of Geebung Villa, Pumpkin (Darling) Point, and is delighted to escape from Possum Gully. Like Rose Scott, Mrs Crasterton is 'a big woman covered in shawls'.

Rose Scott, large-boned and famous for her feather boas and large hats, could have been taken for Mrs Crasterton, but in fact Rose was a far more complex character. She and Miles Franklin met at a crucial moment in each other's lives. Rose was very lonely. Her favourite niece, Rosie, the daughter of her deceased brother, Helenus, had lived at Lynton Villa with Rose for years; tragically, Rosie had died at the age of twenty a few months earlier. And Rose's other protégé, her adopted nephew, Nene, had just left to work in Adelaide. In addition, the elderly aunt who had also lived at Lynton Villa had died. It was at this juncture that Rose became Miles' surrogate mother, finding in her new young protégé a solace for her grief. In letters to Miles she revealed the full extent of that loneliness.[16]

Miles wrote back friendly, sympathetic letters. Miles could be barbed, even malicious about people she disliked, but from the moment they met she loved and admired Rose. Later she wrote:

> Miss Scott ... presided over the only salon in Sydney, in the French sense, in Australia. Beautiful, charming and able, she was of independent but modest means ... a leader in the movement for women's enfranchisement, for the amelioration of the lot of women shop assistants and women prisoners, there was scarcely a humanitarian movement from which the name of 'Rose Scott' was absent ... Lawmakers drafted bills on her dining room table. She had discernment and taste in fostering Australian writing and wrote verse herself.[17]

Rose Scott was indeed a well-preserved, handsome woman, a feminist and the leading light in a committee of Sydney's eastern suburbs ladies who gathered for tea and gossip and raised money to help poor women. Rose was a central figure in the history of feminism in Australia: she and her feminist colleagues played a vital role in obtaining the vote for Australian women as part of the negotiations for Federation, long before their British or American counterparts.

Rose Scott imparted many of her views to Miles. When they met Rose was working on sympathetic politicians to raise the age of sexual consent from fourteen to sixteen, so that men who had sex with younger girls could be prosecuted. To Miles she related hair-raising stories of poverty-stricken, illiterate kitchen maids and parlour maids made pregnant by male employers, whose wives then turned the poor girls out into the streets without a reference. After they had given birth, in despair they often turned to prostitution, which Rose viewed as the ultimate symbol of women's degradation.

Scott, having witnessed the horrendous conditions for women at Long Bay Gaol living among dangerous male prisoners, was also campaigning for a separate gaol for women. She supported shorter working hours for women in factories and shops and was keen to get the New South Wales Parliament to pass a bill whereby widows and children would be entitled to a share in the dead husband's estate.

Rose Scott supported Miles' aim to become a famous author and became far closer to Miles than her mother, who disapproved of her daughter's writing. Rose held literary evenings at Lynton Villa, presiding over these occasions in her famous feather boas, frilly dresses and rope of huge baroque pearls. She had expressive eyes, a finely chiselled profile and the bearing of a *grande dame*; in the distant past Rose Scott had been the most beautiful and intelligent debutante of her year. Another firm bond between the two women was that Rose's father had owned vast tracts of New South Wales but suffered a series of financial failures which had left him in reduced circumstances.

As their friendship deepened Miles wrote letters to 'Dearest Rose'. Rose introduced Miles to a network of influential feminists like Maybanke Anderson and Vida Goldstein and her sisters, who would eventually persuade Miles to go to America (which made Rose very unhappy). Rose was also a good friend of Nellie Melba and was able to reveal details of Melba's love life to Miles that she could not have obtained elsewhere. Scott also passed on to Miles her admiration for the work of the pioneer South Australian novelist-suffragette Catherine Helen Spence.

Rose taught Miles to deplore the prevailing double standard whereby young men with money were allowed to 'sow their wild oats', have affairs with married women, consort with prostitutes or seduce young servant girls. Rose's horror of syphilis was so strong that she was reluctant to help single mothers who had resorted to prostitution.

Eventually she campaigned for the removal of *all* prostitutes from inner Sydney and for harsher laws against them. Her hatred of syphilis and 'male lust' strongly influenced the much younger and impressionable Miles.

At that time the fear of syphilis was as real as the fear of HIV/AIDS is today. The arts were riddled with great names who died of syphilis, from Gauguin, Monet and Conder to Schubert, Schumann, Delius, Donizetti, Smetana and Hugo Wolf. Syphis gave them all terrible deaths. The only man Rose ever loved, David Scott Mitchell, had as a teenager been infected with syphilis by a prostitute. Like Henry Handel Richardson's father and so many men of this era, Scott Mitchell died paralysed, his mind gone. This tragedy was carefully hidden from the world by the Scott family; no one asked questions, and in later years his priceless donation of books, letters, portraits, maps, coins and medals, the collection of a lifetime, to the State Library effectively silenced any discussion about his mysterious illness. Scott Mitchell himself feared his bequest to a public institution might have the opposite effect and start a swarm of questions that would harm Rose and his family. He offered to bequeath to Rose his huge collection of Australiana, but she refused his generous but cumbersome gift. It was she who urged Scott Mitchell to endow what is now the Mitchell Library, at the State Library of New South Wales. The foundation stone was laid in 1906, but in spite of being asked to preside at the occasion Scott Mitchell was far too ill to appear at the ceremony.[18] He died the following year of 'grand paralysis of the insane', the last stage of syphilis.

Rose rejected several other suitors because she was in love with the wealthy David, who was one of the first students to enrol as a law student at Sydney University. In his youth he played cricket and danced well.[19] Sydney society mothers schemed to persuade him to attend their dinner parties and balls. At one stage he became engaged to a 'suitable' girl from the squattocracy, Emily Manning, but eventually he realised that he was much fonder of his cousin Rose and broke off his engagement. He was about to ask Rose's parents for her hand in marriage when he learned from his doctors that the loss of feeling in his lower limbs he was experiencing could be a symptom of tertiary syphilis. Like many young men of the era, Scott Mitchell had frequented prostitutes. The first manifestation of syphilis is a chancre or ulcer which appears a few weeks after contact and then disappears. The symptoms then lie dormant for years.

Aware of the likelihood that he would impart the disease to a wife and unborn children, who risked being born deaf and blind, Scott Mitchell (who was certainly not gay) told the adoring Rose he 'could *never* marry'.[20] The only treatment before the advent of penicillin for the then fatal disease were injections of mercury, which sometimes slowed down its progress but never cured it. He sold up his family home in Cumberland Street and, with an elderly maid to act as his cook-housekeeper, moved to a smaller house in Darlinghurst. He forbade all visitors except for Rose and his doctor. Even the Sydney bookseller who sold him the books he avidly collected was not allowed into the house. Gradually he became partially, then totally, paralysed, and eventually dementia developed.

It was Rose's realisation that her adored cousin was doomed to die a horrible death from this sexually transmitted disease that turned her into a crusader against syphilis. She passed on her revulsion towards prostitutes and the fearsome outcome of sexual intercourse to the adolescent Miles, who was already railing against a male-dominated world. Today, when penicillin can cure syphilis, much of the writings of Rose Scott and Miles Franklin concerning sexually transmitted disease and marriage as a trap for women seem bizarre. However, the shocking story of Rose and her cousin David Scott Mitchell renders their attitudes more understandable. Miles was horrified when Rose took her to visit the reclusive Scott Mitchell. In fact, she was one of very few people to see Scott Mitchell in his paralysed state.

Rose taught Miles that conjugal misery was rife in an era when divorce meant social and financial suicide for women, as well as the loss of their children. Her words echoed Miles' own feelings about her mother's marriage. Rose Scott, influenced by several disastrous marriages of women friends, described the marital bedroom as 'a chamber of horrors', because in the Federation era married women had few rights. They could not open a bank account and handle their own finances, divorce laws were weighted against them, and all contraceptive devices were illegal.

Miles could not have failed to have seen girls as young as thirteen working as prostitutes. It made her just as eager as Rose Scott to have the age of sexual consent raised from fourteen to sixteen at a time when, without any social security for unmarried mothers, illegitimate babies were dumped on doorsteps, abandoned in public parks or murdered by 'baby' farmers with whom single mothers boarded their children. Rose told her that one man in Newcastle had boasted over the dinner table of having seduced over a hundred young domestic servants.[21] She described men who 'would not be ashamed to have diseased harlots at street corners awaiting their patronage and then come [home] to clean [that is, uninfected] girls and blither to *them* about love'.[22]

Clearly neither Rose nor Miles believed in entrusting their lives and chances of happiness to a fellow human being on grounds as irrational as love. A career seemed preferable.

In 1902, after several weeks of loving hospitality at Rose's home, Miles felt she could not continue to accept her mentor's generosity. She could see no way of repaying Rose for her kindness nor did she wish to be seen as taking advantage of Rose, who could afford a reasonably comfortable life but was certainly not wealthy.

In September, desperately short of money, Miles went home to Stillwater. After one of the longest recorded droughts in New South Wales, most of their cattle were dead. In between helping her mother with the younger children and the housework, Miles continued to work on the sequel to *My Brilliant Career*.

The family's debts were soaring. The Franklins realised that their struggling dairy farm would never make money. In March 1903 they moved to a house with a small vineyard at Chesterfield, Penrith, where John Franklin and a friend, Dan Clyne, set up in partnership as Auctioneers and Estate Agents. Unfortunately Miles' father was a dreamer, and was unsuccessful as an auctioneer and wine-grower.

Miles was desperate for financial independence but had no skills whereby she could earn enough income to live on. Then the thought occurred to her: why shouldn't she get paid for the work she was doing already? She could live and work in Sydney as a housemaid and even write a book about her experiences, provided that she wrote under a completely assumed name.

Under the assumed name of 'Sarah Frankling', Miles applied for a housemaid's job on Sydney's North Shore. In spite of her lack of references she was hired. Her new mistress informed her that her duties included washing, cooking the meals, sweeping and polishing the silver. Never afraid of hard physical work, Miles donned her maid's uniform and set to with a will, making notes for her proposed book.

Rose Scott knew Miles was in Sydney but Miles was too embarrassed to tell Rose what she was doing, ashamed that a Franklin of Brindabella and Bin Bin should be found in domestic service. Rose, however, continued to make inquiries about her 'darling girl', having conducted a campaign to get underpaid female shop assistants better pay and conditions.

Eventually Rose discovered where Miles was working and visited her there. She found Miles worn out by cooking and cleaning from dawn to dusk, with only a half-day off each week. Rose, who was well aware how domestic staff were often overworked and underpaid, was worried. She knew Miles suffered on occasions from crippling pain in her lower back, so she found her protégé a far less demanding job in a smaller house. She believed Miles was a talented writer and did not intend to see her worn to a frazzle as a maid.

One night, as Miles served dinner wearing a cap and frilled apron, she was amused to hear a spirited discussion among the guests about Miles Franklin's controversial book and the identity of its central characters, whom some of the guests claimed to know. Miles said nothing but continued to serve the meal, chuckling inwardly as the guests put forward their mistaken theories.[23]

Just as Miles was plotting her novel about life as a servant, she received the devastating news that her younger sister Laurel, of the long fair hair and deep brown eyes, 'the pride of the family', had died from typhoid.

Miles hurried back to Penrith for Laurel's funeral. Those three deaths in her family would leave her permanently insecure about her own health.

When she told Granny Lampe she was writing a book about 'life below stairs' her grandmother, well aware where the money lay, said wryly: 'If you've written one book for the servants, then write another for their employers.'

Early in 1904 Miles decided to move to Melbourne, where the crusading feminist Vida Goldstein was working on improving conditions for women with her sisters Aileen Goldstein and Elsie Belle

Champion. Under the influence of tall, charismatic Vida Goldstein, Miles became concerned with wider issues that affected poverty-stricken women working in sweatshops. Vida had recently returned from America, having been invited to Washington for the founding of the International Women's Suffrage Society and to become its conference secretary. She had helped found the Women's Federal Political Association, and in 1903 stood as its first parliamentary candidate. She and her sisters had strong links to leading American feminists and social reformers, and they supported American suffragettes in their fight to obtain the vote.

The Goldstein sisters lent Miles books about reform of women's working conditions and vainly attempted to convert her to Christian Science. Vida and her sisters (whose father was a very liberal and educated Jew) had recently converted to this fashionable creed. But Miles was far too sceptical of *all* organised religion to take their attempts to convert her seriously, although she played along with the idea, preferring not to upset the Goldstein sisters whom she liked very much and who were supportive of her literary efforts.

On 15 April 1904, in her own newspaper, the *Australian Women's Sphere*, Vida Goldstein published an article on Miles Franklin working as a 'Mary Anne'. Vida firmly believed that, having achieved the vote, Australian women's lives would be transformed, and she passed on this belief to Miles. Both Vida and Miles seem to have spent years hoping women would change the world if they entered parliament, and wondering why so few women tried to get themselves elected. In fact Vida was wrong. Although women had achieved voting rights, they did not embrace political life with much enthusiasm. Vida failed on several occasions to get elected to parliament, although she was an inspiring speaker on public platforms. Women found politics too confrontational or too boring — and life in parliament, with its long hours and male MPs swearing at and abusing each other, was more than they were prepared to put up with.

In Melbourne Miles had an important meeting with the sixty-year-old Australian novelist Joseph Furphy, author of the bush novel *Such is Life* (Ned Kelly's famous last words). Furphy is almost forgotten today but Miles and a teacher named Kate Baker greatly admired his novels. Their meeting, organised through Kate, took place on Good Friday in the National Gallery of Victoria in front of a painting by John Longstaff. Furphy appraised Miles Franklin shrewdly; looking below the surface, he realised that deep down Miles was a troubled young woman, lonely and unsure of herself, desperately wanting his approval but frightened of a close relationship with men of her own age.

As for Miles, her meeting with Furphy affected her deeply. From that day she viewed the elderly and unhappily married Furphy as her ideal of a manly figure. She felt that, unlike other men, Furphy valued her for her mind rather than her body and would make no sexual demands upon her. She never met him again. But Furphy wrote to her, raising her self-esteem by praising her style and telling her that she was a 'brilliant' writer. His admiration was important to her at a time when she could easily have given up the pursuit of a literary career.

At this point Miles received her eagerly awaited royalty statement from Blackwells, dated April 1904, detailing the sales of *My Brilliant Career*. It was accompanied by a cheque for the derisory sum of two pounds, nineteen shillings and sixpence. She could have wept. Should she give up writing?

Vida Goldstein was also experiencing financial problems so was sympathetic. She urged Miles to travel to America. Vida and her sisters pointed out to Miles that as America had a far bigger population than Australia and was more open to new ideas, she would surely stand a better chance of finding an American publisher and earning a reasonable amount. Joseph Furphy bolstered her waning confidence by writing to assure her that her work 'bore the stamp of genius'. She must not give up.

Miles persevered. Desperate to make money, she finished a more 'romantic' novel, *Some Everyday Folk — and Dawn*. Dedicated to 'men who believe in Votes for Women', it was set in a fictitious town called Noonan, based on Penrith, where Miles' parents now lived. Instead of the feisty, lovable teenager Sybylla Melvyn in *My Brilliant Career*, who slashes a man she likes across the face with a riding crop after he has proposed and because he tries to kiss her, Miles chose as her heroine an impossibly pretty but somewhat charmless suffragette 'who yearns for better things'. The winsome whingeing Dawn lacks the fire and dash that makes Sybylla Melvyn so appealing. Dawn throws a bowl of soapy water over a young man who proposes to her to revenge herself on 'all the men who have wronged women'. One can only presume that Miles meant by this men who had jilted women or given them syphilis. Not surprisingly, *The Bulletin* rejected *Some Everyday Folk — and Dawn.* Miles was distraught. Was her career over?

In the spring of 1905, while on holiday with relatives, Miles met Edwin Bridle, a clean-shaven, good-looking young farmer who was a distant cousin of her mother. He was five years older than Miles, shared her interest in family history and was considerate, stable and gentle. They went riding together, were caught in a thunderstorm and took refuge in an old humpy where they talked for hours about their families, life and love. They continued to meet whenever they could arrange it.

Edwin sincerely believed Miles was in love with him. She wrote him witty and flirtatious letters, unwilling to reject him as a husband out of hand because she feared that everyone would see her as an old maid left 'on the shelf'. But whenever Edwin became serious about the prospect of marriage, she would say she was not ready to settle down to rural life. Edwin genuinely loved her, and said he was willing to wait until Miles was ready to settle down on the land.

One cannot blame Miles for being wary; she was terrified of bearing children and all it meant. She had seen her overworked mother bear and raise seven children including herself and become old before her time. She could not imagine herself playing the role of 'wife, mother, cook, laundress, needlewoman, charwoman ... heartbreaking, cruel, tortured slavery'. In an effort to dampen her cousin's enthusiasm and in a fit of despair, she finally admitted the truth to Edwin. She did not want children or sex.

However, this failed to put him off. She chopped and changed, one minute wondering if she *was* in love with Edwin, the next appreciating his kindness and concern for her. He would appear to have had a fairly low sex drive, and for this reason perhaps Miles viewed him as 'controllable'. However, she was not convinced. A visit to America and a job there seemed a good way to escape. Possibly from a distance she could make up her mind; or perhaps that brilliant career would eventuate at last.

The Goldstein sisters provided her with letters of introduction to leading American feminists who could find her work. On 7 April 1906, promising Edwin Bridle that once she had found an American publisher she would return home and marry him, Miles boarded the SS *Ventura* bound for San Francisco. Edwin may even have assisted towards the payment of her fare; it is unclear how she managed to pay for the ticket.

In Miles' cabin trunk were two manuscripts, for the sequel to *My Brilliant Career* and *Some Everyday Folk — and Dawn*, for which she hoped to find American publishers, not realising that American publishers were only interested in works set in America. She also nursed the old dream of having her voice expertly trained.

Miles arrived in San Francisco to find that the hilly city built close to the San Andreas faultline had been shattered by a huge earthquake. Over 500 people had been killed and 300,000 were now homeless. Paid work was out of the question. Miles' humanitarian instincts were aroused. She and a shipboard friend, a nurse who was a Christian Scientist, joined a relief team and were provided with tented accommodation. They worked long hours helping to rehouse and comfort the homeless. Having done all she could, Miles left her female travelling companion and took the train south to Los Angeles.

From there she visited Salt Lake City, travelled through the Rocky Mountains and across the plains of the Midwest to the windy lakeside city of Chicago, newly rich from the meat-packing industry, the lumber trade and real estate, America's wealthiest city after New York. The wealth of Chicago's railroad barons and meat packers meant that the city had an excellent art gallery filled with Monets and Renoirs, a symphony orchestra and several concert halls. The streets were crammed with migrants from Europe and Russia, many of whom lived in deplorable conditions in tenements without running water, heating or sewerage.

However some brave women were attempting to improve the lives of Chicago's poor, something the American government was reluctant to tackle. Miles had a letter of introduction from the Goldstein sisters to the distinguished philanthropist and feminist Jane Addams, an American version of Rose Scott. Jane Addams, who was from a wealthy Quaker background, had gone to Europe to study art history but felt she must do something to help women less fortunate than herself, and had returned to Chicago to start a community education centre for working-class girls. Hull House was a large, red-brick three-storey home on Chicago's teeming West Side staffed by volunteers who ran a music club, a drama group with its own theatre, a science club, gymnasium and childcare centre to help working mothers.

Miles was thrilled by Hull House. Here were American women using their money and intelligence to do good things for other women and help them achieve the right to vote. In the dining room she met social reformers, millionaires' wives, singers, writers and overseas visitors like herself. Among them was the matronly Alice Henry, a journalist from Victoria. Aged forty-nine, Alice Henry was a friend of Rose Scott and the Goldstein girls and, like Miles, a disciple of the feminist Catherine Spence. Alice befriended Miles and showed her around Chicago.

Convinced that she had found the promised land at last, Miles' letters to Edwin Bridle dwindled to brief factual notes.

Hull House offered a refuge and a chance for some self-improvement courses in the evenings and weekends. Miles took a job as a sales clerk in a department store, selling shoes, but found herself overworked and underpaid. Edwin Bridle continued to write loving letters, insisting that he would wait for her. Miles was often cold and miserable in her first winter in snowy, windy Chicago, but at last tasted financial independence.

The American summer of 1907 was swelteringly hot. Edwin, disillusioned by the lack of warmth in her letters, had stopped writing. Miles later heard from her family that he was seeing another girl. A year later he was married, but by then Miles did not care. A new life beckoned.

By October 1907 Miles had left the department store and was earning her living typing in an office, a skill she had perfected in night courses at Hull House. She joined the Stenographers Union, convinced that these skills would help her literary career. Once more she worked long hours at only a slightly higher rate of pay, but Miles was never afraid of hard work. It was the one trait she shared with her mother. By denying herself luxuries and eating at Hull House, where meals were subsidised, she could just balance her budget. She used some of her earnings to take singing lessons from a leading professional, but was dismayed to learn that a teacher in Australia had ruined the timbre of her voice.

Laurel's death had been bad enough; now came a worse blow. A heartbroken letter from her mother informed her that kind, gentle Linda, who had always been Miles' confidante, had died following the birth of her first child. After Miles' feelings of shock and grief came those of guilt as she remembered how jealous she had once been of her younger sister. If only she could have the time over again, how differently she would have behaved! If only Linda had not married and had a child she would still be alive. How terrible childbirth was for women.

Always subject to insomnia, Miles found it harder and harder to sleep. Grieving for Linda, she lost her appetite. She lay awake remembering the past and worrying about the future. Nothing seemed worthwhile: when she did drop off to sleep she awoke just as tired as she had been before. She grew thinner, paler, more depressed. Eventually even the thought of going out and facing other people brought on panic attacks. She was in danger of becoming agoraphobic and could not face the thought of getting out of bed and going out. She spent entire days staring at one wall in her room. Overwrought and lacking sleep, she collapsed. Finally a doctor was called, and he informed her suffragette friends that Miss Franklin was suffering from a 'nervous breakdown'.

Alice Henry and her other American friends arranged for Miles to stay in the country at Winnetka, in a lakeside mansion owned by the wealthy Lloyd family. William Bross Lloyd and his pregnant wife were friends and supporters of Jane Addams and Hull House. At the Lloyds' home, with its army of servants, Miles could rest and relax without financial worries. On a black-and-white picture postcard to her mother she pointed out the house where she was staying and William Bross Lloyd's large collection of cars. There she spent the next three months resting and recovering. She gained some weight, though she was now slimmer than before she left Australia. The colour returned to her cheeks and she regained her previous bright and breezy personality.

When Miles recovered she was offered a part-time job working for the wealthy feminist Margaret Dreiet Robins, a highly respected figure in the trade union movement. Miles proved her competence by helping Mrs Robins with her paperwork, which led in turn to a part-time job of office secretary to the American National Women's Trade Union

League, where she continued to work for Robins, who became the League's president. Two years later, in 1910, Miles was appointed Secretary of the League on a full-time basis. Robins had become another mother figure to Miles.

Initially the office work was carried out in Mrs Robins's home but eventually the League rented office space on Chicago's busy, central Dearborn Street, crowded with horse-drawn wagons, trolley buses, garment sweatshops and market stalls where migrant women wearing long aprons sold salt fish and smoked herring. Miles was concerned with all aspects of the League's program to improve the conditions of working women. In addition to normal office administration she acted as press officer during the great garment workers' strike of 1910–11.

It became apparent to Miles that American publishers were not interested in novels set in Australia. Her job was interesting but underpaid. Once again she started to worry about her financial future and her health suffered.

The winter of 1912 was freezing cold, with thousands of unemployed men lining the streets. The League continued its work for better pay and working conditions in trades that employed women but usually underpaid them. Political activism and the quest to obtain votes for women gave Miles a new goal for her writing, but her inclusion of political theories spoiled her novels. The irony of the situation was that Miles was working long hours for other women but was herself overworked and underpaid.

Alice Henry, tall and severe, had been responsible for persuading numbers of women to join a union to improve their working conditions. In 1913 she oversaw the editorship of the newspaper the *Union Labor Advocate,* and Miles became a staff writer. Although Miles was suffering from insomnia and pain in her lower back after long hours at the typewriter, she fought like a lion for better conditions for oppressed women in the garment trade, standing for hours in picket lines in freezing weather, interviewing strikers and writing articles drawing attention to their cause. She attended court cases where women workers on strike were prosecuted and wrote up their cases. Her devotion to the welfare of oppressed women was heroic.

After several years in America, unable to get her manuscripts published or save any money, Miles Franklin felt justifiably aggrieved by the differences between her way of life, working hard by day and doing her own writing by night, and the cosseted, luxurious lives of the rich American philanthropists who had founded and ran Hull House.

Miles now wrote to make money. She started a romantic novel, *The Net of Circumstance*, which would not be published for several years, using the ridiculous pseudonym 'Mr and Mrs Ogniblat L'Artsau' (an anagram of Old Talbingo, Austral).

'How the Good Lord favours the rich,' Miles sighed enviously. Although she worked hard during the day, went dancing at night with various admirers and wrote her novels whenever she had the time and energy, she had begun to realise she would never be able to save any money.

In 1909 Blackwood & Son of Edinburgh, the publishers of *My Brilliant Career*, decided to accept *Some Everyday Folk — and Dawn*. Before signing the contract Miles insisted that Blackwood & Son stop selling copies of *My Brilliant Career* in England, ship the remaining copies to Australia and *never* republish it, something she claimed to have done years earlier. *Some Everyday Folk — and Dawn* did not sparkle with the wit and irony of *My Brilliant Career*. It sold very few copies, making a minute amount for Miles in royalties and leaving her even more disillusioned with publishers.[24]

In addition to running the Women's Union League's Chicago office with Teutonic efficiency inherited from her German ancestors, Miles had been given another job: assisting Alice Henry to produce a new Union League magazine, *Life and Labor*. Miles wrote a large part of the new journal, but most of her articles appeared under the name of Alice Henry. Later Miles would describe herself as having *'done it all'* (author's italics) behind the scenes. 'I always had to fill in her [Alice Henry's] gaps,' she said.

With her egalitarian Australian way of dealing with people and her quick wit, Miles was popular with her fellow workers and especially good at persuading strikers and union workers to recount their stories for publication. Yet beneath her cheery facade, Miles felt that, like the women she was trying to help, she too was underpaid and overworked. She was homesick and missed her parents, her siblings and her grandmother. And the fact that her books were critical and financial failures annoyed and depressed her. That 'brilliant career' had not materialised.

She wrote in her diary: 'A failure in accomplishment fills me with creeping melancholy'. She even thought about killing herself within a few years time if she did not succeed as an author and wrote a note to this effect, although whether she really meant it or not is open to question.

Fortunately there were compensations: a visit to London with a female fellow activist as companion, with all expenses paid by the League, dinners with wealthy philanthropists in their comfortable homes, visits to the opera and concerts. Miles made friends and attracted people to her by the force of her personality and her ready wit. These attributes opened doors for her wherever she went.

She continued to persevere with writing fiction. However tired she was after a hard day's work in the office she would, if not attending some League function or a course at Hull House, work on her latest novel, revising, editing, imagining dialogue and metamorphosing reality into fiction.

By January 1914 her romantic novel *The Net of Circumstance* was nearing completion. She set it in Chicago among the super-rich and the working poor. However, the beautiful Constance, Franklin's working-class heroine, was as unsympathetic as the nauseatingly winsome Dawn Mudheepe. By now secrets, confusions and pseudonyms had become a passion with Miles Franklin. It would be decades before Australian literary circles realised that Miles Franklin was the author of *The Net of Circumstance*, a novel about American workers going on strike and nouveau riche railroad barons. Although a publisher accepted the novel, sales were poor. Miles typed away half the night but her writing career seemed to be going nowhere. Another American novel, *On Dearborn Street*, failed to achieve publication. The only publishers who would even look at it were Mills and Boon in England (at that period publishers of general fiction rather than the romances issued by their latter-day successors). They agreed to publish if she replaced all the American slang she had so laboriously woven into the book. Angry that the integrity of her writing was threatened, Miles refused. As a result, *On Dearborn Street* would not be published until after her death.

Miles had now been away from her beloved Australia for eight years, and had failed in her quest to become a famous writer. Rejection slips from publishers brought on moods of despair. However, her spirits were lifted by a brief romance with Guido, a handsome, attentive Italian. But her Latin lover's *machismo* made him possessive and sexually demanding and she dropped him like a hot brick.

Next Miles acquired another long-suffering admirer, Fred Pischel, the elder brother of Emma Pischel, another member of the Hull House philanthropic circle. Her friendship with Fred Pischel started to hot up when, urged on by his sister, he offered to teach Miles to drive. Fred was kind and patient, clever and well read. He was a good listener, while Miles loved talking and expounding ideas. Fascinated by the charismatic Miles, he claimed her as 'his precious twin soul'. He made an unusual proposal, a *'mariage blanche'*, which he would not consummate, promising they could sleep in separate rooms. Their offbeat romance reached the stage where she occasionally let him hold her hand ... but no more.

Romance and hard work in Chicago

Fred Pischel wanted a more committed relationship than Miles was prepared to enter into. She was finding her work and private life stressful, had problems sleeping and at times suffered from palpitations of the heart. Years of poorly paid work for the Women's Trade Union League had failed to give Miles the satisfaction she had expected from a career. Each year she seemed to work longer and longer hours while others took the credit.

Margaret Robins paid most of the expenses of the magazines that Miles and Alice Henry edited. But with each new issue Mrs Robins became more worried as the debts to the printer mounted higher. Subscriptions did not cover costs and they had no chance of any paid advertising.

Miles felt she needed a holiday, and leave was due to her. She packed her bags and went to stay in Boston with a feminist friend, Octavia Sprague. At a charity function she met attractive Henry Demerest Lloyd, younger brother of William Bross Lloyd, who owned the house where she had recuperated after her nervous breakdown.

William Bross Lloyd was enormously wealthy. Unlike most of Chicago's meat packers and railroad barons, his wealth gave him a guilty conscience and he had left-wing and philanthropic inclinations.

William Lloyd had been lunching, dining and dancing and talking books and writing with Miles for years with the full knowledge of his wife. Theirs was a three-cornered relationship whose emotional vortexes remain hidden. Miles' diaries and letters to friends fail to reveal her innermost feelings about the complex relationship between Lloyd and his wife, at whose family gatherings she was often a guest. As Miles was known for her advocacy of chastity, Lloyd's wife, heavily involved with two small children and experiencing marriage problems, had no objection to her husband lunching with the girl from the Australian bush and going dancing with her on occasion.

Miles had known William's younger brother, Henry Demerest Lloyd, for years, purely as William's 'kid brother'. Now in his late twenties, Demerest was exceptionally handsome, with a sportsman's lean body, a good brain and a huge trust fund which meant he had no need to work. Demy (as he was called in the family) was drawn towards Miles because he was interested in writing and publishing. (He would eventually become a newspaper editor and owner.)

Miles had used aspects of William's character and lifestyle as the basis for the character of a mega-rich playboy with a social conscience in her novel *The Net of Circumstance*.[25] Now it was Demy's turn to provide material for the male protagonist in her next book.

Like the hero in a Scott Fitzgerald novel, Demy Lloyd's crisp blond hair was immaculately cut while his shoes and his sports cars were imported from Europe. Winters in Florida and summers sailing his yacht at Cape Cod gave him a year-round tan. He had graduated from Harvard Law School, was entertaining and well read and a superb athlete. He enjoyed great success with women. Miles and his elder brother had joked together about his series of girlfriends and the intrigues of society mothers to get him to the altar with their daughters.

In Boston, at the charity function she attended with Octavia Sprague, Demy told her how much he admired the work she did on behalf of the underprivileged. He admitted to being slightly jealous of the friendship between her and his elder brother. It was 1915; Miles was thirty-five but seemed years younger with her supple, sporty figure and bubbly personality. Aware she was facing 'spinsterhood' Miles only admitted to being twenty-nine and was flattered by Demy's attentions.

Back in Chicago she received an invitation to have dinner with Demy. She accepted, appeasing her feminist conscience about dining with a playboy by telling herself that Demerest Lloyd would do very well as a role model for the character of Bobby Hoyne, the American playboy in her next novel, *On Dearborn Street*. She told Demy, who was flattered.

Although Demerest was a qualified lawyer, he found the thought of practising law 'boring'. While he decided what career to follow he was busy sampling the pleasures available to wealthy young Americans. He had a quick and clever mind and, like Miles, loved new ideas, new places, new people. The fact Miles was a published author from a relatively unknown land fascinated him. He liked the fact that she read widely and voraciously and could talk amusingly on a variety of topics. She was a superb dancer, light on her feet and graceful. Demy, an excellent partner, taught her the latest dance craze, the Turkey Trot.

Perhaps William Lloyd was jealous. He warned Miles that his younger brother had had affairs with actresses, dancers and married ladies, that 'he fell in love very easily'. For Demy, 'falling in love was an everyday event, just like taking a bath or a shower', Miles wrote. She treated him like a younger brother, teasing him and refusing to take him seriously when he claimed to be in love with her. She told him he was wasting his talents by acting the playboy, that he should take up writing. She scolded him for his fondness for champagne and teased him about the women who pestered him.

Her rejection only made Demy all the keener. He had never met anyone quite like Miles, and winning her became a challenge. He wrote her romantic letters filled with poetic quotations and called her 'My starlight, starbright girl', signing his letters 'Sinbad the Sailor', a reference to his yacht and love of the sea. In tender, teasing letters accompanied by sheaves of flowers, he also called her his 'dandy ducky', his 'dear little naughty rascal'. He sent her a humorous alphabet describing the ideal suffragette, written by a woman:

Awfully Affable, Brilliantly Blessed,
Cleverly Capable, Daintily Dressed ...
Mentally Masterful, Naturally Neat,
Often Obliging, Polite and Petite ...[26]

The poem continued in this vein to the end of the alphabet. Beside it Demy wrote: 'Thyself to a T. I couldn't have said it better, although I feel I know you rather better than she does.'

In fact just how well *did* Demy know Miles? Miles, the 'fierce virgin', was no longer a girl who lived at home under the watchful eyes of her parents in a small, censorious community. She now moved among Chicago's wealthy inhabitants, who had advanced ideas and tolerated sexual freedom as long as it did not cause a scandal. Society girls might keep their virginity, but Miles was long past the age at which most women went to the altar. Sex was fine as long as conventions were not flouted. Amongst Demy's circle of friends everyone knew obliging doctors who carried out abortions illegally in America or legally in private clinics in Switzerland.[27] This meant that refusing to have sex with Demy was far harder for Miles than it had been with Edwin Bridle or Fred Pischel.

Demy Lloyd, like his elder brother, had recently converted to Christian Science, that popular 'new faith' amongst the free spirits of the period. Miles realised that Demy had a more spiritual side to his nature than he presented to the world. In the summer of 1909 Miles, together with William and Demy Lloyd, attended a summer school at the University of Wisconsin which had some connection with the world of Christian Science.

With the zeal of recent converts, the Lloyd brothers urged the precepts of Christian Science upon Miles as a means of dealing with her worries about finding an American publisher, her headaches and her insomnia. They told her that Christian Scientists believed they became perfect in the image of God. Illness could no longer afflict them and they had no need of doctors. Miles had heard it all before. Just as she had done with the Goldstein sisters in Melbourne, she remained unconvinced by their arguments but said little and kept her options open. After all, Demy *was* a very attractive man.

When the trio returned to Chicago Demy pursued her hotly. This annoyed his elder brother, who regarded Miles as his special confidante over some troubling aspects of his marriage. For years Miles had mocked physical passion as *'amour'*, a passing madness of the flesh. Demy must have known that Miles had never permitted sexual intimacies of any kind with his brother.

What Miles termed 'the dreaded sex question' in her writings was something Demerest Lloyd was experienced at overcoming. Doubtless he saw Miles as a prize, the committed virgin no one had managed to persuade. Possibly he even talked of marriage. Over the next two years he wined and dined Miles but also saw other women. He took her dancing, driving in his sports car and to the opera. Of course they discussed books, writing and politics. He sent her boxes of imported chocolates, bouquets of hot-house flowers. Did he give her a ring as some sort of pledge? In Miles' old age her biographer Marjorie Barnard admired the plain gold ring she wore all the time, queried if it was a present and was sharply rebuffed. Barnard also noted that Miles, secretive as ever, flatly refused to talk about her time in Chicago.[28]

By proceeding slowly and tactfully and arousing Miles' jealousy of other women, Demy captured her careful heart. He was helped by the fact that she had become disillusioned with her 'career'. She had worked extremely hard over the past seven years, but without any qualifications she remained an underpaid, overburdened office worker while the wealthy volunteers or Alice Henry took the credit. Did she wonder if her mother had been right? Was it time to consider marriage? Her literary career was going through a fallow period. Her writing had not yielded the fame she had hoped for.

Miles always viewed flirtation and *amour* as a game played between men and women, unevenly weighted on the side of men. Now in her mid-thirties, perhaps she felt it was not exactly in keeping with the image of the emancipated 'New Woman' to play the fierce virgin. She wanted Demy without sharing him with other women; he wanted sex as a condition for an exclusive long-term relationship. The notion of marrying Demerest Lloyd could have seemed tempting. Miles was tired of living in women's hostels with their petty restrictions. She was insecure, fearing the lonely, impoverished old age which her mother had never ceased to warn her could be her fate.

What did she learn about Demy's other girlfriends? She wrote nothing down.

One night Demy took her to dine at an expensive hotel where they stayed until past midnight. A row erupted. She left the hotel by herself. Demerest had been squiring her around and sending her flowers for two years. He was no Edwin Bridle, content to snatch a chaste kiss and wait until Miles decided she would meet him at the altar. Perhaps he decided the time had come to consummate the relationship with his 'naughty little rascal'. Possibly he had reserved a suite at the hotel where he invited her to dine. Did he become angry when she rejected his advances and walked out, or did she finally relent and let him make love to her? If so, perhaps her fears had made her incapable of making love. She could have suffered vaginismus, an involuntary muscular spasm of the vagina which renders penetration impossible even if the woman desires intercourse. Did Demy accuse her of being frigid? Or did she blame him for forcing the situation? So many questions. All we know is that they quarrelled after their late dinner and Miles left the hotel on foot around midnight and walked home. Demy did not pursue her.

He wrote her a brief, cold letter breaking off their elusive relationship. He did not give an explanation. Probably he had tired of pursuing a virgin with sexual hang-ups. Miles' diary for 1913, the year their romance ended, does not give the reasons for their break-up. Nor does any letter in her vast correspondence.[29]

By now the Trade Union magazine *Life and Labor* was deeply in debt. The organisers had begun to realise that even if each issue sold out completely, with the subscription price set too low it would *still* not cover printing and production costs. Margaret Dreiet Robins felt the WTUL and her wealthy husband could no longer afford to subsidise the magazine. Finally Mrs Robins had had enough. She paid off the magazine's debts and replaced Miss Franklin and Miss Henry with new editors.[30] (Within a few years the debts soared again, and publication was suspended.)

In spite of all her hard work Miles felt that her career as a suffragist and political activist was a failure. Through no fault of her own she had been dismissed like an errant housemaid. It sent her into a spiral of despair, feeling she should not have attempted to mix political activism and a writing career. She had failed at both; all she had was a trunk filled with unpublished plays and novels. Her blighted romance with Demerest marked yet another failure.

It was 1914, World War I had broken out. Miles was a confirmed pacifist who regarded all wars as part of masculine aggression, or 'male madness'. Sad letters from her mother contained news of the deaths of young men Miles had known since childhood. She became intensely aware of Australia's British heritage but felt no loyalty whatsoever towards the Kaiser's Germany, where her Lampe grandfather had hailed from. She wished to prove where her loyalties lay and do something for the war effort. She knew that many of the railroad barons and millionaires were making huge profits out of a war in which Australians were dying, and was angry that the United States insisted on remaining neutral while manufacturing armaments. Miles began to feel an alien in Chicago.

The previous year John Franklin had sold his auction business and the farm at Penrith. This gave him enough money to buy a small wooden house in the unfashionable Sydney suburb of Carlton as well as the freehold of two shops on the North Shore which he planned to rent out. Her mother wanted Miles to return to Australia and care for her parents in their old age, but living with elderly parents in a small house in dreary suburban Carlton did not seem an attractive proposition to Miles. She had left Australia in order to carve out a career. Enlisting as a volunteer in France seemed far more romantic and would provide excellent material for a book. In Miles' farewell speech at a party before she sailed from Chicago, she made a brief reference to the fact that she was disenchanted at 'being used by other people, even my mother'.

On 30 October 1915 Miles left Chicago for New York and took a passage on a transatlantic steamer to Britain. She found wartime London sad and paid jobs hard to find for someone of her age who lacked any qualifications. It was even difficult to enlist as a volunteer cook or nurse. What she needed was a job that would both house and feed her. Through her contacts Miles was welcomed by the Pankhursts' Women's Social and Political Union (WSPU) and met women involved in the struggle for the vote such as Ray Strachey and Dora Black, who would later marry Bertrand Russell.

Emmeline Pankhurst and her eldest daughter Christabel had founded the WSPU. Like Rose Scott, Christabel Pankhurst was horrified to realise how many women were being infected with syphilis and gonorrhoea; she was another who had no wish to marry. Her book *The Great Scourge and How to End It*, published in 1913, reinforced Miles' own opinions on syphilis. However, Miles did not support the pro-conscription sentiments of Emmeline and Christabel Pankhurst, nor the havoc they wreaked in street marches and on golf courses. She preferred Sylvia, the youngest Pankhurst daughter, an artist by profession. Sylvia was against war and was more concerned with helping working-class women in London's East End. Her anti-war stance meant that she fell out with her mother and split the WSPU.

Sylvia Pankhurst's group saw gaining the vote as a pathway to social reform. They did not agree with needless destruction of property in attempts to gain publicity for the WSPU and were shocked to realise how far British women lagged behind their Australian counterparts, who had had the vote for some time. The women of the WSPU talked a great deal,[31] but Miles found them less inspiring than Rose Scott and Vida Goldstein. After a few months she resigned from the WSPU, feeling it had become too violent and too narrow in its aims, and joined a breakaway left-wing group known as the Women's Freedom League led by Teresa Billington Greig and Charlotte Despard.[32]

Miles' funds were running low and London was expensive. Writing seemed very hard in wartime — it was time to enlist. But in what capacity? Miles had no nursing or other qualifications, and the only other skill that was wanted by field hospitals was cooking. To obtain practical training and some British references Miles became a trainee cook at the Minerva Club in High Holborn, which had been established by the Women's Freedom League to provide meals and accommodation for working women. It also served as a training establishment for women who volunteered to join the Scottish Women's Field Ambulance Service. Miles rented a sparsely furnished bedroom at the club with the use of a communal bathroom.

She earned extra money writing articles about votes for women for the *Sydney Morning Herald* and received a tiny royalty cheque for *The Net of Circumstance*. She started work on a play called *Virtue*, which dealt among other things with the dangers of syphilis. But London's theatre scene was suffering badly during the war and she could not find anyone to produce her play.

Now entering her late-thirties, still slim, petite and bright-eyed, Miles lowered her age by seven years when she applied for a passport. She moved from the rather bleak surroundings of the Minerva Club, with its lists of rules and regulations, to Chelsea, a far more attractive part of London.

The passionate pacifist enlists

For years Miles had denounced the horrors of childbirth and the boredom of childcare; ironically, she was now so desperate for money that she was prepared to accept a poorly paid job in an East End baby clinic run by Sylvia Pankhurst. She travelled each day by train to Deptford, a grimy, insalubrious part of south-east London where the docks had been closed down, leaving wharfies without jobs and their families trapped in poverty. The baby clinic occupied a rat-infested building where babies and young children who had been neglected or abused, often by alcoholic parents, were looked after during the day. Some of the children they cared for were brought back next day with broken bones, multiple bruises or cigarette burns. Miles was paid a pittance to bottle-feed undernourished babies, change nappies and mend baby clothes, the very things that had contributed to her rejection of marriage and motherhood.

At night Miles was so tired she could not write. She was desperate to escape this sort of life and go somewhere on the battle front, which would give her material for another novel and revive her dream of a brilliant career. She yearned to write a book about her war experiences that would sell well in Britain, America and Australia. She decided, 'Of all the women's regiments, the famous Scottish Women's Hospitals appealed to me the most, engineered by [politically] evolved women and occupied with humane service among different nations.'

In May 1917, at the start of the fickle English summer, Miles was summoned to an interview at one of the all-female field hospitals run by the Scottish Women's Hospitals Service. Hoping her basic knowledge of French would secure her a job in France, Miles put on her application form that she would also be happy to work as a nurse or a cook in Corsica or Romania.[33] As always she was very conscious of her lack of qualifications, and once again she lopped seven years off her age, fearing she might not be accepted if she revealed her true age as thirty-seven.

Miles' schoolgirl French was not up to standard to work in France, which was a big disappointment. Demerest Lloyd had told her a great deal about France and she longed to visit it. Instead she was offered a job as a cook in northern Greece, an area about which she knew nothing. She was told that the ancient kingdom of Macedonia had been invaded at the start of the war and split in two; the north was held by the Serbs, the south by the Greeks, who allowed the Allies to use the port of Salonika. The Greek King, a relative of the German Kaiser, maintained an uneasy neutrality.

An official of the Appointments Board explained to Miles that fighting between Serb, British and French forces against Austrians and Bulgarians had been continuing in Macedonia for several years. Miles would be working at Ostrovo, on the slopes of snow-covered Mount Kaimaktsalan, where the armies were engaged in trench warfare that produced many casualties, neither side having enough power to make a definitive strike. One of the main dangers that faced the staff at Ostrovo Field Hospital was from bands of armed guerillas, known to the Serbs as *chetniks* and the Bulgarians as *comitajis*. They took no prisoners and tortured and killed anyone on the enemy side, male or female. Malaria had also killed several volunteers, which was why replacements were needed.

The Allies (Britain, France and Italy) had joined in the Balkans war to help the King of Serbia, who was fighting his traditional enemies, the Austrians. Even after her briefing session the details of this remote battle front remained unclear in Miles' mind. She knew that the killing of Archduke Franz Ferdinand, heir to Franz Josef, Emperor of Austria, by a Serbian assassin had started the war in 1914, after Austria had promptly declared war on Serbia. Now she was told that since Austria and Germany were old allies, Britain and France had had no option but to join in on the Serbian side. It all seemed very confusing.

She decided to accept the offer made by the Scottish Women's Hospitals Service. They agreed to pay her passage to Salonika, which acted as a gateway to the Macedonian front lines. For some quixotic reason Miles enlisted under the highly improbable name of 'Franky Doodle'. She received an annual allowance of twenty-five pounds 'all found'; the Service provided her with uniform, accommodation and meals. Her contract required her to serve an initial twelve months without pay or for a nominal salary. She was issued with a grey dress uniform, a tartan badge and scarf and several aprons and white caps for work.

The regulations covering female personnel were strict: 'Only one white silk blouse may be taken for evening wear. Only one suitcase can be taken since staff will be living under canvas. Orderlies must wear their uniform at all times. Underclothing should be of the simplest kind and no white petticoats can be worn. No high heels allowed. No jewellery except a gold tie-pin. Veils as protection against malarial mosquitoes will be provided in camp.'

Miles posed for a photographer wearing a white cap and apron. She cut her thick, chestnut-brown hair so that it would be easy to manage while living under canvas. She was in buoyant spirits at the idea of leaving London, delighted she had been given knee-high boots 'like a bus conductress'. She loved her grey uniform with its 'jolly short skirt, a peach to walk in. All women should be compelled to wear such short skirts', she observed in a letter.[34] In a postscript she explained that her letter was written under difficulties as her arm was in a sling after two smallpox inoculations, making her so full of germs that 'no more of them can get a hearing'. Homesick for the Australian sun after a London winter, she hoped her ship would stop at the British port of Gibraltar so that she would be able to rest and relax. She ended with a typical Miles touch, saying that she would prefer to be torpedoed in a warm sea rather than a cold one.

On the day of her departure Miles wrote to Rose Scott, telling 'Dearest Rose' how much she was looking forward to the voyage through the Aegean. Miles had been told she would be serving under an Australian, Sydney-born Dr Agnes Bennett, an Edinburgh-trained surgeon given command of a Field Ambulance Unit after being turned down by the Australian Medical Corps, who told her to 'stay home and knit'. Dr Agnes sounded like a woman after Miles' own heart.

On 2 July 1917 Assistant Camp Cook Franky Doodle put on her grey uniform with its short skirt, gaiters and leather boots and draped the tartan scarf around her neck. She and two other female orderlies took the boat train to Paris, which she glimpsed only briefly in the bus taking them from the Gare du Nord to the Gare de Lyons. They took a second train to Rome, where she saw the Spanish Steps and the Forum before catching the train south to Taranto. Here they joined thousands of soldiers of many different nations boarding a troopship bound for Salonika. The ship was escorted by two Japanese destroyers (Japan was on the Allies' side in World War I), sailing in convoy through the night, lights shrouded to avoid being shelled by the enemy.

Their voyage through the Greek Islands was breathtaking in its beauty. They stopped at Corfu and at Melos, the island where the statue of Venus de Milo had been excavated. In her journal Miles noted how bare the islands were of trees, the sugar-cube houses of the villages silhouetted against rocky hillsides.

Salonika (Thessaloniki) was built on the side of a hill, its minarets visible from the water. It had once been part of the empire of Philip of Macedon, father of Alexander the Great. The Turks had occupied it for five centuries. Now it was an international port that had been conquered by the Greeks in 1913, hence its Greek name. *Salonique* to the French soldiers quartered there and to Miles, who enjoyed trying to speak French. It was now filled with British, French and Italian troopships and a few destroyers.

The quayside was swarming with British soldiers as well as swarthy French-colonial troops from North Africa, Malays in knee-length khaki shorts, Indian regiments in turbans, kilted Scottish regiments, Sengalese soldiers wearing 'huge fezzes and Italians dapper in dark grey uniforms topped by quaint little Tyrolean hats with feathers'.

Miles was met by a Greek interpreter on the staff of the Scottish Women's Hospitals Service. The plan was for her to see the city and then return to the port area to meet her commanding officer, who was to drive her to Ostrovo. They climbed on a crowded tram that clattered its way through narrow cobbled streets. Miles saw women in long black shapeless dresses bearing trays of unbaked loaves on their heads on their way to the communal ovens. She made a few purchases in 'quaint shops' where British soldiers haggled over goat bells, bracelets and other souvenirs. Miles and her guide visited street markets off Venizelou Street with separate markets for fish, meat and spices. The markets were bisected by what Miles described as 'stinking drains', which were probably open sewers. Later she noted in her journal 'the sanitary arrangements are better not mentioned. They pollute the waterways and distress the nostrils'.[35] Albanian and Macedonian women wearing brightly embroidered costumes stood out among the Greek women dressed from head to toe in black. Beggars thrust out their palms and muttered words Miles could not understand. She was fascinated by it all, but distressed to see tiny donkeys ill-treated, overloaded and underfed, the universal beasts of burden in this part of the world.

Her guide took her to dine at Floka's restaurant, which was filled with portly balding men who ogled Miles' shapely legs, having rarely had a chance to see a short skirt on a woman. The room reeked of garlic, stale tobacco and cheap frying oil. They ate roast goat and rice.

Back at the port Miles met Dr Bennett, her commanding officer, who had come down from Ostrovo to supervise the unloading of a consignment of tinned food. Her guide had explained that Dr Bennett was greatly admired as a skilful surgeon and excellent administrator. By now Miles had admitted that her enlisted name 'Franky Doodle' was false and was introduced to Dr Bennett as 'Miles Franklin'.

Dr Agnes Bennett was a tall, athletic woman in her late thirties or early forties wearing the regulation grey coat and skirt of the Scottish Ambulance Service, with scarlet tabs in the lapels denoting her rank as captain. On her head was a dilapidated Akubra hat, a symbol of Australia that delighted Miles.

A porter loaded Miles' battered suitcase into the boot of the doctor's car, a dilapidated Ford. They drove out of Salonika past a huge triumphal arch built to commemorate the victory of a Roman Emperor over the Persians, then took the dirt road westward bound for the town of Edessa.

As they drove the Vardar River turned to silver in the twilight. Miles glimpsed oxen and water buffaloes yoked to farm carts. They followed a dirt track, where she saw what appeared to be a pyramid of human corpses flanked by the rotting carcases of horses and donkeys. The stench was frightful. Darkness fell as they reached the foothills. The car's headlamps revealed the track was pitted with huge shell holes. In the distance Miles saw the glare of searchlights and heard distant gunfire. 'You'll get used to it,' Dr Bennett said. She chatted away lightheartedly as they bounced over the potholes. Miles, who had travelled over plenty of rough tracks in outback New South Wales, described this as 'the roughest journey I ever underwent. I expected my teeth to be telescoped any moment'.

As they climbed higher, heading for a fold in the Macedonian hills over 160 kilometres west of Salonika, the precipices became vertiginous. Dr Bennett explained that her unit had been staffed by 160 female volunteers, many of whom had died from malaria or typhoid or been invalided home.

The Macedonians' vegetable gardens and orchards had been burned during the recent Balkan wars. Invading Greek and Serb soldiers and

Bulgarian guerillas had burned the barns and confiscated the villagers' corn. Fresh food was very scarce, fresh milk unobtainable.

Miles realised that a falling boulder or a careless lorry bouncing down the narrow mountain road could easily tip them over the edge. She looked over steep precipices 'decorated' with Army lorries and ambulances which 'had somehow or other slid over the edge'.[36] Dr Bennett seemed unconcerned and reassured her passenger that she had driven this particular stretch of road many times. She went on to offer sound advice: 'Never take the netting off your stretcher bed. Always wear high boots or puttees after sundown.' She told Miles that supplies of quinine were low and she was very worried about Sister Cater, who had succumbed to malaria.

They drove through the sleeping villages of Dudular and Pella. Even though the road was pocked by shell holes, Dr Bennett drove rapidly. She was keen to get back to camp as soon as possible.

They passed through a dilapidated village whose battered signpost carried the Bulgarian name of Yenje Vardar and the Greek one of Yiannitsa. Centuries ago the armies of Alexander the Great had gathered here before marching on Persia, Dr Bennett said. She warned Miles to keep a sharp lookout for Bulgarian guerillas, who sometimes lay in wait for cars as they slowed down to cross the high passes. Pointing to a small revolver in the glovebox, she said that she would use it if necessary.

After they left Yiannitsa the road started to climb steeply. The Ford's engine toiled valiantly up the steep mountain pass until the radiator started to steam. Dr Bennett drew close to the side of the mountain and stopped the car on an unstable slope. Miles wondered if the handbrake would hold. Agnes Bennett opened the glovebox, tucked the revolver in her belt and told Miles to look around to see if she could make out any guerilla fighters lurking around before they left the relative safety of the car.

All Miles could see was the sheer drop beside her over the precipice, and above them the towering peak of Mount Kaimaktsalan, which straddled the disputed border. She listened intently for Bulgarian bandits but heard nothing except the call of nightingales. It must be safe, they decided. Both women climbed out of the car and waited until the radiator had cooled down, before they could continue their journey.

They arrived at Ostrovo Field Hospital at 1.30 am to be greeted in an Aussie accent by Sister Dorothy Agnes Kerr, who reported the sad news that Sister Cater had died three hours ago. Due to the heat it would be necessary to bury her in the morning; the British padre from the trenches would be coming over then. Sister Kerr sounded exhausted. Two more of the Serbian orderlies had gone down with fever, one with malaria, the other with typhoid from drinking water which had not been boiled, something which was strictly against the rules. It was scarcely a good introduction to camp life.

Miles was given a candle and directed to a small tent near the end of the first row of tents. She was so exhausted that she lay down under the mosquito net without bothering to take off her uniform and fell asleep immediately.

At dawn she awoke to birdsong. She found herself looking down on the blue waters of Lake Ostrovo, in whose placid depths the snow-covered mountain ranges appeared in reflection silhouetted against an even bluer sky. The sheer beauty of the scene took her breath away. She was surprised that the distant mountain ranges of Macedonia reminded her of the peaks and valleys of her beloved Monaro.

Rat stew and weed soup at Ostrovo

On her first day Miles was given the job of sorting through gift parcels sent from Britain and Australia for wounded Serbians. By midday the heat was sweltering. She rejected piles of woolly gloves and socks but took the tobacco, cigarettes and chocolate (most of which was stale) to give to the patients in the tented hospital. She was distressed to see that some of them were so badly crippled they would never walk again. Many were under eighteen. When she apologised for the stale chocolate and the small quantity of tobacco they smiled wanly, replying: *Ne mari nishta, Sestra* (No matter, Sister).

Miles was so impressed by their bravery that she used this frequently repeated phrase as the title for her projected war novel. She was desperate to help the wounded soldiers, but they could not understand her fractured French. That afternoon she borrowed a Serb-English phrasebook in an attempt to learn a little Serbian.

For the next few days she was rostered on duty as camp cook. In the fierce heat of summer the camp ovens had been moved outside, where they attracted wasps and flies. The volunteers had been issued with beekeepers' veils, but Miles soon found it was impossible to see through them. Even though she and her co-workers knew that without veils they stood a good chance of catching mosquito-borne malaria, they soon discarded them.

Each day was hotter than before. Cooking over an open fire in that heat was a nightmare. When the heatwave ended in a thunderstorm Miles discovered that her tent, along with the others, leaked like a sieve.

Each night lumbering lorry-ambulances arrived from the front line, containing soldiers with bullet wounds or fevered with malaria, driven by courageous female volunteers. The track was so potholed that the wounded were badly jolted around and arrived in agony. Male Serbian orderlies carried the injured to the tents, where they lay groaning until they could get to the operating tent or have their broken limbs splinted.

The unit owned seven lorry-ambulances, and four more had been loaned them by their Serbian allies. As soon as patients were deemed fit to travel they were transported to Ostrovo railway station on stretchers and sent off to the British Military Hospital in Salonika.

By midsummer there were so many blowflies and horseflies that they could not eat their main meal until it was dark. Wasps swarmed over everything and stung them while they tried to eat. They placed jars of jam and water on the table, each jar covered by a tin lid with a hole in it, pierced in such a way that the wasps could not climb out. Stings in the mouth or throat could cause swellings and suffocation. 'Flies, fleas, ants, mosquitoes and snakes — all the realities of Australian bush life were with us but somehow did not impart a sense of "home",' another Australian, Mary Stirling, wrote about life at Ostrovo.

There was no running water. Once a day a bucket of fresh water was brought to each staff tent by the orderlies. Somehow or other earwigs wriggled under the lids of the water jugs and drowned in their precious drinking water. Rats and snakes sometimes entered the tents, desperate for fresh water. There were more cases of malaria and dysentery to nurse than battle injuries.

Camping at Ostrovo reminded Miles of life in the Australian bush, where nothing was ever wasted. Packing crates became washstands, cupboards, tables or stools, and candles were rationed, as their ancient and sometimes unreliable generator was used to power the X-ray machine and provide light and fans in the operating theatre. Two Scots girls and three Macedonian washerwomen operated a laundry by the side of the lake. The women staff were helped by male Serb orderlies, who chopped the wood, carried water and dug the smelly latrine pits. At least they had the luxury of fresh vegetables, provided by a small garden.

At midday Miles had time off. She went swimming with the Serb medical orderlies and rested from the heat under a tree. On 24 July 1917 she sent a photo to her mother showing herself with several orderlies and patients,[37] accompanied by a letter in which she said that the heat reminded her of Australia. Bravely she minimised the danger of attack from the Austrians and the Bulgarian guerillas. She described their usual bathing place: 'a glorious swimming hole, sloping in so gradually at our end that it was safe for beginners, only we hated the snakes.' The lake was known for the poisonous vipers and whipsnakes that lurked around its banks, as well as water snakes whose bites were supposed to be harmless. The Serb orderlies provided a big plank to float on, as well as what Miles called 'a *mia-mia*' (an Aboriginal term for a hut) of boughs to dress in. She and the other nurses were not put off swimming by the assertion (false or otherwise) that the lake was full of corpses from the battle of Kaimaktsalan and the burning and looting of Bulgarian and Turkish villages by invading Greeks and Serbs. Miles found Ostrovo exotic, primitive and beautiful. The drone of distant gunfire mingled with the goat bells and pipes played by itinerant Vlach (Romanian) shepherds.

After a few weeks their supply of tinned corned beef ran out. They were forced to rely on the same diet as the surrounding villagers: rat stew, a soup made from wild herbs and bitter bread (made from a dough to which acorns had been added to bulk out the wheat). The rats were so plentiful that they sometimes ran across immobile patients and gnawed at their bandages.

It took several weeks for the next shipload of tinned food to arrive from Salonika. Sometimes the lorry patrols were able to obtain fresh meat and poultry, which was reserved for the patients. Eggs were as rare as fresh milk. Patients often spent weeks without butter or margarine on the table to make the bitter bread more palatable. Crates of homemade jam and Scottish marmalade had been sent from headquarters in Edinburgh, but most of the crates had been lost in a storm at sea. Sugar, plentiful at first, became very scarce, as did tea. Local goat cheese and milk were welcome additions to their diet. Australian butter, cheese and dried fruits, sent to Australian staff members in food parcels from relatives, were greatly in demand. Cherries, grapes and mulberries appeared in the markets in midsummer as the villagers' orchards were restored. Miles described how for a treat 'French tinned meat, popularly suspected to be horsemeat appeared, as well as dried beans'. They had porridge but as they lacked milk it was almost impossible to eat. Miles and her fellow cooks thought the tinned margarine, regarded as a luxury when it was available, tasted like stale tallow candles.

By 8 am each day, Miles recorded, it was 116°F (47°C) in the 'cooking tent with its two wood-stoves and a hot-water boiler. There was no place to retreat from the heat; the white of the tents attracting the sun rather than affording protection from it. Every single drop of water had to be carried a great many yards in petrol drums by the orderlies, every piece of wood carried by hand'. Their 'beastly little gunyah of a staff kitchen' was pitched in the full glare of the sun; there was no proper protection against flies and wasps, 'not even one trustworthy meat safe'.

As soon as a fresh batch of assistant cooks arrived from Scotland, Mary Stirling and Miles Franklin applied for a transfer from duty as camp cooks to that of nursing assistants. This was granted. Miles was thrilled that the orderlies and patients now called her *Sestra* (Sister) Franklin. A real career at last!

Agnes Bennett ran her field hospital on egalitarian lines totally unlike the British and Australian medical corps, which were rigidly structured by rank. Miles did not want to write anything that would reflect badly on Dr Bennett should it be published. The edited account she intended for publication is at odds with the bleak entries in her private journal which, under a clause in her will, were not to be read until thirty years after her death. Miles' private journal contains entries such as: 'Cooking, cooking and more cooking in *beastly* kitchen'; 'I was made staff cook against my will'; 'Very angry with the Administration, [who are] incapable of protecting staff against flies and wasps'; and 'Oh, the noise of heavy boots and harsh voices! No sleep that night'.

The fear was ever present that the camp might be invaded and the staff taken prisoner or have their throats slit by Bulgarians seeking revenge for the destruction of their villages by the Greeks and Serbs.

Miles was stung by wasps *seven* times in one day. She spent a whole week confined to bed with swollen fingers and a soaring temperature. She had suffered heart palpitations when she first became ill in Chicago, and now the shock of so much quinine brought on the palpitations once more. Three weeks later, drinking a cup of water in the dark, she swallowed another wasp that stung the lining of her throat. The nurse on duty feared Miles' throat might swell and cause suffocation. Dr Bennett was summoned in case a tracheotomy was necessary, but before Miles could be given an anaesthetic the swelling began to subside.

In August more and more staff went down with malaria. As many as a quarter of the staff would be sick at one time; everyone else, in that tremendous heat, was forced to do double and triple duty. Miles wrote: 'Those among us who escaped malaria could be counted on the fingers of one hand, excluding the thumb'. The huge 'Scots Grey' mosquitoes which bred in the marshy reeds by the lake were 'a foe more deadly than the Bulgars'. The only protection they had against mosquito bites was iodine:

> We went about painted as dark as Indians or Maoris with iodine. After 5 pm we wore gaiters to protect our ankles, but it did not prevent us from being stung…through our thin clothing…We dreaded…'bayonet charges', the injection of quinine from a needle about two inches long, plunged into a muscle of the buttocks. The doctors ran an exploding needle of quinine into the region of the sciatic nerve … I never suffered pain like it.[38]

This first anti-malarial injection rendered Miles numb from the hip downwards, so that she did not feel any subsequent ones. Intense pain meant she was unable to sit down for several weeks: 'I ate standing up. It was three months before I could walk without dragging my leg', she claimed. For weeks her upper leg and buttocks were so sore that she was unable to indulge in her favourite recreation, riding thoroughbred horses which some French officers stationed nearby kindly loaned to nurses like Miles who could prove they were good horsewomen.

The massive doses of quinine made her feel 'like a poisoned dingo' and for a few weeks strands of her hair fell out whenever she combed it. A black-humoured joke circulated amongst the hospital staff: in their first year in the Scottish Women's Hospitals Service volunteers lost their hair, in the second year they lost their teeth, in the third their reputations or their virginity.

By the end of November the mosquitoes had fled from their breeding grounds in the marshes. The lake froze over. Winds swept over the plain as though sent direct from Russia; the gusts were so strong that it was feared some of the tents might blow away. In their wake Russian soldiers in need of delousing treatment for louse-borne typhus arrived. Armed with clippers, razors and bottles of disinfectant, the nurses shaved and bathed the infected men, using lighted cigarettes to try to get rid of the typhus-bearing lice that clustered in the seams of their trousers.

It was so bitterly cold at night that the ambulance drivers, mostly London socialites and party girls, arrived at Ostrovo with icicles hanging from their eyebrows. The field hospital staff went to bed in woollen underclothes, reinforced by pyjamas, sweaters, shawls and socks — all the warm clothes they possessed. Dr Bennett wore her fur coat over her uniform in bed and had even been known to operate in it. The temperature was often below zero, and they dined and breakfasted in thick gloves. Knitted woollen balaclavas became the fashion. The sisters were supplied with waistcoats made out of goatskin, but as the skins had not been properly cured 'their odour was of such remarkable individuality that some preferred the cold to the smell', Miles wrote.

As it turned even colder a mouse plague infested their tents, the mice eating holes in their woollen uniforms and nesting in their blankets. To combat sub-zero temperatures, the Slav orderlies made charcoal braziers from old petrol tins. Wood was scarce. Convalescent patients would return from their walks with a treasured piece of firewood. Each tent had a daily ration of charcoal, enough to take the chill off the air and heat a kettle of water. No one bothered much about a morning wash.

A huge storm blew up. The hospital tents still leaked and vital equipment was damaged by water, including their precious thermometers and syringes, which could not be replaced locally so new ones had to be sent out from the Edinburgh headquarters. Wolves howled at night and were rumoured to have eaten village children.

The Field Ambulance hospital was officially for Serbian soldiers, but now they received French-colonial troops from North Africa, a few English, French, Italian and Greek soldiers and Vlach shepherds, who arrived shivering in huge cloaks. What haunted Miles were the groans of dying soldiers, some of them only fifteen or sixteen, boys conscripted into a war they did not understand. Nowadays pharmaceutical drugs are used to control pain but at that time the only painkiller was opium, which was in short supply. Most patients suffered agonies before and after operations. Like the other nurses, Miles held the soldiers' hands when their pain was at its height or to ease their last moments.

One night Bulgarian guerillas broke into the nearby French camp and slit the throats of eleven French officers. Dr Bennett, fearing the same fate for Ostrovo, arranged revolver practice for her staff under the tuition of some newly arrived Italian officers quartered at the French camp. The Italians proved to be even more flirtatious than the French officers. Miles loved riding and flirting with good-looking men; now she had ample opportunity to do both. Unfortunately their skill with firearms was not very impressive.

Christmas was normally a time of religious observance in Macedonia, while New Year was seen as a time of rejoicing and feasting. This year, however, food was in such short supply that there was barely enough for everyday living. Each day the hospital's lorry-ambulances scoured the surrounding countryside and farms for eggs, milk or fowls for wounded patients.

By now Miles, already slim from her bout of depression in America, had lost a great deal of weight. Thoughts of past meals 'at home' occupied much of the conversation at meal breaks as the staff became hungrier and hungrier on their meagre diet of biscuits, bully beef and black tea. No one could bear to discuss the thought of being reduced to rat soup again. Staff Christmas dinner was to be stringy bully beef and a few roast potatoes.

Fortunately Sisters Franklin and Reid found themselves rostered off over Christmas. They were thrilled to receive an invitation for a proper Christmas lunch with roast chicken and all the trimmings from Matron Jessie McHardy White, the heroic Australian in charge of nursing at the British Military Hospital on the outskirts of Salonika. Sister McHardy White was a legend among the nursing sisters for her devoted nursing of Anzacs wounded at Gallipoli.

Miles thoroughly enjoyed all the Christmas parties and staff concerts at the BMH Salonika. Although Salonika had been ravaged by fire at the end of the previous summer, the British hospital was outside the damaged area. The main hospital building was run down and dilapidated but the nurses' quarters were relatively modern. The nurses there had previously been camping outside a desolate village called Hortiack, where terrible atrocities against the Bulgarian inhabitants had been perpetrated and life had been grim. A few comforts had been shipped out to the British nurses by well-wishers in Britain. During her brief time at the Military Hospital Miles appreciated 'Proper beds in real houses made of new boards! Fried ham and two eggs for breakfast! Real bread and real butter! Meals served on table-cloths, with crockery such as plates and cups and *table-napkins*! And *such* dinners and suppers!'

On the way back to Ostrovo she noticed how the village women did all the work in the fields while their menfolk lazed around in dirty cafés, smoking and drinking *ouzo*. She noted that the villagers lived in fear of the armed Bulgarian *comitadji*, 'who still exercise their ancient right of levying tribute in the way of food or livestock on the Macedonians *sans* sanction of parliament', as she wrote ironically. Once again she felt sorry for the donkeys: 'poor little things, much belaboured and labouring bravely'. She was furious to see men riding on donkeys while their wives trudged barefoot behind them and wrote: 'These huge men should be ashamed to ride such tiny beasties; they were covered with swellings and sores from bruises, and when their owners perceived us they invariably indicated their virility by administering an extra walloping'.

Village women admitted to Ostrovo as patients usually arrived on a donkey and were stripped, bathed and disinfected against the lice which were endemic in the poorer villages. One Macedonian who brought his wife to be operated on took her home immediately she had regained consciousness, unwilling to risk leaving his 'property' in the vicinity of soldiers and male orderlies. The Macedonian women, however, were not ungrateful; one, after receiving treatment, drew a chicken from her voluminous skirts and presented it to the nurse who had cared for her.

The 'forgotten campaign' in Macedonia was fought with swords and bayonets which imparted savage wounds. Communications with the outside world were almost nonexistent. The horrors and atrocities committed there would take years to become known, and some remain unrecorded in British and French accounts of the war. For this reason Miles' first-hand account of life in wartorn Macedonia is important.[39]

Miles and her fellow nurses would sometimes joke about how isolated they were in the Balkans with no British or Australian newspapers; they hoped that if the war in Europe ended someone in Whitehall would be kind enough to inform them. They had no idea what was happening elsewhere. 'Although strategists and spies might know; we did not', Miles complained.

She managed to begin writing a short story about her Balkan experiences which she called *By Far Kaimaktsalan* and an article entitled *Somewhere in the Balkans*, but finished neither. Apart from one unpublished article describing a painful but amusing visit to an antiquated dentist's surgery, *Ne Mari Nishta (It Matters Nothing)* would be her only long piece of writing about life in northern Greece. For her, this little phrase represented the stoic bravery of the wounded Serbians she nursed.

As soon as the snow melted, Miles enjoyed hearing once again the cries of newborn lambs and goats which reminded her of childhood at Brindabella. But with the melting snow came insects and disease. Lice-born diseases like typhus, flies which brought dysentery and malarial mosquitoes became as dreaded as the enemy. The diseases these insects carried were impossible to eradicate and killed hundreds of officers, soldiers and nursing staff. The camp turned into a waste of mud and slush. In the trenches, conditions for the soldiers were deplorable. Those who had crouched in shell holes as the snow melted around them and water soaked through their boots were now afflicted with trench foot, which meant blackened toes and suppurating ulcers. Miles wrote: 'I have seen … many men die, heard their shrieks when suffering from wounds which nothing could heal.'

Dr Bennett's workload was enormous and she did not spare herself. Eventually she was bitten by an infected mosquito and succumbed to malaria. Her face became as gaunt and lined as that of an old village woman and she shook with fever. She could not continue at Ostrovo and had to prepare for evacuation while this was still possible. Ironically she caught the infection just as it had been decided by the Edinburgh authorities that the Ostrovo Field Hospital should be moved, as it was situated too close to the mosquito-infested marshes. Most of the nurses and the Serb orderlies were in tears as they watched Dr Agnes climb painfully into the ambulance, determined to leave the camp on her feet rather than by stretcher.

The next day Miles went down with fever. Unable to get out of her camp bed, she stayed there shivering and shaking. As the whole field hospital was now being dismantled, she was evacuated in an ambulance taking patients down to the British Hospital in Salonika, where she was greeted warmly by Matron Jessie Hardy and the nurses she had met at Christmas. She spent several nights at the military hospital before being carried on a stretcher aboard the SS *Lafayette*, a French hospital ship which was taking wounded soldiers back to France.

As the ship drew away from the quay Miles saw for the first time how the great fire had devastated Salonika, destroying ancient Byzantine churches and minarets and leaving much of the ancient port a charred ruin. Seeing the sunlit slopes of Mount Olympus recede into the distance, Miles would describe how 'the city ... with its smells, its sins, its glamour, drops away ... on the horizon. The setting sun outlines Mount Olympus in flame and gold, a vision for the gods'.

A few weeks later the *Lafayette* docked at Toulon. By now Miles was strong enough to take the train to Paris and the boat to Le Havre.

Exhausted and virtually penniless, she arrived back in London on 14 February 1918, her notebooks crammed with notes about her time at Ostrovo.[40] She rented a furnished room from a suffragette friend at 22 Harley Road, Hampstead. She was depressed by the fact that she had returned to London just as penniless as she had been before, and with her health seriously impaired. Air raids and food rationing accentuated the difficulties of life in London. Casting about for a new direction in her life, she found that few people were interested in a forgotten campaign in the Balkans: she was unable to interest any publisher in her projected war novel.

Although many of her feminist friends were interested in communism, which was then seen by many as a daring new experiment, Miles was justifiably cynical about Lenin, the leader of the new Russia that had succeeded the Tsarist regime following the Russian revolution of 1917. It is possible she may have learnt from the Russians she had met at Ostrovo that Lenin had ordered the massacre of 9,000 men and women in eastern Poland and slaughtered thousands of *kulaks* (hard working land-owning peasants and their families) or was working them to death as slave labour, repossessing their land and denying them ration books. Later she learned about Lenin's horrific program of death and destruction in Eastern Poland from her friend Sydney Loch, whose book on Gallipoli, *Straits Impregnable*, Miles succeeded in selling to the London publisher John Murray. Perhaps this explains why she never became a card-carrying communist as many of her friends did.

'Oh dear me, Litvinoff was *very* Russian,' she wrote sarcastically to Alice Henry in America. 'He told us of the *wonderful* democracy they have established overnight, but then we *know* our Russians, don't we. I wouldn't mind betting it will take them a few generations to catch up with England's liberty in some things.'

Miles confided to Alice that her harrowing time in Macedonia had sometimes been 'a lovely experience'. Surprisingly, she wrote: 'I never expected to be so happy again as I was there.' The only thing that seemed to have prevented Miles from returning to Greece was her recurring malaria. Soon she had another bout with high fever and violent attacks of shivering. She lacked the money to pay a doctor. As she was officially on sick leave from Macedonia, the administration division of the Scottish Women's Hospital sent her to see the distinguished Scots physician Sir James Cantlie, a specialist in tropical medicine. By August 1918 her bouts of fever and shaking were so bad that she was admitted to the Merchant Taylor's Convalescent Home in Bognor; she was thoroughly run down and exhausted. The time she spent at the Convalescent Home restored her. When she left Bognor she was even thinking about applying to return to Macedonia, but she was told the war was expected to end soon.

Two months later Miles obtained her official discharge from the Scottish Women's Field Hospitals's service. It was November, the war was over and American aid to the Scottish Field Hospitals' headquarters had ceased. This meant that Miles never received the pay that was due to her. She moved her trunk of clothes, books and manuscripts to No. 1 Milton Chambers in Chelsea's Cheyne Walk, a pleasant spot close to the river.

In between further bouts of malaria Miles managed to write a play as well as two newspaper articles about her time in Macedonia for the London *Daily Herald* and the *Auckland Star*. She continued to offer her war novel to publishers without success.[41] She attempted to earn commissions by acting as a London literary agent for other authors in Australia, but found little profit in this.

By now Miles was disillusioned. She had seen the horrors of war, walked over the rotting bones of fallen soldiers, seen young men maimed in a campaign beyond their comprehension. She called war 'the great idiocy, the unforgettable betrayal', 'a recurring lunacy'. She felt that those who had started and encouraged the war had done so for commercial reasons. Gun dealers, armaments manufacturers, owners of garment factories who had switched into making military uniforms had all become immensely wealthy. England had emerged from the 'war to end all wars' with hundreds of thousands of young men maimed, blinded or so shell-shocked that they had difficulty fitting into society again. Australia had suffered huge casualties to its fighting force at Gallipoli, many killed or seriously weakened by typhoid, like her friend and colleague Sydney Loch, as a result of British administrative blunders. Britain had incurred huge debts to pay for 'The Great War'. The slum dwellers were no better off than they had been. Little had changed.

Yet no matter how disillusioned she was with Britain and its rigid class system, Miles *refused* to return to Australia. The old wounds caused by the publication of *My Brilliant Career* still rankled. She did *not* want to be pitied by her family as the unmarried daughter who had never found a husband and failed to achieve a 'brilliant career'. She would remain in London, continue to write and, if she could, win a scholarship to Oxford University. If this were not possible she would find an office job with an organisation that benefited the poorer members of society.

Secrets, lies, and the 'big prize'

Although Miles was supported by Baron Tennyson (son of the celebrated poet) in her attempt to study English literature at Oxford, at this time there were no scholarships for mature-age female students. Miles could not afford the fees of an Oxford college so she finally gave up her hope of going there.[42]

Instead she found herself a job at the London office of the National Housing Council, a non-profit organisation set up to build cheap housing for workers. This, however, failed to equal the excitement of working with the suffragettes in Chicago. Miles, hard working and idealistic, frequently came into conflict with an autocratic office manager who disliked her spirited approach to life and work and her sense of humour.

She shared a rented apartment at 191c High Street, Kensington, with two feminists whose names were on the lease, the poet Mary Fullerton, and her lesbian lover, widowed Mabel Singleton. However, while she shared an apartment with lesbians, Miles always denied firmly she was one: no letters exist to prove otherwise. Miles became friendly with Mabel's secretary, a witty young English woman named Jean Hamilton, and confided to the three women that, under the pseudonym Brent of Bin Bin, she was writing novels set in rural Australia. Even Blackwood and Son, who agreed to publish the books, were not aware she was their author. The only address Blackwood and Son had for Brent of Bin Bin was the number of a certain desk in the Reading Room of the British Museum from which 'Mr Brent' would reply to readers' queries. Secretive as ever, for the rest of her life Miles would continue to deny that she was Brent of Bin Bin. It gave her a thrill to praise Brent's books to journalists and fellow authors as though they were the work of some other author.[43]

However, there were exceptions. Friends and fellow authors such as Katharine Susannah Prichard, Jean Devanny, Mary Fullerton and Alice Henry were among the favoured few allowed to know the identity of the mysterious 'Mr Brent'. Marjorie Barnard, in her biography of Miles Franklin, relates that Mary Gilmore claimed *her* brother was the author. Doubtless this infuriated Miles, who did not like Mary Gilmore. All these claims and counter-claims prolonged the Brent of Bin Bin mystery; a trifle cynically, Miles thought the mystery helped the sales of the books. Brent's five novels included *Up the Country, a tale of the early Australian squattocracy* (1928), *Ten Creeks Run, a tale of the horse and cattle stations of the Murrumbidgee* (1930) and *Back to Bool Bool* (1931).

On 20 April 1925 Rose Scott died in Sydney, bedridden, stone deaf and almost forgotten. News of her lonely death caused Miles considerable grief. From this time onwards she was haunted by the fear that, like Rose, she too would die alone and forgotten. In 1932 she received a second blow when a telegram arrived from her mother, announcing that her father had died of a heart attack. Susannah Franklin begged Miles to come home and care for her; she had also suffered a mild heart attack.

At the end of that year, after almost thirty years, Miles Franklin finally returned to her beloved Australia to care for her widowed mother. By then her mother's wounding remarks about *My Brilliant Career* had been healed by years of absence from family life.

Miles, the young crusader with the wasp waist and the long chestnut plait, had become a woman in her mid-fifties, her brown eyes hidden behind steel-rimmed glasses. Marooned in an outer suburb of Sydney, Miles felt isolated from all the things in London that interested her passionately and from her closest friends. Fortunately Miles' mother owned the little weatherboard house in Carlton and had also inherited her husband's two small shops. Rented out, they brought in enough money for them both to live on. Miles bottled and pickled plums, apricots and vegetables from the garden and gathered firewood on vacant lots to save money. Returning to London for a visit would be out of the question, even if she had been able to leave her mother in someone else's care while she was away.

Writing for a living in a country with as small a population as Australia remained almost as hazardous a career as tightrope walking. Publishing houses deliberately underpaid their authors in order to survive. In mid-life, like many of her writer friends, Miles was often depressed to think that she had worked so hard and earned so little in terms of monetary reward or literary prizes.[44]

She found the Australia of the 1930s very different to the ultra-conservative Australia of Federation, against which she had so bitterly rebelled. Factors that had previously restricted women's lives had changed. Women could now own property and write cheques. Unmarried girls no longer needed chaperones. They had shortened their skirts, bobbed their hair, learned to type or become telephonists, and held down office jobs. Wasp waists were out, the Charleston was in. The average age of marriage for a woman was now the mid-twenties, and families were smaller. There were far fewer deaths in childbirth. Soon new family planning clinics and progressive-minded women doctors would promote the use of pessaries as contraceptives and condoms to help decrease the spread of sexually transmitted diseases.[45]

Miles still saw herself as a rebel, but by now Australian society had changed so radically that no one was shocked by her ideas. She found this depressing. She had already suffered two bouts of depressive illness in Chicago and London; in today's terms she would be classified by psychiatrists as suffering from cyclothymia.[46] Sufferers of this syndrome are often creative people who write, paint or compose in a frenzy of activity. Once a project is finished they may suffer a depression which manifests itself in loss of appetite and loss of concentration, something often referred to as 'writer's block', the loss of ability to create. Naturally the frequency of such mood swings varies from individual to individual.[47]

On a creative 'high' Miles tapped away from dawn to dusk on her battered portable Corona typewriter, sometimes continuing far into the night. She wrote letters by the score, involved in plans for promoting Australian literature, her own books and those of her alter ego, the mysterious Brent of Bin Bin. What helped Miles to overcome the bouts of depression that followed her periods of intense creativity was her grand aim to save enough money to endow a monetary prize to encourage Australian authors. She also wanted to keep the name 'Miles Franklin' in the public eye. Outwardly she had changed; inwardly she was still the little girl who wanted to be the centre of attention amongst her family.

Through writing hundreds of letters Miles struck up acquaintances with younger authors whose work she admired. She wrote them glowing letters of congratulation when their books appeared in print. Some, like the charismatic, warm-hearted Katharine Susannah Prichard, hard working, loyal Jean Devanny and the perceptive Eleanor Dark, Miles met and felt at ease with. This group of talented left-wing, feminist writers provided her with sympathetic support through letters.[48] Miles extended her penfriendships with young male and female authors by issuing invitations to excellent dinners at Carlton which she cooked herself, with vegetables from the garden and eggs from her own bantams.

In 1930 Miles had made contact by letter with Katharine Susannah Prichard (then in her mid-forties) when she wrote to congratulate her on her prize-winning children's book *The Wild Oats of Han*.[49] Miles advised Katharine that she *must* protect her copyrights and not sell them outright to the publisher, however short of money she might be. After the Great Depression started to bite Prichard replied to Miles, thanking her and saying that although selling a work outright to her publisher might bring her a useful sum, she now realised it would cut her chances of making more money from further editions.[50] The result of this good advice was a long friendship between the two writers. Prichard was a highly sexed woman and very different to Miles; she embraced the writings of D.H. Lawrence and his concept of free love enthusiastically. But both women had parents who had lost all their money, a contributory factor to their left-wing views. (However, unlike Prichard and Devanny, Miles was never a card-carrying communist.) Both Franklin and Katharine Susannah Prichard loved their land with an intense passion and wanted Australia to have a literature of its own.

The beauty of the bush inspired Miles' best descriptive passages. She described its vastness and silence, the bubbling creeks and rivers of the Monaro, the yellow wattles in bloom, the gum trees harbouring green and red parrots and pink galahs, pied magpies with their harsh calls and the kookaburra or jackass, whose laugh was so strong he must never be caged (a phrase she adopted as the title for a later book, *Laughter, not for a cage* (1956)).

Miles also corresponded with the bespectacled academic historian, author, critic and librarian Marjorie Barnard, twenty years younger than herself. Barnard had a first-class arts degree from the University of Sydney, something that made Miles feel distinctly inferior. Barnard had worked as a librarian at the Sydney Technical College and the University of Sydney and received literary acclaim for the novels she wrote with her equally well-qualified colleague, Flora Eldershaw. Their joint novel *A House is Built* had tied with Prichard's *Coonardoo* to win first prize in the *Bulletin's* annual literary competition, a prize Miles dreamed of winning.

Franklin had an uneasy relationship with Barnard, referring to her in private as 'a top notcher in denigrating dead authors'. In public both writers *professed* warm friendship and admiration. On occasions when necessary they wrote pleasant letters to each other, although each could be vitriolic about the other. In private, Miles called Barnard 'the potato wife' for her slavish devotion to her married lover, Frank Dalby Davidson. Miles knew Davidson would never marry Barnard and was merely using her as an unpaid editor and a sexual convenience.[51] For her part, Barnard made no secret of the fact that she did not approve of Miles' verbose literary style, her use of long 'made-up words' or the way she felt Miles' untrained mind was unable to critique literature properly. To students of literature Barnard made scathing criticisms about Miles' prose style.

Barnard's criticisms infuriated Miles, who feared (quite justifiably as it turned out) that the younger Barnard would outlive her and write critically about her after her death. As Miles wryly observed on several occasions, 'prospective biographers lent a new fear to death itself'. Marjorie Barnard, tired of Miles' evasions and lies about the Bin Bin novels, always suspected Miles had written them. She compared Brent's use of made-up words like *orgulous, burstatiously* and *parvanimity* with words Franklin had concocted in other books. But try as she might to trick her into it, Barnard could never get Miles to confirm that she *was* Brent of Bin Bin.

Strangely enough, neither Barnard nor the literary critic Frederick Macartney picked up an important clue that the place name Bin Bin also occurs in *My Brilliant Career*, and was a station that had once belonged to the Franklin family. In 1956 Frederick Macartney, the author of a standard bibliography of Australian literature, who had interviewed Miles Franklin shortly before her death, noted 'striking similarities' between *My Brilliant Career* and the Brent of Bin Bin books, but added wistfully: 'Franklin does *not countenance any such suspicion* [that she is their author]'.[52] It was left to a subsequent biographer, Professor Colin Roderick, to prove that Miles and Brent of Bin Bin *were* one and the same person.

The situation between Miles and her mother could be explosive. The two women had never understood each other and living together did not draw them closer. On Miles' side there was admiration for her mother's 'good' qualities, but Susannah Franklin made it very clear that she had no time for feminist ideas or a writing career and was annoyed her only surviving daughter had not married and given her grandchildren. In *My Brilliant Career*, Miles had summed up their differences when she wrote: 'My mother and I are too unlike ... She no more understood me than I understand the works of a watch'. They argued bitterly. Susannah Franklin resented the hours her daughter spent writing instead of housekeeping or jam making, and that whenever the cooking and housework became too much for her Miles paid for a cleaner to lighten her domestic burden.[53]

In 1935 Miles was awarded the King's Silver Jubilee Medal for Literature, which encouraged her greatly. She was already a member of the Fellowship of Australian Writers and she now joined the Sydney PEN Club, which attempted to protect left-wing authors in countries like Nazi Germany, where freedom of speech was often denied. Miles supported the PEN club and its efforts to raise funds to defend radical Czech journalist Egon Kisch, who had been invited to speak at an anti-war conference but was banned from landing in Australia.

Miles was on firm ground once more as she wrote about Australian pioneers in her last 'big' book, *All That Swagger*, based on a manuscript she had started in London, in which she aimed to produce an Australian version of the famous 'Forsyte' sagas of John Galsworthy. *All That Swagger* described four generations of an Australian-Irish family and incorporated events from the lives of her own forebears. Caring for her mother took up so much of her time that *All That Swagger* took two years to complete, partly in the small cramped house in Carlton and partly in a room in a local hotel that Miles rented to give herself some space. (Her mother railed against this which she regarded as a total waste of money.)

The typescript was submitted for the *Bulletin*'s annual S.H. Prior Memorial Prize for Australian Literature, which Miles had long coveted, under the assumed name of 'Captain Bligh'. The central character, Danny Delacy, was partly modelled on Miles' Irish great-great-grandfather Joseph Franklin and partly on her maternal grandfather, Holtman Lampe. Danny Delacey arrives in Australia at the age of eighteen and settles in the wild country of the Murrumbidgee to breed horses and cattle, but dies as the result of a riding accident (like Holtman Lampe, who lost the use of one leg). Danny's wife, Joanna, was partly based on her mother's early life, including her long ride through the snow to a homestead where a white woman could deliver her child.

All That Swagger, published in 1936, hit a nerve in what was then a very rural society. Australians took Franklin's book to their hearts and it sold well, although without an agent to negotiate her publishing contract Miles made very little money from it. However, the book did win her the coveted S.H. Prior Memorial Prize, which gave her some extra money, and it was serialised in the *Bulletin*.

Winning the prize for *All That Swagger* marked a turning point in what had been for years a less than brilliant career. It vindicated Miles' decision to continue writing in spite of owning a trunk filled with unpublished manuscripts and rejection slips. As the winner of a major literary prize, Miles felt that Barnard and her academic cronies would *have* to respect her work, and to some extent it did change their opinions. However, Barnard saw Miles as a consummate liar and later wrote unflatteringly in her biography of Franklin: 'Who would know from what Miles said, whether it was the truth or not?'

Miles could be a bitter and malicious enemy but she held a special place in her heart for old friends from Ostrovo days. She corresponded with Dr Agnes Bennett, who was now working in a hospital in New Zealand. In 1937 Miles visited Melbourne and friends drove her to Geelong so that she could meet up with warm-hearted Dr Mary de Garis, another former colleague from Ostrovo with whom she enjoyed a very happy reunion and heard news of the volunteer nurses, cooks and ambulance drivers she had worked with.

In 1937 Miles buried the hatchet and contributed an article about Rose Scott for *The Peaceful Army*, a book edited by Barnard and her friend Florence Eldershaw designed to celebrate the achievements of women to mark Australia's sesquicentenary. It was a moving tribute to her mentor explaining in detail Scott's achievements towards raising the status of women in Australia.

Cecil Palmer, one of Miles' British publishers, had gone bankrupt, owing Miles six months' royalties. Miles considered her books to be her children. She bought back all the unsold copies of *Old Blastus of Bandicoot* and the rights to her unpublished detective novel *Bring the Monkey* from Palmer's liquidator, planning to have them republished by the erratic but enthusiastic 'Inky' Stephenson, who was planning to set up a publishing house in Sydney. Inky promised Miles her would employ her London friend, Jean Hamilton.

Life with Inky was never dull. For Miles their relationship as author and publisher involved brilliant talks, long lingering lunches and a trip to Norman Lindsay's home at Springwood to discuss Miles' projected books, Miles' flow of words dazzling Inky and the other guests. Unfortunately for Miles, although Inky's Endeavour Press did publish *Bring the Monkey*, like her London publisher he also went bankrupt.[54] It did not help Inky or Miles that *Bring the Monkey* resembled a third-rate Agatha Christie novel with a touch of burlesque. The plot hinged on a jewel theft in the stately home of Lord and Lady Tattingwood involving a tame monkey and the murder of a police inspector. As Miles knew little about the speech patterns or lives of the English aristocracy, the book is neither funny nor accurate. The monkey, based on the one who had lived in Miles' Kensington apartment, remains the most entertaining character. The book failed along with Inky's publishing ventures, so Jean remained in London and their friendship continued by correspondence.

Susannah Franklin continued to resent the fact that Miles spent so much time and effort writing books that never made any money. She showed a total lack of sympathy to the fact that her childless daughter saw her books as an extension of herself. Miles retaliated by complaining bitterly to friends that she was being used as a cleaning lady by her mother. 'I have to be a charwoman and a nurse ... My mother is very wearing,' she told Alice Henry, adding that Susannah, now bedridden and fretful and demanding due to insomnia, was 'not content with herself and would not allow anyone else to be'.

In this era there were no retirement homes and unmarried daughters usually devoted a large part of their lives to caring for elderly parents. Ironically, Barnard and Franklin both nursed and kept house for ageing and unappreciative parents while they were yearning for free time to write. Miles bravely shouldered the burden of care for her mother, whose kidney problems and insomnia slowly worsened, often keeping Miles up half the night attending to her.

Miles' role as full-time nurse-housekeeper severely limited her writing time and her ability to attend literary functions, as she could not leave her mother alone in the house. 'I have not put in such a year and a half in my life, never one moment off from the strain and stress. It was the purest kind of hell', she wrote. In 1935 she told Alice Henry: 'I am very weary and have no one to stay with my mother, so can only get out by chance.'

The former gadabout feminist now sat at home each evening, the only free time she had to type up her notes or to write long letters to Mary Fullerton, who acted as her London agent, trying to sell her unpublished manuscripts and chase up unpaid royalties. Miles was always very generous in promoting the work of others, carrying pages of their manuscripts around in her 'dilly bag' and showing them to anyone who might help them on the occasions when she did manage to escape from Carlton and attend a literary function.

Her burden of care was lifted when her mother died on 15 June 1938, leaving Miles grief-stricken and remorseful, particularly when she remembered how 'difficult' she had been to her hard working mother as a moody rebellious teenager. She regretted that she had caused her mother so much pain over the publication of *My Brilliant Career* and felt guilty that she had not appreciated her enough while she was alive.

Alone in the little weatherboard house at Carlton, Miles now suffered from insomnia. She had inherited half her mother's money and property, the rest going to her sole surviving brother Norman. As a result of her grief and guilt she suffered yet another bout of reactive depression, losing her appetite and zest for life. About to turn sixty and terrified of ageing and death, she continued the myth that she was years younger than her real age. What pulled Miles through the final months of 1938 and the start of 1939 was having Kate Baker as a house guest. Kate came to stay at Carlton so that she and Miles could work on their joint memoir of the author Joseph Furphy, who had encouraged both women in their chosen careers.

Once Kate had departed, Miles enjoyed a refreshing camping and riding holiday with her cousins Ruby and Leslie Bridle, revisiting scenes of her childhood at Talbingo and reviving childhood memories which she would use in future novels written under her own name and that of Brent of Bin Bin. Kate Baker and Miles Franklin's biographical essay *Who was Joseph Furphy?* was entered for the S.H. Prior Memorial Prize. A biography of Governor Macquarie was awarded the bulk of the prize money, leaving Miles and Kate to share a hundred pounds between them. Fortunately, Miles was given a Commonwealth literary grant to turn the essay on Furphy into a full-length book.

Jean Devanny wrote a joint letter to Miles and Kate praising the book and congratulating them 'for their contributions to the history and achievements of Australia'. Miles responded by telling Devanny that she was torn between many loyalties, saying that she had given 'my love years, my youth, my security' to 'the struggle for freedom' —

by which she presumably meant female freedom. She ended the letter by explaining that only recently had she been able to return to 'my one great abiding love, Australia, our magic land'.[55]

In September 1939 World War II broke out in Europe. Germany invaded Poland, having struck a non-aggression pact with Russia, who also invaded Poland. Britain and France, who had guaranteed Polish neutrality, declared war on Germany. Australia, as a member of the British Commonwealth, dispatched troops to North Africa, although it was Japan that would soon become her greatest threat.

However, Miles was too old to volunteer as a cook or nurse or become deeply involved in the latest hostilities. 'This time I shan't be traipsing around among wolves and Serbs and rats,' she wrote to Jean Hamilton and Mary Fullerton in wartime London.

In 1940 the Battle of Britain, when Britain stood alone against Germany, marked a turning point for Miles the pacifist. She worried about friends in London such as frail Mary Fullerton. In February 1942 Singapore fell, and the Japanese bombed Darwin at the end of the month. America's General Douglas MacArthur set up his command in Brisbane; American troops arrived in large numbers, replacing Australian soldiers who had been sent to fight overseas.

When Miles' remaining sibling, Norman John Franklin, died of a heart attack, she slid into yet another period of depression. Like her previous bouts, this one affected her ability to sleep, her will to live, her powers of concentration and her appetite. She felt ill, old and alone, especially in winter.

What finally lifted her depression was the fact Miles became a broadcasting success. Like her Irish father, she had 'the gift of the blarney'. She was rarely at a loss for words and could, when she felt like it, be extremely witty and entertaining. She loved attention, and popularity on the airwaves made her feel wanted again. In 1943 she was asked to give (unpaid) a broadcast on the ABC called 'The Birth Pangs of the Australian Novel', a topic that interested her passionately. Lacking any lecturing experience or academic qualifications she was nervous about the broadcast, but received a swag of congratulatory letters praising her sparkling delivery and wit.

The ABC considered her an excellent speaker and more broadcasts were commissioned. Eventually there would be radio serialisations of

All That Swagger and the Brent of Bin Bin novels. She also gave a series of broadcasts to schools called 'My Life and My Books'.

By now Miles was frequenting the bare upstairs room that acted as headquarters to the Federation of Australian Writers, an organisation that achieved a great deal in promoting Australian writing before the formation of the Australian Society of Authors (the ASA). (After years of persistence the ASA would eventually persuade the federal government to provide money for the Public Lending Right scheme, to compensate Australian authors for books bought by public libraries, as book-borrowing diminished rather than added to authors' incomes.)

Miles saw feminism as giving women the right to choose between marriage or a career. She had never hated men and still enjoyed their company. However, one male writer she viewed with an ironic eye was Xavier Herbert, who visited her at Carlton. 'You and I are the only two great Australian novelists,' he told her. Miles, who was often in despair because of the poor sales of her books, did not believe him. She knew just how hard Sadie Herbert, Xavier's wife, worked to support him as a writer and was most unimpressed when the self-styled 'Don Juan of northern Queensland' listed the names of all his female conquests. His kiss-and-tell revelations and frequent betrayal of Sadie reinforced what Miles already thought about the male sex drive and the difficulties of matrimony.

A few years later, at the request of the Western Australian writer Henrietta Drake-Brockman and Katharine Susannah Prichard, Miles enlarged her ABC broadcasts and turned them into a series of lectures on Australian literature which she gave in Western Australia. Subsequently they appeared as the book *Laughter, not for a cage* (1956). She started with Australia's first convict novels and went through Australian literature in chronological order, contemporaries she regarded as important included Kylie Tennant, Katharine Susannah Prichard, Jean Devanny, Xavier Herbert and Henrietta Drake-Brockman — and of course Miles included Brent of Bin Bin among them without revealing 'his' true identity.

All this time Miles had been living frugally to save money for her great plan, the Big Prize. In August 1943 she drew up a will making provision for a literary prize that would bear her name.

In October she wrote to Dymphna Cusack, telling her that she had torn up all her love letters, including some that apparently contained proposals of marriage, to 'ensure that there will be no data on my love life'. She was determined to foil the investigations of potential biographers such as Marjorie Barnard and Colin Roderick. (Katharine Susannah Prichard also destroyed significant letters in what she termed 'a rage for privacy'.) According to Miles, an American senator had telephoned her to ask if she remembered how he had proposed to her on board the ship in which she had left Australia for America in her mid-twenties. Miles, who retained her impish sense of humour, demanded, 'And are you proposing *now*?' The Senator replied: 'Yes, provided you are the same radiant creature I knew.'

'Don't be an ass,' Miles retorted. 'How radiant would *you* be after thirty years?'[56]

In 1944 the joint tribute to their friend and mentor Joseph Furphy which she and Kate Baker had written, *Joseph Furphy — The Legend of the Man and his Book*, was published with Miles' name in pride of place on the title page. Relegation to second place infuriated Baker and shattered their long friendship; Miles had insisted to the publishers that her name must be placed first since she was the senior author. Now another friend was gone. Years later, hearing that Kate Baker was ill and knowing that she had little money, Miles sent two anonymous donations of money to her, fearing Baker would refuse them if she knew their source.

Just before Christmas 1943 Miles was asked to give a broadcast on ABC radio on the Australian novel. With deep feeling she spoke about the financial difficulties of being a novelist in a country with a tiny reading population where publishers saw imported 'pulp' fiction as big business and considered bestsellers from England and America their most important products.

In 1944 Miles paid her final visit to the Brindabella ranges, the place she thought the most beautiful in the world.

The following year the war ended. To celebrate, Miles and Dymphna Cusack contributed to a play called *Summon Up Your Ghosts*, which won Melbourne's New Theatre's one-act play competition along with *Sailors Girl* by Ric Throssell, Katharine Susannah Prichard's son, who worked in the Department of Foreign Affairs in Canberra. Miles had entered his play under an assumed name. She adored Ric and, due to his mother's unpopularity over her communist affiliations, she quite often entered his work in competitions in this way.[57]

In *Summon Up Your Ghosts*, both authors expressed their dissatisfaction with Australian publishers who would not publish their work and bookshops that refused to sell it when it *was* published because there was such a small market for Australian books. Their play is set in a bookshop haunted by a talking ghost who keeps plaintively demanding that Australian voices be heard in print. The plot centres on an American ex-serviceman about to return home who tries in vain to buy books about Australia from the saleslady, Miss Gumbootle. She tells him that as no one buys Australian literature, they have used all the remaining unsold Australian novels as sand bags in case of air raids.

Mr Friend, an Australian publisher, claims that, as a businessman, he can't *afford* to publish Australian books: the firm would lose money and alienate their shareholders. He claims that Australians *talk* about buying Australian literature but instead buy books from overseas.

'We haven't the population to make Australian books pay,' observes Professor McChaucer, head of a university department of English literature, who is browsing in the shop. From the attic upstairs the (Australian) ghost can be heard chanting: 'Let our songs be sung and our stories told. Call up your ghosts, Australia. Set them riding far to rouse a sleeping nation.'

The surrender of Germany was followed by that of Japan. Miles' favourite nephew, Norman John Franklin, always known as 'John' to distinguish him from his father, came home after distinguished service in the Pacific as a pilot. He was smoking and drinking too much and claimed the war had taken a considerable toll on his nerves.

Miles was greatly cheered when Melbourne's Georgian House published the long-delayed and much amended sequel to *My Brilliant Career*, now retitled *My Career Goes Bung* instead of Miles' original, more poetic title *The End of the Road*. It appeared in 1946. Henrietta Drake-Brockman wrote to congratulate her, calling it an enchanting and very amusing book.[58]

In February that same year Miles was saddened by news of the death of Alice Henry, her last link with that period of relative freedom in her twenties when they had both worked so hard for women's suffrage and the trade union movement in Chicago.[59]

By this time communist Russia, under Stalin's iron hand, was no longer tolerated as it had been during the war, when communist support was needed against the Germans. America, under McCarthy, was becoming hysterical about 'reds under the bed'. There was less hysteria in Australia, though many conservatives regarded Miles Franklin as being in league with her friends, the communist writers Jean Devanny and Katharine Susannah Prichard.

All Miles wanted to do now was to live cheaply and save any money she might earn from writing to put towards what she hoped would be a handsome literary prize for Australian authors. Her income from the rent of the two little shops decreased as inflation soared. However, habits of thrift taught by her mother were deeply ingrained. She saved candle ends, string and brown paper, and collected free kindling wood. She spent little on herself, mending her worn black dresses and black cotton stockings and wearing her shoes until the soles were paper thin. She did anything and everything to save money, determined to leave as much as possible to found 'The Miles Franklin Award', which would perpetuate her name. This goal helped to console her for the fact that she had not achieved the brilliant career of her dreams.

Fired by encouragement from friends, Miles wrote a sparkling account of her first ten years. *Childhood at Brindabella* was not published until almost a decade after her death, when it became another classic Australian book. Remembering the family furore caused by the publication of *My Brilliant Career*, she was careful to give pseudonyms to the few remittance men, convicts and black sheep in the family. She also changed some place names and called aunts and uncles by their initials.

She learnt that her handsome nephew John, whose visits to Carlton she joyfully anticipated, was now drinking to excess. Miles, who had always been a teetotaller, was horrified. She went to see her nephew's doctor, who told her that if John continued drinking like this his liver would be damaged and he would die of cirrhosis. She found her nephew's violence under the influence of alcohol hard to understand and very depressing.

When John Franklin finally drank himself to death, as his doctor had predicted, Miles realised she was the last surviving member of what had once been a large branch of the Franklin family.

She still attended literary occasions with eyes twinkling behind her wire-rimmed glasses, but there were deep shadows beneath them, the product of sleepless nights, lower back pain and palpitations. Her doctor informed her that she had developed a serious and incurable heart problem.

In her seventies Miles dressed entirely in black and often wore a black velvet ribbon to hide her wattled neck. She did not look like a radical; in fact she looked more like Mary Poppins with her black umbrella, white gloves, long dark skirt and white high-necked blouse. In this outmoded garb she attended meetings and functions held by the Fellowship of Australian Authors in York Street, often wearing an awesomely large hat trimmed with flowers and carrying what she called her 'dilly bag'. The bag bulged with sweets for children and pages of her own and other people's manuscripts, which she would show to anyone who appeared interested. Using a Sydney post office box, she wrote to publishers under the pen name 'William Blake' to try to persuade them to republish the Brent of Bin Bin novels.

At a Commonwealth Literary Fund lecture in 1950 Miles made an important speech, declaring: 'Without an indigenous literature, people can remain alien in their own soil. An unsung country does not fully exist or enjoy adequate international exchange in the inner life.' She continued to save money, but knew the balance to provide a suitable prize would have to be provided by the sale of the Carlton house after her death.

Nancy Keesing, then an unknown young writer, described how Miles inspired terror in some of her contemporaries, for she could be forthright or downright unpleasant to those she did not like. Keesing once accompanied two male authors Miles had invited to dinner out to Carlton. On the walk from the station to Miles' home they were caught in a storm and arrived bedraggled and dripping on Miles' doorstep. Knowing herself to be uninvited, Keesing was scared of Miles' caustic tongue; however, as an aspiring author she was prepared to take the risk in order to meet the writer of one of her favourite books, *My Brilliant Career*.

Much to Keesing's surprise Miles was kindness itself. She insisted on finding a dry towel for the young woman, helped rub her hair dry and sat her down in a large armchair in front of a roaring fire. Miles had cooked one of her excellent roast dinners and plied the trio with food and cups of tea. She insisted Nancy Keesing should write her name in her 'waratah visitors' book' and drink her tea from a china cup with waratahs painted on it. Miles' warmth and encouragement helped young Nancy Keesing to continue writing. In her turn Keesing would become a benefactor to other writers and donate what is now known as the Keesing Studio in Paris for the use of Australian authors — since Keesing's death it has been administered by the Australia Council. She also instigated the Australian Authors' Benefit Fund for impoverished writers.[60]

'Loneliness is a terrible price to pay for independence,' Aunt Lena had warned the adolescent Stella Miles Franklin. Late in life Franklin made the bitter discovery that Aunt Lena had been right. Her almost pathological fear of death caught up with her. Miles, the bush lover who had seen so many animals die in drought and bush fire, who had known the deaths of her brothers, sisters and parents and held the hands of dying soldiers at Ostrovo, was terrified of dying alone.

Early in September 1954 Miles' nightmare was realised when she suffered a heart attack alone in her Carlton house. She lay undiscovered on the floor for a day and a night, unable to crawl to the phone and fearing no one would find her. Eventually a neighbour called; after receiving no reply the police were summoned and then broke down the door. Miles was taken by ambulance to Drummoyne Hospital, where she spent her last few weeks.

She died at Drummoyne on 19 September 1954, a month before her seventy-fifth birthday, surrounded by strangers as she had feared. Her death certificate gives the cause of death as chronic myocarditis (inflammation of the walls of the heart) and pleurisy. She left instructions that she was to be cremated with Anglican rites (she had been confirmed in the Anglican church at Collector, New South Wales, to please her father). As Talbingo homestead was now under water as the result of a conservation scheme, she requested that her ashes be scattered in Talbingo's Jounama Creek. And so Miles Franklin returned home to the place she loved most.

The influence and legacy of Miles Franklin and Rose Scott has been very significant. Today, almost half the young women of Australia aim for some kind of higher education. Their parents no longer tell them that a career rules out marriage, or vice versa. Singledom (called spinsterhood when Miles was young) has lost its connotations of abject failure. Many women now lead productive, happy lives without marrying. Female concern with marriage versus a career, which featured so largely in Franklin's novels, has now been replaced by concerns such as the ubiquitous glass ceiling and/or the availability of good childcare. *My Brilliant Career* has never lost its appeal for female readers and has rarely been out of print, and became even more widely known in Australia and overseas through the film version of the story.

The generous terms of Miles Franklin's bequest astonished authors who had always believed her to be as poor as a church mouse. The Miles Franklin Award has become Australia's answer to Britain's Booker Prize and America's Pulitzer Prize. Miles stipulated that entries, which must be novels (or plays), should reveal 'some aspect of Australian life in all its phases'. Prize-winners include Patrick White (who won with *Voss* in 1957), Xavier Herbert, Thea Astley, Thomas Keneally, David Ireland, Jessica Anderson, Christopher Koch, Tim Winton and Peter Carey. This important prize has provided a boost to the winners' book sales and careers.[61] Today the Miles Franklin Award consists of a cash prize of almost $30,000, thanks to judicious investment of Franklin's original £9000 by the trustees. As she had intended, Miles Franklin's literary prize keeps her name before the public year by year.

CHAPTER TWENTY-TWO

Portrait photograph: Author's collection. Schoolgirl Margaret Sutherland, painted in oils by her cousin, Jane.

Jane Sutherland
(1855–1928)

and

Margaret Sutherland
(1897–1984)

and

Louise Bertha Hanson-Dyer
(1884–1962)

OUTSTANDING WOMEN IN ART AND MUSIC

The parents of Jane Sutherland and those of her niece, Margaret, were hard working Scots who emigrated to Australia. Both women grew up in households where education, art and music were highly valued. In the Sutherland's small home at Kew money was always scarce, for Margaret's father died of a heart attack when she was still a child and there was no widow's pension at that time. Unfortunately, heart disease was the hereditary curse of the Sutherland family.

By the end of her long life Margaret Sutherland would merit an entry in the prestigious *Grove Dictionary of Music,* the bible of the international world of classical music, which describes her as one of 'the first Australian composers to write in an idiom comparable with that of her generation in Europe'. Today some of her chamber music and songs are available on records, on a compact disc and on a video documentary about Australian female composers.[1] But all this was achieved as a result of hardship and struggle.

Margaret Sutherland's father, George, from a working-class Scottish family, had received a sound basic education but was denied a chance to attend university through lack of money. He acquired a passion for art and music after he became a journalist. He married Ada Bowen, a girl with musical talent, and they emigrated to Adelaide where Margaret, their fifth child, was born in 1897. Five years later the family moved to Melbourne, where George was appointed principal lead writer for the Melbourne *Age.* In Melbourne George Sutherland joined his brothers and sisters, who had also emigrated to Australia.

Sadly, the move from Adelaide to Melbourne coincided with the premature death of George's elder brother, who suffered from the family heart complaint. He left a widow and three daughters without much income to support them. One of George's sisters was Jane Sutherland, a brilliant artist. Unfortunately she too had inherited heart problems and suffered a heart attack that left her semi-paralysed shortly before George arrived in Melbourne.

On their arrival in Melbourne, George, Ada and his two sons and three daughters lived for a short time with his brother's widow—as did Jane and her two unmarried sisters, Jessie and Julia Sutherland. Jessie was a talented singer and Julia was an outstanding pianist. Two of their surviving brothers, William and James, were scientists with a love of the arts. The Sutherlands were one of those exceptional Australian families like the Boyds or the MacKerris clan, among whom high intelligence and creative talents abound.

Margaret was only four when she came to live with her cultured and art-loving aunts in Melbourne — a move which proved vital to her musical development. She was an attractive and impressionable child much loved by her unmarried aunts, and Jane Sutherland painted several portraits of her niece in a white frilly pinafore. Margaret recalled how her Aunt Jane's heart attack had left her unable to paint the large oils she had previously produced. Confined to a wheelchair, Jane Sutherland was forced to channel her creative urge into new areas. Previously she had enjoyed working on large, almost 'masculine' canvases; now she painted much smaller works in oils or pastels, a medium in which her technique rivalled that of Degas or Mary Cassatt. Margaret recalled that her Aunt Jane 'did have some sort of pastels and did portraits of me when I was quite small. She would have it [the portrait] on her knee. That was all she could do at the time'.[2]

Jane Sutherland was nine years old when she arrived in Australia in 1863 from America. She had been in New York, as her parents emigrated first to America. Her father, who possessed the typical Sutherland intellectual ability and creativity, married young. Lacking a formal education, he supported his family of three daughters and five sons by carving ship's figureheads, as well as teaching music, painting and producing engravings. When the family settled in Melbourne, Jane's brothers attended the University of Melbourne. Jane's younger brother, William, became a brilliant physicist in the field of molecular dynamics. He too had a passion for music. Both Jane and her niece Margaret adored William, whose devotion to his invalid sister was exemplary.

Jane spent fourteen years studying art at the National Gallery School (now the Victorian College of the Arts), hoping to become a professional artist at a time when most young women studying art were painting purely for pleasure. In 1883 she was awarded the Walker Prize for figure drawing.

Jane and her friend Clara Southern set up a teaching studio in Grosvenor Chambers, the building where Tom Roberts also had his studio. In August 1889 Sutherland produced a few small, rapidly executed oils or 'Impressions' for the famous 9 x 5 exhibition organised by Tom Roberts. Strangely enough, Jane's 'Impressions' were never exhibited.[3] Because of her heart trouble Jane was not a prolific artist; she produced around thirty large oils and the same number of pastel portraits during her lifetime.[4] And she used only her relations as models — her sisters Julia and Jessie or her beautiful nieces Margaret and Dorothy, as Jane could not afford to pay professional models.

Few of Jane Sutherland's paintings remain with family descendants today; most are in public galleries. A portrait of Margaret as a girl emphasises the strong outline of Margaret's lower jaw and suggests strength of character and determination.

Jane Sutherland's weak heart ensured that her artistic output was far smaller than that of Tom Roberts and Arthur Streeton,[5] but she was just as talented as the male members of the Heidelberg School. Sutherland's handling of the colours of the Australian bush is as good as that of McCubbin, her subjects are usually female and her handling of the human figure, although not equal to that of McCubbin or Roberts, is far better than Streeton's. In the late 1880s Jane regularly took part in the famous Heidelberg outdoor painting camps. (Heidelberg and Box Hill were then undeveloped parts of greater Melbourne out in the countryside.) The role of most of the women who were included on these Sunday bush outings was to look decorative in long white muslin skirts and black stockings, pose for the male artists, bring along home-baked cakes and pies, and return home on the late train. Most women of this period believed that 'great art' was for men. In general, middle-class girls were seen as future wives and domesticated guardians of morality. At that period women were the nurturers, the ones who provided the creature comforts — the *subjects* of Heidelberg School paintings rather than their *creators*. Jane Sutherland was the only one seriously intent on taking art outside the confines of the studio and going into the open air to paint the Australian landscape.

Young women were terrified of appearing 'fast' as this would ruin their reputations and marriage prospects. Strict conventions prevented Jane or any of the other female artists from camping in the bush with Roberts and Streeton or staying overnight in the same house with them, at Eaglemont. There were no motorcars and it was too far to bicycle. Instead of staying in the bush camps to paint direct from nature, Jane had to make a tiring and costly journey each day with her paints, canvas and easel.

Her fellow students at these Sundays in the bush, less talented than Jane, wore 'lovely white muslin' and prepared the food while Streeton, Roberts and the rest of the men, accompanied by Miss Sutherland (and sometimes by Clara Southern) departed on their painting jaunt. They discussed art and criticised each other's output, working until late afternoon. Shaded by pine trees, long trestle tables set out by the other girls and laden with what Streeton called 'a feast fit for the gods' awaited their return.

One of Jane's best works, *Obstruction, Box Hill*, showing a young woman gazing at the creek which blocks her path, is as well painted as any work by McCubbin, Roberts or Streeton. Is there some symbolism in the way the creek blocks the path of the young woman in this painting? In 1887 it was exhibited at the Australian Artists' Association and was priced at ten guineas — less than a quarter of the price for a comparable work by Streeton or Roberts in spite of its quality. The painting remained unsold and was exhibited again three years later, at the Victorian Artists' Society show.

Gentler in tone than Roberts and less dramatic than McCubbin, Jane Sutherland's works are excellent for their handling of the human figure and the clever way in which she captured the distinctive colours of the Australian bush. Like other members of the Heidelberg School, Jane's style and subject matter were influenced by artists of the French Barbizon School such as Jules Bastien Lepage and Millet, rather than that of the higher toned French Impressionists such as Monet and Renoir. *Obstruction, Box Hill* is a truly 'Heidelberg' work by a most talented artist who deserves to be just as well known as her male colleagues. But a career in art or music was not easy for either men or women to achieve earlier this century. It was virtually impossible for women to survive professionally, however talented they might be.

When Jane Sutherland suffered a heart attack in her early fifties she was denied the chance to continue painting landscapes, though occasionally her brother William would take her in her wheelchair to the banks of the Yarra, where she made a series of small paintings.

Women were simply not permitted to sell their paintings for the kind of serious money that brings artistic prestige. To bring in additional income, whenever Jane felt well enough she taught art to young women. Her sister Julia earned money by giving piano lessons, while Jessie cared for the ailing Jane and acted as housekeeper.

Margaret Sutherland was only too aware of the hereditary Sutherland heart disease and the brevity of life. Her uncles William, Alexander and James died from the disease; her Aunt Jane was an invalid. And when Margaret's sister Ruth died at a young age from a burst appendix, the news of her death caused George Sutherland, their father, to suffer a fatal heart attack. Margaret was only a child at this time, in her first term at school in Kew. George Sutherland, like his elder brother, suffered a rupture of the aortic valve of the heart; he died spouting a torrent of blood, horrendous for his wife to witness, and she never recovered properly from the shock. After her husband's death, Ada Sutherland became a depressed soul and rarely played the piano or sang *lieder* any more.

Both Margaret and her elder sister, Dorothy, loved the piano. Dorothy dreamed of becoming a concert pianist. They would visit their three aunts — Jane, Julia and Jessie — and perform small pieces for them in their music room, which was hung with Aunt Jane's paintings as well as others by her friend and teacher Frederick McCubbin. These were some of the happiest times in Margaret's childhood.

Margaret Sutherland grew up knowing that a career in the arts was a hard undertaking, but she observed the joy of creativity experienced by her Aunt Jane. At an early age she decided she wanted to be a composer rather than a performer, and she was painfully aware that this path was even more difficult to follow. For the fatherless, penniless Margaret and Dorothy Sutherland, whose mother survived on a widow's pension, it seemed almost impossible to become professional musicians. Dorothy, with her red-gold hair and blue eyes, was the prettier of the two sisters, but she lacked Margaret's iron determination.

In 1905, when Dorothy turned sixteen and shortage of money meant that she had to leave school, she abandoned her dream. She put a notice in a shop window and gave piano lessons to local children in the front room of their modest house in order to provide much needed extra income.

Margaret had a stronger sense of purpose. She knew she had talent and decided to try for a scholarship to the Marshall Hall Conservatorium. In 1914, just as World War I broke out, Margaret's rendering of one of her own compositions won her a scholarship to the Conservatorium. At the time Marshall Hall himself (a close friend of Nellie Melba) was overseas. In his absence Margaret studied piano and composition with two talented European teachers, Edward Goll and Fritz Hart, who would later work with Melba.

At the height of anti-German sentiment during World War I, urchins threw bricks through the windows of migrants with German-sounding names. Due to such intense feeling there were demonstrations against the 'German' Edward Goll as Musical Director of the Conservatorium, and the result was that the unfortunate Goll, like others with German-sounding names, was dismissed from his post. Ironically, Goll — an excellent teacher — was actually a Czech; but to bigoted Hun-haters his name seemed suspiciously foreign. However, in 1915 Goll was appointed as a teacher at the University of Melbourne Conservatorium, and Margaret Sutherland lost no time in following her favourite teacher there. From 1916 when the Belgian conductor and violinist Henri Verbruggen was appointed to the Sydney Conservatorium, his frequent visits to Melbourne with his string quartet stimulated Margaret's lifelong enthusiasm for chamber music. At Verbruggen's invitation, she visited Sydney when she was nineteen to perform as a concert virtuoso pianist playing Beethoven's Piano Concerto in C major.

In 1918 Margaret was appointed to the music staff of the Presbyterian Ladies' College in East Melbourne. Since she was constantly in need of money for living expenses, she also continued to understudy Goll on his concert tours. The war ended and in 1923, her final year of graduate study, Margaret, as Goll's most outstanding pupil, took over his teaching commitments when he went on leave. She still had her own pupils at school, and spent long hours practising for her appearances in country areas on behalf of the Melbourne Conservatorium (later known as the Melba Conservatorium and the Melba Memorial Conservatorium).[6]

Fortunately, Margaret did not inherit the Sutherland family's heart defect — at that time her workload would have felled anyone less physically fit and strong minded. A chance to become a paid pianist in a travelling orchestra under the leadership of Verbruggen brought her the prospect of a professional performing career, but her excitement ebbed away as the proposed orchestra never eventuated.

It was now that Margaret met another strong-minded woman, blonde, extrovert Louisa Bertha Dyer, born Smith. Louise Smith, thirteen years older than Margaret, was blonde ambition personified, a talented pianist who won the gold medal of London's Royal College of Music and continued her music studies in Edinburgh. Extremely attractive, in 1911, three years after returning to Melbourne, the ambitious Louise married an extremely wealthy music lover, twenty-five years older than herself. Jimmy Dyer, known in the newspapers as 'the linoleum king', had made his fortune in linoleum and enjoyed spoiling the beautiful and somewhat bohemian Louise and indulging her interests. The Dyers founded the British Music Society of Victoria in 1921 and out of their own funds paid the performers handsomely and Margaret performed at several of its recitals.

Louise insisted that the programs be designed by leading artists and at the concerts she reigned supreme wearing the latest Paris fashions, delighting in bringing the best of European culture to what was then a very dull and conservative city. Her portrait was painted by Tom Roberts and today hangs in the National Gallery of Victoria.

In 1928 the Dyers left the confining atmosphere of Melbourne (as they saw it) to live in London and a year later set up house in Paris, where Louise used her husband's money to establish her own music publishing house, Lyre Bird Press (Editions l'Oiseau-Lyre, later to become famous as Oiseau-Lyre recordings). Initially Louise published a twelve-volume series of the music of Couperin, which aroused wide admiration internationally for the high quality of its production and impeccable editing.[7]

Louise had no children; she poured her soul and her organising capacities into supporting talented musicians and poets including the Australian poet John Shaw Neilson, and publishing music scores and eventually recordings.

Louise and her linoleum millionaire could well afford to leave in search of greater artistic experience in Britain and Europe but penniless Margaret had to remain in Melbourne, a city indifferent to Australian composers, especially if they were female.

While Margaret's scholarship paid her tuition fees, it did not provide sufficient money to attend concerts and operas to improve her musical knowledge, nor to help her feed and clothe herself. Passionate about becoming a composer as well as a skilled performer, for years Margaret Sutherland paid out money she could ill afford to study composition with a private teacher. She raised extra income by giving poorly paid piano recitals (women performers commanded far lower fees than men) and through her piano teaching.

The examples of her talented aunts Jane and Julia and their lack of public acceptance in a male-dominated world led Margaret to believe that men and women should have equal career opportunities. She maintained that women's creativity, though different, was just as valuable as that of men. Tougher in personality and body than Jane and Julia Sutherland, their niece was driven by a need to succeed. She was truly a woman in advance of her time. She possessed both courage and creativity, but through no fault of her own her career as a composer and performer was failing to materialise.

The premature deaths of so many loved ones, years of financial insecurity and the declining health and deepening depression of Margaret's mother and her aunt Julia, combined with the disparagement she encountered from men in the world of music, only served to strengthen her character and firm up her resolution. She was driven by a passion to create, but frustrated by lack of opportunity; most of Melbourne's classical music lovers were simply not interested in contemporary music. The few who were could not believe that a woman could compose anything worth listening to.

In the end Margaret became disheartened by this lack of opportunity to create. Worry over her future haunted her. Would she *ever* be taken seriously as a composer? Would she end up giving music lessons to untalented children for a few shillings a month like Aunt Julia? She yearned to escape to Europe and visit concerts and operas and see the international performers she had only read about.

Margaret gained her diploma and left the Conservatorium with enough money saved from years of teaching (which she described as 'sweated labour') to enable her to spend the next two years in Europe.

Then, in September 1923, Margaret's mother, now a wan shadow of her former self, died suddenly of Bright's disease, having told no one about her illness.[8] Margaret's sister Dorothy, overcome by her mother's death, collapsed from overwork. Her blighted ambition, financial anxieties and the burden of caring for an ailing mother who was also depressed brought on panic attacks, sleeplessness and despair. Talented Dorothy felt trapped in a life spent teaching small children monotonous scales and exercises in return for a pittance from their parents. She grew pale and listless and could not eat or sleep, nor face going out or meeting strangers. She suffered from agoraphobia and deep depression, for which there was no proper treatment at that time.

Margaret's steamer ticket for London was already booked and paid. Leaving Dorothy in the charge of capable aunt Jessie, who was also caring for her own sisters, Jane and Julia, Margaret embarked on her trip overseas.

In London, the centre of the Empire and springboard for travel to Europe, Margaret Sutherland was thrilled to visit the famous concert halls she had read about. She saved on meals and spent her money attending concerts given by performers she had previously known only through gramophone records. She travelled to Paris and Vienna, often existing on black coffee and dry bread so that she could buy concert tickets, determined to absorb as much as she could of contemporary European orchestral and chamber music. While she was in Paris her friend Louise Dyer gave her some financial support to travel, and great encouragement. Margaret would queue all day for cheap seats to the opera houses of Paris, Vienna and London. Perched high up in 'the gods', she attended concerts and drank in operas she had read about but never had the chance to hear performed. She was overflowing with music, crazy with music, and longed for a piano so that she could work with some of the new ideas that filled her mind. Her strength of purpose to become a composer was reaffirmed.

Back in London, she found a piano and managed to compose. She was still eating poorly and living as cheaply as possible. She was convinced her music was worthy of performance, but had no influential friends to pave the way for her with introductions and words in the right places. She plucked up courage and took what she considered her best pieces to show the great Romantic composer Sir Arnold Bax. She asked him for his comments. He thought her talented and agreed to give her lessons in composition. Bax's tuition was expensive but valuable. Sutherland showed him her *Sonata for Violin and Piano*, composed in 1925. Bax told her patronisingly that the sonata was 'the best work I know written by a *woman*'. He might just as well have remarked that it was the best work ever written by a chimpanzee.

There were times when Margaret Sutherland must have despaired, wondering if anyone would ever take her seriously as a composer because she was a woman and a colonial and, unlike the dazzling Louise Dyer, lacked the acclaim that talent and glamour backed by boundless wealth could bring.

In the initial excitement of actually living overseas Margaret had been able to overlook the cheap, dingy lodging houses which were all she could afford. Her shoes leaked, her clothes were distinctly unfashionable; she had no jewels to wear to the opera. But musically and spiritually she gained great riches from the operas she saw, and from concerts of works by contemporary European composers such as Bartok and Hindemith. For the first time she heard neo-classical works like Stravinsky's *Punchinello,* based on music by Pergolesi, and Ravel's wonderful *Pavane for a Dead Child.* She heard music by Prokofiev, far more avant-garde than anything being performed at that time in Australia.

Margaret's second winter in London was damper and chillier than the first. She realised that living in cheap lodgings smelling of boiled cabbage, stale tobacco and cats' pee during London's freezing winters brought recurrent colds and loneliness. There seemed no chance she would find the fame and financial security she wanted. Her money was fast running out and she had no way of earning more, no social connections to ensure that her truly modern compositions, influenced by contemporary European composers, would ever be performed. The world of musical composition and performance was a tight circle of male power and patronage. The freedom of Margaret Sutherland's sojourn overseas had been liberating and she learned a great deal, but where would it take her?

Margaret did not keep a diary, so it is hard to know whether her decision to return to Melbourne was influenced by her meeting in London with a music-loving doctor from Melbourne who was returning home following a period spent in London acquiring his Diploma of Psychological Medicine.

Towards the end of 1925, Margaret Sutherland's Melbourne friends organised a concert so that they could hear the avant-garde works she had composed overseas. Margaret was well known in Melbourne's musical circles and her concert was well attended — but 'no one seemed to understand what I was driving at', she said afterwards. The appraisal of the male critics (naturally there were no female music critics at this period) was patronising. They concentrated on the fact that she was a woman composer; they regarded her as a freak, an 'oddity', and hinted that her music stemmed from some Freudian unconscious repression. She would, in their opinion, be better off marrying and raising babies. Margaret was deeply discouraged, realising that her new European style of music was totally misunderstood in Australia — that *she* was totally misunderstood.

The doctor whom Margaret had met in London was Norman Albiston. They had previously met a few times at concerts in Melbourne. As two Australians in a foreign city they had been drawn to each other. Little is known about the start of their relationship; some sources state that Dr Albiston followed Miss Sutherland to London, others that they met there merely by chance. Albiston's first marriage to a female doctor had ended in divorce after only one year. He was artistic and had studied art at the George Bell School in Melbourne, and Norman Albiston loved music: he had at one time thought seriously of abandoning medicine in favour of becoming a composer himself but he was deeply interested in psychiatry, and after he gained his post graduate qualifications he became one of Melbourne's first psychiatrists working full-time in private practice.

It was undoubtedly a shared passion for music which drew Norman Albiston and Margaret Sutherland together. She was deeply depressed by her lack of success; as a psychiatrist he had the understanding and the clinical skills to help overcome her depression. Strong willed Margaret might be, but she felt daunted by 'Australia's lack of interest in contemporary music' and experienced periods of self-doubt. She was tired of trying to support herself by giving piano lessons; then she received a proposal of marriage from Norman Albiston. He was interesting, well read, good looking, and was rapidly achieving an excellent reputation in clinical psychiatry. Margaret accepted his proposal. She felt that they had much in common, especially their shared love of music, and she hoped that with a sensitive, supportive partner at her side she would be able to achieve her dream at last and become a successful and respected composer.

Margaret was twenty-nine, sliding into what was then known as 'spinsterhood'. She married Norman Albiston in 1926. Two years later she exchanged a life for a life when her son Mark was born and her adored aunt Jane died.[9] Her aunt's devotion to creativity and her unfailing support had always been a comfort to her niece; her death renewed Margaret's depression. Margaret inherited several of Jane Sutherland's finest paintings, including the delicate oil *The Mushroom Gatherers*, which Margaret would in turn bequeath to the National Gallery of Victoria.

Marriage and motherhood did not bring Margaret Sutherland the contentment she had hoped for, but at least did ensure a measure of financial security. She now lived in an attractive house in the prestigious suburb of Kew. Doubtless Margaret had no understanding of the work a baby would entail in the period before automatic washing machines and other labour-saving devices. It was goodbye to composing and giving recitals once she had her child to look after. Her husband kept long hours at his practice. He had loans outstanding on his medical premises, staff to pay and the need to keep up with a demanding workload as well as the latest developments in psychiatry. Dr Albiston was as dedicated to his patients as his wife was to music; he often did not bill patients who could not afford his services.

Margaret soon discovered she was neither domesticated nor maternal by nature and the marriage became fraught with bitterness. Both husband and wife were driven by a need to succeed; both were highly intelligent, and both had domineering personalities. The marriage had had its conflicts from the beginning, but their relationship finally began to unravel when an exhausted Margaret returned from hospital with their first child. There was no one in her family who could help with the baby. Reliable domestic staff were hard to come by — working-class girls preferred to work in factories and offices rather than help to look after other people's babies. Her husband came home tired and was often on call at night; in any case, it was an era when husbands did not change nappies or help around the house. In the 1920s women's magazines did not run articles about orgasms and infidelity, but advised women to have their husband's slippers ready when he came home, wear a pretty frock and smile brightly at all times.

Margaret detested the mess and noise created by toddlers; she felt caged and cramped by household duties and the never-ending round of what she regarded as boring domestic chores. She resented the weariness and the frustrations connected with bringing up young children — and the guilt she felt because of this resentment. Her husband, tired after a stressful day in the consulting room, wanted the children neatly tucked up in bed, dinner on the table, a shining house and an 'angel of the home'. Instead he found a wife distraught, often at the end of her tether, perpetually frustrated that her talents were going to waste.

Margaret was made to feel 'odd' that she did not enjoy mothering and domesticity. Recriminations followed. She would try to conform to the accepted pattern, but her efforts were often doomed to failure. She wanted time to compose and practise, not to care for two children and a large house and garden. During those first years of marriage Margaret was only able to compose at rare intervals.

As the children grew older she managed to write children's songs and short pieces like *Sebastian the Fox*, designed for them to perform. She enjoyed teaching them the piano and stringed instruments, but the concert halls beckoned and she felt stifled as an artiste. In 1936 she found time to produce *Suite on a Theme of Purcell*, the seventeenth-century Baroque composer whose rich harmonies she much admired. This suite was performed on several occasions by George Szell. That same year she also composed a haunting lament, *Pavane for Orchestra*, influenced by Ravel's neo-classical works. In 1938 she composed *The Soldier* for chorus and strings and *String Quartet*, and in 1939 *Prelude and Jig* as well as small pieces for her children to perform.[10]

On the home front matters deteriorated further. Husband and wife quarrelled fiercely, but they feared that if they separated their children would suffer. Besides, Margaret realised that life for a woman composer trying to bring up children on her own would be worse for all three of them than the disastrous marriage. So the miserable state of affairs, unhappy for both of the Albistons, continued. When their son Mark left home at sixteen rather than going to university (he eventually became an actor), the situation between Margaret and Norman Albiston worsened.

During World War II Margaret threw herself into organising weekly midday concerts for the Red Cross and was an active member of the Council for Education, Music and the Arts which, in conjunction with the Australian Broadcasting Corporation, presented Melbourne's first prom concerts at the Town Hall. As soon as her children were old enough to allow her to return to regular practice sessions, she performed chamber music in Melbourne with Tim and Roy White and their various ensembles. Sutherland's enthusiasm for chamber music was responsible for introducing a great deal of her hitherto unfamiliar repertoire to Australian audiences. Yet to compose as well as perform was still her overriding aim. She wrote: 'To pluck music from the air, that was what made my heart beat faster and that was what I longed passionately to have the opportunity to do.'

It rankled that her husband, during an argument, had actually told her that she was mad for wanting to be a composer. She repeated his accusation with a deepening sense of grievance for the rest of her life.[11] Finally, in 1948, after twenty-two years of marital unhappiness and at a time when divorce was still viewed as scandalous amongst the ultra-conservative medical profession, the Albistons' troubled union was dissolved.[12]

Margaret was now free to lead her own life. Eventually her husband remarried and lived happily with an affluent and talented artist, Valerie Albiston, who was years younger than Margaret. He supported Valerie in her artistic endeavours. The couple had no children, so the same stresses did not arise. It would seem that Margaret received some alimony and she retained the former matrimonial home at Kew, which gave her the sense of financial security she needed in order to be able to write music.[13]

In these final decades of freedom Margaret Sutherland finally came into her own as a composer, and her output of larger-scale works increased dramatically. It must be remembered that up to this time, Sutherland had never been paid any fee to compose relatively long works, something which would have daunted most people's creativity. There were no arts grants to provide time to compose. Everything Margaret did she achieved in her *own* time and at her *own* expense. She showed extraordinary courage and determination in continuing down a lonely road towards her goal.

The international music publishers Boosey and Hawkes raised Margaret's hopes when they wrote to 'M. Sutherland', showing interest in publishing some of her compositions in sheet form. But as soon as they discovered that 'M. Sutherland' was a woman, their interest waned and died.

However, in 1935 Margaret Sutherland's hauntingly beautiful *Sonata for Piano and Violin*, as well as a series of songs she wrote based on poems by Shaw Neilson, was published by the music-loving Louise Dyer, who had followed Margaret's career with admiration for Margaret's tenacity, talent and determination. By now, Louise's Editions de l'Oiseau-Lyre had published superb editions of the works of Purcell. Louise worked with the internationally famous conductor Nadia Boulanger and harpsichordist Wanda Landowska, and these three significant women were key figures in the revival of interest in French and English baroque keyboard music which has since swept the world. In 1934 Louise Dyer received the rare honour for a foreigner and a woman of being appointed a Chevalier de la Légion d'Honneur by the French Government.

When widowed, Louise came home to Melbourne for a year to act as Lady Mayoress for her brother but returned to England and married a youthful admirer, a university teacher almost twenty years younger than herself named Joseph Hanson who shared her passion for music.[14] Naturally, the difference in their respective ages was the subject of much gossip.

Urged on by Louise, who had already published works by the Australian composer Peggy Glanville-Hicks, Margaret chose some of Shaw Neilson's most memorable poems to set to music, including one of Neilson's best poems:

Love cannot sabre us, blood cannot throw,
In the dim counties that wait us below ...

Louise's publishing company brought this out in a handsome format. In neo-classical style, Sutherland set to music other well-loved poems, one of her finest being her setting for John Donne's haunting 'Teach me to hear mermaids singing'. In 1950 she composed one of her most important works, the tone poem 'The Haunted Hills',[15] and also set to music bush ballads written down by Australian writer Vance Palmer.

The following year, when Margaret was in her fifties, she made a second visit to Britain (it was the year of the Festival of Britain, a post war celebration of all aspects of British life including the arts), and once again she indulged herself in a round of concert and opera-going. She met up with Louise Hanson-Dyer, whose company was bringing out long-playing records of various avant-garde composers including major works by Schönberg, Milhaud and Stravinsky.

The next years were fruitful ones for both women. But as a composer of orchestral music Margaret still faced antagonism or indifference to her work and criticism that she, a mere woman, dared to call herself a composer. Besides more chamber music for violin, viola and violoncello she wrote a quartet for cor anglais and strings. She had always drawn on the techniques of Debussy, Stravinsky and Bartok, bringing to them her own ideas, her own voice. She experimented in fresh and wholly original ways, using bi-tonality and inflected scales in innovative works for piano such as her *Chiaroscuro I* and *II,* and *Voices I* and *II*. Other works of this productive period include her unfairly neglected *Violin Concerto,* the *Concerto Grosso* for strings, keyboard and percussion and an orchestral suite *The Three Temperaments*. She also set to music six poems by Judith Wright.

In the more liberated atmosphere of the 1960s, Margaret managed to crash through the barrier of prejudice against the likelihood of women achieving anything in the field of musical composition. Her example opened pathways for other women composers to follow. In 1964 (still at her own expense and without funding from any quarter) she composed a chamber opera, *The Young Kabbarli,* with a libretto by Lady Maie Casey. The opera was based on what was known at that time of the life of the remarkable Daisy Bates — a life which, it now appears, was not exactly as Daisy chose to recount it. Sutherland's well-crafted score concentrates on a couple of events in Daisy's life, exploring the theme of the conflicting worlds of Aboriginal and European culture and Daisy Bates' role in acting as a bridge between the two.

The opera was first performed in Hobart the year after Margaret composed it. She was now seventy-five, but had lost none of her talent. *The Young Kabbarli* won her important recognition and the score was published in book form (though once again she received very little financial reward).

Meanwhile, Louise Hanson-Dyer had survived World War II by moving from Paris to England and then to Monaco, where she died in

1962, leaving her husband to continue the work of l'Oiseau-Lyre with its distinctively Australian bird on the label. Always a proud Australian, the ashes of the remarkable Louise were brought back to Melbourne. L'Oiseau-Lyre editions continued. Hanson remarried, and after his death his second wife also produced fine recordings for many years. L'Oiseau-Lyre has been very important in the history of recorded music, sponsoring among other famous artistes Christopher Hogwood and his Academy of Ancient Music. However, eventually they were taken over by Decca Recordings, although from time to time Louise's distinctive lyrebird logo appears on particular recordings.

In the late 1960s Margaret moved to a small apartment in Hawthorn. At an age when most people are in retirement, the remarkable Margaret was overjoyed to receive her first paid commission to write a string quartet, which she duly completed. *Extension* marked a turning point in her composition, being far more atonal than any of her previous neo-classical works,

In 1969 Margaret was awarded an Honorary Doctorate in music by the University of Melbourne in recognition of her outstanding contribution to Australian music. Commonwealth recognition for her work came the following year with the award of a DBE by Queen Elizabeth II. This was later followed by an Order of Australia.[16]

In 1970 tragedy again visited Margaret Sutherland's life when her daughter was killed in a car accident. Jenny's premature death at the age of forty was a severe shock and Margaret aged considerably after this. She continued to visit her bereaved son-in-law and her grandchildren, and was delighted when her daughter's husband remarried a music-loving young woman whose friendship she enjoyed.

Margaret Sutherland's final decade was filled with activity. With her distinctive aureole of white hair, her characteristic jutting jaw and her forthright manner, Dame Margaret now occupied a very special place in Australian music. She appeared in a starring role in a documentary film about Australian women composers,[17] yet amidst all this activity she always found time for aspiring young musicians and composers if she believed they had talent. She never ceased to give help and encouragement to young composers, believing that music, art and creativity were a vital part of life and must be encouraged in a country obsessed with sport. She did her best to fight the image of an Australia dominated by sport, and at the end of her life saw the country change to one where music and the arts were accorded their rightful place and young musicians received the scholarships to study overseas that she had been denied. Margaret became a highly dedicated member of the Advisory Board of the Australian Music Fund and of the Australian Advisory Committee for UNESCO.

Margaret Sutherland helped fight public indifference to the arts and encouraged what was then an uncaring State bureaucracy to raise funds for the National Gallery of Victoria and the site of what would become the Victorian Arts Centre. At that time the arts did not command the attention they now receive in Australia. Margaret lobbied the State Government of Victoria and organised meetings and concerts to raise money to buy the land on which the Victorian Arts Centre now stands. Her sense of purpose drew others into this worthy cause, and in the end she and her fellow workers succeeded. The noted architect Roy Grounds was commissioned to design Melbourne's Art Gallery and a magnificent Performing Arts Centre took shape. Margaret later became a council member of the National Gallery Society and donated paintings and family portraits by her aunt, Jane, to the National Gallery of Victoria.

In her final years, Dame Margaret was forced to walk with the aid of a silver-topped cane. Old age had its compensations. She experienced great joy at hearing her tone poem *The Haunted Hills*, composed decades previously, incorporated into an award-winning ballet, *Glimpses*, choreographed by Graeme Murphy. Her last days were spent in a nursing home and she died at the age of eighty-six. Up to the end of her life she continued to fight for what both she and Louise Hanson-Dyer believed in: namely the importance of music and its power to draw together peoples of all nations.

CHAPTER TWENTY-THREE

Portrait photograph: Private collection.

(Caroline) Ethel Cooper
(1871–1961)

POLISH GOLD CROSS OF MERIT FOR HELPING REFUGEES

MEMBER OF THE GREEK ORDER OF THE REDEEMER FOR

'EXCEPTIONAL SERVICE TO GREECE'

CONCERT PIANIST, AID WORKER AND INTELLIGENCE AGENT

In her late fifties, so tiny and frail it seemed that a gust of wind might blow her away, a talented concert pianist named Ethel Cooper volunteered to work with thousands of destitute Greek refugees fleeing from ethnic cleansing by the Turkish army. Fearing that the organisers might reject her due to her age Ethel, who had survived famine in wartime Germany, insisted: 'I'm tougher than the lot of you. I survived by eating the elephant from the Leipzig Zoo!'[1]

Ethel's starving friends *had* eaten elephant steak, though animal-loving Ethel refused to share the meal, even though in the last months of World War I she was reduced to living on potato peelings.

Impressed by this feisty Australian woman, Dr Hilda Clarke, Head of Quaker Relief, chose Ethel for the relief team in spite of her frail physique and smoker's cough.

It was an unusual but wise choice. Ethel was tough yet compassionate, with a passionate love of Greece and Greek culture. She worked around the clock to help Greek refugees, saved hundreds of lives, lived very frugally so she could donate most of the money from her trust fund to feed and educate Greek refugee children. She solicited Australian funds from friends and relatives for 'her' refugees after she was appointed Head of Thessaloniki's Refugee Relief Unit in charge of a team of twenty-two aid workers, including two volunteer Scottish doctors. Highly efficient, organised and independent, she ran the Relief Unit very competently because she understood the Greek character and was good at getting the Greek authorities to cooperate with her.[2] She was greatly loved by hundreds of grateful people whose lives she saved and for whose children's education she paid.

What interested me most was learning how Ethel Cooper, a second-generation Australian from an 'establishment' family (her great-uncle was the first judge appointed to the Supreme Court of South Australia), became marooned in war-torn Leipzig at a time when Australia and Britain were at war with Germany.

A lively correspondence written by Ethel in wartime Germany to her older sister in England provided me with the answer.[3]

Caroline Ethel Cooper, always known as Ethel or E, was born in North Adelaide on Christmas Day, 1871. She was the second daughter of hard working, English-born Arthur Cooper, who rose to the position of Deputy Surveyor General of South Australia, and his

Australian-born wife, Harriet (born Woodcock), a talented pianist and music teacher.

Arthur Cooper worked himself into an early grave three months before Ethel was born and her mother Harriet died when Ethel was eight, leaving both her and her sister to be raised by their loving grandmother. The premature death of their parents and the fact there were just the two of them, apart from their grandmother, led to a close bonding of the orphaned sisters which continued throughout their lives. They were educated by a governess and later at Miss Montgomery Martin's, a progressive school at Norwood, where music studies, Latin, ancient Greek, French and German were part of the curriculum.[4]

The girls found a surrogate mother in Mrs Stirling, wife of Dr Edward Stirling, an eminent physician turned State politician, whose four diversely talented daughters became close friends of the lively and intelligent Cooper sisters.[5] Ethel and Emmie Cooper had a wide circle of friends who were well educated and free thinking and did not necessarily conform to the social mores of the period. Dark-haired Emmie, considered a great 'beauty', was tall and reserved while petite Ethel was vivacious and musical. Emmie also had musical talent but no ambition and was besieged by suitors. At a dance she met her Prince Charming, a handsome doctor of Irish extraction who proposed and was accepted. By 1896 Emmie was married[6] and soon after waved goodbye to Ethel and sailed to England, where her husband had bought into a good medical practice.

After leaving school at the age of sixteen, Ethel spent a year with Emmie and her husband in England. Emmie now had a handsome little boy named Howard, who became Ethel's favourite nephew. During her year in England, Ethel (or 'E' as she now styled herself — she hated the name Ethel) acquired a taste for history and archaeology as well as classical music.

On her return to Adelaide she continued her musical studies with Herr Reimann, one of the founders of the Elder Conservatorium of Music at the University of Adelaide. Herr Reimann recognised Ethel's talent and encouraged her to play the piano professionally as well as teach. He suggested further studies at the famous Leipzig Conservatorium, where he himself had studied. Ethel's grandmother agreed that Ethel should attend the Leipzig Conservatorium for further study, but insisted that before doing so she must have a debutante season in Adelaide. Doubtless she hoped that Ethel, like Emmie, would meet a 'suitable' young man and marry well.

Mrs Stirling acted as Ethel's sponsor when she 'came out' at eighteen. She presented Ethel and one of her own daughters, both clad in white tulle ball gowns and long gloves, to the Governor and his lady at a grand ball held in Adelaide's Government House.

Unlike Emmie, no suitors asked for Ethel's hand. This did not disappoint Ethel, who had little taste for what she saw as a dull round of colonial married life, its main excitements whist drives, tennis parties and children's tea parties, with a child at the breast every year. Ethel was passionate about music. She also yearned for Europe, for ancient civilisations, concerts and opera — and to become a better pianist.

As soon as she turned twenty (the age after which an unwed girl was considered unlikely to marry well), it is believed E became the beneficiary of a trust fund set up by the affluent Cooper family to support unmarried daughters. The Australian currency was strong at that period, so Ethel could afford to study and travel in comfort and eventually to take the lease on an apartment in London as a base for her travels.

In 1903, armed with the security of a regular allowance, she returned to England where she stayed with Emmie and her husband and children at first, then toured central and eastern Europe, travelling without a chaperone (a daring thing for a woman of her class at this time). She went by train to Tsarist Moscow, which fascinated her, then took another train over the vast snowy steppes to Siberia. She then backtracked to Vienna, city of music and capital of the Hapsburg Empire, before continuing on to the picturesque university city of Leipzig, surrounded by woods and parks, with its many concert halls and great opera house. Enrolling at the Conservatorium, as her professor in Adelaide had suggested, she rented a room in a pension at No. 2 Braustrasse; her widowed landlady, Frau Ludicke, became a good friend. For over ten years Ethel Cooper spent summers at the Pension Ludicke and the rest of the year at her apartment in Chelsea or back in South Australia.

The bohemian atmosphere of Leipzig resembled the artists' *quartiers* of Montmartre and Montparnasse; here, love affairs among students, teachers, free-spirited concert *virtuosi* and egotistical conductors scarcely raised an eyebrow. The exciting *milieu* of Leipzig's musical world with its love affairs and intrigues was recorded by another great Australian, Ethel Richardson, whose novel *Maurice Guest* centres on Leipzig and its music students. She wrote under the male pen name Henry Handel Richardson, as she knew the novel would be seen as shocking and wished to avoid scandal which might damage her family.[7]

In this bohemian musical paradise Ethel Cooper became friendly with a circle of dedicated music lovers and musicians. They gave recitals together and bought subscription tickets to concerts at Leipzig's famous Gewandhaus and Opera House. The group included Karg-Elert, a teacher from Leipzig Conservatorium who would eventually be appointed Professor there, a music-loving German psychiatrist, a Polish journalist and reviewer, the viola player Emil Telyani ... and the Hungarian pianist Sandor Vaz. Sandor (pronounced 'Chandor' in Hungarian), son of a doctor, was five years younger than Ethel; initially their relationship was that of an indulgent older sister for a talented, amusing young brother. Ethel had a soft spot for this handsome Hungarian and loaned him money from the living allowance sent her from Adelaide each month. Once Sandor was established on the concert circuit he paid her back. E enjoyed giving small dinner parties for close friends, including Sandor and Emil Telyani, in a private room at Frau Ludicke's pension.

Once her studies were over she leased out her London apartment and returned to Adelaide, where she established an all-woman orchestra in which the performers wore long black skirts, black evening jackets and black ties. But getting concert bookings in what was then an ultra-conservative society was a problem.

In 1911 Ethel returned to Leipzig, renting an apartment close to the conservatorium, at No. 11 Grassistrasse, which remained her home for the next six years. E loathed housework but enjoyed cooking for dinner parties. She was a kind and generous friend, helping a pregnant English girl who had been deserted by her German lover; after the baby was born Ethel became godmother to the child. Before Germany declared war on Britain she led a very pleasant existence in Leipzig, performing at small recitals, attending a round of concerts and operas and discussing them with her musical friends. At one time she kept a baby Nile crocodile she named Cheops in the visitors' bathroom, but had to give it to the Leipzig Zoo when it grew too big.

In 1914 everything changed with the assassination of the Archduke Franz Ferdinand, heir to the Austro-Hungarian Empire, by a Serb. The Austrian Emperor declared war on Serbia and the conflict widened to draw in Britain, Germany, Russia, other Balkan states, Italy, Canada, Australia and lastly America. Instead of returning to the safety of her London apartment, E stayed to give financial help to some young English and American music students caught in Germany without adequate funds, as well as two elderly English ladies who did not speak German. Time ran out and the border was closed. By helping them E, who travelled under a British passport, forfeited her own chance of escape across the frontier to France.

Speaking fluent German with only the tiniest hint of a foreign accent, Ethel was perfectly happy to stay on in her beloved Leipzig with her friends believing, like many other Australians and British people, that the war would be over by Christmas, with victory for Britain and her Allies. Her status as a noted concert pianist and music teacher in a city devoted to classical music ensured that she was not interned like other foreigners. She received a pass stating that her presence as an alien 'was agreeable' to the military authorities. Usually enemy aliens were required to move out of German towns with army installations, but E was allowed to remain in Leipzig. In the later years of the war when things were going badly for Germany, on several occasions her apartment was searched by the German police. Ethel hid letters that might have been regarded as incriminating between sheets of music, which the police failed to find.

She gave free piano recitals to wounded German soldiers in *lazarettes*, small military hospitals established by the Government for soldiers injured at the front, and learned from them about the terrible shortages of food in the German trenches and their lack of reinforcements. The soldiers confided to her that the German High Command went to great pains to ensure that the populace at home did not know just *how* short of troops and ammunition the German Army was. This strategic information Ethel passed on to British Military Intelligence via Switzerland.

Each Sunday Ethel wrote a long letter to her sister Emmie. These wartime letters (some 277 in all) reveal her love of literature as well as music. She emerges as a likeable, intelligent bi-lingual observer of Germany and Germans during the war and as such an ideal person or spy for the Allies, although Ethel had few illusions about why the war was being waged.

> We [the British Commonwealth] are fighting for trade reasons, because it was high time to put a stop to a power, which through its enormous energy and expansion, was threatening to take our place in the world. That is a good business reason, but it is not a particularly high ethical one ... The amount of printed hypocrisy one wades through is appalling.[8]

During the first year of the war her letters were smuggled out by a friend through Interlaken in Switzerland. (This friend may also have been the conduit for the strategic information relayed to the British.) Later this route became impossible, but Ethel hints in one letter that there *was* another way of getting information to England. She refers to the German police searching her house and writes that she is delighted that they did not find something she prefers not to name (which would obviously have incriminated her). 'I am convinced they have nothing really against me ... in spite of all denunciations and police surprises, they have found *nothing*. There *was* nothing to find but one thing, and if they had had the *least* inkling of that, I should not be sitting here writing to you now.'[9]

In subsequent letters to her sister Ethel finally admits just how close she and the Hungarian pianist Sandor Vaz have become. Gleefully she recounts how she went with him on one of his concert tours and they spent the night in the same room, booked for them by the Herr Direktor of the local Koncerthalle, who thought that Ethel and Sandor were man and wife and treated her as such during the visit. The Direktor took her slight trace of a foreign accent when speaking German for a Hungarian one. It seems significant that neither Sandor nor Ethel informed the Herr Direktor that he was mistaken and she was Australian.

Like Ethel, Sandor had lost his mother at a young age. Both their mothers had imparted their love of music to their talented offspring. Ethel mentions in one letter how Sandor had become extremely angry and upset when his father, Dr Vaz, talked of marrying again to a much younger woman. Psychiatric literature records that men whose mothers died when they were young can find themselves sexually attracted to an older woman who in some ways remind them of their absent mother. Was this a factor in Sandor's relationship with E? This was not an age when people discussed sex, and Ethel wrote nothing down about this aspect of their relationship.

The fact that Sandor was genuinely fond of Ethel and she of him and that they had a great deal in common shines through her letters to her sister. In February 1915 Sandor refused to go to Berlin, even though he was advised that he should do this for professional opportunities, citing a number of reasons which Ethel quotes in her letter, adding: 'He does not give what I know was the *real* reason, that he would not go while I was here, especially now.'[10] Sandor had returned from a concert tour of neutral Hungary to spend Christmas 1915 with E rather than with his father, showered her with presents at a time when food and clothing were in short supply, and moved into her rented house with his piano. In letters to Emmie, Ethel writes that their friends approved of them moving in together and describes the pair of them settling down in the same apartment and sharing meals 'like an old married couple! We were prepared, as you know, for gossip, but all our friends and acquaintances seem to be delighted, and as even the police and the landlord, who had to be consulted, have expressed their approval, what more can one want?'[11] Later she describes their intention to buy a writing table and a carpet: 'When we settle down permanently, we shall need a few extra things for Sandor's sitting room.'[12] After the war, she wrote, she and Sandor planned a walking tour in Spain. In one letter to Emmie, E describes herself as 'immoral', then in another remarks that she has never considered marriage (possibly because she felt Sandor's father would disapprove since she was now well past child-bearing age, while Sandor himself may have hoped for an heir).

In 1915 Ethel was forty-four, Sandor just thirty-nine. She was small and slim with a mass of dark brown hair, but as the war years dragged on the hardship and stress became etched in her face. Sometimes she was taken for Sandor's wife, at other times for his mother.

Ethel recorded the increasing hardships suffered by the German civilian population as the war continued. Food supplies dwindled until there was practically nothing to buy. Even potatoes became unavailable, as well as firewood and coal. She writes in one letter '...now I am going to make a salad out of the remains of my whale oil, it is beastly, and tastes only of train-oil, but I daren't throw it away.'[13] And a little later: 'Tobacco is beginning to run out, rather a tragedy, for in these days of bad food, we all smoke like chimneys.'[14]

In the middle of winter in an unheated apartment Ethel was often so cold she had to go to bed in her overcoat. She and her friends mended and remade their old clothes. To Emmie she wrote: 'You ask why I don't answer your questions as to why I wear wooden shoes, and what we eat, and so on. I can't in the open letters — nothing about food or such things is allowed by the censor. If I said that I wear wooden shoes because leather is unobtainable or unbuyable, you would not get the card or letter.'

As the war dragged on it was increasingly difficult for E to receive her allowance and she was forced to borrow money from Sandor in order to buy scarce food at greatly inflated prices.

Millions of young men died in the trench warfare on both sides. In one letter to Emmie, Ethel revealed how German soldiers home on leave marched to the Central Railway Station then changed their regimental badges in a closely guarded room, so as to fool the civilian population and foreign observers into believing the Germany Army had more troops than they really did.[15] Her letters also record the serious discontent among civilians, with talk of a Bolshevik workers' revolution in the last year of the war.

As the war worsened, morale amongst Ethel's circle of friends plummeted. A marriage of convenience was celebrated between her psychiatrist friend and his elderly head nurse, to whom the psychiatrist bequeathed the running of his clinic and the care of his private patients should he die. Back in 1915, Connie Jaeger, a wealthy Englishwoman married to a German wool broker, had entertained E and her friends to lavish black-market meals. Towards the end of the war, deprived of her cook, her maid and her wardrobe of Paris fashions, and enduring the stress of being married to a man with whom discussion of the war was impossible, Connie suffered a severe nervous depression and attempted suicide. Fraulein Ludicke, Ethel's former landlady, became catatonic and sat immobile, unable to speak or move. Animals in the Leipzig Zoo were killed for food, including the unfortunate elephant Ethel was to mention in an interview a few years later. Yet she reassured Emmie that she was coping well.

News of events outside Germany was scarce because of censorship. Occasional letters got through to Ethel and sometimes an English newspaper, which was eagerly read and passed around. She fretted about Howard, her adored nephew, who had enlisted in the British Army but she was unable to obtain any news of him.

By the time the war finally ended in November 1918 Ethel was suffering from malnutrition and exhaustion, having been the rock and mainstay of her group of friends throughout the dark days. At last she was able to talk to Emmie by telephone; sorrowfully she learned that Howard had been killed fighting in the trenches over a year previously. His death came as a great shock to her.

She sold her furniture and her precious grand piano at a huge profit — everything was in short supply in post war Germany. Briefly she returned to her Chelsea apartment, which had been let for the duration of the war. In 1921 E sailed back to Adelaide, where she stayed with the Stirling family and caught up with old friends.

The circumstances which ended her relationship with Sandor are not mentioned in Ethel's letters. All we know is that once the war was over, Ethel abandoned music as a career. Her last mention of Sandor, in a letter to her sister dated 19 May 1918, is that he had accepted an appointment to a temporary vacancy at the Conservatorium in Budapest.[16] This was a time when the break-up of a relationship was not written about even to close family members or friends. In Hungary, Sandor eventually married Elizabeth Marek, a glamorous young pianist, and they emigrated to America, where he worked as a concert pianist until his death.

On her return to London from Adelaide Ethel met the renowned Quaker administrator, Miss Ruth Fry, wearing her Quaker uniform of high-necked grey tunic and long grey skirt. Learning that E planned a visit to Poland to see friends, Miss Fry persuaded her to become a volunteer (hence unpaid) aid worker with a Quaker Relief Unit in Warsaw. Due to malaria, many British and American aid workers had been invalided home; several had died, either from malaria or dysentery. Once she arrived in Warsaw, like her fellow aid workers Ethel lived on a semi-starvation diet of tinned sardines, black bread, black tea and corned beef, which seemed lavish compared to the starvation ration of World War I.

In President Pilsudski's new Polish Republic thousands of Poles and Ukrainians were starving. The retreating Germans had burned crops on one side of the country while Lenin's invading Russians had razed the grain-growing villages of the east. Hundreds of women had been raped by the invaders and fallen pregnant, and the Polish Government offered a 'feeding allowance' for the first six months of a baby's life. As a result, six-month-old babies wizened from hunger were often sold by their destitute mothers to foreigners once the allowance had ended.[17] Ethel rescued some of them, using her own money, and placed them in Quaker-run orphanages.

Now in her fifties, Ethel looked older. She had spent years of her life on a severely restricted diet and it showed. Her spirit, however, was as strong and feisty as ever. Like other Quaker and Red Cross workers, she received a Gold Cross of Merit for her work among Polish refugee children.

At this time hundred of thousands of Greek refugees from Turkish ethnic cleansing were being landed at Salonika. As well as Greeks there were white Russian refuges from the Bolshevik revolution and Armenians fleeing from burnt-out Smyrna, where 200,000 Greeks and Armenians had been slaughtered by the troops of Kemal Ataturk. The League of Nations intervened and 1.5 million Greeks in Asia Minor were 'exchanged' for 200,000 Turks residing in Greece; this became known as 'the exchange of populations'. Such vast numbers of refugees were more than the cash-strapped Greek government could cope with, as Greece was one of the poorest countries in Europe. So, having wound up their mission in Warsaw, a new team of volunteer workers was assembled by the Quakers to go to the aid of Greece.

Ethel Cooper was selected by Dr Hilda Clarke as a member of this new Quaker aid team. One of her co-workers who also volunteered to work in Greece was the Australian journalist and author Joice Loch.[18]

After a brief visit to London to see Emmie, Ethel arrived by train at Thessaloniki (then known as Salonika) in May 1923. From the station she took a hansom cab along a dirt road that led from Charilaos to the campus of the American Farm School (near the present-day site of Thessaloniki airport). This was the base for the Quaker mission refugees.

The American Farm School at Thessaloniki is an inspiring story of triumph over adversity. Still operating today, it was started in 1894 by the American-born missionary Dr John House and his wife, who believed that more good would be achieved by introducing Macedonian and Greek village children to advanced farming methods than by giving them Bibles. Dr House and his wife, both in their seventies, ran the Farm School together with their liberal-minded son Charlie and his wife Anne.

The American Farm School had so many refugees to feed and clothe that it was in debt. The House family provided free board and education for as many orphans from the massacre of Smyrna as they could — the refugees slept in tents supplied by the Quakers or the Red Cross or lived in a disused barracks lacking running water or sanitation. Ethel and the other volunteers from Britain, America and Switzerland lived on the same diet as the refugees and slept in sparsely furnished rooms. On arrival they were given a series of lessons in modern Greek, with its totally different alphabet, which Ethel mastered more quickly than any of the other volunteers. Eventually she spoke the language fluently, just as she had mastered German.

At the American Farm School refugees from Asia Minor, whose sole 'crime' was adherence to the Orthodox Church in a strictly Muslim country, found themselves removed from everything they held dear and lives that had once been productive, even affluent. Many of the refugees were widows with frightened children whose husbands had been brutally slaughtered by the Turks. Now they were living behind barbed wire in tented refugee camps where low-cost meals of fried octopus, local fish, black bread bulked out with ground acorns, herb or 'weed' soup and *horta* (greens) were prepared by aid workers until sites for new refugee villages could be found.

The aid teams were overworked and underfed, but everyone did their best under trying circumstances. Each day more and more refugees poured in, many suffering from louse-born typhoid. Ethel and Joice Loch took on the distribution of second-hand clothes and doled out soup, olives and bread to the hundreds of starving refugees, some of whom would die from malaria, blackwater fever or typhoid. Malarial mosquitoes were a huge problem, and hundreds of already weakened refugees died. Many of the aid workers and Farm School staff also went down with malaria.[19] The old barracks on campus where most of the refugees were installed were damp and cold in winter and had leaking roofs. The huge number of orphans meant that girls as young as ten or twelve were caring for younger siblings. Many girls had been gang raped by the Turks and some were pregnant as a result.

After many months, batches of refugees walked out to the new villages selected for them with their few possessions in wheelbarrows or in bundles on their heads. Their only form of government aid was a free issue of two olive saplings and two vine cuttings for farmers, or a trident for those intending to live as fishermen so they could catch octopus from the rocks. They were also given enough tinned food to last for two weeks, after which they had to fend for themselves. In the new villages simple, dirt-floored houses were built by the Greek Army, aided by the refugees themselves.

For transport beyond the Farm School, Joice Loch and Ethel bought starved donkeys and fed them up. Joice named her donkey Menelaus; Ethel's was Agamemnon. Every day for several months they harnessed one or other of the donkeys to an open cart and transported blankets and second-hand clothes donated by well wishers in England, America and Australia to the nearest refugee villages. A faded photograph shows them both in a donkey cart piled high with goods; Ethel holds the reins while Joice shields them both from the sun with a parasol. It is 1923 and both women are wearing ankle-length dresses while Greek refugees crowd around the cart desperate for the goods these two women have brought to one of the newly founded villages.

Ethel, who before World War I was an agnostic, had become interested in Buddhism. Her firm belief in reincarnation, a tenet of the Buddhist religion, tended to shock the more pious members of the Farm School staff and the elderly Quakers who came out from Britain to work as volunteers. However, she kept her views to herself as she wanted to head the Relief Unit. Arthur Bertholf, the current head of the unit, was so inept that Ethel was convinced she could do better. He was a missionary and teacher who was more concerned with saving souls than lives. Ethel got her wish and eventually replaced the impractical Bertholf, whose handling of the cash flow and accounts had been woefully incompetent. She was now in charge of the volunteers, who included Joice Loch and her husband Sydney (he was teaching algebra and history at the Farm School at this time) and the American heiress Nancy Brunton Lauder. Like Ethel, Nancy had a regular income from a trust fund and made substantial donations to assist the work of the Quaker Relief Team.

Never a Quaker herself but a fellow traveller with a strong belief in God, Joice Loch resented the fact that Ethel was only paying lip service to Quaker doctrines in order to be appointed head of the unit. However, Sydney Loch liked and respected Ethel and supported her in her new role. He wrote in his diary: 'Except for the fact she was more probably a pagan than a convinced Quaker, she was suitable for the position, being liked by all staff members and popular with the Greek staff and the refugees.'[20] Sydney was aware of the experience of the physical and psychological effects of famine E had gained in Leipzig. He admired her 'astuteness', and the way she could assume an impressive manner when receiving distinguished visitors and 'spout Quaker phraseology and jargon' when necessary to wealthy Quakers from London who donated funds to the Refugee Unit. He described Ethel as 'cultured, humane and always aware of the human being under the Greek national, though never suffering fools gladly, only occasionally did one hear the creaks in the edifice of her Christianity'.[21]

What jarred on some of the Quakers was Ethel's relaxed attitude to pre-marital or extra-marital sex and the fact that she was believed to have had a lover in Leipzig. E's 'modern' broad-minded approach to life was at variance with the severe doctrines of the Quakers. She also considered that their intention of converting Greek Orthodox refugees to Protestantism was very wrong. By now scandalous stories of how she had lived with a young Hungarian lover in Leipzig were beginning to circulate and some of the Quakers regarded her as 'an immoral woman'. Ethel took no notice. She was Head of the Relief Unit and would do her best for the Greek refugees in her care, whatever anyone thought of her morals and her interest in Buddhist philosophy.

Behind her back some of the aid workers called Ethel 'Pharaoh' because of her passionate interest in Egyptian archaeology. This and her interest in Buddhism was gradually replaced with a fascination for classical Greek history, architecture and archaeology. She vowed that once the refugee situation improved she would visit the most important archaeological sites on the Greek mainland, as well as the island of Crete to view the remains of its ancient Minoan civilisation.

Ethel's life as a musician was over — she never talked about her concert performances and rarely touched a piano in Greece. Her musical sensibilities were bruised by some of the martial music she was asked to play at church services, whenever the Farm School's organist was unable to perform. Finally she felt she could not bear to hear the strains of *Marching to Zion*, Dr House's favourite hymn, a moment longer. When no one was watching, she tore out the page from every copy of *Hymns Ancient and Modern* in the chapel. Her 'sin' was revealed when the number of that particular hymn was announced from the pulpit and none of the congregation could find the correct page. This did nothing to endear E to the more pious members of the Quaker Movement and she had to work very hard to win back their confidence in order to run the refugee mission as she thought it should be run.

Ethel Cooper headed the Quaker Relief Mission in Salonika from 1923 to 1928. During this period hundreds of thousands of refugees passed through the camp and were rehoused in the refugee villages. Running the Refugee Unit was no easy task. Money for feeding the refugees and medicines donated by various overseas missions, including the Quakers, often ran out before the end of the month. To supplement their funds Ethel sent out 'Tin Lizzie', the only truck they had, to scour the foothills for weeds to make soup and acorns to add to the black bread on which they survived.

Ethel worked round the clock on aid programs and administration. She wrote hundreds of letters to Australian companies and private individuals explaining the situation in Greece and asking for funds for food and vaccines, and for second-hand clothing for 'her' refugees. She also had to attend meetings with members of the Greek administration in Salonika, at which her Greek language skills and knowledge of the psychology of the Greek people were vital. Her workload was huge and in the five years she headed up Quaker Relief she took only two holidays, on each occasion staying in England with Emmie and her family.

Gone were the days of tickets to concerts and operas and nights in restaurants and cafes. Ethel spent most of the self-indulgent years of the 1920s Jazz Age struggling with the tough, unpaid job of working with refugees, fundraising and patching up petty disputes that sometimes arose between the overworked and underfed volunteers.

She accomplished so much that by the end of her term in office, the most pious members of the staff were prepared to overlook her approach to religious questions, acknowledging her dedication to the refugees' welfare and her role in establishing good working relations with local Greek authorities. By now most of the refugees had been rehoused in refugee villages built on land requisitioned from large landowners or monasteries.

In her late fifties, exhausted by the years of hardship and work, Ethel (possibly on medical advice) announced it was time to retire. She received high praise from the Quakers for her years of service. An official report to Quaker Headquarters in London noted: 'The development of the Refugee Centre has owed much to her initiative, powers of organisation and knowledge of the Greek language.'[22] The Greek government also recognised Ethel's work and she received the Greek Order of the Redeemer, awarded for 'exceptional services by Greeks or foreigners to the Greek nation'.

At last E was able to indulge her passion for Greek archaeology. Mounted on Agamemnon she set off alone, intending to stay in some of the refugee villages whose inhabitants she had saved and to visit ancient sites: Delphi, seat of the ancient oracle, Sounion with its ruined Temple of Poseidon overlooking the sea, Athens, home of the Acropolis and the Parthenon and the great peaked monasteries of Meteora, perched high on their rocky crags. Sometimes she travelled alone, sometimes with friends she had made in her years at the Farm School, like Dr William Wigram, the classical scholar and British Embassy chaplain.

She spent little on herself, giving away most of the income from her trust fund to those refugees most in need and paying for scholarships for the brightest of their children to attend the Farm School. When Ethel visited the villagers who had passed through the Farm School camp they treated her like a queen. They had little to offer except black bread, olives and goat cheese, which they gladly shared with the woman who had done so much for them.

Ethel had equipped herself with a good camera and was an excellent photographer. She visited Corinth after an earthquake had ravaged the area and killed hundreds of its inhabitants, and photographed the ruined villages around the beautiful Gulf of Corinth.

Photographs in an album held by Cooper descendants bear witness to her travels. She stayed at Megara, Spetsai, Myteleni and Volos, climbed the steep stairs cut in the rock to the great monasteries of Meteora and visited villages like Figaleia and Khania. She took a boat to Crete, where she saw the ancient Venetian buildings of Rethymnion.

Her status as former Head of the Quaker Relief Mission ensured that she was treated with great respect wherever she went. She was thrilled to be shown the excavations of the palace of King Minos by the famous Sir Arthur Evans himself. At Knossos Sir Arthur showed her the oldest known road in the world, used a century before the birth of Christ by merchants arriving to trade with the Minoans, as well as huge Minoan jars or *pithoi* used to store wine and grain under King Minos's palace, the enormous stone chair believed to be the throne of King Minos, and the Queen's bathroom with its dolphin frescoes. In the magnificent throne room she saw the smoke marks on the walls that showed which way the wind was blowing when the palace was engulfed in flames 3000 years ago.

This was the era of the dedicated self-funded archaeologist. Between 1900 and 1906 Sir Arthur, a former curator at the Ashmolean Museum, had personally paid some 350 Cretan peasants to dig out the site, clean the shards and lay bare the foundations of the palace. He had then proceeded to reconstruct it, erecting a series of concrete columns painted red and black and various Minoan frescoes as he imagined they would have looked. He brought out to Knossos brilliant archaeologists from Oxford and Cambridge and housed them in a villa nearby. Ethel was invited to stay there for several days, and was absorbed in conversations with the visiting archaeologists, including the famous John Pendlebury, future hero of World War II in Crete.

Leaving Knossos and returning to the mainland, she travelled in ancient rickety carts and on some of the earliest motorised buses in Greece, equipped with a bedroll. Her Greek was excellent and she was able to talk at length to the old women dressed in black who travelled with hens in wicker baskets on their laps.

She visited the island of Cyprus with its great Crusader Castle and made a special trip to Turkey to see the battlefields of Gallipoli. She rode a mule along the Dalmatian coast to the walled city of Ragusa (Dubrovnik) and spent over six years in constant travel, eventually speaking Greek like a native.

In 1932 Ethel Cooper's life changed once again. Emmie's husband died in London, and Emmie returned to Adelaide, where she bought a large and pleasant house and asked Ethel to join her. It was the end of E's carefree gypsy life. Emmie was conventional and her life as a widow was one of ultra-respectability — all the things Ethel had gone to Europe to avoid. Though the house had space for a grand piano, Ethel declared that she had renounced music. She never played another note for the rest of her life.

The two sisters were devoted but very different. Emmie was the respectable doctor's widow, always beautifully dressed on every social occasion. Ethel cared little for appearances; at times she looked dishevelled and even slightly eccentric. She still sent money to Greek charities, rolled her own cigarettes to save money and wore clothes that looked as if they had come from a jumble sale. Unlike Emmie, Ethel spent very little on herself, renouncing the things women of her class took for granted such as expensive clothes and visits to the hairdresser so she could donate a large part of her income to those in need.

At the outbreak of World War II Ethel was seventy, and mentally as alert as ever. She volunteered her services as a translator and censor to the Military Censor's Office and was put to work reading letters written in German by Germans and Austrians, many of whom lived in the Hahndorf area. Possibly her period of spying for the British during World War I ensured the invitation to work in Military Intelligence in Adelaide. The writers of the letters she censored were distraught: they regarded themselves as patriotic Australians but found themselves interned in special camps in South Australia. E's job was to read the letters in order to see that they contained no strategic information which German relatives could pass to their military authorities. There is a certain irony in the fact that Ethel, who had herself defied the censor in a previous war, was now actively involved in censoring the letters of others. She drove her ancient Ford car to work, invariably smoking her roll-your-own cigarettes. In spite of her erratic driving and outlandish clothes, she earned the respect and affection of all her colleagues. In Military Intelligence she was known affectionately as 'The Gypsy' due to the amusing and fascinating stories she told at morning tea about her travels in Germany, Poland, Hungary and Greece, as well as her former life in wartime Germany.

By the time Ethel was eighty-nine she was suffering from the degenerative nervous disorder known as Parkinson's disease and had difficulty walking and talking clearly. In the early 1960s the pharmaceutical drugs which alleviated symptoms of Parkinson's also produced distressing side-effects. In her final year, Ethel was cared for devotedly at home by Emmie until just before her death, when she was transferred to hospital. Ethel Cooper died a few days before her ninetieth birthday and was buried in North Road Cemetery.

Emmie, realising that her sister's life had been an extraordinary one, donated the collection of letters written during World War I to the State Archives of South Australia. Unfortunately only the postcards Ethel wrote to Emmie when travelling around Greece remain; other letters have been lost.[23]

Ethel Cooper saved the lives of hundreds of Greek refugees and changed the lives of many Greek children by giving them the most priceless gift of all after good health — a good education.[24] Her sister Emmie, who had, in contrast, lived a very comfortable and affluent life, died at the ripe old age of one hundred.

CHAPTER TWENTY-FOUR

Portrait photograph: Art Gallery of New South Wales.

Margaret Rose Preston
(1875–1963)
'I'M NOT GOING THROUGH THE PEARLY GATES
WITH PAINT ON MY WINGS!'

Australia's most famous woman artist was born Margaret Rose McPherson at Port Adelaide during the reign of Queen Victoria. Ambitious to succeed, she started her artistic career by exhibiting under the name 'Rose McPherson', which meant that some of her earliest works, now worth many thousands of dollars, hang unrecognised on walls around Australia.

Margaret Rose's father, David McPherson, a Scottish marine engineer, had married Prudence Lyle. They had two daughters, Margaret Rose (known to her family as Rose and to friends as Maggie) and Ethelwynne Lyle McPherson. Work took David McPherson away from his young family to foreign ports for months at a time. He was earning a good income and Margaret Rose and her sister were sent to a private school. Maggie especially enjoyed her art lessons and went with her class to the Adelaide Art Gallery, where she was fascinated to see art students copying the paintings on the walls. This looked so enjoyable that she decided to become an artist herself.

For some reason their father, usually so kind and pleased to be home with them all, started limping and showing signs of extreme irritability, even eccentricity. If he cut himself the wound refused to heal. These were symptoms of tertiary syphilis (a sexually transmitted disease, incurable before the discovery of penicillin). Eventually David McPherson lost his job and the family lost their income.

His daughters did not know the cause of their father's mysterious illness. Doubtless his wife did, for Mrs McPherson, with both her daughters, moved to Sydney, where she rented lodgings. Margaret Rose was sent to the excellent Fort Street Girls' School in the Rocks area.[1] She also took private art lessons with a young Sydney landscape artist, William Lister Lister. Impressed by the teenage girl's talent and steely determination to become a professional artist at a time when most girls painted for pleasure as a 'lady-like accomplishment', Lister Lister advised Mrs McPherson that the best place in Australia for her elder daughter to study art seriously was the National Gallery School in Victoria.

They returned to Adelaide for Mrs McPherson to sort out her affairs and consult with her husband's doctors, then Margaret Rose was sent to Melbourne to study at the National Gallery School. She had what was then the best art instruction available in Australia under

Bernard Hall, a tonalist, and Frederick McCubbin, the Heidelberg School painter. Margaret Rose described him as 'one of the kindest cleverest artists Australia has produced'.[2]

It was a male-dominated art world and most girls who studied painting were just filling in time till they got married. There were many people in the art world who believed that the famous Professor Hegel was right, that while woman could sketch flowers and pretty landscapes, their limited learning capacity (related, according to some authorities, to the smaller size of the female brain) made them incapable of great art. However, Margaret Rose's intentions were very serious. She won a prize for figure drawing and after submitting a fairly conventional still life was awarded a scholarship which gave her the right to a year's free tuition. This was a godsend.

By now her father was partly paralysed, and had become so violent and hard to live with that he could no longer be cared for at home. His wife, who was not well herself, realised she must admit him to a private nursing home, which would drain their limited savings. In February 1894 David McPherson was admitted to Parkside Lunatic Asylum, where he died a year later from 'grand paralysis of the insane', a term used by the medical profession to denote the final stage of syphilis in which sufferers went blind and became totally paralysed and insane. [3]

Margaret Rose was twenty-three when her father died. As the eldest child she now had to support her ailing mother both emotionally and financially. This turned her into an even stronger and more independent character at a time when women were meant to be meek, gentle and bow to the perceived superior intelligence of men. Although the McPherson family was descending into genteel poverty, Margaret Rose was still determined to become an artist rather than an art teacher. However, she realised that she must do some teaching to help support her mother and younger sister, who was still at school.

In 1898 Maggie McPherson returned to Adelaide and studied under H.P. Gill at the Adelaide School of Design, Painting and Technical Arts. The following year she leased a studio, taught at the Adelaide School of Design and took a few private pupils, hoping to find the time to paint enough works of her own to hold her first exhibition.

By this time her mother had become very frail and needed high-grade care in a nursing home, which Maggie paid for out of her earnings.

Often short of funds, she was invited to spend a long weekend at the home of one of her wealthiest pupils, Bessie Davidson. A very long weekend it became; keen to save money, she moved in with the Davidsons and stayed with them free of charge for two years.[4] Now 'Mad Maggie' could save enough money on food and rent ('penny-piling' she called it) to pay for her fare to Europe.

When Margaret Rose was twenty-nine her mother died, which caused her considerable heartache. She inherited half of what little money remained from her father's estate, and used some of it to rent a larger studio where she continued teaching and painted *Still Life with Eggs,* her best work to date. Unfortunately the painting was rejected by the organisers of an exhibition held in Adelaide, probably because its composition was too 'modern' for conservative Adelaide.

By July 1904 Margaret Rose McPherson had saved enough money to accompany her talented pupil Bessie Davidson to Venice. They studied works by Titian and Veronese in the Gallery of the Academia. Bessie made a series of watercolours of canal scenes, while Margaret Rose seems to have spent her time looking at great art rather than painting the canals and palazzos of Venice.

Subsequently they left for Munich, where they rented rooms and took lessons at the Munich State Art School for Women. At this time Paris, rather than Munich, was the centre of the art world, and soon the two young Australian artists moved there. Paris was at the cutting edge of Modernism, with the new Metro or Underground with its Art Nouveau ironwork decorations and the new picture houses or cinemas created by Monsieur Lumiere. Together Maggie and Bessie ascended the Tour Eiffel and admired the spectacular view over the city.

Margaret Rose attended art classes at the Musée Guimet, with its Oriental collections, where she studied Japanese art. The delicate Japanese woodblocks of the 'floating world' with their line and rhythm opened her eyes to the fact that there was 'more than one vision in art'.[5] The Japanese woodcuts with their strong compositions and their purity of line and colour fascinated her all her life.[6] She also saw the vivid and colourful works by artists considered extremely avant-garde. Used to the dark 'tonal' paintings of artists such as Streeton and Roberts, then at the height of their fame in Australia, she was shocked by the blazing colour of Cézanne. Works by Gauguin and Van Gogh (who was now dead, but whose works were widely promoted by his brother's widow and several dealers) were becoming fashionable and expensive.

Maggie was delighted by the riot of colour and pattern in the paintings of several younger artists who styled themselves 'les Nabis'. One member of les Nabis, Pierre Bonnard, was leading a revival of print-making, something that fascinated her. She also loved the colourful watercolours and oils of Matisse and admired the group of artists known as 'les Fauves' or 'Wild Beasts' for their daring use of colour. Les Fauves were then considered so shocking that very few people bought their work.

Bessie Davidson, Stella Bowen, Hilda Rix Nicholas and other Australian artists working in France received living allowances from home, but Maggie McPherson knew she must earn a living from her art. Much as she longed to shock the stuffy art establishment, she did not want to starve in some chilly unheated studio along with the rest of the avant-garde. She decided that for the present she would exhibit conventional paintings and try to sell them. As a result she had a traditional still life accepted for the annual exhibition of the Paris Salon, where all entries were vetted by the 'establishment' professors of the Ecole des Beaux-Arts. To have a painting hung in the main Salon was a great honour for a woman and a foreigner.

Once the exhibition was over she and Bessie went to Spain to see great art by Velazquez and Goya in Madrid's Prado. At that time Spain was a very primitive and inexpensive country to visit.

In 1907, still the best of friends, the two young women returned to Adelaide where they rented a studio together. Margaret Rose remained in Adelaide for the next five years and longed to exhibit more. To earn her living she was forced to spend most of her time teaching at the Presbyterian Ladies' College, St Peter's Collegiate School and the Adelaide School of Design and Painting.

Now aged thirty-two, exposure to new ideas and new techniques in Paris had changed Margaret Rose, made her more sure of herself and given her a taste for brighter colours. Finally she and Bessie Davidson held a joint exhibition in Adelaide which was reasonably successful.

Miss McPherson did not enjoy the time she spent in the classroom but, according to Stella Bowen, one of her best pupils, she was nevertheless a first-rate teacher. Later in life Stella Bowen described her as 'a red-headed little firebrand of a woman, who was not only an excellent painter, fresh from Paris, but a most inspiring teacher'.[7]

Margaret Rose spotted Stella Bowen's talent and high intelligence and knew her pupil would benefit from time spent in Paris and London. She paid Stella's mother a surprise visit to tell her this. 'You know, Mrs Bowen, you won't be able to keep her,' her teacher said as she told Stella's mother that her daughter showed great artistic promise and urged her to allow Stella to go to Europe.[8] Unknown to Margaret Rose, Mrs Bowen was ill and desperately worried that her daughter might leave her to go overseas.

After the death of her mother Stella became even more determined to go overseas, and her trustees, impressed by Miss Margaret McPherson's opinion of her talent, gave Stella Bowen an allowance to live in Europe.

Unfortunately, gentle unselfish Stella fell in love with Ford Maddox Ford, a married and utterly selfish author who spent her allowance and fathered her child. He demanded she abandon her painting to bring him meals on trays, grow vegetables, clean the house and care for their child, while he wrote his books and edited a literary journal. Maddox Ford repaid Stella for her loyalty and the sacrifice of her own career by conducting an illicit affair with a young writer later to become famous as Jean Rhys, of whom Stella was bitterly jealous. Eventually the situation became so impossible that Stella Bowen left Maddox Ford and raised her daughter alone. Her disillusionment with love caused her to pose a poignant question: 'Why are women encouraged to stake their lives, careers, economic position and hopes of happiness on love?'

Miss McPherson, 'the red-headed firebrand', did *not* stake her career and economic position on love. In fact, although she was surrounded by fellow artists conducting complex liaisons, Margaret Rose seems to have resolutely avoided love affairs heterosexual or lesbian. Perhaps, like the writer Miles Franklin, she was terrified of catching syphilis. At any rate she seems to have avoided emotional entanglements with the opposite sex until she was in her early forties. What she always hoped for was a marriage of equals, something relatively rare then.

In 1912 Margaret Rose left Adelaide for Paris, spending another precious year there. She caught up with her friend and former pupil

Bessie Davidson, who was living and working close to the great art schools of Montparnasse. At last Maggie was able to unfold her wings and soar into new styles and brighter colours. Freed from the constraints of Adelaide, she exhibited works in her new Japanese-influenced style and exhibited with the progressive Société Nationale des Beaux-Arts. At this exhibition Matisse, Bonnard and Vuillard were showing light, bright paintings that reflected their admiration for the work of Cézanne. Cézanne, with his apples seen from unusual angles and multiple viewpoints, profoundly influenced Margaret's work for many years.

In the summer of 1913 Margaret Rose visited Brittany and Normandy on an extended painting trip. On her return to Paris she found her artist friends worried that the Kaiser's troops might invade France. They feared that Paris itself might fall to the Germans, just as it had during the Franco-Prussian war. When it became obvious that war between Germany and the Allies, Britain and France, was inevitable, Maggie took the train for London; she had good friends in Britain. Bessie Davidson, however, decided to remain in Paris.

In London Margaret Rose shared a studio with attractive, dark-haired Gladys Reynell, another former pupil. She exhibited at London's Royal Academy and showed her woodcuts, executed in her new Japanese-influenced style, with the Society of Women Artists. She also showed paintings with Walter Sickert's New English Art Club, whose exhibitions were far more avant-garde and French influenced than the conventional, rather dull Summer Exhibitions of the Royal Academy. No one could ever accuse Margaret Rose of being dull.

Another important source of new ideas were the Omega Workshops run by Roger Fry with the participation of Duncan Grant and his lover Vanessa Bell (sister of Virginia Woolf). Margaret Rose was impressed by the great post-Impressionist exhibition that Roger Fry organised in London, which drew the attention of English art lovers to Cézanne for the first time but aroused the ire of the general public, who simply could not understand the paintings.

Margaret Rose had always shown a broad-based interest in design and craft, and she took a pottery and handicrafts course at the Camberwell School of Arts and Crafts. She was fascinated by the highly original use of colour by Vanessa Bell and Duncan Grant at the Omega Workshops, which offered even more possibilities for her woodcuts. She enjoyed the chance to work with Bell and Grant and their intriguing circle and would have done more with them had war not broken out.

The bright lights of London dimmed. There were no more art exhibitions and few theatres. Art seemed of limited importance once thousands of young men were dying in the trenches. Food was rationed and most people filled their spare time with volunteer work. Many middle-class women became army drivers, camp cooks or served refreshments to soldiers on London stations. Outside the capital, some wealthy landowners allowed their country houses to be used as private hospitals.

Return to Australia was out of the question; due to the hazard of floating mines it was considered far too dangerous to return home by sea. The brother of her former pupil Gladys Reynell was a surgeon at a hospital in Devon; he invited both Margaret Rose and his sister to come and work there, so they retreated to the comparative peace of the rural west of England. At the hospital the two Australian artists did their bit for the war effort by teaching pottery, print-making and basket-weaving to shell-shocked and crippled soldiers in a rehabilitation unit for neuro-psychiatric patients. Handicraft materials were in short supply; sometimes the baskets had to be woven with fresh willow stems or rose stalks instead of osiers. They were sold in the local market to give the wounded soldiers some income. Margaret Rose recorded later that some of the woven baskets amazed their owners by sprouting leaves in spring!

Many of the returned soldiers had been pushed to the edge by living for months in waterlogged trenches filled with rats, where limbs of dead men protruded from a sea of mud. Working with these crippled and often psychologically damaged men involved learning psychiatric procedures. Some of the soldiers had become raving lunatics, others were haunted by nightmares or suffered from constantly twitching limbs or eyes. Many were profoundly depressed, knowing they would never walk again; others had lost the use of their hands or become impotent.

Before the war most women were married by the time they turned twenty-one. By now it was generally agreed that Margaret Rose McPherson, dumpy and frizzy-haired and considered long past the age of child bearing, was well and truly 'on the shelf', a woman dedicated to art who would never marry while men flocked around attractive Gladys Reynell.

However, Margaret Rose amazed everyone by returning to Australia engaged to a tall, broad-shouldered former Artillery officer with the AIF. Handsome, shy Lieutenant William George (Bill) Preston, six years Margaret's junior, had been wounded fighting in France. He was as quiet as she was ebullient. No weakling, he was a man others respected for his intelligence and drive.

Margaret Rose's experience in the neuro-psychiatric hospital for war veterans had made her very understanding about the horrors Bill Preston and other young men had undergone in the trenches; since she was sensitive and highly intelligent she could deal with the problems of shell shock that he was experiencing. Although Bill Preston was slow to anger and seldom raised his voice, it soon became apparent that he had a will as strong as that of Miss McPherson, whom he adored, convinced that she was Australia's greatest living artist.

This somewhat ill-assorted couple had met aboard the ship on which Margaret Rose returned to Australia. Unkind acquaintances would gleefully relate that poor old Bill Preston, who was still recovering from shell shock, didn't stand a chance when firebrand 'Mad Maggie' made up her mind to marry him. He did not care for the names 'Rose' or 'Maggie' and from then onwards she was always 'Margaret'.

By the time the ship docked in Australia Bill Preston had asked Margaret McPherson to marry him, unaware that she was older than he was. She certainly had no intention of enlightening him. For the entry on her wedding certificate Margaret must have falsified the date on her birth certificate, as her age was registered as thirty-six (she was in fact forty-four). She was by no means the only bride of her era to lower her age — the writers Katharine Susannah Prichard and Joice NanKivell Loch both did the same.

The McPherson-Preston wedding took place with a church ceremony on 31 December 1919 and was followed by a lavish wedding reception given by her friends the Reynells at the Chateau Reynella, outside Adelaide, and soon after Gladys married another wounded war veteran.

The gossips did not believe Mad Maggie would change and prophesied doom and disaster for her union with Bill Preston. But the new Mrs Preston, despite the fact that her flaring temper did not make her an easy person to live with, confounded her critics by proving that she could achieve an exceptionally happy marriage. As a convinced feminist it was surprising that Margaret adopted her husband's name and used it to sign her paintings. The only exception was a picture taken from the veranda in their first house overlooking Sydney's Mosman Bay. (The story of this painting, signed 'M.R McPherson', is told at the end of this chapter.)

With Margaret's support and encouragement Bill Preston became a highly successful businessman, a director of Toohey's Brewery and of Anthony Hordern's department store and of several other companies.

A marriage without children freed Margaret Preston from the constant need to teach and gave her, for the first time since she had started to paint, a sense of security. From then, inspired by the Modernistic styles she had seen in Paris and London, her work developed a strength and quality her earlier paintings had lacked. She switched her allegiance from the conservative, rather fuddy-duddy Royal Art Society of New South Wales to the more adventurous Society of Artists, whose members were increasingly influenced by the works of Cézanne, Derain, Bonnard and Léger (often only glimpsed in imported art books).

Margaret was now no longer worried about letting 'modern' influences appear in her work. The 1920s were years of affluence in Australia and she was able to find buyers of like mind. Her *Implement Blue* and other works painted in the late 1920s show just how deeply she had absorbed Cubist and Japanese influences in Paris.

Her contemporaries described Margaret Preston as strong minded and forceful, given to the kind of strong language which shocked some of her friends and patrons. She was relentless in her attempts to promote her own work (a practice now considered normal in the art world but at that time thought shockingly 'pushy' for a woman).

Those who were offended by her sharp tongue and quick temper still called her 'Mad Maggie' behind her back. Few of her critics realised the hard struggle she had undergone to become an artist. In fact, this was the era of the innovative woman artist: she had come into her own. Tom Roberts and Arthur Streeton now seemed staid and old-fashioned. It was women like Preston, Grace Cossington Smith, Grace Crowley and Dorrit Black who brought back new and exciting ideas from the Salon des Beaux-Arts, the Salon d'Autumne and André L'hôte's, the famous summer school held at Mirmande.

In middle age Margaret Preston's originality and her increasing fame ensured that in 1930, just as the Great Depression started to bite, the notoriously conventional Trustees of the Art Gallery of New South Wales commissioned a self-portrait from her. Preston set about painting her own likeness objectively rather than beautifying herself. However, since her adoring husband still did not know her real age, she had to make herself look younger than she really was. So she stares out at us from her self-portrait whey-faced with piercing eyes; her auburn hair fashionably short, clutching her brushes and palette firmly. To make the portrait look 'modern' she placed herself against a bleak wall of concrete blocks, a deliberate Australian touch. Preston's self-portrait made Australian art history by being the first one ever to be commissioned by the Art Gallery of New South Wales, and from a *woman* artist.

Photographs taken in her later years present Margaret as a far softer and more feminine figure. Artists and writers are not known for their happy marriages, but Preston's marriage may well have thrived by *not* having children. The poet Leon Gellert recorded with some amusement that his friend Bill Preston 'regarded it as almost a national duty to keep his beloved Margaret happy and artistically productive'.[9]

Sydney Ure Smith, a talented artist and publisher of the journals *Art and Australia* and *The Home*, admired Preston's work so much that he published her famous Modernist manifesto 'From Eggs to Electrolux' in *Art and Australia*. In 1949 he published the book *Margaret Preston's Monotypes*. But even the gentle, urbane Ure Smith, who owned the Smith and Julius Art Studio as well as his publishing company, sometimes found Preston's strong character and outbursts of temper hard to take. Nevertheless, as a talented etcher himself, Ure Smith had great admiration for her woodcuts and her determination never to repeat herself but always to create new designs. He wrote: '*All* vital artists have enemies. Where they fail to inspire delight they instil terror. Margaret Preston is the natural enemy of the dull'. He proclaimed: 'Margaret Preston strikes a modern note in Australian woodcut. Like her painting it expresses vitality and rebellion … It has personality, ambition, vigour'.[10]

Margaret's essay 'From Eggs to Electrolux' is an important feminist document. The arrival of labour-saving electrical machines in the home did far more practical good for women's independence in servantless Australia than obtaining the vote. Preston was one of the first women to recognise this, hence the title of her article. She declared: 'I would not be without my ironing machine and I am just waiting to get the latest washing machine.'[11]

In 1925 Preston held a joint exhibition of her woodblock prints with her sister-artist Thea Proctor, who contributed thirteen extremely stylish woodcuts. Thea Proctor, highly talented, extremely elegant and with a strong design sense, was a very different character to Margaret Preston, who was never happier than when wearing a paint-spattered smock. Both artists, however, shared dissatisfaction with what they saw as the moribund tradition of Australian national landscape painting. It was Margaret Preston who taught Thea Proctor the art of woodcut, providing her with the special feathery paper she brought back from Japan.

There is a famous story concerning a tea party to celebrate the success of the joint exhibition in which Proctor and Preston displayed their prints in red lacquer frames. Margaret Preston baked some tea cakes for their celebration and took them to Proctor's studio as a gift. When she arrived there she learnt that the Art Gallery of New South Wales had purchased several of Thea Proctor's works but none of her own. Upon hearing this, Preston is reputed to have yelled: '*There's* your present, then!', flung the cakes on the floor and walked out in a rage.

Whether the story is true or exaggerated, Preston did paint Thea Proctor's tea table complete with cakes. (The painting may be seen in the Art Gallery of New South Wales.) She did not exhibit with Proctor again but had three single exhibitions of her work, in 1929, 1936 and in austerity riddled 1953.

Margaret Preston's woodblock prints were extremely popular from the 1920s onwards and have soared in value. Her most popular works, today seen on greeting cards everywhere, are undoubtedly those of flowers, followed by her woodcuts of Circular Quay and the Spit Bridge. Her 'modern' influences ensured that she became the most prominent Australian exponent of Modernism, the movement that in Australia reacted against the landscapes and heroic paintings of the male-dominated Heidelberg School.

* * *

As adventurous and frequent travellers, Bill and Margaret Preston toured New Caledonia and the New Hebrides in 1923, visited Macassar, Bali, Singapore, Thailand and China in 1926 and 1927, and later went to India and Africa. In the 1930s, when Preston was in her mid-fifties, they visited Mexico and South America. In Mexico she was fascinated by the depth of colour in the murals of Diego Rivera, and deeply impressed by the forms of pre-Columbian art. They also visited north Queensland on several occasions and in 1942 toured the Kimberleys and Arnhem Land. There Margaret pursued her deepening interest in Indigenous art and purchased Aboriginal artworks for her own collection.[12] As one of the first artists to appreciate Aboriginal art, she wrote indignantly: 'Australia has ignored a fine simple art that exists at our own backdoor. It has to learn what this art can do to give [Australians] a national culture.'

Margaret positively enjoyed subverting stereotypes and had an impish sense of humour. In her version of *Adam and Eve ejected from the Garden of Eden* (painted in 1950) the Biblical founders of the human race are clearly Aboriginal, while the angel who expels them from Paradise with a flaming sword (a pastiche of Massaccio's famous *Expulsion from the Garden of Eden* from the Brancacci Chapel in Florence) is white, male and Caucasian.

Between 1915–1928 Margaret Preston mainly painted still lifes; her subjects ranged from eggs in baskets to tea sets and flowers and even dead rabbits. She flattened shapes and viewed her subjects from unusual angles, a technique based on works by Léger and Cézanne. Realising how conservative Australia remained at this time, and with a husband to support her, she made little attempt to sell her more 'advanced' paintings, knowing that the conventional public would loathe them.

Intent on solving problems of technique, she continued painting flowers in jugs and cups and saucers. Flower painting was traditionally seen as women's art, but in the hands of Margaret Preston it turned into something far stronger and more dramatic. She believed that Australian native flowers were just as beautiful as any foreign species.

In her fifties and sixties Margaret Preston had five one-woman exhibitions at various galleries and exhibited each year at group shows. During the Prestons' travels in the 1930s around the Far East the strong diagonal compositions of Japanese art were once again to prove yet another influence on her work. With her lively, original mind she wrote numerous articles on art. She was intensely committed to founding a distinctively Australian school of art and wrote perceptively: 'Australia is a country that gives the impression of size and neutral colour. To create this impression on canvas or woodblocks I find it necessary to abandon the regulation yellow sunlight because I feel that Australia is not a golden-glow country but one of harsh, cool light.'

In 1937, when she was in her early sixties, she was honoured by being awarded a Silver Medal at the Paris International Exhibition.

By now the Prestons had moved from their harbourside home in Mosman to a block with fourteen acres of natural bush surrounding a long, low wooden house north-west of Sydney at Stewart Road, Berowra. Here the treasures they had collected from all over the world were displayed. These included a mummified human head which Margaret had boldly smuggled past the Ecuadorian Customs, having hidden the artefact in her knickers beneath her flared petticoat and skirt.

Although the Prestons had no children, she enjoyed their company and used to give children's parties that lasted all day, complete with elaborate games in which she and her husband participated with enjoyment. The Reynell family remained close friends, as did the writers Mary Grant Bruce and Marjorie Barnard.

When Margaret was sixty-four, the Prestons sold their home at Berowra and moved into a Mosman hotel, which simplified their housekeeping. She started lecturing on the techniques of art and craft at the Art Gallery of New South Wales and along with her friend Thea Proctor accepted commissions for woodcut illustrations for Jindyworobak publications. It was during this period that Preston started to make her distinctive woodcuts and monotypes of Australian native wildflowers. In all she made more than 400 prints, some drawn from woodblocks and hand-coloured, others on masonite. Her most popular woodcuts include 'Banksia', a favourite subject. She drew and painted many versions, including one showing these unusual plants in the wild and others with the blossoms arranged in a vase. Her woodcuts of the buildings around Circular Quay and of the Spit Bridge at Mosman have become iconic images of Sydney. Unlike her contemporaries, Grace Cossington Smith, Jessie Traill and Gwen

Barringer, she did not record in paint the building of the Harbour Bridge, which she regarded as ugly; she lamented the loss of rows of historic homes along Cumberland Street which were destroyed to make way for the approaches to the bridge.

Margaret Preston found working with woodblocks hard on her hands. A letter dated June 1941 describes the work as 'pulling her thumbs quite out of shape'. She also made monotypes, a single example of each being 'pulled' from an image on a piece of glass or a copper plate and then painted by hand. She felt that this procedure gave them a softer effect and a greater sense of spontaneity.

Some of her oils are huge, especially those made as decorative panels for ocean liners. She generally made her woodblock prints in three sizes. She was meticulous about the quality of her materials and made her work to endure, so she insisted on using only the finest artist's brushes, watercolours and handmade Japanese paper — another reason why her works are sought by collectors today. (A catalogue raisonné of Preston's work has been made by Roger Butler of the Department of Prints of the Australian National Gallery, because her work has now attracted the attention of the forgers who plague Australian art.)

At sixty-seven Preston shared an exhibition at the Art Gallery of New South Wales with fellow artist William Dobell. One of her Aboriginal-inspired paintings was purchased by Yale University for their art gallery. Towards the end of her life her palette became influenced by the sienna, ochre and grey toning of Aboriginal bark paintings.

Her fascination with Aboriginal art had begun when she was living in the bush at Berowra, surrounded by native flowers and Aboriginal rock paintings. She started painting landscapes such as her Aboriginal-influenced *Flying Over Shoalhaven River* in muted browns, greys and yellows, which showed a respect for Aboriginal art rather than being a slavish copy of a dot painting. She had faith in Australia's future: 'We are a nation of people who are growing up and who should not acquire a counterfeit culture by borrowing the intellect of other countries', she wrote; '...some of [my] monotypes may show the potential of an art that has intellectual differences from that of other countries'.[13]

Preston continued to work furiously. She opened the first exhibition of the Australian Women Artists at the Art Gallery of New South

Wales when aged seventy-one. Three years later she held her first exhibition of stencil prints and monotypes, continuing her immense yet high-quality output for almost another decade.

Her final exhibition took place at the Macquarie Galleries when she was eighty-three. She knew that it would be her last; her eyesight was deteriorating and, like most (although not all) artists, she realised that it was time to give up in order to protect the quality of her *oeuvre*. Very few of her works are below standard, unlike those of some artists who continued on to the end of their lives, producing work of decreasing quality.

Artist James Gleeson, a young struggling painter, spotted Margaret Preston, then in her eighties, coming out of a Sydney framer's shop with a wrapped painting under one arm. 'Is that one of yours?' he asked.

'No, it is *not*!' she replied. '*I'm* not going through the pearly gates with paint on *my* wings!'[14]

She was eighty-eight when she died in a Mosman nursing home.

Her heartbroken husband lived on for another three years. After his death a large proportion of the contents of her studio was donated to the Art Gallery of New South Wales. Margaret Preston remains one of the most loved of Australian artists and print-makers, an inspiration to all women artists today.[15]

Postscript from 'M.R. McPherson' to 'M.R. Preston', a tale of two signatures

Early in 1980, in Brisbane, I was shown a delightful oil painting in post-Impressionist style of a verandah shaded by a pink awning, with a jug of wildflowers and a bowl of oranges on a table overlooking the sea. The work was signed in pencil: 'M.R. McPherson'. Ah-ha, an early Margaret Preston, I thought, painted from the verandah of her matrimonial home in Musgrave Street, Mosman.

The owner told me: 'I bought that painting in a junk shop near Roma Street Station in the 1970s for twenty dollars. I've never heard of an artist called McPherson. Is he any good? If so, I'll sell it.'

'Her real name was Margaret Preston and she was *very* good,' I replied. I made a phone call to Sam Alcorn, then librarian at the Art Gallery of New South Wales, who confirmed that the painting had been exhibited in Sydney in 1928 under the name 'M.R. McPherson'. The instruction 'To be hung on the line', written in Margaret's distinctive bold hand on a label glued to the back of the painting meant that it should not be hung high on the wall. Since she considered it one of her best works, she wanted it hung at eye level. This was typical of flamboyant, fiery Preston, who often issued such instructions to exhibition organisers.

Lawsons the Sydney auctioneers had an art sale scheduled at Brisbane's Park Royal Hotel. The owner agreed to a reserve of $2500, pleased at the prospect of a profit of over $2000 for his twenty dollar painting. Remember this took place in 1980. However, no one in the sale room seemed interested in a work signed 'M.R. McPherson', even though the catalogue stated correctly that it was a genuine Margaret Preston. In the end a group of Sydney dealers acting in concert got one of their number to bid on behalf of all of them, a nasty practice known as 'ringing' that sometimes occurs at auctions. The painting fetched $2600.

Following a major Preston retrospective at the Art Gallery of New South Wales, Preston's prices soared. Some eight months after making $2600, the view from Maggie's verandah made some lucky art entrepreneur $11,500 when the dealers put it up for sale again at Joel's auction rooms in Melbourne. However the pencil signature 'M.R. McPherson' had now been erased in favour of another one proudly proclaiming the name 'M. Preston'.

The painting with its amended signature disappeared to the home of its new owner for twenty years before reappearing in a sale catalogue for a Christie's Melbourne auction in May 2002. Neither the painting nor the frame or added signature had changed, but now the view from the verandah was estimated to fetch between $60,000 and $80,000.

I telephoned Christie's in Melbourne, spoke to Annette Larkin of the Paintings Department and told her the whole story about the group of dealers 'ringing' the painting and the signature which at the dealers' behest had been changed by a clever forger. An official announcement about this was made at the auction. In a blaze of publicity and helped by the escalating prices for paintings by Australian women artists, the now famous Margaret Preston painting of her verandah sold for $55,000, a huge increase on the paltry price it had fetched decades earlier when signed by the relatively unknown 'M.R. McPherson'!

CHAPTER TWENTY-FIVE

Portrait photograph: National Library of Australia, Canberra.

Kylie Tennant, OM
(1912–1988)

A WITTY AND COMPASSIONATE AUTHOR AND
SOCIAL COMMENTATOR

In one of Kylie Tennant's novels a prostitute is gaoled for a week. To understand just what a gaol sentence was like, Kylie got herself arrested for soliciting and spent a week in Long Bay gaol before her embarrassed husband arrived to bail her out. She wrote ten highly realistic novels filled with humour as well as tears. She recorded the harrowing effects of poverty and unemployment on penniless, powerless battlers during the Great Depression of the 1930s. Another recurrent theme in her work is that in a poverty-stricken world, men control what little money is available, something she knew about at first-hand.

Born with a silver spoon in her mouth (it soon tarnished), she was expected to make a brilliant marriage and lead a life of luxury. Instead she renounced all this to be a writer and social commentator. Her maternal grandfather, Tolhurst by name, was a wealthy building contractor who built himself a harbour-front mansion in Mosman, on Sydney's north shore. Her father boasted that he was descended from a long line of British aristocrats. Kylie Tennant's features were distinctly aristocratic but she had a far from privileged childhood. (The current head of the Tennant clan is Lord Colin Glenconner, who gave Princess Margaret a luxurious villa on Mustique, the island he owns in the West Indies.)

Following middle-class custom before World War I, Kylie's father and mother were rarely allowed to meet unchaperoned before their society wedding. Katherine Tolhurst was eighteen when she went to the altar, convinced that she was head over heels in love with Thomas Tennant, a dashing young man with sleek black hair and a film-star moustache. Thomas's upper-crust connections impressed his in-laws, and so did his ownership of a large block of land at Mosman. Katherine Tolhurst was stunningly attractive, with deep blue eyes, short blonde curls and a passion for dancing the Charleston. Initially it seemed as though their marriage would be secure and happy.

What Thomas desperately wanted was a son to carry on the Tennant name. He was severely disappointed when instead of the ardently desired heir, his young wife bore him two *daughters*. Thomas Tennant had little time for girls — his mind-set echoed the philosophy of Hegel; he believed women had considerably less brain power than men, therefore education was wasted on daughters. Soon Thomas and Katherine Tennant began to quarrel violently; he would leave home, threaten divorce, then move back again. It was apparent to everyone around them, including their young daughters, Kylie and Doffie, that they were hopelessly ill-matched.

Kylie's father, known as 'the parent', was arrogant, mean with money and frequently violent. At times Kylie, her mother and little Doffie fled from crockery missiles hurled at them by their furious parent. On one occasion he locked his wife out of the house; she retaliated by smashing down the back door with an axe.

Thomas Tennant constantly reproached his long-suffering wife for failing to produce a son and heir. The 'missing heir' to the Tennant name and money was the dominant theme in their matrimonial rows. Kylie's mother soon had enough of this and retaliated by denying her husband what the lawyers termed his 'conjugal rights'. 'Had "The Parent" been just a little less selfish and overbearing towards my mother, he could possibly have had a flock of sons, but he spoilt his chances' Kylie wrote in her memoirs *The Missing Heir*.[1]

As children, Kylie and Doffie used to dress up in adult clothes and play a game they called 'Divorcees'. Kylie would wear her grandmother's white fur hat, playing the part of a divorce judge in a wig, and award custody of both children to the mother. But in those days divorce was an expensive procedure and created scandal. Thomas and Katherine Tennant would patch up their differences for a while, and for a few days there would be peace and quiet before their matrimonial battles began again.

When their parents finally *did* separate, Kylie, her sister and their mother stayed in her maternal grandmother's house or in a series of cheap rented apartments. Kylie's father, who now had a well-paid managerial post in the steel industry, grudged every penny he had to pay to maintain his wife and daughters. Kylie longed for her parents to divorce, especially after her father was discovered *in flagrante delecto* with his housekeeper.

Not surprisingly, Kylie developed a loathing for everything her father admired, including his wealthy English relatives. She escaped from an unhappy home life into the fantasy world of books and writing. Extremely intelligent, by the time she was six years old she had read most of the leatherbound copies of Charles Dickens's works on her father's bookshelves. Later, Dickens would strongly influence her when she began to create some of the vivid and unusual characters that people her own novels.

In spite of her husband's disapproval of education for girls, Katherine Tennant insisted that he should pay the fees for his daughters to attend Brighton College, a private school in Manly. This was the same school attended by the aviator Nancy Bird Walton; like Kylie, she loathed her time there. Walton notes in her autobiography *Born to Fly* that Kylie was brilliant at sport. The writer Nancy Phelan, who became very close friends with Kylie Tennant, also grew up on Sydney's north shore. She recalls a netball match between Brighton College and the school she herself attended. To Kylie, Brighton College was rigid and ultra-conformist. She spoke of her schooldays as 'my dreary years of conventionality'.

Possibly influenced by Thomas Tennant's attitude, Kylie's teachers were convinced she was stupid. Her spelling was appalling and she was very poor at maths. None of them bothered to enquire if Kylie's chaotic home life was causing problems with her schoolwork. Although initially Kylie's talent for writing went unrecognised, in her final exams she received high marks in English while failing abysmally in Latin and maths. This precluded her from any hope of obtaining a scholarship to go to university. Of course her father refused to pay university fees for her or for private tuition to improve her weak subjects and Kylie left school shortly before her seventeenth birthday.

Her parents' matrimonial battles ensured that Kylie did not believe in romance and had scant interest in finding a husband, the aim of most girls of her day, who sought security and happiness in a 'good marriage'. Her father did manage to find her a job with the Australian Broadcasting Commission, in what where the pioneer days of radio. She started at the bottom as a 'girl Friday' or 'go-fer'. Her quick wit and intelligence led to her promotion to the Publicity Department, where she interviewed celebrities and academics and wrote informative paragraphs about them for the program announcers.

Eventually, her creative flair was recognised and she became an Assistant Producer, which involved a certain amount of scriptwriting for children's radio. She also enjoyed modest success as a freelance journalist and mistakenly believed that she would be able to support herself as a worker. In 1930, after two years with the ABC, she threw away her promising career in radio, telling her section manager that she wanted to leave in order to write a novel.

It was an unfortunate decision in many respects. Kylie was eighteen, had no savings at all and the Depression was about to hit Australia. Against all advice, she left home, took the train to Melbourne and tried to find part-time work as a journalist to support herself while she wrote her first book. This proved impossible.

The Depression was starting to bite and the winter was freezing cold. Kylie had no money and became desperate. She worked briefly as a barmaid before taking a job selling newspapers and cigarettes in a kiosk on Flinders Street Station, working ten hours each day. After paying her board and lodging she was left with a mere two shillings and sixpence at the end of the week.

Kylie had a mop of dark hair, deep brown eyes and an extrovert personality backed by a keen sense of humour. She was wary of men but found many of them were very interested in her. She discovered she could repel unwanted advances by telling her would-be seducers she was a lesbian; however, she had to abandon this excuse when they asked embarrassing questions and it became obvious she had not the faintest idea of the physical intimacy between lesbians.

Kylie was determined she would not be pressured into marriage, as her mother had been. Neither was she interested in pre-marital sex at a time when there was no reliable contraception. (The contraceptive pill did not arrive in Australia until 1952.) She complained that it was impossible to strike up friendships with men because invariably 'they thought you would go to bed with them'. She added indignantly: 'Any young girl with a trace of compassion could find herself pregnant.'

Meanwhile, her father wrote letters ordering her to return to her mother's home, which she threw away. Then one day 'the parent' arrived at the kiosk where she was dispensing newspapers and cigarettes, raging and roaring at her 'like some mad bull elephant'. Kylie stood firm and yelled back. To make his point her father thumped so hard on the counter that he broke its glass top. He refused to pay for new glass, saying his daughter would have to do this out of her wages and stormed off in a rage leaving Kylie to confront the enraged owner of the kiosk. Thomas Tennant next went to the Commissioner of Police, demanding that his wayward daughter be arrested and sent to a home for delinquent girls. He totally overplayed his hand and the Commissioner refused his request, whereupon 'the parent' returned to Sydney having lost the battle.

Eventually Kylie realised that at a time when so many people were being laid off work, it would be desirable to gain a university degree if she wanted an interesting job. This meant taking mathematics, algebra and geometry and Latin exams again so that she could matriculate and gain entrance to the University of Sydney. At this point her maternal grandmother took pity on Kylie and announced that she would pay the fees for her granddaughter's first term at university. Now Kylie *had* to pass her Latin and maths exams. She enrolled for evening classes at a well-known coaching establishment and to earn the fees found a day job selling typewriters. The second time around she passed all her exams.

Accepted as an undergraduate at Sydney University, Kylie enrolled in psychology and economics, convinced that these subjects would be useful for her writing; if she could not make it as a writer she would become a psychologist. By now the part-time job selling typewriters had soured, and Kylie found work as a copywriter in an advertising agency while attending lectures at night.[2]

She soon discovered that she detested economics as much as maths, but gained some help with her assignments from a scholarship student called Lewis Rodd, whose working-class parents were unable to help him financially. Like Kylie, he was putting himself through university by working in an office during the day and attending lectures at night. Quiet, shy Lewis Rodd, who was known as Roddy, adored Kylie from the first moment he met her. In common with other male students, he admired the way she drew people to her by the warmth and magnetism of her personality and her witty and amusing conversation. She was attractive in a boyish way but did not bother too much about her appearance, preferring to wear baggy sweaters, comfortable skirts and flat shoes although her mother and grandmother forced her to wear high heels and a 'frock' to attend family parties.

Ever mindful of her parent's unhappy marriage and the lack of any reliable method of contraception, Kylie was cautious of getting sexually involved with Roddy (or any other man). Since Roddy was in no position to propose marriage, despite his frustration, their friendship remained platonic.

Studying hard and holding down an office job proved exhausting and stressful for Roddy. He seemed responsible and highly organised, but in fact he was plagued by self-doubt and subject to bouts of depression followed by bursts of manic energy. Kylie, like most people of that era, when there were very few psychiatrists in Australia, knew little about psychiatric illness and failed to see the warning signs that Lewis Rodd was afflicted with manic depression, the disease now known as bipolar disorder.

His high intelligence combined with hard work ensured that Roddy graduated with an excellent Arts degree. However, during the Depression, with no friends in high places to pull strings on his behalf, the only permanent work he could find was as a schoolteacher for the New South Wales Education Department, which meant three years in the bush.

Seeing the outcome of Roddy's struggle to put himself through university, Kylie decided she had no wish to get her degree if it meant she too would become a teacher in a bush school. She decided to leave university and write her first book, and to provide a small income she became a country chicken farmer for a while.

Kylie Tennant decided her first novel would be about ordinary 'battlers' during the Depression. To gain material for it she took to the road, like thousands of homeless men and women who wandered about in search of work, lived in shanty settlements and 'jumped the rattler' as boarding a train without a ticket was called. She visited Paddy's Market and bought herself a pair of workmen's baggy trousers, a secondhand sweater, and heavy workmen's boots. A battered felt hat completed her hobo's outfit. In a bout of uncharacteristic generosity, Kylie's father drove her to the Blue Mountains and gave her enough money for a return train fare to Sydney. It seemed that by now he was resigned to his daughter's erratic and unorthodox life. Being Kylie, she donated her father's ten shillings to a destitute tramp and worked as a volunteer helper in a soup kitchen for the unemployed at Bowenfels, where she braved the cold of winter and slept on the verandah at the home of a university friend.

When Kylie had had enough of ladling out bowls of soup at Bowenfels she hitched to Molong, where she boarded a freight train and met more battlers 'jumping the rattler', gathering 'real life stories' from the tramps, drifters and unemployed men seeking work. In her heavy workmen's boots she tramped through the countryside until her feet were sore and blistered; and at Cullen Bullen she attempted to spend a free night in a cell at the police station.

'Surely you *must* have a spare cell,' she pleaded with the police sergeant.

The sergeant told her there was no spare cell, but after talking to Kylie for a few minutes he found her so interesting and entertaining that he invited her to stay in his own home. His wife, horrified by Kylie's blisters, brought her a jug of hot water and helped to bathe her sore feet.

On her travels around New South Wales Kylie called in at Coonabarabran to see her friend Lewis Rodd. This was where he was teaching. She intended to stay with him for a few days then travel further north. However, Roddy had other ideas — he had wanted to marry Kylie since they were students together. Now that he had a steady job (albeit a poorly paid one), he seized his chance of wooing her once more.

Kylie, now in her twentieth year, was still a virgin. In the 1930s, pre-marital virginity was a highly prized virtue. Katherine Tennant had drummed this fact into both her daughters; for Kylie, child bearing and rearing were equated with dependence upon a man, something she did not want. Now, however, carried away by seeing Roddy again and by the full moon overhead, Kylie lost her virginity on the banks of the Castlereagh River. She described the experience as 'very romantic. But by bad luck a moth got into my ear ... I did not think it would be polite to say to Roddy "Could you stop seducing me because I have a moth in my ear?" And so I carried on regardless.'

Although her traumatic experiences of life with 'the parent' and his constant fighting with her mother had put her off matrimony, somehow or other she now agreed to Roddy's persistent demands that they should get married. The wedding took place very quietly in November 1932, shortly before Kylie's twenty-first birthday. In later life, when she was asked why she broke with her principles and agreed to marry so young, Kylie simply explained that the 1930s were an era when 'nice' girls married the man to whom they had given their virginity.

Initially money was tight. Sometimes kind-hearted Roddy had to help out members of his own poverty-stricken family. He adored Kylie and was determined to prove himself a good and loyal husband. He was intelligent, sensitive and very supportive. He too had aspirations to become a writer, but he knew this was impossible; one of them had to earn a regular income. Roddy's memory of childhood as a member of a large family in the brawling, bug-ridden slums of Surry Hills made him well aware that keeping his job was essential.

Their first years of marriage were dedicated to hard work and saving enough money for a trip overseas. At that time London was the place where most 'serious' Australian books were published. They both yearned to visit Britain.

Kylie was aware that Roddy suffered from bouts of depression, but with her optimistic outlook on life she had failed to recognise the full extent of his mood swings from one extreme to the other. Now she realised how during his manic phase Roddy would work away in a frenzy of enthusiasm before collapsing into deep depression, doubting his own abilities, unable to sleep, losing appetite and even threatening to kill himself.

Sustained periods devoted to school administration (which Roddy loathed) made him very tired and brought on his depression. At the time little was known about the crippling effects of bipolar disorder. Antidepressants such as Prozac were not available nor did electroconvulsive therapy (ECT) become available until a few years later. Not until 1949 did Australian-born Dr John Cade discover that a relatively inexpensive, easy to obtain substance called lithium could be used to treat manic depressive disorders. In the 1930s no one knew how to manage these. They caused intense distress to those who suffered them and to those, like Kylie Tennant, who lived with the victims of such disorders.

Having to support Roddy in his bouts of depression strengthened Kylie's already determined character. His mental problems forced her to become even more outgoing than before to compensate for her husband's introverted and at times melancholic personality. As a result of Roddy's rapid mood swings from elation to despair and self-doubt, Kylie spent much of her married life coping with crises. Roddy attempted suicide on several occasions by slashing his wrists or trying to drown himself. In spite of such dramatic difficulties, Kylie remained devoted to Roddy. She nursed him through them and became adept at covering up his suicide attempts to hide them from his fellow teachers, pupils' parents and school trustees to ensure he would not lose his job.

Despite the bouts of manic activity and periods of clinical depression, there were initially long periods of calm, domestic happiness. Basically theirs was a loving union of two highly intelligent, creative people with a great deal in common. Kylie's marriage was in many respects far happier than that of her parents. However, her discovery that the man she had imagined would be her rock and anchor had such huge mental problems was a real shock. 'Marriage,' she wrote with feeling, 'is like coming upon an undiscovered landscape.'

The Rodds had started married life with no money for a rental bond. All they could afford on Roddy's meagre salary was a room at the local pub. However, living in the pub freed Kylie from domestic chores like cooking, cleaning and shopping and she had plenty of time to devote herself to writing.

Before she started on her first novel, Kylie produced a series of articles and short stories and submitted them to *Smith's Weekly* and *The Bulletin*. Many of these were published, which brought in some extra income and helped to persuade her that if she persevered she *could* become an author. She still wrote under the name 'Tennant', refusing to change her name to Kylie Rodd. Keeping her own name was a matter of feminist principle. Such a revolutionary idea for the time won her no friends among her husband's married colleagues, although it pleased her father, offering him a slight compensation for the 'missing heir'. Kylie dreamed of having a son herself, but knew that she and Roddy must wait before starting a family.

They saved enough to move into a modest rented house, and now Kylie's household chores increased hugely. They could not afford domestic help and few of the labour-saving devices we take for granted today were available then. Kylie would far rather have been writing than washing pots and pans, scrubbing wooden workbenches, washing and ironing shirts and lighting wood-fired stoves. In those days that was what wives did, and so she did it.[3]

At the height of the Depression Kylie became involved with the local branch of the Labor Party. With no social security payments for the unemployed, they tramped through the country areas seeking work. Horrified, Kylie saw families evicted from rented accommodation onto the pavement when they could no longer pay the rent or repay loans given them in better days by banks or mortgage companies.

She was determined to include in her book the deplorable conditions in which many thousands of Australians lived during the Depression. She knew that a breadwinner losing his job, usually through no fault of his own, all too often meant eviction due to non-payment of rent. Many went from neat clean homes to insanitary shanty camps, relying on 'susso' — bags of flour and meat handed out at local police stations to men who had been unable to find work after fourteen days and could prove they had no money in the bank. As a result of Kylie's quest for gritty realism, her dialogue captured the racy speech of the average battler. Her readers were drawn into a world peopled by tramps and 'sundowners' and women without hope.

Kylie and a few supporters and friends decided to give a 'slap-up Christmas dinner' for the unemployed. She stood outside pubs rattling a collection box to raise money for food, made puddings, bought turkeys and sacks of vegetables and peeled vast mounds of potatoes and pumpkins for the dinner. She was outraged to learn that the organisers refused permission for the local Aborigines to attend the Labor Party's Christmas dinner. 'We're workers too!' the Aborigines protested. Kylie never forgot the expressions on their faces as they were turned away from the door.

The Mayor and other civic worthies asked Kylie to make a speech at the lunch, expecting the schoolmaster's wife to utter a few conventional platitudes. What she did say shocked them beyond belief.

'Don't feel grateful for this at all!' she told the dust-covered tramps and penniless smallholders whose children sat there wearing patched and ragged clothes . 'People owe each other kindness all the time, not just on one day of the year! Remember that.'

When the Labor League received donations of sides of beef and mutton and boxes of fruit for families in need, Kylie helped to distribute the food. Together with a woman friend, she went into tin-roofed bush humpies with dirt floors and furniture made from old crates. There they found illiterate children, 'shy as bush animals', many of whom never went to school because there was no money for transport.

Describing a visit to one family of battlers living in just such a bush hut, Kylie said that it was like going back one hundred years in time.[4,5] Her description of the forlorn bush wife sitting motionless in an armchair, so depressed that she can scarcely speak, is unforgettable: 'the crude, one-room hut built of bark, the pitifully small clearing, the weary unshaven, man, the wild-eyed, barefoot children, the woman in a shapeless print gown who, as a bright pretty girl, had been brought out from England by her husband and now had become demented by loneliness and privation.'[6]

In 1933 Roddy had fulfilled his three years in the bush for the Education Department. He was moved from tiny Coonabarabran to a much larger school at Canowindra. Once again, at Canowindra, the Rodds moved into the local pub. With Roddy assured of regular meals, a bed with clean sheets and laundered shirts, Kylie returned to Sydney in search of more material for her writing. She stayed with Roddy's family in the working-class suburb of Surry Hills. Outraged by the vermin, filth and despair she found there and the indifference shown by many of Sydney's wealthy eastern suburbs inhabitants, Kylie became sympathetic to the aims of the Australian Communist Party.

Tennant, like other women writers of her day such as Katharine Susannah Prichard, Eleanor Dark and Jean Devanny, each of whom displayed a strong social conscience, came to believe for a time that communism would alleviate the desperate conditions of the unemployed. Briefly (until the party suspended her for a minor breach of discipline), Kylie Tennant became a card-carrying Communist Party member.[7]

By now more than a quarter of all Australians were out of work. To make matters worse the federal government reduced the basic wage for those who did have jobs by 10 per cent. The effects of long-term unemployment were terrible; many families lost their homes, their possessions and their self-respect. Shanty towns of corrugated iron, tents and makeshift dwellings constructed out of cardboard boxes mushroomed around towns and cities, and were inhabited by families evicted by the banks and landlords.

When Kylie returned home to Canowindra after her sojourn in Surry Hills, she found a letter from her father which enclosed a cutting from *The Bulletin* inviting entries for the S.H. Prior Memorial Prize for 'the best novel by an Australian writer'. The winner would receive one hundred pounds, then quite a substantial sum. On the cutting her father had scrawled: '*So get cracking on* your *book right away!*'

Kylie got out the notebooks crammed with ideas for her projected novel and set to work, typing out the pages of her manuscript on a small table in their cramped quarters at the pub. She named this first novel *Tiburon*. ('Shark' in Spanish); it is set in a small fictitious Australian country town of this name. Roddy helped her by reading what she had written when he came home after work and making editorial suggestions. The pages contained many of the stories the tramps and sundowners had told her as they jumped the freight trains together. Having already assembled the raw material of the novel, it took Kylie only four months to write the finished work. Then, with her heart in her mouth, she packed up the manuscript and posted it off.

Early in 1935, Kylie and Roddy were thrilled when a letter arrived informing her that *Tiburon* had won the S.H. Prior Memorial Prize. She duly received a cheque for one hundred pounds. In addition, winning the prize meant that *Tiburon* was serialised in *The Bulletin*, a great honour for any writer and a real boost to her career. While some readers saw a resemblance between Kylie Tennant's novel and the writings of Henry Lawson: others complained that *Tiburon*'s vivid depictions of an underclass of poverty-stricken people and the brutality of Australian men towards Aboriginal women were 'bad advertisements for Australia overseas' exactly the same comments that were levelled against Katharine Susannah Prichard's novels.

During her visit to Surry Hills, Kylie had realised that this underprivileged city suburb would serve as the background for aspects of Sydney life she wanted to expose in her second novel. In order to carry out more research, she insisted that she and Roddy rent a room in Surry Hills which she would use as a base. Roddy, who had escaped from urban poverty through hard work, had no wish to return to the scenes of his slum childhood, but he reluctantly agreed to this plan.

Ironically, just as Kylie obtained her rented room in Surry Hills, Roddy's mother and brother, who had had enough of bed bugs, outdoor privvies and no hot water, moved away to the slightly more salubrious suburb of Paddington. During the school holidays Roddy stayed with them there while Kylie battled on alone in her bug-ridden lodging house, gathering her material and visiting Roddy and her in-laws in Paddington whenever she needed a hot bath.

She contacted the Child Welfare Department of New South Wales, explaining that she was a teacher's wife writing a novel set in Sydney to alert people to what conditions were *really* like amongst the poorest of the population. Keen to cooperate and to draw attention to the living conditions of the poor, an official in the department arranged for Kylie to accompany a government inspector on home visits to some of the worst areas in Sydney. She was shown undernourished, barefoot children playing in rat-infested filthy streets where garbage piled up and was rarely collected and several families shared one cold tap. She talked with gaunt, bedraggled women on their doorsteps and heard stories of backstreet abortionists who operated on pregnant mothers already burdened with a dozen children; many of these women haemorrhaged and bled to death as a result. She witnessed slum landlords in action with their standover men, and the drunken brawls that took place nightly outside the pubs. She immortalised one narrow lane as 'Plug Alley' — an exhilarating, pitiless, gossipy little world of inner city poverty and deprivation.

Both the Rodds were outraged that so little was done by the rich for the poor. In spite of the rhetoric of the Communist Party, Roddy remained unconvinced that they would help anyone or anything except their own cause. Kylie, too, came to regard the leaders of the extreme Left as equally as dogmatic, prejudiced and self-serving as those on the extreme right. She described how 'we were both Reds. But our colouration gradually faded with the years until Roddy even refused to vote for the local Labor candidate if he didn't think he was any good.'

As a country teacher, Roddy was still underpaid but at least his was a tenured position with a pension attached to it. Australian writers earned very little from their books. At Surry Hills Kylie took on various jobs to make ends meet, ranging from social worker to barmaid. She used some of these work experiences in her second novel, *Foveaux* (the name she gave to her imaginary inner city suburb, where she also depicted the dairy run by Roddy's family and their local fish and chip shop). Joseph Foveaux, a soldier and colonial administrator, was a forceful character in Sydney's early history, famous for the role he played following Governor Bligh's arrest.[8] His house, situated in the present-day Foveaux Street in Surry Hills, still stands.

Foveaux was published in 1939 by Macmillan, the London publisher. This second novel was praised by the Australian and British press and hailed as a 'great Australian novel' by both the Melbourne *Argus* and the London *Observer.* In common with Charles Dickens, Emile Zola and Henry Lawson, Kylie Tennant's compassion for human tragedy brought out the best in her writing. She managed to portray the miseries of the human condition with a grim humour typical of the Australian character, writing in a distinctively Australian 'voice'. Frank Swinnerton, the literary critic of the London *Observer* newspaper, gave *Foveaux* a glowing review and described its characters as worthy of Dickens. Tennant never earned very much from her writing. Unfortunately for Kylie, in her day there were no writing grants and only small sums of prize money to be won.

In *Foveaux* she had certainly succeeded in capturing life in the slums — the swarming rats, the harassed women battling in vain against lice and bedbugs. It was very far from the picture of Australia as a sundrenched, caring society concerned with a 'fair go' for everyone — the image the Australian government was trying to promote to prospective British migrants.

Shortly after the novel appeared, the ABC invited Kylie to come in and discuss the notion of a series of paid talks on literary topics.

'What would you *like* to talk about, Miss Tennant?' purred the director, expecting her to nominate the role of women writers or the development of Australian literature.

'Slum life in Sydney,' Kylie replied without hesitation.

The director's jaw twitched nervously. He dropped the idea of a series featuring writer Kylie Tennant.

For her next novel, provisionally titled *The Brown Van*,[9] Kylie went back to the country. With the help of Roddy's family she bought an elderly mare to pull a battered brown laundry cart she had found in a junk yard. The horse was called Violet and Kylie grew very fond of her. Due to Kylie's inexperience with horses, poor Violet was tied up for the night with a slipknot and the unfortunate animal eventually strangled herself.

Before Violet came to her sad end Kylie wandered the roads with her horse and van, sharing meals with battlers who dossed down at night beside rivers or under bridges. On occasions she shared her tent with them — she was amazingly trusting, believing in the basic goodness of people from all walks of life. She talked to tramps who wandered country roads in search of seasonal work at shearing sheds, orchards or canneries, sleeping on the ground with sheepfolds as windbreaks. She witnessed these unfortunate battlers often being treated like criminals, made to produce identification papers by the police in country towns where they arrived seeking work and eventually renamed the novel after them.

The Battlers tells the story of the unemployed who suffered the humiliations of being on the dole, receiving vouchers for food in local shops rather than money. Kylie describes the sense of mateship between battlers: her characters might help themselves to a sheep on occasion or drop a few items into a sack in a shop, but they would *never* rob their mates or dob each other in. In view of her unconventional life among the 'down and outs', tramps and alcoholics, it seems surprising that Kylie was never sexually harassed or raped. Later in her life, one unemployed man with mental problems did attempt to kill her at her home at Dulwich Hill. He knocked on her door asking for work, and Kylie offered him gardening and cleaning jobs in return for money. The man forced his way into the house and almost strangled her, but she managed to escape, pick up a pitchfork and chase him out of the house.

The Battlers, published in 1941, became one of the great classic novels of Australia and won the Australian Literature Society's Gold Medal as well as another S.H. Prior Memorial Prize. Some literary critics dubbed it the Australian equivalent of John Steinbeck's American classic *The Grapes of Wrath*.[10] It is interesting to consider this comparison. While Steinbeck describes undiluted suffering during the Great Depression in America, Tennant's tragedies are mitigated by her Australian characters. Steinbeck's dust-bowl farmers lose their farms and take to the roads in their battered T-model Fords. Tennant's battlers have never had the *chance* to own a farm or a motor car. With little to lose they are not as embittered as Steinbeck's dust-bowl farmers. They keep their distinctive Aussie sense of humour as well as their traditional disrespect for the police and instinctive distrust of success and 'tall poppies', characteristics based on the convict origins of Australian society.

The main characters in *The Battlers* are Dancy, an abused girl from a working-class background, and 'Snow' or 'Snowy', whose straw-coloured hair has earned him that typically Australian name for fair-haired men. 'If Snow became excited, he stuttered,' Kylie wrote. 'He seldom spoke a sentence without three "bloodys" but never even knew he was swearing which [to him] was as natural as his stutter.'

Snow and his dog, Bluey, are expert at stealing sheep to survive 'on the road'. Snow takes odd jobs droving, fencing, shearing. His recreations are fighting, drinking and singing. Dancy has had most of her teeth knocked out by her father, who had escaped from a lunatic asylum, murdered her mother and then cut his own throat, after which young Dancy had been made to mop up the blood. She had been raped repeatedly, her illegitimate child had been taken from her by 'the Welfare', and its father had long since deserted her.

Kylie succeeded brilliantly in conveying the lack of communication between the working-class men and women in her novel. Snow has a wife and children, but is often away on the road for more than nine months at a time and shows little enthusiasm for his family when he does return home. Like many men Kylie met on the road, Snow greatly preferred the company of his mates at the pub. He represents the worst aspects of Australian mateship; all he cares about are his dog, his mates and his grog.[11]

In her autobiography[12] Kylie writes that she 'gravitated naturally to unemployed people, because they had been flung off the industrial wheel and I hated the wheel'.[13] She was very Australian in her support of the underdog and hated the uncaring nature of authority. She claimed that she was not interested in writing about 'how people make a living, because I belong to the generation that *couldn't* get jobs'. Instead, she chose to write about 'true blue' Aussies with their defiant attitude to authority, their tenacity and their sense of humour.

She depicted the harsh reality of the lives of unskilled working-class women in the 1930s, before the days of government allowances and supporting mother's benefits, when single motherhood was feared and young women like Olly, a character in Kylie's third novel *Ride On Stranger*, died as the result of a botched backyard abortion. Among other Australian women writers of her era, only Barbara Baynton and Henry Handel Richardson wrote as well about urban and rural poverty, disease and despair.

While his daughter was hard at work on her novels and chronically short of money, 'the parent' continued to earn his high executive salary in the steel industry. He now lived apart from Kylie's mother and entered into a series of short-term relationships with other women, none of whom satisfied his exacting standards. 'The parent' remained stubborn and hot-tempered, two characteristics Kylie had inherited from him, along with her looks. Her rows with her father were spirited, yet beneath the barbed insults they hurled at one another they respected each other's strength of will and determination.

Thomas Tennant loved having a daughter who was an author. He was intensely proud of her books and their success and the fact that the Tennant name featured on the cover. As father and daughter grew older their relationship mellowed, though it was still fraught with arguments.

Kylie had wanted children for some time; her father longed for 'the missing heir'. Eventually her wish was granted and she had two children, a son named Bim and a daughter, Benison. Thomas Tennant was delighted to become a grandfather.

During World War II and for several years afterwards there was an acute shortage of paper for books, with each publisher receiving only a limited quota. As a result Macmillan were unable to reissue her books.[14] Kylie's father and Roddy raised some capital and formed a company they named Sirius Publishing to reissue Kylie's novels in Sydney. The fact that, like Inky Stephenson, Miles Franklin's publisher, the company never made a profit was largely due to Australia's small population and the consequent size of her book market. Neither Kylie Tennant nor Henry Handel Richardson, Katharine Susannah Prichard or any other Australian writers of this era made enough from royalties to remunerate them adequately for the years they spent researching and writing their books. At that time, of course, the system of writers' fellowships and grants currently offered by the Australia Council and the Arts Departments of the different States had not been instituted.

Kylie's best-known novel (eventually made into an ABC mini series) is *Ride on Stranger*, published in 1943 in London, Sydney and New York to wide acclaim. The plot deals with the life of Shannon, a feisty young woman who in some respects is Kylie's *alter ego*. Shannon is strong-minded and extremely capable but lacks qualifications. Her experiences often mirror those of her creator, as does her cheerful optimism that things will get better. She drifts to the city, going from job to job. Like Kylie herself, Shannon becomes a Girl Friday in a radio station before going to work for a self-important and rather shady 'guru' who heads his own pseudo-religious Order of Human Brotherhood. The self-righteous and hypocritical Vaughan-Quilter, one of Kylie's more memorable characters, was a new phenomenon to Australian readers. (Today we read *ad nauseam* about his present-day equivalents, lecherous TV evangelists and greedy New Age gurus with Rolls Royces.)

Between 1954 and 1955 she wrote *The Honey Flow,* based on the lives of a group of itinerant beekeepers with whom she travelled while gaining background for the book. This time Kylie did receive some financial assistance from the newly-established Commonwealth Literary Fund, and was able to buy herself a motorised van rather than a horse and cart. To escape detection she dressed as inconspicuously as possible in an old pair of men's trousers and an oversized sweater, an outfit that echoed her purchases at Paddy's Market before she first took to the road in her youth.

1967 saw the publication of Kylie Tennant's novel *Tell Morning This,* set in a time when there were few social security benefits for women. The storyline shows how one woman is reduced to prostitution to feed her family. To gain first-hand experience, Kylie bleached her dark hair a brassy blonde, put on a skin-tight dress and high heels and went out to solicit men, pretending she was tipsy. It had been planned that a sailor acquaintance of a friend was to play the role of her client. Unfortunately, the sailor failed to turn up at the appointed time and place and Kylie had to act as a drunken prostitute for a stranger who turned out to be a former boxer. As Kylie had hoped, she was arrested and gaoled for a month.[15] The police failed to recognise her, even though they had often seen her taking notes in court. They booked her under the name of 'Thelma Parker' and gave her a bare cell with six bunk beds and a bucket to act as a lavatory. In the cell Kylie chatted away to her sister prostitutes, noting with sympathy: 'these unfortunate women all had something physically wrong with them — poor eyesight, bad teeth, skin troubles, weak bladders ... To keep our spirits up we sang cheerful bawdy songs after lights out.'[16]

After a few days the police noticed Kylie jotting down her cell mates' conversations in her pocket notebook. They thought she must be deranged and decided to send her away to what was then known as

Darlinghurst Lunatic Asylum. At this juncture Kylie was forced to confess that she was only in gaol to obtain material for her next book. At first the police refused to believe her. To back up her story, Kylie had to telephone Roddy and her mother, both of whom arrived to bail her out. The Sydney *Sunday Sun* published the story and the police were not amused. There was talk of prosecuting Kylie Tennant for creating a public mischief, which worried Roddy. In the end no action was taken against her. However, the story made Kylie Tennant notorious — she had exposed the narrowness and monumental failure of the Department of Moral Rehabilitation. 'I used fact as a foundation for broadening comic fiction, which people would read for entertainment without realising that my stories were penetrating the subsoil of their minds and presenting a true picture of society,' she said, delighted to expose the absurdity, pretension and hypocrisy of Australian society of that period.

Tell Morning This[17] contains a harrowing scene where a mother tries to commit suicide by putting her head in a gas oven but is saved because she does not have enough money for the gas meter. The book was initially called *The Joyful Condemned* and published (like most Australian books of the period) in austerity post war Britain of 1953, when it created considerable scandal. It was republished in Australia a decade later under the title *Tell Morning This*.

Being interviewed by journalists about her life at home and avoiding the revelation that her husband was a suicidal manic-depressive was steadily growing more difficult for Kylie Tennant. She was continually stressed by the demands of being a loyal wife and the mother of two children, having to juggle household duties and writing. At times, she managed to escape and go on a trip to the outback to research fresh material for her novels.

Kylie dreamed of Australia becoming a more compassionate society towards the poor and dispossessed and those of Aboriginal descent. She realised the importance of education to help Aboriginal children. Although the Rodds were far from affluent and had two children to raise, Kylie donated the royalties from her book *Speak You So Gently* (1959) to set up a scholarship fund for Aboriginal education. The book's title was taken from a line in Shakespeare's *As You Like It*, where Orlando says:

Speak you so gently? Pardon me, I pray you.
I thought that all things had been savage here...
If you ... know what 'tis to pity and be pitied,
Let gentleness my strong enforcement be.'

Kylie wrote this book with Roddy's approval. In fact, he asked her to accompany his close friend, the Reverend Alf Clint, the rather unparsonical clergyman appointed as Director of Native Cooperatives, to help Aborigines and Torres Strait Islanders to become self-sufficient and rescue them from poverty, disease and malnutrition.

So Kylie left ten-year-old Benison with Roddy and flew with Bim, now three, to the northernmost tip of Queensland in a series of ancient planes. The final leg of their journey took place in a truck that kept breaking down. They finally reached the Lochart River, where Alf Clint had established the first registered Aboriginal Cooperative in Australia, in an attempt to make trochus diving pay. Here Kylie found a handful of dedicated Europeans who worked themselves almost literally to shadows with 'insufficient manpower, insufficient money, insufficient everything to help the Aborigines establish themselves on a sound and healthy basis'. Kylie lived in the Cooperative for three months and taught a kindergarten class, a class for adults and another for illiterates. She found the Aborigines 'unfailingly courteous, generous and hospitable'.

After this she visited Thursday Island where the proceeds of pearl fishing kept another Cooperative going, and visited remote Moa Island, where she was greeted with great kindness by the local people before she and Bim returned home.

During the 1960s Kylie spent much of her time in Canberra, working for over four years on a biography of the former Australian prime minister, H.V. Evatt titled, *Politics and Justice,* which was published in 1970. (In 1952 she had written a prize-winning play, *Tether A Dragon,* based on the life of Alfred Deakin.)[18] In addition, she worked on a freelance basis as a literary critic for the *Sydney Morning Herald* from 1954–1979, contributing lively and entertaining reviews to the paper.

Things were now going badly with Roddy. He suffered a complete nervous breakdown, brought on by a heavy administrative workload and his bipolar disorder. After surviving another suicide attempt — he threw himself under a train and sustained terrible injuries which resulted in him losing an arm and a leg — he retired from teaching on a small pension. He and Kylie moved to a small red brick villa in the attractive and secluded harbourside suburb of Hunter's Hill, chosen by Roddy rather than Kylie. There, freed from the cares and drudgery of work, they were initially very happy. Roddy was now able to fulfil his own ambition to write and produced his memoir *A Gentle Shipwreck,* the story of his childhood. As he was now retired, in order to help Kylie, who was working as an advisor for her British publisher Macmillan as well as continuing her authorship, Roddy took over the shopping and the cooking.

Australian print runs were still very small in the era before Australia published its own books. Royalty payments for colonial authors published in London or Edinburgh, whose books were exported to Australia, were often based on a mere two, three or four per cent of the selling price.[19] British publishers justified these low payments by claiming that it cost them a great deal to ship the books to Australia.

Kylie was invited to become a member of the board of the Commonwealth Literary Fund, an honorary position which meant travelling to meetings all round Australia to take part in the decision process of awarding grants to younger writers or pensions to ageing or impoverished authors. She also gave lectures on Australian literature and reviewed books, activities which proved more profitable than writing them, although by now she was one of Australia's best-known authors.

Then tragedy struck. Bim, her adored only son who had been a model child at school, gifted, good looking and top of his class, underwent a total personality change in his first year at university — he was afflicted by the onset of schizophrenia. Unknown to his parents, Bim started to take hard drugs to prevent himself from hearing the 'inner voices' which can be a symptom of schizophrenia; in his case, these voices commanded him to perform actions which often caused confrontations with authority.

After a harrowing period of disturbing and disruptive behaviour, Bim was diagnosed as schizophrenic and spent time in and out of psychiatric hospitals. In spite of all Kylie's efforts, care and love, his condition worsened. At times Bim's bizarre, even menacing behaviour frightened the neighbours and the police would take him away in handcuffs and gaol him, as there were insufficient medical facilities to cope with cases of schizophrenia.

Outwardly Kylie appeared to cope well with the mental problems of both her husband and son, but in reality she was devastated. She suffered the guilt and grief experienced by most parents of drug-addicted children. She was angered by what she saw as the medical profession's lack of knowledge about suitable treatment, and in Bim's case by his doctors' failure to communicate with her and Roddy as his parents.

She made plans to take her family away from the city and live in the Blue Mountains, where Bim would not find it so easy to obtain hard drugs. They bought a run-down apple farm called Cliff View at Shipton. Kylie described it as 'sixty-two acres of neglect and desolation', with a weatherboard house that appeared to be on the verge of falling down. Kylie learned that Bim had fathered a child with a fellow student who was a Roman Catholic. The girl's parents refused to let her marry a non-Catholic, especially one suffering from schizophrenia.

Kylie suffered more guilt about this development. She adored her grandson and gave the mother an allowance and tried to become friends with her, but the girl refused to have anything to do with her. Then Kylie attempted to adopt the child, but the baby's mother remained adamant that 'her' child could only be adopted by Catholics. To Kylie's father, in an ironic twist of fate, Bim's son became symbolic of 'the missing heir'; perhaps this is why Kylie eventually bequeathed part of her Blue Mountains apple orchard to her only grandson. Denied the opportunity to raise him, she poured her energy into reclaiming Cliff View and compiling two collections of short stories. She invited some of Bim's hippy friends to stay. The arrangement was that they would help her and Benison to restore and redecorate the dilapidated wooden house on the apple farm in return for some wages and free accommodation.

Roddy was not capable of taking part in this work. His bouts of depression and manic highs had returned with a vengeance and he was receiving electric shock treatment and taking antidepressant drugs prescribed by his psychiatrist.[20] Meanwhile, Bim's friends, who had sworn to Kylie that they were drug free, were procuring illegal supplies of hard drugs for Bim.

Only Kylie's optimistic personality enabled her to survive the double tragedy of Roddy's mental illness and her son's schizophrenia. Her reserves of inner strength, her sense of humour and the fact she could escape into writing gave her the fortitude to cope with these family tragedies. 'Having two negatives in the family, I had to become more positive,' she wrote with magnificent understatement. Kylie ran the orchard, tried to hold the family together and carried on writing. She felt continually frustrated that she could do so little for either of the men she loved.

Tragedy struck again. Roddy was diagnosed with cancer. Then, probably as a result of intolerable stress, Kylie herself developed breast cancer and went into hospital to have her left breast removed. Not even this blow could daunt her unquenchable spirit, and she refused to give way to self-pity. 'Now I know what it was like to be an Amazon,' she told visitors to her hospital bed. She knew she *had* to survive in order to take care of Bim and Roddy and had a long period of remission.

With hard physical work and his removal from the inner city drug scene to the security of the apple farm, Bim appeared to improve. He told his parents he had decided to study law, and so long as he was drug free, he would be accepted back by Sydney University. Kylie did not doubt his word and drove him back to the city. The money he had earned from working in the orchard was sufficient to pay for his accommodation.

Everything seemed to be going well.

Then, just as Kylie thought her problems with Bim were over, she received a phone call from the police. Her son was in hospital, having been pushed out of an upstairs window of a squat in Kings Cross by three people 'involved with the drug trade'. Never one to evade the truth, Kylie asked if her son had gone to the squat to buy drugs. 'Of course. What *else* would he be doing there?' was the reply.

It transpired that a young coloured man had been seen dragging Bim's body into a laundry to steal his wallet. Another was spotted coming out of the laundry wiping bloodstained hands on his shirt. The police arrested all three people living in the squat and decided to prosecute should Bim die. He was only twenty-six.

Bim, the son Kylie had wanted so badly, hovered between life and death on life support but died several days later, having failed to regain consciousness.

Somehow Kylie found the strength to witness the trial of the three people accused of his murder, an Aborigine, a Torres Strait Islander and a Cook Islander, two men and a woman. She tried to contain her feelings against the trio, whose counsel pleaded that they had suffered from hard and difficult childhoods. Kylie had written of human tragedy and the plight of the underclass, which she had witnessed first hand. Now she was confronted by it again in the pointless death of her son.

Only one of the men was convicted — the other man and the girl were acquitted. A lesser woman than Kylie might have sought revenge. Showing extraordinary compassion, she sent money to the Aboriginal girl, who had been acquitted because she was deemed to have given evidence 'obtained under duress'. Kylie told her she did not seek revenge, that nothing could ever bring Bim back. The effect of Bim's death on the whole Rodd family was profound.

A year later Kylie nursed Roddy as he lay dying of cancer. Describing her grief she quoted Mary Gilmore's memorable verse:

Nurse no longer grief,
Lest the heart flower no more,
Grief builds no barns,
His plough rusts at the door.

Once more Kylie's strength of character shone through. She and her daughter threw themselves energetically into making the apple orchard profitable. They produced honey, homemade jams, fruit trees, berries of all kinds, ducks, turkeys and goats. In addition, Kylie finished her autobiography, giving it the ironic title *The Missing Heir*. It was published in 1986.

As a radical and a republican, Kylie Tennant on two separate occasions turned down the offer of an OBE. However, in 1980 she was made AO, the second highest grade of the Order of Australia, for 'outstanding contributions to Australian literature'. Thomas Tennant, proud as a peacock, accompanied her to Sydney's Government House to receive the decoration from Sir Roden Cutler, Governor of New South

Wales. 'The parent' took the decoration home with him to Patonga Beach. 'No use letting Kylie keep it,' he said, 'she'd only lose it.'

Kylie continued to drive all the way from the Blue Mountains to Patonga Beach to visit her father, now aged ninety-four. He had by now resigned himself to living alone. As often as not when she arrived exhausted from the long journey, they would argue fiercely over something trivial, such as her buying him a new mop head — although he was comfortably well off, 'the parent' retained his aversion to spending money. Kylie would cook dinner and stay overnight in the spare room, listening as he coughed himself to sleep. She wanted him to move to the apple orchard, but 'the parent' valued his independence and insisted on living by himself. Local women would visit and minister to him if he got sick, he insisted. Eventually he became seriously ill and was taken to hospital. His daughter rushed to be by his side. At the end of their turbulent relationship one of his last gestures was to kiss Kylie's hand in gratitude.[21]

Kylie did not outlast her father long. By now her breast cancer had spread to other parts of her body. She died in 1988, aged seventy-eight. In the final weeks of her life she was bedridden. Fearing she might linger on as a vegetable, she wrote an open letter to the editor of her favourite newspaper, the *Sydney Morning Herald,* pleading for the right to die with dignity and urging readers of the newspaper to press for changes to the law on euthanasia.

'Cancer cells have gnawed out my ribcage,' she wrote. '…All my friends recoil from discussion of death or cancer. These words never pass their lips until they are up against the desperate situation of the dying. Do what you can to change the social attitude to the terminally ill.'

I regret that I never met Kylie Tennant, but we had a mutual friend, the writer Michael Noonan, who knew her well from the days when they were both members of Sydney's PEN Club. Michael Noonan, a gentle and distinguished man, wrote that Kylie Tennant possessed 'an air of distinction. I remember how her face came alive with warmth when she laughed. She was warm-hearted and generous, modest about her achievements, tolerant and optimistic even in the face of so much tragedy that she confronted so bravely in her own life.'[22]

CHAPTER TWENTY-SIX

Portrait photograph: Private collection.

Oodgeroo Noonuccal
(Kath Walker)
(1920–1993)
AN OUTSTANDING WOMAN WRITER
WHO FOUGHT FOR JUSTICE FOR HER PEOPLE

Any account of the 1967 referendum, which granted a fairer deal to Aboriginal people (at that time they were not able to vote), would have to include the huge contributions made by Oodgeroo of the Noonuccal tribe and several other outstanding women like Faith Bandler, Pearl Gibbs and Jessie Street, women who worked hard to create a more just and equitable society for everyone in Australia.

On 3 November 1920, the child who would become Oodgeroo was born on Stradbroke Island, the largest of the subtropical isles in Queensland's Moreton Bay. She was christened Kathleen Jean Mary Ruska and grew up surrounded by Stradbroke's immense sparkling white sand hills, freshwater lakes and long straight beaches. The Ruskas' Aboriginal family group, the Nunukul or Noonuccal, called the island *Minjerraba* in their language; it was the white explorers who named it 'Stradbroke' in honour of a British colonial official.

On her father's side Kath was part of the Noonuccal tribe; the name she later adopted for herself was the Aboriginal name for the distinctive paperbark tree with its weeping foliage and paper-thin bark, which the tribespeople used as roofing material for their gunyahs.[1]

Kath was one of seven children born to Edward (Ted) and Lucy Ruska. Ted Ruska had Aboriginal, German and Spanish-Philippino ancestors. His grandfather was a Philippino sailor who jumped ship to escape punishment and ended up on Stradbroke Island, where he worked as a dugong fisherman and married an Aboriginal woman.[2] By the time Kath Ruska was born, colonial attitudes and intermarriage had weakened the previously strong tribal life of the Noonuccals; there were only a handful of full-blooded Aborigines left on Stradbroke Island.

Kath's maternal grandfather, Alexander McCulloch, was a Scottish immigrant who married Minnie, an Aboriginal girl he met when she was working as a maid at Marion Downs, a large pastoral station in central Queensland. They had a daughter, Lucy, but Alexander McCulloch died when she was a small child. Against her will the fatherless Lucy McCulloch was taken from her mother and sent to Brisbane to be brought up in a Catholic institution for 'uncontrollable or half-caste' girls. Minnie McCulloch may have been persuaded to place a thumbprint or fingerprint on a government paper as a form of consent, but this does not mean she willingly agreed that her daughter should be removed and sent away. Perhaps she was told that Lucy would receive a good education from the white people, which was certainly *not* the case.

Lucy McCulloch was an intelligent child but was not taught to read or write in her mission school. Like most girls of what has now become known as 'the stolen generation', she was trained by well-meaning nuns to wash clothes, iron, clean and cook in order to find employment as a domestic servant in a white household.

Lucy went to work as a servant at an outback cattle station at Boulia, in Queensland, and it was here she met Edward Ruska, who had left Stradbroke Island in search of paid work. They married and Ted took her to live on Stradbroke Island, where he had grown up. Ted and Lucy raised a large family on this beautiful, unspoiled island.³ All her life Lucy Ruska bitterly resented her lack of literacy and the home life she herself had been deprived of, and she made sure these benefits would not be denied to her own children.

Ted Ruska was employed by the Dunwich Benevolent Asylum, established by the Queensland government to house mentally or physically disabled Aborigines as well as those with an alcohol problem. He was the well-respected and likeable foreman in the gang of Aboriginal labourers, which did everything from wood cutting to road building, sweeping and clearing gutters or unloading cargo from the *Otter,* a rusty old ship that belonged to the Queensland Navy, which made the short journey between Stradbroke's port of Dunwich and the mainland twice a week. In return for working long hours six days a week, Ted Ruska received a minuscule wage and 'rations' to support his family. These consisted of rice, sago, tapioca, matches, flour and one bar of soap, which was handed out every two weeks. Ever since the foundation of the Moreton Bay Colony (renamed Queensland on its separation from New South Wales in 1859), it was traditional that on the Queen's birthday every Aboriginal was issued with a woollen blanket and a plum pudding.

On Stradbroke Kath and her brothers and sisters learned to scale and prepare fish, using the sharp edge of 'eugarie' or pippie shells, and to fish for mackerel, mullet and tailor. She learned that 'Kabool' (the carpet snake) could not be eaten, because this was the totem of the Noonuccal.⁴ Sometimes her father saddled up the horses and they would ride along the shore, then turn inland to climb hills covered with flowering wattles and sweet-scented gums.[5] Just how deeply Kath's childhood influenced her can be seen in her book *Stradbroke Dreamtime*, published in 1972. She wrote how:

> ... at Point Lookout, we would tether our horses ... and take up a position behind the small sandhills that dotted the shore. We would lie full-length upon our stomachs and silently wait for the beautiful nautilus shells to come out of the sea ... Their trumpet-like shells would unfurl to the breeze a sail, mauve-coloured, which caught the sun's rays and shone like satin.

Possibly the fact that Ted Ruska worked for the Queensland government saved Kath and her siblings from the fate of her mother and other part-Aboriginal children, who were taken from their parents and placed in church-run missions.

However, no Aborigines were allowed to join in the social activities of Europeans working on the island. 'We were banned from their dance floors,' Kath remembered. 'When we went to the cinema we were made to sit with the "inmates" of the Dunwich Institution, on hard benches right at the front. The white staff sat on cane chairs at the back of the cinema theatre.'[6]

Before Kath's first day at Dunwich State School her father impressed on her: 'Just 'cos you're Aboriginal doesn't mean you have to be as good as most white children — you have to be *better*.' Her schooldays were unhappy. Her teacher punished her for being left handed by beating her over the knuckles with a ruler, and she was forced to use her right hand; like most left-handed children, she found this very difficult.

Kath was a highly intelligent and creative child who in later life would create art and poetry. But the only future for her was in domestic service or early marriage. At thirteen she left school and started work in the only occupation then available to a part-Aboriginal girl — as a resident domestic employed by the family of a solicitor in Brisbane. She was paid the princely sum of two shillings and sixpence a week in addition to receiving her board and lodging. She had dreamed of becoming a nurse, but knew that her meagre education made such a career impossible.

The outbreak of war gave Kath a chance to escape from the drudgery of poorly paid domestic work. In 1941, when she was almost twenty-one, she presented herself for an interview at Brisbane's Victoria

Barracks, hoping to join the Australian Women's Army Service. Warned she might experience racial prejudice in the armed forces, Kath replied with characteristic forthrightness that she 'could see no difference between a racist in uniform and a civilian racist'. She was accepted for the AWAS, and experienced very little discrimination during her time in the Australian Army, where everyone was known by a number rather than a name. In her khaki uniform she was neat, smart and hard working. In later years, some of the soldiers with whom she served as well as an Army doctor recounted that they had been led to believe Kath came from Ceylon. Such a belief probably helped her to mix and mingle well.[7]

World War II changed Kath's life. Her experiences in the AWAS presented her with opportunities to see how other people lived. She served at Area Signals Headquarters at Chermside, was trained as a telephonist and acquired the rudiments of stenography.[8] She had a lively personality and from her time in the Army acquired a fondness for 'cricko', a female version of cricket. In order to get Aboriginal girls to work together harmoniously, Kath formed a cricko team known as the 'All Blacks'.

During her Army service Kath developed gingivitis, a severe gum infection, as well as an inner ear infection which led to loss of hearing. These ailments caused her to be invalided out of the forces in 1944 on health grounds and ensured she was given a very small pension.[9] At this point she met Bruce Dennis Walker, one of her former schoolmates from Stradbroke Island. A descendant of the Logan and Albert River tribes, Bruce Walker was a good dancer and a flyweight boxer. He worked as a welder at the Kangaroo Point shipyards. Kath and Bruce Walker were married in 1942 and, with a private loan from a friend, acquired a small house in Myrtle Street in the Brisbane suburb of Buranda. In 1946 the couple had their first child, a son whom they named Dennis.

Kath and her husband joined the Australian Communist Party in 1944; they felt it was the only party that was not racist. However, they soon became disillusioned by the communists' lack of action on racial discrimination and resigned. Kath was unhappy about the fact that the party wanted to write her speeches for her and 'tell her what to say'.[10]

Bruce Walker, in an effort to bring in more income to help his family, took up boxing in noisy and often violent tents at local shows. At that time boxing was one of the few ways Aborigines could acquire money and status. Gradually his life became dominated by fights, the excitement they stirred up and by alcohol. By the time their son was born the marriage was in trouble. Kath implored Bruce to give up boxing. Eventually he did so and became a 'wharfie', but he blamed Kath for his loss of status. Soon Bruce Walker's dissatisfaction with the monotony of work on the wharves, his increasing dependence on alcohol and the contrasts in character and ambitions between himself and Kath caused rows. These led to bouts of domestic violence punctuated by periods of remorse on Bruce's part, and led to a complete breakdown of the marriage. After they separated Kath kept little Dennis, whom she adored. Her husband, who was also fond of his son, retained visiting rights. Bruce, in and out of work, soon ceased to contribute to the household and Kath found herself virtually penniless. To support herself and Dennis she had to take in washing and ironing, something she loathed doing. In this bleak period she also took a job at the Dandy Bacon Factory at Murrarrie, but abandoned it in fear that her son would be harmed by her absence while she was working.

During this difficult time in her life Kath replied to an advertisement for domestic help in Brisbane, and joined the family of Sir Raphael and Lady (Phyllis) Cilento, both highly respected doctors. Dr Phyllis Cilento was widely known as the 'Medical Mother', the name she used for her radio broadcasts and newspaper articles. Kath soon became a family friend; although she was paid for her work, she was never regarded as a servant. Sir Raphael and Lady Cilento were an exceptional couple, and Kath helped Dr Phyllis Cilento to look after her elderly mother.[11]

The Cilentos had five highly intelligent children; theirs was a family with a strong interest in the arts. Their daughter Diane would become a world-famous actress, and Ruth and Margaret, their two other talented daughters, followed artistic pursuits. Their sons, David and young Raphael, studied medicine. The family were far more open minded than most members of Brisbane's extremely conventional society of the 1950s.

Sir Raphael Cilento played an important role in Kath's education, encouraging her to browse among his vast library of books and to read poetry. From Margaret Cilento (Maslen), Kath learned to draw and paint.

In 1953, at the age of thirty-two, Kath gave birth to a second son whom she named Vivian. Claims have been made that Dr Raphael Cilento Jnr (known as 'Raff' and the same age as Kath) was Vivian's father. Raff Cilento was unhappily married and visited his parents' home regularly. Eventually he divorced his first wife and remarried. Raff Cilento, now a leading New York neurologist, is cited in Kathie Cochrane's biography of Kath Walker as being Vivian's father. He was also cited in this context in an article about Vivian in *The Bulletin*.[12] However, he has never spoken out in public on the topic.

The year before Vivian's birth, Kath still saw her ex-husband Bruce whenever he visited his son. However, many people commented on how different Vivian was in appearance and character to Bruce Walker and to his elder brother, Dennis.[13]

According to a member of the Cilento household, Kath was extremely fond of all the Cilento family. 'She would not have wanted to cause trouble in our family,' Dr David Cilento told me in a telephone interview.[14] All her life Kath remained great friends with him and other family members. 'She was a very proud and independent woman who would not have wished to have charity from anyone,' Dr Cilento said.[15]

Living in the lively and stimulating Cilento home, Kath experienced a new way of life. Yet to her it seemed impossible that she would ever become part of such a world. How could an Aboriginal woman with two children to support, who had left school at thirteen, find the time and money to develop her own artistic talents? Her first priority was survival for herself and her children. Apart from her small Army pension, she had no other means of financial support. It would be years before there were arts grants and fellowships for indigenous writers.

At the age of thirty-seven, Kath was brave enough to take the first step towards intellectual self-improvement. She took a refresher course in stenography and typing, hoping to obtain some kind of office job. In 1958 she was approached by Kathie Cochrane and her husband to join the newly formed Queensland Council for the Advancement of Aborigines and Torres Strait Islanders (QCAATSI). In 1961 she joined the Queensland Aborigines Advancement League (QAAL). Both organisations aimed to obtain civil rights for Aborigines and to advance their cause.[16]

The *Queensland Aborigines Preservation and Protection Acts*, passed between 1939 and 1946, gave the Queensland government of the day total control over Aboriginal settlements and their inmates. The acts provided for a director to be appointed by the Minister for Native Affairs; the director had almost omnipotent powers over Aborigines.

As legal guardian of *all* Aborigines under the age of twenty-one, the director had the power to remove children from their parents and arrange for their adoption. His permission was necessary for any marriages between Aborigines. He controlled the movement of Aborigines between settlements, and had the right to remove any 'trouble-makers' to Palm Island.

The Office of the Director also had control of money earned by Aborigines. Since no Aborigine could obtain a bank book, their earnings were 'managed' or banked for them. It was therefore relatively easy for any corrupt official to funnel money out of Aborigines' hard-earned savings accounts held by the office.[17]

Some of the reserves and many of the missions were run by concerned staff. Others, however, harboured highly disturbed employees, among them sadists and child abusers. The Office of the Director controlled the entry of visitors to the settlements, making it harder for Australian and foreign journalists to investigate reserves suspected of treating their inmates harshly or inhumanely.

Brisbane psychiatrist Dr Lilian Cameron and North Queensland physician Dr A. Campbell and others wished to draw attention to the plight of Aborigines and Torres Strait Islanders. In conjunction with the United Nations, they wrote and published a booklet detailing treatment of Aborigines that they believed to be unjust.[18] While Lilian Cameron was writing the booklet she met Kath Walker at the home of Kathie Cochrane; she found her to be highly intelligent but at that stage still very shy of speaking out in public.

Close involvement in politics on behalf of her people proved to be the catalyst which would draw Kath into public speaking. Indignation over the treatment of Aborigines and the rape of black women developed her determination and revealed her talent. Concern for others helped her to become well known in her own right at a time when women (black or white) found it very hard to be taken seriously. She became the voice of a voiceless people.

The decade of the 1960s was an important time for Kath Walker, on a political and on a personal level. She was deeply involved in the civil rights movement for Aborigines and stood as the ALP candidate for Greenslopes. However, she subsequently left the Labor Party because of internal racism.

She became Secretary of the QCAATSI, and was subsequently invited to join the Federal Council for the Advancement of Aborigines and Torres Strait Islanders (FCAATSI) in Canberra. She also became an important member of a delegation to the Menzies government that argued the case for constitutional recognition of Aborigines; their efforts culminated in the famous 1967 referendum which gave Aborigines and Torres Strait Islanders official recognition in the census, the right to vote and greater control of the money they earned, previously held in trust for them. By this time much of that money had conveniently 'disappeared';[19] Aborigines who had managed to save up enough money to buy land sometimes found that those savings, supposedly held in trust, had 'evaporated'.

Kath became the first Aboriginal member of the Brisbane Realist Writers' Group and received a great deal of support from her writing colleagues. Praise and encouragement came from writers she respected such as James Devanney and the ageing poet and author Mary Gilmore. Gilmore invited Kath to read some of her poems and told her: 'these poems belong to all mankind. You are the tool that writes them down.'[20]

In 1964, aided by a Commonwealth Literary Grant, Kath Walker published her first collection of poetry, *We are Going*. It was reprinted seven times. She was lionised by other writers who wanted to help the cause of indigenous people. Still writing under the name Kath Walker, she quickly gained some degree of fame although like most Australian poets did not receive much money for her work. The book's title was not intended to indicate that Aborigines were a dying race, as many Europeans had believed them to be in the past. Kath said that her book was intended 'as a warning to the white people that we can go out of existence or, with proper help, we can go on and live in this world in peace and harmony'.

Two years later she published a second collection of poems, *The Dawn is at Hand*, which won the Jessie Litchfield Award. Kath received significant and valuable encouragement from the celebrated poet and conservationist Judith Wright, who first read Kath's early poems at the request of the Brisbane publisher Jacaranda Press. These two talented women became friends and 'shadow sisters'.

The literary world was impressed, recognising that the strength of Kath's poetry lay in the simplicity of her language allied to the fervour of her message.

Kath's poetry and prose carried a potent appeal for social justice for Aborigines, and her poems were an important vehicle for transmitting Aboriginal culture to Australian schoolchildren as well as to the general population. Kath wrote her poems in a simple, direct way spiced with wit. Many were based on Aboriginal chants: simple but direct lines like 'Son of Mine' touched people's hearts with its message of reconciliation. Her overall message with its attendant rhythm, humour and irony caught the imagination of the Australian reading public:

> *No more boomerang, no more spear:*
> *Now all are civilized, colour bar and beer.*
> *No more sharing what the hunter brings,*
> *Now we work for money, pay it back for things.*

Over the years she acquired an international reputation through her poetry, but her work as an activist meant less time for her own writing. She was invited to visit China with members of the Australia–China Society, headed by Professor Manning Clark. The poetry she wrote on her trip to China was later translated into Mandarin and published with Oodgeroo's requiem for those killed in the Tiananmen Square massacre, added at the last moment due to the poet's sense of outrage.

Oodgeroo was awarded major literary honours in several countries. In Australia these included the 1966 Jessie Litchfield Award for Literary Merit, and in 1967 an award from The Fellowship of Australian Writers as well as the Mary Gilmore Medal. In 1970 she received the honour of an MBE (Member of the Order of the British Empire) from Her Majesty the Queen. Eighteen years later, however, at the same time she changed her name to Oodgeroo Noonuccal by deed poll, she made the decision to hand this back as a form of protest against '200 years of unadulterated humiliation'.

She travelled as an official envoy and lecturer to national and international conferences, received a Fulbright Scholarship and a Myer Travel Grant to visit the USA and was poet-in-residence at Bloomsburg State College, Pennsylvania, where she became a source of inspiration for younger women.

From 1970 onwards she dreamed of creating an education centre on her beloved North Stradbroke Island on the site of the old

Presbyterian Moongalba Mission, north of Dunwich. *Moongalba* means 'sitting down place' in the Noonuccal language. Oodgeroo was a keen conservationist who fought to preserve the beauty of Stradbroke in the face of sand mining, developers of holiday resorts and builders intent on putting up blocks of apartments. She was fiercely protective of the unspoiled beauty of her birthplace and also opposed those who wanted permission to build a bridge to link Stradbroke to the mainland, which she feared could easily upset the fragile ecological balance of the island by bringing in hordes of tourists.

Oodgeroo asked for a relatively small sum for her Aboriginal Educational Centre, but this was denied her by the Queensland government and by the Redland Shire Council.[21] Lacking an official commitment to funding, she was unable to create her dream.

At the former Moongalba Mission she lived in a caravan. Always able to see the funny side of things, she joked that life in her caravan meant that she was spared some of the domestic chores she had carried out for others as a domestic servant. 'I can't stand domestic work,' she said. 'As soon as you get a house, you have to do the chores. You could spend your entire life doing the cleaning and I really can't bear housework.'[22]

On Stradbroke, Oodgeroo turned the old bushland mission into a centre for educating children of all races. Her application to the local council for the lease and eventual purchase of the land was refused, so she was not able to establish the permanent museum, library, art gallery and theatre she had dreamed of building. She wasted a great deal of time negotiating with state and federal governments. At one time Lilian Bosch, an American art collector who resided in Queensland, became interested in putting up some of the money.[23] When Ms Bosch learned of the unavailability of a council lease beyond Oodgeroo's lifetime, she changed her mind about investing. Oodgeroo was outraged.

It was extremely shortsighted of the council that administered Stradbroke to grant a lease of the land at a peppercorn rent for Oodgeroo's lifetime only. It was surely a supreme irony that they allowed Oodgeroo's grave to be dug at Moongalba, but denied her request for a building permit for her Noonuccal—Nughie Education and Culture Centre. Since she was denied the right to build any structure of a permanent nature, she continued to live in her small caravan with its open-sided extension. Between 1972 and 1978, 8000 visitors came to Moongalba: academics from the United States, Japan, Germany, Sweden, the former USSR and the Pacific islands, including Papua New Guinea ... after that Oodgeroo stopped counting.

Oodgeroo showed visiting children many of the traditional ways of the Noonuccal. They learnt to fish and discovered which bush foods were good to eat. She proved herself an excellent teacher, never happier than when talking about her beloved island to children. In 1972, Barbara Ker Wilson had eagerly published at Angus and Robertson Oodgeroo's collection of childhood reminiscences and Aboriginal stories contained in *Stradbroke Dreamtime*. The book's cover was based on a painting by a young Aboriginal student. In 1993 a new edition was published, with full colour illustrations by the outstanding Aboriginal artist Bronwyn Bancroft. Oodgeroo wrote most of this book during a visit to Judith Wright at her home on Tambourine Mountain, near Brisbane.

During her lecture tours Oodgeroo often made a series of drawings in a defined style 'as a bit of an escape'.[24] In July 1981 she abandoned her pen in favour of the paint brush and held a one-woman show of her paintings and fabric designs to coincide with National Aboriginal Day at the Brisbane Community Arts Centre. 'Art is a universally understood language,' she said. She hoped that recognition of her work would open the way for other Aboriginal artists. She was proved right: Aboriginal art has become sought after worldwide by a jaded materialistic society in which many people despair of the latest developments in modern art and are searching for the spirituality which they encounter in Aboriginal art.

The success of Oodgeroo's poetry and prose and its acceptance among the Australian writing community provided encouragement to other Aboriginal writers. In 1985, when she was sixty-five, a second exhibition of Oodgeroo Noonuccal's art was held in Sydney at the home of publisher Ulli Beier. In the book *Quandamooka* (the Noonuccal name for Moreton Bay), Oodgeroo explained that she had tried to capture the essence of the island in her brightly coloured drawings in which shells, barnacles, snakes and turtles appear juxtaposed with well-known Aboriginal motifs.

In the early 1980s, Oodgeroo realised that Australian society was changing. 'The best thing that ever happened to Australia was all the other races coming to this country — they improved our eating habits for a start!' she declared. However, she still considered white Australians as racist, saying that 'they tend to see only the black drunks in the street, not the white drunks alongside them'.[25]

In 1977 Oodgeroo received an American acting award for her part in *Shadow Sister,* a film about her life based on poet Judith Wright's name for her friend. Eight years later she gave a second and even more memorable performance in a film directed by Australian Bruce Beresford, based on Nene Gare's book *The Fringe Dwellers.* Oodgeroo threw herself enthusiastically into playing Eva, a tribal elder living in a tiny humpy. She put on a white wig and a faded sundress and smoked a battered pipe. Her portrayal was masterly and revealed her as a highly talented actress.

Bruce Beresford shot his film on the outskirts of Murgon, a small Queensland town that happily styled itself 'The Gateway to Joh Bjelke-Petersen country', and the film crew and actors stayed in the town. Oodgeroo observed that not all inhabitants of Murgon were pleased to receive the *Aboriginal* actors, and that although the townspeople liked the money the film crew spent in the bars and restaurants, the town showed its true racist attitude by refusing to provide accommodation for the film's Aboriginal actors. She caused a furore by naming Murgon as 'possibly the most racist town in Australia'.

Beresford's film has become a classic, depicting Australia just as it was in the 1960s, warts and all. Oodgeroo advised Beresford on the authenticity of the film and one of her grandsons played a small role. She found the days of shooting it 'hard work but enjoyable'. After seeing the completed film, she observed: 'It's very realistic. Some people will probably be embarrassed to see Aborigines portrayed as living on the white man's rubbish dump. But that's what we did to survive during the 1960s. After two hundred years of being belted into the ground, dispossessed and spat on, we're still surviving — and it takes a strong race to do that. Physically we're a mess, but spiritually we'll always be strong.'[26]

On an overseas trip Oodgeroo made in the mid-1970s, a plane in which she was a passenger was hijacked by Palestinian terrorists. She awoke from sleep to find a gun pointed at her head. 'It's a wonder they didn't shoot my ruddy head off,' she said later. Her ordeal and that of the other passengers and crew of the Boeing 707 ended in Tunisia, after the terrorists shot dead one of the passengers, a West German banker, claiming they had to do this to publicise their demands for the release of nine of their fellow terrorists.

In 1987, on a tour of some of the poverty-stricken areas of India, Oodgeroo spoke out about AIDS, foretelling: '... the population of the world is going to be drastically reduced. One half dead from AIDS and a quarter gone from cancer and related diseases ... Man is the most aggressive, dangerous animal ... I'd love to be proved wrong. I don't want to be proved right about this — ever!'

She spoke from the heart, for her son Vivian had been diagnosed as HIV-positive and would later develop AIDS.

Oodgeroo and Vivian Walker shared many interests, including the theatre. At the age of seventeen he had been the first Aborigine to receive a scholarship to NIDA, Australia's National Institute of Dramatic Art. It was shortly before the 1988 Bicentennial celebrations that Oodgeroo visited Brisbane's Government House to return her Imperial honour, the MBE, in a gesture of protest against the federal government's failure to legislate for land rights. In support of his mother, Vivian changed his name to Kabul Noonuccal.

The Queen sent a telegram of congratulations to Oodgeroo when she was awarded an honorary doctorate by Macquarie University in 1989. She also received honorary doctorates from five other universities. The Australian composer Malcolm Williamson, Master of the Queen's Music, paid tribute to Oodgeroo when he composed an extravagant orchestral and choral production based on her poetry. He told the press that he regarded her as 'the greatest living poet in Australia'.[27]

Her son Kabul's premature death from AIDS-related complications was a tragedy for Oodgeroo, but somehow she recovered from her grief. Like his mother, Kabul was a multitalented artist who had worked as a choreographer in Australia and California, and he was also a gifted playwright. His play *Why the Corroboree?* was designed to connect urban and tribal Aborigines. He and his mother had worked together on the script, which was used in the Rainbow Serpent Theatre, the centrepiece of the Australian pavilion at Brisbane's Expo, held to celebrate the Bicentennial of 1988.

Oodgeroo saw no conflict between returning her MBE to Government House and working on a story for the Australian government pavilion at Expo. Although her role at Expo aroused controversy, she and many others hoped Expo would be (like the opening ceremony of the Olympics) what she called 'a marvellous opportunity for Aboriginal people to showcase their own heritage to a wide audience'. She defended her actions by insisting that 'the Bicentenary is the celebration of white settlement. What *we* have written is for the *world's* marketplace'. Oodgeroo and Kabul's show at the Rainbow Serpent Theatre was seen by two million visitors and was one of the highlights of Expo, which was extremely popular with overseas visitors, many of whom knew nothing of Australian indigenous culture.

Oodgeroo and Kabul related the storyline through a mixture of live theatre and colour transparencies, music and spectacular light effects. The concept of the Dreamtime, the core of Aboriginal spirituality, was explained by an Aboriginal elder seated in a cave. He told of his people's love and respect for the bountiful landscape, for Mother Earth, and recited the powerful story of the Rainbow Serpent, the giver and taker of life. As the elder communicated with the spirits they appeared from the smoke — a kangaroo, a goanna and an emu. Oodgeroo and Kabul reminded the audience to: 'Consider the land at all times or else the spirit of the Earth Mother will grow angry and take back what she has provided.' Oodgeroo received congratulations for stressing the need for conservation, to care for Mother Earth.

Only Aboriginal actors took part in the performance. Oodgeroo was firmly convinced that her people were born actors, playwrights and artists, talents that stemmed from the ancient oral tradition of the Aboriginal storyteller. I talked to Oodgeroo when I was researching an article on art events at Expo, aware that before the event opened she had expressed grave reservations, feeling that Aboriginal contributions were being marginalised amid the welter of hype about Expo making millions for Brisbane.

Oodgeroo spoke from the heart. 'I don't give a stuff for Expo or the Bicentennial. What I'm doing is giving fourteen of my people six months' full-time work — and that *is* worth celebrating.' She wondered if all the emphasis on 'entertainment' would detract from the genuine Aboriginal experience she and Kabul wanted to provide. She hoped benefits would flow to her race because the Aboriginal message was being made to all the many visitors in a peaceful manner. She repeated several times: 'Aborigines have proved what I said all along: if you give them a fair go, they can accomplish anything they put their minds to.'[28]

Two years after Expo, Oodgeroo once again spoke out fearlessly about Aboriginal deaths in custody, as she had done before. She described the Royal Commission for Aboriginal Deaths in Custody as a cover-up for criminal acts committed against her people, and a waste of taxpayers' time and money.

At seventy-five she showed the same fire, fortitude and tenacity that had inspired her involvement in Aboriginal rights for nearly forty years. Her determination and strength of purpose were as strong as ever. Although Oodgeroo's detractors claimed she was strident and manipulative, her admirers regarded her as a loyal friend and a powerful force for reconciliation and for Aboriginal education.

Two years later, the end came very suddenly for Oodgeroo. She began to complain of leg pains and she was diagnosed with cancer of the pancreas. It spread rapidly to her liver; unable to eat, she grew thinner and thinner. She died as bravely as she had lived and was buried beside Kabul, her younger son, in a traditional Aboriginal ceremony. Tributes to Oodgeroo were received from all over the world by Dennis Walker, her elder son, her grandchildren and her three remaining sisters. Leading Australian writers from many different backgrounds spoke of their sense of loss at her passing, acknowledging her as the first published Aboriginal author to express her commitment to political equality and education for Aborigines and her deep concern for the environment. Rodney Hall, a fellow member of the Brisbane Realist Writers' Group who knew Oodgeroo for nearly forty years, said: 'She was a woman who could move between two worlds, so she set out to make a bridge between them.'

Hundreds of people, rich and poor, poured onto Stradbroke Island to honour her at a memorial service held in Dunwich Hall. The burial ceremony took place in a clearing among her favourite paperbark trees. Dennis Walker pronounced a fitting epitaph: 'She has done her job. She has set the example here and she needs the rest.'

As Oodgeroo's body was lowered into the earth, two humpback whales swam slowly through the shallow waters of Moreton Bay and out to sea. She would have liked that.

CHAPTER TWENTY-SEVEN

Portrait photograph: Courtesy Nancy de Low Bird Walton.

Nancy de Low Bird Walton, OBE, AO
(1915–)
BORN TO FLY — AUSTRALIA'S FIRST
FEMALE COMMERCIAL PILOT

Nancy Bird was aptly named; a yearning to soar above the clouds took her around the world, fulfilling dreams that began in childhood.

The Birds were of English stock, but Nancy also had French forebears. She was christened Nancy after the capital city of the French province of Lorraine. De Low was the family name of Nancy's maternal grandmother, whose husband, a classical musician, emigrated to Australia, invested money in timber milling and lost most of it.

Nancy was born in the sawmilling and timber town of Kew on the northern coast of New South Wales. At a time when aeroplanes were new and exciting, she enjoyed pretending she was an 'eppyplane'. She would climb fences and jump off them, flapping her arms as though they were wings. Nancy and her five siblings lived in what she described as an 'air conditioned house': the cracks between the weatherboards were so wide that the wind blew in and out quite freely.[1]

Her father, Edward Bird, was concerned that his children should receive a good education, so he bought a house at Manly on Sydney's North Shore, where his children lived with their mother and went to school. (Meanwhile, with his brother, he ran a bush store at Mount George and retained a financial interest in the local sawmill.) Nancy attended several private schools before finishing up at Brighton College, Manly, where the future writer Kylie Tennant was a fellow pupil. Neither Nancy nor Kylie, both spirited and highly intelligent girls, enjoyed their schooldays and neither were good students. They both left without matriculating.

When Nancy was thirteen, she and her sister Gwen were staying with their father when they had their first plane ride at an air pageant at Wingham. The pilot did not have many passengers, and Nancy plucked up her courage and offered him extra money to perform some aerobatics especially for them. The experience thrilled her so much that she decided then and there that flying would become her career. School seemed a complete waste of time; Nancy set herself the goal of earning enough money to pay for flying lessons.

That same year her parents agreed she be allowed to leave school and help her father and his brother run the general store at Mount George. They paid her one pound a week, which helped to support the family. She also acted as housekeeper for her father and uncle and lived with them above the store. Since they worked a sixteen-hour day, Nancy had to do the same. She carted buckets of water from the tank in the backyard, made the beds, cleaned the house, filled kerosene lamps and did the cooking and laundry. Any remaining time was spent serving customers and on bookkeeping.

Nancy worked so hard that her wages were raised to thirty shillings a week. She kept quiet about her ambition to fly and saved up for her flying lessons by going without things most girls of her age considered essential. On a visit to her mother in Sydney, Nancy slipped away and bought herself a leather coat and goggles. Her leather flying helmet had to be made to measure in an extra small size.

Charles Kingsford Smith, widely considered one of the world's greatest airmen, was about to open a flying school. In 1928 he had been the first man to fly across the Pacific Ocean and two years later he was the first aviator to circumnavigate the globe.

One cool spring day in August 1933, out at the old Mascot airport, the petite, auburn-haired teenager took an aptitude test by flying with Charles Kingsford Smith himself. At that time what is now Sydney's Kingsford Smith Airport at Mascot was nothing but an old cow paddock with one dirt runway and a few hangars.[2]

The famous flying ace took the sixteen-year-old girl up in a Cirrus Moth fitted with dual controls to ascertain whether she had the makings of a pilot. Wearing her new flying helmet and jacket, Nancy sat in the rear cockpit. Being so small she had to sit on top of a pile of cushions to be able to see out. Kingsford Smith climbed into the front cockpit, adjusted his headphones and spoke a few words to her to make certain she could hear him before he taxied the Cirrus Moth onto the dirt runway. Nancy's excitement grew when the plane's nose came round into the wind. Then there was a pause as Smithy made the usual checks of the controls, explaining to Nancy over the intercom what their functions were.

With a roar the plane was away, undercarriage clattering over the bumps and ridges on the runway. Nancy felt the tail lift off the ground. Kingsford Smith banked steeply, then pivoted the plane on its wingtip so that Nancy was lying on her side and looking down at the line where the earth met the sea. Her hand went instinctively to her safety straps to make certain they were buckled. She felt no fear, only elation. This was what she had been waiting to do for years. It was wonderful.

Smithy was a brilliant pilot but not a very good flying teacher. He had great difficulty explaining to novices what he was doing and why he did it. 'Kingsford Smith was just too inspired a pilot to be a good instructor,' Nancy reckoned, adding that you'd hardly expect Einstein to shine as a maths coach to a pupil learning something simple like the multiplication tables. 'Charles Kingsford Smith's flying had such beauty and precision that he simply could not understand how a novice pupil would misjudge a gliding angle or let the nose drop beneath the horizon,' she observed. She said Smithy got quite annoyed when his pupils made mistakes.[3]

At the end of Nancy's first attempt at flying he told her: 'All right. Not bad for a first try. You'll learn.'

Nancy was delighted to hear Smithy say this, having heard that he could make very caustic comments indeed to his pupils. His words clearly indicated that the Kingsford Smith Flying School would take her on as a pupil.

In the early 1930s air charter companies were being started up on a shoestring, flying flimsy aircraft with wooden struts covered with cloth, many with worn engines that would certainly not meet the requirements of the Civil Aviation Regulations today.

In her autobiography *Born to Fly* Nancy wrote: '...flying an aircraft isn't as easy as falling off a log. If you have normal intelligence and determination you can learn to do it — you may even do it very well indeed. But the greatest pilots of all, those whose flying is as precise as music — as Kingsford Smith's was — don't fly like that simply because they were born to it: they've also put [into it] heart, intelligence, judgement, patience and spirit.'

In spite of the fact that Nancy spent all her spare time reading Frank Swoffer's textbook *Learning to Fly*, her father regarded her desire to become a pilot as 'only a teenage craze'. When Nancy told him she was going back to the family home at Manly so that she could continue her flying lessons and would not be working for him much longer, Ted Bird was furious. 'You'll spend all your money, crash the plane and come back a cripple,' he thundered.

Nancy didn't care. Of course she would spend all her money, that was why she had been saving it up. But there was no way she would come back. She *had* to make flying her career.

On her second flying lesson she went up with Pat Hall, the flying school's chief instructor, a quiet, patient man who (unlike Smithy) *never* got excited or angry no matter what the pupil did. With Hall at the dual controls Nancy acquired confidence. She learned to keep a watchful eye out for suitable landing sites at all times, just in case she got into trouble. That exciting first landing with the long glissade towards the ground through the shining air, just like a bird, was something she never forgot.

On some days at Mascot Nancy might receive only twenty minutes' flying time in a dual control plane with Pat Hall; the rest of the time she would spend in the offices of the Kingsford Smith Flying School and Aviation Services making herself useful and learning as much as she could.

In addition to learning about radio operation and semaphore, she was taught maintenance techniques. Tommy Pethybridge, Kingsford Smith's chief engineer, did his best to put Nancy off flying by giving her plenty of dirty jobs. He showed Nancy how to scrape black carbon off spark plugs with steel wool and wire brushes, how to grind valves, how to time a magneto and check tappet clearances. But nothing on earth would deter Nancy from her goal of making flying her career.

Pupils of the Kingsford Smith Flying School formed a small and very keen group. They spent hours sitting on the grass outside the hangars watching other pupils make mistakes on landing and 'talking them down' even though the pupils up in the air could not hear them. Nancy's fellow trainees at the Flying School included Smithy's nephew, the daring John Kingsford Smith, and Denzil Macarthur-Onslow, who flew for the fun of it. Two other female pupils were Peggy MacKillop, the blonde, vivacious daughter of a grazier, and the quieter, more serious May Bradford, who several years later was destined to die in a plane taking off from Mascot. Both these young women regarded flying as an exhilarating hobby.[4] The teenage Nancy saw flying as an escape from domestic routine and a career.

Nancy described Kingsford Smith as '…one of the most likeable people I have known. He had a special trick of standing on his head while drinking a glass of beer, without spilling a drop. He was an extremely kind and generous man. Women admired him and sought his company, but he was essentially a man's man. His partners, engineers and his fellow workers at Mascot felt a tremendous affection and loyalty for him.'

The flimsy planes of those days damaged very easily and their maintenance cost a great deal of money: Kingsford Smith Air Services and the Kingsford Smith Flying School were perpetually short of cash. Unlike other famous aviators such as Charles Lindbergh, James Mollison and Amy Johnson, who had newspapers acting as their major sponsors, Smithy had to pay his own way and made his record-breaking flights on a shoestring. He did receive some help from the Vacuum Oil Company but he never received major backing from anyone, not even from the Australian government of the day, which would have been an enormous help to him.

Unlike other female pilots, Nancy had no intention of flying as a hobby. She managed to master simple mechanics, but what caused her a great deal of difficulty was her lack of mathematics, a subject to which she had never paid the slightest attention in her schooldays. Now she realised she must study maths if she was to achieve her aim of becoming a commercial pilot.

Nancy was in her late teens by the time she was allowed to fly solo and was still sitting on cushions in order to see her surroundings. Pat Hall came up with her on that important morning and watched approvingly as she made a smooth landing beside the hangar of Kingsford Smith Air Services. In astonishment Nancy saw her instructor, joystick in hand, climb out of the cockpit.

'You'll be right,' he said with a wave. 'Off you go. Just remember, if you're not satisfied with your approach, open up the throttle and go round again.'

Nancy was trembling with excitement as she took off alone for the first time. *Solo at last!* she thought as she raced the plane across the aerodrome and felt it soar into the air. Without Pat Hall's weight the little plane climbed much faster and Nancy found herself rising to a thousand feet far more quickly than on previous occasions. Now all she had to do was get the plane down safely.

This presented a problem. In 1933 space was in short supply at Mascot aerodrome. Pilots had to come in low over the boundary, clearing a fence to get in.

As Pat Hall was no longer with her, Nancy 'talked' herself down aloud. 'Don't lose speed on your turns!' she reminded herself, just as her instructor used to do. As the plane swooped low over Mascot she told herself: 'Check your glide ... hold her steady, hold her right.' Then, as the controls slackened, she drew the stick back and let the plane settle gently on the grass.

She had done it.

She needed twenty-five hours solo flying for an advanced A licence, which allowed pilots to carry passengers on a non-fee basis. Obtaining this was no problem for her and she gained the licence still sitting on cushions so that she could see out.

What did present a problem was the far more difficult B or commercial licence. To obtain this she needed to record one hundred hours of solo flying, in addition to passing flying tests and written examinations in Navigation, Engines, Air Frames and Meteorology. How Nancy regretted the fact that she had never taken mathematics seriously at school! To fulfil her dream she abandoned her social life and for months spent every evening struggling with angles of incidence, thrust and drag, camshafts and tappet clearances. She learned what the various cloud formations indicated and studied wind velocity and speed.

It was hard but she managed it. The auburn-haired teenager with the sapphire blue eyes who was not afraid to get her hands dirty maintaining aircraft engines was issued with licence number 494 at the age of nineteen, the youngest woman in the British Empire to hold one. The Controller of Civil Aviation was so impressed that he wrote Nancy a letter of congratulation. There was only one problem. Commercial licence or not, in 1935 no airline would employ a woman pilot. Everyone at Mascot shook their heads and said, 'Nancy, there's no room for *women* in commercial aviation.' What she needed was to be self-employed with a plane of her own to charter.

By this time Ted Bird had realised that his daughter was absolutely serious in her aim of becoming a commercial pilot, and he decided to help her. He approached Nancy's great-aunt, Mrs Annie Thomas, who planned to leave Nancy money in her will. Great-aunt Annie agreed to give her the sum immediately and her father added an extra two hundred pounds.

Nancy started hunting about for a suitable plane and finally found a wrecked light aircraft that was within her budget, a De Havilland Gipsy Moth. She worked with the men who virtually rebuilt the plane, which was the usual flimsy affair of wooden spars glued together and covered with cloth. Nancy now knew how to sew up tears in the cloth should future repairs be needed.

To cover her expenses and make a little money Nancy planned to offer 'barnstorming tours', flying around the farming areas of New South Wales and Queensland giving flying exhibitions and joy rides. She would become the first woman pilot to use her commercial licence. She arranged with the Shell Oil Company to advertise her arrival in country areas, so that she could work at the big country shows. There was still a large number of people who had never seen an aircraft, let alone a woman pilot.

Nancy took her friend Peggy MacKillop on as co-pilot. Peggy had acquired her commercial licence at the same time as Nancy but, as the daughter of a wealthy grazier family, unlike Nancy she did not regard flying as a career. Their agreement was that Peg should receive 10 per cent of gross takings, which she hoped would prove sufficient to cover her hairdresser's and dress bills, while Nancy would pay all the expenses. Neither of them would make much, but provided Nancy lived frugally she would be able to pay off the running costs of her plane. Thanks to all her lessons with Tommy Pethybridge, Nancy knew enough about engines to make her own safety checks herself each morning and carry out simple maintenance work, which would save her money.

The girls were interviewed by local papers and radio stations that saw a certain glamour in two stunningly attractive girls touring with a plane. They were treated like VIPs and entertained lavishly on grazing properties around Tamworth, Newcastle, Inverell, Moree, Coonamble and Narromine.

At the country shows people turned out in flocks to see them, but were dismayed when they saw the fragile little plane vibrate as Peg or Nancy revved up the Moth for take-off. As a result not many paying passengers were willing to risk their lives in a light plane piloted by a woman. Persuading customers to part with money to fly for fun was hard work. Nancy soon discovered that she was better at doing this than Peggy, so Peg flew the passengers while Nancy stayed on the ground selling flights to the brave and calming the nervous. Many property owners wanted to fly in order to see their own land from the air; fortunately for Nancy, some of these men were prepared to take the risk of being flown by a woman.

Tom Perry, a Narromine grazier and philanthropist who was the enthusiastic president of the local aero club, told Nancy that she needed a larger plane with a cabin that would take two passengers in order to obtain profitable charter work. Nancy told him this was beyond her means. Tom Perry then offered to guarantee a loan if Nancy would pay him back on a monthly basis at 5 per cent interest. He also offered to pay her life insurance premium. If she were killed in a crash the plane would remain his property. Tom Perry was also providing financial backing to Southern Air Lines, which Wilfrid Kingsford Smith was due to start a few months later, so Nancy could help promote this new venture.

Nancy worried whether she would be able to pay off the loan. Should she take up Tom Perry's kind offer? She spent sleepless nights worrying about it.

The matter was finally settled for her. Her old patched-up Gipsy Moth developed starting problems too serious for Nancy to fix. As a result, she and Peg arrived two and a half hours late for their next show, much to the annoyance of the organisers. So Nancy accepted Tom Perry's proposal to buy a new and greatly improved silver Leopard Moth on credit terms.

The new Leopard Moth eventually arrived from England. It had a cabin with two leather-upholstered passenger seats and a bucket seat up front for the pilot. It was a huge contrast to the ancient, flimsy Gipsy Moth, in which Nancy had to sit with her head and shoulders exposed to the burning sun or freezing wind and wear a flying suit to protect her from the elements.

Out of gratitude to Tom Perry, Nancy tried to interest potential investors in his new company, Southern Air Lines. At Dubbo, which had become her base, she tied her plane to a fence on a property Tom Perry rented out as the landing field for the company. Nancy would always be very grateful to Tom Perry; whenever she flew over his property at Narromine she would land and chat to him.

Just as Nancy achieved her dream of owning such a magnificent monoplane, Australia received distressing news. Sir Charles Kingsford Smith (who is now considered the world's greatest flier) and Tommy

Pethybridge had gone missing in the *Lady Southern Cross* in the area of Rangoon. They had left England bound for Australia on 6 November 1935 in spite of the fact that Kingsford Smith had influenza, knowing that if they postponed the flight they would run into the monsoon season. Everyone watched and waited for more news but none came.

Months later a barnacle-encrusted undercarriage was found washed ashore on remote Aye Island in the Bay of Bengal. It was eventually identified as the undercarriage of the *Lady Southern Cross*. No bodies were ever found. Sorrowfully Nancy knew that she had lost two valued mentors as well as friends. Mascot airport would never be the same without them.

With a heavy heart she left Sydney for Dubbo to resume her country flying. There she met the Reverend Stanley Drummond, who persuaded her to join the Far West Children's Health Scheme, a medical service he had set up to serve people in remote areas of outback Australia. Stanley Drummond was appalled by the number of children suffering from trachoma or sandy blight, a disease brought on by glare, dust and, in the case of Aboriginal children, by malnutrition. These children would eventually go blind as the trachoma progressed. Drummond had bought obsolete railway carriages for conversion into mobile clinics staffed by a nursing sister. Now he realised that a light plane would be far quicker and possibly prove cheaper to transport a nursing sister and her equipment to the outback whenever she was required.

Nancy agreed to act as pilot to the Reverend Drummond's outback medical service in return for a two hundred pound annual retainer. As part of her job she was also to help the nursing sister set up a clinic in the local hotel, where one existed.

Nancy and the nurse also undertook many journeys by car to visit isolated properties way beyond Bourke, where they saw children in desperate need of medical help and families living in corrugated iron shacks on stony ridges without a bush or a tree to break the monotony. Most children were brought up on bread, milkless tea and salt meat, all they could get in the outback.

By plane, Nancy flew nursing sisters to places not yet reached by the Royal Flying Doctor Service. Their timely intervention saved many hundreds of lives over the four years she was with the Far West Children's Health Scheme. It was rewarding but lonely work.

Soon Nancy had to shift her base to Bourke, which unfortunately had no engineer to repair her plane should it have mechanical problems. She rented a room at Fitzgerald's Hotel and set off with Sister Webb on a round of clinics and outback properties at remote places such as Louth, Hungerford, Hantabulla and Ford's Bridge.

In 1935 it was very unusual for a young unmarried woman to live on her own in a country hotel, let alone someone as attractive as Nancy. She wore shorts in the summer and overalls in winter, but her 'modern' attitude scandalised some of the residents. She often risked her life flying over vast, waterless, uninhabited areas where no one could provide details on where she was heading.

Nancy greatly enjoyed the experience of helping people, but she was always aware that if she crashed it could take a long time for help to arrive. As she flew over extensive tracts of the outback one of the things that flashed across her mind was the fact that she could get lost in the Never-Never and die before anyone found her. To understand how very brave Nancy was in carrying out this work, one must remember that she was not flying over open plains where she could land safely if she became lost in a rainstorm or if the engine failed. Instead, she spent most of her time flying over tough mulga scrub which she knew would tear her light plane to shreds were it forced to land there. Nancy experienced violent rainstorms followed by floods, drought and blinding dust storms, conditions that made flying extremely difficult. In high summer the ground heat created turbulence, with the plane thrown about in the air, which sometimes made her air sick.[5] In summer she often wore dark glasses to keep the flies out of her eyes, and if the insects became unbearable she wore a fly veil.

In December 1936 Nancy de Low Bird entered the Adelaide to Brisbane Air Race, which was open to men and women. The entrants, many of whom were hobby fliers, started out from Brisbane on a glorious sunny morning. Their first stop was Coffs Harbour, then they flew on to Mascot, stayed overnight and took off for Wangaratta. On this leg of the race they ran into a heavy storm before going on to Melbourne. The race was won by Reg Ansett, the future founder of Ansett Airlines. Petite Nancy Bird won the Ladies Trophy for the best time flown by a woman.

Soon after this the Far West Children's Health Scheme announced that it could no longer afford to use planes for mercy flights and would go back to using cars and chauffeurs. Nancy moved to Charleville, hoping to persuade the Queensland government to fund an air ambulance service from there. Although she did obtain some paid work in Charleville, her living expenses there were high. The air ambulance service never eventuated.

At this juncture Mrs Davis, president of the Cunnamulla branch of the Red Cross and owner of the Cunnamulla Hotel, made a generous offer and Nancy moved to Cunnamulla and lived in the Royal Hotel. As a very attractive and unattached young woman she received many offers of marriage from graziers, including some by letter from men who had seen her photograph in the local paper. It was flattering, but none of them succeeded in capturing Nancy's careful heart.

The heat took its toll on her strength. After four years of living in the outback and facing the hazards of flying under a wide variety of conditions, Nancy considered it was time for her to take a break and see something of the rest of the world.

Accordingly she sold her plane, paid off her debt to Tom Perry and ended up with roughly the same amount of money she had when she started out chartering the plane. But making money was never the main aim for Nancy; she had proved that she could be a commercial pilot, and that was enough.

In search of a complete change and thrilled by the chance to see the world, Nancy accepted an offer from a major Dutch airline to carry out promotional work in Java and Europe in return for their protection. She was flown around the world, visited twenty-five different countries and was entertained as a VIP by Lufthansa, Air France and other European airlines. In between celebrity functions she lived cheaply and ate in the most inexpensive places she could find. She met ace fliers and other celebrities, was presented to King George VI at Buckingham Palace, and made many speeches. To her surprise, she discovered she had a talent for public speaking.

Nancy Bird sailed steerage class on RMS *Queen Mary* from England to New York, where she was welcomed by the Ninety-Nines, an association of women pilots, and later presented to Eleanor Roosevelt, the journalist wife of President Roosevelt.

Crossing the Pacific Ocean by ship on her way home, Nancy met an English-born businessman, Charles Walton, who was returning to his home in Australia. It was a shipboard romance that went further as their feelings for each other developed into love.

They married in Australia in December 1939, three months after Britain and Australia declared war on Germany. Their marriage produced two children, a boy and a girl. Nancy dedicated all her time and effort to raising her children until they were old enough to manage without her full-time care.

During World War II Nancy Bird was involved with setting up training courses for women pilots to back up men who were flying in the Royal Australian Air Force. This led eventually to the founding of the Women's Auxiliary Australian Air Force. After the war, in 1950, she founded the AWPA (Australian Women Pilots Association). Doing this made her realise just how much she wanted to fly again, so she obtained a co-pilot's licence.

She flew to America and met up once again with the Ninety-Nines. In the USA Nancy Bird Walton made headlines when she became the first woman from overseas to compete in the all-female transcontinental air race, the Powder Puff Derby, organised by women for women from many different backgrounds and ranging in age from seventeen to seventy. Nancy and her American co-pilot Lauretta Foy Savory came in fifth. That same year, Nancy received the Order of the British Empire for her support 'for charities and people in need'.

In 1990 Nancy wrote her second book, *My God! It's a Woman!* — the exclamation made by a man on a remote airstrip as she clambered out of the cockpit wearing flying overalls and carrying a spanner.

Charles Kingsford Smith had several airports named after him. In 1998, Nancy Bird Walton was honoured by Bourke Airport being named after her. She also received the Order of Australia and was asked to take part in Melbourne's official Federation celebrations. Looking far younger than her years, Nancy Bird Walton is always in great demand on speaking platforms. She is an outstanding example of a woman who shows other women that if they persevere they *can* achieve their dreams.

CHAPTER TWENTY-EIGHT

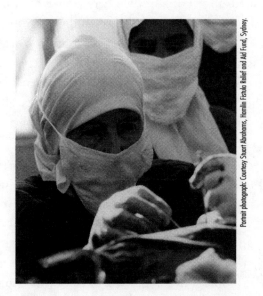

Portrait photograph: Courtesy Stuart Abrahams, Hamlin Fistula Relief and Aid Fund, Sydney.

Dr Catherine Hamlin (Nicholson)
(1924–)
FELLOW OF LONDON'S ROYAL COLLEGE OF SURGEONS;
ORDER OF ST GREGORY; COMPANION OF AUSTRALIA
(AUSTRALIA'S HIGHEST HONOUR),
THE DEDICATED DOCTOR WHO CHANGED WOMEN'S LIVES

Catherine Hamlin is a tall, slim, attractive woman with blue eyes and a warm smile, who looks many years younger than her actual age. She was born in 1924 in Sydney, where her family, the Nicholsons, lived in a pleasant home at Ryde. Catherine was sent as a boarder to Frensham School, near Mittagong, where she proved herself an excellent student.

At a time when most women married in their twenties, while those few who attended university studied arts rather than medicine or law, Catherine Nicholson was accepted into the prestigious medical school of the University of Sydney. In 1946, a year after World War II ended, she qualified as a doctor. She wanted to specialise rather than go into general practice, a brave aim for a woman in that male-dominated era. To this end she worked long hours in hospital as well as studying at night for the examinations which would allow her to become an obstetrician and gynaecologist.

While she was working at Sydney's Crown Street Women's Hospital she met and married a talented and equally dedicated doctor, Reginald Hamlin, also an obstetrician and gynaecologist and, like Catherine, a dedicated Christian. They both wanted to use their medical knowledge to help the underprivileged, and in 1959 they responded to an advertisement in *The Lancet* for two gynaecologists to set up a School of Midwifery in Ethiopia, one of the world's poorest countries, bordered by the Red Sea, the Sudan, Kenya and Somalia and bisected from the north-east to the south-west by the Rift Valley. Friends tried to dissuade them from going there with their six-year-old son, warning that living and working, even for a limited time, in an undeveloped country with rudimentary sanitation and rampant disease could shorten their lives.

The Hamlins ignored such dismal forebodings, convinced their decision to go to Ethiopia was the right one. They left Sydney on a three-year contract to work in Ethiopia's only maternity hospital.

When they arrived at the capital, Addis Ababa, a sprawling city of more than a million souls over 2500 metres above sea level, they found themselves in the midst of thatch-roofed mud huts, tin shanties and scrawny babies with beautiful dark eyes. The Hamlins worked very hard at the Princess Tsahai Maternity Hospital. In what little free time they had they took the opportunity to explore the countryside. Ethiopia is a vast, strangely beautiful land of fertile plains and sandy deserts with a dramatic range of almost impassable mountains. Some seventy-five per cent of the population lives, on average, two and a half days' walk from an all-weather road, making it very hard to reach the capital.[1]

Ethiopia (formerly known as Abyssinia) is a fascinating country whose linguistic roots date back to the Biblical days of King Solomon and the Queen of Sheba. Its rich cultural legacy is based on successive occupations by Egyptian pharaohs, Persians, the Caesars of Ancient Rome, by Moslem incursions and in 1936 by Mussolini's Fascist Italian Army, before being relieved by the British during World War II, which enabled it to regain full independence. Today's Ethiopians speak an ancient language known as Amharic while, in the provinces adjoining Somalia, Somali and Arabic are also spoken.

At the Princess Tsahai Maternity Hospital, where the Hamlins worked with interpreters, they were presented with a gynaecological problem they had not previously encountered. They recognised it as 'fistula', the correct medical name for a condition which may occur in (usually extremely young) pregnant women lacking access to good medical faculties, who go into a prolonged labour which in some cases may last as long as six days. During this time the baby's head does terrible damage to the surrounding tissues as it continually pushes, seeking to exit from the birth canal. The pressure of the baby cuts off the blood supply to the woman's bladder, tissue dies, and the woman is left with a tear or fistula. This problem is averted in the developed world by assisted labour or caesarian section. In countries lacking easily accessed medical facilities, the baby is stillborn and the mother dies. *If* she survives she is left with permanent damage, a tear or fistula in the walls of the birth canal and bladder and, in many cases, the rectum as well, leaves the mother incontinent in one or two ways. The condition is permanent and occurs throughout the Third World.

During their first year at the maternity hospital in Addis Ababa, Reginald and Catherine Hamlin saw thirty young girls suffering from fistulae. These mothers, whose babies had died, were in great pain, leaking urine and faeces. In addition, some of them had badly damaged legs as a result of the positions they were forced to adopt during their agonising days and nights in prolonged labour.

The Hamlins were shocked to learn that in addition to the pain and grief suffered by these poor girls, through no fault of their own they had become outcasts. Their beds were always wet, they reeked of urine and faeces, they could no longer cook, dig in the fields or bear children, all highly valued attributes in rural communities.

No one deliberately wanted to be cruel to these unfortunate girls, but even their closest relatives found they could no longer live with them. Often the husband's family convinced him that he had suffered an 'act of God' for which he had no responsibility and that he should move out of the house. The saddest cases of all were those in which the husband, in a country where women have very few rights, told his wife to leave the family hut then took a second wife. In some cases this meant the fistula sufferer was left to beg for a living. Others were hidden away by embarrassed relatives or banished to the outskirts of the village and treated like mediaeval lepers.

Dr Reg Hamlin described the condition in one of his reports: 'These poor young women are ashamed of their offensiveness; spurned by their families; they exist without friends and without hope. Due to their offensive smell, no one will give them work of any kind. If there is no sister or mother who will care for them they are reduced to begging for food. Death seems preferable to life as a fistula woman.'

The Hamlins realised what a huge medical and social problem they were confronting. This problem occurs throughout the Third World wherever prenatal care and obstetric facilities are poor. As fecundity is a status symbol among illiterate women, many are married off very young indeed and the prevailing cultural patterns of a rural society where fertility is greatly valued in women made birth control seem undesirable. How could they as Christians turn their backs on so much human misery and need?

The Hamlins decided they must do something to help, that God must have sent them to Ethiopia for this special purpose. Accordingly, they set about developing entirely new surgical techniques to repair fistulae. They honed their skills in an incredibly delicate operation that could take as long as three hours for a skilled surgeon to perform on the operating table. A fistula repair demands the utmost precision on the part of the surgeon; if it is successful, as most are, the patient is able to live a normal life and have more children.

After the Hamlins had performed a few of their operations free of charge, word spread like wildfire about the two saintly doctors who could cure the terrible affliction. The number of fistula patients arriving at the Princess Tsahai Maternity Hospital soared. Women in despair came to them from all over Ethiopia seeking the miraculous cure.

In the Hamlins' second year in Ethiopia's capital over 200 fistula women arrived from all parts of the country seeking treatment. Due to the limited capacity of the maternity hospital and the need for beds to be changed so frequently in order to treat fistula patients, it became difficult to treat them on the wards. The Hamlins now aimed to found a free hospital especially for fistula women that would provide them with sanctuary, a safe haven where they would feel welcome.

It is hard to estimate the exact number of Ethiopian women who suffer from fistula, as no statistical records have been kept by any government department there. As a rough comparison, in nearby Nigeria, a country smaller than Ethiopia which also lacks many medical facilities, it is believed some 150,000 women are fistula sufferers.

Ethiopia's population is now estimated at some fifty million and increases annually by as much as 3 to 4 per cent. The remoteness of many Ethiopian villages, the rugged mountainous terrain bisected by ravines, and the lack of surfaced roads and good local medical services indicate that the problem may be even worse there than in Nigeria.

Eventually the numbers of women requiring a fistula operation became so numerous that the Hamlins asked the late Haile Selassie, then Emperor of Ethiopia, to help them. Impressed by their work and their dedication to the welfare of his people, he agreed.

As a result, the two Australian doctors were able to build a small hostel in the grounds of the Princess Tsahai Maternity Hospital where fistula women could be treated. This hostel served as a temporary measure until a proper fistula hospital could be built.

Eventually the Emperor granted special permission for Reg Hamlin to buy land for the new hospital. The Hamlins went on speaking tours to raise donations towards building the new hospital from individuals and philanthropic organisations overseas in Australia, America and New Zealand. By this time the Emperor had been ousted in a military coup and imprisoned in his palace, where he died. This meant that the planning of the new fistula hospital took place against a background of political unrest. It was also the tail end of a period of bad harvests which had given rise to famine in some areas. It was a considerable act of faith on behalf of the Hamlins to proceed with such ambitious plans at such a difficult time. However, they persevered and their brand new fistula hospital finally opened in 1974.[2]

Catherine and Reginald Hamlin intended the new hospital to be 'a place of haven and a place of healing, giving life and hope to thousands of young women'. There are many heart-rending stories of patients who overcame huge difficulties to get there. One woman begged for six years to acquire enough money for her journey to the hospital. Another virtually lived for six months in her local bus shelter, begging money from other passengers to obtain the fare to Addis Ababa. Others sold any remaining possessions they had in order to be treated by the Hamlins.

After a long illness, Dr Reginald Hamlin died of cancer in August 1993. Shortly before his death in Addis Ababa the Hamlins featured in a BBC television film about the fistula hospital and its patients which the BBC titled *Walking back to happiness*.[3] His death came as a bitter blow to his wife. Catherine and Reg Hamlin had enjoyed a long and happy marriage and had been blessed with a son, Richard, who now has a family of his own and works as a computer specialist in London.[4]

The staff at the fistula hospital feared that Dr Catherine might return to Australia or go to London to be near her son. They wondered what would happen to the hospital then. In the event they need not have worried: Catherine Hamlin loved Ethiopia and its people. She felt that Addis Ababa was the place where she was most needed, so she decided to remain there and continue the valuable work she and her husband had started.

In the mid-1990s Australia's then Minister for Foreign Affairs, Gareth Evans, visited Addis Ababa; he was so impressed by the work of the fistula hospital that he arranged for Australia to make a considerable official donation towards the new hospital.[5]

At the time of writing Dr Catherine Hamlin, trim, erect and determined as ever, refuses to talk of retirement in spite of having received a hip replacement. She has a devoted and loyal staff, many of whom are former fistula patients. The hospital now has two young and enthusiastic Ethiopian doctors, an Australian doctor, experienced Ethiopian administrators, nursing sisters and nursing aids. Community education programmes are planned to prevent fistulae by encouraging a rise in the age of marriage, which can take place at ten in some areas, and to bring well-trained help to women in labour

However, desperate fistula patients continue to arrive at the hospital from remote and inaccessible parts of Ethiopia, often journeying by bus or by hitching truck rides. In a mountainous country like Ethiopia, where roads are inadequate or nonexistent, their situation is made even worse by the fact that the journey to the hospital may take days or weeks. Skinny girls with gaunt, emaciated faces, prematurely aged, are sometimes brought in by relatives, their legs so badly bent due to labour contractions that they can scarcely walk. Some take months to reach Addis Ababa. Most find themselves unwelcome on public transport because their smell is highly offensive to the other passengers. Some have been turned off several buses before they finally arrive at their destination. One woman with badly damaged legs crawled fifteen kilometres on hands and knees from her village to the bus stop.

As a result of such disdain and rejection, the young women who pass through the hospital's main gate are anxious and apprehensive about their welcome, having learned to fear the reaction of their fellow human beings to their offensive bodies. They are greeted by a large sign in Amharic and in English that reads: FREE HOSPITAL FOR POOR WOMEN, which ensures that none of them fears she may be turned away due to lack of money. The fistula sufferers are unutterably relieved to find themselves greeted with understanding and affection by the well-trained Ethiopian staff.

Sitting under a tree in the hospital courtyard is a group of young girls, their heads cast down, their clothes dirty and smelly, telltale puddles beneath their chairs. They sit apart, not wanting to offend. A nursing aide comes out to fetch one of them. The girl slinks into the Outpatients Department and is shown into the doctor's consulting room where she huddles forlornly, too ashamed to talk, and responds only in monosyllables. When the doctor shows gentleness and compassion and promises 'We'll make you better,' a flicker of hope illuminates the girl's sadness. She is then presented with one of the beautiful-coloured shawls knitted or crocheted by compassionate women all over the world who work for Dr Catherine Hamlin. After the patient recovers from her operation she receives a new dress and is encouraged to join in a joyful dance to celebrate the start of her new life. She returns to her village with a very different persona, knowing she can remarry and have babies.

The patients' joy when they realise their presence is no longer offensive to others is demonstrated by the BBC's video about the hospital. *Walking back to happiness* shows the loving care with which Dr Hamlin treats these girls and shows her putting her arms around some of the most unhappy when they arrive.

Initially any infections are treated with antibiotics, the patients are given iron for their anaemia, vitamins for deficiencies which might lead to beri-beri and a good diet for weight loss. They then receive the operation that will change their lives *free of charge*. Highly important in the post-operative care of patients with injured leg muscles is the role of a sympathetic physiotherapist to help them regain movement.

From 1993 to 1995 the Australian government, through AusAID, made substantial grants to the fistula hospital to assist in the building of a new ward, a house for another resident doctor and a laboratory. An extensive library of medical journals and books has been provided by the British Hamlin–Churchill Childbirth Injuries Fund. There is no other fistula hospital of this size anywhere in the world. Fistula wards are not needed in the west because with medical care during labour, the problem is rare, but among aid agencies there is now an awareness that in most Third World countries, enormous numbers of women are suffering from this dreadful affliction.

Dr Hamlin is inspired by her strong Christian faith and a determination to see that the best is done for her patients. It is a tribute to her skills as an administrator and surgeon that the Addis Ababa Fistula Hospital has become internationally famous for the psychological and spiritual help it supplies to patients as well as its medical expertise. Patients arrive at the hospital feeling depressed, miserable and isolated from the rest of humanity; once there, they find themselves treated with love and understanding. A former patient acts as cook to produce meals for those who are malnourished based on special high-protein and calorific diets; a clinical specialist is now being trained to undertake nutritional assessment and teaching. Dr Hamlin's practice of medicine is a holistic one that involves treating the whole person: body, mind and spirit. She is one of the few women to be honoured with the Gold Medal and a fellowship from the Royal College of Surgeons, London, which she received recently.

We live in an age of 'manufactured' celebrities prominent in the worlds of entertainment, fashion modelling and sport. Many celebrities throw hissy fits should they suffer a 'bad hair day', lose a football match or a tennis game or if they cannot obtain a supply of their favourite party drug. How refreshing it is to find that a woman truly as great as Dr Catherine Hamlin remains totally unaffected by the fact she has been called a 'saint' by hyperbolic journalists and insists that she is not. However, she is undoubtedly a great humanitarian as well as a brilliant and truly dedicated surgeon. Her people skills are exceptional and she has the ability to speak for those who lack a voice to plead their cause.

Decades spent living in Ethiopia mean that Dr Catherine Hamlin is aware at first hand of the problems of a developing nation. Her fistula hospital provides extra programs such as daily literacy classes for patients and nursing aides, which average twelve students each day. Many patients stay on at the hospital until they have learned to read and write. Not only does reading occupy the girls' minds, but when they do have their own children their literacy will help to ensure that their children will be better fed and cared for. Vocational classes in knitting and sewing are also given to patients awaiting surgery to occupy their minds and teach them useful skills.

'Great oaks from little acorns grow.' The fistula hospital, with its neat thatched buildings, flowerbeds and large operating theatre equipped with four operating tables represents an act of faith and a belief that with love, skill and dedication it is possible to make a difference to the lives of thousands. Through the Internet and the talks Dr Catherine has given in Australia and America, as well as the newsletters the hospital publishes, and her own book *The Hospital by the River*, written with film-maker John Little, the fame of her work has spread.

Dr Hamlin is keen that the Addis Ababa hospital should provide post graduate training in fistula surgery. Ethiopian gynaecology post graduates as well as some overseas physicians have received specialist training at the fistula hospital, and obstetric surgeons come here to train from all over Africa. Several of the hospital's trained specialists are now working in areas of Ethiopia where their skills are desperately needed. One, in Harer, refers the more difficult cases to the Addis Ababa Fistula Hospital, while at Adigrat another specialist trained by Dr Hamlin and her recently appointed medical director, Dr Ambaye Wolde-Michel, has performed over 100 fistula repairs in the last four years. One doctor who came to work with the fistula patients in Addis Ababa has set up a fistula hospital in Nepal, and in Nigeria and the Sudan several doctors who have trained with Dr Hamlin and her team have now set up private clinics.

The upgrading of the fistula hospital's facilities finally took place in 1998; the new and greatly enlarged hospital was opened in January 1999 in the presence of Dr Negasso Gidada, president of Ethiopia, and his wife, the Patriarch of the Ethiopian Orthodox Church, Archbishop and Mrs Goodhew of Sydney and the Australian, British, Canadian and Swedish Ambassadors and their wives. At the ceremony the president made a most important statement, declaring it was time for the ancient Ethiopian custom of child marriages to be revised, which gives hope for the future.

AusAID, the Archbishop of Sydney's Overseas Relief Fund, Rotary, the Hamlin–Churchill Childbirth Injuries Fund and other charities and organisations have helped magnificently to fund the upgrading of the hospital complex, based on plans drawn up by the talented Australian architect Ridley Smith. Thanks to their contributions the hospital's water supply has been improved, there is a new, enlarged kitchen where 200 meals can be prepared each day, and covered pathways have been built between the main buildings to shelter patients from the rain in the three-month-long wet season. A new laundry was built and more toilets provided for 'waiting' patients. Other improvements include a hostel for incoming patients, accommodation for overseas doctors, a pharmacy, a laboratory and an x-ray room, plus an enlarged operating theatre with four operating tables, a scrub room and a sterilising room.

At last a start is being made on prevention programs in the rural regions from where the majority of young patients come, mainly from the Tigrai and the Amhari regions. The health departments of those regions have given Dr Hamlin permission to set up fistula prevention centres where teams from the hospital will visit regularly for operating and teaching in the prevention of childbirth injuries.

The main hospital's operating days are Mondays, Wednesdays and Fridays. Sterilisation of the theatre and the equipment takes place on the other days. Absolute cleanliness and good hygiene are prerequisites but money has to be saved. Needles which in the West would be discarded are sterilised in an autoclave and re-used.[6] (The operation takes place under a local spinal anaesthetic.)

The Hamlins' tireless efforts to perfect their method of fistula surgery have given a second chance of life to many thousands of Ethiopian women. Some patients cry for joy as they thank the staff for removing the stigma of fistula from them and giving them a new life. Many of the former patients remarry and have children, an integral part of the social structure of their rural villages.

Over 1000 women are treated for fistula each year but the hospital is often overcrowded, so great is the need for this operation. Within a few weeks of having their fistula operation the great majority are cured and can return to their villages proudly wearing a new, clean dress, with improved sewing and knitting skills and, in some cases, being able to read and write. Hospital funds provide the money for many of them to return home without begging, even though their villages may be situated 1000 kilometres away.

Roughly 93 per cent of these dark, delicately featured young girls with their expressive eyes, slim as gazelles, are able to resume a normal life. However, a very small number of patients are so damaged by childbirth that they cannot be completely cured. Subsequent operations are performed which sometimes have the required effect but they may also prove unsuccessful, in which case the patient has to wear a urostomy bag for urine, attached to the abdomen. Many have kidney damage, at risk from further complications, they need ongoing medical treatment and should remain within easy access of a hospital. This means it is impossible for them to return to their homes in the countryside, where the nearest doctor is often over 100 kilometres away. If they are not helped they are likely to die or remain outcasts rejected by their families or resort to begging or prostitution.

With care, compassion, and on-going medical supervision these women, physically weakened, can be helped to regain personal dignity and a reasonable lifestyle. They are eager to undertake light work and are capable of producing craft items that can be sold to benefit the group.

Dr Hamlin's plan is to assist them by means of a 'self-help' rural village and farm. When the Ethiopian president spoke at the opening ceremony of the new hospital in 1999 he promised to provide the land for this venture, and the municipality has donated 24 hectares of rural land at Siga Meda in a secluded fertile valley higher in altitude than Addis Ababa, just 30 kilometres north-west of the fistula hospital, surrounded by apple orchards for the women to tend and harvest. A security fence has been erected around it and Ridley Smith, the Australian architect involved with the renovations to the hospital, has designed the buildings. Michael Melles, a volunteer from Belgium, is the on-site manager. The village/farm has a bore and a dam to provide water for irrigation, ten thatched African-style dwellings, each of which houses ten women, and a teaching/meeting centre where they can learn craftwork, attend literacy classes and talks on improved farming practices and hold social gatherings. A huge drinking-water tank has been erected, thanks to the generosity of a Texan engineer who donated his services.7

The overall aim is for incurable fistula patients to live here free from loneliness and want in secure housing, where they can support each other and maintain traditional village life, growing crops, tending chickens and collecting firewood and receiving the regular medical care and attention they need. The village/farm provides the women with a degree of independence, self-sufficiency and self-respect.8 Almost half the amount needed to construct the village/farm has been raised by international and Australian voluntary bodies, including Zonta International, Rotary International and AusAID, the Silverton Foundation and the Archbishop of Sydney's Relief Fund. In 1998 Dr Catherine Hamlin received the Rotary Award for World Understanding; this, together with donations from World Vision, provided funds to establish this valuable project. Like the charismatic (but sometimes controversial) Dr Albert Schweitzer, who ran a Christian hospital in Africa and attracted volunteers of all faiths and nations, the equally charismatic Dr Hamlin draws people from all walks of life to become involved in this inspiring project which has brought new hope to thousands of women. Dr Hamlin's brother and sister-in-law have travelled from Australia to help in the running of the new village. Her inspiring fistula hospital by the river has brought new hope to thousands of young women whose lives would otherwise have been sheer misery.

What inspires Dr Hamlin to continue working so hard at a time when most Australians have retired? 'God put me here for a purpose,' she has said on many occasions. Other motivational forces appear to be her devotion to the memory of her late husband and his work for the people of Ethiopia; his photograph is greatly in evidence around the hospital. Dr Catherine Hamlin is well aware of the need to establish an endowment fund so that the work will continue when she is gone. She has complete confidence in her young Ethiopian surgeon and gynaecologist, Dr Ambaye Wolde-Michel, a much-loved and valued member of the staff, to run the medical side of the hospital. In Australia Stuart Abrahams, an old and trusted friend, runs the Sydney fundraising office with great dedication and Australians have provided generous support.

The greatest worry now occupying Catherine Hamlin's mind is that small percentage of women whom vaginal surgery cannot cure, who need a skilled urologist to make them new bladders from part of the bowel or perform other reconstructive abdominal surgery. A celebrated London urologist, Dr Gordon Williams, of the Hammersmith Hospital, visits the Addis Ababa hospital on a regular basis and is now teaching Dr Wolde-Michel to perform such procedures.

Dr Catherine Hamlin has been nominated for a Nobel Peace Prize. She will go down in history as a brilliant Australian surgeon whose Christian love inspired her to help unfortunate Ethiopian women deprived of most of the things which in the developed world we take for granted.

Anyone wishing to help the valuable work of the fistula hospital and its farm/village is requested to send donations (which are tax deductible) or arrange bequests in their wills to:

The Hamlin Fistula Relief and Aid Fund,
PO Box 965, Wahroonga, NSW 2076;
e-mail: snabra@ozemail.com.au

ENDNOTES

Chapter 1

1 At the time of writing, Sydney's only remaining all-female swimming baths are still at Coogee.
2 Anon, 'Fanny, World Beater', *Sydney Morning Herald*, 29 July 1992.
3 Anon, 'Nude Men and Clothed Women Swam in the Old Domain', *Sydney Morning Herald*, 3 December 1966.
4 See Chapter 2 on Louisa Lawson and her struggles with Rose Scott and Chapter 21 on Rose Scott herself.
5 Fanny's friends, swimmers Peter Murphy and F.C. Lane, had learned the stroke from a visiting seaman, John William Trudgen, who had in turn learned it from South American Indians on a visit to the estuary of the Rio de la Plata in 1904. See also entry under 'trudgen' in the *Shorter Oxford English Dictionary*, Oxford University Press, Oxford, 1973.
6 Hartung, Greg, 'The Kellerman Legend': obituary of Annette Kellerman in the *Australian*, 6 November 1975. See also entry on Annette Kellerman in *The Australian Encyclopedia*, Vol. VI, Grolier Society of Australia, 1977.
7 A copy of Annette Kellerman's *Fairy Tales of the South Seas* is in Sydney with other Kellerman memorabilia in the Performing Arts Collection at the Sydney Opera House Museum.
8 New South Wales Ladies' Amateur Swimming Association *Annual Reports*, 1904–11.
9 Gordon, Harry, 'The First Heroes', article in *Time* magazine, July 1992.
10 Stell, Marion K., *Half the Race. A History of Australian Women in Sport* HarperCollins, Sydney, 1991.
11 King, Helen, entry in ed. Radi, Heather, (ed.) *200 Australian Women* Women's Redress Press, Sydney, 1988. See also King, Helen, entry in *The Australian Dictionary of Biography*, Vol. 8, Melbourne University Press, Melbourne, 1986.
12 Cited by George Blaikie in 'Great Women of History' in the *Australian Women's Weekly*, 3 November 1982. Unsourced quote.
13 Phillips, Dennis H., *Australian Women at the Olympic Games* Kangaroo Press, Sydney, 1992.
14 *Ibid.*

Chapter 2

1 Gilmore, Mary, *Old Days, Old Ways*, Angus & Robertson, Sydney, 1986.
2 The story of Larson's sudden proposal is credited in several sources to family legend. It suggests that Louisa knew very little of her husband's mania for gold before she married him.
3 Details of Henry Lawson's birth are from accounts related by Louisa's daughter, Gertrude, who grew up hearing her mother's reminiscences about this event.
4 Henry Lawson's story *A Child in the Dark* was written to revenge himself on his mother. It presents a portrait of a kind, caring father and a mother 'bad in the head' and 'with nerves', quarrelling with the father in a rundown household without light or running water, unable to cook or clean or do anything except read and write poetry, and neglecting her three (rather than four) children. In his desire for revenge, Henry overplays his theme. Women who are deeply depressed are unable to concentrate, and reading or writing poetry would be impossible.
5 Sheep's intestines were sometimes used for condoms in the bush, but were generally regarded as devices a man would use with a prostitute but not with his wife. See also Chapter 11 on Sister Lillie Goodisson.
6 See Matthews, Brian, *Louisa*, McPhee Gribble, Sydney, 1987, for a moving and well-written but fictionalised account of this distressing period of Louisa Lawson's life; also *Louisa Lawson, Collected Poems with Critical Commentaries*, University of New England Centre for Australian Literary Studies, Armidale, 1996.
7 The destructive relationship between Henry Lawson and his mother is covered in some detail in Lorna Ollif's biography *Louisa Lawson*, Rigby, Sydney, 1978, and in Brian Matthews' *Louisa, op. cit.*
8 Matthews, Brian, entry on Henry Lawson, *The Australian Dictionary of Biography*, Vol. 10, Melbourne University Press, Melbourne, 1986.
9 Radi, Heather, entry on Louisa Lawson, *The Australian Dictionary of Biography op. cit.*
10 *Ibid.*
11 Lawson, Olive, ed., *The First Voice of Australian Feminism*: Excerpts from Louisa Lawson's 'The Dawn', Simon and Schuster, Sydney, 1989.

[12] *The Dawn* was not Australia's first magazine for women, but it was the first to be published entirely by women, with the occasional help of Henry Lawson.

[13] Adelaide, Debra, *A Bright and Fiery Troop*, Penguin Books, Melbourne, 1987.

[14] *The Dawn* issue dated October 1889 informs readers that the paper employs ten women.

[15] The author was shown an issue of *The Dawn* in which the paper was still white and corners had been rounded off to prevent 'dog-earing'.

[16] The first subscription list for *The Dawn* is held in the Lothian Collection of Lawson Papers, La Trobe Library, the State Library of Victoria. It is cited in full in Lawson, Olive, ed., *The First Voice of Australian Feminism*, op. cit.

[17] *Ibid.*

[18] *The Dawn*, January 1889.

[19] Lawson, Olive, ed., *The First Voice of Australian Feminism*, op cit.

[20] *Ibid.*

[21] Wilde, Professor W.H., *Courage a' Grace: A Biography of Dame Mary Gilmore*, Melbourne University Press, 1988 gives an excellent account of Mary and Will Gilmore at Cosme and of her relationship with Henry Lawson.

[22] *Ibid.* Professor Wilde's biography contains Mary's account of her courtship by Henry Lawson, describes her possessive feelings towards him and the decline and breakdown of his marriage to Bertha. See also important sources in Mary Gilmore's letters. Parts of an autobiographical account, *Henry Lawson and I*, appear as footnotes in Wilde, W. H. and Moore, T. Inglis, eds, *Letters of Mary Gilmore*, Melbourne University Press, Melbourne, 1980; in *Mary Gilmore: Tribute*, Australasian Book Society, 1965 and in Professor Colin Roderick's biography *Henry Lawson: A Life*, Angus Robertson, Sydney, 1999

[23] De Vries-Evans, Susanna, *Historic Sydney*, Pandanus Press, Brisbane, 2000.

[24] Matthews, Brian, *op. cit.*

[25] Wilde, Professor W.H, *Courage a' Grace. op. cit.*

[26] Mattews, Brian, *Louisa, op. cit.*

[27] Thanks to psychiatrists Dr Marian Tyrer and Dr Lilian Cameron for discussions about the mental states of Louisa Lawson and her son Charles.
Lawson, Louisa, *Dert and Do*, published Sydney, 1904, followed in 1905 by *The Lonely Crossing*, a collection of her poems.

[28] Matthews, Brian, entry on Henry Lawson, *The Australian Dictionary of Biography*, Vol. 10, *op. cit.*

[29] Louisa Lawson Papers, Mitchell Library, State Library of New South Wales.

[30] Matthews, Brian, *Louisa, op. cit.*

[31] Eyewitness accounts by Gladesville mental patients reveal how bad conditions were. Little was done in Australia for many years to improve conditions for psychiatric patients in State mental institutions.

Chapter 3

[1] De Vries, Susanna, *Strength of Spirit: Australian Women of Achievement*, Pandanus Press, Brisbane 1997, contains the story of Martha's mother, Ann Caldwell.

[2] Gunn, Mrs Aeneas, author of *We of the Never Never*, first published 1907 in London, reprinted Angus & Robertson, Sydney, various editions.

[3] Under the Selection Acts, which sought to break up very large land holdings of squatters, free selectors were able to buy a 'selection' on a mortgage.

[4] Livingstone Gully was named after a tree on the property on which Surveyor-General Thomas Livingstone Mitchell had carved his name when surveying there. A century and a half later, members of the Cox family still live on Livingstone Gully, and run the historic property.

[5] Martha says that Dave 'claimed my hand'.

[6] 'Dummying' meant land-rich squatters rorting a system designed to help working-class selectors. Using the names of poorer relatives or paid agents, squatters would buy land on a cheap mortgage reserved for selectors, thereby deceiving the Lands Department. To 'peacock' or pick the eyes out of the best land, was the practice whereby squatters (sometimes under false names) bought the good blocks around waterholes and creeks, leaving nothing but marginal areas for selectors. When drought occurred and selectors' sheep and cattle died the squatters would simply buy out the selectors at rock-bottom prices. 'Pre-empting' was the practice whereby selectors took up good land on payment of a deposit before it was subdivided (a 'pre-emptive' lease). David and Martha Cox lost their land after it was formally subdivided and gazetted for agistment (to feed cattle travelling through the outback). Sometimes a corrupt Lands Department official would be bribed to do this. Later the land could be rezoned for selection and a neighbouring squatter could purchase it.

[7] Information in this chapter about the effects of scurvy kindly supplied by Emeritus Professor John Tyrer, formerly of the School of Medicine, University of Queensland, who in his early years in the

medical school treated several bushwomen suffering from this terrible disease, caused by lack of vitamin C derived from fresh vegetables and fruits. Today, as a result of improved diet and the use of refrigeration in the bush, scurvy has all but disappeared.

[8] The son of the inspector of stock on Brunet Downs, Australia's second largest cattle station, stated that it was generally the half-caste girls, despised by their full-blood husbands, who were pimped out to white men. See also *Coonardoo* a novel by Katharine Susannah Prichard in which her female protagonist, Coonardoo, dies of syphilis.

[9] Martha would have known little about scurvy. Not until 1928 was lack of vitamin C isolated by Waugh and King as the cause of scurvy (although as early as 1753, ship's surgeon James Lind wrote a treatise naming the disease and advocating the preventive role of oranges, lemons and limes in the diet). After receiving adequate ascorbic acid, the body usually restores fairly quickly. His words were heeded by Cook and other mariners who took limes and lemons on their voyages. Tragically for those in the bush, Lind failed to connect scurvy with the dietary absence of leaf vegetables. Australian farmers often abandoned their vegetable gardens in times of drought and used all available water for drinking, and for cattle and sheep.

[10] Mrs Davidson's diet of raw vegetables was the right treatment for scurvy. Bush diets normally consisted of mutton, well-cooked vegetables and potatoes. Salads were not eaten as no one knew the importance of vitamins, and it was thought that raw foods were too tough on the digestion.

[11] The John Oxley Library, State Library of Queensland, has no separate entry for Caldwell and it has not been possible to trace the exact site where the property was located near Charleville.

[12] A double-seated buggy is a vehicle for two people, drawn by one or two horses.

[13] Martha uses 'milepeg' rather than the English 'milestone': milepegs were used by surveyors to establish boundaries.

[14] The year was 1887 when Priscilla married.

Chapter 4

[1] Bourdillon, Hilary, *Women As Healers*. Cambridge University Press, Cambridge 1988.

[2] Neve, M. Hutton, *This Mad Folly – The History of Australia's Pioneer Women Doctors*, Library of Australian History, Sydney, 1980.

[3] Forster, Margaret, *Significant Sisters*, Penguin, London, 1986.

[4] *Ibid*

[5] Kerr, Charles, entry on medicine in *The Australian Encyclopaedia*, Vol. 6, Grolier Society of Australia, Sydney, 1983. Gandevia, B. Hostler, A. and Simpson, S., *An Annotated Bibliography of the History of Medicine in Australia*, Royal Australasian College of Physicians, Sydney, 1984; and Gandevia, Bryan, *Tears Often Shed – A History of Childbirth in Australia*, Pergamon Press, Sydney, 1978.

[6] Neve, M. Hutton *op. cit* see footnote 2 cites the first medical students in Melbourne as Lilian Alexander, Elizabeth and Annie O'Hara, Helen Sexton, Clara Stone, Grace Vale and Margaret Whyte.

[7] Neve, M. Hutton, *op. cit.*

[8] Bennion, Elizabeth, *Antique Medical Instruments* University of California Press, Berkeley, 1979.

[9] Frances, Raelene and Scales, Bruce, *Women at Work in Australia. From the Gold Rush to World War II*, Cambridge University Press, London, 1993.

[10] Kerr, Charles, entry in *The Australian Encyclopedia*, Vol. 6, *op. cit.*

[11] Frances, Raelene and Scales, Bruce, *Women at Work in Australia, op. cit.*

[12] In the early 1960s Dr Marian Tyrer won the Dagmar Berne Medal but was not told the sad story of Dagmar's brief career. Interview with Dr Tyrer, 1998.

[13] Neve, M. Hutton, *This Mad Folly, op. cit.*

[14] Information supplied to M Hutton Neve by Dagmar Berne's sister, Eugenie Berne, later Mrs E. N. Buswell.

[15] Cited in Neve, M. Hutton, *This Mad Folly, op. cit.*

[16] *The Parkes Examiner*, 27 August 1900 recorded Dr Dagmar Berne's death, stating: 'The deceased lady had long suffered from chest afflictions.'

[17] Russell, Penny, entries on Dr Constance Stone, Dr Clara Stone and Dr Mary Page Stone in *The Australian Dictionary of Biography*, Vol. 12, Melbourne. University Press, Melbourne, 1990 also in Neve, M. Hutton, *This Mad Folly, op. cit.*

Chapter 5

[1] Manson, Cecil and Cecilia, *Dr Agnes Bennett*, Michael Joseph, London, 1969, pp. 22–25.

[2] Curthoys, Ann, © entry on Dr Agnes Bennett in *The Australian Dictionary of Biography*, Vol. 7, Melbourne University Press, 1989. See also Manson, Cecil and Cecilia, *Dr Agnes Bennett, op. cit.* and Agnes Bennett papers, National Library of New Zealand.

³ *Ibid*

⁴ Dr Elsie Dalyell, *Magazine of Women's College* [Sydney], November 1915, pp. 10–13 and November 1920, pp. 37–41.

⁵ De Vries, Susanna, *Blue Ribbons, Bitter Bread: The Life of Joice NanKivell Loch, Australia's Most Decorated Woman*, Hale & Iremonger, Sydney, 2000. This biography covers her childhood in Queensland and Gippsland, her time in Ireland during the Troubles, her period as an aid worker on the Polish-Russian border, 1921–22, her time in Greece before World War II, her spectacular escape from Rumania, after the Nazis entered Bucharest, in Operation Pied Piper, when she and her husband were jointly responsible for saving over 2000 Polish and Jewish people from death camps, escorting them via Constantinople to Palestine. The biography also covers the Lochs' return to post war Greece.

⁶ Byzantine symbols, depicted in manuscripts held in the monastic libraries of Mount Athos, were used by Joice Loch as design motifs for the Pirgos Rugs.

⁷ Australian Nancy Wake, code-named 'The White Mouse', in World War II, worked with the Resistance in France, helping British airmen to escape from the Germans. Her heroism was honoured by the British with a George Cross. Like Joice, Nancy Wake has never received any official recognition in Australia.

Chapter 6

¹ Eileen commissioned portraits from Doris Zinkheisen, Anna Zinkheisen, Augustus John (then London's most expensive portraitist), John Bratby and a host of minor artists as well as a superb bronze bust from Anna Mahler, daughter of composer Gustav Mahler, which were gifted to the University of Western Australia.

² From Abrahall, C.H. (Lady Claire Hoskins Abrahall, *Prelude*, Oxford University Press, London, 1947, pp. 1–48.

³ *Ibid.*, pp. 66–67.

⁴ Eileen's time at Kununoppin is recorded in Abrahall, C.H., *Prelude, op. cit.* She also described her experiences at the bush school to English journalists, often giving the impression to them that she was talking about St Joseph's Primary School at Boulder. This may account for some of the confusions surrounding stories about her childhood.

⁵ Blainey, Geoffrey, *The Golden Mile – The Story of Kalgoorlie and Boulder*, Sydney (n.d.); and Casey, Gavin and Mayman, T., *The Mile that Midas Touched*, Sydney, 1968.

⁶ Eileen's younger sisters, the late Mrs Norma McNabb and Mrs McPherson.

⁷ Telephone interview with Eileen Joyce's friend, Deirdre Prussak, 18 July 2000.

⁸ Felix Hayman told me that when he presented an 'Eileen Joyce Week' for the ABC, listeners from Boulder phoned in saying some of Eileen's stories were inaccurate. Thanks to musical historian Cyrus Metier-Homji (PhD), confirmed by local by local historian Miss R. Eriksson, for information that Joe Joyce owned a buther's shop in Boulder.

⁹ This may or many not be true but appears as a scene in the 1950 film *Wherever She Goes*.

¹⁰ During his ABC 'Eileen Joyce Week', producer Felix Hayman received a call from an elderly Boulder resident informing him that Eileen Joyce had been allowed to practise at Nicholson's piano store.

¹¹ Telephone interviews by the author with Felix Hayman, ABC music producer, 15 May 2000, and with Deirdre Prussak, 18 July 2000, in which Mrs Prussak recalled that Eileen asked her to invite her younger sister, Mrs Norma McNabb, to lunch when Eileen was visiting Perth. Mrs Prussak observed at first hand the huge chasm which separated the Joyce sisters, one accustomed to an international lifestyle, the other having led a sheltered life in Boulder.

¹² Abrahall C.H., *Prelude, op. cit.*, pp. 103, 115.

¹³ Deirdre Prussak, interview with the author.

¹⁴ Abrahall, C.H., *Prelude, op. cit.*, p. 143.

¹⁵ Father Edmund Campion wrote an article about Eileen Joyce titled 'A Most Transcendental Gift', published in the May/June 1998 issue of *Madonna*, citing Sister John and a Sister Veronica's involvement with Eileen's career as well as that of the nuns of her primary school in Boulder. Both convents confirm this involvement.

¹⁶ Details of the pieces from Abrahall, C.H., *Prelude, op. cit.*, p. 177–78.

¹⁷ *Ibid.*

¹⁸ Eileen Joyce obituary, *Sydney Morning Herald*, 9 April1991.

¹⁹ Telephone interview, Sister Ann Carter, archivist, Loreto Convent, Perth, 4 July 2000.

²⁰ Cited by Ava Hubble in the *Sydney Morning Herald*, 9 April 1991, following the death of Eileen Joyce on 25 March 1991.

²¹ Leipzig and its conservatorium are described in H.H. Richardson's novel *Maurice Guest*, published London, 1908, and in her autobiography *Myself When Young*, London, 1948.

Endotes

22 Abrahall, C. J., *op. cit.*, pp. 208–9 and repeated by Eileen Joyce at various press interviews.

23 Eileen Joyce, interview with Peter Ross, ABC 'Arts on Sunday' program, 1988.

24 Abrahall, C.H., *Prelude*, op.cit, 1948, p. 230.

25 Eileen to Mrs Deirdre Prussak

26 John Coomber, London correspondent of the Melbourne *Age*, article dated 12 May 1985.

27 Story from the late Mrs Norma McNabb, Eileen Joyce's sister, as told to Deirdre Prussak and related to the author on 16 July 2000.

28 Eileen to Deirdre Prussak in her later years and related to author on 16 July 2000.

29 As told by Eileen Joyce to Deirdre Prussak.

30 Mathias, Paul, Essay, *op. cit.* in the official program for the opening of the Eileen Joyce Studio at the University of Western Australia, 28 June 1981. Many thanks to Emeritus Professor Sir Frank Callaway, CMG, OBE, for drawing my attention to this program and for help with details about Eileen Joyce's career.

31 Eileen's son, who bore her considerable ill-will, told Richard Davies that Eileen and Christopher were never married but no concrete evidence for this has yet emerged.

32 Details provided by George Cole, former accountant to the Manns, in an interview 28 July 2000.

33 *Ibid.*

34 *Ibid.*

35 Introduction. Abrahall, C.H., *Prelude, op. cit.*

36 Barbara Ker Wilson, editor, worked for Oxford University Press two years after the publication of *Prelude*, by then withdrawn from sale, and remembers complaints about the book. Somehow Eileen managed to salvage her friendship with Lady Abrahall and they were on good terms in the 1980s when Deirdre Prussak stayed with Eileen. Interview, Deirdre Prussak, 16 July 2000.

37 *Ibid.*

38 Details provided by Barbara Ker Wilson.

39 *Ibid.* Parrett was blonde, unlike red-haired Eileen.

40 Margaret Sutherland's life is related in De Vries, Susanna, *Strength of Purpose – Australian Women of Achievement,* HarperCollins, Sydney, 1998, pp. 199–208.

41 Author Richard Davies has written a comprehensive biography of Eileen Joyce's musical career, to be published by the University of Western Australia Press. In a telephone interview, July 2000, he told me he had talked to John Barratt, Eileen's son, who explained that his mother could on occasions be very difficult. Deirdre Prussak and Eileen's Joyce's executor and close friend Zovita Moon were distressed that neither her son nor his wife attended Eileen's funeral or her memorial service and saw little or nothing of Eileen during her last tragic dementia-ridden years. Mrs Moon related that Eileen planned to cut her son and his family out of her will but finally agreed that her grandson Alexander should inherit White Hart Lodge and its contents.

42 Account given to the author by Susan Stratigos, who attended the concert in Brisbane's City Hall as a child.

43 Interview, Deirdre Prussak, 16 July 2000.

44 Eileen Joyce to Deirdre Prussak, 1984.

45 Eileen Joyce obituary, *Sydney Morning Herald*, 9 April 1991.

46 *Ibid.*

47 Cited by Father Edmund Campion in *Madonna*, May/June 1998.

48 Date taken from Christopher Mann's obituary, held in the State Library of Queensland, Arts Library.

49 Deirdre Prussak, telephone interview, 27 July 2000.

50 Eileen Joyce, obituary, *Sydney Morning Herald, op. cit.*

51 Quoted in a London interview with Eileen Joyce by Margaret Jones in the Melbourne *Age*, 26 June 1981, when Eileen was about to visit Australia.

52 Interview, Dierdre Prissack, 16 July 2000.

53 Not all the jurors have been as committed as Eileen Joyce. In the Sydney 2000 Piano Competition a Russian juror was accused of falling asleep and snoring during the competition.

54 White Hart Lodge was built on the site of a former monastery, destroyed in the time of Henry VIII. A small part of the monastery was incorporated into the modern house.

55 John Coomber, London correspondent of the Melbourne *Age*, article dated 12 September 1985.

56 Letter from Emeritus Professor Sir Frank Calloway, CMG, GBE, dated 22 September 1988.

57 Reply by letter from Eileen. Collection of Deirdre Prussak.

58 For dates see entry under Eileen Joyce in the *Monash Biographical Dictionary of 20th Century Australians*, Reed Books, Melbourne, 1994.

59 Deirdre Prussak, telephone interview, 20 July 2000.

60 From a memorial article written by Deirdre Prussak.

61 A letter dated 24 April 1991 to Deirdre Prussak from Eileen's close friend Zovita Moon records Mrs Moon's distress that Eileen's son refused to attend her memorial service and the rector's pious wish that she and her son would eventually be reconciled in heaven.

Chapter 7

1   The banknote featuring Edith Cowan's portrait was first issued in September 1995.
2   In 1990 the Edith Cowan University, Western Australia, was named in her honour.
3   Tolstoy, L., *Anna Karenina*, Moscow, 1877. In his novel Tolstoy questions the institution of marriage when his heroine observes that her husband 'owns' her. She is explaining to her lover why she cannot leave her husband – she would be unable to keep her little son, as her husband legally owns the child. Divorce or legal separation would ensure that she was barred from ever seeing him again.
4   Cowan, Peter, *A Unique Position*, University of Western Australia Press, Perth, 1979. A good but discreet biography by Edith Cowan's grandson.
5   Jull, R., *Papers and History of the Karrakatta Club 1894–1954*, privately published and Lees, Kirsten, *Votes for Women – The Australian Story*, Allen & Unwin, 1995.
6   Children's Protection Society, Annual Reports, 1909–32. Copies in the Battye Library, Perth.
7   *The Dawn*, Bessie Rischbieth's Perth-based paper, had no connection with Louisa Lawson's women's journal of the same name, produced in Sydney.
8   This was the treatment given to artist Paul Gauguin in the French hospital in Tahiti. Gauguin was one of the very few sufferers who described his treatment for syphilis.
9   Hunt, L., ed., *Western Portraits*, cited in entry on Bessie Rischbieth by Steadman, Margaret, Radi, Heather, (ed.) *200 Australian Women*, Women's Redress Press, Sydney, 1988.
10 *Ibid.*
11 Haines, Janine, *Suffrage to Sufferance: 100 Years of women in politics*, Allen & Unwin, Sydney, 1992.
12 Lady Nancy Astor, was elected to the British Parliament as MP for Portsmouth. Her husband, the sitting member, was unable to take his seat because he had inherited his father's title of Viscount, so his wife stood as candidate in his electorate and won by an overwhelming majority.
13 Lees, Kirsten, *Votes for Women – The Australian Story*, op. cit.

Chapter 8

1   Hart, P.R. and Lloyd, C.J., entry on Joseph Lyons, the *Australian Dictionary of Biography*, Vol. 10, Melbourne University Press, Melbourne, 1986. It seems significant that no entry was made for his wife.
2   Anne Sells, entry on Enid Lyons in Radi, Heather (ed.) *200 Australian Women*, Women's Redress Press, Sydney 1988.
3   Hart and Lloyd, *op. cit.*, cite Enid's age as 18, while Anne Sells, in *200 Australian Women, op. cit.*, p. 203, gives Enid's age as 17.
4   Interview with Dame Enid Lyons, *Australian Women's Weekly*, 6 July 1977.
5   In 1973 on the occasion of the publication of Enid Lyons' book *Among the Carrion Crows*, Rigby, Adelaide, she talked freely to correspondent Suzanne Baker in an interview later published in the *Sydney Morning Herald*, 15 April 1977.
6   Hart, P.R. and Lloyd, C.J., *op. cit.*
7   Edith Cowan had been elected to the Western Australian Parliament in 1921 and Millicent Preston Stanley to the NSW Parliament in 1925, Irene Longman to the Queensland Parliament in 1929 and Millie Peacock to the Victorian Parliament in 1933. In 1943 when Edith Lyons was elected both Tasmania and South Australia still had to elect a woman MP.
8   Haines, Janine, *Suffrage to Sufferance: 100 Years of Women in Politics*, Allen a& Unwin, Sydney, 1992.
9   Sells, Anne, *200 Australian Women, op. cit.*
10 A list of Enid Lyons' books and her honours and political and other appointments appears under her name in the *Monash Biographical Dictionary of 20th Century Australia*, Reed Books, Melbourne 1994 and in the *Australian Dictionary of Biography*, Vol 10. Her full biography written by Kate White, *A Political Love Story: Joe and Enid Lyons*, published 1987, is out of print at the time of writing.

Chapter 9

1   The outward signs of tertiary syphilis varied from patient to patient. Ethel Richardson described her father as suffering from premature ageing, delusions, memory loss, partial and then complete paralysis. The artist Edouard Manet had a paralysis of the lower limbs which started with an ulcerated leg; Paul Gauguin's paralysis started with an ulcerated ankle. The composer Robert Schumann suffered from terrifying visions which led to madness, paralysis and death.
2   Richardson Papers, Australian National Library: Dr Richardson's Commonplace Book.
3   Richardson, Henry Handel *Myself When Young*, Heinemann, London, 1948, p. 4.

Endotes

The Fortunes of Richard Mahony, the first volume of Henry Handel Richardson's trilogy *Australia Felix*, partly based on her father's life; part of her hero's character was based 'on my own', she said.

Richardson, Henry Handel, *Myself When Young, op. cit.*

Clark, Axel, *Henry Handel Richardson. Fiction in the Making*, Simon & Schuster, Sydney, [n.d.]. Clark mentions Dr Richardson's attempted surgical removal of the port-wine birthmark, a disfigurement which badly affected Ethel's self-confidence.

Richardson, Henry Handel, *Myself When Young, op.cit.* p. 16.

Ibid. p. 20.

Ibid. p. 25.

10 *Ibid.* p. 25.

11 *Ibid.* pp. 37–38.

12 Richardson, Henry Handel, *The Getting of Wisdom, op, cit.* pp. 71–72, recounts the love story of Evelyn (Connie) and Laura (Ethel).

13 *Ibid.* p. 147.

14 Ethel Carrick Fox, wife of Australian artist Emanuel Phillips Fox, also loathed the name Ethel and flatly refused to use it, signing her paintings 'Carrick Fox' instead.

15 Maugham, Somerset, *Great Novelists and their Novels*, John Winston, New York, 1948.

16 For a discussion about Roncoroni's role in Ettie's life see McLeod, Karen, *Henry Handel Richardson. A Critical Study*, Cambridge University Press, Cambridge, 1985. McLeod met Roncoroni and recorded her talk about agoraphobia.

17 Olga Roncoroni completed the unfinished memoir, *Myself When Young*, published posthumously in London by Heinemann in 1948 with a chapter by Professor Robertson.

18 Olga Ronconi, Preface to *Myself When Young, op. cit.*

19 For a discussion of Ethel Richardson's place in literature, see the following: Wilde, W., Hooton, J. and Andrews, B., The *Oxford Companion to Australian Literature*, Oxford University Press, Melbourne, 1985, pp 584–87; Kramer, Leonie, *Henry Handel Richardson, Some of her Sources*, Melbourne University Press Melbourne, 1954; Clark, Axel, *Henry Handel Richardson. Fiction in the Making, op. cit.*; and McLeod, Karen, *Henry Handel Richardson: A Critical Study, op. cit.* A most perceptive essay on Richardson by Dorothy Green is contained in *Women In Victoria – 150 Years*, edited by Marilyn Lake and Farley Kelly, *Penguin*, Melbourne, 1985.

Chapter 10

1 Elizabeth Kenny was not the only unqualified nurse who continued to use the title 'Sister' after the war, a title many felt she had justly earned.

2 Kenny Treatment Clinics were formed at George Street, Brisbane, the Royal Brisbane Hospital (where Ward 7 was converted into a Kenny Clinic for Children), Cairns, Rockhampton and Townsville. Sister Kenny's most famous patient was a young farm boy of Danish extraction who was greatly helped by her methods. He grew up to become Queensland's controversial premier, Joh Bjelke-Petersen. For a medically based but objective account of Kenny's achievements in Queensland, see Tyrer, Professor John H., *History of the Royal Brisbane Hospital*, Boolarong Publications/Royal Brisbane Hospital, Brisbane, 1993. Other writings on Sister Kenny are *The True Book About Sister Kenny*, Shakespeare Head Press, London, 1965, and Levine, Herbert, *Sister Kenny: A Story of a Great Lady*, Christopher Publishing, Boston, 1954. A short account of her life with excellent source reference is Barren, J. and Hacker, D., *Women in History: Places of Purpose*, Queensland Women's Historical Association, Brisbane, 1994. See also Patrick, Dr Ross, entry on Elizabeth Kenny in The *Australian Dictionary of Biography*, Vol. 12, Melbourne University Press, Melbourne, 1990.

3 See Spearitt, P. and Gammage, B. (eds.), *Australians: A Historical Library*, Fairfax, Syme Weldon, Sydney, 1987, for a discussion of polio epidemics in all Australian States. In 1937 Kenny published her own book, *Infantile Paralysis and Cerebral Diplegia*.

4 Information from interviews with patients treated by the Kenny method, cited in Blaikie, George, 'Women of History', *Australian Women's Weekly*, November 1984.

5 During the 1930s a letter published in the Brisbane *Courier Mail* related how, among polio sufferers, the writer had seen 'cases of paralysis that would make one's heart ache'. He commented: 'Good luck, Sister Kenny, you alone can save these children.'

6 Patrick, Dr Ross, entry on Elizabeth Kenny in the *Australian Dictionary of Biography, op. cit.*

7 Mrs Mary McCracken: interview with Stephen Lamble, Brisbane, *Sunday Mail*, 24 December 1995. Mrs McCracken revealed how her natural mother, the victim of a family break-up, had placed an advertisement in the paper for someone to adopt her nine-year-old daughter. Sister Kenny, who was too old to adopt legally, falsified her age to do this. Mrs McCracken cared for Kenny's widowed mother until she died in 1937. She then worked in Kenny's clinics and was present at Elizabeth

641

Kenny's death. She claimed that Sister Kenny was the equal of Florence Nightingale but said that when she died, not one Australian university would accept custodianship of Kenny's many awards, or Florence Nightingale's bible, given to her by an old soldier. These items were donated to the United Nations Organisation. Additional Kenny papers are in the Fryer Library, The University of Queensland, and with the Countrywomen's Association, Nobby, Darling Downs, Queensland.

8 Blaikie, George, *op. cit.*

9 Production of the anti-polio vaccine developed by Dr J. Salk began in Australia in July 1955. In the following years children all over Australia were vaccinated and the battle against polio was gradually won with this and the Sabin vaccine. In 1964 Tasmania was the first State to immunise children using live Sabin vaccine given to children on a sugar lump. For further information on polio in Australia, see Camm, J.C.R. and McQuilton, J. (eds.), *Australians. A Historical Atlas* Fairfax, Sydney & Weldon, Sydney, 1987.

Chapter 11

1 Dr Aletta Jacobs, writing in 1828 to fellow suffragette, American-born Carrie Chapman Catt.

2 Brindle, David, 'Baby Boom for Women over Forty', The *Guardian,* 20 March 1995. Australian Bureau of Statistics, Canberra, Census figures, 1996.

3 Interestingly enough, in the year 2000 a leading Sydney IVF clinic, where gender selection is carried out, claims that more women are now asking for girls than boys. See also *Parenting Girls,* Pandanus Press, 1999 by Dr Janet Irwin, Susanna de Vries and Susanne Stratigos Wilson.

4 Sheehy, Gail, *New Passages,* HarperCollins, London and Sydney, 1996.

5 *Inter-colonial Medical Journal of Australia,* 20 February 1907.

6 Foley, Meredith, entry on Lillie Goodisson, in the *Australian Dictionary of Biography*, Vol. 9, Melbourne University Press, Melbourne, 1983.

7 During the 1960s the author lived in Spain, where all contraceptives were banned. Female friends implored her to bring a supply from Britain – an offence which carried a heavy fine. In 1971 she worked for a time in a birth control clinic run by the Newcastle Health Authority, Nor-thumberland, England in a working-class dockside and factory area with high unemployment. The clinic was set up to monitor patients with large families who were on control trials to compare the efficacy of contraceptive pills and IUDs. Both gave rise to problems, but the majority of patients found them better than the alternative, having another child.

Chapter 12

1 When Ella was born the NSW Aboriginal Protection Board under their chairman (who happened also to be Inspector of Police) had the right to remove paler skinned Aborigines (if they were deemed 'neglected') from their mothers. In 1910 the NSW Aborigines changed. Proof of 'neglect' was no longer required before removing any Aboriginal child to a mission or a training school. All that was required was for the child's surroundings to be deemed 'unsuitable' to white eyes. The children were forcibly removed by police from their mothers or as they left school and taken to two training institutions – Cootamundra for girls and Kinchela for boys. They were worked extremely hard, denied affection and received no instruction in reading or writing.

2 Purfleet Mission, outside Taree, was founded in 1902 (the year of Ella's birth) on twelve acres of land later designated a government reserve. The United Aborigines Mission in Sydney, an inter-denominational organisation, sent a Missionary to run Purfleet. The Aborigines on the mission worked as a cooperative and built their own houses, a church, a school (unfortunately with an indifferent teacher) and a mission house. Work was plentiful in country areas at that time; male Aborigines worked as stockmen and station hands for less than award wages. Jealousy by white union members ensured many lost their jobs and the Great Depression of the 1930s completed the process of job loss. By 1932 so many Aborigines were on welfare that the Aborigines Protection Board changed the set up at Purfleet. The kindly missionary was removed and a stern manager appointed. So many adult Aborigines and 'stolen' children were being sent to Purfleet that the land was increased to fifty-one acres. Reserves such as Burnt Bridge, Bellbrook, near Kempsey, Stony Gully and Woodenbong were all created at this time. The morale of the Aborigines reached a low ebb as a result of being denied work and land and because of their new regimentation. In 1978, information on poor conditions at Purfleet provided by Professor A.P. Elkin of the University of Sydney (who was a friend of Ella Simon) did a great deal to help Aboriginal people raising white consciousness of the wrongs done to them.

3 By now the Aboriginal Protection Board had been renamed the Aboriginal Welfare Board. In the 1940s the NSW Government closed segregated schools and placed Aboriginal education under the control of the Education Department. The white manager had the right to issue certificates or 'identity cards' to Aborigines like Ella, granting them freedom of movement and access to places such as hotels, from which they had been banned. Aboriginal children were now sent to Homes as wards of the State.

[4] For a fuller description of the background to Aboriginal missions and the assimilation problem, see the entry under Aborigines – The Early Missions and the Big Reserves in *The Australian Encyclopaedia*, Vol. 1, pp. 205–212, Grolier Society, 1983.

[5] Ella Simon, Foreword to *Through My Eyes*, Rigby, Adelaide, 1978.

[6] Ella's life story in *Through My Eyes, op. cit.* She dedicated her autobiography to 'my grandmother, who taught me about being both Aboriginal and Christian and who cared for all people. And to my father for his honesty with the people he knew he had wronged.'

Chapter 13

[1] Information kindly provided by the Board of Architects, Sydney, in September 1996. The NSW Board was set up by an Act of Parliament in 1923 to regulate the profession.

[2] The *Australian Dictionary of Biography*, Vol. 12, Melbourne University Press, Melbourne, 1990, gives John Parsons as starting working life as a labourer.

[3] The *Australian Dictionary of Biography*, Vol. 12, *op. cit.*, gives the year of Florence Parsons' immigration to Australia as 1884, while her entry by King, Helen, *200 Australian Women*, in Radi, Heather (ed.) Women's Redress Press, Sydney, 1988, quotes the date of arrival as 1888, which seems more likely.

[4] According to Bronwyn Hanna's entry on Florence Taylor in the *Dictionary of Women Artists*, Sydney, 1995, Florence became an orphan at the age of nineteen, which may imply that her mother had died before her father, leaving her to support her three younger sisters.

[5] Although no itinerary remains of the Taylors' journey, they probably visited the Panama Canal, which was opened for shipping in 1914.

[6] Berger, John, art critic, in *Ways of Seeing*, Penguin Books, London, 1972.

[7] Hanna, Bronwyn, extract from article 'Hats' in the *Architecture Bulletin*, October 1994 (referring to the *Australian Women's Weekly*, 8 July 1933).

[8] Article on Florence Taylor, in the *Australian Women's Weekly*, 8 July 1933.

[9] *Ibid*

[10] Unreferenced newspaper article from Florence Taylor's Papers in the Mitchell Library, State Library of New South Wales, cited by Bronwyn Hanna in her article 'Hats', *op. cit.*

[11] King, Helen, *200 Australian Women*, entry in Radi, Heather (ed.), *op. cit.*

Chapter 14

[1] Carter, Isabel, *Woman in a Wig. Joan Rosanove, QC*, Lansdowne Press Melbourne, 1970.

[2] Interview with Joan Rosanove in *Table Talk*, Melbourne, 28 November 1929.

[3] Nairn, Bede and Serle, Geoffrey, entry in *The Australian Dictionary of Biography*, Vol. 9. entry in *Melbourne University Press, Melbourne*, 1990. Also Campbell, R.J., *A History of the Melbourne Law School 1857–1973*, Melbourne University Press, Melbourne, 1973.

[4] Interview with Joan Rosanove (Lazarus) in *Table Talk*, 28 November 1929.

[5] A full account of Joan Lazarus's role in the celebrated Ozanne libel case is provided by lawyer Arthur Dean. See Dean, Arthur, *A Multitude of Counsellors*, Cheshire, Melbourne, 1968.

[6] Carter, Isabel, *Woman in a Wig. Joan Rosanove, QC, op. cit.*

[7] *Ibid.*

[8] Joan Rosanove's article *My Outlook on Life*, dated 1936, from the *Melbourne Herald* is cited by Isabel Carter in *Woman in a Wig. Joan Rosanove, QC, op. cit.* However, the date and month of the article are not given.

[9] Carter, Isabel, *Woman in a Wig. Joan Rosanove, QC, op. cit.*

[10] Mitchell, Susan, *The Matriarchs*, Penguin Books, Melbourne, 1987; paine, Jonathan, *Taken on Oath: a seneration of lawyers*, Federation Press, Sydney, 1992.

[11] Joan Rosanove's obituary in the Melbourne *Sun* is dated 10 April 1974. I am indebted for the story of Joan Rosanove to her daughter, Judge Peg Lusink, who also checked my manuscript for errors and kindly gave permission to reproduce photographs of her mother.

[12] The remarkable Dr Mannie Rosanove remarried at the age of eighty and died ten years later.

Chapter 15

[1] Dame Roma Mitchell in a speech at the 1984 Woman of the Year Luncheon, Canberra.

[2] *Ibid.*

[3] Dame Roma Mitchell to the author. Telephone interview, 1997.

[4] *Ibid.*

[5] *Ibid.*
[6] *Ibid.*
[7] *Ibid.*
[8] *Ibid.*
[9] *Ibid.*
[10] Mitchell, Susan, *The Matriarchs,* Penguin Books, Melbourne, 1987, p.29..
[11] An important article on this topic by barrister and anti-discrimination commissioner, Jocelyn Scutt, 'No merit to endemic sexism in the legal system' was published in *The Australian,* 19 July 2000.
[12] Extract from Sir William Deane's address quoted in the May 2000 newsletter of the Churchill Fellowship Association of Queensland.

Chapter 16

[1] *Australian Dictionary of Biography,* Douglas Pike (ed.), Vol 5, Melbourne University Press, 1974. Entry on Dr Christopher Rawson Penfold (1811–70), written by D.I. MacDonald, refers to Mary Penfold in the last three paragraphs but she received no entry under her own name in spite of her importance in Australian wine-making history. See also Mills, S.A. ed., *Wine Story of Australia,* Sydney, 1908; Keane, B. ed., *The Penfold Story,* Sydney, 1951; Mayo, Oliver, *The Wines of South Australia,* Penguin Books, Ringwood, Vic., 1986; Lake, Dr Max, *Vine and Scalpel,* Brisbane, 1967.
[2] Jolly, B., *The Penfold Cottage Story,* Adelaide, n.d.
[3] *Adelaide Register,* 8 August 1842.
[4] Warburton, Elizabeth, *The Paddocks Beneath,* Burnside City Council, Burnside, SA, 1981.
[5] Cited in *The Penfold Cottage Story, op. cit.*
[6] *Adelaide Register,* 4 June 1874. Story headed 'Mrs Penfold's Wine Manufactory'.
[7] 'The Phylloxera Scare', supplement to the *Adelaide Chronicle,* 15 November 1879.
[8] Norrie, Dr Phillip, *Penfold Time Honoured,* Apollo Books, Sydney, 1994. This book, written to celebrate the 150th anniversary of the establishment of the Grange winery at Magill, follows the Australian tradition of minimising the contributions of women to Australia's development. The aim seems to be to establish the fact that since Australia is unique in having some of its best wines initially cultivated by male Australian doctors, then wine (mainly red) must surely be good medicine for those who drink it, which is all well and good in an era when high lipid levels and vascular disease are known to be major killers of Australians. However, there is no need to tinker with history to make a point. Dr Penfold did *not* found what became Australia's largest wine group: his wife did.

Chapter 17

[1] *Australian Dictionary of Biography.* Vol. 5, entry on Lucy Osburn by John Griffith, Melbourne University Press, Melbourne.
[2] Watson, J.E., *History of the Sydney Hospital 1811–1911,* Sydney, 1911, and Florence Nightingale Papers, British Museum, London.
[3] Prostitutes were employed in several Australian colonial hospitals. Former prostitutes employed as nurses at the Woogatoo Asylum are detailed in Evans, S., *Historic Brisbane and its early Artists,* Boolarong Publications, Brisbane, 1982; this also happened in some British hospitals prior to Florence Nightingale's reforms.
[4] Borowski, Eva, A Nice Staff of Nurses, *This Australia,* Australian Consolidated Press, Sydney, 1988.
[5] Lucy Osburn's letter describing the poor standards of nursing staff to Florence Nightingale was dated 4 December 1864. Florence Nightingale Papers, British Museum, London.
[6] *Australian Dictionary of Biography,* Vol. 6, entry on Sir Alfred Roberts by Martha Rutledge, Melbourne University Press, Melbourne, 1974. Borowski, A Nice Staff of Nurses, *op. cit.*
[7] See also Evans, E.P., Nursing in Australia in *International Nursing Review,* 12, 1936 and Sussman, M.P., Lucy Osburn and her five Nightingale Nurses in *Medical Journal of Australia,* 1 May 1965 and Watson, *op. cit.*

Chapter 18

[1] McConnel, David Cannon, *Facts and Traditions collected for a Family Record,* Edinburgh, 1861. This book gives a history of the McConnel family.
[2] Fox, M.J., *The History of Queensland,* Brisbane, 1921.
[3] All extracts are from McConnel, Mary, *Memories of Days Long Gone By,* London, 1905. These are Mary's memoirs.

4 *Ibid.*
5 Banks, Mary McLeod, *Pioneering Life in Queensland*, London, 1931. This book, written by Mary McConnel's daughter, whose married name was Banks, describes her mother's heroism in saving the life of a domestic servant.
6 Australian Council of National Trusts, *Historic Homesteads of Australia*, Vol. 1, Reed, Sydney, 1985. This book contains photographs of Cressbrook Station.
7 McConnel, Mary, *op. cit.*

Chapter 19

1 Twenty-eight of Australia's great achievers were listed in The *Australian* newspaper dated 10 May 2001. The small number of women selected by popular vote included three who are featured in this book, Dame Nellie Melba, Miles Franklin and Mother Mary MacKillop.
2 Some dates and references are taken from Osmund Thorpe's entry on Mary MacKillop in the 1984 edition of *The Dictionary of Australian Biography*, Volume 5, from Thorpe's *Life of Mother Mary, Foundress of the Sacred Heart*, Sydney, 1916, and Lesley O'Brien's *Mary MacKillop Unveiled*, HarperCollins, Melbourne, 1994, all of them written with the cooperation of the Sisters of St Joseph and from information supplied by Father Paul Gardener. (See footnote five). However research on many aspects of Mary's life continues and there is still much work on her waiting to be published. In the brief space available here I am concerned with presenting a lively but abbreviated outline of her life as a role model for young women with a social conscience today.
3 Father Julian Tenison Woods was ten years older than Mary and had only been ordained for three years when they met.
4 Campion, Father Edmund, 'How Mary MacKillop has become a role model', *The Bulletin*, Sydney, 1995.
5 I am greatly indebted to Father Paul Gardner, SJ, author of the authorised biography *An Extraordinary Australian, Mary MacKillop*, E.J. Dwyer and David Ell, Sydney, 1994, for reading through and making amendments to my account of Mary MacKillop's somewhat complex early life. I have drawn on his expertise for this and other parts of the story, for which I thank him.
6 See O'Brien, Lesley, *Mary MacKillop Unveiled, op. cit.* and Father Paul Gardner, SJ. *An Extraordinary Australian, Mary MacKillop, op. cit.*
7 Gardner, Father Paul, SJ, *An Extraordinary Australian, Mary MacKillop*, EJ. Dwyer and David Ell, Sydney 1994, pp. 85–87, and pp. 98–110.
8 Campion, Father Edmund, *op. cit.*
9 For a full account of Mary's teaching career see O'Brien, Lesley, *Mary MacKillop Unveiled, op. cit.* pp. 85–94.
10 Campion, Father Edmund, *op. cit.*
11 For a full account of the Generalate of Mother Bernard see Father Paul Gardner's authorised biography of Mary MacKillop, Op cit., pp. 416–438.

Chapter 20

1 Melba, Nellie, *Melodies and Memories,* London, Thornton Butterworth, 1925, a biography ghosted by Beverley Nichols.
2 De Vries, Susanna, *Great Australian Women. From Federation to Freedom,* HarperCollins, Sydney, 2001.
3 Hetherington, John, *Melba, A Memory*, Melbourne University Press, Melbourne, 1995, p. 20.
4 *Ibid*, p. 25.
5 Melba, Nellie, *op. cit.*
6 Madame Elsie Wiedermann-Pinschof was a former opera singer married to the Austro-Hungarian consul in Melbourne.
7 *Ibid.*
8 Quotation from conductor Sir Thomas Beecham cited in Wechsberg, Joseph, *Red Plush and Black Velvet*, Little, Brown, Boston, 1961. Wechsberg studied at the Vienna Conservatorium before fleeing from Europe to America in 1939, where he became a New York journalist. His book makes delightful reading but while he has some wonderful anecdotes about Melba, many drawn from her own memoirs or told to the author by her friends, Wechsberg is inaccurate about many details of Nellie's Australian years. Other memorable Melba biographies are by Thérèse Radic, *Melba: the Voice of Australia*, MacMillan, 1986 and John Hetherington, *Melba, A Memory*, published by Melbourne University Press in 1995 and the Lady Pamela Vestey, *Melba: A Family Memoir*, Phoebe Publishing, Melbourne, 1996 which is a marvellously warm and personalised account of Melba and her family.
9 Prichard, Katharine Susannah, *Child of the Cyclone*, Angus and Robertson, Sydney, 1963.

[10] Marchiesi, Mathilde, *Marchiesi and Music. Passages from the life of a famous singing teacher*, Harper & Brothers, New York, 1898.

[11] Wechsberg, Joseph, *op. cit.*

[12] Blanche Marchiesi, Madame Marchiesi's jealous daughter, took great delight in chronicling Melba's distress when her love affair became public knowledge. See Blanche's autobiography, *A Singer's Pilgrimage*, published, London, 1923.

[13] Davidson, Jim, entry on Melba in the *Australian Dictionary of Biography*, Vol. 10, Melbourne University Press, Melbourne, 1986.

[14] Wechsberg, Joseph, *op cit.*

[15] Melba's affair with the Duke has been written about by all her biographers but the most comprehensive and believable account is the one by Thérèse Radic in *Melba: The Voice of Australia*, Macmillan, Melbourne, 1986.

[16] Dates from Melba's entry in Grove's *Dictionary of Music*, MacMillan, London, 1998, p. 478.

[17] Radic, T., *op. cit.* P. 147.

[18] Davidson, Jim, *op. cit.*

[19] Davidson, Jim, *op. cit.*

[20] Information provided by Oliver Streeton, grandson of Sir Arthur Streeton and his wife Norma Clench.

[21] Telephone interview with Lady Pamela Vestey, 1994, from which it was apparent how much she loved her grandmother.

[22] Lady Pamela Vestey, *Melba: A Family Memoir*, Phoebe Publishing, Melbourne, 1996.

Chapter 21

[1] Miles Franklin provided many details about her ancestors but omitted their convict origins. See Colin Roderick's biography, *Miles Franklin*, Rigby, Adelaide, 1983.

[2] Kinross Smith G., *Australia's Writers*, Nelson, Melbourne, 1980.

[3] Franklin, Miles, *Childhood at Brindabella. My First Ten Years*, Angus and Robertson, Sydney, 1963.

[4] Franklin, Miles, *Childhood at Brindabella, op. cit.*

[5] Franklin Papers, Mitchell Library.

[6] See Irwin, Dr J. et al, *Parenting Girls*, Pandanus Press, Brisbane, 1999, in which girls' greatly changed attitudes to virginity before marriage are extensively discussed.

[7] Kinross, Hugh, *Australia's Writers* (which includes a chapter on Miles Franklin), Nelson, Edinburgh, 1980.

[8] See de Vries, Susanna, *Great Australian Women: From Federation to Freedom*, chapter on Mary Gilmore and Henry Lawson, HarperCollins, Sydney, 2001.

[9] *200 Australian Women*, Women's Redress Press, 1988. Entry by Jill Roe for Miles Franklin, p. 117.

[10] Franklin, Miles, from the joint edition of *My Brilliant Career* and *My Career Goes Bung*, Angus and Robertson, Sydney, 1994, p. 309.

[11] *Ibid.*

[12] A letter to Franklin's literary agent James Pinker in London dated 7 April 1904 shows sales of three impressions of *My Brilliant Career* dating from 1901–04 for several thousand copies. Franklin Papers, Mitchell Library, Sydney. Almost a century later Franklin's novel was chosen for inclusion in Geoffrey Dutton's *Great Books of Australia*, published in 1992.

[13] Description of Banjo Paterson by his friend Norman Lindsay in Lindsay's series of essays, *Bohemians of the Bulletin*, Sydney, 1965.

[14] See de Vries, Susanna, *Strength of Purpose: Australian Women of Achievement*, HarperCollins, Sydney.

[15] Allen, Judith A., *Rose Scott: Vision and Revision in Feminism*, Oxford University Press, Melbourne, 1994, pp. 140–1.

[16] *Ibid.*, pp. 174–5.

[17] Franklin, Miles, *Laughter, not for a cage*, Angus and Robertson, Sydney, 1956, pp. 99–100.

[18] *Australian Encyclopaedia*, Vol. 7, Grolier Society, 1983. Entry for David Scott Mitchell, p. 12.

[19] *Ibid*, edition dated 1926.

[20] Allen, Judith, *ibid*, and in a telephone interview with the author, 1997. Allen stated that she and other authors had drawn the same conclusions about Scott Mitchell dying of syphilis but had not liked to publish the fact for fear it would offend the Mitchell Library, to whom they were indebted. Emeritus Professor of Medicine John Tyrer, who has made a study of syphilis, confirms that the details of Scott Mitchell's illness fit with the pattern of syphilis.

[21] Allen, Judith A., *op. cit.*, p. 97.

[22] Franklin, Miles, *My Career Goes Bung*, Angus and Robertson, Sydney, 1946.

[23] *Ibid.* p. 61.

[24] In 1968 the book was reprinted in Australia with an introduction by Jill Roe.

[25] Published under the pseudonym of Mr and Mrs Ogniblat L'Artisau, (an anagram based on Miles' grandmother's property of Old Talbingo).

[26] This poem was written by the suffragette Carolyn Wells.

[27] Correspondence from Henry Demarest Lloyd in Miles Franklin Papers, Mitchell Library, vol 12.

[28] Barnard, Marjorie, *op. cit.*

[29] Some 8,000 letters archived in the Mitchell Library and in libraries in America do not appear to give the real reason for the breakup with Demy Lloyd. It seems likely that Miles destroyed any that did. Miles in a letter to Dymphna Cusack dated 13 October 1943 admitted to burning scores of letters and left instructions that other letters were to be destroyed by her executors, observing that biographers 'brought an entirely new fear to death.'

[30] The story of the Lloyd brothers and Franklin's relations with Alice Henry and Margaret Drier Robins are related by Verna Coleman in *Miles Franklin in America, op. cit.*

[31] See Spender, Dale. *Women of Ideas & what men have done to them.* Pandora Press, London, 1990, pp. 682–3.

[32] Purvis, June. (ed) *Women's history in Britain 1850–1945,* University College London Press, London, 1995, pp 294–296.

[33] Details of Miles Franklin's time at Ostrovo are from her own writings and from the comprehensive chapter on the Scottish Women's Hospitals in Gilchrist, Hugh, *Australians and Greeks. Volume 2, The Middle Years,* Halstead Press, Sydney, 1997, pp. 129–152.

[34] Letter held by the Chicago Historical Society in the Agnes Nestor papers is cited in full in Roe, Jill. *Op. cit.,* p. 119.

[35] Most of Salonika's Jews were sent by the invading Germans to Auschwitz during World War II and died there.

[36] Descriptions of the Scottish Women's Hospital at Ostrovo are from Miles Franklin's writing and from the story of Dr Agnes Bennett's Hospital. See Susanna de Vries, *Strength of Purpose, Australian Women of Achievement* and *Great Australian Women, op. cit.,* both HarperCollins.

[37] Letter in Franklin Papers, Mitchell Library ref. P 108 cited in full in Roe, Jill, *My Congenials, op. cit.,* p. 121.

[38] Franklin's letters to Alice Henry contained details about the Macedonian campaign but most of them have disappeared. Mary Stirling, Olive King and other volunteers described life at Ostrovo and other camps in letters and diaries. For more information on life with the Scottish Women's Hospital Service see Gilchrist, Hugh. *Australians and Greeks. Volume 2, The Middle Years,* Halstead Press, Sydney, 1997.

[39] See footnote no. 2.

[40] Roe, Jill, (ed.), *My Congenials. Miles Franklin and Friends in Letters,* Vol l, Angus & Robertson, 1993, p. 103. Hugh Gilchrist in *Greeks and Australians, op. cit.* cites Franklin leaving Greece in February 1917 but the Mitchell Library contains letters from Franklin written in Greece long past this date so this is clearly inaccurate.

[41] This unpublished work was rejected by the London publishers Watt and Company and presumably by other publishers.

[42] Baron Tennyson was a former Governor General of Australia.

[43] Other pen names Miles used at various times were Jay Verney, S. Frankling, Mr and Mrs Ogniblat L'Artisau and H.M. Baker.

[44] Alvarez, A. *The Savage God: a study of depression and suicide among creative people.*

[45] For the story of Sister Lillie Goodisson and Sydney's first family planning clinic see de Vries, Susanna, *Great Australian Women from Federation to Freedom,* HarperCollins, Sydney, 2000.

[46] Three psychiatrists to whom I have shown this chapter agree with this diagnosis of Miles' depressions and insist she was not strictly speaking a manic depressive. She never reached the point where she became suicidal.

[47] See Harris, Beth, MA., *Bipolar Disorder,* Lippincott, Williams and Wilkins, New York, 1999 which refers to cyclothymia as distinct from bipolar disorder and the standard work, Fieve, R.R., *Moodswings,* William Morrow, New York, 1989.

[48] See Ferrier, Carole, *As Good as a Yarn with you,* Cambridge University Press, Cambridge, 1992 for a fascinating series of letters which show these friendships developing between the years 1930 and Franklin's death in which the women discuss their work and their personal lives.

[49] Prichard's correspondence indicates the visit took place in 1930. See also North, M., *Yarnspinners,* UQP., St. Lucia, 2001.

[50] Letter dated June 1, 1930 from K.S. Prichard, Franklin Papers, Mitchell Library, ref. FP 21 cited in full in Ferrier, Carole, *As Good as a Yarn with you* and in Roe, Jill, *op. cit.*

[51] Miles was right. When Dalby Davidson's wife died, he lost no time in marrying a much younger and prettier woman he had also been paying court to. Marjorie Barnard was devastated by his duplicity.

[52] Miller, E. Morris and Macartney, Frederick, *Australian Literature,* Angus & Robertson, Sydney, 1956, pp. 184–185.

[53] Roderick, Colin, *Miles Franklin, her brilliant career,* Rigby, Adelaide, 1982, p. 191.

[54] See Munro, Craig, *P.R. Stephens, wild man of letters,* Melbourne, 1984.

[55] Letter dated 30 August, 1939 in Franklin Papers, Mitchell Library, cited in full in Roe, Jill, *op. cit.*, p. 17.

[56] Letter from Dymphna Cusack Papers. Cited in full in Roe, Jill, *op. cit.*, Vol 2, p. 101.

[57] Phone conversations between the author and Ric Throssell in the year before his death confirmed this and the extent of his fondness for Miles who he saw as a 'very special person indeed.'

[58] Letter cited in Roe, Jill, *op. cit.*, p. 169.

[59] Cited in Roe, Jill, *op. cit.*, Vol 2, p. 5.

[60] Her dinner with Miles Franklin is cited in Keesing, Nancy, *Riding the Elephant,* Allen and Unwin, Sydney, 1988.

[61] Figure quoted by Stuart Glover, former Manager of Literature for the Queensland Arts Council, in an article 'Why Writers Need Grants' in the *Courier-Mail,* 16 December 2000.

Chapter 22

[1] Australian Women Composers, video, Australian Film Institute, Sydney, 1983.

[2] Anon, interview with Dr Margaret Sutherland, undated, Women's Art Register Files, Melbourne.

[3] Peers, Julie and Hammond, Victoria, *Completing the Picture: Women Artists and the Heidelberg School,* Artmoves, Melbourne, 1982.

[4] A total for Jane Sutherland's paintings has been estimated after talks with Geoffrey Smith of the National Gallery of Victoria and the staff of various auction houses. Several of Sutherland's works are in private collections.

[5] Interview with Oliver Streeton at the Art Gallery of Queensland, July 1996; also passage cited by Geoffrey Smith in *Arthur Streeton,* National Gallery of Victoria, Melbourne, 1996.

[6] Radic, Therese, Lake, M. and Kelly, F., entry on Margaret Sutherland in *Double Time,* Penguin Books, Melbourne, 1985.

[7] Entry by Jim Davidson on Louise Hanson-Dyer in Vol. 9, *Australian Dictionary of Biography,* Melbourne University Press, Melbourne, 1981.

[8] *Op. Cit.*

[9] Lindsay, Frances, entry on Jane Sutherland in *The Australian Dictionary of Biography,* Vol. 12, Melbourne University Press, Melbourne, 1990. Frances Lindsay curated an exhibition of Jane Sutherland's work held at the Victorian College of the Arts, Melbourne, September 1977.

[10] At various periods in her life Margaret Sutherland composed works for children. These include: *Simple string pieces: a set of twelve short string quartets for early grade classwork,* n.d.; *Land of Ours,* printed 1934, for which she composed words and music; *First Suite for Piano,* 1937; *Sebastian the Fox,* with words by Robert Garran, 1948. *Rush, the Story of Sebastian the Fox,* was recorded by Move Records in 1948.

[11] The entry for Margaret Sutherland in *200 Australian Women* by Helen King, ed. Heather Radi, Women's Redress Press, Sydney, 1988, states that 'she was dogged by the awareness that her husband doubted her sanity in wanting to compose'. According to Norman Albiston's third wife, artist Valerie Albiston, her late husband did attempt early in his previous marriage to support Margaret Sutherland's efforts to compose. Valerie Albiston told me in July 1996 that the real problem in the second marriage stemmed from Margaret's disillusionment with motherhood.

[12] I am indebted to Valerie Albiston for her account of her husband's marriage to Margaret Sutherland. Valerie Albiston told me during our two telephone interviews in July 1996 that her husband's second marriage had been disastrous from the start. Fiercely loyal to her late husband, Mrs Albiston insisted that Margaret was 'a most difficult woman' and said that during the final years of that marriage their rows were so severe that Norman Albiston often spent nights at his club to avoid going home.

[13] Interview with Valerie Albiston, July 1996.

[14] For the full story of Louise Hanson-Dyer see Davidson, Jim, *Lyrebird Rising,* Miegunyah Press, Melbourne University Press, Melbourne, 1994.

[15] Entry on Margaret Sutherland, *Grove Concise Dictionary of Music,* ed. Stanley, S., Macmillan, London, 1988.

[16] See also Murdoch, James, *Australia's Contemporary Composers,* Macmillan, Melbourne, 1972, and Harris, Laughton, 'Margaret Sutherland' in Callaway, Frank and Tunly, David (eds), *Australian Composers of the Twentieth Century,* Oxford University Press, Melbourne, 1972.

[17] Australian Women Composers, video, *op. cit.*

Chapter 23

[1] This story is related in Loch, Joice, *A Fringe of Blue*, John Murray, London, 1968, and in Gilchrist, Hugh, *Australians and Greeks,* Vol. 2, Halstead Press, Sydney, 1997, and in de Vries, Susanna, *Blue Ribbons, Bitter Bread, the story of Joice Loch, Australia's most decorated woman,* Hale and Iremonger, Sydney, 2000, 2nd edition 2001.

2 Facts cited by Sydney Loch in his unpublished autobiography, held in the Manuscripts Department of of the National Library of Australia in Canberra. Joice Loch, decades younger than Ethel, was annoyed that Ethel had been chosen to head the unit when she was clearly an atheist. Sydney Loch, Joice's husband, saw that Ethel had the seniority and the organising skills that were needed to hold together a diverse section of volunteers during the stressful work they had undertaken and was approving of Ethel, unlike Joice who had resented the fact Ethel had been chosen to head the mission rather than herself and instituted a move to the village of Ouranopoulis.

3 These letters are now in the South Australian Archives.

4 Details from entry on Ethel Cooper by Decie Denholm in Vol. 13 of *The Australian Dictionary of Biography*, Melbourne University Press, Melbourne, 1993.

5 Letters transcribed in Decie Denholm (ed), *Behind the Lines, Ethel Cooper's Letters from Germany*, Sydney, Collins, 1982.

6 *The Australian Dictionary of Biography*, Melbourne University Press, Melbourne, 1993, entry for Ethel Cooper by Decie Denholm.

7 For the story of Henry Handel Richardson see de Vries, Susanna, *Great Australian Women: From Federation to Freedom*, Harper Collins, Sydney, 2001.

8 *Behind the Lines, op. cit.*, p. 59, Letter 29.

9 *Ibid.*, p. 197, Letter 42B.

10 *Ibid.*, p. 54, Letter 26.

11 *Ibid.*, p. 78, Letter 43.

12 *Ibid.*, p. 70, Letter 37.

13 *Ibid.*, p. 166, Letter 15B.

14 *Ibid.*, p. 168, Letter 16B.

15 *Ibid.*, p. 185, Letter 31B.

16 *Ibid.*, p. 256, Letter 42C.

17 Described by Joice Loch in *Blue Ribbons, Bitter Bread, op. cit.*, p. 121.

18 The full story of this period at the refugee centre in the grounds of the campus of the American Farm School is related in *Blue Ribbons, Bitter Bread, op. cit.*

19 Subsequently Joice Loch would learn to speak 'village' rather than demotic Greek but she was never as fluent as Ethel Cooper, who had an exceptional flair for languages.

20 Extract from Sydney Loch's autobiography, one copy held in the National Library of Australia, Manuscripts Section and another copy held privately.

21 *Ibid.*

22 Cited in Gilchrist, Hugh, *op. cit.*, p. 175.

23 In a telephone interview with Decie Denholm, transcriber and editor of Ethel's letters from Germany, in March 2001 she confirmed that the correspondence Ethel sent to Emmie from Greece is missing with the exception of some postcards.

24 Details of Ethel's childhood and later years from Decie Denholm's entry on Ethel Cooper in *The Australian Dictionary of Biography, op. cit.*

Chapter 24

1 Entry on Margaret Preston by Isobel Sievl in *The Australian Dictionary of Biography*, Vol. 11, Melbourne University Press, Melbourne.

2 Preston, Margaret, From Eggs to Electrolux, *Art in Australia*, Sydney, December 1927.

3 The *Australian Dictionary of Biography* cites Parkside Lunatic Asylum, while Elizabeth Butel in her biography of the artist calls it Glenside.

4 Story related in Butel, Elizabeth, *Margaret Preston*, Penguin Books, Melbourne, 1985, p. 12.

5 Preston, Margaret, 'From Eggs to Electrolux', *op. cit.*

6 Sister Wendy Beckett, *The Story of Painting*, Dorling Kindersley, New York, p. 603.

7 Information on Stella Bowen from her autobiography *Drawn from Life*, Virago, London, 1999.

8 Modjeska, Drusilla, *Stravinsky's Lunch*, Picador, Pan MacMillan, Sydney, 1999, p. 10.

9 Cited by Isobel Sievl in *The Australian Dictionary of Biography, op. cit.* Original quote about the Prestons' marriage from the poet Leon Gellert, 'Margaret Preston was one of the Greats', *Sunday Telegraph*, 8 January 1967.

10 Ure Smith, Sydney, The Revival of the Woodcut, *Art and Australia*, Sydney, May 1923.

11 Cited in *Australian Women Artists 1840–1940*, Greenhouse Publications, Sydney, 1980, p. 47.

12 Burke, Janine, *op. cit.*, pp 46–7. Burke's work on Preston helped make Preston better known to Australians just as an Australian art boom started, and this coupled with an exhibition at the Art Gallery of New South Wales meant Preston's fame and prices soared.

13 Preston, Margaret, *Margaret Preston's Monotypes*, Ure Smith, Sydney, undated.

14 Modjeska, Drusilla, *op. cit.*, p. 174.

15 Much of this chapter is based on an article by Susanna de Vries in the *Australian Collector's Quarterly*, Consolidated Press, Sydney, Feb–April, 1991, pp. 36–45.

Chapter 25

1 Tennant, Kylie, *The Missing Heir,* MacMillan, Melbourne, 1986.

2 Kylie Tennant in an interview with Elizabeth Riddell in 1987, filmed by the Australia Council.

3 Housework was a continual problem for women writers who could not afford domestic staff. Eleanor Dark, married to a doctor and considerably more affluent than Tennant, complained in a letter to Miles Franklin how 'nearly half-way through a new novel I have had to shut it away in a drawer and grapple with brooms and pots and pans'. Eleanor Dark to Miles Franklin, 19 September 1936, Mitchell Library, MSS 364/26/427.

4 Eldershaw, Flora, *The Peaceful Army*, Women's Executive Committee, Sydney, 1938, reprinted 1988 (re-edited by Dale Spender) is a collection of essays and poems by prominent writers of the 1930s including Mary Gilmore, Miles Franklin, Eleanor Dark and Helen Simpson praising Australian women of the past and has a chapter by Miles Franklin on Rose Scott. Kylie Tennant contributed the final chapter and the book was intended to coincide with Australia's sesquicentenary.

5 See Eldershaw, Flora, *The Peaceful Army, op. cit.*, in which Tennant describes her visit to the Hassall family.

6 Like Barbara Baynton in *Bush Studies*, Kylie Tennant does not subscribe to the myth that *all* pioneer woman (or in her case women in the Depression) were heroic. Baynton records many who committed suicide when life became too terrible for them to bear. See also de Vries, *Pioneer Women, Pioneer Land*, Angus and Robertson, Sydney, 1987 and E.J. Dwyer, *Strength of Spirit: Australian Women of Achievement*, Sydney, 1992. In the days before antidepressants evidence suggests that many women went mad and drowned themselves in creeks or wells by filling their pockets with stones when the strain of isolation, rural poverty and the deaths of young children became too much for them.

7 Tennant to Elizabeth Riddell, *op. cit.*

8 Details on Joseph Foveaux from Vol. 1 *The Australian Dictionary of Biography*, Melbourne University Press, Melbourne, 1966.

9 Kylie Tennant won the S.H. Prior prize for the second time with her novel titled *The Brown Van*, which was serialised in *The Bulletin*. In 1941 when published in book form the publishers changed the title to *The Battlers*.

10 Green, H.M., *A History of Australian Literature*, Angus and Robertson, Sydney, 1962.

11 Baynton, Barbara, *Bush Studies*, published in London in 1902 and subsequently reissued in several further editions in Australia contains stories of grim realism in which her female characters are seen as the victims of predatory brutal men, who work them hard and then abandon or abuse them. Baynton grew up in the bush near Scone. Her father was a bush carpenter and although she left her roots to marry a doctor and later an English lord, her writing contains harsh realism about the loneliness and isolation of bush women. Her vivid detail and accuracy of dialogue greatly influenced Tennant.

12 Tennant, Kylie, *The Missing Heir, op. cit.*

13 Cited in Dutton, Geoffrey, *The Australian Collection. Australia's Greatest Books*, Angus and Robertson, Sydney, 1985. Due to its popularity *The Battlers* has been reprinted several times.

14 A bibliography of Kylie Tennant's works appears at the end of *The Missing Heir*. Tennant was a prolific writer and wrote short stories, plays and a popular history entitled *Australia, her Story, Notes on a Nation* (1953) with subsequent editions in 1964 and 1971. She also wrote books on Australian literature such as *The Development of the Australian Novel* (1958). With her husband she wrote *The Australian Essay* (1968). She also wrote articles on Australian literature in *Australian Literary Studies*, Vol. 10 (2), 1981 and edited two books for other authors. Her novels are *Tiburon* (1935 and 1981); *Foveaux* (1968 and 1981); *Ride on Stranger*, published worldwide by Macmillan (1943, 1979, 1989) and by Sirius in 1945; *Time Enough Later* (1943, 1945, 1961); *Lost Haven* (1943, 1945 and 1961); *Lost Haven* (1946, 1947 and 1968); *The Joyful Condemned* (condensed version published in 1953 republished in full as *Tell Morning This*) (1968, 1970); *The Honey Flow* (1956, 1974); *Tantavallon* (1983). Her children's books include *All the Proud Tribesmen* (1958), winner of the 1960 Children's Book Award and a collection of children's short stories, *Ma Jones and the White Cannibals* (1967). Her plays include *Tether a White Dragon* (about Arthur Deakin) (1952). Non-fiction works include *Speak You So Gently*, an account of Aboriginal cooperatives.

15 Tennant's week in jail is cited in Kerryn Goldsworthy's foreword to Tennant's book *Ride on Stranger*, 1943, reprinted by Angus and Robertson, Sydney, 1990 and in Tennant's entry in the *Oxford Companion to Australian Literature*, Oxford University Press, 1985. However, Tennant's autobiography does cite how many days she spent in jail before being bailed out.

Endotes

[16] Tennant, Kylie, *The Missing Heir, op. cit.*

[17] Tennant, Kylie, *Tell Morning This* was published in Sydney in 1967 but had been previously published in an abridged format in London in 1953 as *The Joyful Condemned.*

[18] See entry on Kylie Tennant, p. 1063 of the *Feminist Companion to Literature in English*, Batsford, London, 1990.

[19] Miles Franklin received only two per cent in royalties for some of her books published in London, while Katharine Susannah Prichard's London publishers paid her three to four per cent for books as a colonial author when the normal rate is ten per cent.

[20] There are many similarities in the careers of Prichard and Tennant. Both were champions of the poor and homeless, both were members of the Communist Party (albeit briefly in Tennant's case), both shared the S.H. Prior prize for their novels and both were deeply affected by the depression and suicide of loved ones.

[21] Most of Kylie Tennant's papers and some of her letters are held in the Manuscripts Department of the National Library of Australia in Canberra. A filmed interview with Elizabeth Riddell funded by the Australia Council made in 1985 is available from the National and other libraries. In it she claimed that the difference between herself and other writers of social realism was that 'I was always an entertainer. I gave them fun.'

[22] The late Michael Noonan to Susanna de Vries, Brisbane, 1994.

Chapter 26

[1] In 1988, Kath Walker adopted 'Oodgeroo' Noonuccal as her official name.

[2] *The Collected Works of Thomas Welsby*, Vols 1 and 2. Reprints of this standard history of Moreton Bay by Jacaranda Press, Brisbane, n.d., gives details of Felipe Gonzales and his Spanish Philipino descendants on Stradbroke. I am indebted to Dr David Cilento, a friend of Oodgeroo's for many years, for telling me about this connection with Kath Walker's father and for details about her mother being a matriarch of the Noonuccal tribe.

[3] Cochrane, Kathleen, J., *Oodgeroo,* University of Queensland Press, St Lucia, 1994. A comprehensive coverage of Kath Walker's life and ancestry by a close friend. See also Wright, Judith, *Oodgeroo's Story*, ANU, Canberra, 1994

[4] Durbidge, Ellie and Covacevich, Jeanette, *North Stradbroke Island,* Stradbroke Management Association, 1981.

[5] The author's name changed to Oodgeroo Noonuccal in 1988.

[6] From Oodgeroo's article explaining her change of name titled, *Why I am now Oodgeroo Noonuccal, op. cit.*

[7] The doctor who told me this prefers to remain anonymous.

[8] Durbidge, Ellie and Covacevich, Jeanette, *op. cit.*

[9] Oodgeroo's friend and biographer, Kathie Cochrane, described these symptoms as stemming from Oodgeroo's Army service in the *Sydney Morning Herald* of 18 September 1993 and in her biography *Oodgeroo, op. cit.*

[10] Oodgeroo to Isabel Lukas, 23 January 1977, reported in the *Sydney Morning Herald.*

[11] The late Dr Phyllis Cilento would become famous for her vitamin supplement treatments.

[12] Claims of Dr Raphael Cilento's paternity of Kath's second son, Vivian Walker (later Kabul Oodgeroo Noonuccal), appeared in an article in *The Bulletin* dated 5 October 1993 by Greg Roberts, who was described as 'a close friend of the poet and activist'. In Roberts's article Dr Raphael Cilento, Jnr, speaking from New York, acknowledged paternity of Vivian Walker (Kabul). Dr Cilento added that other members of his family had not been told that he had fathered a child by Kath because 'I haven't been living in Australia.' Katharine Cochrane stated in this article that the day Vivian/Kabul died, Dr Cilento telephoned from America and offered to pay for a monument at Vivian's grave, and admitted to having kept a close watch on his son's progress. However, Oodgeroo refused the offer, saying that the young Dr Raphael had never done anything to help his son when he was alive, 'so he needn't bother now'. In the same article Cilento claims that in the early 1980s Dr Cilento met his son in San Francisco and tried to persuade Vivian to live with him in New York but Vivian refused. Members of the Cilento family say that Dr Raphael Jnr and Oodgeroo were friends and for that reason he kindly offered to pay for Vivian's education.

[13] In her biography, *Oodgeroo, op. cit.*, Kathie Cochrane states that Dr Raphael Cilento Jnr was Vivian's father..

[14] Telephone interviews in 1997 and 1998 between the author and Dr David Cilento, who works as a GP in Brisbane.

[15] *Ibid.*

[16] *Feminist Companion to Literature, op. cit.*, entry for Oodgeroo Noonuccal, *op. cit.*

[17] See Cochrane, *Oodgeroo, op. cit.*

[18] Cameron, Campbell et al., *Aboriginal and Torres Strait Islanders of North Queensland*, United Nations Association of Queensland, 1958. Thanks to Dr Lilian Cameron for her recollections of meetings with Oodgeroo.

[19] Oodgeroo Noonuccal, obituary, *The Australian*, 17 September 1993.

[20] Cited in Cochrane, *Oodgeroo, op. cit.*

[21] For the full account of Oodgeroo's attempts to obtain funding see Cochrane, *Oodgeroo, op. cit.*

[22] Oodgeroo Noonuccal. Interview with Christine Hogan, *Portfolio Magazine*, Sydney, July 1987.

[23] Raoul Mellish, a former director of the Queensland Art Gallery, and James MacCormick, former University of Queensland architect, visited the site of the proposed education centre at Kath's invitation to discuss the layout of the projected buildings with her. However, the venture failed when both state and federal governments and Lilian Bosch, a wealthy American artist with a fortune derived from California, pulled out of the venture claiming that without security of tenure beyond Kath's lifetime the project was not feasible.

[24] Oodgeroo Noonuccal to Andrew Urban, 24 November 1985, reported in *The Australian* on the occasion of an exhibition of her art in the house of her publisher, Ulli Beier, in his Annandale home in Sydney.

[25] *Ibid.*

[26] Oodgeroo Noonuccal to Shelly Neller, *The Bulletin,* 3 December 1985.

[27] *Sydney Morning Herald*, 19 October 1989.

[28] Oodgeroo Noonuccal to Brad Forrest, correspondent for the *Sydney Morning Herald*; her statements appeared in that paper on 8 June 1998 under the title, 'Blacks use Expo to get the other message across'.

Chapter 27

[1] Bird, Nancy Walton, *Born to Fly*, Angus and Robertson, Sydney, 1961, and *My God! It's a Woman*, Angus and Robertson, Sydney, 1990.

[2] Details of the old Mascot airport and Nancy Bird Walton's first lesson with Kingsford Smith come from her brilliant autobiography *Born to Fly, op. cit.* I am most grateful to her for permission to quote from this book, one of the best I have read by any aviator including *Westward the Night* written by the remarkable Beryl Markham, pioneer aviator in Kenya. Nancy Bird's skill as a writer and her poetic descriptions of flying deserve to be widely acknowledged.

[3] At the celebrations for Federation held in Melbourne in May 2001 Nancy was asked to repeat her praise of Charles Kingsford Smith, who was chosen as one of Australia's most eminent achievers.

[4] Bird, Nancy, *Born to Fly, op. cit.*, p. 23.

[5] The facts about outback aviation are from Sir Richard Boyer's foreword to Nancy Bird's book *Born to Fly.*

Chapter 28

[1] From a fact sheet put out by the Hamlin–Churchill Childbirth Injuries Fund.

[2] Entry on Emperor Haile Selassie, born Ras Tafari Makonen, from *Who's Who in Modern History* by Alan Palmer, Weidenfeld and Nicolson, London, 1980.

[3] Video casssette, *Walking back to happiness*, made by the BBC Education and Training Service, British Broadcasting Corporation, London WC1 1993. Narrator Ann Diamond, producer Fiona Holmes, VHS format is available in most Australian State Libraries and some public libraries.

[4] Information kindly provided by Stuart N. Abrahams, who acts in a voluntary capacity as fundraiser for the Fistula Hospital in Sydney.

[5] Figures taken from Dr Catherine's Newsletter for the Addis Ababa Fistula Hospital dated June 1996.

[6] Information from the Hamlin–Churchill Childbirth Injuries Fund.

[7] Latest details of the farm/village from the March 2001 newsletter of the Addis Ababa Fistula Hospital, courtesy Stuart N. Abrahams.

[8] Details of the village/farm project can be found in the book *The Hospital by the River* by Dr Catherine Hamlin and John Little, Pan Macmillan, Sydney, 2001.